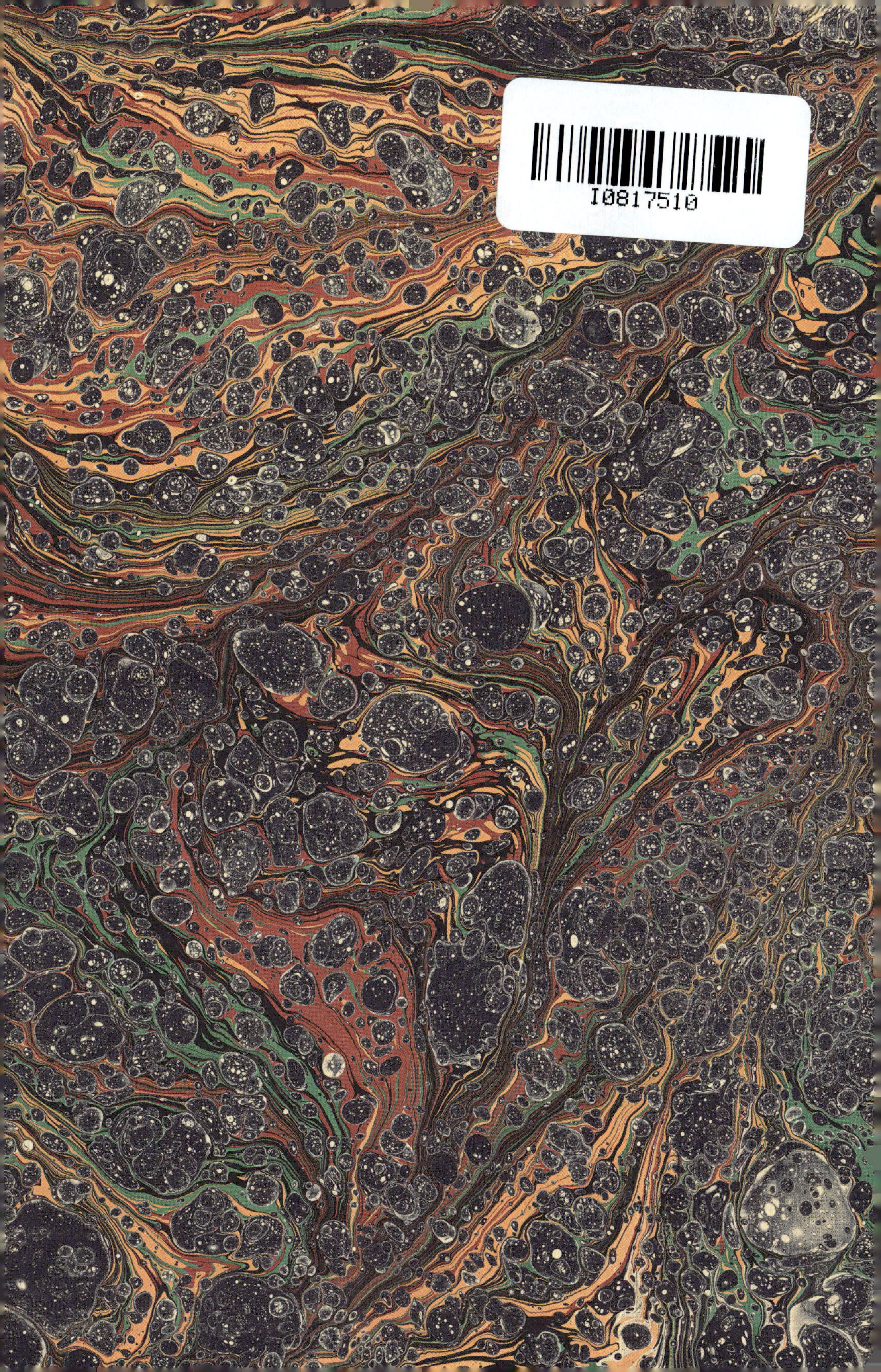
I0817510

Oskar Dirlewanger

Oskar Dirlewanger

The Infamous War Criminal and His SS Sonderkommando

Dr. Soraya Kuklińska

Library of Congress Control Number: 2025930661

Designed by Jack Chappell
Cover design by Jack Chappell
Type set in Tahoma/Liberteen/Bradley/Times New Roman
Translated from the Polish by Krystyna Kupiszewska
Front cover illustration: Włodzimierz Kukliński

ISBN: 978-0-7643-6988-9
ePub: 978-1-5073-0587-4

Printed in India
10 9 8 7 6 5 4 3 2 1

Published by Schiffer Publishing, Ltd.
4880 Lower Valley Road
Atglen, PA 19310
Phone: (610) 593-1777; Fax: (610) 593-2002
Email: Info@schifferbooks.com
Web: www.schifferbooks.com

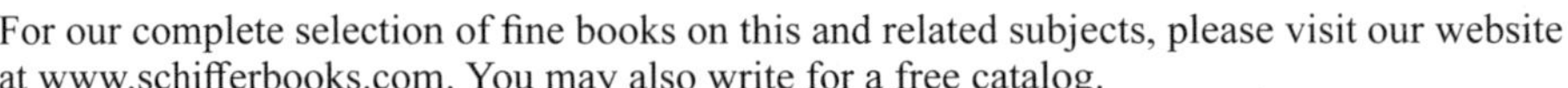

Contents

Introduction

People have always been fascinated by the sad, the terrifying, and even the monstrous. Thus, the interest in Oskar Dirlewanger, one of the Second World War's blackest figures. He became infamous as the commander of SS-Sonderkommando Dirlewanger, of which Heinrich Himmler said after the start of the Warsaw Uprising, on August 3, 1944,

> In 1941, I organized a poachers' regiment under Dirlewanger's command. Dirlewanger is a "nice Swabian," wounded ten times, tough character, slightly strange. I received the Führer's permission to collect poachers who used weapons or traps from all the prisons in Germany: around 2,000 men in total. Unfortunately, only 400 of those "valuable" individuals are still alive today. I replenished the regiment with people from SS schools who infringed the code of conduct of those schools. I told Dirlewanger: And now, why not look around for suitable candidates among the rascals and real criminals in concentration camps? The atmosphere in that regiment is truly mediaeval due to the use of corporal punishment and other similar educational methods. If anybody winces when he hears the question if we will win the war, he will be erased from the rollcall . . . because the others will shoot him on the spot.[1]

Together with his soldiers, Dirlewanger was responsible for the brutal pacification of villages in Belarus and the suppression of the Warsaw Uprising. They were not the only penal battalion in Belarus to commit mass crimes, and they were also not the only ones to murder civilians and insurgents during the uprising; however, history "remembers" only Dirlewanger's unit. In his book *Przemarsz przez piekło*, Stanisław Podlewski describes it as follows:

> It is infamous in the brown army. They are recruited from Volksdeutsch of various countries, army deserters, urban and port scum, knifers, repeat offenders, dangerous felons, criminals of the Jack the Ripper or Vampire of Düsseldorf type, released from the prisons, concentration camps, and correctional facilities of the great Reich. They knew how to mass murder in a refined manner and having been given an order and the hope of freedom, they committed monstrous crimes previously unknown to the world.[2]

In his publication *Stare Miasto 1944*, Stanisław Ozimek describes Dirlewanger thus: "A repulsive, scar-covered, thin face. He knows that the commander of the battle group [von dem Bach] is aware of his lawless past, and still . . . puts his greatest hopes in him and his people."[3]

In the 1960s, the *Frankfurter Illustrierte* magazine, on a wave of interest in Heinz Reinefarth's trial, published a pseudo-documentary account from the Warsaw Uprising, presenting Dirlewanger as follows:

> Himmler's pal holds his soldiers together with barbarian strictness. The thin bird-of-prey-faced figure rules through the gallows and the whip. All too often, privates would line up at the crack of dawn and their own colleagues had to hang convicts. Dirlewanger metes justice out himself, and anyone who was only tied at the whipping post and flogged can consider himself lucky. This former lawyer who threatens to shoot SS judges and Wehrmacht officers is in the habit of holding orgies in his headquarters, and his slavishly devoted NCOs bring him beautiful young girls so as not to fall out of his graces. . . . New loot beckons in Warsaw![4]

This vivid description is to this day repeated in publications and journals under different forms.

What is it about Oskar Dirlewanger's phenomenon that causes tales about him and his unit to fire so many people's imaginations even today? Was he in fact only a drunken bandit and gangster hated even by his own subordinates? Was he a "mentally unstable, rabidly fanatical alcoholic with a tendency to episodes of violence under the influence of drugs"[5] and was his Sonderkommando famous only for "constant abuse of alcohol, pillaging, sadistic cruelty, rapes, and murders,"[6] achieving nothing beyond this? Was Oskar Dirlewanger a common criminal and emotionally unstable hoodlum whom Himmler took "under his wing"?[7] He himself wrote in an *Untersuchungsbogen* (SS-UB) form of May 18, 1940, that he smoked twenty cigarettes per day and drank moderately (*mäßig*).[8]

This publication aims to present Oskar Dirlewanger as he was and as he was seen by his contemporaries. I set myself the task of unraveling—to the extent possible—the mystery of this man's personality. To this end, we need to go beyond the fixed model of a war criminal's biography and take into account individual stages of Dirlewanger's life and the different spheres and areas of his activity.

Despite the emotion- and prejudice-filled discussion, not much is really known about him. It is certain that he was a Nazi war criminal. The offenses committed by his unit are very well documented. Nevertheless, numerous historians and writers add many untrue details of their own invention. One example is Jesús Hernández, who in the book *Nazistowskie bestie* described one of Dirlewanger's operations in Lublin thus (on the basis of the testimony of the lawyer Konrad Morgen in Nuremberg):

> On one occasion, Dirlewanger unlawfully and arbitrarily arrested several people. In the case of several young Jewish women, he proceeded as follows: he stood them in the middle of a circle formed of himself, some of his people and an auxiliary Wehrmacht unit. He then conducted what he called a "scientific experiment," which in this case involved stripping the victims of their clothes and injecting them with strychnine. After that Dirlewanger lit a cigarette and smoked it calmly, looking on the slow agony of the naked girls together with the others. Immediately afterwards the bodies were cut up into small pieces, mixed with horse flesh, and cooked in a soup.[9]

In fact, Morgen stated,

> Together with a group of friends, 5–8 people, Dirlewanger organized a regular binge. First, they drank significant amounts of schnapps.

> Then Dirlewanger forced the arrested Jewish women to undress and dance naked. Ultimately, they were killed with strychnine injections.[10]

The murder of fifty-seven Jews (dressed) with strychnine injection is a fact, but the remaining parts of the tale are only a flight of the imagination. Despite having investigated the matter in the 1940s, Morgen was unable to indicate who applied the poison or where it had been obtained (for more on the strychnine injections, see the chapter "Tasks of the Unit in the General Government," subchapter "Lublin").

Konrad Morgen kept adding to the stories about poisoning Jews. During his interrogation, Gottlob Berger was asked if he knew that Dirlewanger gave poison to Jews and then fed their bodies to dogs or perhaps made soup out of them. Berger was surprised by these revelations. Even thc investigators themselves judged Morgen's testimony to be so improbable and ridiculous that it was not taken into account during the Nuremberg trial.[11] This makes the fact that they are quoted by historians all the more shocking.

The emergence of many incredible and terrifying tales about Oskar Dirlewanger was also influenced by the postwar testimony of commanders who attempted to avoid prison or the death penalty at his expense. SS-Gruppenführer Heinz Reinefarth and SS-Obergruppenführer Erich von dem Bach-Zelewski offer excellent examples.

In Nuremberg, in 1946, von dem Bach-Zelewski said of Dirlewanger:

> A veterinary doctor by profession, typical brutal soldierly character. . . . There was a rumor that Dirlewanger had been punished for various offenses already during his civilian activity. . . . He maintained his authority only through the greatest brutality. A heavy drunkard and liar. . . . Although he knew he had many enemies among decent people, he nevertheless knew how to cover all evidence of crimes, so that nothing could ever be proved against him. . . . False reports became a kind of second nature to him.[12]

During the war, his opinion of Dirlewanger as a man and commander had been completely different. They worked together for many years, starting from antipartisan operations in Belarus, up to the suppression of the Warsaw Uprising. Von dem Bach personally supported motions to decorate Dirlewanger, highly appreciating his abilities. An example may be seen in his letter of September 10, 1944, in which he refers to Reinefarth's motion to award Dirlewanger the Knight's Cross of the Iron Cross:

> I most warmly support the motion. The successes achieved are chiefly the result of SS-Oberführer Dirlewanger's personal merits, he always being a shining example of personal courage and battle spirit for his people.[13]

After the war, Heinz Reinefarth pushed all responsibility for crimes committed in Warsaw onto Dirlewanger. He even gave an untrue date of his own arrival in Warsaw and claimed that before he appeared there, Dirlewanger had already started committing crimes against the civilian population. He testified that he himself had had no impact on the actions of Dirlewanger's unit whatsoever. As regards the motion to award Dirlewanger the Knight's Cross for putting down the Warsaw Uprising, Reinefarth claimed that he probably signed the recommendation without previously reading the text, which had been prepared by somebody else. Von dem Bach even maintained that it was a staff officer who used a stamp with a facsimile of his signature, and that the decoration was surely awarded upon Himmler's personal request[14] (for more, see the chapter "Participation in Suppressing the Warsaw Uprising," Kampfgruppe Reinefarth, Wola).

The goal that I have set myself is to start somewhat "from scratch": without prejudice and preserving some distance from Dirlewanger's image as presented in the press and various publications. I have attempted to investigate him and describe his life as objectively as possible, and above all to show what kind of man he was.

The chronological boundaries of this book extend beyond Dirlewanger's lifetime (1895–1945). What also needs to be shown is events of later years: In the 1960s and 1970s, investigative proceedings were conducted before various courts; for instance, pertaining to crimes committed by the unit in Belarus. Separate court proceedings were instituted in Germany concerning Dirlewanger's death (this includes case files concerning his exhumation from 1960). In the years 2000–09, the Institute of National Remembrance's (IPN) Commission for the Prosecution of Crimes Against the Polish Nation started investigating crimes committed in Warsaw in 1944. The gigantic documentation of crimes committed by the unit and Oskar Dirlewanger includes material from an investigation against Dirlewanger held by the Gestapo in 1941 (currently located in the IPN) and from post-1945 court investigations (in German archives).

A special role in my book is played by little-known sources originating from German archives, including the Central Office of the Land Judicial Authorities for Investigation of National Socialist Crimes (Zentrale Stelle der

Landesjustizverwaltungen zur Aufklärung nationalsozialistischer Verbrechen), located in the Bundesarchiv in Ludwigsburg (where I found valuable material about the operations in Belarus in the years 1942–44, the circumstances of Dirlewanger's death and postwar investigations against members of his unit); from Landesarchiv Baden-Württemberg (Staatsarchiv Ludwigsburg) in Ludwigsburg; from Stadtarchiv Esslingen (documents concerning his youth and family); from Stadtarchiv Heilbronn (files on Dirlewanger's professional career before the Second World War); and from the Yad Vashem Institute in Israel. Extremely interesting material about young Oskar Dirlewanger's military career during the First World War was provided by Hauptstaatsarchiv Stuttgart. Furthermore, I used documents obtained from Bundesarchiv Berlin-Lichterfelde (formerly the American Berlin Document Center). I also conducted searches in Staatarchiv München, Archiv Gedenkstätte und Museum Sachsenhausen, the Military History Archive in Bratislava (M.H. Arch.), and the Institute of National Remembrance's Commission for the Prosecution of Crimes Against the Polish Nation, Bydgoszcz Branch.

I additionally examined court reports from postwar investigations into the operations of SS units commanded by Oskar Dirlewanger, testimonies of soldiers who were part of the units' whole combat history (from 1940 to 1945), their opinions about their commander, court judgments, testimonies of witnesses of the crimes in Belarus, war diaries from antipartisan operations (including Cottbus, June 1943), and also war diaries of the von Gottberg Battle Group (SS Kampfgruppe "von Gottberg").

For historians, court records are a particular challenge. It is often hard to decide which testimonies to believe and which should be rejected or treated with some reserve. Obviously, all those involved in Nazi crimes had significant reasons to downplay their role and distance themselves from such crimes. Moreover, soldiers and other witnesses were questioned twenty, thirty, and sometimes even more years after the war, and thus their memories were not always very reliable, leading to many inaccuracies and discrepancies.

Additionally, German investigators did not always seek to reveal the truth about German crimes committed during the war by German soldiers. Many factors contributed to this. Some of those questioned held important positions in their country, while others were friends of the investigators. The unwillingness to reveal the full scale of the crimes was also due to personal factors: Some prosecutors, judges, and investigators had also been highly placed in the Nazi system, and so diligent probing of some topics could have brought them down too.[15] When reading the transcripts of the questioning of Oskar Dirlewanger's subordinates, one often has the impression that the investigator preferred to avoid certain topics (particularly those connected to massacres of civilians).

In addition to the abovementioned sources, in my work I drew on literature about the combat operations in which Oskar Dirlewanger and his subordinates took part. Books from the interwar period describing the activity of regiments in which Dirlewanger served offer very valuable material about the First World War.[16]

This book consists of ten chapters. In the first, I discuss Oskar Dirlewanger's childhood and youth and the interwar period, from 1918 to 1939. I attempt to show the origins of the Dirlewanger family, the environment in which Oskar was raised, and his school years. Right after matriculation, he joined the army and took part in the First World War. In the years 1914–18 he fought on the Western and Eastern Fronts. After the war ended, he went on to study and work. During all this time, he was active in several Freikorps volunteer units and participated in fighting against the Communists. In this chapter, I further present Dirlewanger's numerous encounters with the law and his prison stay. He spent the last years before the start of the Second World War in Spain. As a soldier of the Condor Legion, he took part in the Spanish Civil War (1936–39), which was likely when he became fluent in Spanish.[17]

In chapter 2, I present the order of battle of the units under Dirlewanger's command, and their evolution and growth: from the small Oranienburg Poacher's Unit (SS-Wilddiebkommando Oranienburg); through SS-Sonderkommando Dirlewanger, SS-Sonderbataillon Dirlewanger, SS-Sonderregiment Dirlewanger, and SS-Sturmbrigade Dirlewanger, up to the 36th Waffen-SS Grenadier Division Dirlewanger (36. Waffen Grenadier Division der SS).

Chapter 3 contains a description of the operations of SS-Sonderkommando Dirlewanger (this was the name used by the German command for most of the war) in the General Government (in the Stary Dzików labor camp and in Lublin).

In chapter 4, I study the fighting against partisans (*Bandenbekämpfung*) in Belarus (1942–44), where the unit stayed for thirty months. It participated in at least thirty-eight major operations there, and in more-minor combat actions. For this reason, this chapter is more extensive than the others.

Chapter 5 presents the role of Dirlewanger's unit in suppressing the Warsaw Uprising (1944). Although it was present in Warsaw for "only" (compared with Belarus) two months, the fighting there was very fierce. The suppression of the Warsaw Uprising has great significance for Polish historiography, which is reflected in the length of the chapter.

The suppression of the national uprising in Slovakia (1944) is described in chapter 6. It is shorter than the previous ones, among other reasons due to fewer archival resources.

At the end of chapter 7, I write about the fighting at Ipolysag in Hungary (1944). There, Dirlewanger's subordinates faced the Red Army in frontline combat. Political prisoners had been conscripted into the unit from concentration camps, and most of them went over to the enemy side as soon as they had the chance. This was the first and last such situation under Dirlewanger's command.

In chapter 8, I present the late activity of Dirlewanger's subordinates at Gubin and Halbe in 1945. In the final days of the war, extremely intense fighting took place, and some settlements changed hands several times.

Chapter 9 contains the memories and reports of Dirlewanger's subordinates and his friends and acquaintances, and also commanders and soldiers who encountered him at various stages of his military career. This allowed me to show how he was seen by his contemporaries.

In the final chapter, I describe the arrest and last days of the commander of SS-Sonderkommando Dirlewanger. Using memories and testimonies, I reconstruct the events in the Ostarrest prison in Altshausen, Baden-Württemberg, and the circumstances in which Dirlewanger died. I present the 1960s investigation into his death and the conjectures that he managed to survive the war. I also discuss reports from the exhumation carried out in 1960.

At the end of the publication, I enclose maps from Gubin in 1945 and photographs of Oskar Dirlewanger and his subordinates.

Note for readers: Various names (place-names, surnames, etc.), many of them Polish or Belarusian, appear throughout the text. Where an English equivalent could not be established, the source spelling was used.

Acknowledgments

The preparation of this book would not have been possible without the very kind aid of many people. Much credit goes to my supervisor, Prof. Aleksander Lasik, from Kazimierz Wielki University in Bydgoszcz. Apart from offering me his great support, he also pointed me to the necessary literature, which broadened my horizons and provided knowledge about Waffen-SS operations and structure.

My heartfelt thanks go to the employees of the archives I searched. I am particularly grateful to Abdullah Toptanci of Bundesarchiv Ludwigsburg. With a great deal of patience and understanding, he explained to me how to find materials and was able to locate every file, even if the reference number I gave was incorrect. I wish to express my gratitude to the Bundesarchiv Berlin-Lichterfelde team and especially Sven Schneidereit for his determination and stoic calm as he explained to me the intricacies of order system functioning in the archive. Even today, I am impressed by the kind welcome and help I received from the employees of Stadtarchiv Heilbronn, who found for me the original photographs of Dirlewanger from the period in which he commanded Panzerzug Dirlewanger. The ladies in Archiv Gedenkstätte und Museum Sachsenhausen also gave me a very warm welcome. Not only did they prepare the files I needed, but they also allowed me to browse the library in the camp archive, which I am very grateful for. Much appreciation goes also to the employees of the Bydgoszcz branch of the Institute of National Remembrance for their help.

Furthermore, I wish to greatly thank the employees of the Yad Vashem Archive in Jerusalem, Hauptstaatsarchiv Stuttgart, Staatsarchiv München in Germany, and the Military History Archive in Bratislava for carrying out searches for me and sending me the material necessary for my work.

Completing the chapter about Oskar Dirlewanger's childhood and school years would have been impossible without the help of Rolf Laschet, a teacher at Schelztor-Gymnasium in Esslingen, who shared his knowledge with me. I am extremely grateful to him for his kind welcome in Esslingen and showing me Dirlewanger's family house.

This publication would not have been so detailed were it not for the aid of regional historians and enthusiasts, who are often underappreciated. They allowed me to discover information that is not widely known, among others about the camp in Stary Dzików. Moreover, my thanks go to Norbert Drupi, since without his help, many issues concerning the fighting in the Gubin area would have remained unexplained. I thank Andrzej Skorupski, who provided me with several interesting facts about SS-Sonderkommando Dirlewanger during conversations about the Totenkopf Division.

I also wish to thank my nearest and dearest. Much gratitude goes to my parents for their great encouragement, help, and faith in me. My husband also deserves great thanks for his patience, support, and understanding for my work, and for lugging heavy books from libraries.

1

Oskar Dirlewanger's Youth (1895–1939)

The youth and childhood of Oskar Dirlewanger fell in a stormy time, full of change and political turmoil. The year 1918 saw the end of the belle époque, a period of flourishing, progress, and peace in Europe. In 1888, Kaiser Wilhelm II ascended to the German throne. One of his first decisions was to remove Otto von Bismarck from his position as chancellor. This blocked the extension of the June 1887 secret agreement with Russia, which in the event of war gave Germany freedom of decision and took into account Russian interests in the Balkans.[1] Bismarck's successor, Leo von Caprivi, believed the agreement to be a betrayal of Austria-Hungary and advised the kaiser not to renew it. German policy was reoriented to consider the needs of Austria-Hungary. Meanwhile, at that time Serbia increasingly strived to unite all nations held to be part of the Serbian cultural world; that is, to form a Greater Serbian state. One obstacle was Archduke Franz Ferdinand d'Este, who wished to repartition the Austro-Hungarian monarchy and institute German as the official language in the fifteen new states. This was why the Serbian assassin Gavrilo Princip selected him for his victim.

In the interwar period, public feeling in Germany did not settle. In November 1918, Kaiser Wilhelm II was forced to abdicate and left the country almost unnoticed. On November 9, 1918, SPD (Social Democratic Party of Germany) deputy Philipp Scheidemann announced, from a Reichstag balcony, the fall of the monarchy and the birth of a republic. The provisions of the Treaty of Versailles caused discontent in the country to grow drastically. Germany was required to reduce its military to a minimum (the professional army could number 100,000 people and could not comprise tanks, airplanes, or heavy artillery, while the general staff was to be dissolved). Building of fortifications was forbidden, and the release of significant territories mandated: Alsace and Lorraine were returned to France, and Poland obtained Poznań, Western Prussia (Pomerania), and part of the Upper Silesian plebiscite area. Gdańsk became a free city. The towns of Eupen and Malmedy were annexed to Belgium as a result of plebiscites. Germany lost all its colonies. Moreover, the economic burdens were stifling for the young republic.

As a result of these decisions, nationalist feeling in Germany increased, counterrevolutionary organizations formed, retaliatory action was called for, and extreme nationalist views spread. The theory of the "stab in the back" was popular, and the need to win living space in the East was emphasized. City streets saw constant protest marches, while worker strikes were brutally put down by Friedrich Ebert's government. Unemployment kept rising, and more and more people were pushed to the margins of society. Growing inflation compounded the young republic's instability. War veterans were unable to find work and adapt themselves to the new situation. Universal unrest contributed to general uncertainty, and newly emerging political movements took advantage of this.

It was at this point that the Nazi movement appeared. In 1919, Adolf Hitler, employed in Munich as an agent of the Reichswehr counterintelligence, made contact with a chauvinist group going by the name of Deutsche Arbeiterpartei (German Workers' Party), which numbered several people and pushed anticapitalist slogans.[2] He relatively rapidly came to be the leading figure of this movement, becoming its führer (leader) by 1921, and the name of the organization was changed to Nationalsozialistische Deutsche Arbeiterpartei (National Socialist German Workers' Party, or NSDAP). The party did not write detailed political manifestos but primarily built emotional engagement, rejecting democracy and advocating for revolution. It demanded that the injuries done to Germany at the end of the First World War be remedied, and the guilty parties punished, and that the Marxist worldview be opposed.[3] The party's first program of February 24, 1920, was "a mishmash of vague economic promises intended to protect the middle class and small businesses, coupled a clear commitment to exclude Jews from full German citizenship."[4]

The NSDAP's symbols were as unoriginal as its program. The swastika had previously been used by other right-wing groups, the *Totenkopf* (death's head) skull and crossbones later adopted by the SS had been worn by the German cavalry, while the extended-right-hand salute was borrowed from Benito Mussolini's Fascists.[5]

1.1. Early Years

The Dirlewangers were a well-known, respected, and well-to-do family. Oskar's paternal grandfather worked in Stuttgart as a surgeon and a doctor specializing in vaccination, and his maternal grandfather was a primary-school teacher. Oskar's parents were in trade: His father, August Dirlewanger, was a merchant, and later an attorney in Esslingen.[6] From Oskar's school documents it seems that August came from Mannheim.[7] Little is known about his mother, Pauline, née Herrlinger. It is hard to say how Oskar's parents met, but they married in December 1893, in Esslingen am Neckar. The wedding was held just in time, since on June 7, 1894, their first daughter, Mathilde, was born. Just before her birth, the young couple moved to the Bavarian Würzburg, larger than Esslingen and situated around 160 km away. That was where on September 26, 1895, Oskar Anton Paul Dirlewanger,[8] future commander of the SS-Sonderkommando Dirlewanger special unit, first saw the light of day. A second daughter, Elfriede, was born on December 26, 1898. Würzburg offered the siblings a peaceful childhood in a family atmosphere, and Oskar spent the first six years of his life there. He was remembered as an able and talented child.[9]

On July 1, 1901, August Dirlewanger gave up his job as a merchant and became an attorney, which involved a move to Stuttgart.[10] The rest of the family joined him in October.[11] On December 9, 1901, Pauline gave birth to her second son, Paul. The four siblings were raised in Stuttgart until 1906. In 1901, Oskar started his primary education (*Elementarschule*) there and was enrolled in a *Vorklasse* in 1903. He then started learning in a *Realgymnasium* in Stuttgart.[12]

In 1906 the Dirlewangers returned to Esslingen.[13] The location they settled in, at Kesselwasen 16 near the old town, was quite picturesque.[14] The house (Gräßle Haus) still stands, overlooking the charming Wehrneckar canal, which can be accessed by a footbridge. The family occupied one floor. In May 1906, Oskar was enrolled in Georgii-Gymnasium at Abt-Fulrad Strasse, and in the 1910–11 school year he transferred to Schelztor-Oberrealschule at Berliner Strasse, like many of his peers.[15] He did not have far to school: around six minutes' walk through the lovely streets of Esslingen.

In the 1910–11 school year, Oskar was a pupil of the seventh form, and his tutor was Professor Dietmann. For unknown reasons, on September 16, 1910, Dirlewanger was enrolled as a pupil "for a trial period" and obtained full rights only on November 1. His grades were not outstanding. Initially, his results in three subjects were termed, on an eight-point scale, "not fully satisfactory" (3). His performance improved in the ninth, final form. His class tutor at the time was Professor Schirmer. Dirlewanger's favorite subject, in which he received the best marks over these three years of education, was history. He achieved the grade of 6.

The young people (the first girl was enrolled in 1908) attending the Schelztor-Oberrealschule together with Dirlewanger came from Esslingen's leading families. In Oskar's final year, there were twenty-nine boys in his class, three of them from the most-renowned families: Oskar Bechtle (b. 1895), Otto Boley (b. 1895), and Eugen Mangold (b. 1891).[16] Dirlewanger's matriculation certificate of June 30, 1913, indicates that he was interested in history. His highest grade, 7 (very good), was for the history of German literature, and he received a 6 (good) in history and geography. His results in several subjects—introduction to philosophy, French language, religion, and physics and chemistry—were satisfactory (5). Mathematics was more of a challenge: In analysis, he had a satisfactory (5) grade, but only a sufficient (4) one in geometry. Neither were English language, nature, and drawing Dirlewanger's strong points, and for them he also received sufficient (4) marks.[17] His matriculation examination results placed him eleventh of twenty-nine pupils. After sitting the examination, Dirlewanger stated that he was planning legal studies, and his certificate of June 30, 1913, lists "administrative lawyer" as his preferred profession.[18]

For unknown reasons, Oskar Dirlewanger did not decide to go on to further study immediately after matriculation. He chose a military career instead. Both his sisters married quickly, and his brother, Paul, lived with their parents in Esslingen.[19] Paul probably also chose a military career. In the 1920s he fought against Communists in Sangerhausen together with Oskar. From letters and memoirs, it seems he spent the period of the Second World War in the family home in Esslingen.

1.2. Participation in the First World War

Oskar Dirlewanger tied his life and career with the military from the very start. On October 1, 1913, he enlisted as a volunteer in the machine gun company of the 123rd (5th Württemberg) Grenadier Regiment "König Karl"

(Grenadier-Regiment "König Karl" [5. Württembergisches] Nr. 123) in Ulm.[20] He received the rank of lance corporal (*Gefreiter*).[21]

On June 28, 1914, Gavrilo Princip assassinated the archduke and his wife, Sophie, of Hohenberg. Dirlewanger was then nineteen years old. The First World War resulted in the fall of the empire, a period of political turmoil, and the establishment of the Weimar Republic. However, in 1914, soldiers, including the teenage Oskar, went to war gleefully and full of faith in a swift victory. The mood was uplifted, and newspapers published patriotic articles; militaristic and chauvinist slogans were even preached from pulpits. More and more countries declared war. On Austria-Hungary's side stood Germany, Turkey, and Bulgaria, forming the block of Central powers. Their opponent was the Entente; that is, France, Russia, Serbia, the United Kingdom, Japan, Italy (from 1915), Romania (from 1916), and the United States (from 1917).

The German Graf Alfred von Schlieffen prepared a campaign plan according to which Germany was to avoid fighting on two fronts, and France was to be swiftly overcome, but his successor, Colonel General Helmuth von Moltke, changed the plan and did not manage to realize those assumptions. Clashes on the Eastern and Western Fronts became extremely heavy and bloody, bringing more and more victims. In the last days of September 1914, the offensive on the Western Front ended and positional warfare began. Its main causes included defenders outnumbering the attackers, exhaustion of both sides' soldiers, lack of personnel and material reserves, and the incapability of the arms industry to satisfy frontline needs within a short time.

From August 2, 1914 to September 9, 1915, Dirlewanger fought in the machine gunners' company of the 123rd Grenadier Regiment (Grenadier Regiment 123, MG-Kompanie) in Belgium and France.[22] On August 2, 1914, together with his unit he entered Belgium as a one-year corporal (*Einj.-Unteroffizier*)[23] (he was promoted to corporal on July 2, 1914).[24]

Dirlewanger fought his first encounters at Longwy-Longuyon in Belgium.[25] The German army's victorious march was arrested at the Longwy fortress.[26] Combat in this region lasted from August 21 to 27, 1914[27] (Dirlewanger participated in it from August 21 to 22).[28] The fighting has been described as extremely fierce. The storming German troops came under heavy bombardment and artillery fire. In the initial period of the battle, they had many wounded.[29]

On August 22, 1914, the assault on Bleid started.[30] The attack was launched from an elevation northeast of the town. The grenadier regiment (*Grenadierregiment*) set off from the brigade's right flank, while the 124th Infantry Regiment (Infanterieregiment 124, I.R. 124) moved from the left.[31]

Although the machine gun company (*MG Kompanie*) was excellently positioned to fire at their opponents, it did not manage to hold back the counterattacking French soldiers. As a result, it suffered significant casualties in both killed and wounded and was forced to save itself by drawing back to a forest. The soldiers were unlucky and ended up in a gorge during their retreat, where they suffered further casualties.[32] This is probably when Dirlewanger was seriously wounded in his foot and left arm. These were the first injuries that he sustained in combat. His convalescence took a long time: From August 22 to December 18, 1914, he stayed in several hospitals.[33]

After leaving the Esslingen hospital, he was promoted[34] and in 1915 was appointed lieutenant (*Leutnant*). Dirlewanger was also decorated for the first time (Iron Cross, 2nd Class).[35] From that point up to November 30, 1916, he commanded a platoon.[36]

Fighting in the Forest of Argonne had already started in 1914. Due to his injuries, Dirlewanger did not take part in them. He returned to the 123rd Grenadier Regiment in only mid-1915 and participated in military action from July 27 to September 8.

At 8:00 a.m. on September 8, heavy fighting started. A hailstorm of bullets and grenades fell both on German and French trenches.[37] In one of the strikes, Oskar Dirlewanger was wounded once again. During hand-to-hand fighting, grenade shrapnel tore a tendon in his left hand, and his opponent bayoneted him in the shoulder. He was sent to a hospital again, where he stayed until January 26, 1916.[38] The 123rd Grenadier Regiment fought in the Forest of Argonne until the end of 1915.[39] Dirlewanger's left hand was scarred, and according to his brother, Paul, his left palm stayed stiff forever, and Oskar was able to bend only his thumb. As a result, a medical commission found him to have a disability of 40 percent.[40] For his heroic deeds, he was decorated with a Gold Württemberg Medal for Bravery on October 4, 1915.

On April 22, 1915, during the fighting at Ypres in France, the Germans used chemical weapons for the first time. None of the soldiers from the French colonial troops or the Canadian infantry had a gas mask, even though the higher command knew of the forthcoming gas attack. Fifteen thousand soldiers died as its result. Germany's violation of the 1907 Hague Convention by using chemical warfare agents would cause other armies to employ that technology in the future. Soon the war was to have a giant impact on the daily lives of the civilian population. In 1915 the Allies managed to cause the first significant supply problems through blockades, and rationing of food articles was introduced as a result. At the beginning of the year, it was decreed that bread and flour (the daily ration being 225 grams per person) would be available only with rationing cards. Economizing as far as possible during cooking was ordered, and the use of kitchen waste was suggested. Hunger was present in many homes. We do not know how Dirlewanger's family in Essen survived this difficult period.

In 1916, the most important action on the Western Front was the heavy fighting for Verdun, which lasted from February to June 1916 and ultimately brought no success to the German side. The second important battle took place by the Somme (from June to November 1916). It involved the first use of tanks (by the British side). The Germans lost 500,000 people in total; the French, 200,000; and the British around 555,000. The battle of Verdun frustrated German plans to end the war in 1916. It was the greatest German defeat since the Battle of the Marne.

In September 1916, due to the permanent damage to his health, Dirlewanger was assigned to staff work in the 7th Landwehr Division (7. Ldw. Division) and was employed there until February 1917.[41] From November 1, 1916, he taught a training course for this division as a machine gun instructor.[42]

He was not the type of person who liked to spend his time "sitting at a desk." Vitality and the need to act were his chief characteristics, and so staff work did not turn out to be a sufficient challenge for him. He volunteered to go to the front once again.[43] On December 30, 1916, he was appointed the commander of an assault company of the 7th Infantry Division (7. Inf. Div.), which he led until March 26, 1917.[44] He probably stayed in Lorraine with his company until mid-February.[45]

In 1917 the situation in czarist Russia changed drastically. Discontent among Russian soldiers was so great that whole units refused to carry out orders. Strikes erupted in Petrograd (St. Petersburg), with demonstrations against the tragic supply situation. Revolution broke out. On March 10, martial law was declared in Petrograd and a general strike began in all of Russia. Czar Nicholas II abdicated on March 15. At this time, Dirlewanger was probably already fighting on the Eastern Front.

Christian Ingrao wrote, "We have no information about his [Dirlewanger's] experiences . . . during the last part of the war."[46] He is wrong. Dirlewanger's military service book, listing all the battles he took part in, has been preserved. From March 27, 1917 to October 1, 1918, he commanded the 2nd Machine Gun Company of the 121st Infantry Regiment (2. M. G. K. Ldw. Inf. Regts. 121), belonging to the 7th Landwehr Division.[47] At that time he was in Ukraine, where between May 19 and December 1, 1917, he took part in the fighting on the Stokhid. After these clashes ended, the company rested there until February 1918.[48]

From February 18 to mid-June 1918, Dirlewanger was still fighting in Ukraine.[49] Between April 28 and 30, there were clashes north of Taganrog, near the town of "Potrovstaya"[50] (probably Pokrovskoye, Покровское). On the last day of combat, Dirlewanger was wounded for the fourth time. He suffered a light bullet wound to his left arm.[51] In addition to smaller battles, he also fought at Taganrog and Bataysk.[52]

From June 22 to October 29, 1918, his unit took part in the occupation of Ukraine.[53] During this time, he was decorated again, receiving the Iron Cross, 1st Class, in July and the Black Wound Badge in September.[54] On October 2, he took command of the 2nd Battalion of the 121st Infantry Regiment (2. Btl. 121.) and commanded it until the end of the war.[55]

After the end of the action in Ukraine, from October 30 to November 25, 1918, the battalion commanded by Dirlewanger took part in the occupation of Romania.[56] On November 11, 1918, the armistice between the Allies and Germany was signed in a staff wagon in the French Compiègne. Many Germans perceived the war that ended in capitulation to be a national catastrophe, a "stab in the back." In consequence, the kaiser abdicated, and the Weimar Republic was proclaimed. On June 28, 1919, in the Hall of Mirrors at the Palace of Versailles, the countries of the victorious coalition signed a peace treaty with Germany.[57]

Because of the Russian October Revolution, Dirlewanger's division was in danger of being interned in Romania. A 1932 edition of the newspaper *Sangerhäuser Kreiszeitung* quoted a statement by a former soldier from Dirlewanger's regiment, describing his memories about the end of the war:

> When the revolution broke out, our battalion was on a road leading from south Russia towards the fatherland and was to be interned in Romania. Lieutenant Dirlewanger decided that we would push through and go back to our fatherland. Soldiers from other companies which were—at last some of them—dissatisfied with their officers voluntarily placed themselves under the command of lieutenant D. He led the people back to their fatherland, all the while preserving the previous discipline, despite great dangers, and sparing no effort. It is a rare situation for an officer to be honoured as much as our comrade in arms Dirlewanger was after the successful return, which the soldiers owe only to him. He saved six hundred people from internment, which was the experience of so many military formations before us and after us.[58]

From Romania, Dirlewanger led the soldiers through Hungary and Austria. The group started out on November 26 and reached Germany on December 28, 1918.[59]

The end of the First World War met Dirlewanger as a lieutenant of reserves (*Oberleutnant der Reserve*).[60] In June 1919, his service was very positively assessed, with the statement that his "resourcefulness, bravery, and personal courage were an excellent model for soldiers."[61]

1.3. Studies, and Professional and Military Career

Studies

At the turn of 1918 and 1919, Oskar Dirlewanger passed the entrance examinations to the Mannheim School of Commerce and studied trade and business administration (*Handels- und Betriebswirtschaftslehre*).[62] Due to his participation in anti-Semitic incidents, he had some problems with the college authorities;[63] despite this, in March 1921 he was awarded the professional title of qualified economist (*Diplomkaufmann*).[64] He was already then a great proponent of *volkism*. As Ingrao wrote, from 1919 he belonged to the organization Deutschvölkische Schutz und Trutzbund,[65] which propagated revolutionary nationalist ideas and hatred for Jews.[66]

Dirlewanger then went on to study in Frankfurt am Mein at the Johann Wolfgang Goethe University.[67] In 1922, he lived there at Leipzigerstrasse.[68] In August 1925, he earned a doctorate in political sciences on the basis of the thesis "On the Critique of the Theory of Planned Control of the Economy" ("Zur Kritik des Gedankens einer planmässigen Leitung der Wirtschaft").[69] It numbered over a hundred pages, making it slightly longer than other works from the period.[70] In his introduction, Dirlewanger presented the economic and political history of the Reich from 1871. He stated that between 1870 and 1914, the number of inhabitants of the German state increased from thirty to seventy million, which was due to an improvement in living standards resulting from economic development, which was halted by the outbreak of the First World War. He indicated that the developmental economy "then transformed into a deficit economy, which required a rapid change in the state's economic policy. The latter then resorted to mechanisms such as command organization, requisition, [and] setting and control of prices; that is, to a system of state intervention, which was synonymous with centralization and bureaucratization."[71]

Dirlewanger described the First World War and the peace settlement according to the received view of the time: Germany had suffered an injustice and had been "stabbed in the back." His work combined memories of the bygone war, fears of an economic nature, and anti-Communist beliefs. He criticized the Communist project of collectivization and claimed that economic planning could be done only in wartime.[72] He wrote, "It is beneficial to investigate the matter of planned control of the economy, if such a one is to be implemented when the vital need of the nation (for example, the defense of the country's territory) leads to the necessity of planned organization and centralized management of the economy. If the condition for the appearance of such a phenomenon is an attitude of the people resembling the one from 1914, when minds were filled with a pure and true love for the fatherland, then the ethical conditions for a planned economy would be partially met."[73] In the summary he indicated that economic centralization and planning were the main conditions of victory: "During a future war, because of the geographical situation of our fatherland we must reckon with a deficit economy despite all possible preparations. And any objections against planned control of the economy should be relegated to the background, given the nationwide goal of creating, through planned control of the economy, of economic conditions conducive to the waging of war."[74]

The university authorities ordered Dirlewanger to change the conclusions of his thesis by January 9, 1924, threatening to void his diploma otherwise. He had not done so by early 1925. So, the deadline was moved to April 15, 1925.[75] This changed nothing.

On October 1, 1922, he joined the NSDAP, with the number 12,517,[76] but was not a member long, since he was soon expelled. Around this time, he was arrested for failing to comply with the disarmament laws.[77]

The situation in the country was becoming increasingly favorable to the NSDAP. In January 1923, France, using a delay in war reparation payments by Germany as a pretext, occupied the Ruhr. After an appeal by Chancellor Wilhelm Cuno, the Germans used passive resistance, striking and seeking to decrease production. The region became economically isolated, and the fall in the value of the reichsmark slipped out of control. It was only in September that the new government headed by Gustav Stresemann called for an end to passive resistance.

In Bavaria the right became increasingly radicalized. In September 1923, the SA (Sturmabteilungen der NSDAP), a Freikorps division from Oberland, and the paramilitary organization Reichsflagge (Imperial War Flag Society) led by Ernst Röhm formed the German Battle League (Deutsche Kampfbund).[78] The first NSDAP militias emerged in mid-1921.[79] They were initially supposed to protect Nazi meetings and disperse rival parties' rallies. Soon, leadership of the German Battle League was assumed by Adolf Hitler, and behind the scenes stood General Erich Ludendorff, former quartermaster general of the Imperial Army and chief of the general staff. Around this time, the Bavarian government announced a state of emergency.[80]

The *Kampfbund* planned to proclaim a dictatorship in Munich led by Hitler and Ludendorff. On the evening of November 8, 1923, in Bürgerbräukeller in that city, an opportunity for carrying out the putsch arose. Accompanied by armed supporters, Hitler forced his way into a rally,[81] announced that the Bavarian government was overthrown, and declared that he was taking power as the chief of a temporary national government. The next day, his supporters attempted to take control of the Munich city center, but the coup ultimately failed in Feldernhalle,[82] when the police started shooting at the revolutionaries.[83] Oskar Dirlewanger tried to join the putschists, traveling with gendarmerie from Stuttgart.[84]

Freikorps, Panzerzug Dirlewanger

During his time as a student (1919–21), Dirlewanger was deeply involved in the activity of the Freikorps[85] and the fight against the Communists. In the years 1919–23 he belonged to Freikorps Epp, Haas, and Sprösser.[86] He participated in putting down many Communist uprisings in Württemberg, Westphalia, and Thuringia.[87] In that period he was penalized twice for concealing weapons. In the district court in Nordhausen in Thuringia, proceedings were started against him for illegal arms possession and use, allegedly in self-defense.[88] Moreover, he was briefly imprisoned in Mosbach in Baden, and after being released he left for Silesia to fight in one of the Freikorps units there.[89]

In 1919, Dirlewanger formed a temporary defense platoon and fought as its leader against Communists in various parts of the republic.[90] In that same year, he suppressed a Communist general strike in the towns of Backnang, Kornwestheim, Esslingen, Untertürkheim, Aalen, and Schorndorf, and a year later in Heidenheim,[91] and also Communist revolts during the so-called Bloody May (Mai-Unruhen) unrest in Stuttgart and Esslingen.

In 1920, he participated in clashes in the Ruhr, Dortmund, and Essen,[92] which has been described as follows: "Like during earlier riots, on March 13, 1920, he once again stepped forward to keep peace and order."[93]

In 1920, Dirlewanger was active in units protecting stations and railways in Stuttgart. In this time of crises and frequent strikes, special defense units were formed, which made sure that trains could pass through safely and that the mail was delivered. Dirlewanger held the function of commander of a railway protection platoon (Geschützter Zug Dirlewanger) in Stuttgart at least from March 18, 1920: he assigned provisions, arms, and ammunition to his subordinates.[94] There were several platoons of this type operating in Stuttgart. According to orders from March 18 and 23, the unit protecting railways in Stuttgart comprised the following sections:

1. Main Railway Station Group, commanded by Scharführer Bücheler (later called Bücheler's Group):

"Hofmann" platoon

"Ruf" platoon

"Strobel" platoon

"Fahrion" platoon (at Kronenstrasse, first mentioned in the order of March 23, 1920)

"Bühler" platoon (assault platoon)

"Kirchner" platoon (machine guns, M.G.)

2. Group in the General Directorate building, commanded by Scharführer Kurz (later called Kurz's Group):

"Entenmann" platoon

"Löble" platoon (not mentioned in the order of March 23, 1920)

"Baumgärtner" platoon (first mentioned in the order of March 23, 1920)

"Böhm" platoon, at the New Railway Station / Neuer Bahnhof (first mentioned in the order of March 23, 1920)

3. "Neuer Bahnhof" platoon (Zugführer Gaggstetter), incorporated on March 23, 1920, into the Kurz Group and moved to the post of New Railway Station, Tower

4. Defense Platoon, Führer Dirlewanger[95]

As a distinguishing sign, persons belonging to these units wore special green armbands.[96]

In March 1920, after the Kapp Putsch was put down,[97] Communist rioting broke out in the Ruhr. In his book *Antifaschisten in SS-Uniform*, Hans Peter Klausch states that an armored train commanded by Dirlewanger was directed to suppress it. The Württemberg Reichswehr-Brigade 13 under the command of Gen. Otto Haas was sent into action, as was a volunteer unit commanded by Sprösser. Freikorps Haas, of which Dirlewanger was a member, was incorporated into the Reichswehr-Brigade. Next, the armored train commanded by Dirlewanger was merged into Gruppe Division Haas: it operated in Dortmund, Iserlohn, and Essen. Dirlewanger participated in the Freikorps and Reichswehr operations known as the "white terror" (*weißen Terror*). Over their course, members of Reichswehr-Schützen-Brigade 21, previously known as Freikorps Epp, together with soldiers of Reichswehr-Schützen-Regiment 41, carried out a massacre at Pelkum, during which three hundred Communist workers were shot. Klausch states that a unit commanded by Dirlewanger (Panzerzug IV) took part in this.[98]

In August 1920 the station and railway defense divisions in Stuttgart were ordered to maintain battle readiness and sentry patrols before buildings were strengthened.[99] On August 29, Dirlewanger's troops were ordered to transfer to the station at Untertürkheim, near Stuttgart (now a part of Stuttgart). He was to protect the cars of another defense platoon there.[100] Untertürkheim was the location of Daimler-Motoren-Gesellschaft, a company that faced numerous problems (economic crisis, worker strikes) in the 1920s.

On August 30, Dirlewanger and his subordinates were quartered in the village of Kornwestheim, between Ludwigsburg and Stuttgart.[101] They stationed there until September 1 and then were transferred to Heilbronn by order no. 8 of September 2.[102]

Because of the tempestuous situation and numerous strikes, in 1920 railway and station defense units were constantly being enlarged and expanded. New soldiers were drafted, and individual platoons were regularly moved about. The platoon commanded by Oskar Dirlewanger was transferred from Heilbronn to Aalen on September 3, 1920.[103] It did not stay there long, stationing in Stuttgart from September 4 to 7.[104]

In September 1920 the situation in Stuttgart and its neighboring area was tense. Strikes and mutinies kept breaking out, including among workers of Daimler-Motoren-Gesellschaft.[105] According to order 13 of September 5, 1920, Dirlewanger's and Eckart's defense platoons were to oversee trains and keep them under steam at Post 3 in Stuttgart.[106] On the next day, Eckart's platoon was freed from this duty, and half of the people were released. The remaining thirty-five stayed under Dirlewanger's command. Those released from duty were to clean arms, while Dirlewanger's people were still charged with keeping trains in readiness.[107]

On September 7, 1920, Dirlewanger and his subordinates were once again transferred, this time to the area of the railway yard in "Engl. [Englisch] Garten."[108] Two days later, they were awarded time to rest from duty from 8:00 to 11:00 a.m.[109]

Oskar Dirlewanger particularly distinguished himself while putting down the Communist uprising in Sangerhausen in Saxony on Easter Saturday, March 26, 1921. The Communists fought under the command of Max Hölz, who in 1920 had formed a "Red Guard" of around 350 people and together with them took part in the Kapp Putsch. The workers' emotions did not abate after the revolt failed. Their strike intensified until it led to an outbreak of a workers' revolution.

In March 1921, Communist revolts erupted in central Germany: This was the so-called March Action, caused by the workers' dissatisfaction with the situation. In towns of the Vogtland region (Bavaria, Saxony, and Thuringia), posters appeared with appeals to join the ranks of the unit led by Hölz, who was arming workers, the unemployed, and miners and calling for them to start fighting the police. Around five hundred people joined his unit. He organized them into assault groups, which in that region plundered, stole, committed arson, blew up railway lines and derailed trains, and called for a Soviet Republic to be formed. The escalating acts of violence and growth of his forces caused Hölz to gradually lose control over the revolution, which was bloodily suppressed in late March 1921. On April 1, in Beesenstedt the last group of revolutionists led by Hölz was destroyed and the strike collapsed. Hölz himself fled to Berlin and was arrested there on April 15, 1921.[110]

The final battle at the Sangerhausen railway station on Easter Saturday was very tough, with machine guns and grenades being used. Not only Oskar Dirlewanger, but also his brother, Paul, took part in the action. German regiments attracted mainly railway employees—workers, shunters, train drivers, but not exclusively; there were also many students (such as the two Dirlewangers), a notarial trainee, and salesmen. In total, 158 men assembled for battle on the anti-Communist side.[111] Heavy fighting lasted until 2:00 a.m. and ended in the defeat of the Communists, who fled. In May 1934 the *Heilbronner Tagblatt* newspaper wrote that of Dirlewanger's forty-two comrades, twenty-two (including him) were injured, and one was killed.[112] These data are in accordance with the list of dead and wounded in the Sangerhausen fighting. The mortal victim was train driver Wilhelm Müller. Oskar Dirlewanger sustained a light bullet wound to the head and buttock during the campaign, on April 12, 1921. He was not hospitalized and remained with his troops.[113]

In June 1932 the mayor of Sangerhausen invited the veterans of the battle to celebrations of the victory. Oskar Dirlewanger also wrote a letter to his companions in arms who fought in his regiment, inviting them and asking them to confirm their presence. On the first day of the event, the program included a visit to the Rose Garden and a meeting with the mayor at the

Prussian Station (Preussischen Hof). Dirlewanger stated that on the next day, the veterans would be driven in private cars to the Kyffhäuser Monument,[114] located at the top of Kyffhäuser Hill in Thuringia.[115]

As a reward for his heroic actions, in 1934 Dirlewanger was granted honorary citizenship of Sangerhausen,[116] and the main square of the town was named after him. The ceremony took place on Saturday, June 10, 1934, in the Heilbronn Town Hall. The Sunday paper described it as a short but very solemn occasion, which was presided over by Heilbronn's mayor, Gültig. He was accompanied by Sangerhausen mayor Dr. Heß. Its participants included important party members from the region: Zeller, Captain Schmidt, and the chief of police, Ortsgruppenleiter[117] Reppmann. Dirlewanger was visibly moved.[118]

Freikorps Holz, Uprising in Upper Silesia

Because of his rakish and rebellious character, Oskar Dirlewanger constantly walked a fine line versus the law. His activity in the Freikorps and the SA brought him many problems. After the First World War, great anxiety was caused in the Weimar Republic by the fact that many social groups owned arms, and thus laws regulating this issue were instituted. The disarmament act was adopted. As a militia activist, Dirlewanger broke the prohibition on possession of arms and was arrested as a result. Proceedings were instigated against him in Nordhausen, and he was imprisoned in the Bavarian Mosbach.[119] In the years 1919–21, he was punished at least twice for possessing arms. After the Sangerhausen action in 1921, he was arrested for the third time and imprisoned for two weeks for owning arms. These were not his only encounters with the judicial system.

Right after his release from prison, in June 1921, Dirlewanger joined Freikorps Holz, and as part of that unit he participated in the suppression of the Polish uprising in Upper Silesia.[120] He fought against miners and smelter workers in Gleiwitz (Gliwice).[121] Neither his prison term nor his activity in Freikorps Holz impeded him in his studies: he completed them and obtained the professional title of qualified economist (*Diplomkaufmann*).

The atmosphere in Silesia had been tense since the end of the First World War. In 1919, a special regulation was issued, according to which any activity promoting the annexation of Upper Silesia to Poland was to be deemed treason. This did not prevent further strikes and workers' manifestations. On August 17, 1919, at 2:00 a.m., the First Silesian Uprising broke out. The fighting spread through the Pszczyna, Rybnik, and Katowice Districts, and those that had a large percentage of Polish population. It did not last long: On August

24, 1919, because of the tragic situation of the insurgents, increasing reprisals against the populace by the German authorities, and the overwhelming, better-armed German forces, the struggle was discontinued.

The future of Upper Silesia was to be decided in a plebiscite; however, before it was held, on the night of August 19, 1920, the Second Silesian Uprising erupted. Its goal was achieved, the strength of Polish military organizations was demonstrated, and, most importantly, the German system of control over the plebiscite area was demolished.

The plebiscite that was to decide about the possession of Upper Silesia was held on March 20, 1921. There were 1,190,637 votes cast; 479,365 Silesians (40.3 percent) voted for Poland, and 707,393 (59.4 percent) for Germany. This outcome did not satisfy either of the sides. According to the results, Poland was to take 25 percent of the plebiscite area, mainly parts with no heavy industry. This situation led to the outbreak of the Third Silesian Uprising on the night of May 2, 1921. It lasted two months. First, nine railway bridges were blown up, which made it impossible for the Germans to bring in reinforcements. The insurgent forces initially numbered 39,000, and later even 45,000. They were divided into three operational groups: "East," "North," and "South." Within a week, they managed to seize the whole plebiscite area. The heavy fighting ended in a military draw. On June 25, 1921, in Błotnica Strzelecka (Blottnitz) an armistice was signed, and in effect part of the region with strategically significant industry fell to the Second Republic.[122]

For one day of fighting as a soldier of Freikorps Holz, Dirlewanger received a salary of fifty German marks. He is said to have drunk it all away.[123]

Professional Career, NSDAP, SA

After the end of operations in Upper Silesia, Dirlewanger was dismissed from the Freikorps because of his negative and disparaging attitude toward the Weimar Republic. He then joined Organization Consul, a group that attacked leading figures of the democratic Weimar system.[124] It was founded in 1921 by Hermann Ehrhardt and Manfred von Killinger.[125] Initially, it was called the Association of Ehrhardt's Former Officers. Ehrhardt[126] was a right-wing radical who wished for the Republican order to be overthrown, and hated Jews, Communists, and Socialists.[127] The formation included mainly former members of the Freikorps, also those who had operated in Upper Silesia.[128] They swore an oath of loyalty, and revealing the organization's secrets was punished by death.[129]

Organization Consul primarily attempted to destabilize the democratic system of the Weimar Republic. To this end, its members carried out assassinations of well-known politicians who in their opinion were a danger to Germany's interests. On June 5, 1921, they murdered Karl Gereis, the leader of Bavaria's Independent Social Democratic Party of Germany (USPD).[130] The most-spectacular actions conducted by Organization Consul were the assassinations of Minister of Finance Matthias Erzberger (August 26, 1921) and Minister of Foreign Affairs Walther Rathenau, a democrat of Jewish heritage (June 24, 1922).[131] As investigators in the 1970s noted, Dirlewanger supported these activities and even defended them. It was discovered that in 1923 at the School of Commerce in Mannheim, where he was studying, he gave a lecture in which he justified these actions by referring to the terror of the Weimar provisions.[132] However, in 1923 he was already living in Frankfurt am Mein, so these events likely took place at the university there.[133]

After completing his studies, Dirlewanger worked as a volunteer in banks in Osterburken and Stuttgart.[134] He often changed positions and place of residence. In 1925, he was employed by Schwäbische Treuhand AG in Stuttgart.[135] Next, he became an administrative employee[136] or managing director[137] at the Kornicker Jewish textile warehouse in Erfurt. He worked there from September 1, 1928, to December 31, 1931.[138] At the end of 1931, he became an independent tax advisor in Esslingen.[139] At Kornicker he defrauded a large amount of money. Instead of using these sums to participate in tenders, he transferred them to the SA. He was arraigned on this charge in the district court in Erfurt and banned from working in commerce.[140]

Nothing in 1928 indicated the NSDAP's impending success and seizure of power. In the elections the party won only 2.6 percent of votes. It was believed that the NSDAP had no influence over the masses.[141] However, public sentiment in the declining Weimar Republic was radicalizing. Economic problems, the consequences of the global crisis, unemployment, inflation, and the unstable political situation pushed many people toward Hitler and his party. Moreover, many former soldiers could not understand Germany's defeat in the war. As the veteran Herbert Richter remembered,

> We did wonder, because we didn't feel beaten at all. The frontline soldiers didn't feel themselves beaten, and we were wondering why the armistice was happening so quickly, and why we had to vacate all our positions in such a hurry, because we were still standing in enemy territory, and we thought all this was strange. . . . We were angry because we did not feel we had come to the end of our strength.[142]

Dirlewanger was no stranger to these feelings. The myth of the "stab in the back" was becoming increasingly popular with the populace.

With his speeches, Hitler resonated with the prevailing mood of the time and fascinated millions of Germans, whom he promised a bright future for Great Germany. His performances drew new members. In the 1930s, thanks to the success of the NSDAP in the Reichstag elections, Hitler won a political platform. The Nazis obtained 18.3 percent of votes, and the Communist Party of Germany 13.1 percent. Chancellor Heinrich Brüning, not wanting to work with a Reichstag divided between Nazis and Communists, started to circumvent it. He ruled the country through Article 48 of the constitution: He issued emergency decrees, which were signed by President Paul von Hindenburg.[143] German democracy had entered its decline. In the April 1932 election, Hindenburg defeated Hitler by a majority of six million votes, but the leader of the national Socialist Party entrenched his political position. He was aiming to become chancellor of the Reich.

On March 1, 1932, Dirlewanger joined the NSDAP for the second time (with the number 1,098,716),[144] and on April 1, he became a member of the SA as *SA-Sturmführer*.[145] On July 31, 1932, the NSDAP won 37.4 percent of votes in the Reichstag election and became the largest parliamentary force.[146] The victory was secured through gigantic expenditure on a propaganda campaign and activity of all party and SA members.

A day after the Reichstag election, on August 1, 1932, the SA and SS carried out a series of bomb attacks and assassinations of NSDAP opponents in Königsberg. Over the next days, the terror spread to all East Prussia and Silesia.[147]

Oskar Dirlewanger worked actively toward this victory. Together with other SA militia members, in July 1932 he participated in storming the headquarters of a trade union in Esslingen. Several Communist and social-democratic activists were then arrested. They were imprisoned in the cellar of the local SA headquarters and beaten. Many of these people were later sent to penal (concentration) camps in Esterwegen and Börgermoor (Börger-Moor).[148] Interestingly, no mention of this incident may be found in July 1932 issues of the *Esslinger Zeitung*.

Dirlewanger's third encounter with the courts, this time in Stuttgart, happened in connection with this attack. Thanks to the intervention of the commander of the Southwest SS regional command (*SS-Oberabschnittsführer Südwest*) in Stuttgart, SS-Brigadeführer Dr. Werner Best, he managed to avoid punishment. The proceedings, which concerned a serious breach of the peace, were discontinued.[149]

At the start of the 1930s, Dirlewanger was completely committed to the NSDAP. In 1932 in the Brown House,[150] he reported to Heinrich Himmler that he and his people were ready to fight for the party at any time.[151]

In December 1932, he was charged with "affray" before the district court in Stuttgart.[152] We do not know if he was convicted.

On January 30, 1933, Hitler became the chancellor of a coalition government, and half a year later the Nazis gained control of the whole state apparatus, changed the constitution, and became the dominant political force in the country. By July 1933 they had seized full power.

Dirlewanger was a very energetic activist of the Esslingen SA and climbed rapidly in the hierarchy. On August 2, 1933, he was appointed *SA-Scharführer*, and two days later, *Truppführer*. In August he took command of SA Battalion I/122 (Sturmbanne I/122), and on November 9, 1933, he was promoted to *Sturmführer*.[153]

His activity in the SA was a big help in his career. In September 1933, he became deputy director and, for several months, member of the managing board of the Heilbronn Labor Office.[154] His career, both administrative and military, gradually advanced. As the head of the Labor Office, he achieved propaganda successes that were extolled in the local press, the *Heilbronner Tagblatt* and the *Neckar-Zeitung*. Their headlines suggest that Oskar Dirlewanger was an important personage in the Heilbronn community. Issue no. 86 of the *Heilbronner Tagblatt* devoted two articles to him.

In the large headline of the first text, the newspaper tells of another great success by the Heilbronn Labor Office. The anonymous author

> wholeheartedly congratulates the "tireless director Dr. Dirlewanger" for the wonderful achievement of decreasing the number of unemployed from 4,260 to 2,206 and thanks him for his help in finding work for unemployed war veterans: the office could thus "proudly report to the Führer that the order had been carried out!"[155]

The second article mentions fighting against Communists commanded by Max Hölz, including in Sangerhausen. Thirteen years after those events, the national-socialist press honored party member Oskar Dirlewanger.[156]

While he was employed by the Labor Office, Dirlewanger lived in Heilbronn at Kaiserstrasse 50,[157] in photographer Fleischmann's house. The building had been erected at the turn of the years 1905 and 1906 according to a design by the renowned architects Emil Beutinger and Adolf Steiner. It was topped by two monumental statues and was a very exclusive location. Its construction cost five thousand German marks. The ground floor hosted shops, an office, and cloakroom space; the first floor held five rooms, including a bathroom and a kitchen; and the second floor contained a photographer's atelier, three rooms, a bathroom, and a kitchen. The stairwell contained a lift.[158] The fact that Dirlewanger moved into such a luxurious building located on Heilbronn's main thoroughfare indicates his high social status in that period. The building did not survive to the present. It was destroyed on December 4, 1944, in the Allied bombing of Heilbronn, together with all the town center. Today, the Klosterhof shopping center stands in its place.

Problems with the Law

Dirlewanger was very attracted to women, and that feeling was reciprocated. His female acquaintances described him as a handsome figure and gallant gentleman. Dirlewanger's interest in the fair sex became apparent in his youth and was later the cause of many problems with the judiciary. In 1936, court records stated that "the only weakness of his character is his liking for the female sex."[159]

This weakness, and the connected court case, have caused authors to paint Dirlewanger as a rapist and a sadist. The case files do not confirm the sexual perversions attributed to him. French MacLean, frequently quoted by other authors (e.g., Alexandra Richie), has written that Dirlewanger "repeatedly had sex in the official car of the Labor Office with girls who were less than 14 years old" and sexually abused fourteen-year-old Anneliese "four or five times in the period of February to mid-July 1934 in order to satisfy his sexual appetite." He indicated that during one of these meetings, the girl was dressed in a BDM (Bund Deutscher Mädel, Band of German Maidens) uniform.[160] Below I present court records, from which a slightly different picture emerges.

Furthermore, according to MacLean, on April 14, 1934, Dirlewanger "drove the official car of the Labor Office into a ditch while completely drunk; on this occasion a female passenger was severely hurt and he fled the scene of the accident."[161] The accident did take place, but its course was completely different, which I also describe further on.

While carrying out his duties for the SA, Dirlewanger met many BDM members. In February 1934, four of them were delegated to the SA in order to sew tabs and armbands onto SA members' uniforms. As a reward and to thank them for their work, Dirlewanger invited them to café Eyth for coffee, cake, and whipped cream. Among them was Anneliese B., who was then not quite fourteen. Dirlewanger formed a closer relationship with her. In the following weeks, they often passed each other in the street, exchanging greetings and polite conversation. The case files draw a picture of a gradually deepening acquaintance, which in May or early June 1934 became closer. Court documents contain many details concerning the intimate relations and behaviors of Dirlewanger and Annelise B. They describe joint trips to neighboring towns: Neuenstadt am Kocher, Stuttgart, and Öhringen. Annelise's friend Alma G. took part in one of these excursions. Anneliese's parents agreed to these trips, and the girl received presents from Dirlewanger, including a bathing suit for her birthday.[162]

The court hearing caused quite a stir in Heilbronn and likely the whole region. Dirlewanger was a very well-known and respected figure, and so the proceeding was a source of much controversy and interest. The matter gained wide coverage in the press. For at least three days in a row, the *Heilbronner Tagblatt* and *Neckar-Zeitung* published articles on the subject: "Heute vor der Großen Strafkammer: Prozeß gegen Dr. Dirlewanger"; "Prozeß Dr. Dirlewanger: Der Mann, der an der Türe horchte; Wird das Gericht diesem Zeugen glauben?"; "2 Jahre Zuchthaus: Das Urteil gegen Dr. Dirlewanger"; and "2 Jahre Zuchthaus für Dr. Dirlewanger: Die Plädoyers."[163] They wrote that two court experts and as many as forty-one witnesses had been called on for the case. Dirlewanger was accused of an offense against public decency and two minor offences involving road transport. Dr. Schliz was in charge of the case as public prosecutor general, with Dr. Stubbe acting for the defense. The court case aroused such great interest among Heilbronn inhabitants that the hearing room in the criminal court was filled to the very last seat.

Dirlewanger did not deny before the court that he had maintained a close relationship with Annelise, and he even described more meetings than she had. According to their testimonies, they probably met from May to July 1934. To defend himself against the charges, Dirlewanger stated that he had thought Annelise to be sixteen, almost seventeen years old, and that he had been misled by her. He added that the girl had told him she attended the School of Commerce. The defense called on two witnesses. The first was an acquaintance of Dirlewanger's from Esslingen, the mechanic Eichbauer, who testified that he had heard Annelise tell Dirlewanger that her seventeenth birthday was approaching, and that in response the latter had hummed a fragment of "Schön sind die Mädchen von 17, 18 Jahr," a well-known song in those times. The other witness, Willi Rosenfeld, lived in a room next to Dirlewanger's and also stated that he had heard a conversation in which Annelise claimed to be seventeen. Their testimonies were not deemed reliable.[164] Many people spoke in Dirlewanger's defense, emphasizing his merits as a soldier, commander of the armored train, and NSDAP activist. Some stated that Dirlewanger "is not choosy when it comes to women" and "just takes what is offered to him."[165]

During the trial, two of Dirlewanger's previous partners gave testimonies against him: Rosa M., then a twenty-year-old leader in the BDM and Frida S., a twenty-year-old saleswoman. So did Annelise's sixteen-year-old friend, Alma G. (she stated that during their joint trip to Stuttgart on June 16, 1934, Dirlewanger tried to molest her). Also, fourteen-year-old Gertrud W. testified against Dirlewanger, indicating that he had given her a lift from Flein to Heilbronn and tried to touch her.[166] In accordance with §154 StPO, Gertrud W. and Alma G. filed separate complaints with the prosecution.[167]

Court documents and the detailed opinion of a court-appointed medical doctor, Dr. Graner, indicate that Annelise B. was not raped. Testimonies state that she had a close, intimate relationship with Dirlewanger, and as a result of it he molested her sexually. The court-appointed doctor's opinion undermined Dirlewanger's line of defense that he could have believed Annelise to be sixteen. The doctor stated that the girl's behavior, looks, and figure suggested her age of fourteen years.[168]

As a person accused of a sexual crime, Dirlewanger was held in detention by July 22, 1934.[169] Although he had previously committed various misdemeanors, he had never been convicted, always evading the justice system.

Before going into detention, on Saturday, July 14, 1934, Dirlewanger organized an event in Flein near Heilbronn for thirty-eight of his colleagues from the Heilbronn Labor Office. He did this to thank them for their support and to celebrate the reception of the honorary citizenship of Sangerhausen.[170] The party was long, and its participants returned to their homes between 2:00 and 4:00 a.m. Dirlewanger demonstrated a particular propensity for trouble, and over the course of that night he was responsible for two separate car accidents under the influence of alcohol. He caused the first as he was returning from Flein between 2:00 and 3:00 a.m. in his government car with the number plate III D 7472. He turned so sharply left into Fleinerstrasse from Kiliansplatz that he hit a woman who had been standing there, knocking her about. He did not even notice and later explained that he turned so sharply because he wanted to avoid a cyclist. Nobody apart from Dirlewanger had actually seen a cyclist.

Around an hour later, Dirlewanger was driving a different car, also official, with the number plate III D 10313. He was taking four participants of the Flein party home. This time he fell out of the Heilbronnerstrasse road on a rut, flew over a meter-wide, 50 cm deep ditch, and then over a small garden, stopping on a concrete pillar. All the passengers were injured, and Dirlewanger himself was wounded in the head by a shard of glass from the windshield. During the investigation, it turned out that over the course of the celebration, he had drunk around 1.5 liters of wine ("six-quarters of a liter of wine"), one beer, and a glass of schnapps.[171]

A further investigation against Oskar Dirlewanger was launched at that time. The district court in Heilbronn opened preliminary investigation no. 84/34 against him, concerning unauthorized use of the Heilbronn Labor Office's car for private purposes. It also turned out that Dirlewanger had provided false information in the register of trips, and the court additionally looked into the matter of his embezzlement of money while employed at Kornicker in Erfurt.

The Penal Chamber session that took place on September 20–21, 1934, was presided over by prosecutor general Dr Schliz.[172] On September 21, shortly after 11:00 a.m., Dirlewanger was convicted of an offense of a sexual nature with a person under fourteen years of age and was sentenced to two years' heavy imprisonment.[173] In consequence, he was stripped of his academic title, expelled from the SA, and deprived of his military functions. He was forbidden to wear the uniform of the 123rd Grenadier Regiment (Gren. Regts. König Karl Nr. 123) and to use the military rank of lieutenant of reserves (*Oberleutnant der Reserve*).[174]

While serving his sentence, Dirlewanger still maintained that he had not been aware of Annelise's young age, and that the girl had misled him in that respect. He underlined that the conviction was the effect of political infighting and personal animosity from other party officials. He wrote that he had fallen victim to a conspiracy by local NSDAP officers: Kreisleiter Richard Drauz,[175] whose superior was Gauleiter Wilhelm Murr,[176] had accused Dirlewanger of stealing money from the "Winter Help" (Winterhilfswerk) project.[177]

While serving his sentence, Dirlewanger sent off appeals.[178] Already on November 13, 1934, he wrote to the prosecutor's office that Dr. Schliz had bent the regulations in his disfavor. The Ministry of Justice of the Third Reich did not respond to that appeal.[179] A year later, Dirlewanger wrote a denunciation to the Stuttgart prosecutor's office, claiming that during the hearing, an "unknown official" had committed malfeasance in office.[180] Many years later, during the Nuremberg trials, these allegations were confirmed by Gottlob Berger, who testified that the proceeding and the sentence were caused by a personal feud between Dirlewanger and another state official.[181]

Overall, during his period of activity in Heilbronn, Dirlewanger participated in infighting between the SA and NSDAP, where corruption and intrigue abounded. Within a short time, for reasons including excessive drinking and "mockery and garrulousness" (*Stänkerer und Schwätzer*), he was "got rid of" (*abzuservieren*) and he lost the position of leader of SA-Brigade 155. Because of his misbehavior while under the influence of alcohol, he was called the "evil spirit of Heilbronn" (der böse Geist in Heilbronn).[182]

Some time earlier, in April 1934, Dirlewanger also incensed the commanders of other SA units. On April 28, 1934, in Heilbronn he spoke negatively about the promotion of the brigade chief of staff (*Stabsführer der Brigade*), Sturmführer Garbsch. Dirlewanger believed that he had been awarded the honorary dagger wrongly.[183] As may be expected, this was badly received in Heilbronn SA circles, and, in effect, on May 5, disciplinary proceedings were initiated against Dirlewanger for "insulting remarks" (*abfällige Bemerkungen*) about brigade members, and he was sent on mandatory leave.[184] Dirlewanger objected to all the allegations made against him. He described the course of conversations in detail and presented his own witnesses.[185] This changed little. On August 3, 1934, the chief of the party district temporarily suspended him from the party.[186] In the SA, Dirlewanger had reached the rank of *Sturmführer*. A document of August 8 states that "Dirlewanger is destroying the reputation and discipline of the SA in Heilbronn. With his lifestyle he gives a very bad example, and so in the interest of the SA [he should be] immediately excluded from the SA."[187] On August 30, 1934, the SA court in Munich expelled him from the SA and condemned him for having committed a "reprehensible act."[188] This was in accordance with a regulation of June 30, 1934, in which Hitler commanded members of the SA, the party, and Hitlerjugend to observe moral principles, and ordered that any violations of these principles be punished by unconditional removal from the SA.[189] There was therefore no possibility of reducing the sentence.

It is possible that this situation contributed to Dirlewanger's removal from the ranks of the SA and NSDAP and had an impact on the course of the court proceedings and the issuing of a "guilty" verdict. Furthermore, Dirlewanger's statements and behavior resulted in a negative assessment of discipline within the SA in Heilbronn.[190]

Meanwhile, the investigation into the car accidents caused by Dirlewanger was suspended. He was ordered to pay the court fees and punished with a fine of a thousand marks or six months' imprisonment.[191]

Thanks to a conditional suspension of his sentence, he was freed from prison three months before the end of his term: on October 12, 1936, at 6:45 p.m.[192] A report from December 1936 that summed up the trial and the conditional release stated that Dirlewanger took the verdict calmly and caused no problems for officials. He was assessed to be a reasonable, decent, honest, and virtuous man. The report indicated that he had the nature of a warrior who was ready to make sacrifices for his fatherland, but that as a result of a false and unjust ruling, he had become embittered. There was therefore no certainty as to how the judgment could impact Dirlewanger's future life. However, the specialists were convinced that he was aware of the judgment's consequences and the weaknesses of his character.[193]

Before Dirlewanger was conditionally released from prison, the court of the NSDAP Württemberg-Hohenzollern District (Gaugericht Württemberg-Hohenzollern der N.S.D.A.P.) decided on February 26, 1936, that the judgment removing him from the SA and the party should be upheld. The conclusion emphasizes

> his bad lifestyle and punishable acts (offences against § 176 . . . , car accidents under the influence of alcohol, including injuries [suffered by] a passerby and leaving [the place of the accident] show him to be unworthy of [holding the position] of SA commander. . . . There is no place in the NSDAP for those who hurt teenage girls so shamelessly.[194]

In July 1937, it was decided that Dirlewanger did not have the right to wear the uniform of the 123rd Grenadier Regiment (Grend. Rgts. König Karl [5. württ.] No. 123) and to use the military rank of lieutenant of reserves (*Oberleutnant d.Res.a.D.*).[195]

After being released from the high-security prison in Ludwigsburg, Dirlewanger endeavored to have the trial repeated, since he did not agree with the verdict. These actions and the animosity of a gauleiter and imperial lieutenant (*Reichsstatthalter*) caused him to be imprisoned in a small concentration camp in Welzheim near Stuttgart. He was placed under preventive detention (*Sicherheitsverwahrung*), the main reason given being "disturbing the peace with vicious complaints."[196] The aforementioned camp was created in 1935 on the initiative of the Stuttgart Gestapo and operated until 1945. Inmates included German political prisoners and Jews. It functioned mainly as a transit camp—from it, prisoners were transported, among other places, to the Dachau concentration camp. Dirlewanger was not held there long: from February 14, to March 10, 1937.[197] The head of the Recruiting Office (Ergänzungsamt), SS-Brigadeführer Hanz B., intervened, and as he himself stated, it was only thanks to him that a further infringement of the law did not occur.[198] Thanks to the support of Hanz B. and Dirlewanger's friend Gottlob Berger, Oskar was released.

1.4. Spanish Civil War (1937–39)

In March 1937, Oskar Dirlewanger set off for the civil war in Spain.[199] He remained there until June 1939. Initially, he fought in the Spanish Foreign Legion and later transferred to the Condor Legion.[200] He was helped by the previously mentioned SS-Brigadeführer Hanz B.[201] In the Condor Legion, he served as an instructor and trainer in the Imker unit, among other positions. Most likely from November or December 1937 to March 1938, he was assigned to work in Special Staff "W" (Sonderstab "W").[202]

In the 1930s the whole world experienced a crisis, which also affected Spain. The monarchy became the target of numerous political attacks, and many conspiracies were formed, which led to its fall. On April 12, 1931, King Alphonse XIII organized municipal elections in which Republicans and Socialists won. A so-called Revolutionary Committee was formed, which took power on April 13, 1931, and transformed into a Provisional Government. A day later the republic was proclaimed. Alphonse XIII left the country.

Like in other countries in that period, rising unemployment and lack of hope for the future resulted in a radicalization of public sentiment. In Spain, many regions also strived for autonomy, which was achieved in Basque Country, Galicia, and Catalonia. Radical political forces demanded religious freedom; monasteries and churches were destroyed.

At the end of 1933, as a result of increasingly intensive fighting for power, a new parliamentary election was called, in which the Republicans lost a significant part of votes to the Confederation of Right-Wing Groups. Fascist parties such as Spanish Phalanx and National Syndicalists also appeared. Demonstrations and clashes with the police took place. In October 1934 in Catalonia, Basque Country, and Asturias, worker uprisings erupted, bloodily put down by Moroccan divisions commanded by Gen. Francisco Franco. After the pacification came mass arrests and numerous proceedings ending in death sentences.

The turmoil in Spain lasted over the next several years. A new parliamentary election was set for February 16, 1936. On January 15, left-wing groups formed a joint Popular Front, which won the majority of the votes. The III Republic was formed as a result. President Niceto Alcalá-Zamora decided that the cabinet would be headed by Manuel Azaña. The new government did not carry out a purge among the higher military leaders, which turned out to be a mistake. At the end of February 1936, the right-wing parties started preparing to seize power by force. The main role in the coup was to be played by higher officers of the military junta. Initially the start of the revolt was planned for April 20, 1936, but disagreements within the leadership of the conspiracy and a leak of information to the republic's government caused the date to be moved.

The situation in Spain became increasingly tense. The economic crisis deepened, unemployment rose, food production dropped, and political murders occurred. It is estimated that between February and July 1936, over 250 people died.

The putsch was planned for 5:00 p.m. on July 17, and the sign for its start was to be a sentence transmitted by a Ceuta station: "Over all of Spain the sky is clear." Gen. José Sanjurjo was to command the coup, and Gen. Franco was to take control of the Spanish Foreign Legion and native troops in Morocco. Next, he was to transfer them from Africa to the European continent. Gen. Emilio Mola, meanwhile, was to command action in northern Spain and cooperate with the monarchists, who had a particularly strong position in Navarre.

Despite successes achieved in the north and in Morocco, the rebels did not achieve an immediate victory. The Republican government kept around two-thirds of the country's territory under its rule.[203]

Through the whole Spanish Civil War, the Republicans maintained that German and Italian involvement in the war had been planned, and if it had not been for their earlier guarantees of help for the conspiracy, fighting would not have broken out. Actually, however, before July 1936 the Third Reich's interest in the situation in Spain had been small. On July 22, Gen. Franco made an attempt to contact the Germans. The reaction of diplomats, including Minister of Foreign Affairs Konstantin von Neurath, was negative. Franco decided to circumvent diplomatic channels and turned directly to Adolf Hitler, requesting support for the rebellion. Without hesitation, the führer decided to lend aid to the rebels. For ideological reasons, supporting the forces fighting against the Popular Front ruling in Spain was a given. He was also counting on potential support from Spain in the event of a conflict with Great Britain and France. Despite this, he was aware that Germany was not yet ready for confrontation with other European countries, and thus the aid was to be provided in secret. Furthermore, there were around fifteen thousand Germans living in Spain at the time, and Hitler did not want to leave them under Communist rule.[204] The war allowed the German armed forces to test equipment, arms, and training of their soldiers and officers. Furthermore, the Third Reich could obtain resources such as wolfram, copper, and tin from Spain.[205]

Germany's primary discovery of the Spanish Civil War was that tanks should be more heavily armed and concentrated in armored divisions, since this allowed them to break through a front line using the *Schwerpunkt* method. They also established the precision and strength of their 88 mm antiaircraft guns (later installed on Tiger tanks).[206]

The conflict created enormous opportunities for testing new arms and tactics. Hitler realized this at the very start of the fighting. The Condor Legion, subordinate to the Luftwaffe, very scrupulously reported on the effects of using new armament systems. The legion's divisions quite rapidly discovered that shooting at enemy trenches as soon as its soldiers put their heads out after artillery fire was a very effective method. Furthermore, enemy artillery positions were attacked in order to stifle their firepower. The bomber divisions focused on regions where units were formed and on communication lines behind the front, so as to prevent reinforcements from being brought in.[207]

The first contingents of the Condor Legion arrived in Spain in mid-November 1937. Antitank units, heavy machine gun units, and the equivalent of two armored battalions commanded by Col. Wilhelm Ritter von Thoma were sent there. These units were formed in Cubas, north of Toledo, and equipped with 106 Panzer I tanks. The soldiers serving in them wore black berets with a skull motif, which was a reference to the hussars of the old Prussian army. These units were supported by batteries of 20 mm antiaircraft artillery and 88 mm antiaircraft guns. Furthermore, a contingent of engineers and civilian instructors were sent to area of the fighting.[208]

By September 1936, a small, armored company under the cryptonym Drohne started to be formed, with the purpose of training Spanish tankists and antitank artillerists. From September 23, 1936, at its head (and that of the Imker group) stood Col. Wilhelm Ritter von Thoma (later commander of the Afrikakorps). On September 20, the commanders of the 4th Schweinfurt Armored Regiment and the 6th Neuruppin Armored Regiment were ordered to select volunteers who would undertake special tasks. Because of the secrecy of operations, volunteers were formally enlisted in the Luftwaffe for the duration of the mission. They were to obtain civilian clothing and travel to Spain as "tourists." The first group of soldiers from armored formations assembled in Döberitz numbered 120 officers, NCOs, and soldiers. Panzergruppe Drohne consisted of two companies of PzKpfw. I Ausf. A and B light tanks, an antitank company armed with 37 mm Pak 35/36 guns, a transport company, a technical company, and a signals platoon.[209]

Franco's army was supported by two German heavy machine gun battalions, von Thoma's tanks, six artillery batteries with 155 mm guns, and the Condor Legion, equipped with 88 mm guns (which were being tested under fire for the first time).[210]

From March 1937 to May 1939, Dirlewanger served in the Imker German armored unit (Panzer-Einheit) under Ritter von Thoma.[211] In November 1939, von Thoma wrote,

> D[octo]r. Oskar Dirlewanger was with me in a training camp in Spain from April to October 1937 and from July 1938 to the end of May 1939, mostly serving as a company commander, and over his 17 months of activity distinguished himself in training work. In particular, he was also at the front, where he always behaved impeccably. Dr. Dirlewanger, a former warrior of the world war and machine gun company commander, is a decorated soldier and because of his training and sense of soldierly duty is suited [to fighting] at the front.[212]

In Spain, Dirlewanger spent nine months establishing training camps, working mainly as the commander of a company.[213] He later wrote of those operations:

> When my old opponents heard about my military activity in Spain as part of the Condor Legion, they ordered my arrest in November 1937 in Toledo, giving my political uncertainty as the motive, and my transport to the Fatherland together with a Gestapo operative. After I arrived in Berlin, Gen. Willber explained in R.L.M. that he was sorry that I had left the Condor Legion, particularly as I had proved my good service by presenting certificates from my military superiors in Spain, I immediately turned, despite a recent ban from the Gestapo, to the Führer's office with a request for a complete investigation of all of my case after the end of the war and to make it possible for me to return to the Condor Legion—because the commander of the German armored division, Col. von Thoma, also appealed for my return to Spain. Via the Office of the Führer (SS-Sta[ndarten]f[ührer] Brack) I was transferred once again in March from Special Staff "W" to the Condor Legion, which caused the renewal of my duty and the return to the fatherland together with the Legion at the start of recent months.[214]

Imker was a small land unit formed by the Wehrmacht for the needs of the Spanish Civil War. Imker was also the pseudonym used by its commander, Lt. Col. Hans Freiherr von Funck. He held this function until spring 1939. Additionally, he had under him Panzergruppe Drohne, a training group whose main task was to help form nationalist armored divisions.[215]

As the nationalist armored units grew, the numbers in Panzergruppe Drohne fell. German panzer soldiers are estimated to have trained around 6,200 Spanish soldiers during the civil war. They occasionally also took an active part in the fighting. Furthermore, the Imker group included a special radio reconnaissance group under the cryptonym Horch, in which around two hundred German soldiers served.[216]

For fighting in Spain, Dirlewanger was decorated with the Spanish Cross with Swords[217] and the Military Merit Cross[218] (Spanisches Mil. Verdienstkreuz).[219] The activity of German military instructors from the Imker group had no little impact on the nationalist army. In 1937, around 130 of them were active in Spain. In cooperation with the Spanish command, a network of training centers was formed. At the start of 1939, the following were in operation:

Cubas de la Sagra (Madrid province)	Panzergruppe Drohne center
Casarrubuelos (Madrid province)	training center for German and captured equipment, including antitank guns and flamethrowers
Brisiesca near, Burgos	trainee artillery division
Cordoba	mortarmen school
Salamanca	antigas defense school
Monasterio near Burgos	signal corps school
Toledo	infantry training camp
Avilla, Granada, and Pampeluna	officer candidate schools
Miranda de Ebra, Vitoria, San Roque near Gibraltar	NCO schools

By February 1939 these centers had trained 56,000 Spanish soldiers.[220] From March 1937, Dirlewanger served as an instructor and company commandant in the Condor Legion's NCO school in San Roque.[221] As he mentioned, in November 1937 the Gestapo arrested him in Toledo and sent him back to his homeland. He was then employed in Special Staff "W" for some time.[222]

The Spanish Civil War caused the death of around 500,000 people from the twenty-four-million-strong Spanish population. Its last shots were fired on March 31, 1939, in Alicante, but for the Condor Legion the civil war ended on March 28, when Madrid and Aranjuez surrendered.[223] Over the course of the conflict, Germany learned, for example, that in combat, closer communication was needed between the attacking land forces and their aerial support.[224] All through the war, Luftwaffe and Wehrmacht operations were kept secret. Even the German public was not informed about the endeavor. Legionnaires were well paid: They received wages not only in Germany, but also in Spain.[225]

On April 17, 1939, in Seville, May 3 in Valencia, and May 12 in Barajas (near Madrid), parades were held. During the last of them, an "Honor Standard" funded for the Condor Legion was presented. Several days later, the largest ceremonies were organized in Madrid. The parades, which lasted many hours, were opened by Spanish units and closed by the Italian Corpo Truppe Volontarie and the Condor Legion. In total, 5,500 members of the legion took part in it, marching in their parent units: airmen from J/88, K/88, and A/88; ground personnel from P/88, F/88, and LN/88; the Drohne groups; Ausbilder Imker, Artilleriegruppe Lucht, and Anker rear units; and an honor company with ship crews. After returning to Germany, on June 4 in Döberitz, soldiers of the Condor Legion were decorated with the Spanish Cross. Two days later, an official parade with all forces from the legion marched down Unter den Linden.[226]

After returning from the Spanish Civil War and taking a short rest, Dirlewanger appealed for his court judgment to be reconsidered. This time he was acquitted.[227] He found employment as an independent account book auditor.[228]

2

The Second World War, from the Oranienburg Poacher's Unit to the 36th Waffen-SS Grenadier Division Dirlewanger

On July 4, 1939, Oskar Dirlewanger wrote a letter to Heinrich Himmler concerning his endeavors to clear his name, and his imprisonment in the Welzheim camp. He was a man of action and abhorred idleness. He thus requested that Himmler accept him into the ranks of the SS and send him to the front:

> I would like to ask . . . to be allowed to march with the SS. . . . I was convicted for personal and political reasons. It is true that I have sinned, but I did not commit a crime. When after serving my sentence I attempted to have the proceedings reopened, and at the same time I provided, to high-standing party officers, documents presenting the background of the proceedings against me and the true reasons for

my conviction due to shortcomings of higher-standing party officers, the Gestapo forbade me to further apply, in person or in writing, to the Führer's Chancellery or to a common court to bring action for defamation. Even though I observed this curious ban, three days later I was transported to the camp at Welzheim. . . . Thanks to his [SS-Oberführer Berger's] recommendation, I left for Spain in March 1937 [and was assigned] at first to the Spanish Foreign Legion, then I managed to transfer to the Condor Legion. My commander there, Col. Ritter von Thoma, and the commander of my battalion in the world war, Col. Knörzer, whom I met in Spain, are ready to confirm that I fulfilled my soldierly duty there. . . . A reopening of proceedings concerning my full rehabilitation is currently being considered by the Führer's Chancellery (SS-Sta[ndarten]f[ührer] Brack). According to lawyers, another two–three months may go by before the verdict is reviewed and the injustice that I suffered is remedied.

I did my duty during the war and the fighting of the revolution and later as an SA member, and I was always there where men [soldiers] were needed. I find inaction unbearable in a situation where German soldiers are setting out [for combat]. For this reason, I make my request to be allowed to join the SS. . . .

Finally, I would also like to add that in 1932 I had the honor of meeting you, Reichsführer, personally. I was then summoned to the Brown House, and I reported to you that in the event of internal conflict during the takeover of power, my armored railway security train and my comrades were unreservedly at your disposal.[1]

On July 28, 1939, Gottlob Berger[2] also wrote a letter to Himmler, supporting Dirlewanger's request as follows:

3. Since 1918, D[octo]r. Dirlewanger has undeniably been engaged in activity against the "Reds" and has achieved particular merit. For this reason and because he helped me to arm the SA and SS in Württemberg, Baden, and the Palatinate in 1931, I believe it my duty to speak on his behalf and not allow him to be destroyed. . . .

4. The motion to review the case was heard.

The guilty verdict that was issued at the time was completely unjust due to "political reasons." D[octo]r Dirlewanger somehow came up against the Kreisleiter of Heilbronn and the latter accused him of defrauding NSV funds.[3]

The Reichsführer-SS's staff responded to Dirlewanger, stating that Himmler was unable to take the decision to allow him into the ranks of the SS until Dirlewanger's conviction was reviewed and he was absolved of guilt. Moreover, it was suggested that he join the Wehrmacht as a volunteer.[4]

The wait for the next letter from the Reichsführer-SS's staff lasted almost a year. As the *Stuttgarter NS-Kurier* reported, on April 29 and 30, 1940, a hearing to review the 1934 verdict was held, and during it the latter was annulled.[5] It was only on May 17, 1940, that the Chancellery of the Third Reich sent a response, in which it indicated that Dirlewanger "had become the victim of a court mistake" (*einem Justizirrtum zum Opfer gefallen*), and "due to his exemplary engagement in the German cause . . . he is immediately transferred to the Waffen-SS and further to his wish he will go to a frontline unit within the shortest possible time."[6] On May 20, 1940, after the verdict was reviewed, he was again accepted into the NSDAP under his old membership number (1,098,716).[7] In the SS he received the number 357,267. He was drafted on July 1, 1940,[8] and immediately released from service in the Wehrmacht.[9] He became the commander of SS-Sonderkommando Dirlewanger in the 2nd Oranienburg SS Infantry Regiment (2. SS-Infanterie Regiment Oranienburg).[10] Furthermore, he was appointed *SS-Führer im Stab der Inspektion der SS-Totenkopfstandarten*.[11]

On May 25, 1940, Berger wrote Dirlewanger a letter in which he expressed his joy at his rehabilitation and the restoring of his honor.[12] In response, Dirlewanger owned to his friend that it had been a "happy fluke" (*Dusel*), because the doctor assessing his military capability had been his comrade from the SA and a school friend. For that reason, he issued a certificate stating he was "only conditionally capable of military service and useful for work for the fatherland."[13]

Berger suggested to Himmler that Dirlewanger be entrusted with training prisoners convicted of poaching, and lead them to the front.[14] In response to the letter of June 4, 1940, concerning Dirlewanger's joining the Waffen-SS, on June 15, Rudolf Brandt wrote to Berger on behalf of Himmler:

> The Reichsführer-SS supports the admission of Dr. Oskar Dirlewanger to the Waffen-SS and granting him the rank of *SS-Obersturmführer*. At the same time, the Reichsführer-SS grants permission for Dr. D[irlewanger] to take over training of those convicted of poaching.[15]

To SS-Gruppenführer Walter Schmitt, Berger wrote,

> D[octo]r. D[irlewanger] is trained in the modern way and particularly distinguished himself during the fighting of the Condor Legion in Spain. He is to choose [men for his unit] from among those convicted of poaching, in order to train them and send them to the front.[16]

On August 19, Dirlewanger was promoted to *SS-Hauptsturmführer*.[17]

2.1. Formation and Evolution of Special Units (Including SS-Sonderkommando Dirlewanger)[18]

Adolf Hitler abhorred hunting and did not believe it to be a sport. As his friend and photographer Heinrich Hoffmann remembered, he had nothing against hunting as a profession or those who hunted from an early age. Despite disapproving of killing animals for sport and entertainment, he respected poachers, appreciating their knowledge of the wilderness and their skills. During a dinner in the company of Hermann Göring and Hoffmann, he stated,

> I will instruct the Minister of Justice to appropriately change the penalties for poaching! I will also order Himmler to release imprisoned poachers and form them into a corps of accurately shooting foresters, for the protection of wild animals![19]

Allegedly, after he calmed down, he forgot about the whole issue.

During interrogations in the 1960s, Gottlob Berger also said that Dirlewanger's unit had been formed further to the expressed wish of Adolf Hitler in 1940.[20] On March 23, 1940, Heinrich Himmler's adjutant *SS-Gruppenführer*, Karl Wolff, dictated a memo in which he informed that Hitler wished persons imprisoned for poaching who came from Bavaria or the Austrian Ostmärkisch region[21] to be sent to the front. This way they were to receive the opportunity to redeem themselves and be amnestied.[22]

Himmler was delighted by Hitler's idea.[23] Taking Henry the Fowler as his model,[24] he wished to establish a unit consisting of criminals, whom he promised liberty if they fought for him. Such troops also operated in the nineteenth century. In 1882, the Austrian-Hungarian army used penal companies to guard the border and prevent arms smuggling to Montenegro. During the First World War, the Austrian-Hungarian army used penal companies, so-called *Strafunis*, composed of poachers, to protect its borders in mountainous areas.[25] A contribution toward the creation of this type of formation was also made by the wife of one of the prisoners. In a letter to Himmler, she asked for her husband, an NSDAP member, to be released from prison. He had been sent there for shooting a deer in a state forest. The woman suggested that instead of being held in prison, he should get the opportunity to rehabilitate himself by fighting at the front for the führer.[26]

Himmler immediately demanded to be provided a list of all imprisoned poachers. They were to form a special unit composed of sharpshooters under the auspices of the SS. Problems appeared during the selection of poachers: What traits should such people have, and what conditions and requirements should they meet?

From 1925, the name SS (*Schutzstaffeln*, protection squadron) was borne by groups of party activists formed by the party. They were mainly responsible for protecting meetings and public appearances of important NSDAP figures. In January 1929, Himmler took over a small security unit and soon formed it into a paramilitary organization with "elite pretensions," which answered to the highest party command. SS members wore brown shirts, black ties, black caps with a death's head, black-white-red ribbons, horse-riding breeches, and swastika armbands.[27]

In the early 1930s, Himmler quite rapidly climbed subsequent rungs of the career ladder, ultimately reaching the position of *Reichsführer-SS*. His objective was to create a state protection corps (*Staatsschutzkorps*) and ensure full internal security. At the end of the 1930s, he expanded the Waffen-SS. In 1941, he implemented a race-based policy of systematic mass murder. He thus wanted to form a new power structure, the Great German Reich.[28]

Thanks to Himmler's endeavors, SS membership ensured one's status. The SS were an elite whom not everyone could join. SS members had to be in excellent physical and medical form. They had to be aged twenty-three to twenty-five, thin and powerfully built, and at least 1.70 meters tall. Candidates were checked in terms of "hereditary health" and "Aryan heritage." It was stated that "they have to be comrades who profess the old maxim: 'One for all and all for one.'"[29] They had to prove that since 1750, their family tree had not featured any "non-Aryan" ancestors, demonstrate their obedience to the führer, and fulfill many criteria. Training material published by the SS Main Office (SS-Hauptamt)[30] defined the following specific features that characterized the internal connection shared by SS members:

> 1. Spiritual community, the foundations of which are formed by the principles of national socialism; 2. absolute and unconditional loyalty

> and obedience to orders, expressed in the words "My honor means loyalty" [*Meine Ehre heißt Treue*]; 3. constant promotion and maintaining of a battle spirit (*Kampfgeist*), leading to the creation of a German soldiery (*Soldatentum*); 4. cooperation within the SS for the creation of a community of all German nations.[31]

Tightening the racial criteria was to make young men aware that they belonged to the avant-garde of the *Übermenschen* and confirm them in their contempt of ethnic groups believed less valuable, which justified the use of the most-brutal measures of terror and violence.[32]

"Racial examinations" involved the inspection of a candidate's general presentation according to criteria of "body structure" and "racial assessment" (joint category of "appearance"). Negative features could be compensated for by "general appearance" and "mental attitude," and the general assessment was capped with an intelligence test and sports trials. If the "confirmed proof of ancestry" was accepted, but there were doubts as to "general appearance," Himmler decided that a "racial and biological test" be conducted.[33]

It was not completely clear how the SS requirements and criteria should be applied to poachers. Questions arose: Should poachers undergoing sentences for serious offenses become part of the unit, and should they be free from addictions? Himmler set no age limit or maximum penalty for qualifying a poacher for the unit.[34] Racial selection and the system of anthropological assessment conducted by the SS Race and Settlement Main Office (Rasse- und Siedlungshauptamt, or RuSHA) did not apply to candidates for SS-Sonderkommando Dirlewanger.[35]

Himmler shortlisted over three hundred poachers.[36] Ultimately, eighty-eight of them were released from prison on his order and transported to the Sachsenhausen concentration camp in Oranienburg.[37] These were people born between 1894 and 1921. Around 12 percent came from Austria and 8 percent from Bavaria. Most of them had been sent to prisons and camps for poaching, the shortest sentence being four months, and the longest two and a half years. The group also included petty thieves, goods fencers, and fraudsters.[38] In the Oranienburg barracks, they all were quartered in block 36, where they remained under special supervision of the criminal police.[39]

Around seventy to eighty poachers underwent military training in the SS barracks at the Sachsenhausen camp and received uniforms.[40] The camp was built in 1936 and was the first concentration camp formed after Heinrich Himmler's appointment as chief of the German police. It was built mainly by prisoners from the Emsland camp, according to new guidelines by the

Concentration Camps Inspectorate. It was intended to become "an architectural expression of the national socialist worldview in which prisoners were also symbolically subject to the absolute power of the SS."[41] It gained a special position in Nazi concentration camp structures.[42]

Its location was very picturesque. Previously, under Eicke's command, his villa had been erected in "a copse of oaks surrounded by a pine forest," while

> the prisoners' camp proper [was surrounded] by a protective row of utility buildings that blocked the view. What is more, along the main street that lay next to the KL, idyllic one-and-a-half-floor detached houses with deep-set, steep gable roofs had been built, and their stone walls were covered with wooden siding. The *Heimatschutz*-style houses built for SS officers, surrounded by old pine trees, looked like foresters' huts on kitschy postcards.[43]

It was next to these "idyllic houses," in the SS military training area, that the training of the poachers selected for Dirlewanger's unit was conducted. Currently, these areas are outside the camp zone and are not available for sightseeing.

Within the restricted Sachsenhausen building complex, separate functional centers were planned: the camp itself, command offices and living quarters for their personnel, and barracks for guards. During his visitation at the end of 1936, Himmler assessed Sachsenhausen to be a "completely new, modern and contemporary concentration camp (cc), which could be expanded."[44] He added that this type of camp protected "the Reich against enemies of the state in peacetime and also in the event of mobilisation."[45]

In the years 1936–45, over 200,000 people were held there. Initially, these were political prisoners who opposed the regime, and later also members of groups deemed racially or biologically inferior. From 1939 onward, citizens of the occupied countries of Europe also were imprisoned there.[46] "Volunteers" for Dirlewanger's unit were selected from among the inmates up to 1945. In late 1944 and early 1945, many political prisoners were conscripted into SS-Sturmbrigade Dirlewanger and the later 36th Waffen-SS Grenadier Division (36. Grenadier Division der Waffen-SS).

By 1939, further camps had been formed, modeled on the ones in Dachau and Sachsenhausen: in Flössenburg in eastern Bavaria (May 1938), in Mauthausen near Linz (August 1938), in Neuengamme near Hamburg (December 1938), and, for women, in Ravensbrück (May 1939). Prisoner numbers grew slowly from the end of 1936. As a result of Theodor Eicke's[47] activity, some subordinate functions in the camps were assigned to inmates—

often criminal prisoners—who were granted privileges in exchange. Thus, the SS included specific incarcerated groups as a tool in its system of terror. Furthermore, prisoners were used in projects that drew on forced labor, and factories were built in camps. From 1937 the "work-shy" and antisocial individuals were likewise imprisoned. When the Second World War began, Himmler started using these people also for other purposes. In subsequent years, as the unit commanded by Dirlewanger grew, more and more "volunteers" were recruited from the camps then formed (apart from Ravensbrück).

As Georg Kraus and Peter Gossens, convicted of breaking the hunting law (*Verstoßes gegen das Jagdgesetz*), remembered, in the summer of 1940 all incarcerated poachers were assembled in the Sachsenhausen camp.[48] Around a hundred of them underwent military training. Although the exercises took place outside the camp area, these people were still quartered in camp barracks. During training they wore uniforms with the SS runes, and their instructors were SS personnel from the 5th SS-Totenkopfverbände.[49] The assumption was that poachers would become highly trained sharpshooters to fight against partisans.[50]

Dirlewanger was likely sent to Oranienburg by May 1940 to select and train these people.[51] On July 1, 1940, a letter was sent from the Reichsführer's staff to the SS-Totenkopfstandarten Inspectorate, informing them that

> upon the order of the SS Reichsführer, Obersturmführer d.R. Waffen-SS Dirlewanger has been charged with the training of those convicted of poaching to prepare them to be sent to the front. Dirlewanger has been ordered to report immediately to the *SS*-Totenkopfstandarten Inspectorate in Oranienburg to start service.[52]

After arriving, he was quartered in the SS barracks in Oranienburg.[53]

Thanks to the preserved later log of the 2nd Battalion of SS-Sonderregiment Dirlewanger of June 12, 1944, we can find out what the training in Oranienburg consisted of:

Time and type of duty	
05:00	Wake-up call
05:05–05:25	Morning exercise
05:45–06:00	Coffee dispensed
06:30–07:30	Lesson about arms

(a) advanced: MG34[54]

(b) beginners: Gew98k rifle[55]

07:35–08:45	Shooting lessons: Use of weapons during shooting, elements of the bullet flight path
09:00–12:00	Practical shooting exercises: Aiming and leveling a gun, shooting-position types

At this time, each company carried out [the following]:

Shooting 1:150 meters from a lying position

12:30	Lunch
14:00–16:00	General training

Forms from general order, according to H. Dv. 130/2 a, point. 246–303.

16:30–17:15	Lesson: Lying in ambush and standing on guard duty, position defense
17:15–18:00	Weapon cleaning, simultaneous learning of new marching songs, ending in a muster with weapons
19:00	Issuing of orders
19:30–20:00	Dinner
22:00	Last post[56]

The creation of the unit was supported by Dirlewanger's friend from Esslingen, the head of the SS Main Office (SS-Hauptamt), Gottlob Berger, who was responsible for recruitment to Waffen-SS divisions and supervision over them.[57] It was likely he who carried out the initial selection of poachers, which Dirlewanger then approved.[58] Upon Himmler's order of July 1, 1940, the Oranienburg Poacher's Unit (SS-Wilddiebkommando Oranienburg) was formed in the Sachsenhausen concentration camp.[59]

Ultimately Dirlewanger selected only fifty-five people.[60] The prisoners he rejected bore no consequences apart from being sent back to the institutions they had previously been held in, and continued their sentences. According to initial assumptions, the company was to train sharpshooters for SS divisions. By "using the special skills of poachers," the unit was intended for combat against partisans.[61]

On September 1, 1940, it was renamed SS-Sonderkommando Dirlewanger (Truppenteil 00512).[62] In orders and other documents, it was referred to under various names (e.g., SS-Sonderformation Dirlewanger, Einheit Dirlewanger, etc.) until 1942, but usually SS-Sonderkommando Dirlewanger was used. In

Oranienburg it was trained by the 5th Totenkopf SS Regiment (5. SS-Totenkopf Regiment).[63] It was likely still in Oranienburg that five further poachers joined the unit, thus bringing its total number to sixty.[64] Initially, the members of SS-Sonderkommando Dirlewanger were "only" poachers, with no military rank. Only soldiers of the *Unterführer* rank and above were SS men.[65]

SS-Hauptascharführer Wilhelm Schlauter, a soldier of Leibstandarte SS Adolf Hitler (LAH) since May 1933, was in October 1940 delegated to SS-Sonderkommando Dirlewanger, where, as he mentioned, thirty poachers served. In the LAH barracks in Berlin-Lichterfelde, he received written orders to transfer to Oranienburg. There he reported to Oskar Dirlewanger. When he understood what unit he had been assigned to, he was outraged. He telephoned Sturmbannführer Willi Schinke, who had given him this order, but Schinke claimed the task brought him no dishonor. Schlauter's duties included training the poachers, and he reported on his progress every so often. In LAH, his task since 1934 had been training new recruits.[66]

Despite Hitler and Himmler's support for the idea of forming a division composed of poachers, its inclusion in the elite SS elicited protests. The idea of granting its insignia to convicts provoked hostility. It thus held a special status, operating within the Waffen-SS but not officially part of it. At first, depending on the situation and needs, it was subject to orders from the Waffen-SS, the police, and the army.[67] SS insignia were cut off the old SS uniforms that its members were given. Only the Nazi eagle remained on the left sleeve.

It was only in 1943 that they were granted, instead of the SS runes, a patch with crossed grenades and a rifle.[68] This was confirmed by one of Dirlewanger's first soldiers, Franz Wegscheider. He indicated that in the summer of 1940 in Sachsenhausen, he was assigned to the poacher unit (Wildschützen-Einheit), which was then renamed Dirlewanger-Einheit. In the 1960s he mentioned that its members were part of the SS and wore SS uniforms, but without SS insignia.[69]

Right after training, four *Unterführer* from the SS Germania Regiment (Ers.-Btl.SS Germania) were assigned to the unit and were joined a year later by an *Oberscharführer* from SS-Leibstandarte Adolf Hitler, unknown by name, who in 1939 completed a monthly prison sentence, probably for embezzlement.[70]

Oskar Dirlewanger had special powers from the start of the unit's life. Further to Himmler's decision, without turning to the military courts he could punish his men as he saw fit: flog them, send them back to the camp, or even mete out the death penalty. All the soldiers were aware that he was "master of life and death" (*Herr über Leben und Tod*). Erich von dem Bach-

Zelewski remembered: "When Dirlewanger reported to me [in 1942], he presented me with instructions from Himmler. According to these orders, Dirlewanger was a sovereign judge over his subordinates. . . . Dirlewanger had the right to immediately, without extended proceedings, issue death sentences for his soldiers."[71]

3

Tasks of the Unit in the General Government

SS-Sonderkommando Dirlewanger was intended for special tasks. Because of their skills, poachers could move through the forests quickly, efficiently, and unobserved. Their primary assignment was combating partisans and banditry (*Partisanenbekämpfung* and *Bandenbekämpfung*). They were prepared by specialists in training recruits from the best Waffen-SS units.

Before being sent to Belarus, they continued training in the General Government (GG), taking on guard duty in labor camps for Jews and combating smuggling and black-market trade. As some soldiers stated after the war, they also prepared for their later operations in Lviv (Lemberg).[1] On August 5, 1941, Odilo Lotario Globocnik, the SS and police leader (*SSPF*) in the Lublin District, summed up their tasks there as follows:[2]

> As the commander of the unit, Dirlewanger did some excellent work while [supervising] digging of trenches by the Bug River and as the commander of the camp for Jews in Dzików. After the end of the works by the Bug, he received a special task from the Lublin District SS and police leader. Dirlewanger demonstrated extraordinary skills in combating smuggling and black-market trading; he was similarly

> able to apply the appropriate means to combat the Polish resistance movement; moreover, he always achieves positive results in all tasks assigned to him.[3]

From October 1940 to the start of 1942, SS-Sonderkommando Dirlewanger stayed in the GG.[4] Apart from training and acquiring skills useful in clashes with partisans, the unit had guard duties in a labor camp for Jews in Stary Dzików and operated in Lublin. It focused on combating illegal trading. Its members perpetrated many requisitions and committed various infractions, and so explanatory proceedings were initiated against them.[5]

3.1. Stary Dzików

Training in Sachsenhausen most likely ended in 1940. From Oranienburg, SS-Sonderkommando Dirlewanger was transferred to Lublin in the GG, where its members were quartered together with other SS units in a school building in the town center.[6] They spent a day there and set off for Stary Dzików.[7] They operated in the Stary Dzików, Bełżec, and Narol communes.[8] The field post office of SS-Sonderkommando Dirlewanger was in Bełżec and was received in the Polish post office.[9]

At that time, the unit was divided into smaller groups of several persons each, which were assigned different tasks. They were commanded by *SS-Unterscharführer*.[10] Some poachers stayed in Stary Dzików, others supervised the building of trenches and fortifications on the Bug River, and still others served in Bełżec, near Chełm,[11] and near Dęblin,[12] while several were sent to Riga[13] and Lviv.

No doctors or dentists were assigned to SS-Sonderkommando Dirlewanger. As Wilhelm Schlauter stated, Dirlewanger himself provided medical care to his subordinates.[14] This was confirmed by Friedrich Walter, who remembered that it was only during operations in Belarus that the unit was joined by the medical orderly Engelage. In the event of more-serious illnesses or wounds, soldiers were sent to the nearest hospital.[15]

Franz Wegscheider indicated that he was sent to Lublin together with three other soldiers. They were commanded by SS-Unterscharführer Schneidt. Thence, their small unit was transferred straight to Riga, where it was supposed to report to the local SS and police leader (SSPF), Walter Schröder.[16] Wegscheider operated in the area of Lake Peipus, and his tasks included hunting and providing the game thus obtained to Schröder.[17] Wegscheider mentioned that they stayed in Riga until Christmas 1942, when they returned to Lublin.[18] We can assume that he meant Christmas 1941, because in 1942 the unit was already stationed in Belarus. In Riga, Dirlewanger's soldiers likely supervised a "large warehouse."[19]

Gustav Brusberg, Georg Kraus, and Peter Gossens stated that in early autumn 1940, they were sent to Lviv. Erich Illing testified that this happened at the beginning of 1941.[20] They did not indicate what they did there, saying only that they continued training. However, putting this information together with the tasks of Dirlewanger's other subordinates, we can assume that this group also supervised a Jewish labor camp. Apart from SS guards, also Ukrainians oversaw the prisoners. The date given by Illing seems the most likely. In June 1941, in Lviv at Janowska Street, Odilo Globocnik's men (the Deutsche Ausrüstungswerke company, or DAW) took over a Jewish factory that manufactured mill machinery, owned by Steinhaus. Like in Lublin, a labor camp for Jews was formed there.[21]

In September 1941, a barrack complex was built, and the whole camp was surrounded by barbed-wire fencing and guard towers. No sanitary or heating infrastructure was included, and only few latrines and washrooms were located there. The inmates slept on long shared bunks, without blankets or bedding. Terror reigned, with beatings, torture, and executions occurring daily.[22]

Josef Rau claimed that in early 1941, he arrived in Dęblin, located north of Lublin. There their tasks included supervising bridge building and protecting unspecified facilities. After around eight weeks, they were sent to Lublin.[23] He added that in winter 1940, they were also sent from Lublin to Stary Dzików, near Bełżec and Narol. They returned to Lublin at the start of 1941.[24]

Four of Dirlewanger's soldiers were sent as sentries to Krasno, a labor camp for the Jewish population housed in a seminary in western Ukraine, near Lutsk. Initially, few Jews were held there, but gradually, following SS-Oberscharführer Heinz Feiertag's orders, around four hundred forced laborers were imprisoned there. Numerous workshops, including a shoemaker's and a tailor's, operating for the benefit of the Third Reich, were established within it.[25] Feiertag described their tasks in 1942 thus:

> I arrived in Lutsk with three other soldiers to train units that protected farms in Ukraine. . . . Around five hundred Jews were working in it [the camp]. First, together with my three people, I fenced off the camp area, then I brought in Jews from the ghetto to work in the camp. In the warehouse the following items were produced: shoe polish, floor polish, soap, and brushes. Around 6–8 people were employed in one

> facility. Also, part of the camp was a tailor's workshop, in which 40 laborers were employed and which housed 60 confiscated sewing machines; one shoemaker and one quilter worked there. . . . The German Workshops, as I called this enterprise, are achieving big financial success. Over the first 2.5 months, the facility brought in a net income of 25,000 marks. Unfortunately, the facility was taken over by the civilian administration.[26]

According to a document from 1967, Feiertag's subordinates from Dirlewanger's unit were Franz Hunke and brothers Gottlieb and Franz Zalski. Their tasks also included training the Ukrainians who supervised the Jewish workers.[27]

During a postwar proceeding, a Jewish witness who was a laborer in the camp thus described the activity of SS-Oberscharführer Feiertag:

> F. visited the workshop several times a day. Not a day went by without him beating one of the workers. . . .
>
> I remember exactly how once in the shoemakers' workshop a pair of boots was made upon his order. F. was very pleased with them. As proof of his delight, he commanded the foreman, the Jew Wydra, to be given 15–20 blows of the stick. F. knew perfectly how to torment prisoners. . . .
>
> There was no day that somebody did not get a thrashing. . . . For the beatings, a stick was used on the naked body. Two SS men would carry out the beatings.
>
> They reveled in [torturing] the victim all day long. They called him [the prisoner] names, ordered him about, made him sing songs, and then they had him undress completely [and] dig himself a grave in the camp yard. The torture lasted several hours. . . . In the end, they shot him.[28]

Prisoners in the Stary Dzików labor camp received similar treatment.

According to my findings, SS-Sonderkommando Dirlewanger arrived in Stary Dzików in October 1940 and had guard duty there in the labor camp for Jews. This camp was established in October 1940 and, under the Otto plan,[29] was the farthest away from the central camp in Bełżec.[30] In Stary Dzików, members of SS-Sonderkommando Dirlewanger, numbering around sixty to seventy men, primarily underwent further training; for instance, they were taught to ride.[31]

According to information provided by the Ośrodek "Brama Grodzka-Teatr NN" center, the labor camp in Stary Dzików operated very briefly, only several weeks. This institution bases its findings on the recollections of a Jewish Olmer (leader of the camp council) inmate from Częstochowa, according to whose description the

> conditions were quite inadequate. Like in Cieszanów [where another labor camp subordinate to the one in Bełżec was located], also here the distance from Bełżec of 45 km played the deciding role. Luckily, however, this Camp lasted relatively briefly, so the consequences for us were less painful.

According to his information, the Dzików camp was dismantled in November 1940,[32] which does not correspond to the testimony of soldiers from SS-Sonderkommando Dirlewanger made in the 1940s, 1960s, and 1970s. The information that it stopped operations at the end of 1940 can also be derived from the fact that Odilo Globocnik dismantled the labor camp network near Bełżec at that time. Despite this, thousands of Jews continued working in other camps of the Lublin District in 1941 and even into 1942.[33]

The unit was stationed in Stary Dzików until the spring of 1941, which confirms that the camp operated until that period. This is supported by the testimony provided in 1941 to the Gestapo by the Jews Sara Bergmann (employed by Dirlewanger as an interpreter), Mendel Rosenberg (sent to the Stary Dzików camp in January 1941, which Izaak Flomenbaum mentioned), Josef Tintenfisch, and Moszek Wassermann (also incarcerated in Stary Dzików in January 1941).[34] On the basis of their accounts, the camp functioned at least until January 1941 and was closed most likely in early spring of that year. Jews held in labor camps built roads, bridges, airfields, and fortifications along the border with the Soviet Union, regulated riverbeds, and carried out water melioration work.

According to SS-Rottenführer Erich Selzer, who belonged to SS-Sonderkommando Dirlewanger from June 1940 onward, the main task of the unit in Stary Dzików was to supervise Jews who were carrying out roadworks and erecting the Panther–Wotan line. He mentioned that the incarcerated Jews came from all over the GG and that in Stary Dzików, they were placed in two large camps.[35] The Panther–Wotan line was a completely pointless project by Odilo Globocnik built along the frontier of the Soviet occupation zone. Globocnik's activity in that area caused the Lublin District to become the center of slave labor in the GG. Near Lublin, Jews from other districts were usually employed in large projects and placed in special camps, in primitive and inadequate conditions.[36]

Around one thousand Jews were transferred to the Stary Dzików camp, which was under Oskar Dirlewanger's command, from the neighboring camp in Cieszanów. They were put in two barns, one on land belonging to the Greek Catholic parish, and the other belonging to the Roman Catholic parish. The camp was surrounded by a fence of barbed wire.[37] The guards were men from SS-Sonderkommando Dirlewanger, who were quartered in the local schoolhouse.[38] Oskar Dirlewanger lived in a different building, in which also the canteen was located.[39] Between Bełżec and Stary Dzików, a defensive rampart of around 50 km was supposed to be built. To carry out this task, the camps in Stary Dzików, Bełżec, Lipsk, Płazów, and Cieszanów were established. They were officially known as Labor Camp No. 1, the Bełżec camps, or the SS-Grenzsicherungs-Baukommando camps.[40] Like in other camps, also here the forced laborers were abused: For instance, "bathing" in a local pond was organized. Prisoners who tried to escape or were unfit for work (being too ill or old) were sometimes shot.

The investigation conducted by the Gestapo in 1941 indicated that Oskar Dirlewanger released some forced laborers from the camp in exchange for money. Interestingly, the interrogated prisoners confirmed that after payment, they received (or were supposed to receive) a receipt from him and really were released home.[41] According to the Gestapo investigation, embezzlement occurred. Dirlewanger was characterized by extraordinary cunning and guile in financial matters.

SS-Rottenführer Erich Selzer mentioned that in Stary Dzików, the unit cooperated with the Ukrainian police, from which it received reports about criminals and bandits present in the area. According to him, Dirlewanger delegated some of his people to arrest such people and place them in the labor camp.[42]

The tasks of SS-Sonderkommando Dirlewanger in the Stary Dzików and Lublin areas also included patrolling the forests in search of partisan groups and camps. According to Gottlob Berger, partisan units often attacked and killed German officials (likely guards) and the Poles working for them. Moreover, timber theft occurred. Dirlewanger's subordinates oversaw an area within a radius of 40–50 km.[43]

During their stay in Stary Dzików, there was a shortage of officers in Dirlewanger's unit. For this reason, his deputy at the time was SS-Hauptscharführer Wilhelm Schlauter. During a period of around eight weeks, Dirlewanger was on leave or had to take care of something in Berlin. Command of SS-Sonderkommando Dirlewanger was then also taken over by Schlauter.[44]

In this period, part of SS-Sonderkommando Dirlewanger operated in the Narol commune, where they probably guarded Roma who were held in a large barn and its adjoining granary, a part of a former manor farm belonging to the Lewandowski family. Once the Roma had been deported to the concentration camp in Auschwitz, the unit guarded Jewish laborers, who were made to build fortifications along the newly demarcated border.[45] Dirlewanger's soldiers also oversaw Jewish laborers in Bełżec.[46]

At the turn of 1940 and 1941, Gottlob Berger inspected Stary Dzików. He assessed not only the camp's functioning, but also the progress in the training of soldiers from SS-Sonderkommando Dirlewanger. Shortly afterward, in February 1941, Wilhelm Schlauter was released from the duty of training Dirlewanger's subordinates, since he had achieved his task. The order to this effect had to be sent twice because Oskar Dirlewanger ignored it.[47]

3.2. Lublin

From Stary Dzików, SS-Sonderkommando Dirlewanger was transferred to Lublin in February or March 1941.[48] This happened gradually, with single small groups and detachments being sent there. The whole unit, or most of it, was assembled in the city only at the start of summer 1941.[49] It was stationed at "Szopena" Street 18, in an "old house." This was a large, four-floor tenement building comprising six to eight flats and a coal cellar. The courtyard housed a kitchen and a canteen.[50]

The SS-man Alfred Koziel,[51] who supervised guards in the labor camp at Lipowa Street, was quartered on the ground floor of this building together with members of Dirlewanger's unit. He remembered that only part of the unit, numbering a company, was stationed there. The rest were accommodated in a school belonging to the Bernardine Monastery. The office and canteen of SS-Sonderkommando Dirlewanger were located on Chopin Street. The canteen was situated in a small room, in which a tiny counter and two tables were set. Dirlewanger's office and flat were on the ground floor of that house.[52]

At the time, there were sixty-two soldiers and eleven or twelve *Unterführer* in SS-Sonderkommando Dirlewanger.[53] In Lublin, as Franz Wegscheider and Josef Rau remembered, the focus was on further training. Sentry and other duties were performed by soldiers who had previously been in the army.[54]

Josef Rau testified that in Lublin, SS-Sonderkommando Dirlewanger was transformed into a motorized unit. They received motorcycles and trucks, which they used among other vehicles to deliver supplies.[55] Motorcyclist units were formed, and Rau was assigned to one of them. There were three soldiers per motorcycle: the driver and two gunners. They were initially armed with pistols; over time they received machine guns. At that time, the motorcycle unit numbered twelve teams in total.[56] In turn, Franz Wegscheider stated that in Lublin SS-Sonderkommando Dirlewanger did not have its own trucks or drivers yet. When necessary, it cooperated with Lublin police forces. The unit did not have a high combat strength: it consisted of only sixty to seventy men.[57]

Interviewed by Berndt Rieger, Irmgard Rickheim (Odilo Globocnik's fiancée) described Lublin in 1940 as a town that did not differ significantly from Berlin, and stated that "Lublin belonged to the SS." The central Litewski Square was renamed Adolf-Hitler Platz; the main barracks were called after Hitler's former driver, Julius Schreck. Lublin also had a Reinhard-Heydrich Strasse and an Ostland Strasse, and its center housed offices and flats of SS members and the families of the German civilian administration. Poles and Jews were relocated to the suburban districts, and Lublin became a typical German town. All Polish and Jewish traces were erased, and the principal buildings flew German flags on their facades.[58] On March 20, 1941, Ernst Emil Zörner, governor of the Lublin District, announced the following order:

> For the public good, a closed Jewish residential district (ghetto) is created with immediate effect, for the purpose of which I order:
>
> The borders of the ghetto in Lublin shall follow the streets: from the corner of Kowalska along Kowalska, through Krawiecka along the block of buildings marked on the plan, cutting across the free plot on Sienna to Kalinowszczyza up to the corner of Franciszkańska, down Franciszkańska, through Unicka to the corner of Lubartowska, down Lubartowska to the corner of Kowalska. Public utility buildings, other buildings occupied by offices and formations, and churches are not subject to this order.
>
> All Jews settled in Lublin shall reside in this Jewish district. Jews are forbidden to remain outside the ghetto.[59]

The date for transferring Jews to the Jewish district was set for April 5, 1941; the first ghetto in Podzamcze was also formed then. It did not exist very long: it was liquidated only a year later during Operation Reinhard. The liquidation started on the night of March 16, 1942, and on April 15, 1942, the area was already "free from Jews."[60]

In the Lublin District, SS-Sonderkommando Dirlewanger was subordinate to Odilo Globocnik, who held the post of SS and police leader (SSPF) in the

Lublin District for almost four years. He was also the head of the local NSDAP office as the *Distriktsstandortführer* (highest-ranking party administrator in the district), and the chief representative of Heinrich Himmler as the Reich commissioner for the consolidation of German nationhood (*Reichkomissar für die Festigung deutschen Volkstums*).[61] Himmler commanded him to "create a system of SS and police bases in the new eastern regions" and authorized him to expand the operation of "searching for German blood" to cover all of the GG.[62] Globocnik also became a central figure of GG settlement policy.

Globocnik supervised all penal institutions and camps operating in the district. In December 1939, at Lipowa Street 7 and 9, one of the largest labor camps for Jews in Lublin was established. That was also when the building of the first barracks started, intended to house workshops and quarters for the Jewish prisoners. In 1941, the camp was taken over by the company Deutsche Ausrüstungswerke (German Equipment Works), and the complex grew to include workshops, warehouses, a stable, camp administration, and SS barracks.[63]

In the camp, craftsmen's workshops were built and equipped with gear appropriated during requisitions conducted in Jewish businesses. This camp was the first one to function as an efficient business, which allowed Globocnik to get rich. It profited from the handcrafting skills of its Jewish inmates.[64] It also held a warehouse with looted valuable objects, which were sent there as a result of the operations of Dirlewanger's unit,[65] among other reasons. The Jewish laborers were supervised alternately by Selbstschutz, SS-Sonderkommando Dirlewanger, and the Kluß unit. When between late 1941 and early 1942 SS-Sonderkommando Dirlewanger was withdrawn from the GG, guards from the Lublin concentration camp and later Trawniki men took over guard duties.

Living conditions in the camp were atrocious, the prisoners being quartered in dilapidated stable buildings. The backbreaking labor together with meager food rations reaped a fatal harvest. Laborers were beaten and abused, and executions occurred.

Dirlewanger's soldiers carried out requisitions; for example, taking sewing machines required for work in the camp.[66] According to the testimony of Werner Schindler,[67] an inmate of the labor camp at Lipowa Street, and information provided on the basis of the so-called Michalsen files, in the summer of 1942, soldiers from SS-Sonderkommando Dirlewanger participated in the liquidation of the abovementioned ghetto and the camp at Lipowa Street.[68] However, this is impossible, since in late 1941–early 1942 the unit was transferred to Belarus and was already quartered in the Mogilev area in summer 1942.

On August 5, 1941, Oskar Dirlewanger was promoted from *SS-Hauptsturmführer* to *SS-Sturmbannführer der Reserve*, in recognition of his achievements during operations in the GG (supervising forced laborers during trench digging near Bełżec, commanding the Stary Dzików camp for Jews, and combating smuggling and black-market trading).[69] SS-Brigadeführer Odilo Globocnik noted that Dirlewanger was irreplaceable in his work. The nomination was supported by SS-Oberguppenführer Friedrich Wilhelm Krüger, higher SS and police leader "East" (General Government).[70]

In Lublin, Dirlewanger's subordinates frequently violated the law: They traded with Poles on the black market, selling German goods unavailable to them (food, cigarettes, alcohol) and also clothes.[71] Apart from overseeing the camp in Stary Dzików, they also operated in the Majdanek concentration camp.[72] They engaged in blackmail and fraud, extorted money from the populace, and molested Jewish women. The proverbial "last straw" was injecting fifty-seven Jews in the Stary Dzików camp with strychnine,[73] which Dr. Konrad Morgen described:[74] "I remember from the files that Jewish women were killed with strychnine injections, and soap was made from the corpses."[75] However, Konrad Morgen's testimony should be taken with a grain of salt. As I stated in the introduction, even investigators during the Nuremberg trial rejected his testimony as too ridiculous.

Nevertheless, the administration of poisoned injections to fifty-seven Jews did take place in Lublin.[76] In a letter of March 20, 1942, to SS-Untersturmführer Dr. Friedrich of the SS Main Office (SS-Hauptamt, Amt I), Dirlewanger wrote,

> It is true that I allowed an SS doctor to poison Jews (57) instead of shooting them. I did it to save the clothes (boots, etc.), which I gave to SS-Hauptsturmführer Streibel for his forced laborers. The golden teeth of the Jews killed were pulled out by the commander of the SS and Police Reserves [Reserviers der SS- und Polizeiführers Lublin], for proper dentures for SS men.[77]

Because the principle of discretion had been violated, this caused great indignation among other Nazis. Karl Streiber, interrogated in the 1960s, denied everything. He wanted to have nothing to do with suspected war crimes.[78]

SS-Unterscharführer Peter Erretkamps added that this incident took place in the summer of 1941. He described that later, the bodies of around fifty men and women were brought out from the cellar of their quarters—he earlier testified that he had been one of the "porters."[79] He indicated that together with six other soldiers (including Karl Kunz), he drove the corpses away in a truck,[80] and that one of the women killed had been around twenty-five years old and was at an advanced stage of pregnancy. Dirlewanger kicked her in the stomach with his shoe, observing to his two companions that a "bastard" would have been born in a month.[81]

The duties of SS-Sonderkommando Dirlewanger also included supervising the civilian population and enforcing the curfew:

> If at night we met Poles breaking curfew, we had to detain them and take them to where we were quartered. We shut them in the cellar and the next day they were released in the morning, usually after a flogging. The detainees were usually interrogated. The interrogations were conducted personally by Dirlewanger in the presence of Strumpf and several other *Unterführer*. I remember the names: Feiertag, Haag, and Eckert. During the interrogations [the people] were beaten. Screams could often be heard from the interrogation room.

Dirlewanger's soldiers were also responsible for road inspections: They checked documents and vehicles.[82]

As Peter Longerich and Martin Winstone stated, in November 1941, upon Globocnik's order, SS-Sonderkommando Dirlewanger helped deport around two thousand Poles from seven villages in the Lublin District to make room for 105 Volksdeutsch families from the Radom District. This was one of the great resettlement actions planned by Himmler, intended to clear the area for ethnic Germans (a prelude to operations in Zamojszczyzna). At the same time, a "general review" of the Polish population and its assets was begun. The operation itself was unsuccessful, however, as indicated in the report of November 20 by Helmuth Weihenmaier, chief of the Zamość District. The plan to transport the deported peasants farther east was frustrated by the occupying authorities in Volhynia, while the population, both Polish and Ukrainian, began to fear that they would be resettled next. They thus started to abandon their home villages.[83]

In Lublin, Dirlewanger's soldiers had no overly strenuous or dangerous duties. However, they made a lot of trouble, also causing denunciations of the unit to be written. As a result, on October 24, 1941, Oskar Dirlewanger issued an order concerning "law and order" (*Zucht und Ordnung*) in their quarters:

> Further to the order of the SS and police leader I am responsible for order and cleanliness in the building at Chopin Street 19. The stairs

> and corridor leading to the upper floor are grimy with dirt. . . . Drunken men often break windows and intentionally destroy doors and furnishings. Not only singing and music, but also shouting, dancing, and altercations may be heard in the building into the early hours of the morning; it has become the norm for men to return late at night and early in the morning, shouting and screaming.
>
> Visits by women have reached a scale that is unacceptable in the case of military quarters. . . . The courtyard and garden are treated like a rubbish tip, even though a chest for refuse has been prepared there. . . . After the failure of all attempts to limit this gypsy life through admonishments and warnings, I order as follows:
>
> . . . In the event of future nighttime incidents (noise—violent shooting—destruction of property, shooting at lighting casings, etc.), the perpetrators will be placed by me in the lockup and punished the next day. The same concerns violations of quiet hours after 22.00.
>
> The U.v.D. [*Unteroffizier vom Dienst*] of my unit has been ordered to take out the staircase lighting fuse at 22.00 every evening; if lights are still on after 22.00, I will remove them.[84]

The unit was probably stationed at Chopin Street until Christmas 1941. Before their transfer, they lived in unspecified barracks.[85]

In Stary Dzików, Oskar Dirlewanger employed a Jew, Sara Bergmann, as his interpreter; she moved to Lublin together with SS-Sonderkommando Dirlewanger. Gossip about a romance between them circulated at the time.[86]

Gottlob Berger, who had been friends with Oskar Dirlewanger many years before the start of the Second World War, testified in 1965 that Dirlewanger did indeed have romances with Jews. He declared that while visiting Stary Dzików (a social hunt had been organized), he had seen Dirlewanger in the company of two Jewish women, and he was undoubtedly in an intimate relationship with them.[87]

Disciplinary Proceeding Against Oskar Dirlewanger

In 1941, in connection with the offences of Dirlewanger and members of his unit, and the resulting numerous complaints and denunciations (mostly anonymous), the Gestapo initiated an investigation and criminal proceedings. Friedrich Krüger made a statement in which he wrote, "If this band of criminals does not vanish from this region [GG] within a week, I will arrest him [Dirlewanger] personally."[88] Over a brief period, Krüger had diametrically changed his opinion about the unit and its commander. Back in September

1941, he had supported Berger's motion to promote Dirlewanger from *SS-Hauptsturmführer* to *SS-Sturmbannführer* and agreed with Globocnik's positive assessment of him.[89]

SS-Sturmbannführer Johannes Müller,[90] head of the Lublin Gestapo, called SS-Sonderkommando Dirlewanger a "plague." He claimed that they observed no rules and blackmailed, stole from, and shot the Jews they arrested. Furthermore, he accused them of looting the Lublin ghetto.[91] In response, on February 6, 1942, the *Reichsführer*'s staff sent him the information that SS-Sonderkommando Dirlewanger was subordinate to him.[92]

As I mentioned earlier, while serving in Stary Dzików, Dirlewanger released some forced laborers from the camp for an appropriate fee. Captured by the Gestapo, the prisoners testified that after making the payment, they received a receipt from Dirlewanger and were actually allowed to go home.[93] Embezzlement and financial scams also occurred. Dirlewanger showed extraordinary cunning and guile in financial matters, which was actually already apparent in the 1920s.

One of the many anonymous letters about Oskar Dirlewanger was sent on July 23, 1941. Its author claimed that since September 1940, Dirlewanger had been ordering supplies for his subordinates that included chocolate, schnapps, and cigarettes. However, according to the letter, these items were not provided to the soldiers but sold in the canteen at inflated prices. The money allegedly lined Dirlewanger's pocket. According to the writer of the anonymous note, the unit's commander sent part of the goods and money to his mother and sister.[94] In a letter dated August 3, the informer continued his list of allegations, which included trading in leather for shoes with Poles. Moreover, the author claimed that Dirlewanger forced his people to sign letters for supplies *in blanco* and kept for himself part of the money he later received to pay for food. Dirlewanger was also accused of a sexual relationship with a Jew[95] and of employing the Jew Rosa (Sara Bergmann was meant) as a home help and interpreter. The author was indignant that a Jew was living in the same place as Dirlewanger.[96]

After acquainting himself with the anonymous letters, Heinrich Himmler ordered SS-Hauptsturmführer Ullbrich to investigate them. The latter stated that the information contained in the letter described above was false.[97] Dirlewanger's problems with denunciations, and thus also with investigations, did not end there. The Gestapo inquiry concerned intimate relations with the Jew Sara Bergmann, releasing Jews from the Stary Dzików camp in exchange for money, embezzlement, trading with Poles in confiscated goods, organizing hunts, giving presents to Jewish women, and bringing Jewish prostitutes to his quarters in Lublin.

The most controversy was engendered by Sara Bergmann, whom Oskar Dirlewanger employed while serving in the Stary Dzików camp. Bergmann was Dirlewanger's interpreter and housekeeper. As I mentioned above, Oskar Dirlewanger's subordinates and soldiers from other similar units gossiped about a romance between him and Sara Bergmann. Nothing was proved against him, however. She herself denied it vigorously, and also testified that she had a fiancé in Józefów.[98]

Sara Bergmann was born on November 11, 1924, in Józefów in the Biłgoraj poviat.[99] During questioning, she was asked about the situation in the Stary Dzików camp and her relationship with Dirlewanger. She stated that she was not employed in the camp, but by SS-Hauptsturmführer Dirlewanger. Having no livelihood, she had come to him in early 1941, asking for work, which she obtained after a trial period. Dirlewanger paid her PLN 32 per month, and she also had free food and lodging. She insisted that she did not receive presents from him. She once got stockings and a manicure device from Dirlewanger's sister when the latter visited.[100]

A Jew she knew from Józefów, Isak Flaumenbaum (Izaak Flomenbaum), gave Bergmann PLN 1,500 while she was already working for Dirlewanger, with the request that she deliver this money to him. This was a payment for releasing another Jew, Rosenberg. Interestingly, Dirlewanger accepted the money, issued a receipt for Flaumenbaum and then released Rosenberg from the camp. At the start of September 1941, while the investigation was ongoing, Rosenberg was living in his house in Józefów.[101] On September 23, he was interrogated in connection with his release from the camp by Dirlewanger. He confirmed that Dirlewanger let him go in exchange for PLN 1,500. He was supposed to receive a receipt later by mail. After the interrogation, he was sent back to prison with two other Jews (sixty-six-year-old Moszek Wassermann and seventy-year-old Josef Tintenfisch). Tintenfisch and Wassermann had paid Dirlewanger PLN 1,000 each to be released from the Stary Dzików camp. Wassermann received a receipt immediately, which he showed to the Gestapo during the interrogation. According to a note of September 24, all three of them attempted to escape and were shot.[102]

The Gestapo also interrogated members of SS-Sonderkommando Dirlewanger concerning both the release of prisoners in exchange for money and command of the unit. The Gestapo had the most questions for Hugo Kannegießer, who was then Dirlewanger's already former batman, and Erich Selzer, his batman at the time. Selzer's testimony differs diametrically on many matters from Kannegießer's testimony, and this is visible in many of the most-important points. This was most likely caused by the dislike that Kannegießer had for Dirlewanger and Selzer's liking for his commander. Furthermore, the former was envious that his position at Dirlewanger's side had been taken by Selzer. When making his testimony, Kannegießer was in Riga, and, as he stated, he was afraid of going back to serve under Dirlewanger. He explained that Dirlewanger was authorized to punish his subordinates with death and often sent culprits back to concentration camps for their faults.[103] Due to the above, in both testimonies many things may be exaggerated or concealed.

Hugo Kannegießer testified that Dirlewanger did indeed release Jews from the camp, but did not mention that the commander took money in exchange. He added that in Stary Dzików, Jews were shot very rarely and then only as a result of escape attempts.[104]

Erich Selzer denied that prisoners were let go for a fee. As he claimed, sometimes some prisoners were beaten as a punishment and then released. According to him, the ones whom the Gestapo mentioned had been accused of something, which was why they were transported to Zamość. Dirlewanger simply released those who had proven their innocence.[105] When the Gestapo showed Selzer the receipt of February 7, 1941, for the release of the Jewish woman Wasserman, he said that he had remembered that this type of situation did sometimes occur.[106] He added,

> Next I remember that when Dirlewanger was not present in Stary Dzików or when he left it, he explained to me that some Jews had fines to pay and this might be carried out in his absence. I should accept the money and issue a receipt. I did so four or five times.[107]

Another of Dirlewanger's subordinates to be questioned by the Gestapo was Franz Hunke, who denied that Dirlewanger released Jews.[108]

As regards sale of goods in the canteen by Dirlewanger, Kannegießer indicated that it was true that soldiers had to buy various products (e.g., chocolate, cigarettes, beer, schnapps), but that the prices were not inflated. Neither did he confirm that the commander kept products for himself. Although as a batman he also performed personal commands for him, he could not cite any irregularities.[109] Kannegießer's words were fully confirmed by Selzer.[110]

Kannegießer testified that Dirlewanger obtained money from unknown sources. When going on leave in the Reich, some soldiers in the unit received various amounts to be deposited into his bank account in Stuttgart.[111] Selzer completely denied these words.[112] Given that in the 1920s, Dirlewanger was accused of embezzlement, such situations may have taken place.

Kannegießer did not deny that Dirlewanger traded with Poles. He testified that upon his order, Gustav Strumpf, the unit's treasurer, traded in confiscated goods.[113]

In May 1941, Sara Bergmann moved to Lublin along with SS-Sonderkommando Dirlewanger. There, Dirlewanger "arranged" for her to have a flat at Grodzka Street 8/10, along with furniture and equipment, since it was brought in from Stary Dzików.[114] As the owner of the premises, a Jewish woman named Sara Elka Rozencwajg, testified, one day she was ordered to prepare a room for an important person. Soon seventeen-year-old Sara Bergmann arrived. Rozencwajg stated that no rent was paid for this room.[115] Moreover, Sara Elka Rozencwajg told investigators that Bergmann spent some nights away from home. She was also sometimes picked up at night by an SS soldier, allegedly to make coffee for the chief.[116]

Hugo Kannegießer testified that Sara Bergmann had taken his place at Dirlewanger's side. He stated that she was conceited, slovenly, and lazy, but his description may have been due to jealousy. She had an influence on Dirlewanger, who protected her, and often accompanied him in his official car.[117]

The overly close and unclear relationship between Dirlewanger and Sara Bergmann gave rise to general displeasure and irritation among SS-Sonderkommando Dirlewanger members. According to numerous testimonies, it caused a sudden deterioration in the relationship between commander and soldiers. Richard Eibl stated, "In January 1941, the Jew Sara Bergmann from Józefów took a position as a servant with Dirlewanger, and from this point on, general unease and discontent reigned among the comrades [of the unit]."[118]

Erich Selzer categorically denied that Dirlewanger and Bergmann were in an intimate relationship. He said,

> Because Dirlewanger's room is directly opposite the canteen, I was able to supervise the Jewish woman's work. If D. is suspected of an intimate relationship with the Jew, then this is a vile and outrageous suspicion. The Jew was employed by D. only during the day and she left our house every evening as arranged. In the daytime, as I have already mentioned, she was always under my supervision, so I had to see everything and would have seen everything. Dirlewanger was too severe on the Jew, if this can even be said about such a slob. I remember that D. often beat the Jew and deprived her of food for several days. This was because of minor offenses.[119]

In the context of the allegation that Dirlewanger organized numerous hunts for fun, Kannegießer testified that the commander did not participate in them. He did remember that SS-Brigadeführer Berger's visit was the exception.[120] This was confirmed by Richard Eibl and Erich Selzer, who indicated that the meat of the animals killed was served in the canteen.[121]

SS-Hauptsturmführer Oskar Dirlewanger was interrogated on October 14, 1941. He briefly responded to questions concerning the allegations of the anonymous letters, stating that he had already talked about this during his stay in Berlin in a conversation with an officer from the SS Main Office.[122] He added that he had no knowledge about trade in objects from the camp. He indicated that the camp was subordinated to SS-Untersturmführer Riedel.[123]

Dirlewanger was accused of giving gifts to Jews. In his response to the Gestapo's question if he had given a purple scarf to a Jewish woman called Epelbaum, Dirlewanger made no denial. He stated that she used it as a rag to clean windows, and when she asked if she could take it, he agreed. A Jewish woman called Mandelbaum, meanwhile, received shoe polish from him. He explained that she polished his shoes, and so he had to provide her the means to do so.[124] In both cases the explanations were very businesslike, and the so-called presents not particularly expensive. Looking at the arguments used by the anonymous informer, it is apparent that the letter's author intended to smear Dirlewanger and spoil his already rather tarnished reputation. It was impossible to build charges on the basis of such information.

Concerning Sara Bergmann, Dirlewanger stated that he employed her as an interpreter for SS-Sonderkommando Dirlewanger. She was additionally supposed to help in the kitchen and the canteen. She had been ordered to move from Lublin to Stary Dzików together with the unit. He justified renting her a flat by citing matters of hygiene. He did not want a person who worked for SS-Sonderkommando Dirlewanger to stay in the ghetto, where diseases were rampant.[125]

Dirlewanger did not deny letting Jews out of the camp for a fee. He stated that it was true that Sara Bergmann had given him PLN 1,500 as a fine for the Jew Rosenberg. Also, other Jews were released from the camp for a fee. He judged that this was a normal procedure and a punishment for some offenses. What is more, he claimed that he had arranged this with the SS and police leader in Lublin, Odilo Globocnik, and that the money was collected according to regulations and then transferred to the police and SS treasury.[126]

Two weeks after Dirlewanger's interrogation, Sara Bergmann testified again. She confirmed what she had said earlier. Despite pressure, she still denied being in an intimate relationship with Dirlewanger. To her previous testimony, she added that Dirlewanger was often violent toward her. If she failed to do something or lied, he hit her with a whip or a stick—even minor issues (such as dusting badly) or a bad mood were enough. She mentioned that she once shared some bread with a Polish prisoner who worked in the quarters of SS-Sonderkommando Dirlewanger. Dirlewanger also punished her for this, having one of the soldiers whip her and then shut her in the cellar until the next day.[127] Dirlewanger treated and punished Sara Bergmann just like he treated his soldiers.

Also, soldiers of units stationed in the neighborhood of Dirlewanger's unit were interrogated. On November 4, 1941, in Groß-Rosen, SS-Hauptscharführer Rheinhold Kluss[128] from 1. SS Sturmbann Groß-Rosen was interviewed. He said that he was familiar with Dirlewanger only by sight and maintained no contact with him. The only link between them was the units' quarters at Chopin Street in Lublin.[129] He did, however, state that one day a mutiny had broken out in SS-Sonderkommando Dirlewanger, with many soldiers drunk, but Dirlewanger did not react. Nobody from that unit was on duty. As he testified, he had found out all this from Dirlewanger's five subordinates, who asked him to assume command. He could not do so without the permission of his superiors, although as he admitted, he would have been glad to take over. Despite the lack of reaction on Dirlewanger's part, on the next day the unit functioned without any problems.[130]

In the context of Sara Bergmann, he stated that he had seen the girl being brought to Dirlewanger's quarters at night once. He also said that Dirlewanger's subordinates told him that this was nothing out of the ordinary. Furthermore, he once met Bergmann around midnight in SS-Sonderkommando Dirlewanger's quarters, where she was waiting for the commander in the corridor. However, he was unable to say whether they were in an intimate relationship.[131]

Reinhold Kluss's testimony does not seem particularly credible. At the start of the interrogation, he indicated that he did not know Oskar Dirlewanger personally and maintained no contact with him. This suggests he was not quartered with him. Several sentences later, he describes how in the middle of the night, in a corridor of SS-Sonderkommando Dirlewanger's headquarters, next to the door to the commander's room he met Sara Bergmann. He did not explain what he had been doing there. In each statement, he emphasized that Dirlewanger's soldiers had come complaining to him and asked him to take command of the unit, but on the other hand, he gave no specific details or names (he himself owned that he did not know them and knew Dirlewanger's subordinates only by sight).[132] He had no evidence to support his words. None of the people interrogated by the Gestapo confirmed his testimony or mentioned a mutiny in SS-Sonderkommando Dirlewanger. The most inconsistent part of his statement is the claim that Dirlewanger did not react in any way to the unrest, almost mutiny in his unit, and despite this, everybody went back to work. Kluss most likely just wanted to take over the unit (which he mentioned) and profit from its leadership and the unit's operations.

On November 10, 1941, Oswald Egger, an *SS-Unterscharführer* from SS-Sonderkommando Dirlewanger, was questioned about Kluss's testimony. He denied everything and even stated that the soldiers had no reservations about the way Dirlewanger commanded. The only thing they had been unhappy with in the recent period was the employment of Sara Bergmann, of which they had informed Dirlewanger point blank (*unverblümt*). Despite this, Egger said he had nothing against the girl and even had a positive attitude toward her. He added that he did not know and had never heard of any intimate relationship between Dirlewanger and Bergmann. Moreover, it was quite unclear to him whom Kluss may have talked to and how he could have drawn the above conclusions.[133]

Next to be interrogated was Gustav Strumpf, the accountant (*Rechnungsführer*) of SS-Sonderkommando Dirlewanger. He stated that the accusations contained in the anonymous letters were very much exaggerated. He testified that Dirlewanger always divided the provisions in a way that was beneficial to his subordinates, did not embezzle money, and had even opened a special account for the whole unit. He said that the soldiers were paid PLN 100, while the rest was transferred to the account. Strumpf noted that not everybody was pleased with this solution.[134]

It could be said that the testimony of the unit's members was partisan and intentionally undermined Rheinhold Kluss's words. Kluss's statement was also called into question by a soldier not in SS-Sonderkommando Dirlewanger who was close to SS-Hauptscharführer Kluss and a member of Kommando Kluss. SS-Hauptscharführer Hermann Tetzel testified that in the period between June and July 1941, the relationship between Dirlewanger and Kluss kept deteriorating. He described Kluss as an awful man, self-absorbed, malicious, and extremely hypocritical.[135]

The aim of all the investigations was, among other things, to draw attention away from Odilo Globocnik's wrongdoings. As Gottlob Berger ascertained, there was a lot of tension between Dirlewanger and Globocnik. It subsided after the unit was transferred to Belarus and may have been due to the fact that Dirlewanger had two "friends" (of Russian or Jewish origin) who accompanied him in particular during his drunken sprees.[136] Globocnik himself wrote on January 22, 1942:

> I thank SS-Sturmbannführer Dirlewanger and his men for their work, often performed in difficult conditions.
>
> I would like to use this occasion to emphasize that all the accusations leveled in recent times against SS-Sturmbannführer Dirlewanger are

> groundless, and SS-Sturmbannführer Dirlewanger is leaving us after one and a half years' service in Stary Dzików, which was not easy.[137]

In consequence of the explanatory proceedings, on February 25, 1942, SS-Sonderkommando Dirlewanger was withdrawn from the GG and sent to occupied eastern Belarus. The unit was made part of HSSPF Russland-Mitte under Erich von dem Bach-Zelewski. Further to Heinrich Himmler's order, Oskar Dirlewanger remained its commander.[138]

4

Fighting Against Partisans and Banditry in the Belarusian Soviet Socialist Republic: *Partisanenbekämpfung* and *Bandenbekämpfung*

June 22, 1941, saw the start of Operation Barbarossa, the Third Reich's attack on the Soviet Union. It was the largest German action during the Second World War. With the support of Romanian, Finnish, Hungarian, and Slovak forces, three army groups entered the USSR. German panzer groups were supposed to destroy the Red Army in Belarus; take Leningrad, Moscow, and Kyiv; and reach the line of the Ural and the Volga.[1]

It was intended as a genocidal war. During a conference in Wewelsburg held on June 11–15, 1941, Hitler stated that the population of the USSR should be reduced by thirty million.[2] Two weeks before the attack, an order was issued to shoot all Soviet political commissars taken into captivity and to form special-operation groups that would push through to the Ural. Their tasks would include "on the one hand, the elimination in areas behind the lines of actively operating opponents" and, on the other, "preventive eradication of elements who due to their views or past would be able in conducive circumstances to undertake hostile activity."[3] In practice, this order meant the extermination of population groups that could be accused of hostile activity.

Hitler ordered the military justice system not to prosecute criminal offenses committed by Wehrmacht soldiers against the civilian population in eastern territories (they were thus to remain unpunished), military courts did not handle crimes that enemy civilians committed against each other, and offenders were to be killed on the spot. He also granted consent to "mass acts of violence against Communists."[4]

According to the "Guidelines for the Treatment of Political Commissars" signed by the chief of the Supreme Command of the Armed Forces (Oberkommando der Wehrmacht, or OKW), Field Marshal Wilhelm Keitel,[5] as the "initiators of barbarian Asian combat methods," Soviet commissars were to be eliminated by the fighting units. Bolsheviks were believed to be "deadly enemies of the national socialist German nation," and thus "merciless and energetic methods of combating Bolshevik agitators, partisans, saboteurs, and Jews" were necessary. Furthermore, it was planned that "all forms of active and passive resistance" would be stifled, and the death penalty would be used as a form of repression, involving the killing of fifty or a hundred hostages, because "in those areas life has no value."[6]

Himmler's attitude toward the population residing in eastern regions is best shown in the illustrated brochure called "Subhuman" published by the SS Main Office: "These are terrifying creatures . . . , with barely any resemblance to true human beings . . . , and intellectually and spiritually they remain at animal level."[7]

In Belarus the Germans initially used the tactic of *Partisanenbekämpfung*, which they later changed to *Bandenbekämpfung*. The difference lay in how the opponent was viewed. People from SS-Sonderkommando Dirlewanger were trained and prepared for clashes with partisans (*Partisanenbekämpfung*), who according to military law were soldiers and combatants under legal protection. At the turn of 1941 and 1942, the perception of the fighting against partisans changed and thus so did the whole military doctrine. This was why SS-Sonderkommando Dirlewanger and other units participating in the fighting operated under the principles of *Bandenbekämpfung* (i.e., combating banditry). In German, *Banden* means bandits and criminal groups. Such people may be treated as pariahs and offenders, which means they are not under any legal protection. The change in the doctrine had no significance for the fighting methods and soldiers' training. The difference lay in radicalization and brutalization during pacifications of areas suspected of favoring the partisans.[8]

The Germans managed to surprise the USSR and initially achieved great successes. In summer 1941, they took Belarus within a few weeks. Gradually, however, Soviet resistance hardened and German losses grew. The acute heat, great distances, and ubiquitous dust brought soldiers to the limits of endurance, while tanks and trucks broke down regularly.

The coming of autumn brought no respite. On October 6, 1941, came a snowfall, and starting on October 9, sleet fell constantly.[9] All vehicles kept getting stuck in the waterlogged roads, and infantry waded knee-deep in mud. In mid-November, freezing temperatures started, which brought new challenges. Few soldiers had winter clothing and white camouflage suits; furthermore, the low temperatures caused numerous malfunctions in German tanks and trucks. Bringing in supplies became an enormous problem.[10]

After taking Belarus, the Germans formed the Generalbezirk Weissruthenien (General District White Ruthenia) in the western and central part of the republic, with its seat in Minsk. The areas around Białystok and Łomża were annexed to East Prussia as the Białystok District, while the lands around Kobryn, Pinsk, and Brest belonged to Reich Commissariat Ukraine until early 1944 (afterward, they were under the authority of the general commissioner in Minsk for six months). Generalbezirk Weissruthenien was part of Reich Commissariat Ostland. The Gauleiter of the Kurmark District and supreme president of Brandenburg and West Prussia, Wilhelm Kube, was appointed general commissar, with headquarters in Minsk (he was assassinated in 1943). From 1943 onward, this position was held by Kurt von Gottberg, higher SS and police leader.[11] Generalbezirk Weissruthenien was divided into eleven areas: Baranavichy, Barysaw, Hlybokaye, Hantsavichy, Lida, Minsk–rural district, Minsk–urban district, Navahrudak, Slonim, Slutsk, and Vileyka. Many Belarusians (and initially also Poles) were employed in offices. From 1942 onward, collaborators of the administrative bodies became a frequent target of partisan attacks.[12]

In these conditions, numerous partisan units formed behind the front lines. They were composed of civilians (often drafted by force) and Red Army soldiers who had managed to avoid captivity. In combat, their members used their acquaintance with the land and were able to mask themselves very well. They attacked German supply columns, blew up railway lines, and killed marauders. This lowered morale among soldiers fighting on the eastern front. To prevent these types of partisan operations, SS-Sonderkommando Dirlewanger was sent to Belarus.[13]

The authorities of the Generalbezirk Weissruthenien obligated the civilian population to help combat the resistance movement. The principle of collective responsibility for attacks on German soldiers and representatives of the occupant's administration was introduced. This meant that homes, settlements, villages, and even whole areas of land that were deemed to harbor partisans were destroyed and burned down completely. The inhabitants were usually murdered, resettled, or transported as laborers to the Reich. During operations, the concept of "dead zones" (*Tote Zonen*) was introduced, which Himmler had advocated in July 1941. Through these actions, individual areas were systematically depopulated via murder and deportation.

In Belarus, fifty-five large antipartisan operations were conducted, during which at least 150,000 people died. To this should be added smaller operations with an unknown number of victims. It is estimated that around 200,000–300,000 people were killed,[14] mainly Belarusians, but also Jews and Poles.

4.1. Antipartisan Operations in Belarus (1942)

Formation of Partisan Units in the Belarusian Soviet Socialist Republic

According to Russian estimates from the Second World War period, in December 1942, 49.1 percent of its partisans were fighting in Belarus, while they amounted to 39.4 percent in the Russian Soviet Federative Socialist Republic, 8.7 percent in the Ukrainian Soviet Socialist Republic, and 2.8 percent in the remaining republics.[15] In 1944, the Central Headquarters of the Partisan Movement (CHPM) wrote that on the territory of the Soviet Union occupied by the German army there operated 1,156 units and groups, numbering 187,571 people in total, most of whom were in Belarus: 23 units and 121,903 fighters.[16]

By 1941, German commanders were aware that the most effective method of combating partisans would be an extensive military operation:

> Pacification of an area with evenly distributed partisan positions is the most effective via a rapid incursion with a broad front, its maximally fast occupation with as great a scattering of [partisan] units as possible. . . . The military should be located in closed buildings, schools, or barns and equipped with means of defense. Each unit then starts to thoroughly search the area assigned to it, including the settlements and individual peasant homesteads located within it, in order to expose strangers and check that the local population does not support the partisans.[17]

SS-Sonderkommando Dirlewanger was sent to Belarus for this very purpose. In that period, there was a lack of units that could carry out such an operation on a broad scale. A temporary solution was chosen, and small motorized units were brought in. Dirlewanger's soldiers were sent there due to their "special poachers' skills."[18] They would supposedly locate partisan encampments more easily in cooperation with the local people; moreover, their particular abilities would help them make the life of partisan groups harder and to put pressure on them. In Nuremberg, Erich von dem Bach-Zelewski[19] testified that the battalion-sized unit commanded by Dirlewanger reporting to him was incorporated into Army Group Center at the turn of 1941 and 1942.[20] In military terms, they were under von dem Bach's orders.

The Soviet Union had been preparing to conduct partisan activity on its own territory by the early 1930s. At that time, organizational structures were developed that later were able to engage in surprise combat and carry out sabotage operations. This was due to Stalin's fears of a Polish preventive attack, among other reasons. All over the USSR, special schools were established to train future partisans and saboteurs. Moreover, the Red Army and the State Political Directorate (Gosudarstvennoe politicheskoe upravlenie, or GPU)[21] built secret warehouses with arms, ammunition, and explosives. These operations were abandoned in 1937, at the latest, because Stalin and his collaborators concluded that preparing for a partisan war was a manifestation of defeatism. As a result, most of those who had trained for partisan operations (school instructors, graduates, et al.) were shot in the "great purges." Only a few managed to survive. In the years 1937–38, arms and ammunition warehouses were also destroyed. Several years later, these structures had to be rebuilt with great effort.[22]

The concept was revisited on June 29, 1941. On that day, Stalin signed directive no. P509, in which he called for all state and party structures to form partisan units and saboteur groups. Two days later, directive no. 2 was published, according to which all party, Komsomol, and state organizations were to undertake the following operations:

> On all territories of Belarus occupied by the enemy, a dense network of partisan units should be formed immediately, which should unceasingly and relentlessly fight the enemy for the purpose of its destruction. . . . All Communists and Komsomol members able to bear arms are to remain in the occupied areas . . . , to mobilize the populace to mercilessly combat the enemy.[23]

In a radio speech of July 3, Stalin personally called the nation to relentlessly oppose the enemy:

> In areas occupied by the enemy, it is essential to form cavalry and infantry partisan units, form groups of saboteurs to fight the enemy's army units, undertake partisan warfare everywhere, blow up bridges, destroy roads, interrupt telephone and telegraph connections, [and] set fire to forests, warehouses, and rolling stock. In occupied areas a situation should be created that is unbearable for the enemy and all its supporters; they should be hunted and destroyed at each step and all their endeavors should be frustrated.[24]

On July 18, 1941, in a directive organizing combat in the German army's rear areas, the Central Committee of the Communist Party of the Soviet Union (Bolsheviks)—CC CPSU(B) commanded underground party committees to be formed in occupied areas. Their aim was to ensure the development of partisan and saboteur activity.[25]

In the forests and marshes of Belarus, partisan groups very soon started to form, composed, among others, of Red Army soldiers and Soviet activists who had not managed to escape the approaching front but survived the first German attacks. Initially, their operations came down to attempts to survive, obtain food, and hide from German soldiers. However, by the end of 1941, few groups engaged in active combat against the Germans were left in Belarus. Until the start of 1942, only small detachments operated in the Minsk District. It was not until the spring of 1942 that these groups transformed into active partisan or criminal groups that attacked and looted the local population.

The partisan units were also joined by civilians from areas occupied by Germans, including those escaping from destroyed and burned villages and fleeing persecution. Contrary to appearances, a large part of Belarusians had a hostile, negative, or neutral attitude to the partisans. Local populations cooperated with the German army, which to a large extent contributed to their successes.

In many cases, German armies would not have managed without the aid and support of the civilian population. In 1941, Belarusians were sympathetic toward the German military. This is confirmed by a report of Gen. Maximilian von Schenckendorff, commander of the Rear Area of Army Group Center: "The best information about the location of partisans always comes from the local population,"[26] and also by a report of September 30, 1941:

> Many times while fighting against partisans we had friendly cooperation of the local population. This help would have been far larger it if it were not for the fear of the Red Army's return, which is maintained among the population via leaflets and whispered propaganda.[27]

A similar opinion was expressed by Filip Piestrak, a Soviet activist who hid between summer 1941 and spring 1943 in the Lyelchytsy District:

> In all their operations, the Germans take advantage of support from the local population. These are mostly the sons of kulaks, former soldiers, bandits, and other criminals, who were deported by the Soviet authorities for their harmful activities. They formed the Germans' personnel. . . . They did more work than the Germans. Some testified before the district commissar that they were persecuted during Soviet rule, that they were kulaks, and now they should have privileges. . . . In some instances these recruits betrayed partisans.[28]

On July 2, 1941, Reinhard Heydrich, the chief of security police, issued "Additional written guidelines for four higher commanders of the SS and the police: SS-Obergruppenführer [Friedrich] Jeckeln, SS-Gruppenführers [Erich] von dem Bach-Zelewski and [Adolf] Prützmann, and SS-Oberführer [Gerret] Korsemann—in the East," in which he indicated that

> the following will be executed: all officials of the Comintern (as well as all the Communist career politicians); senior, middle-ranking and radical lower-level functionaries in the Party, the Central Committee, and the provincial and district committees; the People's Commissars; Jews in Party and State positions; other extremist elements (saboteurs, propagandists, snipers, assassins, agitators, et al.); in so far as in individual cases there are not required, or are no longer required, for political intelligence of special importance, for future security police measures, or for the economic reconstruction of the occupied territories. . . . No steps will be taken to interfere with any purges that may be initiated by anti-Communist or anti-Jewish elements in the newly occupied territories. On the contrary, these are to be secretly encouraged.[29]

Oskar Dirlewanger's unit also operated in accordance with these instructions.

SS-Sonderkommando Dirlewanger: *Bandenbekämpfung*

In an order of January 29, 1942, Himmler finally regularized the unit's status. According to this decree, Kommando Dirlewanger became a volunteer unit (*Freiwilligen-Abteilung*), recognized by the Waffen-SS. They thus came under the orders of SS Leadership Main Office (SS-Führungshauptamt).[30] In February 1942, they were sent to the Babruysk region and then to Mogilev. As Gerhard Hellkamp, one of Dirlewanger's soldiers remembered, that winter was very harsh.[31] A year earlier, in 1941, a forced-labor camp had operated in Mogilev, and Himmler had considered expanding it. In mid-November 1941, the construction of a large crematorium was even ordered there.[32]

Dirlewanger's soldiers stayed around four to six weeks in Babruysk, and at the end of summer 1942 they left for Mogilev. They spent around a year there.[33] They were quartered in a former old people's home,[34] near a field hospital commanded by Dr. Heinz Hartlieb. This was extremely important to the facility for security reasons, particularly since its personnel were composed only of several German doctors, and among the wounded there were around a hundred German soldiers and a thousand wounded Russian patients.[35] By February 10, 1942, SS-Sonderkommando Dirlewanger had been fully equipped and uniformed by Higher SS and Police Leader Russland-Mitte.

In Nuremberg, von dem Bach-Zelewski testified,

> Among the units that were deemed suitable for fighting partisans at the start of 1942 was one battalion commanded by Dirlewanger, which was incorporated into Army Group Center; this battalion was gradually enlarged until it reached the size first of a regiment, then a brigade. "Dirlewanger's brigade" consisted mostly of convicted criminal offenders officially called poachers, although they actually included offenders convicted of break-ins, murders, etc.[36]

In 1942, Heinrich Himmler's racial ideals, which were a precondition for joining the Waffen-SS, started to blur due to the lack of soldiers for the Eastern Front. Thus, the need to recruit volunteers from conquered territories was born.[37] The first so-called eastern units were formed at the end of 1941. They were used in frontline fighting and in antipartisan operations. Initially, the soldiers of the eastern divisions were recruited from POWs, and later among young men from western Belarus and other occupied areas of the USSR. It is estimated that in July 1943, these units numbered around seventy thousand people.[38]

When there were no more native German poachers left, Dirlewanger started enlisting offenders and criminals, and also Russians and Slavs. In late April and early May 1942, SS-Sonderkommando Dirlewanger was still a small unit of around seventy poachers.[39] It was only in May 1942 that sixty Ukrainian volunteers recruited from POWs were assigned to Dirlewanger's orders.[40] He was able to form a motorcyclist platoon in Mogilev,[41] though not a very numerous one as of yet. As Friedrich Walter mentioned, the team consisted of three people and twelve motorcycles.[42]

Starting on March 23, 1942, Dirlewanger repeatedly requested that Himmler assign him more men. On June 19, 1942, he wrote another letter to the SS-Führungshauptamt, and in a letter to Gottlob Berger of July 27, 1942, he asked the unit to be enlarged to 250 men; that is, for around two companies to be formed, and for the appropriate equipment. As a result, on September 20, SS-Sonderkommando Dirlewanger was joined by 115 men convicted of poaching, from Mogilev.[43]

Dirlewanger constantly demanded replenishments, further "volunteers" and soldiers from prisons belonging to the police and SS. He would personally decide whether their character and skills were right for his needs. Preparatory proceedings against all the individuals selected for the unit were to be deferred, while convicts were to have the opportunity to rehabilitate themselves and erase their sins.[44]

By July 1942, Sigmund Rascher wrote in a letter to Willy Suchanek about three prisoners of the Dachau camp who were to be released and transferred under Dirlewanger's orders. They were Willi Mürdter (born March 8, 1903, in Stuttgart; camp no. 24538), Bruno Förstner (born September 9, 1903, in Reutlingen; camp no. 61) and Wilhelm Sobota (born May 27, 1906, in Vienna; camp no. 2963).[45] Mürdter deserted in 1943. It is unknown what the further fates of the remaining two were and whether they ultimately found their way to Dirlewanger's unit.

Erich von dem Bach-Zelewski testified that Berger was responsible for the unit's provisioning, armaments, and equipment, as well as for appointing officers.[46]

After obtaining consent from Higher SS and Police Leader Russland-Mitte (HSSPF Russland-Mitte) and von dem Bach-Zelewski, Dirlewanger formed two additional companies composed of Ukrainians (Belarusians). Their command was held by Russian officers, supervised by Germans: SS-Oberscharführer Engel-Niedermeier and SS-Hauptascharführer Paul Zimmermann.[47]

By the end of 1942, Dirlewanger had formed two companies composed of Russian, Ukrainian, and Belarusian POWs—*Hilfswillige* (so-called *Hiwis*). One of the companies, according to what Gustav Brusberg remembered, was commanded by SS-Hauptsturmführer Schreier.[48] Moreover, three hundred more prisoners from the Sachsenhausen concentration camp were transferred to the unit.[49] The recruits were provided uniforms and trained briefly in Lahoysk, where the unit was stationed. In that period SS-Sonderkommando Dirlewanger consisted of three German and two Russian companies. Dirlewanger additionally assigned an *SS-Unterführer* of Russian origin to each German commander of a Russian company to defuse problems and conflicts.[50] The companies numbered around 180 soldiers each.[51]

Zimmermann mentioned that he was transferred to the Minsk region from Lahoysk together with his company, which was assigned to the 2nd Battalion, commanded by Steinhauer. It then had to retreat to the Łomża (Lomscha) region due to severe losses.[52]

As a result of later losses, the two Russian companies were merged into one.[53] Ultimately, the Russian company was disbanded completely in Łomża. The *Hiwis* who could drive wagons and ride were incorporated into the company and battalion transport groups of Dirlewanger's unit.[54] Men for the unit were selected according to criteria provided by Dirlewanger on October 9, 1942:

> Persons . . . who . . . are subject to investigation or undergoing imprisonment for poaching with firearms. Not to be taken into account are
>
> (a) poachers who are often recorded for punishable offenses other than poaching, particularly those previously sentenced to heavy imprisonment
>
> (b) foreigners, the stateless, and persons of non-German blood
>
> (c) persons above the age of 55, and,
>
> (d) persons who are not fully capable of performing duties due to physical and mental illness or physical handicaps.[55]

In 1968, a trial was held in Moscow of "former Soviet collaborators" who worked with Dirlewanger's soldiers during the war. Eleven *Hiwis* were sentenced to eleven to fifteen years' imprisonment for crimes committed against civilians during the pacification of villages carried out by SS-Sonderkommando Dirlewanger in Belarus.[56]

The tasks of Dirlewanger's soldiers in Belarus included patrolling (*Streifen*) and fighting partisans (*Bandenbekämpfung*).[57] As they remembered, actions and operations there were particularly difficult. *Bandenbekämpfung* primarily involved surrounding the enemy. As a result, partisans had practically no chance of escaping and getting out of the encirclement, while German losses were not that large. During combat against partisans, there was no time to consider one's actions. In a letter to his sister, Paul Lau wrote that in this type of unit, combat was conducted "without pardon": either the partisan or the German soldier had to die.[58] The historian Philip W. Blood stated that there were four ways of destroying partisans:

- "Crushing the encirclement" (*Kesseltrieben*): After surrounding the partisan group, German forces moved forward toward its center, killing everybody in their way.
- "Drive hunt" (*Vorstehtreiben*): pushing the enemy into the field of fire ("like a 'partridge drive' where beaters scare birds toward the hunter's gunfire").
- Driving a wedge into "heart of the enemy" (*Vortreiben starker Stosskeile*): In this method, "a wedge formed out of a combined arms team of infantry and armor or self-propelled artillery was held in reserve until an opportunity opened for to smash their way into the heart of the band."
- Deployment of an assault group (*Bildung einer Stossgruppe*): The *Stossgruppe* would attack the encircled group, relying "on accurate intelligence and the correct assumption of the band's intended breakout point." They mainly hunted down those who attempted to escape.

The units participating in the operation were supposed to confuse the enemy. Even if the commander heard from the interrogated deserters or captured partisans that a group had been destroyed, he should not stop the "hunt."[59] The fighting was extremely fierce. In the course of one day, German soldiers moved around 5 km.[60]

Antipartisan Operations

Dirlewanger's soldiers stayed in Belarus for thirty months. During that time, fifty-five major operations of combing the area were conducted, and the unit participated in at least thirty-eight of them,[61] both independently and as a formation that was a part of battle groups fighting against the partisans. It also conducted smaller combat operations that included combing the area near Babruysk, Mogilev, and Lahoysk.[62]

The situation was made more difficult by omnipresent marshes. Heinz Feiertag, one of Dirlewanger's soldiers, mentioned that the partisans had excellent training and suitable equipment and weapons. These people were superbly prepared for fighting in marshy areas and knew how to hide there and how best to build their positions. Feiertag described the 1942 antipartisan fighting in the Pripyat Marshes:

> It was a summer operation. Around early spring. In that respect, it was quite a hard operation; fighting with partisans is generally quite hard. But because of the marshy area it became even harder. The partisans were well trained; they had the right armaments and good positions in the marshes. They stood immersed in the marsh up to their necks, covered with fern leaves. . . . They allowed us to approach as close as possible and then they opened fire from every side. The partisans kept surprising us completely. For a moment we lost our heads completely.[63]

Dirlewanger's soldiers sustained great losses in such clashes. Partisans took advantage of their acquaintance with the land, and thus it was easier for them to hide and mask their dwellings. Only when the first shock passed did the Germans start to gain control. They gradually adapted to this type of combat. Dirlewanger ordered the following:

> We will not discover the enemy's camp by following comfortable paths, but by forcing our way through the marshes. . . . The marsh is no obstacle to bandits; what bandits can do, poachers can do as well.[64]

They learned to recognize ambushes and limited the amount of equipment they took along. On this type of action, they took machine guns and were accompanied by snipers. The first clash usually took place around 30–40 km away from the partisans' headquarters.[65]

Not only the partisans knew how to camouflage themselves well. German forces kept improving their masking methods throughout the war. The first experiments with camouflaging clothes and masks were initiated in 1936. Heinrich Himmler waited with great impatience for the newest camo and face shields, but other commanders were more skeptical toward this idea. Camo was sewn in concentration camps: in Dachau, Buchenwald, Ravensbrück, Majdanek, and Trawniki. There were two types of patterns on the masking shirts: spring-summer, in which the color green was dominant, and autumnal, with mostly browns and yellows. Sometimes the colors seeped to the other side of the material and formed new sets of colors, patterns, and shades. The most-usual patterns were those imitating the foliage of trees such as the plane (sycamore), aspen, and oak, but a polka-dot pattern (until the end of 1943) and a palm leaf pattern (until the turn of 1941 and 1942) were also used.[66] During the fighting, the masks fell off or obstructed the field of vision at the most-undesirable moments. Despite these inconveniences, they were supposed to supplement Waffen-SS soldiers' camouflage dress and helmet covers. They were made of cotton and viscose. Thongs were used to secure them to the head, and they covered the whole face. In Belarus, SS-Sonderkommando Dirlewanger soldiers used them to conceal themselves in forest thickets as thoroughly and completely as possible. Masks were also worn by snipers.[67]

Some soldiers were entitled to wear chevrons (*Ehrenwinkel*). This was the privilege of those who had joined the SS or NSDAP before Hitler's rise to power; that is, before January 30, 1933. Also, policemen and soldiers serving before July 25, 1935 (i.e. before the remilitarization of Germany), had such a right (they wore a chevron with a star on the inside). The right to wear a chevron was also held by NSDAP members in Austria who had belonged to the organization before February 12, 1935. Chevrons were sewn onto the right uniform sleeve.[68] As a long-term NSDAP member, Oskar Dirlewanger also wore a chevron on his sleeve.[69] Some soldiers from Dirlewanger's unit wore armbands (*Ärmelstreifen*) announcing their membership in a given unit. These distinctions had the nature of souvenirs and could be worn by soldiers serving in a given formation.[70]

Partisans usually tried to avoid regular combat. They made surprise attacks, with the whole action lasting practically only seconds: Clashes took from five to ten minutes. As far as possible, they tried to avoid longer and more-direct fighting with the Germans:

> Partisans received instructions to act destructively, tie down the [enemy's] forces, but never to engage in direct combat unless this was necessary. They were to attack railway lines, trucks, etc.[71]

Their advantage lay in their better acquaintance with the land. As Feiertag mentioned, many roads were not marked on German maps, while the partisans knew them perfectly. They could disappear before the eyes of Dirlewanger's soldiers and vanish without a trace.[72] The objective of the partisan attacks was railway lines and trains. Railway workers attempted to protect trains: For instance, the locomotive would push a freight car filled with sand intended to dampen the strength of a possible explosion.[73] Partisans also attacked German supply units and couriers on motorcycles and blew up bridges and fuel, ammunition, and food depots. They inflicted massive damage, destroying telephone lines, telegraph stations, and airfields.[74]

German soldiers taken prisoner by the partisans were as a rule sentenced to death. Captives were shot almost immediately or after several days. If the aspects of antispy psychosis present among partisans are disregarded, this was primarily due to the lack of space for holding prisoners over an extended time; neither could they allow such persons to go free, and sending prisoners to the rear was too problematic. Execution was the only option. German combat groups did the same, since they could not hold prisoners either.

In order to find partisan settlements, special small combat groups were sent out. They were to perform reconnaissance, find out the enemy's strength, and establish the precise location of the headquarters or camp. In forming this type of small combat group, the Germans drew on hunting customs: They acted like hunters tracking wildlife.[75] On September 4, 1942, the Supreme Command of Army Group B issued instructions for the Wehrmacht's so-called hunting units. According to these guidelines, the units were to move only by night and hide in forested areas during the day. Furthermore, they were to behave "the same as enemy bandit groups"; that is,

> (2.a) After thorough reconnaissance of the land, traps for the enemy are to be laid everywhere where his appearance may be expected (e.g., next to roads where the enemy tends to place mines). Next to bridges that he has tried to burn many times, or on the edge of the forest near a village that according to its inhabitants' reports is a food base for bandit groups. (b) Hunting divisions destroy all enemies caught in a trap. Combat with an enemy that has a large advantage should not be engaged in. . . . (d) In situations where the effect of surprise fails (e.g., due to the coincidental appearance of local inhabitants), if it is impossible to soundlessly remove unwanted witnesses, the place in question should be left immediately.[76]

During antipartisan operations, special flying squads (*fliegenden Verbänden*) were organized.[77] Such groups were formed of soldiers belonging to *Einsatzkommandos*, police units, Wehrmacht, and SS units. Small detachments formed by Dirlewanger's soldiers were composed of four, sometimes five people: soldiers (shooters) and an officer. To lead them through inaccessible forest and marsh areas, they employed a trusted local guide (sometimes these were the local foresters).[78] The German soldiers were supported both by

Belarusians and by some Russians. Not only Dirlewanger's unit looked to them for help. An order by the command of the 403rd Security Division indicates that

> once again, attention is drawn to the fact that due to a lack of sufficient [combat] forces, it is indispensable to recruit trusted collaborators from the local population, who will lead us to find traces of bandit and partisan hideouts.[79]

Operations in other areas were similar. A report of February 6, 1942, on the situation in the Oryol and Kursk region stated,

> As far as possible, the population should take part in the observation and combating of partisans. Cooperation with Russian inhabitants has so far usually brought good results. . . . Should it turn out that the population is not cooperating fully in combating the partisans, the most-severe measures should be used against it, and action should follow the principle that fear of German reprisals must be greater than fear of threats from the partisans.[80]

Groups composed of Dirlewanger's soldiers moved mainly by night and crept up to partisan camps unobserved. In this way they could estimate the size of the enemy force and find the best place for fighting, unnoticed. They attempted to perfect their techniques of tracking and neutralizing their opponent. These were simultaneously reconnaissance and combat units. Only the necessary equipment was taken on this kind of operation: submachine guns, ammunition, food, and water. Anything that might restrict movement was left behind.[81]

> Radio stations stayed behind because they were too heavy and sank. We could not have heavy weapons. We were accompanied by many sharpshooters with telescopic sights, and besides that we had submachine guns, which formed [illegible word] of our company's firepower.[82]

Patrols disappeared into the forests even for several weeks and covered an area within a radius of 20 km.[83] As Gustav Brusberg remembers, they were on the road for weeks, combing the forests.[84]

Small combat groups usually consisted of poachers and experienced hunters, which undoubtedly made it easier for them to move about the forest unnoticed. During combat, experience and rapid responses were the mainstay. Soldiers had no time to contact commanders. Because of the activity of Dirlewanger's unit, partisan units had no time to regenerate and rest. The destruction of their camps may be described on the basis of a report of September 3, 1941, by the 1st SS Cavalry Regiment:

> The report was confirmed by a Belarusian head forester, who volunteered as a guide familiar with that area. . . . On August 26, 1941, and August 27, 1941, the planned movement of the regiment took place. On August 27, 1941, in the evening the partisan group was surrounded. On August 28, 1941, at 13.45, the partisans attempted to escape the encirclement. They were liquidated by the 4th squadron (using machine guns). There were 21 killed. No own losses.[85]

Reconnaissance patrols were also conducted with the use of motorcycle platoons. An action of this type lasted up to fourteen days.[86] It was carried out not only by Dirlewanger's forces, but also by police divisions and *Hiwis*. Like in the case of foot patrols, the aim was to encircle and fight with partisans and to control the local population.[87] As Friedrich Walter remembered, skirmishes with partisan groups often occurred, and the task of motorcycle patrols was to maintain communications between individual small German units.[88] Moreover, motorcyclist platoons were, particularly during the initial period of antipartisan fighting, rapid-reaction forces.

> Wherever partisans appeared, we had to gather intelligence or stand and fight. We were mostly on the road. Later, large-scale antipartisan operations were carried out. Other units like the police and SS also took part in them.[89]

Only after smaller skirmishes had been fought and reconnaissance patrols carried out was an assault group gathered and a great operation conducted, with the participation of eight thousand to ten thousand soldiers[90] (including Wehrmacht units, police forces, Waffen-SS and Luftwaffe units, etc.). In this way, partisan units were encircled and attacked from all sides. They were unable to escape. According to Feiertag's estimates, during an operation that lasted two to three weeks, four thousand to five thousand partisans were killed.[91] Not only Dirlewanger's subordinates took part in such operations, but also other land troops. Such operations occurred in the following way:

> At 2:00 or 3:00 in the morning we set out for the meeting point, and at dawn we were so far along that we could start. The first clash with the enemy took place at 9:00. The first fight took place after an attack from north, east, south, and west, there was shooting from all sides, and we were right in the center. [. . .] Surprisingly, at midday peace fell, and in the afternoon, as we pulled out, there was shooting from all sides for two hours once again; this was partly massed fire and partly single shots. Close hand-to-hand combat occurred only in some places.[92]

Operation Bamberg

Conducted from March 16 to April 1, 1942, in an area situated north and south of Babruysk (Бобруйск), this was one of the first large antipartisan operations. Apart from Dirlewanger's unit, the 707th Infantry Division, the Slovak 102th Infantry Regiment, the 307th Police Battalion (I. Batl. [Pol. Batl. 307]) and the 32nd Police Battalion (Pol. Batl. 32) participated in it.[93]

The Germans surrounded an area with a radius of 20–30 km. Encircled, the partisans of Fyodor Pavlovsky's brigade split up into smaller groups and tried to pass through the German barrier lines without the need to fight.[94] Among the "partisans and their helpers" killed, civilians formed the majority. Before the start of the operation, the Germans were aware that the locals were not hostile and would readily cooperate in the liquidation of the partisans. The civilians' position was extremely difficult: What German soldiers did not take, the partisans requisitioned. Despite this, German, Slovak, and eastern units murdered several thousand inhabitants during the operation.

The civilian population was trapped between a rock and a hard place: The Germans killed those who supported partisans, and partisans murdered those who refused to help them. A glimpse of the situation is offered by a report of March 10, 1942:

> Numerous . . . larger bandit groups are moving from place to place and requisitioning cattle and food. In doing so, they also shoot pro-German individuals, primarily mayors and kolkhoz administrators, and also force young men aged 15 years and older to join the ranks of the partisans.[95]

In turn, the Germans terrorized those who aided the partisans, as shown in a report on the action of the 102nd Cossack Regiment conducted south of Babruysk within Operation Bamberg:

> In the settlement of Semla, which was taken on 29.03, partisans had been staying shortly before. However, they were warned by the inhabitants and managed to escape. . . . Before leaving quarters on 1 April, after carrying out a thorough control, around 10 homesteads belonging to partisan supporters were burned down. . . . On April 5, an SD and OD [Order Service] group arrived. On the night of April 5, together with this unit, the village Kowszyce was surrounded, where partisans were sleeping according to reports received. However, they must have been warned earlier, because they were not found there. After the whole settlement was searched, it was established who the farmers that usually sheltered the partisans were. The Order Service liquidated those peasants and burned down their houses. In Kowszyce the Cossacks themselves discovered 5 helpers of the partisans and handed them over to the SD. . . . In areas with a partisan presence, it [the population] is incited against Germans. That is why particularly hostile attitudes can often be encountered there. Inhabitants also often warn the partisans. In some villages, for example in the village of Protasy, their active participation in partisan units has been observed. As a result, the squadron command in cooperation with the 10th [Company] of the 727th [Infantry Regiment] decided to undertake an energetic intervention in the village of Protasy, where a particularly large number of men turned out to be partisans. They were destroyed together with their families and all their belongings.[96]

From March 2 to 10, SS-Sonderkommando Dirlewanger engaged in combat with partisans northeast of a settlement called Asipovichy. They reported that a "strong bandit group" had been liquidated and "rich spoils" obtained. On March 12, the unit repulsed a partisan attack at Klichaw, and at Czerwaków (Tscherwakow) it defeated and liquidated another unit.[97] From March 16 to 28, it clashed with partisans in forests and on a road south of Mogilev, toward Babruysk.[98] Next, a report was made that it had cleared partisan settlements along the route between Mogilev and Babruysk.[99]

In the first days of April, Dirlewanger's soldiers clashed with partisans in marshy areas around the settlements "Selleri," "Lushiza," and "Bazewischi,"[100] and between April 8 and 15, fighting took place near Chachevichy (Mogilev District).

For the period of combat, SS-Sonderkommando Dirlewanger was supplied with food that was to last for five days. In the following days, they were supposed to obtain provisions by themselves. They were ordered to make three reports a day: the morning report by 7:00 a.m., the middle one by 12:00 a.m., and the daily report by 1:00 p.m.[101]

An order concerning combat with partisans of March 31, 1942, stated that heavily armed "partisan bands" were moving between the villages of "Drut" and Berezino. According to the German order, a group of six hundred partisans had been seen there.[102] These data might not be exaggerated. Pavlovsky's brigade, which was active in that area, numbered around 1,300 people, but when the operation started it split into smaller groups.[103] Furthermore, several independent partisan groups (including a unit commanded by Vladimir Nichiporovich) operated there, and on March 20 they attacked German administration facilities in Klichaw. According to partisan reports, around 140 "policemen" were killed.[104] This is confirmed in German reports: "The village of Klichaw (33 kilometers north of Babruysk) was taken by partisans. A warehouse with 100 tons of grain was set on fire there."[105] As a result, Klichaw was bombed by the Luftwaffe.[106]

On April 5, 1942, the Wehrmacht Supreme Command proclaimed Operation Bamberg a great success: "During the clearing of the Rear Area in the central part of the front, a group of 3,000 partisans was destroyed."[107] The operation was deemed a model for later great campaigns conducted in the years 1942–43 in Belarus and on Russian and Ukrainian occupied territories.

Stalin Partisan Unit No. 208

Among the groups Dirlewanger's soldiers encountered was the unit commanded by Col. Vladimir Nichiporovich. On June 22, 1941, he had been in command of the 28th Motorized Division, which in the first weeks of fighting succumbed to German forces west of Minsk. At the turn of 1941 and 1942, together with his subordinates he joined a partisan unit operating in the region of Uzda (south of Minsk). Soon afterward, he was in command of Stalin Partisan Unit No. 208.[108] In that period, many similar groups formed in the Minsk region.

From January 1942, Stalin Partisan Unit No. 208[109] was active in an area around 60–100 km south and east of Minsk, near Uzda, Rudziensk, Cherven, Asipovichy, and Smilavichy. The partisans destroyed bridges, attacked local policemen and their families, dispersed offices of the occupational administration, and killed mayors and local and village administrators appointed by the Germans.

As mentioned earlier, from March 2 to 10, 1942, Dirlewanger's unit fought against a strong partisan group under Nichiporovich in the Asipovichy area. According to German documents, the whole "band" was destroyed.[110] However, this must have been only a small partisan unit, since Nichiporovich's group continued to fight.

From January to March 1942, his unit already numbered around five hundred men: former Red Army soldiers, activists, and peasants hiding from the Germans. Nichiporovich took control of smaller partisan groups operating in the Klichaw region relatively rapidly. By early June, Nichiporovich's forces had grown to 670 men,[111] who controlled the whole Klichaw region and carried out numerous attacks on surrounding areas. The Germans attempted to destroy the whole group many times, but without success.

On April 26, SS-Sonderkommando Dirlewanger reconnoitered and gathered intelligence on enemy numbers in the so-called Usakino Partisan Republic (Banditenrepublik Usakino).[112] Oskar Dirlewanger was personally in command during the fighting.[113] In April 1942, he was awarded the Clasp to the Iron Cross 2nd Class,[114] which he was presented on July 16.

To pacify these territories, in early May 1942 the 1st Police Regiment Mitte was dispatched. However, the German units encountered a strong partisan group that managed to withstand them and even moved to counterattack and defeated the 2nd Company of the police battalion. On May 10, Erich von dem Bach landed in Chachevichy in his private Fieseler Storch plane and assumed command.[115] In May, he sent SS-Sonderkommando Dirlewanger and a battalion of Ukrainian auxiliary police, among others, to destroy Nichiporovich's group. From May 8 to 13, there was heavy fighting around the villages of Usakino and Susha. Also participating in them was Kampfgruppe Schimana, over which Dirlewanger assumed command.[116] On May 12, the Germans attacked the settlements occupied by partisans. The fighting was fierce and balanced. After heavy clashes, the German forces took Usakino. Further attacks on Olkhovka brought no effects, however.

Due to lack of progress, von dem Bach decided to bomb Susha, where the main partisan forces were concentrated.[117] As a result, German troops managed to breach enemy resistance, and thanks to Dirlewanger's "energetic" leadership they were able to capture the fortified station in Susha and severely weaken the enemy.[118] Von dem Bach observed the whole attack from a plane.[119] The partisans sustained heavy losses and had to withdraw to the forests and marshes. The Germans took Rozwada, Usakino, Olkhovka, and Susha,[120] and Dirlewanger's soldiers burned down the latter two.[121]

The following enemy losses were reported on May 16, 1942: in Voevichi, 120 people; on May 9 in Susha, 80; in Usakino, 120; and on May 12, as a result of the bombardment of Susha, 200.[122] Civilians made up most of the dead.

In a report of May 25, 1942, the staff of Gen. Maximilian von Schenckendorff informed Oberkommando des Heeres (OKH):[123]

> In the area between Babruysk and Mogilev the number of partisans was . . . horrific. The village of Susha (50 km north of Babruysk), one of the main strongholds of the partisans, was taken by the police after heavy fighting and with aerial support. The village was completely burned down. The troops remaining at our disposal were, however, too weak to achieve complete destruction of the enemy. The Babruysk–Mogilev road, on which attacks on Wehrmacht vehicles occur almost daily, should be closed to all traffic.[124]

The 1st Police Regiment Mitte assessed enemy losses at "520 people," of whom around two hundred died as a result of the bombing. Their own losses were seven killed and seventeen wounded on May 9, and three killed and six wounded on May 12.[125] The number of 520 killed included peasants liquidated during the pacification and burning of villages.

At the time, Nichiporovich's group had no support from the Soviet side. Three months later, Nichiporovich reported the following losses sustained by German soldiers: 138 killed on May 9, and 120 killed on May 12. He indicated that during the bombing, two company commanders and a platoon leader were killed in his unit, and thirty-three partisans were wounded. He confirmed that the local units panicked and ran away into the forests and marshes.[126]

From May 24 to 29, 1942, Dirlewanger's forces were constantly in combat. Near Dolgoe (Nichiporovich's area of operation, around 18 km from Susha), thanks to his "undaunted and daring" command, further partisan units were liquidated.[127] The clashes did not always go according to Dirlewanger's plan. On May 25, Erich von dem Bach recorded the following in his diary:

> Another truck attacked by partisans on the road from Mogilev to Babruysk. Three of Dirlewanger's SS men are dead, several are wounded, 4 Wehrmacht soldiers are dead. That is why I am going personally to the area, to Chachevichy.[128]

From the first days of June, SS-Sonderkommando Dirlewanger participated in smaller clashes with partisan units in the Orsha region.

On June 15, 1942, von dem Bach noted,

> Today is a disastrous day. A 19-strong platoon of the 51st police battalion took over escort tasks of Wehrmacht signal corps on the Mogilev-Babruysk route. In a well-known place, in the forest, south

> of Sukhinichy, [our] people walked into a partisan trap. Sixteen policemen were brutally massacred. . . . Also today, on the Susha stretch,[129] partisans attacked a platoon of the 122nd police battalion. The platoon commander and 1 soldier are dead, 2 people are missing, 6 heavily wounded. A later report: 5 people are dead.[130]

On June 16, SS-Sonderkommando Dirlewanger conducted a larger action on the Mogilev–Babruysk road in revenge for the killing of seventeen policemen. Three days later, they destroyed a forest camp of the partisans near the village of "Stochowtschina." On June 22, with the help of police troops, they destroyed a group near Nowy Gródek, and on June 16, after Luftwaffe bombardment, they took Stary Bykhov and Lubyanka in the Mogilev District.[131] The partisans whom they fought in this area belonged to Nichiporovich's group.

Nichiporovich's fighters had the whole area under their control and did not avoid combat even with large German units. In May and June, they were active in the extensive forested and marshy areas between Minsk and Mogilev, in the Klichaw-Berezino-Byalynichy-Rahachow quadrant. Apart from open combat, their operations included attacking German cars. They also blew up railway lines, carried out executions of so-called traitors (members of the Order Service and the administration), and pressed the local population into the resistance movement.[132]

The Germans treated local civilians mercilessly. According to information from partisans operating in the Klichaw region, from July 1942 onward, German soldiers burned eleven villages to the ground, and in three of them they murdered almost all the inhabitants.[133] Dirlewanger's unit burned down two villages: Kostrichskaya Slobodka on June 12 and Borki on June 15.

Borki (Борки)

On July 17, Ponomarienko reported to Stalin, Molotov, and Beria that

> at the end of June, a German pacification unit encircled the village of Borki in the Kirawsk region and then burned it down and shot its inhabitants, including children and the elderly.

He believed this to be a reprisal for an attack carried out by partisans on a German column of thirty-three vehicles. As Bogdan Musiał states, forty-two airmen were killed in the raid. This was most likely an ambush carried out on June 6 by the 277th Unit, near Kirowsk.[134]

One of Dirlewanger's soldiers, Albin V., testified about the pacification operations carried out by SS-Sonderkommando Dirlewanger in June 1942 in Borki, located around 18 km east of Klichaw:

> During the march—we were 200 km from Smolensk—the villages were surrounded. No one could get in or out of them. The fields were searched, and the people sent to the villages. Next morning, around 6, all the inhabitants—it was a large settlement, around 2,500 inhabitants—children, women, old people, were crammed into 4–5 barns. . . . At that point, Dirlewanger appeared with ten people, officers and so on, and said: "Shoot everybody right away." He placed four SD officials with submachine guns in front of the barns. The barns were opened and Dirlewanger commanded: "Open fire." They shot the rifles . . . at the people, children, women, and so on, regardless. Something terrifying happened. Magazines were pulled out, new ones kept appearing in their place. It was not planned. Then the barns were shut. The SD men took the hay from the roofs and set fire to the barns. What I saw was the most terrible image in my life. The barns burned with a bright flame. No one could get out until the barns collapsed. Meanwhile, Dirlewanger and his staff positioned themselves with Russian rapid-fire rifles around the barns at 50 meters. Then they dragged out the lightly and heavily wounded and the people who had not been shot yet, people who were burning like torches. Those beasts shot only those who were looking for a way to escape, and Dirlewanger was at their head, until there was nobody left. I lived through examples like the one I am telling you about now in at least 4–5 actions. . . . Every single settlement was destroyed like that.[135]

The destruction of Borki and the shooting of all its inhabitants has been confirmed by another of Dirlewanger's soldiers: Gustav Brusberg. He stated that the inhabitants of the village of Studenka met the same fate. Apart from Dirlewanger's men, also SD divisions took part in both pacifications.[136] Brusberg said,

> In the villages of Borki and Studenka it happened like this: we had to encircle the village with my platoon. The Germans killed the villages' inhabitants; the houses were set on fire. *Hiwis* were not involved in this type of task.[137]

He added that he had not heard about village people being herded into barns and burned alive. He testified that before a village was destroyed, the people were shot.[138] Brusberg made his testimony only in 1975, likely wanting to avoid a conviction, and probably did not describe the true course of pacification operations.

A day after the pacification (June 16), Dirlewanger reported,

> Yesterday's operation carried out in Borki took place without contact with the enemy. . . . The inhabitants who tried to run away were shot, and three of them were armed. A search of the settlement revealed support for the partisans. The men were mostly not present, few horses, almost no wagons. We found 7 Russian automatic rifles, 3 grenades, ammunition, and 2 pistols. The inhabitants were shot; the village was burned down.[139]

A handwritten note on the document gives the numbers:

> Inhabitants shot: 1,112
> + killed by the SD: 633
> In total: 1,745
> additionally for running away from the village: 282
> Total: 2,027[140]

In the years 1942–44, various German units conducted similar actions all over Belarus. Pacification units were instructed on how to conduct themselves and what methods to use. One example is a letter by Col. Knecht, who was in command of Operation Winterzauber in 1943:

> The necessary executions should as far as possible be left to the SD, so as not to leave any traces. If it becomes needful for a unit to carry out executions because the SD is not in the neighborhood, this should be done inside. Bodies should be covered in straw and hay and burned together with the buildings.[141]

SD functionaries had orders to kill all Communists in occupied USSR territories, even if there was no proof that they had been actively resisting the German authorities. The practice became routine.[142]

From July 3 to 11, Dirlewanger's unit fought together with Wehrmacht troops against strong partisan groups in the area of Klichaw.[143] SS-Sonderkommando Dirlewanger also proved itself in combat near Voinevichi.[144] On July 9, 1942, Oskar Dirlewanger was wounded in the left arm. As he himself said, it was a surface scratch that healed quickly.[145] He was decorated with the Gold Wound Badge,[146] and as I have already written above, on July 16, he received the Clasp to the Iron Cross 2nd Class that he had been awarded in April.[147]

At the end of July 1942, Dirlewanger went on leave to his family in Esslingen, but he did not stop seeking to obtain better military equipment for his unit. In a letter of July 27, 1942, most likely addressed to Gottlob Berger, he complained that SS-Brigadeführer Graf Pückler[148] refused to give him weapons and cars to make up for losses. Rather irritated, he wrote,

> Every construction inspection, economic inspection, command offices, courier offices, and so on have more than enough vehicles at their disposal. In our unit, two trucks, three B-motorcycles, and one car went to hell during an action; we get nothing![149]

Still more annoying to Dirlewanger was that

> we are specialists in fighting from concealment and we have rich experience. Does it thus make sense to field new formations to fight the bandit groups and fully equip them, if they will start achieving success only after long months and a plentiful tribute of blood, or is it better to give us the arms and vehicles necessary for this type of war? In Oranienburg many captured tanks stand ready to roll. Four or five with drivers would greatly help us. They are standing there, and we feel their lack. The security division in Pobrujsk [Babruysk] has two Russian battalions. Formed and equipped, their experience in fighting banditry should be used. With the permission of the SS and Police Leader, I have established a Ukrainian company and formed a Russian battalion. Why have I not received any arms?[150]

From July 1942 onward, overall command of antipartisan operations was assumed by Heinrich Himmler in consultation with the OKW. In the relevant areas, operations were conducted in his name by Higher SS and Police Leaders.[151]

Operation Adler

In July 1942, Schenckendorff decided to start a "wide-scale special action of cleansing the whole neighborhood [of partisans]."[152] He gave the order to start Operation Adler on July 10. Before this occurred, SS-Sonderkommando Dirlewanger was in constant combat against smaller partisan units, among others on July 19, in Krasnitsa.[153]

Operation Adler was conducted between July 20 and August 7, 1942, in the area around Chachevichy.[154] The participants of the action, under the command of Gen. Johann-Georg Richert,[155] were

- 3 battalions and the 8th Artillery Unit of the 286th Security Division
- 102nd Cossack Regiment
- SS-Sonderkommando Dirlewanger
- 2nd Police Regiment (Pol.Rgt.2)
- The eastern battalions Dnjepr and Beresina (formed in April upon the order of Gen. Schenckendorff; they were composed of Soviet POWs commanded by German NCOs and officers)
- 9th Smolensk artillery unit[156]

Unlike the earlier Operation Maikäfer (June 30, 1942), during which single attacks on partisan settlements were organized, Adler was centrally commanded. It did not involve the participation of single battalions and companies, but of thousands of policemen, soldiers, and members of eastern battalions. The Luftwaffe and artillery provided support.[157] Adler was one of the great operations of combing the land during which a strong strike group aimed to encircle partisan units and then destroy them. The German action was carried out with precision and methodically. Partisan positions were not stormed. Villages were encircled, searched, and then burned down. In this way, through caution and foresight, German soldiers reduced their own losses. The partisans were commanded by Col. Nichiporovich, who assigned each unit a specific stretch to defend.[158]

On the first day of the operation, the Germans lost one plane, which fell on Susha while making a bomb run. During the attempt to bury the deceased pilots, mines attached to the bodies by partisans exploded. As a result, one policeman died, and two Ukrainians and an SS man were heavily wounded.[159]

After July 22, the partisans left their fortified bases in villages and dug in in the forests. On July 26, German units took Klichaw. Fighting was fierce, and the settlements taken by the Germans were sometimes recaptured by the partisans.

The German units had to fight for them anew. The partisans also encircled smaller units and destroyed them. Von dem Bach noted,

> On 21.7 the Russian battalion "Beresina" took the village Voevichi after an aerial attack. Following a nighttime counterattack, the settlement was recaptured. On 22.07 in the morning, Voevichi was retaken. Own losses: 5 killed, 30 wounded.[160]

Sergey Mazur, one of the partisans and commander of the 227th unit, describes the fighting as follows:

> I fought against them [the Beresina battalion] . . . on the 8, 13, and 20 July in the area of the village of Voevichi, which they captured three times, and then we retook it. They forced us out in the daytime; at night it was we who attacked and pushed them [out of their positions].[161]

Dirlewanger's soldiers took part in the fighting. On July 28, von dem Bach reported to Gen. Schenckendorff:

> SS-Sonderkommando Dirlewanger, commanded by Lieutenant Colonel Kölbinger, after an exchange of fire . . . took by storm the camp [of the partisan headquarters] 9 km southwest of Knajczyce, on the road to Chachevichy. Enemy losses in the fighting: 9 killed, including 1 officer and 1 political commissar. . . . Own losses: 1 killed.[162]

The partisans' situation gradually deteriorated; only three groups escaped the encirclement: those commanded by Sviridin, Mikholap, and Perestenko. The remaining formations of the 208th unit were caught in the encirclement; the partisans lost their positions around Klichaw. They lacked drugs, ammunition, and food. Their situation became tragic. On July 25, Nichiporovich ordered an attempt to get out of the encirclement, which, however, in most cases ended in failure. On the last day of July, the Germans made Nichiporovich an offer of surrender talks, but he refused. Three days later, at 8:00 p.m., he carried out an attack with all his forces in order to break the encirclement. After an hour and a half of fighting in the forest north of Susha, Nichoporovich's men managed to break out of the encirclement.[163]

In a report of September 14, 1942, Unit Ia reported in Schenckendorff's headquarters that during Operation Adler, 1,809 partisans were "neutralized."[164]

Both Schenckendorff and von dem Bach stated that as its result, 1,381 partisans were killed and 428 captured: 1,809 in total.[165] The dead also included the civilian population of the neighboring villages. All men encountered were treated as partisans.

> The enemy is attempting to transfer most of its people over the barrier lines disguised as simple peasants but is failing. All men living in the region are being detained.[166]

This was how victims among peasants from the neighboring villages were justified. According to data provided by the partisans, during Operation Adler the Germans burned several villages: In Usakino, they killed around 150 families, and in Klichaw, around 300 people.[167] All the victims were described as "partisans and their helpers." As Musiał wrote,

> None of the partisan units were destroyed; they all managed to escape the encirclement without greater losses and move to other operating areas assigned to them earlier by Nichiporovich, who thus wanted to avoid a concentration of forces in the Klichaw region that was irrational from a military perspective, and at the same time to intensify sabotage operations along strategic lines located outside the Klichaw region. . . . Immediately after Operation Adler, [Nichiporovich's] group was stronger than before its start.[168]

After the operation ended, the commander of the 2nd Police Regiment (Pol.Rgt.2) wrote to Dirlewanger:

> I would like to take the opportunity offered by the end of Operation Adler to say that during the action, the people under the command of the 2nd Police Regiment were in constant combat readiness and [presented] an extraordinary fighting spirit in the performance of the tasks assigned to them. They contributed significantly to the operation's success.
>
> Together with my thanks and appreciation, I express the hope of working with such people during future operations.[169]

Operation Greif

After Operation Adler, upon the command of the chief of the Red Army's general staff, Georgy Zhukov, partisan units were deconcentrated. Focus was placed on sabotage operations that disorganized movement along strategic German communication lines (both rail and road). The actions were to be carried out simultaneously in several places to make restoring communication on a given stretch as difficult as possible. Railway sabotage was very dangerous to German supply routes. Nichiporovich's units were assigned new operating areas in the region of Babruysk Barysaw, Mogilev, Orsha, Asipovichy, Rahachow, and Zhlobin. The partisans operated in an area spread over 20,000 km^2; that is, 10 percent of the territory of today's Belarus.[170]

The next great action was Operation Greif. It was carried out between August 14 and 20, 1942, east and west of the road connecting Orsha and Vitebsk.[171] Its participants were the 286th Security Division, SS-Sonderkommando Dirlewanger, and police and SS units, commanded by Erich von dem Bach-Zelewski. Due to a wound sustained earlier by Dirlewanger, SS-Sonderkommando Dirlewanger was to be led into attack by SS-Obersturmführer Meyer-Mahrendorf.[172] On the Soviet side, the following partisan groups were operating between Orsha and Vitebsk in August:

- Aleksey Brigade, commanded by Aleksey Danukalov (1,085 people, Liozna region)
- Boyko Brigade, led by Vasiliy Boyko (392 or around 1,000 people, Bogushevsk region)
- Chekist Brigade (600 partisans, Orsha and Shklov area)
- Diadia Kostia Brigade, commanded by Zaslonov (352 or around 600 people, Osintorf area, around 30 km northeast of Orsha)
- Sokolov's unit (110 people)
- Furthermore, individual saboteur groups and unregistered units that fought independently[173]

The objective of Operation Greif was mass pacification, and its participants were large, well-armed German units. The partisans were taken entirely unaware by its scope. They fought in a completely uncoordinated manner, which was criticized by Ivan Andreevich Stulov, secretary of the oblast committee of the Communist Party (bolshevik) of Belarus (CP(b)B) in Vitebsk:

> The leadership there, comrades Boyko, Riesnikov, and Wojciechowski, foolhardily and contrary to our regulations allowed the formation of a great partisan group (numbering over 2,000 people), which was stationed in one place and conducted no intelligence activities concerning the movements of enemy forces.[174]

The Germans scrupulously took advantage of all the partisan commanders' mistakes. The partisans led by Boyko did not make a stand and were destroyed. A similar end met the Orsha grouping. Meanwhile, Danukalov described the fates of his brigade thus:

> On August 16, the Germans sent around 10,000–15,000 soldiers against us, against the Orsha group. . . . They were merciless. They killed part [of the partisans], took others prisoner, and the rest of the brigade dispersed around the area. I was unable to gather them together afterward. Of 10 units, 8 were left.[175]

On September 3, the Germans destroyed the Chekist Brigade, which operated north of Orsha. As its leaders reported, the partisans managed to escape without losses. This allowed the unit to re-form, and they were assigned the Krupki region between Orsha and Barysaw as their operating area.[176]

During Operation Greif, a lower number of partisans were reported killed. This is likely because most of those killed were really partisans, and not random civilians. The operation was a far-greater success than Adler. It is possible that for this reason, German soldiers were not so frustrated and did not take their anger out on the locals.[177]

Activity by German Units and Partisans

In the last days of August, SS-Sonderkommando Dirlewanger carried out smaller antipartisan actions in the Usakino (August 23) and Rahachow (August 25–28, 1942) regions, among others.[178] As German documents report, wherever they went they were characterized by "reliability" (*Zuverlässigkeit*).[179]

On September 5, Stalin issued order no. 189 on the "tasks of the partisan movement," which commanded them to disorganize the enemy's rear area, in particular by destroying railway lines. He also called for them to gather intelligence for the needs of the Red Army. On September 6, Marshal Kliment Voroshilov was appointed commander in chief of the partisans.[180] From that point on, partisan groups became an element of Soviet military structures, and the Red Army gained a greater influence on the development of the resistance movement.[181] As a result, in October 1942 the sabotage activity of partisan groups intensified.

German units that had so far fought against the partisans were assigned to the defense of railway lines. In the first days of September, Schenckendorff alarmed the Command of Army Group Center:

> In the report of June 1942 to the OKH/quartermaster general . . . it was indicated that Stalin's order mentioning the "creation of circumstances unbearable for the enemy behind German army lines" is not actually far from reality. . . . Meanwhile the Russians have escalated their efforts even further to spread unrest in the Rear Areas. . . . Directing almost all troops to defensive protection of railway lines increases the chances that this type of success [partisan attacks] will be achieved. The absolutely necessary combating of partisans through great antipartisan operations has been abandoned. Areas with economic significance have already been left to the opponent. . . . Settlements whose inhabitants cooperated with the Germans are being burned to the ground by bandits, and population that is friendly to Germans is being murdered. . . . With brutal ruthlessness, the bandits will force the still-passive Russian masses to maintain an attitude hostile to Germans.[182]

The situation of the German forces was dire. Therefore, in October, Hermann Göring issued a decree establishing a kilometer-wide strip of so-called no-man's-and on both sides of the railway and introducing greater reprisals for attacks (burning of villages and executing their inhabitants). Schenckendorff believed that this would bring an effect opposite to the one intended and was against the decree. Ultimately it was decided that the strip of no-man's-land would be 100 m wide on both sides of railway lines.[183]

All this caused German repressions of the civilian population in Belarus to increase in cruelty. According to the principles of *Bandenbekämpfung*, partisans caught under arms and showing resistance were to be shot immediately. Dirlewanger's soldiers used firearms primarily to kill partisans: this was probably the honorable form of execution.

The civilian population inhabiting villages suspected of aiding and supporting partisans was treated quite differently. The principle of collective responsibility was applied. Adolf Hitler stated,

> When combating partisans, everything that is effective is allowed and I want everyone to get this principle firmly into their heads. This way, everybody gains the necessary freedom of action. . . . When the partisans use women and children as human shields, each officer and NCO must open fire on them without the least hesitation. This is because it is paramount that he himself break through, destroying the opponent.[184]

On July 28, 1941, Heinrich Himmler defined the guidelines for combating partisans by the SS Cavalry Brigade on marshy areas in the Pińsk and Polesie oblasts:

> **(2)** In cases where the population is hostile in terms of nationality and qualitatively of low value or even, as it often happens in marshy areas, is composed only of the criminals settled there, all those suspected of supporting partisans shall be shot; women and children should be transported, cattle and food should be requisitioned and secured, and the villages should be burned down completely.
>
> **(3)** Villages and settlements will either form a network of bases whose inhabitants will in and of themselves [bolded in original] kill every partisan and marauder and inform us about them all, or they will cease to exist. No enemy in the area shall find it possible to receive support or the means necessary to live.[185]

In the coming years, Himmler would further tighten these guidelines. In June 1942, he ordered,

> 3. The action has to cause the liquidation of all inhabitants who by showing good will supported the bandits, providing them with supplies, arms, and shelter. Men from accused families, in many cases even whole families, are as a rule [designated] for execution; women from these families should be arrested and sent to camps; children are to be taken from their homeland and gathered in the Old Reich. I expect separate reports on the numbers and racial value. The property and assets of guilty families will be confiscated.
>
> Another objective is to release inhabitants of good will from under bandit pressure and to ensure them safety in the German Reich.[186]

The same orders also pertained to other pacification units, including SS-Sonderkommando Dirlewanger. The rule was that fear of German repression should be greater than that of partisan reprisals.

In February 1943, Erich von dem Bach attempted to ease these orders slightly, though this had no impact on further operations in Belarus. In his guidelines for fighting partisans, he wrote,

> The most important principle of combat against partisans is their complete destruction.
>
> However, this is not synonymous with the destruction of all people inhabiting areas occupied by partisans. Only bandits and their accomplices deserve death.
>
> Uninvolved old people, women, and children should be spared, even in the immediate area of partisan operations. Uninvolved men should be assembled for labor. . . .
>
> Repressions against members of partisan groups will be applied after checking their appropriateness. Every individual case must be documented with the name, cause, and evidential material.[187]

The softening of Himmler's previous guidelines was not the result of humanitarian concerns, as the next fragment indicates:

> Belarus is the source of food for the whole army. This source should never dry up. . . . Each ton of grain, each cow, each horse are worth more than one bandit killed.[188]

Dirlewanger's soldiers themselves mentioned that the unit committed crimes against civilians and burned down whole villages. SS-Sonderkommando Dirlewanger covertly surrounded villages deemed a real or suspected dwelling place of partisans, and destroyed them unexpectedly. Inhabitants were forced into a barn, school, or other large building. To calm them down, they were told that they would be transported to the Reich as laborers. Next, the building was surrounded by positions with automatic weapons and set on fire. Nobody was able to escape such a trap. Killing the inhabitants of villages thus saved ammunition. Burning of villages was also a way in which small combat groups ensured their safety. By doing so, they made sure that partisans would not find out about them. Of course, most of those questioned in the 1960s and 1970s claimed that they had only heard of such events (being on leave or in hospital at the time). If they were eyewitnesses (and thus participants of a pacification operation), they testified that their company had been charged with surrounding the village and making certain nobody escaped. However, they themselves did not directly take part in the executions. Among Dirlewanger's soldiers, eyewitnesses included SS-Untersturmführer Paul Illing and SS-Unterscharführer Johannes Stein. Illing testified that

> I saw single cases where during the search of a village, inhabitants were gathered in one place and then shot. Later it was said that these people were partisans or suspected of partisan activity. Among those shot, old men, women, and children were the most numerous. In one instance I was an eyewitness to how the inhabitants of a kolkhoz were hustled into a barn, which was then set on fire. I could hear the screams of the people in that barn from some distance away. Whether anyone escaped whole from that barn and was later shot, I don't know.[189]

Meanwhile, Johannes Stein said,

> It is true that whole villages were burned during our operations. I remember three situations in which villages burned while the 3rd Company searched them. The civilians who came out of the burning houses—men, women, and children—were shot as soon as they appeared. To my knowledge, the corpses lay [there where the people died].[190]

If investigators asked more-detailed questions (which was rare), the interrogated admitted to seeing burned-down villages and murdered inhabitants. For example, in 1978 Friedrich Noweck stated,

> I saw burning villages myself; namely, in the Babruysk region. I heard that Dirlewanger's unit committed such acts. It was commonly said: "Where there is fire, Dirlewanger is at work."[191]

His words were confirmed by Wilfried Höfling, who was on the staff of a similar unit: "I know that it was said that if the glow of fire appeared on the horizon, Dirlewanger was in action."[192]

Thus spread the view that if a village had been burned and its inhabitants killed, it was the work of Dirlewanger's unit. A member of the 13th Police Regiment (Pol.-Regt. 13) mentioned that the leader of one of the police battalions (Schuma-Bat.) stated that Dirlewanger's subordinates "needed no weapons, only matches."[193] Also, Werner Weber-Bergfeldt from the staff of Kampfgruppe von Gottberg spoke of burning villages in which SS-Sonderkommando Dirlewanger operated. When he pointed this out to von Gottberg, the latter told him not to concern himself with the matter again.[194]

Most German units taking part in antipartisan operations in Belarus treated the civilian population like this, as did Soviet partisans, as will be seen further in this chapter. Moreover, at least one other German penal unit operated in the area in question. Dirlewanger also had SD troops under his command.

Gen. Schenckendorff was an opponent of brutal methods, claiming,

> Responding to partisan terror with German terror will only increase the danger, which will ultimately destroy all our work toward rebuilding, and thus the basis of our troops' existence. I therefore order—in consultation with the Higher SS and Police Leader [Russia Center]—the following:
>
> (1) Means of reprisals, as far as they include executions of the civilian population and burning of villages, shall in principle be allowed only upon the order of an officer in the rank of battalion commander at the least, and only when *it has been conclusively proved* that the civilian population or specific persons supported partisans. . . .
>
> (2) *I forbid women and children to be shot, with the exception of armed women* [both fragments in bold in original]. . . . We are not at war with the civilian population, particularly as it is generally willing to cooperate.[195]

This order was not respected, and Himmler and von dem Bach disagreed with it. According to them, terror, murder, and engendering fear were the most effective.

An argument for the burning of villages together with their inhabitants was also provided by the German forces' fear that the locals would turn against them and join the partisan groups. At the start of 1942, the Wehrmacht informed,

> Belarus: During an operation combating partisans in the last week it turned out that the population tends not to be in a pact with the banditry and is ready to provide us with useful information. However, it should be noted that a large part of them will immediately go over to the partisan side in the event of a larger uprising attempt. This is because in Russian propaganda they are told that they really must be ready for a return of the Red Army and thus of Bolshevism! Most Belarusians who are now working peacefully will certainly turn against Germans in such circumstances,

> fearing they will later be suspected of favoring German soldiers. This part of society, even if it does not hold any combat value, could significantly strengthen the partisans in terms of numbers. . . . antipropaganda is a very effective measure. . . . The Belarusian population can best be won over through politeness and good-naturedness. But where necessary, considerable strictness should be demonstrated.[196]

Sanctions meted out by various units against the civilian population in Belarus also included the public hanging of women accused of helping and supporting partisans.[197] The inhabitants of villages were registered, to facilitate sending them to forced labor and transporting them to the Reich. All property was confiscated.

Burning of houses, neighborhoods, and whole villages was not the exclusive domain of Dirlewanger's unit. It was a method universally used to intimidate and punish civilians both in Belarus and in Russia. In Belarus in 1941 and at the start of 1942, such operations were still a rarity, but from the very start, in Russian territory, German extermination groups pacified whole villages in revenge for aid given to partisans. This is confirmed by reports of October and December 1941 by the commander of the Rear Area of Army Group Center: "Along the Vielikiye Luki–Toropets railway line, several villages burned down for helping partisans"; "In the Velizh area, various settlements burned down for helping partisans"; "In response to the attack on Pogoreltsy the neighboring villages were burned down."[198]

In 1942, partisans stepped up their activity: they attacked, killed, and robbed individual German soldiers and policemen, and also officials, mayors, and local and estate administrators, accusing them of collaborating with the Germans. The civilian population suffered both from German reprisals and from partisan action. The partisan activity was painfully felt by owners of agricultural estates and farms, which were regularly attacked, devastated, looted, and set on fire. Attempts were made to draft peasants by force, and if they refused, they were shot as enemies and collaborators. Leaflets were distributed among policemen and POWs working for the Germans, intended to convince them to go over to the Soviet side. To "encourage" them, they stated that everyone would be killed irrespective of whether they were working for the occupier of their own free will or under duress.

Very frequently, instead of fighting the Germans the partisans conducted "economic operations" (*bambioshki*).[199] According to the local population, during supply operations partisans became regular groups of looters:

> The unit (group) is assigned a given village or two villages by the command. They set out at night and from each house they take everything they can find: lard, butter, sour cream, bread, and other food. That is why the peasants hide everything they can. It often happens that such "partisans" not only take food but also plunder cupboards and chests in search of clothing and shoes, and even luxury goods: eau de toilette, watches, and other items. They confiscate horses and carts to transport food. They promise to return everything, but in practice they never do so. They do this with no regard to the social and economic consequences for the family in question. It is no chance that as soon as partisans appear on the horizon, children playing in the yard run home shouting: "Mum! The partisans are coming!" And the mother hurries to hide everything she owns.[200]

The methods used by partisans toward those who were reluctant to fight the occupier can be compared to pacification operations by the German side. They not only killed individuals but also destroyed whole villages. A report on the activity of the 2nd Belarusian Partisan Brigade states,

> 20.5.42. . . . The deserter Sinigeriev ran away, was stopped, shot. . . . 28.5.42: Attack on a police Station in the village of Kholuy. The policemen scattered. No losses on the partisan side. The partisans broke up a group of deserters. . . . 12.6.42: . . . group of 35 policemen and deserters destroyed in the village of Kholuy. As a result of the fighting, the village burned down completely, 1 policeman was taken prisoner. . . . 16.6.42 . . . In the village of Satchin, deserters insidiously murdered the partisan Piotr Sztukin.[201]

"Deserters" and "bandits" were labels used by partisans in their reports for peasants from surrounding villages who did not voluntarily want to join their units or ran away from them.

The civilian population of Belarus was forced to join partisan units; some were recruited into self-defense groups, and others were to work "from home" to fulfill partisan needs. For example, in the Baranavichy oblast, drafting was done on the basis of an oral command or an order:

Order no. 322
Further to the orders of the people's commissar of defense, leader of the nations of the USSR, head of the Bolshevik party and the Soviet government, comrade Stalin!!!

I order!!!

Mobilization to be carried out and the following comrades, inhabitants of the village Novoe Selo, to be conscripted into partisan units for the purpose of fighting a deciding battle against fascist dogs and protecting our homeland: Sincia Paweł Sacharowicz, Czeriedolio Siergiej Nikołajewicz, Kieda Władimir Antonowicz, Kieda Nikołaj.

In the event of a refusal to join the partisans by the comrades listed above or their running away from the unit, they should be treated as traitors of the fatherland and supporters of the looters of this land, [for] which each of them will be severely punished by the partisan movement.

Each of those Hitlerite dogs will be shot.

To the full eradication of the German occupiers!!!

Death to German occupiers!!!

Long live our glorious fatherland, to its freedom, to its independence!!!

Unit commander (Dieniscenko).[202]

In 1942, the partisans used collective responsibility. General Schenckendorff wrote to the OKH:

In settlements where our troops are not present, the partisans shoot the mayors, members of administrative bodies, and policemen installed by us, together with their families. They thus intimidate the population, which is behaving differently toward the Wehrmacht than before. This is seen in low efficiency of labor, and also refusal to cooperate.[203]

Four months later he informed that

so far [in the Rear Area of Army Group Center], partisans have killed around 500 mayors and village heads. Relatives of the deceased were shut in spaces for animals and burned alive.[204]

Also between January and March 1943, partisan units destroyed whole villages. In the area of the settlements Asveya-Rossony and Surazh, the Germans carried out five large antipartisan operations, during which around 11,800 people were killed and 9,800 were transported as laborers to the Reich. People were burned alive together with the villages. Soviet propaganda informed about the massacre but did not state that the Germans were not responsible for all the village burnings. Some of the villages in the Asveya-Rossony zone were razed to the ground by partisans. On March 14, 1943, during a session of the bureau of the oblast CP(b)B committee in Vitebsk, it was noted that

> the issue of village burning by units of the Stalin Partisan Brigade and the 1st Belarussian Partisan Brigade is being discussed. In winter 1942–43, during combat with German pacification units, upon the order of Okhotin and Zakharov, a number of villages in the Surazh and Rossony regions were burned down. The justification was that Germans might establish their garrisons and bases in these villages. The Germans used these facts for propaganda purposes. The following was decided:
>
> (1) Burning down villages is forbidden unless it is necessary due to the course of the operation. New incidents of village burning will be punished with full severity.
>
> (2) This resolution does not pertain to those settlements where the enemy's bases and warehouses or other facilities used by the occupiers are located.[205]

Despite the ban, in spring 1943, partisans from the Vitebsk oblast burned down many villages. Burning was done not only to "punish" alleged traitors and their families, but also to make it impossible for the Germans to establish outposts in partisan zones. This caused great dissatisfaction and bitterness among the local population, who said that "the Germans did not burn us, and now the partisans are doing it."[206]

Together with partisans, the NKVD conducted operations against so-called German agents. These were peasants, often previously persecuted by the Soviet regime, "kulaks," and farmers, whom the Germans formed into auxiliary police battalions. When "German agents" were liquidated, the principle of collective responsibility was applied. Apart from the "agent" himself, his relatives and any helpers were also punished and killed. Potential "offenders" were tortured during interrogations to force confessions of guilt.

The civilian population was in the worst position. On the one hand, the peasants had to feed the partisans, who mistreated, looted, and even killed them. Furthermore, partisans often presented the policemen and civilians they killed as "liquidated German soldiers and officers" in their reports. They most likely understated the number of "policemen" and "traitors" and their families killed.[207] On the other hand, civilians suffered at the hands of German units, which burned down villages and houses, wanting to deprive the partisans of their food base and protect small combat groups. Moreover, the Germans also looted and murdered, and they transported those capable of work to be forced laborers in the Reich.

Discipline problems among the partisans were enormous. This is indicated by the establishment of special forces that were to maintain discipline and combat capability in partisan units. From summer 1943 onward, they operated within all groups of the Mogilev oblast. They were to punish all instances of insubordination: theft, looting, rape, drunkenness. It was forbidden to "carry out unauthorized executions and abuse the civilian population and to commit arson."[208]

Before this decree came into force, partisans sometimes burned down whole villages. Moreover, the special units were tasked with preventing panic, betrayal, and espionage. During German antipartisan operations in the Mogilev oblast, four to seven members of a unit would go over to the enemy side, and the deserters would reveal the location of the partisan camp.[209]

On September 6, 1942, Hitler's instructions "concerning increased combating of the plague of banditry in the East" appeared, which were expanded by the OKW:

> Anyone who supports partisans, shelters them, conceals information about their hiding places, etc. shall be put to death. Women, girls, and children suspected of being "partisan agents" shall be killed "immediately after capture."[210]

After a five-day break following Operation Nordsee, SS-Sonderkommando Dirlewanger together with SS-Polizei Regiment 14 (SS-Pol. Rgt. 14) carried out operations south of Mogilev (Stary Bykhov-Chachevichy). The action lasted from September 10 to 14, 1942.[211] On these days, Dirlewanger's unit "cleansed" the Chachevichy region. In September, Oskar Dirlewanger was decorated yet again: He was awarded the Clasp to the Iron Cross 1st Class.

Thanks to Dirlewanger's cooperation with SS-Gruppenführer Arthur Nebe,[212] 115 more prisoners convicted of poaching joined the unit. After a brief training, on September 20, 1942, they were sent to Mogilev.[213]

On October 4, 1942, it was reported that SS-Sonderkommando Dirlewanger was composed of three officers (führer) and 165 soldiers:

- Armaments: 9 MG34 machine guns, 6 light machine guns (LMG, [tsch.]), 4 submachine guns (SMG), 130 rifles (Karabiner 98k), 45 Parabellum pistols (Pistolen 08), 22 M.Pi rifles (Suromi), 2 flare guns (*Leuchtpistole*), 2 antitank guns (Pak 4.5 cm), 1 mortar (*Granatwerfer* 8.1 cm), 1 mortar (*Granatwerfer* 5.2 cm)
- Attached Order Service (*OD-Männer*), Bartschke Group: (officer and 233 people); armaments: 1 4.5 cm antitank gun, 17 light machine guns (Russian), 6 submachine guns, 180 rifles, 20 pistols (Russian)
- Attached Ukrainians (officer and 53 people); armaments: 6 light machine guns, 45 rifles (Russian), and 10 pistols (Russian)[214]

On October 23, 1942, Himmler created the position of *Reichsführer-SS*'s Plenipotentiary for Combating Bandit Groups (*Bevollmächtigter des Reichsführer-SS für die Bandenbekämpfung*). Effectiveness in fighting partisans was achieved through central planning and the direction of the *Reichsführer-SS*'s staff. Over time, he transformed the office of plenipotentiary into that of *Chef der Bandenkampfverbände*, which was given to Erich von dem Bach-Zelewski:[215] "I assign him the task of pacifying individual areas, specifically defined each time."[216] Himmler, meanwhile was *Chef der Bandenbekämpfung*.[217] Von dem Bach was to organize and supervise antipartisan operations. On October 30, Himmler ordered that during antipartisan operations, "each member of the local population who can be kept alive and is capable of work should be imprisoned and then sent to labor in Germany."[218]

Operation Nürnberg

This action was conducted in the environs of Hlybokaye from November 22 to 26, 1942.[219] It was commanded by Kurt von Gottberg, higher SS and police leader (HSSPF) in Belarus. Order no. 1 defined the groups of persons who were to be exterminated during Operation Nürnberg: "Every bandit, Jew, Gypsy, and person suspected of banditry should be viewed as an enemy."[220] The action targeted mainly the civilian population.[221]

Such activity is confirmed by an entry in the war diary of the commander of the Rear Area of Army Group Center of December 4; that is, already after the end of Operation Nürnberg:

> Report of the 1st SS Infantry Brigade concerning Operation Nürnberg in the Hlybokaye District. The numbers cited in it give a shocking depiction of methods used also in some part against the local population. Many settlements were burned down, and all inhabitants, including women and children, received special treatment [were killed]. This is the best focal point for new bandit areas.[222]

On the German side, apart from Dirlewanger's unit, the participants of the action were

1st SS Infantry Brigade (mot.) (1. SS-Inf. Brig. [mot]):
- 8th SS Infantry Regiment (SS-Inf. Rgt. 8)
- 10th SS Infantry Regiment (SS-Inf. Rgt. 10)
- 14th Police Regiment (Pol. Rgt. 14)

Barkholt security group (Sicherungsgruppe "Barkholt")
- part of Landesschützenbataillon 75 (Lds. Schtz. Btl. 75)
- Lithuanian auxiliary police forces 254 E (lit. Schutzm. Btl. 254 E)
- Kern gendarmerie troop (Gen. Truppe Kern)

SD units were commanded by SS-Hauptsturmführer Artur Wilke.[223] At this time, SS-Sonderkommando Dirlewanger was composed of the following:

German company (commander, 130 soldiers)
motorcyclist platoon (commander, 35 soldiers)
Russian company (Russian commander, 200 soldiers)
Ukrainian platoon (Ukrainian commander, 53 soldiers)[224]

On November 30, 1942, it was reported that during Operation Nürnberg, 789 bandits, 353 people suspected of belonging to partisan groups, and 1,826 Jews and Gypsies (2,975 in total) were liquidated, with German losses of two killed and ten wounded. The provided statistics do not include Jews and partisans (and potential partisans) burned in houses or bunkers.[225]

Moreover, during Operation Nürnberg, from November 21 to 23, 1942, SD groups liquidated the ghettos in the area, including in Pastavy (Поставы) and Dunilavichy (Дунілавічы).[226] The Germans captured Pastavy on July 6, 1941, and formed a ghetto there for around four thousand people from the surrounding area. When the Jewish quarter was liquidated, the ghetto was burned down and all Jews were killed. This is how inhabitants of Pastavy remembered the actions of the German soldiers: "The liquidation of the ghetto lasted almost a week. In the end, to smoke out those in hiding, often in attics, the whole district was burned" (Stanisław Jurkowlaniec).

> It was terrible; the Germans disliked Jews very much. God, those people were so wretched. Why didn't they escape to the forests, drop everything. . . . Why did they wait there for death? Maybe now they wouldn't have waited like that for the Germans to take them away and shoot them. Why, there was a ghetto here in Pastavy; they herded all the Jews together and shot them. My parents knew Jews. I remember how they said that they always bought flour and everything else that had to be bought from Jewish acquaintances, in Zarechna Street (it's been renamed Gagarin Street now). There, along Leninskaya Street, there on the right they resettled people and everything up to the railway road was a ghetto, surrounded by Germans, and they settled those Jews there. There are graves there now, where they shot and buried them. An unpleasant memory, but well, that's how it was. Everyone was shocked that it was so terrible; they were afraid they would kill those Jews, and later maybe they would shoot Poles too . . . Anything might happen. (Janina Owsiuk)[227]

It was reported that on November 21, 1942, in Dunilavichy, SD troops commanded by SS-Haupsturmführer Artur Wilke exterminated around 1,300 Jews.[228]

End of Fighting in 1942

Despite such great losses, at the turn of 1942 and 1943, partisan units were becoming increasingly strong and well organized. This was an effect of orders from Moscow. On May 30, 1942, the State Defense Committee of the USSR (GKO, Государственный Комитет Обороны СССР–ГКО) established the Central Headquarters of the Partisan Movement (CSPD)[229] and appointed Panteleimon Ponomarenko as its chief. The Central Headquarters reported directly to the Headquarters of the Supreme High Command of the USSR Armed Forces.[230]

The CSPD's objective was to initiate a resistance movement that would engage the whole nation, and its tasks included directing the movement and ensuring its growth. The following partisan headquarters were created at the same time: Ukrainian, Bryansk (Bryansk Front), Western (Western Front), Kalinin (Kalinin Front), and Leningrad (Leningrad Front). Later the following were also established: Southern (on the North Caucasian part of the front, August 3), Belarusian (September 9), Voronezh (October), Estonian (November 11), Lithuanian (November 26), Latvian (January 8, 1943), and Crimean (July 1943).[231] From September 9, 1942, the chief of the Belarusian headquarters was Pyotr Kalinin, second secretary of the CP(b)B CC.[232]

At first, partisan groups in Belarus formed spontaneously. Their composition changed frequently, leaders were selected via resolutions of the partisans themselves, and their activity was uncoordinated. It was only in the spring of 1943 that a Soviet partisan command structure took shape:

- Central Headquarters of the Partisan Movement
- Headquarters of individual republics
- Oblast headquarters
- Supraregional centers (each covered several neighboring regions)
- Regional centers[233]

From June to December 1942, SS-Sonderkommando Dirlewanger fought practically ceaselessly. The first leaves were granted to its members only in December. As Oskar Dirlewanger stated, his subordinates were unable to see a dentist or doctor. Due to bad health and uninterrupted service, they constantly suffered from disease and colds. He thus demanded that a dentist and a doctor be assigned to the unit. Furthermore, he requested that the "recruits" who were going to be sent from the camps in the near future be better equipped with uniforms and boots.[234]

During the period of the unit's activity in Belarus, the commander's parents profited significantly from his service. According to a denunciation of July 24, 1942, by Karl B., an engineer from Esslingen, Dirlewanger often went on leave, during which he organized drinking parties and banquets. At one such event he received around a thousand eggs (partly damaged) from supplies intended for the Wehrmacht. Wasting food and this type of behavior by Waffen-SS officers and NSDAP members decorated with the honorary party badge outraged the engineer. Also, members of Esslingen elites, such as Frank, a factory owner's son, took part in the banquets.[235] Dirlewanger sent parcels with luxury goods to his family. A neighbor of the Dirlewanger family said that the servants in their house were allegedly forced laborers from Ukraine, age fifteen or sixteen.[236]

4.2. Activity of Kampfgruppe von Gottberg (1943)

From November 1942 to November 1943, SS-Sonderkommando Dirlewanger was part of Kampfgruppe von Gottberg.[237] A *Kampfgruppe* was a basic tactical formation. It was usually composed of infantry, tanks, and artillery. Leadership of Kampfgruppe von Gottberg was assumed by an experienced commander, Kurt von Gottberg,[238] who was stationed in Minsk at Gartenstraße[239] in the so-called Lenin House (Leninhaus).[240]

Between November 1942 and the start of May 1943, the SS, police, and Wehrmacht conducted eighteen extensive operations, during which over forty thousand people were killed in Poland and Belarus.[241] Over the period of a year, Dirlewanger's soldiers participated in fifteen large actions; one a month long, but, on average, most of them lasted around two weeks.[242]

At the start of 1943, SS-Sonderkommando Dirlewanger was reorganized into SS-Sonderbataillon Dirlewanger[243] and stationed in the Pleshchanitsy region. In January 1943, Erwin Walser was transferred to the unit from the SS Main Office. He mentioned that at this time, Dirlewanger was on sick leave, having sustained a wound. In his absence, SS-Sonderbataillon Dirlewanger was commanded by SS-Sturmbannführer Franz Magil.[244]

Gradually the battalion was replenished by soldiers recruited from concentration camp prisoners and Russian POWs: *Hiwis*. As of June 8, 1943, the unit reported the following structure:

- German company: 150 soldiers
- Motorcyclist platoon: 40 soldiers
- 3 Russian companies: 450 soldiers
- 1 artillery battery: 40 Germans and 40 Russians[245]

In 1943, many skirmishes initiated by German units took place. However, the Germans themselves rarely participated in them, and partisans most often clashed with eastern units: Ukrainian, Belarusian, Latvian, and Russian police battalions; Cossacks; and other units composed of former prisoners of various nationalities and citizens of the USSR. The belief in the Belarusian headquarters was that the Germans conducted their operations using mixed forces, composed of 30 percent Germans and 70 percent "traitors." The share of Germans was actually smaller still.

In 1943, a hunting unit composed of Latvians was formed near Lahoysk. Its tasks and nature (finding and destroying partisan habitations) were very similar to the profile of activity of Dirlewanger's subordinates. It numbered around thirty soldiers, led by Hans Wiechert, a member of the Command of the Security Police (KdS). Dirlewanger talked with him about the activity of the Latvian unit, interrogating village inhabitants and gathering information about partisan groups (their size and armaments).[246]

In March 1944, Kampfgruppe von Gottberg numbered twenty thousand people, of whom only three thousand were Germans. Eastern units were always commanded by German officers and NCOs.[247]

In 1943, there were around fifty thousand officers of the order police (OrPo) serving in Belarus under the command of the military administration, and of the auxiliary police (Schuma), under civilian administration orders.

> In spring 1943, there were 55 gendarmerie stations and 72 Schuma stations in the territory of Belarus. Each of them was manned by around 50 people (later, many Schuma stations numbered even up to 200 people each). In regions under the military administration there functioned from 4 to 6 police districts. Each of them had 60 OrPo order police members, which means that there were around 300 people originating from the local, mainly Belarusian population, per region.
>
> To this were added non-Belarusian auxiliary police battalions. In March 1943, 7 Ukrainian, 4 Lithuanian, and 2 Latvian battalions were active in this area. In the spring of the next year, Kurt von Gottberg's battle group, whose main goal was combating partisans, was formed from "eastern" units. These units included Bronislav Kaminski's Russian National Liberation Army (15,000 men); the Eastern Muslim SS Regiment (3,000 men); 1 Latvian and 1 Estonian security battalion; 5 Lithuanian, 5 Ukrainian, 11 Belarusian, 2 Caucasian police battalions (1,000 men each); and 4 Cossack cavalry divisions.[248]

After the war, SS-Oberführer Hermann Pister[249] testified that in 1943 he received an order from SS-Gruppenführer Richard Glücks, head of Office D–Concentration Camps,[250] to separate prisoners categorized as "repeat offenders" (*Berufsverbrecher*) and "asocials" (*Asozialen*). Repeat offenders included burglars, sexual offenders with the exception of homosexuals, and those convicted of premeditated murder or serious offences. The asocial group comprised the lazy and pimps. Oskar Dirlewanger personally went to the Buchenwald camp to assess these inmates.[251]

On July 2, 1943, a transport of prisoners from the Sachsenhausen concentration camp arrived. A total of 321 convicts, who no longer included poachers, were drafted into SS-Sonderbataillon Dirlewanger. In the camp, most of them had received the green triangle of professional criminals (*Berufsverbrecher*), or a black one as asocials. Transports were also sent from Dachau (48 people), Buchenwald (59), Auschwitz (17), Groß-Rosen (9), Lublin (3), Natzweiler (15), Neuengamme (25), Flossenbürg (19), Mannheim (34), Sachsenhausen (a further 49), and Ravensbrück (16).[252] Not all of them stayed with the unit. On August 21, 1943, Dirlewanger reported to the SS Main Office that he was sending back forty-four prisoners due to racial reasons.[253]

In summer 1943 the unit had the following composition:

Staff company with motorcyclist platoon
1st (German) Company (composed of poachers); they received white epaulettes (as a privileged group)
2nd Company (recruits) (concentration camp prisoners), red epaulettes
3rd Company (recruits) (concentration camp prisoners), red epaulettes
4th (Russian) Company
5th (Russian) Company

The average age of German soldiers was around forty, and of *Hiwis*, around twenty-five.[254] At the start of 1943, the 1st Police Artillery Battery (1. Batterie einer Polizei-Artillerie-Abteilung, labeled as 1. Batterie Schutzmannschaft-Ari.-Abt. 56) was placed under Dirlewanger's orders, remaining so until the end of the war.[255]

On January 26, 1943, new patches were introduced for SS-Sonderbataillon Dirlewanger by order of Reichsführer-SS Himmler. After looking at four proposals for the patches, Himmler finally reached a decision.[256] Instead of the crossed SS runes, Dirlewanger's soldiers started wearing crossed rifles with a horizontally placed stick grenade on their patches.[257] As Josef Rau mentioned, during operations in Belarus they also had their blood groups tattooed under their left arms.[258] SS men had their blood groups tattooed to allow easier and faster help in the event of injury.

In January 1943, the battalion was transferred from Mogilev to Lahoysk. It was replenished with men from prisons and concentration camps, but they did not include only poachers and criminals. Also, soldiers from elite SS units such as the 2nd Das Reich SS Panzer Division (2. SS Panzer Division "Das Reich"), or the 1st Leibstandarte SS Adolf Hitler Panzer Division (1. SS Panzer Division "Leibstandarte SS Adolf Hitler") were drafted into SS-Sonderbataillon Dirlewanger. Furthermore, Wehrmacht soldiers and policemen degraded as a punishment were also placed under Dirlewanger's command during operations in Belarus. According to Friedrich Walter, the unit's strength had grown tenfold from the moment of its formation in Oranienburg.[259]

Men were drafted into Dirlewanger's penal battalion for the slightest misdemeanor. Herbert Koeber was sent there in July 1944, from the French front, as a result of a denunciation: He was accused of being politically unreliable. For him, the war ended a year later, on April 6, 1945, when, further to a military court sentence, he was shot at Schmiden.[260] Fighting under Dirlewanger gave such soldiers the opportunity to erase their guilt for the crimes they had committed.

Franz Schmuckerschlag's story offers an interesting case. During the Second World War, he served in various regiments in the Netherlands and France. From summer 1942 onward, he worked in the SS Recruitment Office (SS-Ergänzungseinheit) in Vienna and in Lviv. He was sent on official business to Preßburg (Bratislava), where he met a woman. His offense was going on a walk with her and kissing. He had to show his papers immediately, and as a result, he was demoted to *SS-Obersturmführer* and transferred between November and December 1944 to SS-Sturmbrigade Dirlewanger as a punishment.[261]

Also, people suspected of plotting against Hitler who were sent to concentration camps in the 1930s and 1940s were transferred to Dirlewanger's unit by Himmler.[262] In a later period, so were people suspected of taking part in the attempt on Hitler's life on July 20, 1944.[263]

In March 1943, Himmler gave the order to make the following units directly subordinate to Erich von dem Bach-Zelewski, the *Reichsführer-SS*'s plenipotentiary for combating banditry:

Higher SS and Police Leader Rußland-Mitte in Mogilev (*Höhere SS- und Polizeiführer Rußland-Mitte*)
SS and police leader in Belarus (*SS- und Polizeiführer in Weißruthenien*)
The following SS and police units:
2nd Police Regiment (Polizei-Regiment 2)
13th Police Regiment (Polizei-Regiment 13)
I./Pol.23
12. verst. Pol. Pzkw. Komp.
112th Signals Company (Nachr. Komp. 112)
Radio reconnaissance company (*Funkaufklärungskompanie*)
Security police unit from Vitebsk (Kdo.d.Sch.Witebsk)

SS-Sonderbataillon Dirlewanger
Foreign security police units (*Kdr.d.fremdv.Schutzmmanschaften*)
Schm.Art.Abtlg.56
57th Police Battalion (Schm.Batl.57)
Fv. Arbeitskomp.2
Drushina unit (Drushina Verbände)[264]

In May 1943, the rear areas of Army Group Center covered 110,000 km^2, mainly in eastern Belarus. This territory was inhabited by 4.32 million people. Traversing it were railway lines (2,205 km) and roads (1,015 km) with military significance, which had to be protected from partisan activity. Furthermore, supply warehouses and military and economic bases had to be safeguarded. The commander of the rear area of Army Group Center had fifty-nine battalions (around 20,650 people) under his jurisdiction, which included fifteen Hungarian, thirteen Eastern, one French, and four police battalions. Railway lines were protected by thirty-seven battalions (one per 60 km on average), and railways by eight battalions (one per 125 km). A further twelve battalions secured the approaches to roads and railways and facilities with economic significance. Two units were assigned to carry out so-called mobile operations.[265]

In May, around fifty thousand Soviet partisans were located on Belarusian territory in the Rear Area of Army Group Center. However, they were poorly armed and lacked competent command and adequate military reconnaissance.[266]

From 1943 onward, so-called dead zones (*Tote Zonen*) were formed in Belarus: Mass deportations of locals to factories in the Reich, the Lublin region, and the Auschwitz labor camp took place. The motivation was both economic and pragmatic. It was believed that "dead zones" would be an extremely effective method of combating partisan activity.

On July 10, 1943, Himmler announced in an order that Hitler had decided that the territories of northern Ukraine and "central" Russia "affected by the plague of banditry" should be "cleansed of all population." All men capable of working were to be transferred to Fritz Sauckel[267] as "prisoners of war." The plan was to place part of the women and children without parents in holding camps. Himmler intended to use the vacated area to cultivate the Kazakh dandelion kok-saghyz, a source of rubber.

> On the edges of these zones, children's camps should be established, so that the children will be able to work on cultivation of kok-saghyz and other plants.[268]

Everybody who remained in "dead zones" was to be treated as a bandit and shot on sight.

In the General Commissariat of Belarus, in August 1943, adjoining "dead zones" covered 16 percent of agricultural land, and the respective number under military administration in eastern Belarus in July 1944 was 75 percent.[269]

Civilians in Belarus were used to clear mines: They were driven through mined areas until an explosion took place. Thousands of people were killed in this way.[270] Dirlewanger's soldiers were the first to invent and use the so-called mine detector method. First, inhabitants of neighboring villages were "hunted and assembled." Next,

> these people were to march in close rank along roads, with the next row walking after them exactly between the tracks left behind by the first row. Thus, there was no inch of land on which these people did not set foot. The rows set off . . . and were completely ripped to pieces.[271]

On May 25, 1943, Dirlewanger reported,

> Roadblocks and artificial barriers are almost always mined. Losses during their removal so far: 1 killed, 4 wounded. This is why as a rule we do not remove blockades, but they are destroyed by the locals. The blood saved justifies the loss of time.[272]

This practice was officially accepted by Erich von dem Bach-Zelewski and used by all units operating in Belarus. During Operation Cottbus, which lasted from May 22 to June 21, 1943, two thousand to three thousand people were killed as "mine detectors" north of Barysaw (Борисов).[273] In his diary, von dem Bach noted, "Between 2,000 and 3,000 people were probably blown up during the clearing of minefields."[274] In areas within the scope of antipartisan actions, villages were burned and food products, furnishings, and all useful objects were "registered" (i.e., looted).

Antipartisan Operations

Near Smalyavichy and Lahoysk, larger and smaller partisan units were very active. They attacked small groups of German soldiers on roads and blew up tracks and trains. It was for this reason that Dirlewanger's unit was transferred to Lahoysk. Dirlewanger's soldiers were joined by three translators and four members of Latvian volunteer companies.[275] They were also assigned members of SD units. As Gerhard Hellkamp remembered, these were people who provoked fear.[276] In Lahoysk, soldiers were placed in the school building, while the staff, officers, and Dirlewanger himself had quarters in the Tyszkiewicz palace.[277] In 1943, SS-Sonderbataillon Dirlewanger participated in over a dozen major antipartisan hunts.

Operation Erntefest I and II

At the turn of January and February 1943, the unit took part in Operation Erntefest. The operation itself was divided into two stages: Erntefest I (January 18–27, northeast of Slutsk) and Erntefest II (January 30–February 15, west of the Minsk–Slutsk road).[278]

One of the operation's participants was Kampfgruppe von Gottberg, which included eleven police and security battalions (*Polizei- und Schutzmannschaftsbataillone*). Apart from Dirlewanger's unit, these were, among others, the 13th Police Regiment (Pol. Rgt. 13), 57th Security Battalion (Schutzmannschaftsbataillon 57), and the Lithuanian 12th Security Battalion (lit. Schutzmannschaftsbataillon 12). Moreover, three security police (*Sicherheitspolizei*) units and SD units took part.[279]

In a report, SS-Hauptsturmführer Artur Wilke (from I./Pol. Rgt.13.) presented his people's activity as follows:

> 22.1. Friday: Unit sets off for Wolossatsch at 7.00. . . . 15 men, 41 women, 50 children—in total 106 people suspected of partisan activity or its support received special treatment.[280]

In von dem Bach-Zelewski's diary, "special treatment" (*Sonderbehandelte*) was synonymous with shooting (*Erschossenen*) and served to conceal the real data. We know that partisans and their collaborators were shot with a pistol.

On January 26, the Germans were attacked by a strong partisan group. Dirlewanger's unit dealt with them rapidly, killing 230 people.[281] The people termed partisans were most likely civilians.

One of the successes proclaimed after Operation Erntefest I was that 805 armed enemies were eliminated (including two officers and two commissars), 1,165 people received "special treatment," and thirty-four people were captured. After Erntefest II, 2,325 dead enemies were reported.[282] Most of the victims were civilians.

Operation Hornung

This action was conducted from January 8 or 10 to 26, 1943, in the area of Slutsk (Слуцк), Lenin (Лéнін), and the Pripyat marshes.[283] Dirlewanger's unit took part in it from February 16 to 26.[284] The operation's participants numbered 9,031, including 6,991 Germans—units from central oblasts:

2nd Police Regiment (Polizeiregiment 2)
31st Police Rifle Regiment
SS-Sonderbataillon Dirlewanger
Delegated SD group
23rd Police Regiment (Polizeiregiment 23)
18th Latvian Auxiliary Police Battalion (18. Lett. Schutzmannschafts Bataillon "Kurzeme")
12th SS Police Grenadier Division[285]

During Operation Hornung, units were under the orders of four field commands: Ost, Nord, West, and Süd, which indicates that an attempt was made to surround the enemy.[286] As SS-Hauptsturmführer Artur Wilke testified, the Command of the Security Police (KdS), which was responsible for "cleansing" the Slutsk ghetto, took part in the operation.[287]

On February 11, Oskar Dirlewanger and the 1st Company were cut off from the other German forces and surrounded by partisan groups 2 km southwest of Starobin. The situation was serious: Ammunition was running out, and they could not count on supplies. As stated in the motion to award Dirlewanger the German Cross in Gold, it was only thanks to the "cold blood" and composure of the commander that the company escaped intact.[288]

Whole villages suspected of supporting partisans were burned down during Operation Hornung also. On February 13, 1943, the 18th Latvian Auxiliary Police Battalion (Schutzmannschaftsbataillon 18) drove all the inhabitants of Pusicze into a barn and then shot at and set fire to the building. A report states that seven hundred people were killed. The battalion also destroyed neighboring villages in the same way.[289]

The whole action started with the liquidation of the Slutsk ghetto, inhabited by around three thousand people: 1,600 Jews were shot.[290] The fighting against partisans went on until February 26. Its objective was to eliminate the resistance of trained partisan groups and destroy the civilian population that was sympathetic to them. According to reports, "enemy losses" numbered "2,219 killed, 7,378 with special treatment" (these people were most likely transported to death camps),

"65 prisoners of war, and 3,300 Jews." Meanwhile, their own losses were estimated at two Germans and twenty-seven people from foreigner units (*Fremdvölkische*) killed, and twelve Germans and twenty-six foreigners wounded.[291]

"Cleansing" of the Lahoysk Area

While stationed in Lahoysk, SS-Sonderbataillon Dirlewanger not only participated in large actions but also operated locally. After the end of Operation Hornung and before the start of Zauberflöte, the unit took part in numerous pacifications and "cleansing" of the Lahoysk region. This lasted from February 27 to April 16, 1943.

Operation Dirlewanger

At the start of March 1943, SS-Sonderbataillon Dirlewanger was assigned the task of locating and destroying partisan groups and their camps between Lahoysk and Smalyavichy (Смалявічы). According to German reports, the partisans were very active, blowing up railways and trains east of Minsk.[292]

For the duration of the operation, Dirlewanger's unit was assigned an SD unit commanded by SS-Hauptsturmführer Wilke. It was composed of SS-Oberscharführer Weinhöfer, SS-Oberscharführer Semke, SS-Scharführer Rüssel, SS-Unterscharführer Konetzni, and three local translators (Simanowitsch, Sokolowski, Aisupe). Furthermore, SS-Sonderbataillon Dirlewanger was assigned four soldiers from a Latvian company and SS-Oberscharführer Gahlow from a signal group. The members of the unit were supposed to obtain provisions on their own.[293]

The Villages of Kozyri and Khatyn (Хатынь)

On March 22, 1943, SS-Sonderbataillon Dirlewanger and the 118th Auxiliary Police Battalion (Schutzmannschaft Btl. 118) destroyed Khatyn, a village near Lahoysk. This was done in revenge for a partisan attack on a German convoy, in which four German soldiers from the 118th Police Battalion died, one of the victims being Hans Woellke, a German athlete.[294] Pjotr Grigorjewitsch Lis[295] was living in the village of Kozyri in 1943. He said that he had heard about this event:

> Near us, the partisans opened fire [at the Germans], and one SS soldier died and another was wounded. For this reason, the SS soldiers returned to us and part of the village's inhabitants (around 25 people) were shot. On that same day, the village of Khatyn, where the partisans who shot at them had allegedly been staying earlier, was burned down.

> I was later told . . . that the Germans shot and burned alive almost all the inhabitants of that village: that village doesn't exist anymore today.[296]

Józef Kamiński[297] testified after the war that on March 21, 1943, a group of partisans came to Khatyn. They spent the night there in peace. They quietly left the village in the morning, before it was light. On the next day at dinner time, the inhabitants of Khatyn heard shots from the village of Kozyri, located 5 km away. As Kamiński remembered, the partisans returned to Khatyn for food most likely around 3:00 p.m.[298]

Pjotr Grigorjewitsch Lis described that in March, the village administrator Aljeksandre Lis gathered the inhabitants together. The Germans ordered them to clear the side of the Pleshchanitsy–Lahoysk road of bushes and undergrowth with axes. Around forty to fifty people (men and young women) were selected to carry out this task. While they were working, three or four trucks with German and Ukrainian soldiers drove up. Part of the soldiers wore SS uniforms with skulls on their hats, while the others had German uniforms without insignia. As Lis remembered, the people were divided into several columns of four people and led along the road.[299] He testified that

> when we reached the edge of the forest behind the village of Guba, part of the inhabitants ran away into the forest, as a result of which the bandits opened fire on them and almost all those who tried to escape were shot. I remember that Lis Jada Pjetrowna, an inhabitant of the village of Kozyri who was wounded in the arm, managed to get away. Raschjkjewitsch Antjuk, two inhabitants called Lis . . . and many others . . . were killed, however.
>
> When the oppressors saw that we were running away individually, they surrounded us and chased us into one place on the road and ordered us to lie down. . . .
>
> Those who did not want to lie down on the road were mercilessly beaten with rifle butts. . . .
>
> While we lay on the road, the bandits started shooting at us. I lay still, face down, and I heard the oppressors call a truck, to shoot us with a machine gun. The others were still firing their rifles. You could hear the groans of the wounded. . . . Soon afterward I felt that I had been wounded in the right buttock. . . . When I got up, I saw that around twenty of my companions were lying dead in the road, and around twenty were getting up.[300]

Around an hour and a half later, soon after the partisans came to Khatyn, Dirlewanger's unit and the Schuma battalion surrounded the village. Fighting and an exchange of fire ensued, during which many partisans were killed. After around an hour of combat, the partisans retreated and the German soldiers started to load wagons with all the goods found in the village.[301] Next, all the inhabitants were driven into a barn belonging to Kamiński. His homestead was located to the right of Khatyn's center, in the direction of Lahoysk. He remembered that part of the soldiers were dressed in German uniforms, while others had gray military cloaks similar to the Russian ones.[302] In the barn, 12 by 6 m in size, 160 people were crowded[303] and the barn was set alight. Those who tried to get out were shot.

Five children survived the massacre. Three (Volodia Yaskevicz, his sister Sonia, and Sasha Zhelobkovich) managed to hide from the Germans. Of the persons in the burning barn, twelve-year-old Anton Baranovsky and seven-year-old Viktor Zhelobkovich were saved. Anna Zhelobkovich, the mother of the latter, was shot while attempting to escape and, in falling, crushed her son underneath herself. The boy waited under her body until the soldiers had gone. Anton, meanwhile, was wounded when he tried to get away, and Dirlewanger's soldiers thought him dead. Two more girls, Maria Fedorovich and Yulia Klimovich, managed to get out of the burning barn. They got to the nearby village Khvorosteny, which, however, was destroyed several days later. The girls died together with its inhabitants. The children who were saved ended up in a children's home in Pleshchanitsy and lived to see the end of the war there.[304]

Of the village's adult residents, only Józef Kamiński, a fifty-six-year-old smith, survived. He described that day as follows:

> I too was thrown into the barn. My small daughter, my son, and my wife were already there. And many, many others. . . . Such a lot of people had been crowded in there that you couldn't even breathe freely or raise your hand. People shouted, children! . . .
>
> The hay and straw there had been brought in for cows. They set fire up above. They set fire to the barns from above. The roof burned, fire fell on the people, and the hay and straw started to burn, people fought for air, panting, and pushed against each other, until it was impossible to breathe anymore. Unbearable. I told my boy: "Lean with your hands and feet against the wall, lean against them!" Then the doors opened. The doors were opened, but people did not go out, did not run outside. Why? Yes, I state that they started shooting at

> the door. The screaming was so loud that those shots, that banging was not audible. It's understandable; people burned, fire fell, and also the children—there was such screaming!
>
> I told my boy: "Watch out so that you don't stick out above the heads in any way!" I helped him. I tried to pass between legs myself. There the dead fell on me. Dead, I could hardly breathe. I threw them off—I was even stronger then—and crawled. I almost reached the threshold when the roof collapsed, fell, and fire covered everything. Before I went outside, a German came, hit me with the butt of his gun so that my teeth fell out. My son also managed to get out; his hair was only a little singed. He ran five meters and then they shot him with a machine gun. . . . They shot him. . . . Our neighbor Taddej, tottering in the fire, fell on me, sat up; he was burning like a log of wood, red, and his blood flowed onto me. . . . "Save me!" he shouted. "Save me!"
>
> Then the Germans moved on. I grabbed the boy, pulled him away, but his guts were dragging after him. . . .
>
> He only asked if his mother was alive, his sister. . . . God save everybody on earth from this. So that nobody will see or hear such suffering![305]

Józef Kamiński was treated for the wounds he sustained at Bogdanówka farm and later in Lahoysk, where he lived to see the liberation by the Red Army. During the pacification of the village, his whole family was killed: his wife, Adelija; four children (including a daughter, Jadwiga, and a son, Adam) aged between 12 and 18; his brother Iwan (killed during the fighting with partisans); and his brother's son, Wladislaw.[306]

In Khatyn, 149 people, including seventy-five children, were killed: The youngest was seven weeks old. A memorial complex commemorating the events is now located there; it was unveiled on July 5, 1969. In the center is a monument depicting Józef Kamiński carrying his son's corpse in his arms. The space left behind each of the twenty-six burned-down houses is surrounded by symbolic foundations, and in the center of each, an obelisk topped with a bell is placed. The bells symbolize the chimneys of the houses burned. Individual bells ring every thirty seconds to show that in Belarus, one citizen died every half a minute during the Second World War. Another symbol of this place is three birch trees planted in a square: The fourth missing one is to indicate that every fourth inhabitant of Belarus died during the war. The complex commemorates not only Khatyn, but also other settlements burned down and destroyed during the war.[307]

Some suggest that the Khatyn atrocity was committed by "Soviet partisans commanded by NKVD officers in German uniforms." Marek Koprowski, a journalist specializing in eastern affairs, stated,

> The main reason why the inhabitants of Chatyń [Khatyn] were murdered was the fact that in English Chatyń is spelled Khatyn; that is the same as Katyń [Katyn]. It is symptomatic that the massacre was carried out right after the graves of Polish officers were discovered in Katyń.

The chairwoman of the regional Union of Poles in Belarus in Slonim, Leonarda Rewkowska, stated that she had met, in Khatyn,

> the last living witness of the tragedy that had played out there. His name was Józef Kamiński, and he told excursions about what had happened there. When he heard that I spoke Polish, he approached me and surreptitiously told me that the crime in Chatyń had been committed not by Germans but by Soviet partisans dressed in German uniforms. The Chatyń victims were simply supposed to cover the Katyń massacre. Everybody who was to encounter the word "Katyń" was supposed to associate it with the German massacre of Chatyń.[308]

Archival documents such as the orders of Kampfgruppe von Gottberg, the soldiers' use of methods identical to those used in other villages of Belarus, postwar testimonies by soldiers of SS-Sonderbataillon Dirlewanger, and, above all, the postwar testimonies of the six witnesses saved from the pacification of Khatyn (two, Sonia Yaskevicz and Viktor Zhelobkovich, are still alive today) unequivocally point to men from SS-Sonderbataillon Dirlewanger and the 118th Auxiliary Police Battalion as the guilty parties.

From March 24 to mid-April 1943, SS-Sonderbataillon Dirlewanger was assigned to Kampfgruppe Schimana, commanded by SS-Brigadeführer Walter Schimana.[309] The *Kampfgruppe* was moreover composed of the following units:

2nd Police Regiment (Pol.-Rgt.2)
13th Police Regiment (Pol.Rgt.13)
57 Schutzmannschaft Battalion (Schm.Btl.57)
12. verst. Pol.Pz.Kp[310]

Operation Zauberflöte

Between April 1 and 24, 1943, Dirlewanger's soldiers participated in an urban operation in Minsk code-named Zauberflöte (magic flute), during which a manhunt and a blockade were carried out in the Jewish ghetto.[311]

During this operation, 130,000 houses were searched (including those ruined as a result of military action) for deserters, "Bolshevik bandits, terrorists, and saboteurs." The manhunt was extremely well coordinated. Subunits of the 141st Wehrmacht Reserve Division and the Minsk garrison established a closed outer ring. Inner cordons were formed by SS and police units, including Dirlewanger's.[312] One of Dirlewanger's soldiers remembered that six thousand men took part in the operation, while in that period, five thousand Jews were living in the ghetto in terrible conditions.[313] Human memory is fallible: According to official data, within the operation, 76,000 people were controlled, 52,000 were placed in assembly points to wait for further proceedings, and 22,400 railway passengers were arrested. In total, 5,500 people were deported to the Reich as forced laborers. Moreover, 720 people were kept in Minsk as slaves, thirty-nine were arrested, and two received "special treatment."[314]

After the end of Operation Zauberflöte, on April 23, 1943, von dem Bach organized an assembly and parade with the participation of

- 2nd Police Regiment (SS-Pol.Rgt.2)
- 13th Police Regiment (SS-Pol.Rgt.13), including the 12th Panzer Company (Pz.Komp.12), subordinate to it
- SS-Sonderbataillon Dirlewanger
- Special-purpose staff company (Stabskompanie z.b.V.)
- The Security Police and the Security Service (Sicherheitspolizei und SD)
- Security Police Orchestra platoon from Lipsk (Musikzug der Schutzpolizei Leipzig)[315]

Operation Draufgänger I and II

This was conducted between April 26 and May 10, 1943,[316] in the Maladzyechna (April 23–30) and Rudnya (Рудня) (May 1–10) regions.[317] In the second part of the action, the 2nd SS Police Regiment (SS-Pol. Rgt. 2), SS-Sonderbataillon Dirlewanger, and the 118th Police Battalion (Schutzmannschafts-Btl. 118) participated.[318]

Brigidovo

On May 4, in Brigidovo a pacification action was conducted during which around sixty men, women, and children were killed. The report of Company D (German) provides more-precise data on the following days:

> On May 5, 1943, at 15.30, the village of Starzynski was destroyed. While retreating we were fired on from the northeast part of the settlement. (One part is located in the forest.) 75 people suspected of belonging to bandit groups and a further 65 women and children were shot.
>
> The number of people suspected of cooperating with bandits shot in Brygidowo on May 4, 1943, has risen to 90.[319]

Maladzyechna (Молодечно)

From April 28 to May 10, 1943, SS-Sonderbataillon Dirlewanger took part in action Draufgänger I and II in the Maladzyechna and Manila regions. A large part of Maladzyechna was destroyed, and around thirty thousand of its inhabitants were sent to concentration camps.[320] To this day, people are living in the town who survived the action conducted by Dirlewanger's soldiers, and also their descendants. Interestingly, in 1988 the German Esslingen became Maladzyechna's partner city: this is the town where Oskar Dirlewanger, the commander of SS-Sonderbataillon Dirlewanger, grew up and was educated.[321]

After the end of Operation Draufgänger II, on May 12, 1943, Oskar Dirlewanger was promoted to *SS-Obersturmbannführer*.[322] In a report summarizing the action, his unit declared that on May 5–6, thirty-three bunkers were demolished, 386 "bandits" were killed, and 294 suspects were "finished off." Furthermore, it was reported that 3 men, 30 women, and 248 children were captured and 117 horses, 140 sheep, 14 pigs, and 120 tons of food were seized. During Operation Draufgänger II, Starinki, Brygidovo, Lubon, Baturino, Kremenets, and Yanushkavichy were destroyed.[323]

In a report covering two weeks' activity during Operation Draufgänger I and II, Dirlewanger listed that fourteen thousand enemies had been eliminated. Moreover, thirty-nine had been captured as a result of encirclement. He declared the following own losses: one officer and two privates killed and twelve wounded, and among *Hiwis*, seven killed and twenty-one wounded.[324]

Operation Cottbus (Kottbus)

Operation Cottbus was a continuation of Draufgänger I and II and was the largest antipartisan operation to take place in 1943.[325] It was conducted at the turn of May and June in the area of the settlements of Barysaw, Lepel, Begoml, Ushachy, and

Berezino, around 140 km northeast of Minsk, and it ended on June 21.[326] The German and Eastern forces of 16,662 (police, Wehrmacht, Luftwaffe) were commanded by Kurt von Gottberg.[327] Their composition was as follows:

2nd SS Police Regiment (SS-Pol. Rgt. 2)
13th SS Police Regiment (SS-Pol. Rgt. 13)
SS-Sonderbataillon Dirlewanger
Polizei-Schützen-Regiment 31 (I./Pol. Schtz. Rgt. 31)
I./Flak-Abt. Kdo. Stab RFSS
12. Polizei Panzer Kompanie (12. Pol. Pz. Kompanie)
6th, 11th, 12th Gendarmerie Platoons (mot) (Gend. Züge (mot) 6, 11, 12)
Gendarmerie Einsatzkommando z.b.V. (zur besonderen Verwendung–"special purpose") Kreikenbom
SS-Drushina Verbände
15th, 54th, 57th, 102nd, 118th Auxiliary Police Battalions (Schutzmannschafts-Btle. 15, 54, 57, 102, 118)[328]

In the Begoml and Lepel regions around Lake Palik, partisans had been gathering since spring 1942, because the lay of the land made it possible for them to hide there. In the autumn of 1942, eighteen of their units were located in that area (including "Diadia Kolia," "Starik" Brigade, "Za Rodinu" Brigade, "Mstitel," "Smiert," "Fashizmu," "Zheleznyak" Brigade). These groups terrorized and stole from the local population, which had to feed them.[329] The situation of peasants in these areas is depicted in a report on "Mstitel":

> Drunkenness reigned in the unit. Vodka was delivered to the unit not in liters, but in barrels, which were used in the headquarters as chairs. . . . The drunkenness of the leaders also spread to the partisan rank and file, which caused relations with the local population to deteriorate. . . . Kobylkin, the commander of the 5th Company, . . . drank, looted, and was generally demoralized. He raped women and allowed his partisans to do the same.[330]

The situation was similar in the whole area controlled by partisan units. Drunkenness, looting, rapes, theft, shootings, and murders of civilians occurred on a daily basis. A report from the Lahoysk region for the period from May

15 to June 15, 1943, states, "There is great dissatisfaction among the peasantry due to the behavior of the partisans, who demand too much for themselves, drink, and revel."[331] Another indicates that

> all the brigades [Begoml-Lepel zones] have stripped the population of the Ilya, Kurenets, and Krivichi [in the western part of the zone] regions to such an extent that a strong antipartisan mood is currently prevalent there. . . . If decided steps are not undertaken shortly, hostile incidents against the partisans on the part of the local population may occur.[332]

In this period, SS-Sonderbataillon Dirlewanger was stationed in Lahoysk. Interestingly, in the 1960s and 1970s, its soldiers testified that the inhabitants of the village trusted their commander. They called him "Major" and came to him with information and complaints about the partisans, and also about members of the unit.[333] They certainly were not people from villages pacified by the unit, but it is likely that they did so. Dirlewanger ruled his people with an iron fist. Despite the cruel pacifications conducted in the environs of Lahoysk and during Operation Cottbus, civilians turned to German soldiers for help in combating partisans.

The partisans' intelligence gatherers noticed in mid-April 1943 that German and eastern forces had started to concentrate around the zone controlled by them. Smaller German groups organized strikes against partisan-occupied areas. In May, ten brigades (forty-three units) and an independent detachment, 8,598 partisans in total, were present there.[334] There was no centralized command, however.

On May 20, Operation Cottbus proper started. From May 28 onward, Dirlewanger's unit (supplemented by foreign volunteers) began building fortifications and trenches. On June 1, Dirlewanger's headquarters were attacked by a partisan unit. Hand-to-hand combat ensued, in which Dirlewanger personally participated.[335]

A report observes that

> moreover, during actions such as Operation Cottbus, all humane care for the civilian population should be extinguished, because it has frequently turned out that the local population, including women and children, constantly mine the roads behind our lines.

Thus the German command justified the high number of victims among civilians, including women and children. It is quite unlikely that partisans placed mines, which they lacked, on roads on a large scale.[336]

On June 8, Dirlewanger reported,

> SS-Sonderbataillon Dirlewanger currently comprises one German company of 150 people, one German motorcyclist platoon of 40 people, 3 Russian companies of 150 people each, a Ukrainian platoon of 40 people, one battery with 40 Germans and 40 Russians; 760 people in total.[337]

In June he was decorated with the Infantry Assault Badge.[338]

On June 18, 1943, SS-Hauptsturmführer Artur Wilke informed of the following "result of the operation" (*Ergebnis des Unternehmens*):

> Enemy losses:
> May 11–June 7, 1943, in combat 4,799
> June 8–June 17, 1943, in combat 851
> May 11–June 7, 1943, eliminated 3,379
> June 8–June 17, 1943, eliminated 237
> June 11–May 7 [should be May 11–June 7], 1943, in combat 280
> June 8–June 17, 1943, in combat 272
> total enemy losses: 9,818[339]

Finally, on June 23, 1943, Wilke provided the following data in his report:

> Enemy losses:
> 9,751 (6,042 fallen in battle, 3,709 eliminated), 599 prisoners
> Labor force 5,500 (4,900 men, 600 women)
>
> Own losses:
> German losses: 88 dead (3 officers, 85 *Unterführers* and soldiers), 383 wounded (10 officers, 373 *Unterführers* and soldiers)
> Foreign units: 39 killed, 152 wounded, 4 missing[340]

Meanwhile, the Belarusian Headquarters of the Partisan Movement (BSPD) reported that during Operation Cottbus, the partisans killed 1,968 German soldiers and one hundred officers in total and also destroyed fifteen tanks, seven tankettes, and two armored cars. Their own losses were eighty-eight killed, fifty-seven wounded, and fourteen missing, the ratio of forces being eight thousand partisans to forty-five thousand enemy soldiers and officers.[341] In reality, the partisans faced 16,662 German soldiers and did not achieve any particular successes during the fighting. They hid in forests and recorded many desertions, some units attempted to pass through German lines, and they burned villages (e.g., Kvetcha) so that the Germans would be unable to create their own bases there.[342]

The German troops did not manage to eradicate all the partisan units stationing in the neighborhood of Barysaw, Lepel, Begoml, and Ushachy during Operation Cottbus. None of the units were completely eliminated. In June, the command of Army Group Center reported,

> The destruction of the great bandit groups concentrated in the area west of Lepel was not achieved. Their masses have passed through to the north. It was necessary to interrupt the operation because the forces under HSSPF command have been assigned elsewhere; neither could forces of the general commanding [the Rear Area of Army Group Center] remain available.[343]

Numerous villages were destroyed during Operation Cottbus. On May 28, 467 inhabitants of the villages Ikony, Bolskaja, and Maloje Pustomstisch were burned alive and murdered. Also, in this instance they were driven into a barn, which was then fired upon and subsequently set on fire.[344] On June 2, in a settlement called Pijany Las, six men were shot while ninety women and children were burned in a barn. On June 5, in the village of "Schunjawka" (this may have been Shunevtsy, Шунеўцы) twenty-eight men, women, and children were burned and drowned in a well.[345] These are only some examples of settlements pacified by Kampfgruppe von Gottberg units during Operation Cottbus.

Many of the villages that were then destroyed, together with their inhabitants, currently hold monuments to remind visitors of the crimes committed there. Once again, the civilian population suffered the most. First, partisans looted and murdered. Next, during the operation itself, German troops had orders to systematically exterminate civilians and to create "dead zones" in the areas covered by fighting. The Germans burned whole villages together with their inhabitants, while those capable of working were transported as laborers to the Reich. The only chance for survival was running away into the forests and marshes. After Cottbus ended and the German units had retreated, the people who had survived tried to return to their villages. Soon afterward the partisans reappeared, while the German Luftwaffe bombed and fired on the temporary homesteads, killing both locals and partisans.

Operation Günther

It was conducted between July 2 and 7, 1943, in the area of the settlements Besjady, Januschkowitschi (Yanushkavichy?), and Kalatschi.[346] Before its start, it was reported that in the forests of Rudnja and Manila, the organized groups Diadia Vasya and Fürs Vaterland (commanded by Walodje Tschitschyo[347]) were operating. Furthermore, the unit Kotov (commanded by Romanov) and the Raykov group had been located.[348]

The decision to conduct Operation Günther was made under the influence of information from confidants (*V-Männer*) who lived in those areas. The pretext was allegedly a report that in the settlement of Januschkowitsche, around 200–250 wounded or sick "bandits" were hiding after the fighting in the area of Lake Palik (Палік).[349] It was also stated that the unit Fürs Vaterland, numbering around eighty people (including twenty-five women), was stationed there.[350] It was estimated that around six hundred to eight hundred partisans were present in the area to be affected by the action.[351]

The following units were sent to carry it out:

Griep Regiment (Regt. Griep, SS-Pol.Rgt.2)
von der Goltz Regiment (Regiment von der Goltz, Wehrmacht)
SS-Sonderbataillon Dirlewanger
1 SD-Kommando
motorized gendarmerie platoon (*Gandarmeriezug mot.*)[352]

The operation was commanded by SS-Hauptsturmführer Wilke, and all units were assigned line commanders. To SS-Sonderbataillon Dirlewanger, SS-Untersturmführer Ammann was assigned, together with four people from a unit stationing in Lahoysk. Ammann was to report to SS-Obersturmbannführer Dirlewanger immediately. After the action ended, these people were to return to their original unit. The operation was planned for July 1–4, 1943.[353] During it, all the units were to obtain supplies on their own.[354]

SS-Sonderbataillon Dirlewanger together with SS-Pol.Rgt.2 was tasked with destroying a camp located most probably south of the village of Kapusszin.

On July 2, Dirlewanger's soldiers set off from Lahoysk toward Yanushkavichi (Januschkowitschi), and at 6:00 p.m. they reportedly occupied a position near Dmitrowo. Next, it was planned that they would establish a connection with the Griep group.[355]

As a result of Operation Günther, inhabitants were "evacuated" to transit camps as labor force, while livestock was "secured" for the needs of the Third Reich. Valuables found in villages suspected of supporting partisans were confiscated.[356]

After numerous massacres of the local population, on July 6 an administrator from the Minsk forestry district reported the aftermath of the "action to combat banditry" in his oblast:

> All these operations have not reduced the danger. So, for example, the region of Lahoysk and Pleshchanitsy, and also of Uzda, are completely dead to us apart from communication routes and the immediate environs of several garrisons. In the first two regions, this is primarily the result of the activity of SS-Sonderbataillon Dirlewanger, which surely does not contribute to calming the situation. Mass burning of villages leads only to the extermination of the remnants of the population that is on our side or at least is not obstructive, because those who really are guilty have managed to run away to the forest. In time, even decent people follow in their footsteps since they are currently far safer with the partisans. Unfortunately, SS-Sonderbataillon Dirlewanger believes its task to be pure annihilation. . . . This war of extermination conducted north of Minsk pursuant to special orders, which in fact affects only innocent people and their property, brings the opposite result and has an impact like the most effective enemy propaganda.[357]

On June 29, 1943, Commissar General Wilhelm Kube also condemned this type of activity:

> After every large operation it may be observed that true bandits, who are usually able to escape to the forest in time, disperse around the country in small groups, while the population from the burned settlements, if it has managed to save itself, goes over to the partisan side. Women and children are killed in mass shootings, villages are burned, and bitterness grows among the part of the population so far loyal to us.[358]

As a result of escalating criticism, the murder of all civilians was limited or in some places abolished. Instead, the locals were deported to the Reich as forced laborers.

Operation Hermann

This was conducted by SS-Sonderbataillon Dirlewanger in the region of the Naliboki Forest, near the village of Naliboki, three weeks after the end of Operation Cottbus. The forest was surrounded by an encirclement that included Naliboki (Налібакі), Rubiazhevichi (Рубяжэвічы), Rakaw (Ракаў), Bahdanaw (Багданаў), Iwye (Іўе), Pudzina (Пудзіна), and Karelichy (Карэлічы).[359] The headquarters of Kampfgruppe von Gottberg were located in Navahrudak (Новогрудок). One of the commanding officers was SS-Hauptsturmführer Artur Wilke. The position of the officer of Ia was held by Weber, and of Ib by Rohde. Moreover, Kurt von Gottberg and his adjutant Hauptmann der Polizei Schröder were part of the staff.[360]

Operation Hermann lasted from August 5 to 15.[361] Besides Dirlewanger's soldiers, the units that took part in the action were the 1st SS Infantry Brigade, police regiments and battalions, and auxiliary police battalions (Latvian, Lithuanian, and Belarusian). In total, 8,820 people fought on the German side.[362] They were commanded by Kurt von Gottberg.

The partisans appeared in this region in spring 1942, and in June the 125th Stalin Unit destroyed in Naliboki a German unit on its way to an "anti-Jewish action." According to a German report, the events took the following course:

> The "Baranowitsche" unit, remaining under the orders of the commander of the SS Security Police and the Security Service, set off on an anti-Jewish action in the strength of 8 German officers and NCOs, 2 members of the district commissariat in Navahrudak, 1 second lieutenant, 1 wachtmeister of the gendarmerie, and 15 Lithuanians and Russians. On June 9, 1942, around 17.00 they reached Walliboki [Naliboki], north of Stowbtsy. The village is situated deep in a forest; however, on its outskirts there is quite a lot of clear space. As soon as the cars, one passenger car and one truck, emerged from the forest and wanted to drive into the village, they were fired upon from two sides [with machine guns]. . . . In this unequal battle, all members of the unit gradually fell; only the SS-Oberscharführer and 1 SS man and 4 translators or drivers managed to retreat and escape with their lives. . . . On June 10, 1942, the commander of the SS Security Police and the Security Service in Belarus immediately set off from Baranavichy

> with almost all the forces in his unit. . . . In Naliboki he found 15 people fallen in battle. All the fallen had had their boots taken off, while the SS men were stripped to their undergarments. A swastika and the Soviet star had been burned onto the SS-Obersturmführer's breast. During the interrogation of the village's inhabitants, it was ascertained that 4 . . . Germans had been captured and taken away from Naliboki in the passenger car seized from the Germans. . . . The bandit group comprised 90–100 Russians, including paratroopers in Russian uniform. The bandit group had heavy weapons and possessed a radio station.[363]

In fact, the unit did not have a radio station, nor did it include paratroopers. It comprised former Red Army officers and soldiers.[364] German intelligence estimated that around two hundred partisans were located in this area, but one of the groups was estimated at a thousand.[365]

Fighting against German units during Operation Hermann were the 125th Stalin Unit, already mentioned, and also Nikitin's unit, the Chkalov unit,[366] the Dzerzhinsky unit, "Bolshevik," and the Suvorov unit.[367] During the previous winter of 1942 and 1943, all these groups had become a plague to the civilian population. Vasily Chernishov "Platon" had been delegated to the forest as their commander.[368]

Aware that the Germans were preparing an operation, the partisans took action. They felled trees in all of Naliboki Forest to block the entrances to it. They dug fire trenches on the edge of the forest and mined access roads.

The objective of Operation Hermann was "the liquidation of bandit groups, destruction of their camps and bunkers, and securing of their provisions." Furthermore, the Germans intended to "secure" crops and livestock and obtain forced laborers.[369] The Naliboki Forest was to become another "dead zone." The action was aimed not only against Soviet but also against Polish partisans:

> Special attention is drawn to the fact that in the area mentioned we encounter two types of bandit groups. First, there are Bolshevik bandit groups, and second, nationalist Polish bandit groups, which fight both against German units and against Bolshevik bandit groups.[370]

"Polish bandit groups" meant the so-called Polish Legions (Home Army, AK) stationing near the village of Bielitsa in the southern part of the Naliboki Forest. They numbered around 650 people and were commanded by Kacper Miłaszewski, second lieutenant of the Polish army. There were at least two more Polish partisan groups in the area besides them.[371] SS-Hauptsturmführer Wilke stated that they were destroyed at the start of the operation.[372]

Around 15 km from Naliboki, in the very heart of the forest, there operated a large group of Jewish partisans and escapees from local ghettos, commanded by the Bielski brothers (Tuvia, Zus, and Asael).[373]

Unlike during Operation Cottbus, whose goal was to exterminate the civilian population, in Hermann the objective was to acquire as many forced laborers as possible. This resulted from Adolf Hitler's decree, communicated on July 10 by Heinrich Himmler:

(1) The Führer has decided that the areas of North Ukraine and central Russia contaminated by bandits must be cleansed of all population.
(2) All men capable of work should be, on the basis of decrees that are yet to be drawn up, assigned to the Reich commissar for labor issues, but as prisoners of war.
(3) Women should be assigned to the Reich commissar for labor issues, to work in the Reich.
(4) Part of the women and all orphaned children are to go to our transit camps for children.[374]

Constant reminders about this order were made during the operation, and it was emphasized that the population should not be murdered but assigned to forced labor. On July 7, an order was issued stating that "partisan groups are to be exterminated, their camps and bunkers destroyed, and all provisions appropriated."[375]

During Operation Hermann, the individual German units moved closer to each other from the directions of various settlements located around the Naliboki Forest. The partisans were thus shut in an encirclement. Resistance was relatively weak, but the partisans remained constantly active. Wilke remembered that they attacked a police platoon and killed around fourteen people.[376]

Forming Einsatzkommando Dirlewanger were

Kreikenbom Special-Purpose Unit (Gend. Kdo. z.b.V. Kreikenbom), which by July 19 was to arrive in Rakaw from the settlement of Ivyanets (bel. Івянец):

Valozhin (bel. Валожын) gendarmerie station (Gend. Posten Wolozyn), 8 Germans and 60 locals

Rakaw Police Battalion station (Schm. Posten Rakow), 1 German and 41 locals

Koydanava (Dzyarzhynsk) gendarmerie station (Gend. Posten Kojdanov) (biel. Дзяржынск, Койданаў), 3 Germans and 60 locals

Radashkovichy (bel. Радашковічы) Police Battalion station (Schm. Posten Radoszkowice), 1 German and 25 locals

Zaslawye (bel. Заслаўе) gendarmerie station (Gend. Posten Zaslaw), 6 Germans and 108 locals[377]

It was decided that Einsatzgruppe Griep, attacking from the west, would be subordinate to Einsatzkommando Dirlewanger, which until July 26 also had under it a platoon of antiaircraft guns, the 57th Schuma Battalion, until July 27, two battalions of land troops from the 392nd Higher Field Command (Oberfeldkommandantur 392) from Bahdanau (bel. Багданаў) and the 2nd Battalion of the SS Police Regiment (SS-Pol.Rgt.2),[378] and, until August 6, the 31st Regiment of the Police Battalion (Pol. Schtz. Regt. 31).[379]

SS-Sonderbataillon Dirlewanger was to arrive in Zaslawye from Lahoysk on July 18, 1943. Two days later, at 6:00 a.m., Einsatzgruppe Dirlewanger commenced its attack on partisan lines from the settlements of Haradok (Гарадок)–Mikhalovo (bel. Міхалова)–Duszkava (Душкава).[380]

The commander of the unit was wounded during the operations:

> The cartridge went through the cloak sleeve, [Dirlewanger] sustained a light bullet wound in the chest, and the third bullet knocked the cigarette out of his lips.[381]

After this action, he was probably transported in the company of a nurse from Minsk to the hospital in Wolkowycze (Vawkavysk was probably meant) in an airplane piloted by Johann Görgen.[382]

The partisans tried to escape the encirclement. In its eastern part, increased activity by members of the Polish resistance movement was observed. Einsatzgruppe Dirlewanger was fighting on that side, and its task was to prevent partisans from breaking out. To achieve this, they were to close the circle by establishing a connection with SS-Pol.Rgt.2 and Pol.Sch.Rgt.31.[383] According to orders, the soldiers were supposed to have provisions for the whole period of the operation with them.[384]

Despite the information provided to them by Polish intelligence, the Soviets realized that they were dealing with a large pacification operation only after several days.[385] In July, all the partisan units were surrounded and the liquidation of the encirclement began. "There ensued very violent and heavy fighting on extremely marshy and inaccessible terrain."[386] The partisans attempted to escape the encirclement in smaller groups. On August 4, the action ended in "complete extermination of the bandits trapped in it [the encirclement]."[387] German units did not destroy all the surrounded partisan groups. The Bielski brothers' group, among others, survived, having managed to get to the island of Krasna Horka, which was surrounded by marshes on all sides, and they stayed there until the end of German operations.[388]

After the operation ended, the Germans provided the following data:

> Enemy losses: killed in fighting: 4,280 (including 6 bandit group commanders and 2 commissars); prisoners: 654 (including 1 officer of the Polish resistance movement); . . . Own losses: Germans: 46 killed; 112 wounded (including 9 officers); missing: 3. Foreigners: killed: 6; wounded 43; missing: 1.[389]

According to Vasily Chernishov "Platon," his partisans achieved significant successes. Furthermore, he informed that the partisans had managed to save "thousands of people" from being murdered, and even to destroy the "staff of the military group" of Oskar Dirlewanger, who was allegedly killed in the action. Chernishov reported this information to Ponomarienko, and the latter to Stalin. As I mentioned above, Oskar Dirlewanger was wounded during the fighting in Operation Hermann, but the wound was not dangerous. Further, "Platon" gave the losses of the Germans as three thousand killed and wounded, twenty-nine prisoners, sixty destroyed passenger cars and trucks, three tanks, and four armored cars. According to him, own losses were 129 killed, fifty wounded, and twenty-four desertions to the enemy side.[390]

After the end of Operation Hermann, the Germans commenced with the creation of a "dead zone" in the Naliboki Forest. By August 1, 1943, von Gottberg gave the order to "evacuate" the area:

> All people (men, women, children) and live and dead livestock should be expelled from . . . the area in question. Men capable of work will be secured [for labor in the Reich] by government councillor Tuschen from the employment affairs headquarters. The fate of the remaining population is the responsibility of the relevant civil administration bodies [district commissariats]. However, leaving them near the evacuated area is disadvantageous. . . . Villages and all other buildings, and also bridges and crops, if they cannot be secured [by us], should

> be destroyed and burned. If possible, the forests located in this area should also be burned. In the future, people found in this area should be treated as wild game.[391]

After the end of the fighting, Einsatzgruppe Dirlewanger was to gather people intended for "evacuation" in a transit camp in Ivyanets and was afterward dissolved.[392]

By August 11, 1943, the combing of the area and creation of a "dead zone" were complete. According to a report of August 20, 9,065 men, 7,701 women, and 4,178 children had been detained.[393] This means that 20,944 people were deported as laborers to the Reich. In this respect, Operation Hermann was the largest such endeavor carried out by German units in Belarus.

Ponomarienko informed Stalin that 150 villages were burned down during the action.[394] Like in other parts of Belarus after pacification actions, some were never rebuilt. The population transported as laborers to the Reich was mostly unable to return to their homes after the war. For example, in summer 1943, Rudnya Nalibotskaya comprised 170 households, but only sixty families returned there after the war, and currently the village no longer exists (two houses remain).

The Germans assessed enemy losses during Operation Hermann at 4,280 killed in action and 654 taken prisoner. As their own losses, they listed forty-six German soldiers and six foreigners killed, and 112 German and forty-three foreign wounded.[395] After the operation, SS-Sonderbataillon Dirlewanger returned to its quarters in Lahoysk.[396]

Due its scale, it was decided that Hermann should be presented to the general public. The activity of German troops—SS units (including SS-Sonderbataillon Dirlewanger) and police units—was immortalized by war correspondents. The publication of a photo album was planned, and a copy was to be presented to Himmler.[397]

Naliboki

In the largest settlement in the Naliboki Forest, Naliboki, were seven hundred homesteads. Many inhabitants hid in the forests or marshes, often joining the partisans or establishing so-called family camps. To the Germans they were "game," and for partisans, victims to be looted. Those who did not want to leave their homes were killed on the spot or burned in barns, and others were transported as laborers. Ten people were murdered in Naliboki. Of the village, only smoldering ruins remained.[398] Maria Chilicka, born in 1926, remembered German operations in Naliboki during Hermann thus:

> In the month of August 1943, after the Ivyanets uprising, Germans entered the village. They also looted our belongings then. They gathered us in the square and said we would be resettled. Many people ran away to the forest. Later I found out that the Germans burned Naliboki.
>
> They took us by rail to Stowbtsy, and from there to Białystok. They transported me and my sister Jadzia farther, to Germany. Our parents and four siblings stayed in a German camp in Białystok. On August 6, 1943, I arrived in Westphalia in Baden Hausen. There I worked in a factory producing antiaircraft guns and tanks. I got sick with trachoma, but thanks to a good foreman I got better. Uncle Wacław Grygorcewicz was in Buchenwald.[399]

She never returned to her farm. Naliboki was rebuilt and exists to this day.

Settlement of Juzefowo (Yuzefovo)

Erich Koedel, one of Dirlewanger's soldiers, remembered that in autumn 1943 the unit occupied a Belarusian village as its quarters. His testimony was summarized thus:

> Dirlewanger personally ordered him to guard around twenty men and women, whom other members of the unit had gathered for labor in the Reich. The witness heard shots from the barn that was located around 200 meters away and saw that the barn was burning. When the witness later approached the barn, he ascertained that charred bodies were lying there.[400]

This event may have occurred during the next operation, Fritz, which took place at the turn of September and October 1943. At that time, an unspecified penal company stationing in Lahoysk burned Yuzefovo down and killed most of its inhabitants.

Anna Iwanowna Zhdanowitsch survived the massacre.[401] After the war, she testified that on September 19, 1943, several trucks and motorcycles with German soldiers arrived in the village. When the inhabitants started running away in panic, the soldiers opened fire on them. Those who survived the first attack were herded into the largest barn, belonging to Stepan Razhewskij. All those who hid in houses were shot, and the whole village was set on fire.[402]

In the next hours, as Anna Zhdanowitsch remembered, the neighboring villages of Parkhovo and Swidno were burned down.[403] Anna Aleksandrowna

Tichonowitsch[404] was an inhabitant of Swidnoje and confirmed the description of events presented by Anna Zhdanowitsch. Also here, trucks carrying SS men from a penal company (*Strafeinheit*) arrived from the Lahoysk area. Anna Tichonowitsch's whole family and most of the residents were shot in the nearby pine woods. In the village, the houses, a mill, and forty to fifty people were burned.[405]

Operation Heinrich and Fighting on the Front

The operation took place between November 1 and 9, 1943, in the region of the settlements Idritsa (Идрица, now in Russia) and Polotsk (Полацк).[406] Kampfgruppe von dem Bach, under the command of Erich von dem Bach, was formed in order to perform it.[407] Two *Einsatzgruppen* operated within it: the first commanded by SS-Obergruppenführer Friedrich Jeckeln,[408] and the second by Kurt von Gottberg.[409]

The units of Kampfgruppe von Gottberg were SS Police Regiments 2, 13, and 24 (SS-Pol. Rgt. 2, 13, 24); SS-Sonderbataillon Dirlewanger; 64. Sicherung Regiment z.b.V. (zur besonderen Verwendung, special purpose);[410] Gendarmerie Einsatzkommando z.b.V. Kreikenbom; Schutzmannschaft (Schuma) Btle. 57; 255. SS-Abteilung Pannier; 12. Pol. Pz. Kompanie; and Gendarmerie Platoons (Gend. Züge mot.) 13, 19, and 49.[411]

The operation was interrupted because of the movements of Soviet troops. The groups participating in it, including SS-Sonderbataillon Dirlewanger, were sent to the first line of the front. Dirlewanger's soldiers fought in the area of Nevel, Dretun, and Polotsk[412] as part of Gruppe Nickel, commanded by Lieut. (Oberleutnant der Schutzpolizei) Nickel, who stood at the head of the 13th SS Police Regiment (SS-Pol. Rgt. 13).[413] The attack on Polotsk was initiated from Dokhnary (Дохнары).[414] Next, the fighting moved to Konnyi Bor (Конны Бор).[415]

Due to a lack of coordination and cooperation between individual commands operating in the region, stopping the march of the Red Army and launching a counteroffensive on Nevel were unsuccessful.[416] As Johannes Stein mentioned, snow lay everywhere.[417] Commanders had serious fears concerning the weather: They were worried that a sudden drop in temperature would occur, hindering operations.[418] Left of Dirlewanger's unit, Latvian troops were located, and to the right, German police units. SS-Sonderbataillon Dirlewanger pushed into the positions of Soviet troops like a wedge, suffering heavy losses as a result.[419]

Before the fighting in the Nevel region started, Dirlewanger received quite a large transport of prisoners from the Ravensbrück concentration camp. Most of them died at the front.[420]

Summary of Fighting in 1942 and 1943

At the end of May 1942, Schenckendorff reported that since June 1941, eighty thousand partisans had been eliminated in the rear area of Army Group Center. By January 1943, this number had risen to 100,000 (this included civilians and former Red Army soldiers).[421] In 1942, numerous massacres of the local population were committed as part of antipartisan operations. The crimes reached their apogee a year later. It is impossible now to establish and separate the civilian victims (women, children, older people, the disabled, and men) from partisan losses. To magnify their successes, many German commanders overstated data about the number of people killed in antipartisan fighting, and they also added the civilian population. Nevertheless, partisan losses were far higher than what they themselves officially reported.

Klaus Jochen Arnold estimated that until May 10, 1942, the number of people killed on the German side in the rear areas of Army Group Center was 3,248, and in the period from June 1942 to June 1944, around 25,130. To this, losses among members of eastern units of 10,543 should be added. The total German losses in Belarus were 39,568.[422] Christian Gerlach, meanwhile, estimates German losses in the rear area of Army Group Center to have been between fifty-four thousand and fifty-seven thousand people, including members of eastern units.[423]

According to a summary of the antipartisan fighting by SS-Sonderkommando Dirlewanger and the later SS-Sonderbataillon Dirlewanger, the unit achieved significant success thanks to the leadership of Oskar Dirlewanger. During attacks, he led his people into combat personally, demonstrating courage and infallibility. It was emphasized that it was because of his skills, qualities as a leader, good situational assessment, and effective tactics that the unit was so effective in battle.[424] Furthermore, the report indicated that the unit's successes were accompanied by low losses. Officially, it was stated that Dirlewanger's battalion eliminated 15,000 partisans, recording very low own losses of 92 killed, 218 wounded, and 8 missing.[425] Furthermore, it captured or destroyed 20 mortars, 8 antitank guns (Pak), 2 tanks, 62 AMGs, 112 LMGs, 70 automatic guns, 82 machine guns, 1,100 rifles, and also radio stations, parachutes, ammunition, mines, explosives, etc.[426] It is estimated that in Belarus, Dirlewanger's soldiers destroyed and burned around two hundred villages and murdered over 120,000 inhabitants.

From the start of 1942 to August 1943, Oskar Dirlewanger not only led his own unit but also took command of other battalions. He demonstrated courage and audacity in every action.[427] For his achievements in antipartisan fighting, a motion was made on August 9, 1943, to decorate Oskar Dirlewanger with the

German Cross in Gold, which he was awarded on December 5.[428] Gottlob Berger remembered: "Dirlewanger was an excellent and venturesome soldier, and together with his unit he achieved great successes in fighting partisans."[429]

Contrary to what was stated in the 1970s, Dirlewanger did not receive the SS ring[430] or honor sword[431] for his activity in Belarus, unlike some of his subordinates; for example, Kurt Weisse.[432]

The unit grew constantly; by order of Heinrich Himmler of August 10, 1943, SS-Sonderbataillon Dirlewanger was changed into SS-Sonderregiment Dirlewanger. As a result, the *SS-Sonderregiment* was to have the following composition:

1st Staff Infantry Regiment (1 Stb. Inf. Rgts.) from November 1, 1941

1st Staff Company of the Infantry Regiment, group B2 (1 Stbs. Kp. Inf. Rgts. Zusammenstellung B2) from March 1, 1943

3rd Staff Infantry Battalion (supply troops) (3 Stb. Inf. Btbs. Verpflegungs-u. Gepäcktross besp.) from February 1, 1942

9th Security Company (9 Schütz. Kp.) from February 1, 1941

3rd Machine Gun Company (3 M.G.Kp.) from January 22, 1943

According to the order, uniforms and equipment for soldiers recruited from concentration camp prisoners were to be provided from camp warehouses. However, members of the unit were to obtain other material equipment (arms, military equipment, horses, etc.) on their own as loot.[433]

In September 1943, SS-Sonderregiment Dirlewanger numbered 391 Germans and 309 foreigners, to which twenty-five Germans and eight foreigners on leave and sixty-two Germans and fifteen foreigners in hospitals should be added.[434]

At the end of 1943, they were transferred from Lahoysk to the Minsk area. According to what Franz Stümpfl remembered, in Minsk they were quartered in barracks.[435] In a letter to von Gottberg, Dirlewanger wrote that pursuant to Himmler's order of December 30, 1943, the unit had been withdrawn from duty on the front. Nevertheless, even in February 1944, von Gottberg used the artillery unit commanded by Steinhauer (1. Batterie Schutzmannschaft-Ari.-Abt. 56), composed of fifty-eight soldiers, in combat. On February 26, 1944, Dirlewanger requested von Gottberg to release his people and send them to Uzda.[436]

SS-Sonderregiment Dirlewanger was divided into two battalions—the 1st (stationing in Uzda and commanded by SS-Hauptsturmführer Herbert Meyer), and the 2nd (in Sabalodje, under the command of SS-Sturmbannführer Josef Steinhauer).[437] The staff of the brigade, battalion, and regiment remained with the 1st Battalion in Uzda.[438] The 1st Company was also stationed there.[439]

4.3. Retreat from Belarus (1944)

At the start of January 1944, the Germans gradually pushed partisan units away from the front toward the west. From January to March the Wehrmacht were informed of the fighting against them and about the destruction of bunkers, winter camps, and warehouses. Most clashes took place on the central stretch of the front, in Belarus. By March, almost all partisan units had been forced toward the west and out of areas in which fighting was taking place. As a result, giant groups of partisans formed near Minsk: north of Minsk, in the region of Begoml, Lepel, and Ushachy; to the south, in the Luban and Slutsk area; and in the Polesia and Pinsk oblasts.[440]

In February 1944, Himmler decided to replenish SS-Sonderregiment Dirlewanger. He wanted the unit to reach the strength of one thousand men.[441] He thus wrote to Higher SS and Police Leader Rußland Mitte, SS-Gruppenführer von Gottberg:

> Dear Mr. Gottberg, I have just given the order and undertaken measures for Battalion Dirlewanger to once again number one thousand soldiers. Please convey my greetings to Mr. Field Marshal Busch, and also my request for Army Group Mitte to equip Battalion Dirlewanger with a sufficient quantity of weapons and vehicles. The battalion will be of use also to Army Group Mitte.[442]

In January the first transports of "volunteers" and "recruits" from camps were prepared. One of them was Paul Dorn, an inmate of Auschwitz since September 1943. As he remembered, on January 2 or 3, 1944, he was released, and his striped camp uniform was replaced with an SS uniform. Together with three hundred other former Auschwitz prisoners, he was sent to SS-Sonderregiment Dirlewanger. At the same time, transports from other camps were prepared. Dorn reached Minsk by train, and thence he was transferred to Uzda.[443]

On February 8, 1944, the unit numbered six officers, forty-four *Unterführers*, 209 German soldiers, and 201 *Hiwis*.[444]

The Waffen-SS was unable to carry out Himmler's order. As a result, Himmler decided to include repeat offenders and antisocials in the unit. He made everyone between the ages of seventeen and thirty-five eligible. To rehabilitate themselves by fighting at the front, they were supposed to volunteer for service.[445] On February 19, 1944, Himmler issued special instructions for the SS Main Command:

> I wish for SS-Obersturmführer Dirlewanger to personally seek out in concentration camps, among asocials and repeat offenders aged 17 to 35, in individual cases up to 40, those who volunteer to fight at the front to rehabilitate themselves. The following shall be excluded: (1) political criminals; (2) persons who hold key positions for the functioning of concentration camps.
>
> I request all heads of main offices whom the issue concerns to consider the problem and remember that it is at the front that every individual may best be used, and if avoiding victims is impossible, it is better for people with criminal records to die; and German youths can thus be saved. Three heads of main offices, SS-Obergruppenführer Berger, SS-Oberstgruppenführer Pohl, and SS-Obergruppenführer Dr. Kaltenbrunner, shall report on the success of the operation. However, I believe the most important thing is for Dirlewanger to be able to see and inspect his people in the camps himself. The maximum number of recruits to be accepted is 800.[446]

Oskar Dirlewanger constantly strived to enlarge the unit. Despite the possibility of obtaining eight hundred recruits from concentration camps, he kept trying to find further recruits, particularly from among trained soldiers.[447] On February 20, 1944, Himmler issued another order:

> Dirlewanger's battalion is composed of German soldiers who were convicted of poaching. On the whole, we can assess this group positively, even very positively: both the prisoners of concentration camps who were suitable for the unit and the former SS members who due to the sentence they were undergoing were called to the front to rehabilitate themselves.
>
> During combat operations, the commander has the right to decide about the life and death of all battalion members.
>
> Rehabilitation of poachers takes place without the participation of the SS Supreme Court and with the participation of SS-Obergruppenführer Berger and SS-Gruppenführer Nebe in the Reich Security Main Office via the Reich Ministry of Justice. The SS Supreme Court will be informed of the rehabilitation by SS-Obergruppenführer Berger.
>
> The commander of the battalion, SS-Obersturmführer Dirlewanger, is authorized to decide about the life and death of concentration camp prisoners both in quarters and in the field garrison.

> Poachers who have been rehabilitated are subject to the SS justice system. Until they have rehabilitated themselves, Dirlewanger has the right to decide about their life and death both in quarters and in the field garrison.
>
> Former SS members are subject to SS courts until their rehabilitation.[448]

Since the unit was growing, in February 1944 Himmler decided to assign it a field doctor. Up to that point, medical aid had been provided by Dirlewanger himself and a paramedic, Engelage. Back in autumn 1943, Dirlewanger tried to have Doctor Heinz Hartlieb, whom he had encountered already in Mogilev, assigned to the unit. In March 1944, Hartlieb officially became the doctor of SS-Sonderregiment Dirlewanger and accompanied Dirlewanger until the fighting near Budapest.[449] Many soldiers stated that an SS doctor in the rank of *SS-Sturmmann* had been assigned to the unit as punishment for embezzlement, thus receiving the chance to rehabilitate himself.[450] This could not have been Doctor Hartlieb, however, because the latter had held the position of front doctor in police battalions from September 1940 onward and later managed a hospital in Mogilev. Nowhere have I found information about his punishment and demotion. In 1943, two SS dentists were also assigned to Dirlewanger's orders as punishment for "incitement to abortion" (Walter Zeppenfeld) and "drunkenness" (Walter Escher).[451]

On March 14, 1944, Dirlewanger turned to Himmler with a request for convicts from the SS and police criminal camp in Maćkowe near Gdańsk (SS und Polizei Strafvollzugslager Danzig-Matzkau) to be drafted into the unit.[452] SS and police members were imprisoned there for desertion, homosexuality, defeatism, fraud, theft, and even murder, among other reasons. Dirlewanger gave the following motivation for his request:

> During constant fighting at the front and against partisan bands, the unit suffered grievous losses, so that the companies are missing two-thirds of their strength.
>
> Replenishing the unit with eight hundred recruits from concentration camps would not mean increasing the unit's combat strength in the next 3–4 months as these people have to be trained first and then additionally have to be subjected to detailed observation for an extended period. The people transferred to the unit so far are not a guarantee of adequate reserves.

> I thus request an order to be issued for the transfer of convicts who after completion or partial completion of their sentence in an SS and Police Penal Camp were sent to the Probation Camp in Prague, and for them to be transferred here on probation after four weeks' training.
>
> Similarly, I request that the Labor Unit in Babruysk be dissolved, and the men transferred along with arms and equipment—apart from the SS members with no criminal record—so that they will be able to prove their usefulness in combat against the enemy.
>
> My request results also from the observation that despite all their diversity, unit members have mostly, thanks to the appropriate military training and psychological resilience, turned out to be good soldiers.
>
> The right education and training, taking into account the rich experience gathered so far, would guarantee members of the Probation Camp in Prague and the Labor Unit in Babruysk the opportunity to rehabilitate themselves in combat. In the case of the Labor Unit in Babruysk, the opportunity for rehabilitation is not ensured as its members mainly undertake construction work. So far, the military successes of this unit remain unknown.[453]

He achieved his objective and on September 24, 1944, 1,500 prisoners from the Matzkau camp joined SS-Sturmbrigade Dirlewanger.[454] They took part in the fighting in Warsaw. Dirlewanger also managed to make foreign units whose soldiers had no criminal records tactically subordinate to himself. These included the 450th Turkestan Grenadier Battalion.[455]

On March 18, 1944, Dirlewanger prepared a list containing 337 names of unit members with an appeal for rehabilitation and sent it to the SS Main Office.[456] Also in March 1944, an application was made for fourteen Iron Crosses 2nd Class to be awarded to soldiers of SS-Sonderregiment Dirlewanger.[457]

The unit still required replenishment. On March 20, 1944, SS-Obergruppenführer Gottlob Berger turned to Heinrich Himmler with a request for convicted, imprisoned SS members to be transferred to Dirlewanger:

> SS-Obersturmbannführer Dr. Dirlewanger has filed the attached application with a request that is close to the SS Reichsführer's heart. . . .
>
> Sometime previously I was informed that in a certain facility in the settlement of Marienfelde, former SS soldiers are employed in prison. . . .
>
> I would like to propose that all those SS members . . . join Dirlewanger.[458]

On April 17, 1944, another transport with twenty-seven prisoners was sent from the camp in Sachsenhausen to Dirlewanger's unit. One of the inmates, the Norwegian Odd Nansen, wrote,

> Yesterday a large group of repeat offenders was sent away. They were released to be sent to the front. Criminals and rag-tag are now greeted as comrades. They were given gifts and flowers, and before leaving they were filmed before the main entrance. Murderers and death row prisoners, dangerous enemies of society: they are now comrades who should fight for their great fatherland and German honor![459]

Until mid-1944, Dirlewanger's unit operated in Belarus and occupied itself with antipartisan actions, protecting field labor, and pacifying villages.

Operations Regenschauer and Frühlingsfest

In the first half of 1944, further antipartisan operations were carried out: Regenshauer ("Rain Shower"), lasting from April 11 to 16, and Frühlingsfest ("Spring Festival"), which was a continuation of Regenschauer. The objective of the former was to prepare an encirclement in the Ushachy zone. Next, as part of Frühlingsfest a concentrated attack on the partisan units trapped in the encirclement was carried out. In these actions, the unit commanded by Bronislaw Kaminski distinguished itself.

Caught in the encirclement were sixteen partisan brigades; that is seventeen thousand people commanded by Lobanok. Also within the encirclement were around 100,000 civilians. Drops with arms and ammunition for the partisans were made, but their position was very difficult. The commander of one of the units encircled, Sadchikov, reported,

> The ring of the encirclement is tightening. We lack ammunition; there are many wounded. If the Red Army does not come with aid within 2–3 days, the regiment faces inevitable disaster. I request permission to escape the encirclement toward Maladzyechna-Baranavichy.[460]

On April 23, the partisan line of defense partly collapsed, with partisans fleeing their positions in panic. It was reported that German soldiers used barbaric methods, and "in front of their own attacking units they led the civilians they had apprehended, women, old people, and children, as protective shields."[461] German armies repeated this while putting down the Warsaw Uprising in 1944, where civilians were driven before the forces assailing barricades.

On April 29, the Germans broke through the left wing and pressed onward. A day later, the decision was taken to push through the encirclement on the western and southwestern sides. In May 1944, the partisan grouping of the Polotsk-Ushachy zone ceased to exist.[462]

Operation Kormoran

Units of the 3rd Panzer Army, 4th Army, SS and police units, and eastern battalions started the operation on May 22, 1944. The Germans, having no precise data about the number of partisans encircled in the Begoml and Lepel regions, assumed they numbered from fifteen thousand to sixteen thousand. In fact, twenty-one brigades—that is, around twenty-two thousand people—were present there.[463]

The surrounded units had no joint command. Ten local brigades were under the leadership of Maczulski, but the other units did not want to submit to his orders.[464] Trapped in the encirclement were, among others, the Shturmovaya, Frunze,[465] and Zheleznyak (commanded by Titkov) Brigades; the brigades commanded by Kiłłow, Celiszczewski-Pietrowicz, Kuksienok, Misunow, and Smoleński; units commanded by Romanov, Alexey, and Lobanok; the Dubow brigade; and the Gvardeyetz detachment (belonging to Za Rodinu).[466]

The partisans' situation was tragically bad: hunger reigned, and they lacked ammunition and weapons. The Germans moved forward gradually. They took control of all local settlements and roads. Partisan camps were shelled by planes and artillery.

On the night of June 15, the encircled units attempted to escape, some of them successfully. Their losses were enormous. The Germans provided the following summary of Operation Kormoran: 7,697 killed, 5,286 captured, 342 partisan camps leveled, and 900 bunkers destroyed.[467]

The success of Operation Kormoran did not last long. In mid-June 1944, the German units operating in this area were encircled by the Red Army.

Summary of the Fighting in Belarus in 1944

It is estimated that during operations in Belarus, Dirlewanger's unit burned down around 150–200 villages and killed around 120,000 people.[468] Pawel Beljagow, a *Hiwi* fighting in an eastern company under Dirlewanger's orders, remembered after the war: "In the territory of Belarus, over one hundred inhabited settlements were destroyed together with their residents by this SS formation."[469]

From April 15, 1944, SS-Sonderregiment Dirlewanger had its own reserve company, commanded by SS-Untersturmführer Zimmermann. This company was stationed in Krakow.

In May 1944, more prisoners sent from concentration camps were drafted into the unit. From the Sachsenhausen camp, 287 were sent, and 182 from Auschwitz, while from Buchenwald came a transport with an unknown number of people.[470] In June, seven hundred further recruits arrived in Uzda.

During action in Belarus, an Azerbaijani battalion, the 1st Eastern Muslim SS Regiment, numbering almost eight hundred people (Ostmuselmanische SS-Regiment),[471] and the 1st Finnish SS Police Regiment (1./Finnische SS-Polizeiregiment)[472] were placed under Dirlewanger's orders. Later the two first units took part in suppressing the Warsaw Uprising under his command.

The unit's route of retreat from Belarus led from Minsk to Lida, where it fought heavy battles with the Red Army. Part of SS-Sonderregiment Dirlewanger commanded by Dirlewanger was tasked with securing and defending the stretch south of Lida. Thanks to his operations, part of the German forces present on that stretch were able to retreat to Grodno with practically no losses.[473]

During the retreat through Grodno and Łomża, Dirlewanger's soldiers were to regain their strength in East Prussia, in a training camp in Orzysz. During that time, the unit was to be reorganized and expanded to a brigade (SS-Sturmbrigade Dirlewanger). However, in terms of combat strength, according to what Albert Venderbusch remembered, they remained a regiment of two battalions.[474] In fact, the unit comprised two regiments composed of three battalions.[475]

On July 30–31, consultations took place in the *Reichsführer-SS*'s headquarters in Kruglanki. Its participants were Lt. Gen. Heinz Guderian (newly appointed chief of the OKH), SS-Obergruppenführer Erich von dem Bach-Zelewski, and Bronislaw Kaminski. Oskar Dirlewanger was likely also there, as a telegram from Himmler of August 4, 1944, indicates (at the time, SS-Sonderregiment Dirlewanger was located in the Olecko area). In it, Himmler mentioned their "recent personal" meeting.[476] It is uncertain what was discussed, but it likely concerned the unstable situation in Warsaw. Several days prior, on July 27, in response to information coming in from Warsaw, Hitler had appointed Generalleutnant (Lieutenant General) Reiner Stahel military commander of the city.[477]

5

Participation in Suppressing the Warsaw Uprising

The start of the Warsaw Uprising came as no surprise to the Germans. Their intelligence service had long informed them that the Home Army (Armia Krajowa, or AK) might join the battle. At the end of July 1944, Generalleutnant (Lieutenant General) Reiner Stahel and SS-Brigadeführer Paul Geibel[1] ordered their units to be placed in combat readiness.[2] When the uprising started, the German garrison numbered around thirteen thousand soldiers, including

approximately 5,600–6,000 Wehrmacht soldiers,
4,300 in SS and police units, and
approximately 3,000 soldiers in aviation ground crews.

Also located in Warsaw were antiaircraft artillery batteries and smoke generator units, which were part of the 80th Regiment of the 10th Antiaircraft Artillery Brigade stationed there. The city was divided into so-called defense sectors: "A," "B," "C," "D" (left-bank Warsaw), and "E" (Praga on the right bank). Each of them had their own leadership and command structure, allotted resources and forces, and had their also own system of food and ammunition supply.[3] Wehrmacht units were primarily stationed in the Żoliborz, Bielany, and Okęcie Districts and the so-called government district (the area around Piłsudski Square and Krakowskie Przedmieście Street). Most of them were dispersed throughout Warsaw, primarily near the main communication routes. SS and police units were concentrated in the police district (i.e., in Szuch Avenue, South Śródmieście, and Mokotów).[4] Moreover, when the uprising started, Warsaw was in the area of operations of the German 9th Army, commanded by Nikolaus von Vormann.[5] Frontline units constantly moved through the city; they included the 3rd SS Panzer Division Totenkopf, the 1st Paratrooper Panzer Division Hermann Göring, and the 5th SS Panzer Division Wiking.[6]

The Home Army, meanwhile, was unprepared for the start of the fighting. According to Jerzy Kirchmayer, "The general state of armament and ammunition at the moment when the Warsaw District was put on alert would have sufficed to normally arm around 3,500 soldiers; that is around seventy insurgent platoons for two days' fighting, if not for the lack of heavy infantry weapons and the complete lack of field and antiaircraft artillery and almost complete lack of antitank weapons. The armaments possessed were sufficient for around 10 percent of the personnel count of the Warsaw District actually mobilized at the 'W' hour (36,500 soldiers). The rest (that is, 90 percent) had to be treated as defenseless personnel reserves."[7]

Around twenty-three thousand soldiers took part in the first clashes, even though around fifty thousand were available to the AK. Only around 10 percent were armed, mostly with small arms. AK soldiers were joined by units of the National Armed Forces (Narodowe Siły Zbrojne; according to various estimates, 740 to 3,500 soldiers), the People's Army (Armia Ludowa) and Union of Youth Struggle (Związek Walki Młodych, from 270 to 800 in total), the Security Corpus (Korpus Bezpieczeństwa, around 600 to 700), and the Polish People's Army (Polska Armia Ludowa, from 120 to 500); moreover, the civilian population took an active part in the uprising.[8] The commander of the AK stated, "By giving soldiers a rifle, a pistol, or two grenades each, at the end of July we were able to arm 70 percent of them."[9] Col. Antoni Chruściel "Monter" believed that the resources held would last for two or three days of fighting and might suffice for even up to two weeks in defense. He argued that for the insurgents, the wish for revenge would replace weapons. At the commanders' briefing, he ordered them to "throw all forces into combat, arming the insurgents who do not have arms with axes, pickaxes, and crowbars."[10] All through August 1944, until the fall of the Old Town (Starówka), despite having no reserves, he laid plans of "completely ejecting the Germans from the city."[11]

The Warsaw Uprising was to start on Tuesday, August 1, 1944, at the "W" hour (5:00 p.m.). In some spots, fighting broke out several hours earlier. In the area of Napoleon Square (currently Powstańcy Warszawy Square), the first shots were fired at 4:30 p.m. Action in Żoliborz started still earlier, by 1:50 p.m.[12] At 4:30 p.m., Paul Geibel announced an alert, and Gen. Stahel ordered the teams in important facilities such as the Main Post to be strengthened. Half an hour after the start of the revolt, Stahel sent the following report to Himmler:

> Riots have broken out in Warsaw. Several police stations have been attacked. The post also. So far, it seems we are dealing with Communist rebels, because they are wearing red armbands.[13]

At 8:15 p.m., Gen. Stahel proclaimed Warsaw to be in a state of siege, thus formally assuming executive power over all German military units, the police, the SS, and the civilian administration. However, the German response was ineffective, and Stahel himself was blockaded in the government district by the insurgents.

Adolf Hitler assigned the task of suppressing the revolt to Heinrich Himmler, and not to the newly appointed supreme commander in the east, Gen. Heinz Guderian.[14] When the Warsaw Uprising started, Himmler traveled to Poznań from his headquarters in the East Prussian Grossgarten.[15] At a meeting with army officers, he mentioned that he had told Hitler,

> Mein Führer, we have trouble. From a historical point of view, what the Poles have done is a blessing. After five, six weeks we will retreat. But by then, Warsaw, the capital, the heart of this formerly 17 million nation will have been destroyed, a nation that has been stopping us in our drive toward the East for 700 years and standing in our way since the first battle at Tannenberg. Then the Polish problem will cease to be a historical problem for our children, and also for us.[16]

He summed up his statement as follows:

> I have given the order for Warsaw to be completely demolished. You may now think, gentlemen, that I am a terrible barbarian. As you wish, gentlemen, yes, I am that, if I have to be. The order was: every house should be set on fire and blown up.[17]

He also added, "Those several staff headquarters that really have to operate somewhere can move to cellars without obstacle."[18]

On August 2, Gen. Stahel informed that the insurgents were first attacking smaller and then increasingly larger points of resistance and were "well organized and trained." He also stated that "freeing the city seems possible only with the use of significant forces brought in from outside" and that

> external reinforcements should definitely include assault sapper troops, flamethrowers, infantry support guns, mortars, [and] incendiary material to set houses on fire, as well as axes for breaking down doors.[19]

The Germans started mobilizing forces to put down the uprising. At the railway station in Poznań, in his Steiermark train, the *Reichsführer-SS* met with Heinz Reinefarth. He commanded him to go to Warsaw and mercilessly suppress the uprising. Reinefarth hesitated. He was no military man, but a lawyer who had achieved the high rank of SS and police *Gruppenführer*. He said that he had never commanded a unit of more than 150 people in the field and thus was insufficiently qualified. He proposed that Wilhelm Koppe (higher SS and police leader in the GG) take his place, but Himmler had already made his decision.[20] According to Hitler's oral command, Warsaw was to be razed to the ground and its inhabitants liquidated. Poland's capital was to become a deterrent for all of Europe.[21] The order was not confirmed in writing. After the war, Police General Ernst Rode testified, "Knowing Dirlewanger, I can safely say that on the basis of this order, he believed himself authorized to do everything; that is, to kill, loot, etc."[22]

In the first days, insurgents in Śródmieście, Powiśle, and the Old Town successfully attacked many targets whose capture had been planned, among them the Main Post building in Napoleon Square and the Prudential skyscraper, Warsaw's tallest building at the time. The latter was visible from afar, also from distant suburbs, and thus the fact that, thanks to units of the Kiliński Battalion, the red-and-white flag flew on its roof already in the first hours of the uprising had a substantial impact on the mood and morale of the populace. Attempts to capture the Citadel, Traugutt Fort, Gdańsk Railway Station, the police district, and Okęcie Airport brought great losses and ultimately failed. Fighting for the SS barracks in Mokotów at the junction of Kazimierzowska and Narbutt Streets and for the barracks at Rakowiecka Street also ended in a fiasco. Taking the electric plant and thus the district of Powiśle was a large success. The Germans held on to both airports, in Okęcie (southwestern

Warsaw) and in Bielany (northern Żoliborz), and also to the strategically vital bridges on the Vistula. The Polish assault on the bridges failed in the first hours of the uprising.[23]

As regards significant facilities, the Poles captured only the food and uniform warehouses in Stawki Street, the barracks in the Święta Kinga school building at Okopowa Street, the Military Geographical Institute in Jerozolimskie Avenue, the Municipal Transport Company building on the corner of Swiętokrzyska and Marszałkowska Streets, and the State Railway Directorate building at the junction of Targowa and Wileńska Streets in the Praga District. The only large area taken by the insurgents and free from enemy forces was the Old Town. Insurgent Warsaw was composed of several separate points of fighting separated by enemy forces. Due to a lack of communication, several thousand soldiers left Żoliborz, Wola, Ochota, and Mokotów, heading for nearby forests at night.[24]

5.1. Kampfgruppe Reinefarth

Wola

On the second day of the uprising, street megaphones broadcast an announcement in which the city's commander informed the populace that it was forbidden to go out into the streets. Any Pole failing to observe the ban would be shot, and all buildings from which German soldiers were fired upon would be razed to the ground.[25]

Also on that day, Heinrich Himmler arrived in Poznań by plane from his quarters in East Prussia, and in cooperation with the *Reichsstatthalter* of the Wartheland, Arthur Greiser, and the chief of the local military district, he ordered that a group of sixteen police companies commanded by SS-Gruppenführer Heinz Reinefarth and the 608th Special Regiment (Posener Ersatz Regiment) commanded by Col. Willy Schmidt be directed posthaste to Warsaw. From the Częstochowa region, the RONA (Russkaya Osvoboditelnaya Narodnaya Armiya, Russian National Liberation Army) assault brigade, led by Bronislaw Kaminski, was to be sent. After returning to East Prussia from Poznań, Himmler also commanded Oskar Dirlewanger to set off for Warsaw.[26]

During the afternoon of August 3, Reinefarth started recruiting a personal staff and an operations group from the 21st Military District and police outposts in the Wartheland. Two battalions, Reck and Peterburs, were formed thus. The position of first operational officer (Ia) in Reinefarth's staff was given to Security Police Major Kurt Fischer.[27]

On August 5, Battalion Reck (later Assault Group North) consisted of a staff company of the Waffen-SS officer school in Owińska (Treskau) and three cadet companies from the 5th Infantry School in Poznań, with the addition of an assault gun unit (*Sturmgeschützabteilung*). Battalion Peterburs, meanwhile, was composed of the Mounted Police Reserve Unit from Poznań and a guard unit of the Łódź Security Police (5. Wach-Abteilung der Schutzpolizei Litzmannstadt). When the commander changed, its name was changed to Battalion Sarnow, but this unit was not very visible during the uprising.[28]

On August 3, German forces started to form a ring to separate Wola from potential external aid. The access route to the Kampinos Forest in the north and the retreat route from Wola on the northwest side were to be guarded by the 3rd Regiment and 572th Cossack Battalion.[29]

On August 4, a battalion of the 608th Special Regiment commanded by Col. Schmidt, part of SS-Gruppenführer Reinefarth's group, arrived in Warsaw. Moreover, the 1st Police Company from Poznań and the 1st Police Company from Łódź were brought in by road. The rest of the formation reached Warsaw over the next two days by express rail transport.[30] Reinefarth himself arrived in Warsaw in the early hours of the morning on August 4, in the company of Fischer and his own adjutant, SS-Hauptsturmführer Helmut Stühmer. He reported to Gen. Nikolaus von Vormann.[31]

At this time, Kampfgruppe Reinefarth was formed in Warsaw under the command of SS-Gruppenführer Heinz Reinefarth;[32] it numbered around five thousand soldiers:

South: 72nd Waffen-SS Grenadier Regiment (SS-Sturmbrigade RONA, initially commanded by Major Ivan Frolov):[33] 1,700 soldiers

Center: SS-Sonderregiment Dirlewanger: 865 soldiers; part of Special Unit Bergmann: 228 soldiers; part of gendarmerie group Posen: 341 soldiers

North: part of gendarmerie group Posen: 155 soldiers; company from the SS Academy in Brunswick: 116

Reserves: part of the 608th Security Regiment: 292 soldiers; Reserve Field Battalion Hermann Göring: 800 soldiers; 6th Field Gendarmerie Company: 600 soldiers[34]

By August 5, Reinefarth's Poznań units numbered 2,750 soldiers:

Rifle company from Biedrusko (2 officers, 125 NCOs and soldiers)
Heavy-weapons company from Biedrusko (1 officer, 199 NCOs and soldiers)
Company of the gendarmerie operational unit Walter from Biedrusko (4 officers, 142 NCOs and soldiers)
Company of the gendarmerie operational unit Walter from Biedrusko (4 officers, 146 NCOs and soldiers)
Company of the gendarmerie operational unit Walter from Biedrusko (4 officers, 131 NCOs and soldiers)
Rifle company Liebisch from Gniezno (1 officer, 138 NCOs and soldiers)
Rifle company Liebisch from Rawicz (1 officer, 139 NCOs and soldiers)
MMG platoon (Poznań SS company) Röntgen (1 officer, 37 NCOs and soldiers)
Sapper platoon Liebisch (1 officer, 38 NCOs and soldiers)
Cavalry platoon (1 officer, 31 NCOs and soldiers)
Motorized antitank platoon Liebisch from Gniezno (1 officer, 38 NCOs and soldiers)
Rifle company (5th Panzer Grenadier School Battalion) (1 officer, 134 NCOs and soldiers)
Rifle company (2 officers, 152 NCOs and soldiers)
Rifle company (2 sapper platoons and 1 criminal platoon) (2 officers, 163 NCOs and soldiers)
Heavy-weapons company (1 officer, 137 NCOs and soldiers)
Police battalion Burkhard (10 officers, 366 NCOs and soldiers)
Police battalion Peterburs (8 officers, 489 NCOs and soldiers)[35]

The formation's central axis was formed by Wolska Street. Near the junction of Górczewska and Wolska Streets were located Col. Schmidt's 608th Special Regiment and SS-Sonderregiment Dirlewanger. The police company was deployed south of Wolska Street.[36]

SS-Sonderregiment Dirlewanger did not reach Warsaw as a single group. The first to arrive was the 1st Battalion (365 soldiers), under SS-Obersturmführer Meyer (Kampfgruppe Meyer), on August 4. Additionally, Himmler sent two Azerbaijani units of Battalion Bergmann and the 1st Battalion of the 111th Regiment from East Prussia in emergency mode.[37]

On August 5, Dirlewanger's unit was replenished to a strength comprising a command group, two battalions, an MMG company, a mortar company, and an antitank artillery company. It then numbered 16 officers and 865 soldiers.[38] As Dirlewanger's subordinate Heinrich Kraus stated, SS-Sonderregiment Dirlewanger had a motorcycle company at the time with around sixty to seventy people and thirty to thirty-five vehicles.[39]

On August 5, 1944, Dirlewanger's unit swung into action. Its soldiers remembered that they were transported in groups. Karl Vieregge testified:

> At the start of August 1944, Dirlewanger's brigade traveled from the Minsk region to Treuburg [Olecko] in East Prussia . . . first we were to assemble and rest. This came to nothing because on August 1, 1944, the uprising in Warsaw started. The brigade, but not all of it, set off from Treuburg for Warsaw. Various means of transport were used (railway, trucks). My battalion was transported to Warsaw from East Prussia by truck.[40]

They drove to Warsaw from Olecko through Modlin, Wyszogród, and Sochaczew.[41]

In the first days of the uprising, the fully motorized 13th Company (Postschutzeneinheit) formed in Seesen in Lower Saxony was placed under Dirlewanger's orders. It arrived in Wolska Street (Litzmannstädter Straße). As a result of violent fighting and heavy gunfire, it was withdrawn to the airport and awaited further orders there. Over the course of operations, Dirlewanger divided it into three platoons and deployed each of them in a different part of Warsaw. It was reunited only after the capitulation, and it was then possible to estimate the losses it had incurred.[42]

Karl Jochheim-Armin remembered that they arrived at Okęcie Airport on August 4, late in the afternoon,[43] and were thence transported to Wolska Street. The journey from East Prussia took around two days and they rested along the way in Modlin.[44] Jochheim-Armin described what he saw after arrival:

> On the north side of Wolska Street was a high red wall. Under this wall, within an area of 18 to 20 meters, bodies lay; not in one layer, but in several. The pile of corpses was maybe a meter high. I did not know how the bodies had ended up there. However, I got the impression that the people under that red wall had been shot, particularly as from the pile of bodies there stuck out the upper part of the body of a child who was still alive. I saw this during transport by truck. . . .

> In the place where we got out of the trucks, there was a[n entrance] gate . . . to the factory area. . . . Through this gate, soldiers led civilians into the factory site, the gate was closed, [then] I heard screams and shots; after some time, soldiers came out of the factory gate but now without civilians.
>
> According to me, the civilians were shot in the yard. Afterward, I also entered the factory yard. I saw many bodies there. It wasn't 10–100 bodies, but several hundreds.[45]

Karl Vieregge's battalion was also sent to Litzmannstädter Straße[46] (Wolska). Meanwhile, the 2nd Battalion, in which Gustav Strumpf and the brigade staff served, arrived in Warsaw from East Prussia on August 5, 1944, via Łomża and Modlin. Paul Zimmermann remembered that his company (2nd Battalion) traveled to Giżycko (Lötzen) from Łomża (Lomscha) and then to Warsaw. He and his men (around fifteen people) reached the city two or three days later than the rest of Steinhauer's battalion (around August 8–9) as a result of a breakdown of the truck they were to travel in.[47] Strumpf described how together with SS-Oberscharführer Daub (who died on August 8, 1944, near the Saxon Garden) and SS-Sturmführer Weisse, they were the first people from Dirlewanger's unit to reach Warsaw. According to Strumpf, Dirlewanger arrived on-site on August 15 at the earliest.[48] This was partly confirmed by Adolf Katz, who at the time of the retreat from Belarus and the start of the uprising was on leave in Germany. In the first days of August, on the second or third, he met Dirlewanger and his driver, SS-Rottenführer Erich Ködel, in the SS Main Office (SS-Hauptamt) in Berlin. Dirlewanger was dealing with some matters with SS-Obergruppenführer Berger. Katz ate lunch with them in the Main Office casino. The issue of the uprising was not mentioned. In the afternoon, Katz talked with Dirlewanger again, and the latter stated only that the unit had to regain its strength in East Prussia and would then be transferred to the Warsaw region.[49]

Meanwhile, Erich von dem Bach-Zelewski noted in his diary that Dirlewanger joined him in the command post in Sochaczew on August 8. In the evening, he headed for his staff headquarters, located in the Infectious Diseases Hospital in Wola, and spent the night of August 8 in the Brühl Palace.[50] These dates were confirmed in the testimony of Oberleutnant (Lieutenant) von Riesen, commander of the 1st Company of the I/111 Azerbaijani Battalion. He stated that he reported to Dirlewanger in the Saxon Garden on August 9.[51]

Oskar Henning mentioned that after reaching the Saxon Garden, he noticed a group of Muslim soldiers: "They wore curved daggers, and on their heads, they had Turkish fezzes as their head coverings. Apart from that, they were in German uniform."[52]

SS-Sonderregiment Dirlewanger was initially commanded by Kurt Weisse, Dirlewanger himself being still in Berlin on August 4, which outraged Heinrich Himmler, who wrote to him:

> While I am very pleased with your action, as I recently told you personally, I nevertheless have to express my displeasure with the fact that despite the admonition about immediately returning to your regiment in the plane prepared for you, you still wasted time in Berlin.
>
> I am accustomed to rapid and immediate obedience.
>
> (–) H. Himmler.[53]

Despite this, Dirlewanger together with Adolf Katz and his driver, Ködel, went to East Prussia. There they found the unit ready to set off and awaiting orders. Dirlewanger did not start for Warsaw together with his people. He first wanted to acquire additional equipment for his soldiers.[54] He also focused on finding new members for the unit. He obtained more "volunteers" from the camps and prisons in Glatz (Kłodzko), Anklam, Torgau, and Matzkau near Gdańsk.[55] Additionally, before reaching Warsaw he went on a personal visit to his family in Esslingen.[56]

After the war, Reinefarth maintained that Dirlewanger did not want to place himself under his command and accepted orders only from Heinrich Himmler.[57] Gustav Strumpf testified similarly in the 1960s, remembering that Reinefarth had no particular influence on the direction in which Dirlewanger would attack, and that these two commanders did not especially like each other. Arguments and tension between them were commonplace.[58] Dirlewanger's officers prepared for combat separately, without consulting Reinefarth.

Even before Himmler arrived in Poznań, he met with Dirlewanger in East Prussia. He also then assigned him his tasks. From Himmler, Dirlewanger received "all authorization to kill who he wants, at his discretion."[59] Ernst Rode stated, "I received a copy [written] in pencil of an order issued by Himmler to Dirlewanger. On the basis of that order, Warsaw was to be razed to the ground."[60]

All through the uprising, Dirlewanger refused to submit to Reinefarth's orders, and conflicts between them were frequent. Dirlewanger caused him a lot of problems by opposing his commands. Von dem Bach-Zelewski stated that Reinefarth "hated Dirlewanger and Kaminski with all his heart and often would not maintain direct contact with them. At one point, it almost came to a duel between them."[61] During Dirlewanger's sumptuously celebrated birthday in September, a duel between and Reinefarth nearly did occur.

Lieutenant Kurt B., commander of the staff of a company within the battle group, described the difficulties he encountered when an order from the staff had to be communicated to Dirlewanger:

> Mr. Dirlewanger got rid of us using profanities; agitated, he claimed that he did not need any battle group. During another visit to this unit, I was not even allowed to go in to see him, and Mr. Dirlewanger had one of his soldiers tell me that he would order every officer sent by Reinefarth who once again tried to give him instructions from Reinefarth to be shot.[62]

Dirlewanger caused problems not only for Reinefarth. As Alexey Pishenkov stated,

> Dirlewanger was very firmly convinced that he was subordinate directly to Reichsführer-SS Himmler, and thus he ignored orders from the local command. In the presence of von dem Bach-Zelewski, he once threatened the chief, SS-Standartenführer Holtz, that he would kill Holtz if the latter kept interfering in his affairs. . . . It should be added that this was no empty threat: after this incident, the headquarters of von dem Bach's staff was fired upon several times with machine guns from the positions of the *Sonderkommando* [SS-Sonderregiment Dirlewanger].[63]

The *Kampfgruppe* was commanded by Reinefarth, whose task in the first days of August, according to von Vormann's plan, was to assemble troops around St. John Climacus Orthodox Church in the Orthodox cemetery at Wolska Street. From there he was to lead an attack along this street. The starting point of the attack was the location at which Wolska Street and a railway bridge crossed. On August 5, Governor-General Hans Frank reported to the chief of the Reich Chancellery Hans Lammers: "This morning at 10:00 a.m., the German relief began combat activity in three points on the edge of the city."[64]

The main forces were to set out through Wola: SS-Sonderregiment Dirlewanger along Wolska Street and south of it, while Reinefarth's policemen were to attack through the districts in its northern part. Next, the attack was to proceed along Chłodna Street, which started where Wolska Street ended, directly through the Saxon Garden to Brühl Palace and the government district, where the city's commander Stahel and Governor Fischer were defending themselves.[65] At the time, Wolska and Chłodna Streets were the main access routes to the center of Warsaw. The number of German soldiers and policemen taking part in the assault along Wolska Street and in the north part of Wola was 2,300. Against them stood 1,650 insurgents belonging to the Radosław Group.[66]

According to the report of SS-Hauptsturmführer A. Feucht of August 13, 1944, the military situation in the first days of the uprising was as follows:

> The German side started the assault in three wedges. Group "North": Major Reck, group "Center": SS-Standartenführer Dirlewanger, group "South": SS-Brigadeführer Kaminski.
>
> Group "North" has reached the Catholic cemetery [Powązki] and the western side of the Jewish cemetery and is now continuing to attack. Group "Center" has moved along Wolska and Chłodna Streets through the Saxon Garden to Teatralny Square. Group "South" captured the Tobacco Factories, which had resisted for an extended period, after shelling from heavy mortars.
>
> The situation of the police district is allegedly unchanged.[67]

The assault groups had the following structure:

"South": SS-Sturmbrigade RONA (4 T-34 tanks and a Russian self-propelled gun)

"Middle" (subordinate directly to SS-Gruppenführer Reinefarth):

Part A: two battalions of SS-Sonderregiment Dirlewanger, 4 75 mm antitank guns, 1 37 mm gun, part of the 2nd Azerbaijani Battalion / Bergmann and the 1st Battalion of the 111th Infantry Regiment

Part B: Poznań police company, Łódź police company, Vistula Field Gendarmerie Company (motorized), Pabianice Field Gendarmerie Company (motorized), Vistula Field Gendarmerie School Company

"North": two rifle companies, heavy-weapons company, Junker School Company, SS Brunswick

Reserves: 608th Security Regiment, Hermann Göring Reserve Field Battalion, six field gendarmerie companies

In transport: SS brigade Siegling[68]

On August 5, Reinefarth's formation was replenished with men arriving on successive rail transports. Cooperating with it were the bomber aviation of Air Fleet 6 and an armored train. The offensive commenced around 6:00 a.m. on August 5 after an air raid. Wolska and Górczewska Streets formed the center of the assault. Dirlewanger's first company was to attack along the southern side of Wolska Street.[69] The second attack moved from Tarnowska and Prądzyński Streets through Dworska and Przyokopowa Streets toward Kerceli Square.

On August 5, a mortar platoon (*Granatwerferzug*) from the 8th Company / II Bergmann (Azerbaijani) (8. Kp. des II/Bergmann [Aserb.]) was attached to Kampfgruppe Meyer. The group was commanded by Col. (Oberleutnant, Kompanieführer) Schulz, and he was accompanied by Staff Sergeant (Oberfeldwebel, Kompanietruppführer) Weißkopf and Sergeant (Feldwebel, Granatwerferzug-Führer) Metzger.[70]

Against the German units there fought the battalions Czata 49, Wigry, and Pięść; the 3rd Company under the command of Jerzy Gebert "Lot"; and a team from the 2nd Company commanded by Andrzej Wojnicz "Andrzej" from the Parasol Battalion. Between Górczewska and Wolska Streets, the German attack was repelled by a group commanded by Jerzy Zborowski "Jeremi."[71]

On August 4–5, Dirlewanger's soldiers attacked Michler's Palace, occupied by Parasol Battalion. It was the site of heavy fighting. Dirlewanger's subordinates suffered high losses when they were drawn into an ambush laid by people commanded by Janusz Brochwicz-Lewiński "Gryf."[72] In Kronika obrony Pałacyku Michla, the events of August 5 are described thus:

> First assault
>
> August 5. At 6:00 a formation of around 40 Heinkel He 111K bombers flies in from the west at an altitude of around 500 meters. In the beautiful morning sun, the details of the planes and the bombs falling out of the holds are clearly visible. After a moment there is increasing whistling, hits, bangs, rocking of the building, dust, and the stench of the explosion. The detonations move toward Chłodna Street. . . .
>
> After a moment, "Gryf" and his boys delightedly inform us again that from their bay windows they can see the German assault force positioning themselves. "Gryf" reminds us that we will let the Germans into Staszyc [Street] and that gunfire will start from the Palace.
>
> Now time is dragging. It is completely quiet. Finally, German commands may be heard. One more moment and the "Gryf" MG screams. Everybody jumps up and, standing in the windows, they

have what they dreamed of for so long: Their sights are on a row of Germans around 30 m away. They stand calmly every several meters by the houses on both sides of Wolska Street, their sleeves are rolled up, [and] they have no helmets; the coats, open at the neck, have black facings and armbands: it is the SS, and as it will later turn out, one of the companies from Dirlewanger's brigade.

"Jacek" as MG42 gun aimer and "Józek" [Józef Hoppe] and "Jur" as loaders are now hard at work and cover with fire the region of Franaszek and Skierniewicka Streets, blocking the enemy's retreat at the same time. With SMGs, "Gryf," "Brzoza" [Zbigniew Rylski], and "Krzych" destroy an MG emplacement in the gate of no. 39 and those standing next to the hospital wall. "Ziutek" [Józef Szczepański], "Kuba," and "Wołłowicz" shoot at the now-solitary SS soldiers with rifles.

On the other side of Wolska Street, "Kruk" disperses an MG emplacement in the Palace gate with SMG fire. . . . "Czarny" fires at Wolska 42 with a rifle, and "Siódemka," at a group of SS men between the Palace and the Staszyc corner from a Sten. . . .

The SS men incur serious losses but do not retreat. They stand calmly and return fire toward the windows. They are commanded via parabellum movements by an SS officer who strolls under the walls of the Michler buildings. The obedience and training of the SS are admirable. Fire is concentrated on the SS officer. . . . However, "Jur" gets him from a Smith-Wesson. The SS men start to regroup. The shooting reaches its peak. The strong fire from the Palace has overwhelmed the SS, inflicting heavy losses, and pushes the SS out from the southern side of Wolska Street without own losses. The Wolska 39 team, weaker in terms of firepower, incurs losses after initial success and is stifled. . . . The SS men retreat, leaving behind the wounded crying for help. . . .

As a result of over a dozen minutes' fighting, the enemy recorded losses. . . . We count: in gateway 39: 2 and an abandoned MG34, 2 by the hospital wall, 5 by Franaszek, 3 including 1 officer by Michler's mill, 1 in gateway 40, 1 and an abandoned MG by no. 42. In total, 14 definitely killed and more seriously wounded. . . .

Second assault

The weapons lying in the street become the object of our next activity. . . . A wounded SS man tries to defend himself and is finished off. . . .

Around 8 the second assault takes place. On the basis of reconnaissance by fire in the first attack, the enemy improve their tactics. They now attack as one column on the Palace side. On the other side of Wolska Street, a Panther [tank] crunches along. Thus, the SS infantry, being in the blind spot of the Palace, which is stronger in terms of firepower, rapidly reaches our positions. . . .

The Panther, drawing increasingly close, stifles "Gryf" and his boys in the Palace. . . . The fighting becomes more intense amid dust and explosions. Under the cover of the Panther's gun, which blasts missiles directly into the Palace's first-floor windows, the SS men try to force their way into the ground floor. Their training and commanders are once again to be admired. . . .

Meanwhile "Gryf," "Brzoza," "Krzych," and a limping "Jacek" are already directly among the surprised SS men and open very effective fire, which literally cuts down—an inimitable sight—the SS men near the gate. . . . The remaining SS men, unable to shoot for fear of hitting their own, jump behind the tank, from behind which they try to return fire. …

The second attack is repulsed, but the situation has become difficult. [. . .]

3rd assault

. . .

Around 10 the enemy commences another assault. Just as before, the SS men move along the northern side of Wolska. On the south side, two Panthers approach and with very heavy fire from their guns they repel "Jeremi" [Jerzy Zborowski] from the windows. The first Panther stops near Franaszek's factory and fires at the windows of the Palace while the other drives up to Michler's and positions itself to ram the gate. . . . The SS men are furious. They break the ground floor windows with rifle butts and throw grenades into the Palace. A larger group gathers round the Panther, waiting for the gate to be broken down. . . .

The Panther is set alight and withdraws, but after several dozen meters the flames unfortunately die out. Despite being under fire, the SS men engage in combat. A heavy exchange of fire ensues. . . . The SS men suffer losses. . . . After some time, the firing on the SS side weakens and there is a retreat among terrible shouts of "Hilfe, Kameraden" from the wounded. Some of the Germans use a transporter, which, however, offers no protection from above. . . .

Although the third assault has been repulsed, the situation changes from difficult to critical. Once again, the enemy has incurred losses estimated at around ten killed and seriously wounded. Wolska Street is a macabre sight. Lying in it are the corpses of SS men killed in the first assault, the wounded finished off by their own tank fire after the first and before the second assault, the killed and wounded from the second assault, and finally the dead from the third assault. While fighting, the SS men used the bodies of their comrades as shields, and so some of the corpses lie one on top of the other, while others are flat as pancakes after the Panthers maneuvering next to Franaszek and the Michler gate drove over them. . . .

Defense and loss of the mill

Around 11 the enemy appears for the fourth time, preceded by particularly intensive shelling of the now-empty Palace and warehouse by a Panther. The tanks come no further. Several attempts to enter the mill yard take place. . . . Despite the SS men's fury, their efforts are not as decided as before and are easily frustrated by several long rounds from "Józek's" MG and from SMGs. After some time, a Panther appears and, without approaching the gate, opens fire at the mill front through the gate. The missiles explode inside the steel structures of ceilings and equipment. . . . Unexpectedly, amid great rumbling, breaches form in the western sidewall of the mill. It is the other Panther in Działdowska Street that opened fire. . . . The German tankists have already become very familiar with the lay of the land and are solidly at work. Under their cover, the SS soldiers move from Działdowska through a ruined area and reach a large breach skillfully knocked in the wall by many Panther missiles, and throw stick grenades into the mill. . . .

Around noon, "Gryf" receives the order from "Dyrektor" to leave Michler's because Górczewska Street is in danger. The Germans have forced out Czwartacy and Oddziały Wolskie from the Wawelsberg buildings and Działdowska Street and are approaching Staszyc. . . .

Attack on Wenecja

From our windows we see that despite efforts, the assault scatters in the open area of the garden and returns to its initial positions. Enemy silhouettes now clearly appear in the setting sun on the tram car barricade near Młynarska Street. These are our old friends from

> Wolska Street, the same SS men from Dirlewanger's brigade. They are just as calm as before. Unhurriedly, they settle themselves into positions despite fire from our windows and being targeted by grenades. . . .
>
> A rather chaotic exchange of fire broken up by longer series from MGs takes place, the SS soldiers occupy the corner building of Wolska 34 on the opposite corner of Młynarska.
>
> Twilight causes the gunfire to partly die down. The Germans set fire to the tram car barricade and several buildings in Wolska.[73]

Ultimately, SS-Sonderregiment Dirlewanger captured the palace area on August 5 only after 3:00 p.m., once the Parasol soldiers had already abandoned it.[74]

As Piotr Stachiewicz stated, losses among the insurgents on August 5 only during the defense of Wolska Street numbered seventeen soldiers from Parasol killed and around fifteen wounded. As a whole, Radosław Group recorded twenty killed and forty wounded. In the region of Dworska Street, Reinefarth's battle group lost six killed, and twenty-four seriously and twelve lightly wounded. SS-Sonderregiment Dirlewanger, which attacked along Wolska Street, bought 200 m with thirty-four killed, and eighteen seriously and fifteen lightly wounded.[75] The assault progressed very slowly. On August 5, only around 800 meters of the planned 4–5 km were captured.[76]

On August 6, 1944, Reinefarth's group was released from under the command of von Vormann's 9th Army. It was to operate individually under the orders of von dem Bach-Zelewski. On August 6, Col. Schmidt's group held initial positions for a frontal attack from the northwest in a belt between Wawrzyszewska and Długosz Streets. The group commanded by Reinefarth and SS-Sonderregiment Dirlewanger was to press on along Wolska, Chłodna, and Grzybowska Streets from the west in an easterly direction; along Staszica, Szlenkierów, Młynarska, and Karolkowa Streets from Wolska Street toward the north; and from Leszno Street toward Żytnia Street.[77] The war diary of the 9th Army notes the following about the fighting by Kampfgruppe Meyer on August 6: "The troops starting out from the west gain only 400 m of terrain in fierce fighting on barricades."[78]

During the uprising, Dirlewanger's main forces were divided between two battle groups, Kampfgruppe Meyer and Kampfgruppe Steinhauer.[79] The 2nd Battalion—that is, Kampfgruppe Steinhauer—reached Warsaw on the evening of August 7. Within a short time, Dirlewanger's units managed to forge a thoroughfare along the Wolska-Chłodna-Kierbedź Bridge route.

According to what the soldier Vieregge remembered, his battalion (I) was commanded by SS-Obersturmführer Herbert Mayer (Maier). The 2nd Battalion was not yet in Warsaw at the time. According to Vieregge, the 1st Battalion numbered around four hundred men.[80] In his wartime notes, Karl Jochheim-Armin recorded that on August 6, Dirlewanger's soldiers moved along Wolska Street.[81] RONA units attacked the Ochota District, around 1 km south of the main forces.

At dawn on August 6, dive-bombers started dropping bombs on houses and barricades on Chłodna Street. During the fighting, the whole street was razed to the ground. The Germans did not manage to clear any of the corridors leading to the Vistula River that day. The greatest effectiveness was demonstrated by Dirlewanger's soldiers led by Weisse, who managed to push 400 m into the ruins. In the afternoon they reached the edge of Saxon Garden, whence they set off toward the besieged Brühl Palace, where Stahel was located. They achieved the Brühl Palace "in the evening of the second day [of combat]; that is, August 6, 1944."[82] Karl Jochheim-Armin wrote that they captured the Brühl Palace on August 7 (he kept notes all through the fighting).[83] At that point, they made contact with the Germans fighting in the government district. It was only on the following day that Dirlewanger's units secured the Wola thoroughfare up to Bankowy Square.[84] Thus the area controlled by the insurgents was divided into two parts.

Karl Vieregge remembered that in the first days, the clashes were exceptionally fierce, and he estimated losses in his battalion at 324 killed or wounded ("I know precisely that after 2 days of fighting there remained 41 people in Obersturmführer Meyer's battalion, while on August 5, 1944, 365 people set off for combat from that unit").[85] Such high losses were confirmed by Adolf Katz:

> The losses during that three-day march through Litzmannstädter Straße to the Brühl Palace were exceptionally high. . . . Upon reaching Brühl Palace, Meier [Meyer] had around 40 out of his more or less 400 people.[86]

Peter Erretkamps indicated that

> on the first day, we were in the area of the railway flyover . . . we moved forward by only 100 meters. I know we reached a barricade. We spent the first night somewhere in the ruins of buildings. On the second day, we moved another 100 meters. We spent the next night

> outside again. On the third day, we reached the market halls. There we had to retreat slightly because our aviation carried out a raid on the halls and bombed us too; we suffered losses. When the Stuka attack ended, we entered the Mirowskie Halls, and from there the park, and reached the Brühl Palace.[87]

Oskar Henning described that he saw a Polish girl who had been detained take out a pistol from under her skirt and shoot an officer of the Criminal Police. She was killed immediately, of course.[88]

Dirlewanger's unit pushed through to Chłodna Street and via the Mirowskie Halls and the Saxon Garden reached Gen. Stahel, who was surrounded in the Brühl Palace. For the insurgents fighting in the Wola and Old Town Districts, this meant the loss of communications with Śródmieście.[89] The following was recorded on August 7, in the diary of the 9th Army: "Units attacking from the west managed to make a connection with the commander's headquarters, located in Adolf Hitler Square."[90]

Weisse, Dirlewanger's deputy, allegedly stood on the first tank that rolled into the courtyard of the palace, driving soldiers before him during the fighting.[91] These are only rumors, however: Weisse was disliked by his subordinates, who called him a "giant pig."

Vieregge assessed the insurgents as difficult opponents. He said, "After we pushed through to the Brühl Palace—that is, the Saxon Garden—the insurgents surrounded us."

On the night of August 6, SS-Sonderregiment Dirlewanger completely cut off the insurgent units fighting in the Wola and Old Town Districts from Śródmieście. On August 7, the firestorm intensified and the main German attack commenced from Wolska and Chłodna Streets to the north: toward Leszno Street. In the morning hours, an assault by German infantry set out under tank cover.[92]

From August 7, Dirlewanger's 2nd Battalion, under the orders of Steinhauer (Kampfgruppe Steinhauer), waited in combat readiness in Wolska Street. They likely numbered around 350 soldiers.[93]

The Germans were shot at from buildings in neighboring streets; the insurgents crept through sewers to surprise them.[94] On August 8, Reinefarth and Col. Schmidt's group attacked the Radosław Group from three directions: Col. Schmidt attacked the Evangelical Cemetery frontally from the west, Reinefarth's police from the south along the axis of Karolkowa and Okopowa Streets toward the Calvinist Cemetery, and the German crew of the Pawiak Prison hit Radosław from the rear.[95] The insurgents blocked the assault, and bloody fighting for each grave, each square meter of land ensued. The Germans had been repulsed for the time being, but as a result of the counterattack the German soldiers managed to capture the Calvinist cemetery. At that point, Dirlewanger's sharpshooters (former poachers) stepped up their fire from machine weapons positioned on the towers of St. Augustine's Church and St. Charles Borromeo's Church, which significantly impeded movement behind Radosław Group battle lines.

> It was extraordinarily accurate, and thus regardless of the losses inflicted it caused great nervousness, particularly while moving along Gęsia Street, which was the only connection between Wola and the Old Town.[96]

Also, Janusz Brochwicz-Lewiński "Gryf" spoke about the sniper skills of Dirlewanger's soldiers. He described the battle in the Evangelical-Augsburg Cemetery as follows:

> On August 8, at dawn, I entered the evangelical cemetery with my platoon, the assault group, and I had the feeling I would not leave the cemetery alive. That silence, the graves, cemetery atmosphere, and the enemy, who were so well concealed that I could hardly see them, could not see them. They were very experienced soldiers from the Eastern Front who knew how to camouflage themselves by pinning bits of trees, leaves, some bits of greenery to helmets and uniforms, which were field uniforms, of course—they wore field uniforms and so did we—and had a number of sharpshooters hidden in the trees or somewhere in crannies between graves, who accurately, with telescopes on special rifles for sharpshooters, looked for their target. And I became the victim of such a sharpshooter, who got me in his sights and almost finished me off. It is a miracle that I am alive. I should not be living normally; I should be a corpse, but somehow, I managed to survive. During the assault on the German positions, I attempted to push them out by storm near the Halpert Chapel, and I scrambled my people for the attack. I was leading that attack; at the moment when I was next to one of the graves, that sharpshooter, seeing that I was in command, took action against me on purpose and shot me right in the chin. I was lucky because I must have turned my head slightly to the right at that moment, so that the bullet went in where it was supposed to go in but went out sideways—it did not go out through the back of my head, because then it would have killed me.[97]

He also stated that

> the Germans had their sharpshooters in position, who did not shoot at ordinary soldiers but waited for commanders. When they recognized a commander, they shot at him right away. Killing a commander spells catastrophe for a unit because there is no one to lead.[98]

Here is a fragment of an interview in which he talked with Piotr Zychowicz about this part of the fighting:

> Janusz Brochwicz-Lewiński "Gryf": Dirlewanger's soldiers wore camouflage uniforms, had covers on helmets. They covered themselves with twigs and leaves, which made them very difficult to notice. They shot not only directly at us, but also at gravestones. Thus, a hail of stone chips exploded into the air in all directions, and the chips were just as dangerous as bullets. They killed people with equal effectiveness.
>
> Zychowicz: So, you encountered a difficult opponent?
>
> Janusz Brochwicz-Lewiński "Gryf": Oh, undoubtedly. They lay there unmoving, patient, excellently trained. Before, they had spent the last three years on the Eastern Front. They were not only excellent shots but also hardened soldiers; they could keep their cool until the end. They approached their soldierly tasks professionally. And I had eighteen-year-old boys. Very heroic, brave, but without the enemy's experience. Over the last three months before the uprising, I had trained these young boys, but it was too little. They had to learn the rest already during the uprising.[99]

According to Vieregge's testimony, the fighting there lasted around three or four days. Only after several days did they "clear" the area to such an extent that Stahel and Fischer could safely leave the palace.[100] The Brühl Palace was prepared to be Dirlewanger's headquarters, but he moved into it only around a week later.[101] It was only on August 17 that the Germans could report that the Wolska-Chłodna-Saxon Garden-Kierbedź Bridge route was completely unblocked.[102]

In 1958, while collecting material for a documentary about Heinz Reinefarth, Andrew Thorndike conducted interviews with inhabitants of Warsaw who had lived through the uprising. One of the women claimed to have met Reinefarth during a nighttime orgy in the German headquarters in the city, but her statement does not indicate what she was doing there. The events she describes cannot be precisely located in time or confirmed. However, they are quite interesting:

> Thorndike: Mrs. Witkowska, you told me that you understand a little of our language, the German language.
>
> Witkowska: Yes, I understand a little, but I spoke German many years ago, so I find it a bit difficult.
>
> Thorndike: All right—you told me recently, when we met, that you know SS-Gruppenführer Reinefarth from the Warsaw Uprising period. Is that right?
>
> Witkowska: Yes, that's right. I was in the Brühl Palace every day and every night because Dirlewanger's headquarters were located there.
>
> Thorndike: Dirlewanger's?
>
> Witkowska: Yes! I also saw Reinefarth there, when orgies were held at night.
>
> Thorndike: You said that nighttime orgies were held in the Brühl Palace?
>
> Witkowska: Yes, because that is the only name you can call it!
>
> Thorndike: What happened there?
>
> Witkowska: I find it hard to talk about it today. Anyway, there was no lack of alcohol. They brought in women to dance there. And it all happened at a time when terrible scenes were playing out in the city. The whole city was on fire. Tanks were crushing human bodies, and in the Brühl Palace there was dancing. Oberführer Dirlewanger often went up to the window, and one time he said: Look how pretty it is, just like in Madrid.
>
> Thorndike: Please tell me, what role did SS-Gruppenführer Reinefarth play in this company?
>
> Witkowska: Reinefarth sat in an armchair at the table, just like a king. At first I thought that maybe Hitler himself had come, the officers paid court to him so. When I later looked at him more closely, I saw that it wasn't Hitler.
>
> Thorndike: And it was definitely SS-Gruppenführer Reinefarth? No possibility of a mistake?
>
> Witkowska: Yes, it was Reinefarth. Dirlewanger's batman whispered in my ear that it was Reinefarth.

> Thorndike: And at nights, when these orgies were organized, were executions held then or did they just have fun? How was it?
>
> Witkowska: At night the soldiers took care of such matters on their own, because the officers were busy drinking vodka. And in the daytime they returned to their companies, which were busy shooting people.[103]

In the early stage of the Warsaw Uprising's suppression, mass crimes were committed in Wola and Ochota. Gustav Strumpf remembered that he received an order from Kurt Weisse stating that "no stone on stone is to be left standing in Warsaw."[104] Walter Hardt testified:

> Before we set off for battle on the first day, they told us that we were to leave scorched earth behind. We were told this by our platoon leader. . . . Next the platoon leader told us that in the battle area we were to shoot at everything that "creeps and runs," without pardon. I understood this to mean that in the area of the fighting, we were to shoot at men, women, and children. My companions also understood [the order] like that, I believe. I am deeply convinced that the basis of the order issued by the platoon leader about scorched earth and shooting in all circumstances coincides with Hitler's decree.[105]

Hardt emphasized that wherever possible, the soldiers did not obey it. He also testified that by the first week of the fighting, this order was rescinded, and they were to shoot only at insurgents who carried weapons.[106]

Dirlewanger's soldiers mostly denied having been ordered to murder all the inhabitants of the capital. They were interrogated in the 1960s, and to avoid a possible penalty, they preferred not to say everything. Peter Erretkamps admitted that they were ordered to treat men, women, children, and older people like partisans and shoot them.[107] As a result of such instructions, all buildings were set on fire. This was confirmed by Franz Haschäcker. He also mentioned that when they reached the Brühl Palace, they received the order to spare women and children from that point onward, and that insurgents should be sent as POWs to the rear areas.[108]

The order to destroy all of Warsaw had been issued at the start of the Warsaw Uprising by Heinrich Himmler. The head of the Reich Chancellery in Berlin, Dr. Hans Lammers, remembered that "in Warsaw the conducting of an action to destroy the city was ordered." Nobody is capable of quoting the exact wording of the order. When interrogated on January 26 and 28, 1946, Erich von dem Bach-Zelewski recalled it as follows: "Every inhabitant of the city is to be killed, taking prisoners is forbidden, [and] Warsaw should be razed to the ground to give an example intimidating all of Europe."[109] Moreover:

> 1. Captive insurgents are to be killed regardless of whether they fought in accordance with the Geneva Convention or violated it.
> 2. The part of the population not participating in the fighting, including women and children, is also to be killed.
> 3. The whole city is to be razed to the ground, and thus the buildings, streets, municipal facilities, and everything located within it.[110]

On August 10, the SS and police leader in the Warsaw District, SS-Brigadeführer Paul Geibel, received a telex from Himmler stating that "tens of thousands [of people] are to be liquidated!"[111] Meanwhile, Dr. Ludwig Hahn, the chief of security police in the city, testified on July 12, 1961, in Hamburg:

> From what I remember, on August 2, 1944, I received via the order police a telegram informing me that the uprising was to be put down using all the most brutal methods, that all the districts were to be burned down, and Poles murdered whether they took part in the uprising or not. I don't remember the contents of the telegram, however, particularly the fragment about the murder of the civilian population. I believe, however, that I remember the spirit of the telegram's contents.[112]

That such an order was issued was confirmed at the start of the 1960s by Peterburs, a gendarmerie officer and commander of a police battalion. As a witness in Reinefarth's proceeding, he testified that "commanders of units who do not achieve the right energy will be put on trial before a military court for cowardice." He further said that "everyone who shows themselves along the route of troop movements shall be treated as a participant of the uprising."[113]

Peterburs's testimony was confirmed by Max Reck, who, having some doubts as to the interpretation of the order to treat everybody "without pardon," sent a courier to Reinefarth. He was sent away with the comment that "asking about it again is probably . . . unnecessary; the issued order is after all clear and explicit."[114]

This is how Dr Hartlieb, a doctor in Dirlewanger's unit, recollected the order:

> All inhabitants of Warsaw regardless of age and sex shall be killed; it is not allowed to take any prisoners. Warsaw is to be razed to the ground, and thus Europe should be shown what organizing an uprising against the Germans means.[115]

In the first week of the uprising, mass shootings of the local population took place in Litzmannstädter Straße (Wolska) in the Wola District. During the so-called Wola massacre, according to various estimates from thirty thousand to sixty-five thousand men, women, and children were murdered. It is commonly accepted that this massacre was carried out by Oskar Dirlewanger's soldiers. While they were responsible for many crimes (also during the uprising), they did not play a large part in the shooting of Wola residents. They committed crimes in Wolski Hospital and St. Lazarus Hospital,[116] where they shot most of the personnel and patients, and burned the buildings down along with those patients who could not move. This will be discussed in a further part of this chapter.

The chief perpetrators of the Wola massacre were Reinefarth's police units, while Dirlewanger's soldiers were engaged in heavy clashes with insurgents (including units from the Radosław Group) at the time. Apart from Reinefarth's police units, the participants of the mass shootings included the following:

- Police divisions of Warsaw's garrison
- Subordinates (SD and Ukrainian auxiliary units) of SS-Hauptsturmführer Alfred Spilker[117]
- A company from the Poznań police's cavalry squadron
- 9th Police Guard Battalion
- Company from the Walter special police unit
- Police company from Łódź
- 12th Belarusian Guard Battalion from the Minsk Security Police
- 209th Cossack Battalion
- Ukrainian industrial guard[118]

Moreover, at that time, Sonderkommando 7a, belonging to Einsatzgruppe B and subject to the orders of SS-Sturmbannführer Gerhard Bast,[119] was located near Warsaw.[120] The fact that it was the police units that were responsible for the shootings is confirmed also in the recollections of insurgents and Wola inhabitants who survived the massacre, and also in the testimonies of soldiers. Over subsequent days, special units such as Reinefarth's police units

(Einsatzkommando der Sicherheitspolizei bei Kampfgruppe Reinefarth) were designated to conduct the organized shootings. Detachments of these units were assigned to individual assault groups.[121]

The Peterburs Police Battalion also participated in the executions:

> The start of the mass murders on the eastern edge of the city of Warsaw around 9 coincides in time and space with the start of an action by police forces that had practically no military tasks here, west of the railway line. On the basis of their composition, these were police troops that partly had experience with "combating banditry" and partly, as Volksdeutsche, may have harbored more or less pronounced national resentment against Poles.[122]

In the region of operations of Assault Group North (Angriffsgruppe Nord), executions were started around noon and were most likely continued by a special security police operational unit.[123]

In the context of crimes committed by Dirlewanger's soldiers in Wola, the recollections of Mathias Schenk are referred to the most often. They were also cited by Alexandra Richie: "One of the most terrible features of the Dirlewanger Brigade was the wilful [*sic*] murder of children."[124] She repeated after Schenk's account the story of a massacre carried out on August 5, in an Orthodox orphanage at Wolska Street 149:

> A lot of children were standing on the stairs with their hands up. Lots of children. All with their little hands in the air. We looked at them for a while until Dirlewanger appeared. He ordered them all to be killed. They killed them and then stepped on the children's bodies, smashing their little heads with the butts of their guns. The stairs were covered in blood.[125]

On August 5, 1944, Oskar Dirlewanger had not yet arrived in Warsaw.

Adolf Katz stated that Dirlewanger's unit was to be followed by police units, whose tasks included checking that there were no insurgents or civilians left in buildings.[126] The members of these units drove the civilian population into the streets; assembled them in public spaces, squares, parks, and yards; and then shot them with machine guns and killed them with grenades they threw. The policeman Josef V., who followed behind Dirlewanger's unit, heard the sound of shots behind his back and wondered, "Why are they still shooting there? There is no more work left there."[127] The soldier Aloys T., conscripted into Reinefarth's police units, remembered:

> I heard heavy machine guns shooting ceaselessly nearby, and because there were no bullets flying about, I couldn't understand what it meant. I decided to check and then I found out that the SD was constantly shooting Poles. And because I assumed they had been caught armed, I didn't investigate further. After a moment the policeman G. came up to me and said that he had recently been in the courtyard of a building in one of the blocks and had seen shot women and children lying on the ground. . . . In Wolska I suddenly saw a large column of people coming from the city center, escorted by soldiers. Our mood immediately fell and you could hear among others the words "They're leading priests as well." . . . After around 10 minutes I suddenly saw 15 or 20 Catholic priests stop in the glow of a burning house. They stood in single file. Suddenly two SD soldiers armed with machine guns ran up to them from behind and killed them all with shots to the neck. When they finished, the turn came for around 20 Poles, among whom there was also a boy aged 14–15.[128]

Rudi Fiedler, one of Dirlewanger's subordinates who was part of Kampfgruppe Steinhauer (2nd Battalion, 5th Company), remembered that after arriving in Warsaw he saw many bodies of people killed in executions. On one of the first evenings, he witnessed the following scene:

> Uniformed civilians who came out of houses were shot immediately. Those people were led into the hall and shot there. I want to say that thirty people in total were shot like that before my eyes. They were not only men, but mostly women and children. . . .
>
> Those were not SD people. Because of my long stay in the concentration camp, I know the uniforms of people from the SD. The SD served in the Oranienburg-Sachsenhausen concentration camp. I also know the SD wore a diamond with the letters SD on their sleeves.
>
> It wasn't the Wehrmacht either. I was also familiar with Wehrmacht uniforms.
>
> It was the police. They wore green police uniforms, whose shade was more intensive than the Wehrmacht's feldgrau. They were uniformed like the policemen whom we fought together with in the Beresino region [in Belarus].[129]

The shootings conducted by police and SD units find confirmation in the recollections of surviving inhabitants of Wola. Wacława Szlacheta described the extermination of the residents of the tenement house at Wolska 129; that is, the Hankiewicz building. On the night before the shooting, soldiers in police uniforms ran into the building.

> They spread out into the flats, where they carried out a search. Three of them burst into our flat, ordering those present to put their hands in the air; they searched the flats, opening wardrobes and rummaging through the things. They didn't take anything from our house.[130]

The German soldiers returned before 10:00 a.m. They were uniformed similarly to the ones who searched the tenement at night:

> I came out of the flat with my husband, two sons, and two daughters. Together with other residents of the building, the gendarmes told us to go out into Wolska Street, cross the road, and stop next to Park Sowińskiego.[131]

These people were shot. Everything indicates that the perpetrators were German soldiers under Reinefarth's command, brought to Warsaw from Warthegau. Similar events played out in other tenement buildings in Wola.[132]

Many historians state that police units operated behind the lines of the fighting and that they were the ones who shot civilians. At the same time, they place responsibility for the massacres on Dirlewanger's subordinates only because they were deemed a "band of criminals." An example of such a description is offered by a fragment of the book *Powstanie Warszawskie*, which is frequently quoted by other authors. Jerzy Kirchmayer wrote,

> As soon as Reinefarth and Dirlewanger's units moved deeper into Wolska Street, *special groups of policemen immediately dragged people out from buildings in the rear of the attack* [author's emphasis] and with no regard for age or sex, from the young to the elderly, shot the innocent and defenseless en masse. . . . At the same time, in the rear of the progressing attack, the Germans systematically burned the captured houses and even those occupied without combat, thus taking revenge on the population and making it easier to clear the captured area. *In this sea of blood and fire spilling across Wola in the footsteps*

> *of the German assault, Himmler wanted to drown the uprising, using the hands of Reinefarth's policemen and Dirlewanger's criminals, armed to the teeth, to do so* [author's emphasis].[133]

Adalbert Daschner, one of Dirlewanger's soldiers who came to Warsaw in late August or early September 1944 (that is, after the Wola events), remembered that Dirlewanger's subordinates had received an order to send all "partisans" behind the lines. There they were to be taken care of by people from the SD.[134] Also, Emil Bauer testified that people who surrendered and prisoners were to be sent to the rear to the gendarmerie and SD.[135] Artur Schuldt stated that he had seen police units lead civilians behind the lines and then shoot them, describing such events as follows:

> Anyway, we had no doubt that the police were shooting the civilian population in courtyards. We did not see them [the shootings]. However, in the course of further operations . . . we saw the bodies of civilians, we also partly saw policeman move the bodies, undoubtedly to loot them.[136]

Both in the initial stage of the uprising and in subsequent weeks, most soldiers from Dirlewanger's unit fought on the front lines and so could not have dealt with "prisoners" and the civilian population. The eastern units subordinate to Dirlewanger—the Azerbaijani Battalion and part of the 1st Eastern Muslim Regiment—did take part in the executions.

Dirlewanger's soldiers testified that during combat, there was no time or possibility to take prisoners. In such instances, they did shoot everyone who was in the combat area. They opened fire at anybody who opposed them in any way, and particularly anybody who was armed. Of course, each of them underlined that if people did not have weapons, they were not killed even if they were insurgents and wore armbands.[137] We know this to be untrue. However, the interrogations of the soldiers took place in the 1960s, and they all tried to save themselves from prison. Meanwhile, for various reasons, prosecutors and investigators were not interested in a thorough explanation of all war crimes.

An additional impediment in establishing the scale of crimes committed during the uprising by Dirlewanger's unit is the "dispersal" of its members. As I mentioned above, not all of Dirlewanger's soldiers arrived in Warsaw at the same time. Subsequent transports arrived in Warsaw during the fighting. The units that arrived in the city in the first week of combat fought mostly on the front lines as Dirlewanger's unit. However, further transports were split up as needed. Thus, smaller combat groups (*Kampfgruppe*) scattered about the city were formed and assigned to various forces, both Wehrmacht and police. Part of them remained under Dirlewanger's orders, and some were subordinate to other commanders. Some had no contact with Dirlewanger in Warsaw.

One of the soldiers who was assigned to a completely different unit was Wilhelm Rass, who joined Dirlewanger's forces around February 1944 in the Minsk region and participated in antipartisan operations. In Warsaw he was assigned to the Polizei-Schützendivision, which was under Dirlewanger's orders. The commander of Pol-Schützendiv. was police colonel "Kubitschek." Rass arrived in the Praga District around August 11–12. Since the fighting there had already ended, he was sent to the Citadel to block communications between AK soldiers in the Old Town and Żoliborz. According to him, the Germans were cut off in the Citadel for around fourteen days. There, he was in charge of armor and grenade launchers. He commanded a heavy grenade launcher and stood at the head of a company of around a hundred people. He claimed that he was not subordinate to any platoon or battalion and received orders from Weisse, Dirlewanger's deputy. He did not meet the commander himself in Warsaw.[138]

Franz Haschäcker testified that in the first days of the uprising, while moving toward the Brühl Palace, he set fire to all tenement buildings. The inhabitants encountered were shot regardless of age and sex. The same occurred in the rear area of his unit. Of course, he stressed that he had a "clear conscience" (*reines Gewissen*) because he had not participated in the executions himself. He said, however, that anyone could participate in them if only they wanted to. It was also possible to decline participation in executions.[139]

The corpses of execution victims were burned. Some, as Dirlewanger's soldiers also mentioned, were told to pull boards off fences and hold them by their bodies during the shooting. This, they claimed, made it easier to burn the bodies. Such a method was used all through the uprising.

Haschäcker stated that during the uprising, he witnessed the shooting of a group of doctors and nurses:

> I also saw a group of doctors and nurses being shot. This happened next to a wooden fence. You could tell that they were doctors and nurses by their white aprons; they also had medical bags and containers with them. The shooting was done by Dirlewanger's men.[140]

The wounded in insurgent hospitals were also shot, after which the hospitals were set on fire. Nurses were raped and murdered. Soldiers from the Azerbaijani Regiment, which was subordinate to Dirlewanger, took part in executions in the Wolski Hospital at Płocka Street 26. After the barricade next to Górczewska and Działdowska Streets had been captured and the insurgents had withdrawn, the German soldiers entered the hospital area.[141] Stefan Wesołowski, a surgeon in the facility, remembered the attack as follows:

> The tragic day of August 5 approaches. The weather is beautiful. Terrible shooting since the morning. The German assault begins. Before noon, two German soldiers run into the hospital. Dusty, dirty, black with smoke, wrapped in bullet belts, they ask about wounded German soldiers. . . . One of the arrivals, short, thin, slim, rat-faced, calmed him down: "Don't worry! We will come here soon, take you away, *und das alles wird gesprengt!*" He concluded, "The hospital will be blown up!"[142]

Also, Leokadia Ciekanowska was present in the Wolski Hospital that day and remembered the moment when the Germans attacked:

> Around two in the afternoon [on August 5], with a cannonade of shots, German and Ukrainian soldiers rushed into the hospital. They shot at people, spread out around the hospital, ordering those present to leave the hospital. Those who could went to the ground floor, even patients who could barely drag themselves out of bed. Here, on the ground floor, they killed Prof. Zeyland,[143] the director of the hospital, Dr Piasecki,[144] and the hospital chaplain [Fr. Kazimierz Ciecierski].
>
> We were herded into Górczewska Street to the corner of Moczydło Street and placed in a gigantic hall with a large, open doorway. At this time, they kept taking male doctors and even patients away in groups of 25 and led them out to be executed. After we had been standing as a huddled group for some time, I noticed through the open doorway of the hall—I was standing in their direct vicinity—that at some point a group of German officers had come and stopped before them. One of the arrivals must have held a high rank, because he had red lapels on his uniform.
>
> At one point, one of the officers shouted in a loud voice, "*Hunde setzen!*" It became quite tight. The officers talked among themselves, and again the loud voice of one of them was heard in German, "All men come out!"

> There was a commotion in the crowd of seated people, and screams and crying could be heard. Directly next to me there sat a man who wanted to stand up, but at that moment a woman who was sitting next to him hit him on the back to make him hunch down and pulled a kerchief over his head so that from some distance away, it was impossible to tell him apart in the crowd of sitting women and children, and thanks to this he was saved for the present. I also saw nuns save a priest the same way, putting a wimple on his head and a shawl on his shoulders. The men, among whom there were doctors in white coats and also those patients who were able to leave the hospital, were led out of the hall in groups of twenty-five to be shot.[145]

After the hospital was captured, the soldiers turned to looting and stealing; meanwhile, the patients and personnel were driven into the yard. Stefan Wesołowski remembered:

> Right after lunch I heard a noise. I ran out. The corridor was swarming with German uniforms. They were SS men, and among them many with Asiatic features. "*Alles raus! Los! Los!*" They drove us all out of the hospital rooms into the hall. As I was walking along the corridor, as we were about to go downstairs, I looked at the staircase leading upward. "Maybe the attic?" I thought. But Germans were also coming down the stairs. "Too late! Too late!"
>
> We go into the hall, where everybody driven out of the ward and cellars is gathering. A crowd of people, the wounded and personnel, is milling around. Further in, I noticed my patient Schliffacke lying on a stretcher, some officer standing next to him. I push my way through to the stretcher, bend down and say to the wounded, "Tell this officer that we operated on you; tell him that Polish doctors looked after you." Schliffacke looks at me unthinkingly and is just as terrified as I am.
>
> The soldiers herd us out of the hall into Płocka Street and start putting us in fours. Civilians come out, men, women with children, Daughters of Charity, ward sisters, a group of doctors and lightly wounded. . . .
>
> The head of our column is already turning left into Górczewska Street. When we go round the corner of the hospital building, the Asians start shouting something at us and make us lie down in a shallow trench formed when the pavements were pulled up to make barricades. We lie down on the ground, thinking that this is the end. . . .

> We stand on the slope by the street, which lies lower down because of the dugout that was made under the railway track to let the road through; we are located slightly behind the railway crossing. In the field behind us stands the crowd swept out of the hospital. Around us houses burn; machine guns, artillery shots, and the banging of bombs may be heard. A machine gun has been placed on the other bank across from us.[146]

Patients and doctors from this facility were shot on Górczewska Street where it crosses the railway flyover.[147] Those who survived the execution were brought back to the hospital. In mid-August it was still operating as an establishment, merging several neighboring hospitals. Part of the building was occupied by Germans, while in the other part, Polish civilian patients and wounded insurgents in hiding were treated.[148]

On that same day, Jerzy Górski, who was then sixteen, was thrown out of a house on Górczewska Street. He described that initially, civilians were used in the German attack on a school on Gostyńska Street:

> It happened on August 5, 1944, in Wola. I stood among the numerous residents of Górczewska Street and nearby streets under the flyover, waiting my turn to be shot. I was 16 years old then; I didn't know where my parents and siblings were, because when the Germans threw us out and drove us before them like a shield, we lost each other. They drove several tens of us in front, wanting to capture the school in Gostyńska Street. Quite a lot of people were killed then. Later they turned us about and led us with hands in the air under the flyover to Górczewska, where several hundred people were already standing. Some German officer spoke, saying we would all be shot. Crying and screaming started, mothers hugged children to themselves, families said goodbye, there was a priest with us who blessed us, and the execution started; drunken Vlasovites took people in groups of ten and went into Moczydło and Zagłoba Streets to shoot them. They robbed people of gold. . . . I thought that maybe I would run away somehow, but that could not succeed because we were guarded on all sides by drunken Vlasovites. . . . At one point, some German officers arrived on a motorcycle from the direction of Płocka Street, and the execution was called off.[149]

The Germans needed surgeons to operate on their own wounded. That was why Doctors Wesołowski and Leon Manteuffel were not shot. The former remembered:

> After some time a German paramedic takes us away in a three-person motorcycle. . . . In the open air, at a table abundantly laden with bottles of alcohol, sit SS officers. . . . After a longer period of waiting, at one point a corporal whom I had noticed earlier, and who bustled between the table and the nearby building that remained standing, brought us a bucket of cold soup.[150]

Both doctors were sent to the Provincial Hospital for Infectious Diseases (St. Stanislaus Municipal Hospital for Infectious Diseases) at Wolska Street 37. Dr. Joanna Kryńska "Elżbieta," who later became Dirlewanger's interpreter, was sent there together with them. Despite initial reluctance and an attempt to send them back to be executed, they were saved by the battalion doctor from SS-Sonderregiment Dirlewanger, Major Hartlieb:[151]

> At one of the tables sat Major Staff Doctor Hartlieb from Kampfgruppe Reinefarth. He turned to our guards and asked why we had been brought there; there was no need for any Poles, and they should only be shot. Near the table sat Dr. Manteuffel and Dr. Wesołowski from the group that was being led from the hospital from Wola to the locomotive factory.[152]

SS-Sonderregiment Dirlewanger took part in the fighting and the shootings in the area of the St. Stanislaus Provincial Hospital for Infectious Diseases, which it captured on August 5, 1944, during the fighting to take the barricade across Wolska Street near the junction with Młynarska Street. Immediately after entering the area of this facility, soldiers from Dirlewanger's unit shot the doorman.

Bronisław Paczyński, a fourteen-year-old boy at the time, remembered the events of August 5, 1944, in the St. Stanislaus Hospital as follows:

> I mean, when the Germans got me and my guardian, he still wanted to save himself; he showed them, "I am a train driver." He had German passes. They hesitated. They hesitated whether to shoot us right away or not. They even took us under guard to their commander, who was

sitting at the corner of Młynarska and Wolska. We arrived before him with the guard, and he said something to him—I did not know German well yet. He just barked something. As it turns out, he just answered: "And what is the order?" The end. Goodbye. There was an order, a clear order that at this time everybody had to be shot, just like that.[153]

In the book *Rzeź Woli*, Piotr Gursztyn wrote that Paczyński was sent "to the commander, to St. Stanislaus Hospital. The commander, a tall older officer—Dirlewanger himself, perhaps—barked something briefly. Remembering the situation after many years, Paczyński decided that the words spoken were 'And what is the order?'"[154] However, the commander whom Gursztyn wrote about cannot have been Dirlewanger. As I mentioned above, Dirlewanger arrived in Warsaw around August 8–10, 1944, at the earliest, and according to the memories of Gustav Strumpf, a soldier from his unit, around August 15.[155] On August 5, Dirlewanger was on his way from Berlin to East Prussia, which is confirmed by Himmler's order of August 4, which I quoted above, and Adolf Katz's testimony. He set off for insurgent Warsaw from East Prussia only after several days.[156]

Around August 10, Dirlewanger arrived at the quarters in the hospital:[157]

At this time the commander of one of the SS groups attacking Warsaw, Sturmbahnführer Oskar Dirlewanger, came to live in our hospital. In his batman I recognized the NCO who on that memorable day, the fifth of August, brought us that soup. One day I witnessed the batman bringing out an enormous suitcase loaded with silver out into the corridor, and he started sorting through it under Dirlewanger's directions.[158]

From August 6 onward, the Infectious Diseases Hospital housed the staff and chancellery of SS-Sonderregiment Dirlewanger, as well as the dressing and first-aid station of Reinefarth's group. Heinrich Arndt stated that he organized the chancellery in the barracks located on hospital grounds. In one of the rooms, the belongings of deceased comrades in arms were sorted and sent off.[159] Moreover, Arndt remembered:

In the Infectious Diseases Hospital I saw two Poles hanged on a tree, a red-and-white flag flying between them. The hanged wore red-and-white armbands. There was no doubt that these were insurgents, and

> they had not been shot but hanged for the purpose of intimidation, and they had been left there for a longer time. I don't know who gave the order to hang them. I don't know whether "Oskar" gave that order either. Of course, he was staying at the Infectious Diseases Hospital at the time. Neither do I know if "Oskar" had seen the hanged.[160]

Franz Haschäcker confirmed the information about insurgents hanged in the Infectious Diseases Hospital courtyard. He testified that Dirlewanger interrogated them personally in his quarters. The insurgents refused to speak, and so Dirlewanger gave the order for them to be hanged, to serve as an example. Haschäcker denied that a red-and-white flag had been flown between them. He stated that the insurgents showed no signs of mistreatment and beating. Furthermore, he mentioned that Dirlewanger also interrogated other captured insurgents. Ten of them were hanged.[161]

The conviction that it was Dirlewanger's unit that carried out the massacre of Wola results from a number of unverified pieces of information about the "bloodthirstiness" of Oskar Dirlewanger and his subordinates. During the postwar trials of Nazi criminals, the defendants pushed the blame on others in order to show themselves in the best possible light. In the case of crimes committed during the Warsaw Uprising, the most convenient solution was to place responsibility on two commanders who were already dead: Dirlewanger and Kaminski. Depending on his needs, von dem Bach blamed Kaminski ("When I saw that soldiers from Kaminski's brigade were shooting civilians, I received the following explanation: 'This is Hitler's order'"),[162] Dirlewanger, Reinefarth, police units, and even Guderian, who did not want to help him get Hitler's order rescinded. He often changed and withdrew his testimony. In 1958, when testifying in Reinefarth's favor, he claimed that the massacre had been carried out not in Wola but in Ochota, and placed the blame on Kaminski's soldiers.[163] He backed out of this in 1961, when he stated that these events did play out in Wola after all.[164] As a result, the proceedings concerning his participation in the Wola massacre were discontinued. Frequent changes in testimonies contributed to information chaos, and the blame for all the crimes was laid on the best-known unit to fight in the uprising: Dirlewanger's soldiers.

Also, the postwar testimony and trials of Heinz Reinefarth contributed to the dissemination of accounts about crimes committed by Dirlewanger during the uprising. In 1964, while making a statement before the Subsequent Proceedings Division of the American Chief of Counsel for War Crimes (OCCWC), he distorted facts in his own favor, pushing blame onto Dirlewanger.

He claimed, for example, that he received the order to suppress the uprising only on August 5 (or even 6), 1944, and heard about the order to murder the civilian population from von dem Bach only in Warsaw. He even stated that Dirlewanger's unit was already engaged in combat when he arrived there, and was never subordinate to him in any way.[165]

In 1958, Reinefarth asserted that he came to Warsaw on August 7; during the next interrogation, he claimed that on August 5, he forced his way in an armored car to the encircled commander Reiner Stahel to discuss the situation. All the while, he firmly emphasized that Dirlewanger's soldiers had never been under his command. To push away all allegations, he indicated that he had not carried out Hitler's order to "raze Warsaw to the ground." He explained:

> Senseless cruelty would only have strengthened the opponent's will to resist and would have been a direct impediment to a rapid end of combat, which was our goal.

He laid all crimes against civilians at Dirlewanger's and Kamiński's door, presenting himself as a perfect commander who had almost nothing to reproach himself with.

> As far as possible, I conducted the fighting in Warsaw, which for me was a purely military operation, according to the principles of traditional military law. I instructed my officers and the units under me many times that they were to observe those principles and in no event take revenge for any possible cruelty perpetrated by the enemy. I consider—and have so far considered—that this attitude brought me the appreciation of my Polish opponents, particularly Gen. Count Bór-Komorowski. I am not aware of any fault.[166]

All through his proceeding in 1958, he vehemently attempted to emphasize Dirlewanger's criminal personality. Witnesses and friends testifying for Reinefarth, such as Günther Bock, underlined his unimpeachable soldierly attitude and claimed that apart from the conduct of Dirlewanger's unit, no war crimes had been committed in Warsaw by the German side.[167] Thus the vision of Dirlewanger as a criminal responsible for the murder of Warsaw's civilian population became entrenched in popular consciousness, even though he was not present in the city at the time. All other German units operating in Warsaw in 1944 were ignored. Reinefarth, meanwhile, could continue to hold important posts in German society.

In 1967, Reinefarth was once again accused of the crimes committed in Warsaw. The impulse for restarting the process was provided by a file with documents from the Warsaw Uprising possessed by Günther Rohr and by the research of historian Hanns von Krannhals.[168] Reinefarth defended himself by testifying that Dirlewanger's and Kaminski's units were not under his orders and committed the massacres of the civilian population unauthorized. Despite abundant proof of his guilt, he was found innocent, and in popular consciousness it was Dirlewanger who became the cruelest figure of the Warsaw Uprising. The court in Flensburg decided that Dirlewanger's and Kaminski's units were subordinate to Reinefarth only as regards tactical matters, while as regards discipline, they were subordinate to Himmler and only he could hold them responsible. Nevertheless, in the verdict the court wrote,

> It seems doubtful, however, and is impossible to establish that members of Dirlewanger's special unit took part in the massacres of the Polish civilian population outside the area of combat. This group was engaged in heavy fighting against the insurgents, particularly during the first three days, until they reached the Brühl Palace on August 7, 1944, . . . suffering heavy losses (almost 90 percent) at the time. Members of this unit would thus have had practically no time or opportunity to carry out such executions of civilians outside combat. On the basis of testimonies, one may, rather, expect that they shot only those civilians whom they encountered in the combat zone, and particularly in buildings from which they were fired upon.[169]

Still, contrary to postwar testimonies, Reinefarth and Dirlewanger formed a closely cooperating team, which may be seen when analyzing documents from 1944. On September 10, Reinefarth wrote a motion for Dirlewanger to be granted the Knight's Cross.

> On 5.8.1944, Dirlewanger's special SS regiment was sent into action on the western edge of the city of Warsaw to put down the uprising of Polish and Bolshevik banditry in Poland. Right after it set off from its initial position, heavy street fighting ensued. The well-masked and heavily barricaded firing positions of the bandits had to be forced into silence. It is solely thanks to the tactical skills, courage, and cold blood of SS-Oberführer Dirlewanger that it was possible to smoothly carry out the attack and achieve the set daily goals. Also, in this

> respect SS-Oberführer Dirlewanger demonstrated the greatest fervor and led his soldiers with weapon in hand to destroy pockets of resistance. . . . SS-Oberführer Dirlewanger . . . frequently demonstrated by his actions that he is the bravest of the brave.[170]

During the uprising, Dirlewanger's weakness for women revealed itself once again. Around August 10, the twenty-nine-year-old doctor Joanna Kryńska, who spoke excellent German, became his interpreter.[171] As she herself owned, she talked both with Dirlewanger and with other officers:

> From those conversations I found out that Wola had been taken by German and Vlasov units[172] from Kampfgruppe Reinefarth, which arrived there together with the Herman Göring Division.[173]

Kryńska was a pretty woman, and her beauty and good German made an impression on Germans. Dirlewanger tried to awe her, boasting that he was a friend of Himmler's.[174] In the first week of the fighting, she worked at St. Stanislaus Hospital, where an emergency medical station had been organized just before the start of the uprising, with Kryńska "Elżbieta" becoming its commander. She had fifteen paramedics age seventeen to eighteen under her.[175]

When testifying in 1947, Kryńska quoted conversations she had had with Dirlewanger during the uprising. Even though she was questioned three years after the events, her testimony shows many postwar influences, such as mentions of "Vlasovites" and tales purportedly about Dirlewanger's soldiers. Given Oskar Dirlewanger's weakness for women, it may also be assumed that he tried to impress Kryńska in his conversations with her. Nevertheless, in the testimonies we still find much interesting information that is confirmed in other sources:

> In the first half of August 1944, in a conversation with me and Dr. Kubica, Dirlewanger observed that what was happening to the civilian population in Warsaw was nothing compared to what had happened in Russia, where his subordinates had left no people alive and murdered and raped the women. He said that this had been necessary for Germany's victory, particularly as it happened to a nation that was beneath Germany in all respects. Slavs were simply *Untermenschen*, Vlasovites would not come to Germany either. He also said that his unit was specially trained to fight partisans. Dirlewanger cooperated very closely with the Warsaw Gestapo, which was located in one of

> the buildings near St. Adalbert's Church. There the head of the intelligence cell invigilating inhabitants, Spile[r] of Szuch Avenue, was staying, who [ordered] Dirlewanger to carry out multiple purges in the hospital.[176]

In the second half of August and all through September, upon Dirlewanger's order, Gestapo men from Sonderkommando Spilker carried out a triage of patients in severe condition and men who were staying in St. Stanislaus Hospital. Selected men were moved to St. Adalbert's Church. Some of them ended up in Pruszków, while of others all traces disappeared.[177]

During the fighting, Polish units had no mercy for German soldiers and prisoners either. The insurgents sometimes killed prisoners, particularly SS members and policemen. They liquidated a whole unit of Azerbaijanis from the 111th Azerbaijani Regiment serving in the German army under Dirlewanger, although they had surrendered and been promised to be let free.[178]

Heinrich Arndt remembered witnessing crimes perpetrated on members of SS-Sonderregiment Dirlewanger:

> I once experienced two old members of Dirlewanger's unit being mistreated in some courtyard. These people were beaten and hit with rifle butts. Why this happened I don't know. Maybe they wanted to force them to talk.[179]

He also told of an incident that occurred in the cellar of a music school:

> I saw Obersturmbannführer Weis[s]e go down into the cellar with several officers and grenadiers, and they came back with seven civilians. Then Weis[s]e called one of the soldiers and ordered him to shoot those seven civilians. I heard this with my own ears. Later I also saw that soldier go away with those seven civilians. I didn't see the shooting itself. I don't doubt, however, that those seven civilians were shot.[180]

Dirlewanger's unit cannot be considered completely innocent of the crimes committed in Wola in the first week of the Warsaw Uprising: It did play a role in them. Nevertheless, the Wola massacre cannot be ascribed mainly to this unit, as is commonly held. Dirlewanger's soldiers bore the brunt of the main assault along Wolska Street and combat against the insurgents, and for this reason they could not have taken part in the systematic shootings of the civilian population.

In 1963 the Flensburg prosecutor's office declared,

> It may be assumed that this unit fought fiercely and mercilessly. It may have frequently occurred that this unit, seasoned in fighting with banditry, destroyed its opponent during combat even when from the military point of view this was unnecessary. . . . However, so far it has not been possible to establish whether parts of this unit found the time and opportunity to participate in mass planned shootings outside of combat.[181]

Even though the participation of SS-Sonderregiment Dirlewanger in the mass shootings of civilians in Wola in 1944 has not been confirmed in war diaries, the testimonies of Dirlewanger's soldiers, or the memories of survivors, full responsibility is laid on them because of their questionable reputation.

5.2. Korpsgruppe von dem Bach

When it turned out that the Germans would not be able to suppress the Warsaw Uprising rapidly, Himmler gave command to Erich von dem Bach-Zelewski.[182] During the proceeding of Governor Fischer in February 1947, von dem Bach stated before the Supreme National Tribunal in Warsaw that he had applied for this function himself. He believed that in this case, passing over a specialist in combating partisans "would have been a kind of degradation."[183] Von dem Bach received the order by telephone while in Sopot[184] and set off for Krakow immediately. Governor General Hans Frank and Obergruppenführer and Police Gen. Wilhelm Koppe gave him little information about the situation in Warsaw.[185] He thus moved to Sochaczew and established his headquarters there. SS-Obersturmbannführer Herbert Golz became his chief of staff.[186] From August 5 onward, all Wehrmacht, SS, and police units in Warsaw (including Kampfgruppe Reinefarth) were subordinate to him. Furthermore, he assumed command over the German civilian administration. Thus, Korpsgruppe von dem Bach came into being on August 14. Von dem Bach's plan assumed the application of *Zangenbewegung*: the surrounding of insurgent forces from two sides, north and south.

On August 5, von dem Bach toned down Hitler's command to murder all residents of the Polish capital. He issued an order forbidding the murder of women and children. From that point on, only men were to be shot. He claimed that he could not shoot all residents because he would run out of ammunition. This was confirmed by Peter Erretkamps, who testified,

> After three days we were told that from now on we should shoot at Poles who were armed. We thus understood that we were not to shoot at Poles who surrendered with hands up, but were to send them to the rear and deport them.[187]

On January 26, 1946, in Nuremberg von dem Bach indicated that

> when I arrived and was acquainted with the state of the fighting, I ascertained that there was great confusion. Each unit was shooting in a different direction, nobody knew who to shoot at, and from the military point of view the whole situation had become difficult to solve. In a cemetery, I myself saw a group of civilians being taken away and shot in situ by members of Reinefarth's combat group. . . . I personally went up to Reinefarth, met him in his position. . . . I informed him of the whole situation, and then I drew his attention to the fact that his units were shooting innocent civilians.[188]

At his disposal, Erich von dem Bach had artillery, including the heaviest 60 cm mortars, which fired missiles weighing 2,200 kg that could punch through 2.5 m thick walls. Also available to him were flamethrowers, gas generators for combat in sewers, MG42 machine guns, and remote-controlled miniature tanks called Goliaths[189] that could carry 100 kg of explosive material to the enemy's barricades. Goliaths were around 1.5 m long, equipped with tracks for moving, and were controlled via a cable or by radio. Raids by Luftwaffe dive-bombers offered great support to German soldiers.[190]

The Old Town

After the Saxon Garden, Brühl Palace, and Saxon Palace had been taken, an offensive was launched toward the town hall and the Blank Palace. This was to be a preliminary to the attack on the Old Town, which Dirlewanger's unit commenced with sixteen officers and 865 soldiers.[191] On August 7, the offensive reached the area of Teatralny Square. Dirlewanger's soldiers started to expel civilians living in the neighborhood of Teatralny Square. They shot those unable to walk where they were, and marched the rest to Piłsudski Square and the Saxon Garden. Thence, these people were directed to St. Adalbert's

Church in Wola and then transported to the transit camp in Pruszków from the Western Railway Station.[192]

Erich von dem Bach decided to precede the attack on the Old Town, where around six thousand insurgents were barricaded (only a third were armed),[193] with heavy shelling. Among others, Goliaths and a massive mortar that fired 610 mm caliber concrete-piercing shells were used. From August 5 onward, an armored train was used to support attacks by Dirlewanger's and Kaminski's units.[194]

The insurgents had already captured the Old Town in the first hours of the uprising, and so a great mass of civilians were located there: over eighty thousand inhabitants. People built barricades, which in the narrow, labyrinthine streets created convenient positions that allowed defense against attacks by the enemy's tanks. By August 6, the forces in the Old Town were completely cut off from Śródmieście and Żoliborz. Communications were maintained only via the sewers.

Joanna Kryńska, mentioned above, testified that Dirlewanger cooperated with SS-Hauptsturmführer Alfred Spilker:

> Dirlewanger cooperated very closely with the Warsaw Gestapo, which had its seat in one of the buildings near St. Adalbert's Church. There the chief of invigilation and monitoring public sentiment from Szuch Avenue, Spilke[r], was located, who brought Dirlewanger in to carry out multiple purges in the hospital. As a result, German soldiers frequently selected the seriously ill (of tuberculosis) and young men, whom we hid in beds. The Gestapo took them away and often led them to St. Adalbert's Church, where they usually disappeared without a trace. The Gestapo searched air-raid shelters located in cellars, where some from among the civilian population were sent, on the basis of looks or documents, to the Pruszków camp, and others disappeared without a trace. The Gestapo called Dirlewanger three or four times to carry out a purge in the hospital.[195]

As Emil Bauer testified, Dirlewanger's unit captured the National Opera building (Grand Theatre) in Teatralny Square.[196] Part of the civilian population was herded there, and the others were expelled from the air-raid shelter below the building where they had been hiding.[197] Women and children were separated from the men. The women were placed in the cellar of the building; many of them were raped or used as live shields during attacks on insurgent positions.[198] The men were shot on August 8–9, 1944.[199]

SS-Untersturmführer Paul Zimmermann, who commanded one of the companies of the 2nd Battalion (Kampfgruppe Steinhauer), stated that during combat in Teatralny Square (Theaterplatz) and Ratusz Square (Rathausplatz), high losses were incurred: One day, his company lost fifteen soldiers (killed and wounded). They therefore received numerous replenishments from concentration camps and SS and Wehrmacht prisons. He stated, "Before we even managed to register the new people, part of them had already managed to drop out [die or be wounded]."[200] For this reason, it is very difficult to estimate the total losses that Dirlewanger's unit sustained in Warsaw.

Von dem Bach used all available forces to put down the uprising. He was aware that the units he had at his disposal were insufficient, as von Vormann's report to the command of Army Group Center from August 9 indicates:

> The resistance in Warsaw is increasing. The uprising, improvised at first, is now being directed in a strictly military fashion. With the forces available to us, it is not possible to crush it within a foreseeable time. There is increasing danger that as a result, it will spread and even cover the whole country.
>
> The ongoing fighting involves street combat on the territory of a large city in the most difficult meaning of this word. Own losses are high. The current situation is unbearable in the long term for units fighting east of the Vistula. The supplies sent via a very circular route through Modlin can at any time be seized by insurgents, and we lack forces to secure them. The danger posed to the bridgehead teams in the event of a failure should be underlined.
>
> SS-Obergruppenführer von dem Bach has reported the same to the Reichsführer-SS. For the situation to be brought under control, a full division abundantly equipped with heavy weapons is needed.[201]

Furthermore, it was noted that no success had been achieved in combat on August 9.[202]

Also in the following days, no specific progress was made. On August 10, Schmidt's and Reck's assault groups took two cemeteries in Wola: the Jewish and the Calvinist. Kaminski's units were still fighting in Ochota, but the assault sapper company assigned to them broke through toward Jerozolimskie Avenue and reached Zamkowy Square in the evening.[203] On August 11, the diary of the 9th Army recorded that

> north of the city, Dirlewanger's group is fighting for [illegible word] and securing access to Adolf-Hitler-Platz [Piłsudski Square], but this is not yet a fully usable connection.[204]

Very heavy fighting was still ongoing in the area of Teatralny and Zamkowy Squares.[205]

On August 11, SS-Sonderregiment Dirlewanger breached the weak insurgent positions in the Bankowy Square area. Its members reached the barricade at Bielańska Street that protected an outpost in Bank Polski.[206] On August 12, after heavy artillery fire and aerial bombardment, an attack on the Old Town began. It was planned that district after district would be destroyed. German forces numbering twenty-six thousand soldiers, preceded by a wave of Goliaths and self-propelled guns, set out from the southwest edge of the district and from the Citadel in the north toward the center of the Old Town. They moved forward very slowly due to strong resistance by the insurgents.[207] The attack did not bring the expected results: Dirlewanger's soldiers were pushed out of Bankowy Square.

The next, better-prepared offensive was launched along a broad front stretching from Bankowy Square through Teatralny Square and Zamkowy Square up to Wybrzeże Gdańskie Street near Boleść Street. The nature of these operations was to engage the enemy, drawing Polish forces away from the most important, western direction of the Old Town's defense, which was attacked by a group composed of students of the Poznań officer school, commanded by Maj. Max Reck,[208] and a group under the orders of Col. Schmidt.[209] On the following day, it was reported that part of the Old Town between the area of the former ghetto and the bridge had been captured, and thus at night, communication would be possible via that route.[210]

On August 12, a council was held in the headquarters of the 9th Army, during which it was decided that the main part of the attacking forces, equipped with special technical firing assets, would launch an attack toward Kierbedź Bridge to reestablish this major thoroughfare. Moreover, RONA would continue to push through toward the Main Railway Station and fight against insurgent units between the station and Ochota. Kaminski's group was thus supposed to reopen a second east–west communication axis and cut Śródmieście into two parts. Next, the German troops would start to eradicate the insurgent army in Śródmieście. The staff expected that as soon as these objectives were achieved, the insurgents would surrender.[211]

On August 13 at 10:00 a.m., SS-Sonderregiment Dirlewanger launched an all-out attack. The assault set off from the direction of Wierzbowa Street and the ruins of the Grand Theater toward the City Hall and the barricade at the end of Długa and Bielańska Streets, and also from the ghetto toward the Arsenal-Krasiński Garden-Mostowski Palace line of defense.[212]

On August 14, Dirlewanger's subordinates took the Maltese Hospital[213] and the surrounding buildings. SS-Obersturmführer Lagana gave the order for the hospital to be abandoned immediately. After a conversation with the commander of the hospital, Dr. Leon Strehl, the wounded and the personnel were formed into a column that set off from the Resursa Rzemieślnicza (Craftsmen's Club) building on Senatorska Street. Under German protection, the wounded were evacuated and moved to Śródmieście. They passed through the insurgent barricades in Marszałkowska Street near Królewska Street. The procession of the wounded was stretched out and slow. In Śródmieście, all the patients were housed in hospitals, and part of the personnel established a new hospital at Zgoda 17. The others were assigned to the hospital at Śniadeckich 12. In the Maltese Hospital, thirty to thirty-five seriously wounded patients were left behind. They were not shot. On the following day, the Germans ordered the hospital to be completely evacuated. Dr. Dreyza assembled some civilians who helped carry the wounded. Protected by a soldier from Dirlewanger's unit, who saved them from attacks by the soldiers they passed along the way, they went to the Wolski Hospital at Płocka Street. This group was not aware of the fate of the column that set off for Śródmieście: They were convinced that everybody had been shot. The evacuation of the Maltese Hospital was an unprecedented event during the Warsaw Uprising. The hospital, after another transfer from Zgoda Street to Śniadeckich 17, survived until the capitulation and as a civilian hospital was evacuated to Piastów with full equipment for 120 patients.[214]

At the time of its formation, Korpsgruppe von dem Bach numbered almost twenty-six thousand soldiers, twenty-six tanks, and thirty-eight assault guns.[215] All through August, its forces were gradually increased and were composed of

Kampfgruppe Reinefarth (including SS-Sturmbrigade RONA and SS-Sonderregiment Dirlewanger, transformed in August 1944 into SS-Sturmbrigade Dirlewanger)

Sonderverband Bergmann (2nd Azerbaijani Battalion), under Dirlewanger's command

1st/3rd Azerbaijani Field Battalion Dönmec, under Dirlewanger's command

75th School armored train

384th Railway Security Battalion, 3rd Cossack Regiment, and 572nd Cossack Battalion
608th Security Regiment (commander, Willi Schmidt[216]), 618 people
5th Panzer Grenadiers' Training Battalion from Kalisz
48th Panzer Grenadiers' Training Battalion from Gniezno
458th Panzer Grenadiers' Training Battalion from Rawicz
3rd Cossack Regiment (commander: Maj. Jacob)
500th Motorized Assault Sapper Battalion
501st Waffen-SS Assault Gun Unit[217]

Von Krannhals also listed

200th Assault Gun Reserve Battalion
302nd Panzer Battalion
218th Assault Tank Company Sturmpanzer IV
638th Heavy-Artillery Battery (Karl mortar, 600 mm)
201st Heavy Positional Mortar Battery (*Nebelwerfer*)
1000th Fassault Mortar Company
Krone flamethrower Battalion[218]

The Old Town, under daily heavy fire, gradually succumbed to German military might. The encircled area shrank from day to day, attacked from the south and east by Dirlewanger, from the north by Schmidt's assault group, and from the west by Reck's group. The insurgents' situation was tragic. Despite this, German progress could be considered marginal.

For ten days there was no rainfall, and there was a growing shortage of drinking water. The incredible heat caused the asphalt to melt, and corpses buried in shallow graves to decay rapidly. The air was rank with the bland odor of death, which drew thousands of fat flies, bringing an epidemic of dysentery. Moreover, the insurgents and the civilian population were running out of food supplies.[219]

By mid-August, half of the buildings in the Old Town had been destroyed as a result of fighting and bombing. On August 17, five thousand surviving insurgents were crowded into an area of 1,200 by 600–1,000 m. Besides them, around 75,000–100,000 civilians were present in the Old Town.[220]

On August 18, a general offensive was launched, which was intended to ultimately destroy the "North" group. However, the fighting lasted another fifteen days. In a secret order of August 18, Reinefarth wrote,

> For the most rapid and complete destruction of the banditry enclosed by the regiments Schmidt, Reck, and Dirlewanger in the northeast of Warsaw's center (Old Town), the Dirlewanger group is formed under the command of SS-Oberführer O. Dirlewanger, composed of all the infantry and heavy-weapons forces at my disposal. The objective of the offensive is complete destruction of the encirclement via a broad-front attack from west to east.[221]

As Stachiewicz stated, the order of battle of the Dirlewanger group thus formed was as follows:

Group commander: SS-Oberführer Oskar Dirlewanger
Chief signals officer: Maj. Grevemeyer (Willbrand)
Liaison officer between the group and Gen. Reinefarth: Capt. Krabbe

A. Units so far under Dirlewanger's direct command:
2 battalions from the SS Brigade Dirlewanger (4 75 mm class quick-firing antitank guns, 1 37 mm cal. antitank gun), 19/1,306 (numerical strength: officers/soldiers)
218th Assault Panzer Company (8 tanks), 1/60, commander: Capt. Kellermann

B. Units commanded by Col. Schmidt:
608th Special Regiment, 20/598
Benthin Grenadier Battalion (without one company), 9/536
Antitank platoon, 1/36
Medium grenade launcher platoon from the 1st/111 Azerbaijani Regiment, 1/60
Burkhardt Police Battalion, 7/180

B. Units commanded by Maj. Reck (which later moved to the southern area of the fighting, Mokotów):

Arzberg Infantry Battalion (1 heavy-weapons company and 3 infantry companies), commander: Maj. Arzberg

5th Panzer Grenadier Battalion, 11/888, commander: Capt. Schöning

Police company, 3/360, commander: Capt. Kirchhubel

MMG platoon from the SS Posen Company, 3/74, commander: Capt. Röntgen

Warsaw police guard company, 3/163, commander: Capt. Fersemann

D. Units also subordinate to Dirlewanger:

69th Cossack Division, 14/759, commander: Lieut. Schlatermund

200th Assault Gun Division (6 guns), 3/157, commander: Capt. Früchtenich

96th Motorized Sapper Battalion, 10/192, commander: Capt. Wollenweber

500th Panzer Sapper Battalion (without one company), 4/281, commander: Capt. Zielke

1000th Assault Mortar Company (2 38 mm cannons), 2/54, commander: Lieut. Kodar

Heavy Battery no. 688 (1 600 mm mortar), 1/22

201st Heavy Battery of positional mortars (2 280 mm mortars), 2/62, commander: Lieut. Mathy

302nd Panzer Division (20 assault guns and 50 Goliaths), 3/157

Platoon of pneumatic trench mortars, 3/67, commander: Lieut. Schmuke

Moreover, all mortars that could be released on the day of the offensive (10/292) and training armored train no. 5, commanded by Capt. Edom (12/94), were provided and the cooperation of close-support bomber aviation from the 6th Aerial Fleet was assured[222]

The German group numbered 145 officers and 6,300 soldiers. The individual units of the Dirlewanger group were positioned as follows:

The 69th Cossack Division cut off the contact route with group "North" from the northwest, having the region of the Duchnicka and Przasnyska Streets as a foothold

Col. Schmidt's group occupied the area from the railway bridge on the Vistula (eastern boundary) in a semicircle to Gęsia Street in the ghetto (western boundary)

Maj. Reck's group covered the area from Gęsia Street in the ghetto (northern boundary) to Bielański Square (southern boundary)

The group directly subordinate to Dirlewanger occupied the area from Bankowy Square (western boundary) up to and including Wybrzeże Gdańskie Street (eastern boundary)[223]

Group North was surrounded and shut in the encirclement. On August 19, German forces launched an all-out attack. The assault was intended to rapidly break down insurgent resistance, but the fighting went on for two weeks.[224] The combat diary of the 9th Army reports the following:

> 19 August: "Dirlewanger's group achieved little with large resources; under [Major General] Rohr, much achieved with small resources." 20 August, 9.45: "Situation in Warsaw: numerous command mistakes are increasingly clearly visible. Bach is good, Reinefarth lacks tact. [tactical] training, as do many NCOs. Brave but have not mastered the detailed technique of street combat." 18.25: "Warsaw at a standstill. Command shortcomings. Soldiers and commanders untrained in this respect. Lack of detailed preparation; where it existed (Rohr) things went well. Situation: proletarian war."[225]

On August 30, 1944, the part of Dirlewanger's staff that was staying in the Brühl Palace and was responsible for administration was withdrawn due to Polish gunfire. The command headquarters under the Ia officer, Weisse, remained there.[226] The administration of SS-Sturmbrigade Dirlewanger was moved to the Infectious Diseases Hospital on Wolska Street, where it took up several rooms. Oskar Dirlewanger also moved in there, living under this address until the surrender of the Warsaw Uprising.[227] As I mentioned above, the Infectious Diseases Hospital had already been captured by German units on August 6, and an operation and dressing station of Kampfgruppe Reinefarth had been established there.[228]

Dirlewanger's soldiers attacked again and again from the direction of the Vistula along Boleść Street. Their objective was to reach Mostowa Street, and thus to create a breach in the defense of the Old Town and approach the rear of the units defending its southern edge. On August 21, the main defensive positions of insurgents from the Czwartacy Battalion,[229] who clashed with Dirlewanger's unit along this stretch, were limited to the block of buildings between Wisłostrada Street, Boleść Street, Rybaki Street, and the building referred to as Pekin. The most-important positions were the so-called Prochownia building at the junction of Rybaki and Boleść Streets, the tannery (Quebracho factory), and the barricade at the junction of Mostowa, Rybaki, and Boleść Streets.[230] Under the pressure of SS-Sturmbrigade Dirlewanger, the insurgents gradually retreated.

Although the German troops made progress, on August 21 it was reported that

> the bandits are still maintaining an obstinate defense. It seems that thanks to Stuka attacks and fire from heavy weapons, the bandits have been encircled by Kampfgruppe Dirlewanger. Attempts by smaller groups to push through toward the south between Krakowskie Przedmieście Street and Teatralny Square were repulsed.[231]

The next days brought success for the Germans: Above all, they managed to take control of the Vistula bank north of Kierbedź Bridge. They thus created "a north–south corridor on the eastern edge of the Old Town encirclement." In the south part of the Old Town, Dirlewanger's units crossed Długa Street and moved toward Krasińscy Square. The insurgents responded with counterattacks from Miodowa Street toward the stock exchange.[232]

On August 25, it became clear that the downfall of the Old Town was close. Reinforcements were constantly being sent to Warsaw: For instance, on that day, seventy of Dirlewanger's soldiers arrived, reporting to the staff headquarters in the Brühl Palace.[233] Among them was Otto Ruch, who served as a courier in Warsaw. He remembered that like the Varsovian insurgents, he traveled most of the route between destinations by moving through the sewers and holes smashed in the walls between tenement buildings. His duties involved carrying reports between Dirlewanger's staff and Reinefarth's command post.[234]

On the night of August 25, the staff of the AK left the Old Town area via relatively safe sewer canals, evacuating to Śródmieście. Dirlewanger's soldiers, meanwhile, pushed into Nowe Miasto and reported the capture of the "church with two towers" (St. Francis Seraph Church). At this time, Schmidt's group captured the building of the Polish Security Printing Works and buildings situated to its south and southeast up to Samborska Street.[235] The Germans encountered fierce resistance of the insurgents everywhere.

According to data from the 9th Army staff, from August 10 to 27, German forces lost ninety-one officers and 3,770 NCOs and soldiers, of whom twenty-eight officers and 629 NCOs and soldiers were killed. The summary of the report stated as follows:

> Even given a lack of change in enemy numbers, without bringing in sufficient reinforcements we cannot count on capturing Warsaw within a foreseeable period.[236]

On August 29, von dem Bach confirmed these data. He also stated that

> Kaminski's regiment had to be withdrawn as unsuitable. The enemy constantly recruits from the area and obtains supplies via air. If the combat strength of the insurgents does not suddenly collapse or significantly weaken due to some political event, we cannot count on the possibility of capturing Warsaw within the nearest weeks using those units that are currently at our disposal. So far there is no indication that Polish combat strength is dropping.[237]

At the end of August, the unit was strengthened by 120 soldiers returning from leave and hospital or transferred to Dirlewanger's command. Additionally, transports from the Aklam Wehrmacht prison (300 prisoners), Glatz prison (Kłodzko, 600 people) and the camp at Sachsenhausen (around 120 people) arrived in Warsaw.[238] The fighting in the Old Town ended on September 2. On that day, the Sigismund column, the symbol of Warsaw, was felled by missiles from a German tank. Around 4,500 of 7,000 insurgents retreated via the sewers to Śródmieście and Żoliborz. It is estimated that around thirty thousand people died in the Old Town.

Reports from August 30 indicate that the attack by Col. Schmidt's assault group in the area west of Freta Street toward Franciszkańska Street went on all day, as did that by Dirlewanger's assault group from the corner of Senatorska Street and Daniłowska Street northward. Schmidt's units encountered fierce opposition, while SS-Sturmbrigade Dirlewanger achieved some success.[239] Von dem Bach observed the fighting, which he reported in his diary:

> Today before noon on the north bank of the Vistula in Warsaw, I observed the attack of Schmidt and Dirlewanger's assault group on a block of houses in the Old Town encirclement.[240]

On September 1, Col. Schmidt's soldiers approached Krasiński Square and took St. Benno's Church, located south of Piwna Street. At the same time, SS-Sturmbrigade Dirlewanger captured the Old Town Market Square, coming in from the south. However, the insurgents continued to counterattack to keep the area that contained the sewer entrances in their hands.[241] On the night of September 1, they retreated via the sewers from the Old Town to other districts. Nevertheless, morning reports of September 2 stated that fighting in the Old Town was still ongoing. At night, an attempt was made to escape the encirclement, and in the morning a counterattack took place between Długa Street and Krasińscy Square. The Germans achieved complete control of the Old Town only in the evening.[242]

In the Old Town, the German soldiers found burned-out ruins, civilians, and wounded insurgents in the hospitals. Many of the wounded were murdered: For example, in the hospital at Długa Street, 430 patients were killed.[243] Zofia Krauze, a doctor in this institution, remembered the Germans coming in:

> Early in the morning, after dressing all the wounded, we finally sat down on a blanket to rest. There was no shooting, no bombs fell, no "cows" shook the ground. We could doze. . . . Sudden screaming in the yard: "*Heraus! Heraus!*," and gunshots from a rifle. Somebody went out to look and returned, saying:
>
> "It's the Germans; they're making us all go outside. '*Schneller heraus!*' . . . Line up in fours!" We lined up with my husband, holding hands. Quite a lot of people from all the hospital cellars assembled. We had marched into the middle of the yard when behind us there came the explosions of grenades thrown into the cellars of the left wing, which housed the heavily wounded. They were all wiped out, including the boys operated on that night.
>
> We walked, driven through the ruined, nonexistent city. We passed the demolished Sigismund's Column and a Christ [statue] lying next to the rubble of the Holy Cross Church; we could not believe and did not know why we were alive, why we had not been shot as well. They started robbing us, beggars, of the watches and rings remaining on our hands. . . .
>
> We were led to a church in Wola, and there the men were separated from the women. First the men and then the women were driven into the unknown. . . . That was the worst, what we had feared the most: separation.[244]

Stefania Krosnowska, a paramedic, remembered this moment similarly:

> In the yard I met the SS unit coming in. They turn to me in Polish:

"Where are the wounded Polish bandits lying?"

"They were taken away within the last three days by the army."

. . .

After three hours the decision is made that the hospital will still operate for our wounded and those who are in the houses. Soon the Germans rush in again.

"All nurses upstairs! *Schnell! Raus!*"

We go, convinced that they are calling us for a briefing.

"The lightly wounded can come out too!"

We understand. We want to go back to save as many wounded as possible. Unfortunately, the Germans drive us out into the yard; a dozen people come out after us . . . The rest? We hear crazy bursts of pistols underground, and when having been led out into Podwale Street we look back at the hospital, we see the building in flames.[245]

The staff of Army Group Center reported that around thirty-five thousand civilians, including eight thousand to nine thousand men, were removed from the Old Town.[246] A September 2 report of the 9th Army states,

> Today in Warsaw in the north encirclement, under constant barrage of the infantry and assault sappers, the Polish resistance broke after three weeks. The whole area north of Adolf Hitler [Piłsudski] Square is now in our hands.[247]

According to von dem Bach's reports, his own losses during the assault on the Old Town were 150 people per day. This is very high, especially given that when the fighting for the Old Town started on August 12, both sides numbered seven thousand to eight thousand each. These numbers may be compared to the first twenty days of fighting in Normandy, where the Germans lost forty-three thousand soldiers (i.e., slightly over two thousand per day).[248] On average, on each day of the fighting for the Old Town, the German side lost one company. The greatest losses were in Dirlewanger's unit.[249]

The fall of the Old Town opened the route through Wybrzeże Gdańskie Street and Zamkowy Square to Kierbedź Bridge to the Germans. After taking the Old Town, they were ensured a free, unimpeded, and secure connection between the reserves and frontline units.[250]

Czerniaków and Powiśle

Walter Fentzahn, who returned under Dirlewanger's command from the hospital in late August or early September, testified that the train carrying soldiers stopped in the western railway station. From the station, a paramedic brought him to Dirlewanger's unit.[251] At the start of September, the staff headquarters of SS-Sturmbrigade Dirlewanger was located in the police district at Szuch Avenue.[252] Fentzahn mentioned that he did not meet most of his companions after coming to Warsaw because they were either in action or lying wounded in the hospital.[253]

After the fall of the Old Town in the north and Sadyba Czerniaków[254] in the south on September 2, von dem Bach sent his forces to Powiśle (the area between Poniatowski and Kierbedź Bridges). Von dem Bach's plan envisaged enveloping the area affected by fighting from two sides, north and south, along the Vistula, in order to cut the insurgents off from the river.[255] The decision to attack Powiśle was the result of Gen. (Generalleutnant) Helmut Staedtke's report: "Frontline situation: Russky is taking everything before Praga. Political, operational, and tactical issue. Therefore, Vistula bank to be taken fast."[256]

On September 4–5, Powiśle was subjected to intensive air raids and artillery fire. After this prelude, Dirlewanger's and Schmidt's units attacked toward the south while Rohr's group set off from the south through Sadyba and lower Mokotów. The fighting took place in the region around the cannery and the electric plant.[257] A report by the 9th Army of September 4 informed that Schmidt's and Dirlewanger's assault groups, progressing from the area east of Piłsudski Square and "overcoming extremely fierce resistance by the enemy," had captured the Vistula bank up to Poniatowski Bridge, including the new building located between Karolkowa and Gęsta Streets. Maj. Reck's assault group, meanwhile, blocked Śródmieście in the north.[258]

Initially, the operations in Powiśle brought only slight progress. Von dem Bach himself wrote that the attack on Powiśle "is unfortunately not progressing well." He also stated, "The Poles are fighting like heroes. Time is pressing because of the Bolsheviks, but it cannot be hurried."[259] Moreover, the report of September 4 turned out to be exaggerated. In reality, Dirlewanger's and Schmidt's offensive had reached only

> the block between Czacki and Traugutt Streets, the church west of Oboźna Street [Holy Cross Church], the high-rise building south of Oboźna Street [National Mutual Insurance Institution building at Kopernik Street], [and] Leszczyńska Street.[260]

Nevertheless, within three days they managed to capture all of Powiśle, which fell on September 7. Leszek Łacheta, who was present there on September 6, described the final combat as follows:

> On the sixth, artillery and mortars pounded Tamka Street since dawn; Stuka bombers flew in waves and dropped bombs. A moment of silence after yet another raid, and grenades explode in cellars. Screams of the wounded and fire: Germans above us. After one of the older men, a sailor shipping on the Vistula, calls out saying that there are only women, children, and old men in the cellar, the Germans order us to come out. . . . The Germans set the ground floor on fire with grenades. . . . They march us some way down toward the Vistula and immediately turn into Topiel Street, which is on fire on both sides. Rows of SS men, sleeves rolled up, are looting, beating, shooting. . . . We hear a tank rolling up, which stops behind us. A stir among the Germans; the loud chatter gives the impression of a quarrel; I can't catch even single words . . . this lasts a very long time, until finally the tank rolls away. We are in Browarna Street . . . there are a lot of wounded and burned. . . . SS men move among us; they continue to loot and catch insurgents, who are mostly wounded and dressed in gray drill from the Electric Plant.[261]

All reports about the capture of Warsaw contained similar information:

> After very heavy combat, in which both sides suffered large losses, all Powiśle was captured, delimited from the east by the Vistula, from the west by Krakowskie Przedmieście and Nowy Świat Streets, from the south by Jerozolimskie Avenue. From 11:00 until dark, columns of prisoners and civilians leave the city.[262]

The doctor Jerzy Rowiński, who on August 2 organized a hospital in the orphanage run by the Ursuline sisters at Tamka Street 30, described the events of September 6 and the fall of Powiśle as follows:

> On September 6, 1944, around 14:00, the Germans entered Tamka and a patrol that burst into the hospital wanted to shoot us all as bandits, but when I mentioned I had a heavily wounded German soldier in my care, taken captive by the insurgents, after talking to

> him and his statement that he had been treated well and cared for by the doctor and personnel, the German desisted from this intention. . . . The Germans forced inhabitants out of houses and led them to an assembly point in Wola, burned the houses down with flamethrowers after looting them, and we were left alone for twenty-five days until we left Warsaw; in Tamka among the burned-out buildings and unsure what tomorrow would bring, as the Germans kept bursting in, their faces far from friendly, we had to explain ourselves to each one, appease him. . . . And so, one day five German soldiers came, former prisoners of the Mauthausen and Sachsenhausen camps, who after looking at the wounded not only did not shoot us but after a few hours brought us loaves of bread, tinned meat, and cigarettes. It turns out that they were from Dirlewanger's units, which elsewhere brutally murdered Poles.[263]

After Powiśle was taken, part of the attacking Kampfgruppe Reinefarth separated. Schmidt's group stayed in Powiśle, extending the front on the Vistula from Wybrzeże Gdańskie Street through Wybrzeże Kościuszkowskie Street to Poniatowski Bridge. The main forces of Dirlewanger's group, meanwhile, attacked in the direction of Nowy Świat and Napoleon Square.[264] This led to bitter fighting. The soldiers reached the Prudential building at Warecka Street. Combat ensued also in the area of Nowogrodzka Street and along Marszałkowska Street.[265]

From September 2 to 9, the German side was positioned as follows: Gen. Reinefarth's combat group operated in the north. Next, the battle line along Książęca Street–3 Maja Avenue–the Poniatowski Bridge viaduct up to the Vistula was manned by Dirlewanger's troops, organized into seven replenished battalions:

2 battalions of the Dirlewanger Regiment with a heavy-infantry company

2 battalions of the Azerbaijan Regiment

2 battalions of the East Muslim Regiment

Walter Gendarmerie Battalion

5 20 mm antiaircraft guns

Tracked assault gun unit

2 companies of tanks

This was around 2,500 people in total.[266]

From the south, units subordinate to Gen. Rohr attacked. The light cavalry barracks–Sobieski Park–Czerniakowska Street battle line was assailed by Col. Schaper's troops. From the west, the offensive was conducted by a *Schutzpolizei* group under Lt. Col. Wilhelm Rodewald, supported by several tanks (axis: Na Skarpie Avenue–Sejm buildings–Książęca Street). It was supported by assault airplanes, pneumatic trench mortar batteries, and a 600 mm mortar. The size of these forces may be estimated at around five thousand people.[267] The fighting in Czerniaków took place in the area of the riverside hostel in Port Czerniakowski on the Vistula, among other locations.[268]

At the same time, the local population and those suspected of helping the insurgents were still being shot in Warsaw. In the 1960s, Fentzahn testified that in September he worked in Dirlewanger's staff quarters at Szuch Avenue and could see the playing court from his window. In this court, Polish civilians were shot, and afterward their bodies were set on fire.[269] He described:

> I went to this sports court once. . . . On the court I stood practically unnoticed by the hedge. With my own eyes, I saw the following. On the side where the fire barrier was located, graves sized 5 times 3 m had been dug. . . . From the edge of the graves there ran a board walkway. . . . In the corners of the court, SD outposts stood. . . . On the left sleeve were sewn black diamonds, on which the letters SD were embroidered in silver. . . . Groups of thirty Poles were led onto the court. These were not only men but also women and children. They all had to undress completely. Next they had to go onto the walkway one by one. They lay down on an iron beam and were killed with a shot to the neck. . . . When the piles of dead Poles lying on the beams reached a given height, the bodies were doused with petrol or another flammable substance and set on fire, causing massive clouds of smoke. Next, the bodies were tipped into the graves with rods.

Fentzahn indicated that he observed the mass executions for about half an hour, and in that time over two hundred people were killed.[270]

Between September 11 and 23, Dirlewanger's subordinates fought further heavy battles in Upper Czerniaków, attacking from the north. The main offensive was directed along Czerniakowska (Hafenstrasse) and Solec (Salzstrasse) Streets.[271] Karl Vieregge testified that in the neighborhood of Wilanowska and Fabryczna Streets, the clashes lasted a very long time. In this period, the Russians were concentrating their forces on the east bank of the Vistula, near the Praga beachhead. Viktor Zerfaß stated that the combat in Warsaw was extremely difficult: "The unpleasant thing about this fighting was that we never saw the opponents' faces; we never knew where the shots would come from."[272]

As Adalbert Daschner remembered, every tenement building had to be fought for:

> The commanders informed us that partisans were staying in specified houses and firing on us from those buildings. . . . When we approached the houses, we threw grenades and fire bottles into the cellars through holes. We usually heard the screams of women and children, who were forced by the partisans to remain with them to make fighting harder for us. When we entered those houses, it turned out that the insurgents had had time to leave the building, thanks to special passages in the cellars connecting those houses.[273]

In Czerniaków, units of Radosław Group (around five hundred people) fought against the Germans, and for uprising conditions they were comparatively well armed. They were supported by a group commanded by Maj. Zygmunt Netzer "Kryska" (around six hundred people), far more badly armed.[274]

During the clashes in Czerniaków, von dem Bach motioned for Reinefarth to be decorated with the Knight's Cross of the Iron Cross with Oak Leaves. Despite mutual hostility, on September 10, Reinefarth petitioned for Dirlewanger to be awarded the Knight's Cross.

Also on September 10, in the Praga District the Russians commenced the battle for the beachhead. After several days, Praga and the right bank of the Vistula were in Russian hands. The Germans blew up the bridges, destroying the roads connecting the banks.

Kedyw soldier Stanisław Likiernik "Stach" remembered the encounter with Dirlewanger's soldiers in Czerniaków thus. Wounded, he was staying in the cellar of the hospital at Wilanowska Street 14, where he lay together with two other insurgents who were unfit for combat. They were accompanied by two paramedics: Irka Minkiewicz and a girl whose name is unknown. After the insurgent units left, he ordered his companions to take off and hide everything "that resembled German uniforms, because death is certain if they see it." After several hours the Germans came in. Everybody who was able to move was to go outside.

A simultaneous thump of steel-capped boots, shots, screams of the wounded being finished off in the room next door. Irka and the other paramedic did not come out despite a formal order. Some soldier saw them, stood in the doorway, signaled for the girls not to move, and told the others, "*Schön fertig*," already done. I found out after the war from Irka that she knew his name: Freitag.

After some time, the next German soldiers came into their cellar:

He saw me first. . . . He took a revolver out of its holster and pointed to my head to finish me off. But before he pulled the trigger, he saw the other wounded man. . . . It was lucky for me that this was a man with bad, for a German, organizational skills. Before he finished the first job (with me), he was distracted by the next task: the other wounded. The third of us, much older and speaking excellent German, said in response to the shout of *Zweite Bandit*, "But no, we are all civilians."

A cow speaking in a human tongue would not have made a greater impression on the feldfebel than this sentence did. "You are German?" "No, but I speak German." "Your documents." Mr. Burhardt had his; we other two did not have any. "Your name is German." Here commenced a drawing-room conversation on the origins of the Burhardt family, their arrival in Poland, etc.

The feldfebel and other soldiers would come visit us. It turned out they were a *Strafkompanie*; that is, a penal company composed of the politically suspect or those convicted of serious crimes.

My "would-be murderer" told me in French (this was our only common tongue, though we spoke it badly) that his parents had a hotel in the Rhineland. He was hiding the fact that he was fighting in Warsaw from them. He knew French better than I did, because he lived right on the French border. He had been sent to the penal company for slapping his lieutenant's face in Normandy. His French fiancée had cheated on him with that officer. As a punishment, he was sent to the Russian front and now to Warsaw.

Other soldiers came too. One of them, a Silesian, spoke Polish and was called Romanowski. This one, it seems, was negatively perceived as politically "unreliable."

My face, unshaven for several days, was starting to become bearded. . . . I was shaved [by a German soldier] and he almost cried over me because the razor was blunt and he hurt me. . . .

> That same man had been finishing off the wounded the day before upon the order of the penal company's chief, a gendarmerie officer.
>
> Another German left several hand grenades behind in our cellar, which we politely returned to him. A third one sat down on my pallet, slightly drunk, and said in German, "It's a pity I'm not Polish, because I would have been a partisan too." Naturally, I protested: I was a civilian and not a partisan at all. He just patted my arm and left.[275]

After the fighting of September 13, the Germans ultimately lost Praga. Warsaw thus found itself on the front line, and Korpsgruppe von dem Bach was tasked with defending the left bank of the Vistula. The defense of its bank between Żoliborz and Siekierki was assigned to the provisionally formed Regiment Nöthe. It was composed of units taken from the assault groups of Col. Schmidt, Maj. Reck, and Dirlewanger.[276] The remaining forces continued their assault on Powiśle Czerniakowskie under von dem Bach. The attack set off from the north, between Nowy Świat Street and the Vistula. It reached Książęca and Ludna Streets, and on the left wing, along the Vistula bank, also Wilanowska Street.[277]

On September 14, the offensive against Powiśle Czerniakowskie continued. Reinefarth's forces attacking from the north came into contact with Gen. Rohr's, which hit from the south, and occupied the area around the junction of Książęca and Rozbrat Streets. Lieut. Col. Radosław's units put up heavy resistance, and so Dirlewanger's group captured only one block between Okrąg Street and Ludna Street, and the church at Solec Street.[278]

At dawn on September 17, Gen. Rohr's combat group, strengthened by detachments from the 146th Panzer Grenadier Regiment, and SS-Sturmbrigade Dirlewanger reprised their attacks on Powiśle Czerniakowskie. At 9:35, Maj. Voekel reported to the chief of staff of the 9th Army: "In the southern encirclement, only smaller blocks and the undeveloped factory area remain outside our hands."[279] That day, Dirlewanger's units captured the factory areas south of Wilanowska Street.[280]

On September 18, the group commanded by Dirlewanger was strengthened to include the 2nd and 3rd Battalions of the 34th Schutzpolizei Regiment, numbering over a thousand people, and also other smaller units.[281] On that day, Rohr's combat group managed, "after heavy fighting bought with heavy losses, to capture the fortified" factory area located east of Idzikowski Street. Meanwhile, SS-Sturmbrigade Dirlewanger fought in the neighborhood of the block between Okrąg and Wilanowska Streets and due to "the enemy's fierce resistance" reported "only insignificant progress."[282]

Oskar Dirlewanger's family home at 16 Kesselwasen St. The house ("Gräßle Haus") is located on the Wehrneckar canal and can be accessed by crossing a bridge. The Dirlewanger family occupied one floor. *Soraya Kuklińska*

Starting in the 1910–11 school year, Dirlewanger attended the Schelztor-Oberrealschule in Berliner Straße. *Soraya Kuklińska*

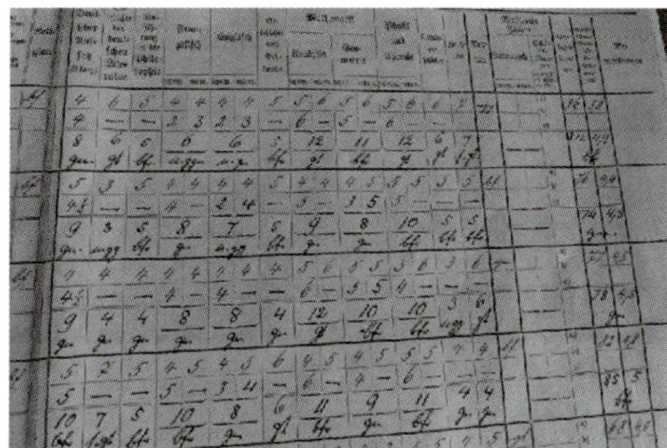

List of grades on the 1913 high school diploma. *Rolf Laschet*

Oskar Dirlewanger together with the crew of the armored train he commanded (Panzerzug Dirlewanger), 1920s. Dirlewanger stands sixth from the left. *D027-3, "Materialsammlung zur Geschichte des Bahnschutzes in Württemberg von Reichsbahnoberinspektor Rudolf Behn," Stadtarchiv Heilbronn*

Panzerzug Dirlewanger. Dirlewanger is seated at top (*second from left*).

Panzerzug Dirlewanger. Dirlewanger sits in the middle.

Der Württembergischen Bahnschutztruppe

[Schutzzug „Uhland"]

zum ehrenden Andenken

für die Errettung des Bahnhofs Sangerhausen vor dem Kommunistenüberfall in dem Gefecht am 26. März 1921.

Führer: Gaugenmaier, b/Stab: Hofmann, Knoll Alois.

Zug Plochingen:
Bauerle,
Schienle,
Siegler,
Schür,
Weißinger,
Reiger,
Brücker,
Mangold, verw.
Wenzelburger,
Lütze,
Eitel,
Grupp,
Zacher
Weiß,
Narr,
Linder,
Held,
Volz,
Weitl,
Nussbaum,
Zapp,
Esslinger, W.
Esslinger, E.
Bauer, W.
Bauer, K.

Lokpersonal:
Müller, gefallen,
Leirer, schw. verw.
Aupperle, verw.
Steffan, verw.
Guter, schw. verw.
Veil, verw.
Kohler, verw.
Geiselmann,
Dölfel.

Sanitätspersonal:
Martini,
Klump,
Junk.

Zug Aulendorf:
Strobel,
Jäck,
Bohner, Franz.
Bohner, Eug.
Lämmle,
Friedmann,
Amendinger,
Weber,
Bäder,
Kaiser,
Briechle.
Wirth,
Wöllhaf, verw.
Schmid, Jos.
Seyfried,
Bossenmaier,
Habnitt,
Buck,
Gaßner,
Stotz,
Huber,
Bauknecht,
Diem,
Vogel,
Wolfgang,
Spieß,
Schleweck,
Heinzelmann,
Müller, X.
Bettenmann,
Baur, A.
Kiene,
Dilper,
Fuß,
Wäschle,
Fürst.

Küche:
Reuter, H.

Zug Sigmaringen:
Seespeck,
Westhauser I,
Westhauser II.
Beck,
Zettel, schw. verw.
Heppeler,
Fränkel, K.
Fränkel, A.
Küchenhoff,
Eisemann,
Moll,
Saupp,
Briehl,
Hörter,
Mors,
Fröhlich,
Niederer,
Späth,
Heinemann,
Wahr,
Leiprecht,
Lutz,
Eberhard,
Keßler,
Bösch,
Schmid, F.
Schönle,
Kuner,
Schlarbaum,
Maier, C.
Bolter,
Fiederer,
Hund,
Bauer, A.
Luibrand,
Geiger, U.
Hummel,
Hugger.

Zug Dirlewanger, verw.:
Lundie, schw. verw.
Pfeiffer,
Wulz,
Gänzle,
Zeller,
Köppritz,
Knoll, A.
Hutzenlaub, verw.
Wüllnitz,
Ehlers,
Schenk,
Mühlbeyer, verw.
de Thierry,
Ruppmann,
Hellge,
Füßenhäuser,
Mickeler,
Neumeister,
Bauer,
Dirlewanger II,
Hammer,
Straßburg, schw. verw.
Schmitt,
Zarges,
Schiele,
Gamer, schw. verw.
Bauer, J.
Dausch,
Aißlinger,
Combe,
Locher, schw. verw.
Rhein, verw.
Knauß, verw.
Reuscher,
Weber,
Römmler,
Gißer, schw. verw.
von Kapff,
Hohnecker.

Bahnhof Sangerhausen.

Bauer,
Dirlewanger II,
Hammer,
Straßburg, schw. verw.
Schmitt,
Zarges,
Schiele,
Gamer, schw. verw.

A roster of troops taking part in the battles against the Communists commanded by Max Hölz on March 26, 1921, in Sangerhausen. Dirlewanger's platoon is listed in the first column at right. Visible entry Dirlewanger II; Oskar took part in the fighting together with his brother, Paul.

While Dirlewanger was working at the labor office, he lived in Heilbronn on Kaiserstraße 50 in the Fleischmann (photographer) house. It was an exclusive townhouse on Heilbronn's main street. *Public domain*

Kaiserstraβe today. *Soraya Kuklińska*

31/5/34

Heilbronner S

Pg. Dirlewanger zum Ehrenbürger der Stadt Sangerhausen ernannt

Heute erinnert man sich wohl in weiten Kreis[illegible] nicht mehr der Zeiten, in denen rote Ban[illegible] und Kommunisten in unserem Lande hausten.

So hatte am Ostersamstag des Jahres 1921 der Kommunistenführer Max Hölz die Diktatur des Proletariats in Sangerhausen errichtet. Diese Diktatur bestand zunächst einmal im Plündern sämtlicher öffentlichen Kassen und der Verhängung des Standrechts, der Gefangennahme und Verschleppung zahlreicher Geiseln. Die gesamte Sangerhauser Bürgerschaft wurde unter Todesandrohung zur Ablieferung sämtlicher Waffen, Motorfahrzeuge und Fahrräder aufgefordert. Im Falle eines Widerstandes der Polizei wurde angedroht, die Stadt anzuzünden.

Die damalige Regierung, die diesen Banditen, wie allgemein bekannt, nahezu wehrlos gegenüberstand, erinnerte sich in solchen Fällen gerne alter, verdienter Frontoffiziere und erprobter Kämpfer. So wurde in jenen Tagen der Panzerzug Dirlewanger, der nebe[illegible] bemerkt die erste militärische Formati[illegible] war, die bereits 1921 die Hakenkreuzflagge führte, aufgefordert, nach Sangerhausen zu fahren.

Dirlewanger bereitete auch der „Diktatur des Proletariats" ein rasches Ende. Nach hartnäckigen, schweren Kämpfen mit Handgranaten und Maschinengewehren, bei denen Dirlewanger selbst verwundet wurde, die bis nachts um 2 Uhr dauerten und mit der größten Erbitterung geführt wurden, war es dem Panzerzug Dirlewanger gelungen, die Hölz-Banditen in die Flucht zu schlagen. Dabei wurden von 42 Kameraden 22 verwundet und einer getötet.

Diese einzigartige Tat, die den Einsatz der ganzen Person, jedes einzelnen forderte, namentlich unter den damaligen Verhältnissen fast sicher auch die Vernichtung der Existenz der Betreffenden bedeutete, hat den Rat der Stadt Sangerhausen veranlaßt, nunmehr den Führer des Panzerzuges, Pg. Oberleutnant a. D. Dirlewanger, mit Zustimmung des preußischen Ministerpräsidenten zum Ehrenbürger zu ernennen.

Nur kurz sei noch erwähnt, daß, wie so oft im Leben, wie es namentlich damals allen Kämpfern für ihr Vaterland ergangen ist, auch Dirlewanger seine Tat schlecht gelohnt wurde. Kurz nach seiner Rückkehr von Sangerhausen wurde er, der im Weltkrieg dreimal und auch in Sangerhausen verwundet wurde, wegen Vergehens gegen das Entwaffnungsgesetz ins Amtsgefängnis in Mosbach (Baden) eingesperrt. Aber derartige Strafen konnten Dirlewanger von seinen Plänen und seinem festen Willen, an der Befreiung des Vaterlandes zu arbeiten, nicht abbringen. Zwei Tage nach seiner Entlassung aus dem Gefängnis eilte er wieder nach Oberschlesie[illegible] um dort als Freikorpskämpfer seiner Sc[illegible]enpflicht zu genügen.

Zweifellos hat sich Pg. Dirlewanger bleibende Verdienste um die nachrevolutionäre Geschichte Württembergs erworben. Ueberall, wo Kommunisten-Unruhen auftauchten, erschien der Panzerzug Dirlewanger und bekämpfte diese mit der Waffe in der Hand und schlug sie nieder.

Bis zum Jahre 1933 tat Dirlewanger späterhin Dienste als einfacher SA.-Mann in den Reihen der braunen Armee Adolf Hitlers.

Wir beglückwünschen unseren Parteigenossen zu der Ernennung zum Ehrenbürger und hoffen, daß er im alten Geist lange in unseren Reihen seine Dienste tun wird. Gerade solche Männer, die, wenn es gilt, das Leben und die eigene Existenz aufs Spiel setzen, brauchen wir, um das große Ziel unseres Führers zu verwirklichen.

A press release announcing that Dirlewanger has been named an honorary citizen of the city of Sangerhausen. *Bundesarchiv Berlin, R/9361/III*

Oskar Dirlewanger, ca. 1920s–'30s. SS personal folder (*Personalnachweis*). *Bundesarchiv Berlin, R/9361/III*

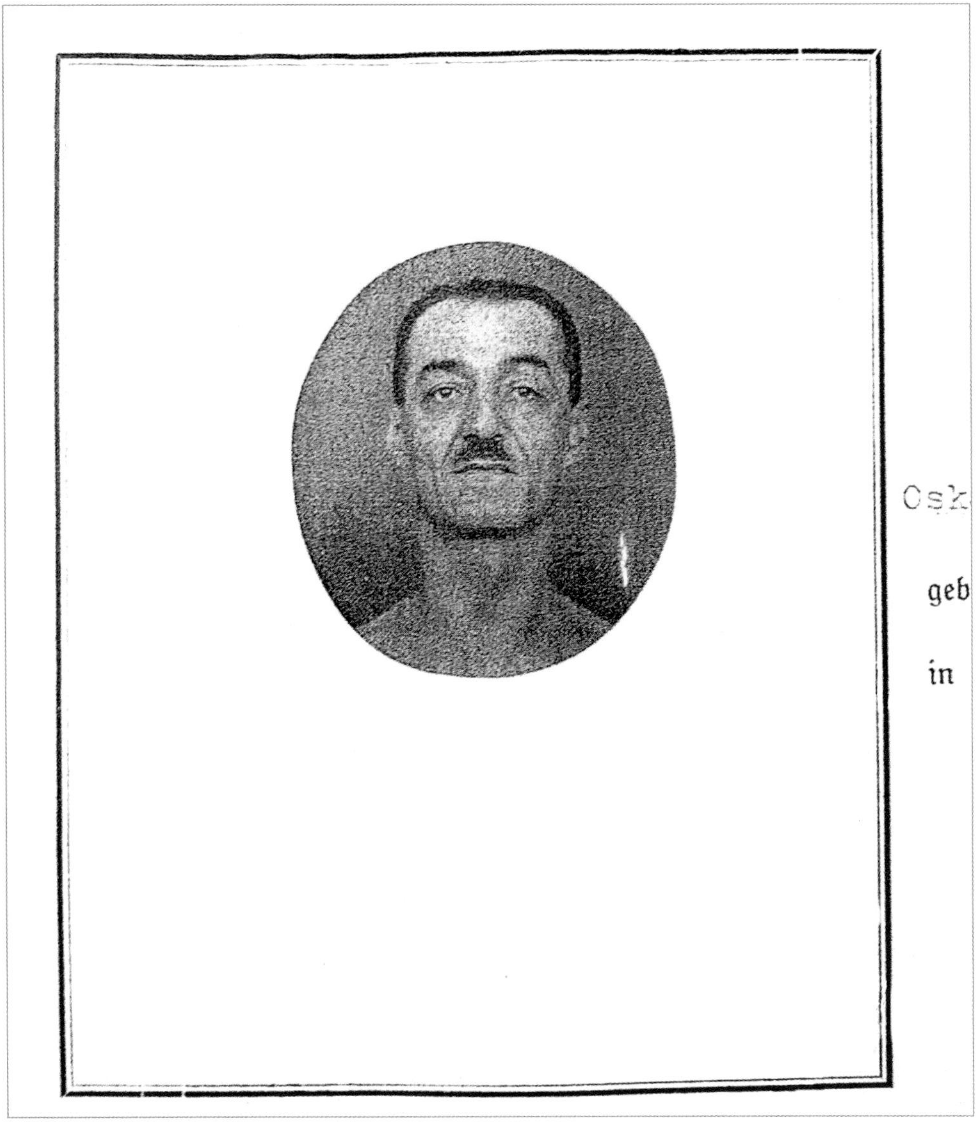

Photo from Ludwigsburg prison or Welzheim concentration camp. *Staatsarchiv Ludwigsburg*

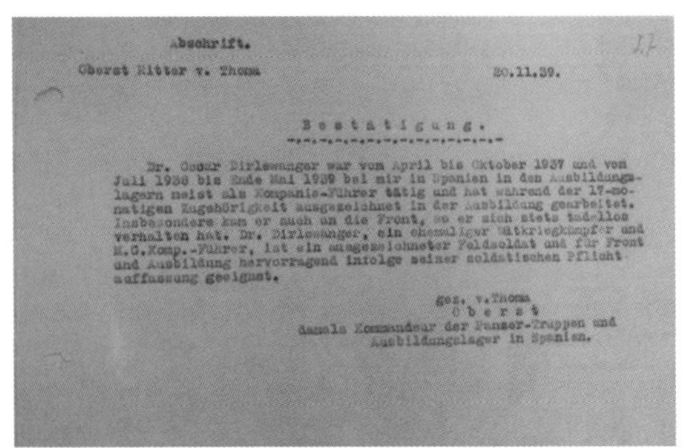

Abschrift.

Oberst Ritter v. Thoma 20.11.39.

B e s t ä t i g u n g .

Dr. Oscar Dirlewanger war vom April bis Oktober 1937 und vom Juli 1938 bis Ende Mai 1939 bei mir in Spanien in den Ausbildungslagern meist als Kompanie-Führer tätig und hat während der 17-monatigen Zugehörigkeit ausgezeichnet in der Ausbildung gearbeitet. Insbesondere kam er auch an die Front, wo er sich stets tadellos verhalten hat. Dr. Dirlewanger, ein ehemaliger Weltkriegkämpfer und M.G.Komp.-Führer, ist ein ausgezeichneter Feldsoldat und für Front und Ausbildung hervorragend infolge seiner soldatischen Pflicht auffassung geeignet.

gez. v.Thoma
O b e r s t
damals Kommandeur der Panzer-Truppen und Ausbildungslager in Spanien.

Information written by Ritter von Thoma about Dirlewanger's assignments during the Spanish Civil War. *Bundesarchiv Berlin, R/9361/III*

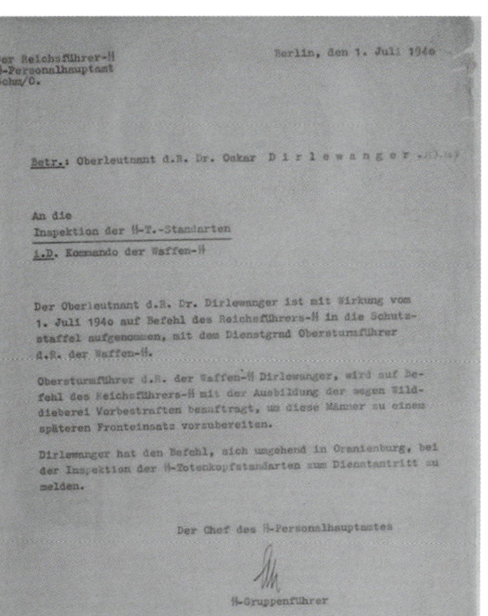

Der Reichsführer-ᛋᛋ
ᛋᛋ-Personalhauptamt
Schm/C.

Berlin, den 1. Juli 194o

<u>Betr.:</u> Oberleutnant d.R. Dr. Oskar D i r l e w a n g e r

An die
<u>Inspektion der ᛋᛋ-T.-Standarten</u>
<u>i.D</u>. Kommando der Waffen-ᛋᛋ

Der Oberleutnant d.R. Dr. Dirlewanger ist mit Wirkung vom 1. Juli 194o auf Befehl des Reichsführers-ᛋᛋ in die Schutzstaffel aufgenommen, mit dem Dienstgrad Obersturmführer d.R. der Waffen-ᛋᛋ.

Obersturmführer d.R. der Waffen-ᛋᛋ Dirlewanger, wird auf Befehl des Reichsführers-ᛋᛋ mit der Ausbildung der wegen Wilddieberei Vorbestraften beauftragt, um diese Männer zu einem späteren Fronteinsatz vorzubereiten.

Dirlewanger hat den Befehl, sich umgehend in Oranienburg, bei der Inspektion der ᛋᛋ-Totenkopfstandarten zum Dienstantritt zu melden.

Der Chef des ᛋᛋ-Personalhauptamtes

ᛋᛋ-Gruppenführer

Himmler's order on training poachers to fight at the front, Berlin, July 1,1940. *Bundesarchiv Berlin, R/9361/III*

The main gate of the Sachsenhausen camp and the roll call square. *Soraya Kuklińska*

Sachsenhausen concentration camp. The square currently outside the camp is visible. According to descriptions and accounts of Dirlewanger soldiers, military training was conducted here in 1940.

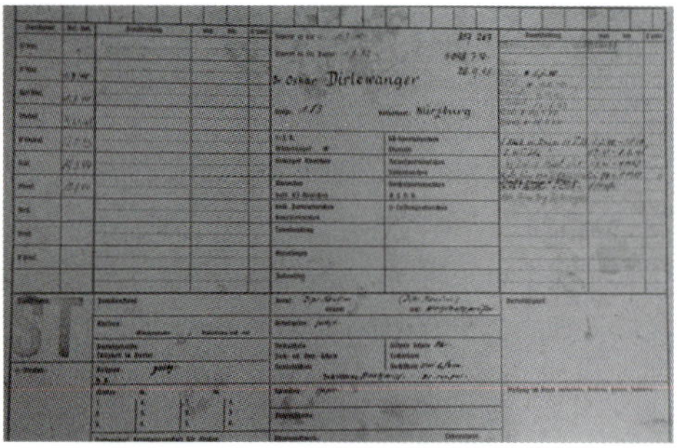

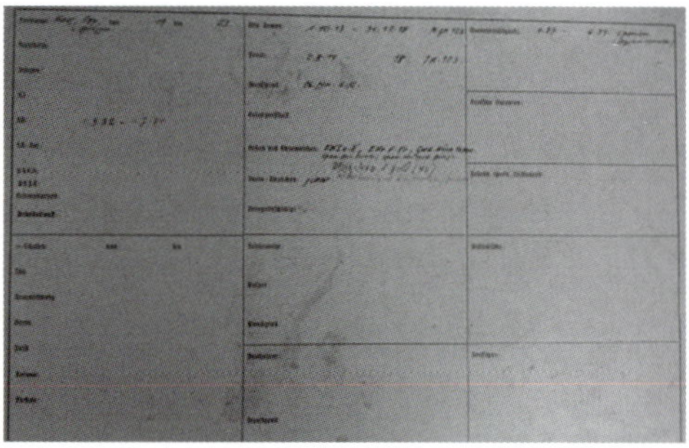

An excerpt from the SS personal file of Oskar Dirlewanger. *Bundesarchiv Berlin, R/9361/III*

In Lublin they were stationed at 18 "Szopen" Street, in the "old house." It was a large, four-story tenement house, in which there were six to eight apartments. In the courtyard there was a kitchen and a canteen. The tenement also had a coal cellar. Its current appearance is shown here. *Soraya Kuklińska*

Oskar Dirlewanger (*left*) with his staff near his quarters in Lohojsk (Tyszkiewicz Palace). Probably 1943. Fourth from the left stands Heinz Feiertag. *Staatsarchiv Ludwigsburg EL 317 III, 142, p. 17*

Soldiers from the "Miotła" Battalion after going through the canals from the Old Town to Warecka Street (Śródmieście). *From left*: Tadeusz Rajszczak "Maszynka," Kazimierz Gabara "Łuk," and Mieczysław (Ryszard) Lach "Pestka." *Photo by Jerzy Tomaszewski, public domain*

Dirlewanger stands at right, ca. 1943. *Douglas E. Nash Sr.*

Oskar Dirlewanger (links) 1943 in einer "Kampfpause" in Belorußland

Dirlewanger during a break in antipartisan fighting in Belarus, 1943. *H. P. Klausch,* Antifaschisten in SS-Uniform*, Bremen 1993 (Edition Temmen)*

Dirlewanger soldiers during fighting in Belarus. In the top photo, they are dressed in SS camouflage jackets, and their caps and sniper masks are made of Wehrmacht camouflage material. The weapon is a pepesha. In the bottom photo is a subordinate of Dirlewanger, probably during operations in Belarus. He is dressed in SS camouflage and mask, is additionally camouflaged with branches, and is armed with an MP40.
Public domain

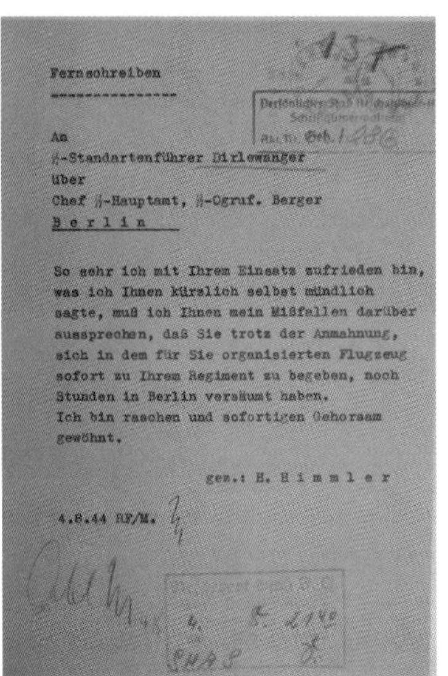

Fernschreiben

An
ϟϟ-Standartenführer Dirlewanger
über
Chef ϟϟ-Hauptamt, ϟϟ-Ogruf. Berger
B e r l i n

So sehr ich mit Ihrem Einsatz zufrieden bin, was ich Ihnen kürzlich selbst mündlich sagte, muß ich Ihnen mein Mißfallen darüber aussprechen, daß Sie trotz der Anmahnung, sich in dem für Sie organisierten Flugzeug sofort zu Ihrem Regiment zu begeben, noch Stunden in Berlin versäumt haben.
Ich bin raschen und sofortigen Gehorsam gewöhnt.

gez.: H. H i m m l e r

4.8.44 RF/M.

Heinrich Himmler's letter of August 4, 1944, ordering Dirlewanger to leave for Warsaw.
Bundesarchiv Berlin, R/9361/III

An assault group from Dirlewanger's unit in the courtyard of one of the tenements in Warsaw. The soldiers are probably going around insurgent positions. In the background, a soldier armed only with a Walther P.38 pistol, which is better than a long gun for fighting inside buildings. A shrine typical of insurgent Warsaw is visible in the background.
Public domain

A break during antipartisan actions in Belarus. *Bundesarchiv Ludwigsburg*

Sturmpanzer IV from Stu.Pz.Kp. 218 z.b.V. on Pankiewicza Street, August 1944, supporting Dirlewanger soldiers. Between the soldiers is a monkey, which was the unit "mascot" and accompanied Dirlewanger and his soldiers since they were stationed in Lublin until the battles in Hungary. *Public domain*

Dirlewanger soldiers at the barricade on Chlodna St., St. Kopf, Dni Powstania. *Warszawa 1984 (PAX)*

Dirlewanger soldiers preparing a flamethrower for action.
Author's collection

SS-Sonderregiment "Dirlewanger," Kampfgruppe "Steinhauer." The photo was taken in a store window on 9 Focha Street (today Molier Street) and is posed. A reflection of the building from Focha 8 can be seen in the windows. The soldier in the foreground has crossed rifles and a grenade on his collar insignia and is armed with an MP40 (Schmeisser). The others are holding Kar 98 (Mauser) rifles. *Coloring: Mikołaj Kaczmarek; public domain (https://ipn.gov.pl/pl/multimedia-1/74983,Fotografie-z-Powstania-Warszawskiego.html)*

Visible are two StuG III assault guns from Pz. Abt. (Fkl) 302 on Theater Square working with Dirlewanger's unit.
Public domain

Soldiers of "Zośka" Battalion after going through the canals from the Old Town to Warecka Street (Sródmieście). Zofia Dąbrowska "Zośka" can be seen in the foreground. Heavily wounded in Czerniaków, she died of her wounds a few days after this photo was taken on September 5, 1944. *On the right*, Waldemar Papiński "Pancerz" (with the submachine gun "Błyskawica"). *Colorization: Mikolaj Kaczmarek; photo: Jerzy Tomaszewski; public domain (https://ipn.gov.pl/pl/multimedia-1/74983,Fotografie-z-Powstania-Warszawskiego.html)*

Soldiers of "Giewont" company of "Zośka" Battalion on August 5, 1944, after capturing Gęsiówka prison during the Warsaw Uprising. At center stands Stanisław Kozicki "Howerla"; on the right, Wacław Cyniak "Orlicz." *Wikipedia/NAC, public domain*

Dirlewanger soldiers on Theater Square. The second photo shows that the fighters were supported by StuG III from 3./Pz.Abt.302. Blanka Palace from Focha Street (today Molier Street) was attacked. Warsaw, August 1944, St. Kopf, Dni Powstania. *Warszawa 1984 (PAX)*

T. Sawicki, Rozkaz zdławić powstanie. *Bellona*

Kampfgruppe "Meyer." The attack on Blanka Palace. The photo shows SS men under fire from the insurgents. *Schremmer. This file is licensed under the Creative Commons Attribution-Share Alike 3.0 Germany license; attribution: Bundesarchiv, Bild 183-J27793 / Schremmer / CC-BY-SA 3.0, https://commons.wikimedia.org/wiki/File:Bundesarchiv_Bild_183-J27793,_Warschauer_Aufstand,_Stra%C3%9Fenk%C3%A4mpfe.jpg*

Ivan Frolov is visible at left. On the right stands Kurt Weisse and Heinz Reinefarth. *Public domain*

Resting soldiers of SS-Sonderbrigade "Dirlewanger" in Czerniakow in September 1944. *Leher. This file is licensed under the Creative Commons Attribution-Share Alike 3.0 Germany license; attribution: Bundesarchiv, Bild 101I-696-0426-21 / Leher / CC-BY-SA 3.0, https://commons.wikimedia.org/wiki/File:Bundesarchiv_Bild_101I-696-0426-21,_Warschauer_Aufstand,_Waffen-SS_bei_Rast.jpg*

Leher. This file is licensed under the Creative Commons Attribution-Share Alike 3.0 Germany license; attribution: Bundesarchiv, Bild 101I-696-0426-25 / Leher / CC-BY-SA 3.0, https://commons.wikimedia.org/wiki/File:Bundesarchiv_Bild_101I-696-0426-25,_Warschauer_Aufstand,_Soldat_beim_Essen.jpg

Sturmgeschütz Ausf. G from Panzer-Abteilung 302 (FKL) sits in front of Brühl Palace. *Public domain*

Kampfgruppe “Steinhauer” marching through Warsaw in August 1944. The 2nd Battalion of the SS-Sonderregiment “Dirlewanger” was commanded by Joseph Steinhauer. The battalion’s strength in Warsaw was about 350 men and was better equipped and uniformed than the 1st Battalion (Kampfgruppe Meyer). Kampfgruppe “Steinhauer” arrived in Warsaw on August 7, 1944. *TVP*

The original caption read as follows: Squad or platoon leader from SS-Sonderregiment Dirlewanger (*third from left*) outside the Brühl Palace, Warsaw, early August 1944. On his left breast pocket he wears the Bandenkampfabzeichen, awarded for repeated engagements against so-called bandits. The StuG III assault gun in the background is most likely from Sturmgeschütz-Ersatz-Abt. 200, which was briefly attached to Kampfgruppe Dirlewanger during this period. *Douglas E. Nash Sr.*

Dirlewanger's subordinates. Both photos show the same officer and soldier with a pitcher. The first photo is at 15 Krakowskie Przedmieście Street, corner of Ossolińskich Street. The commanding officer was decorated with the Iron Cross Second Class and wears a divisional armband on his sleeve—he had previously served in one of the elite SS formations. He is armed with an MP40 and dressed in the new M43 uniform. The 54th photo was taken near the Potocki Palace. The soldier on the right is armed with a "pepesha." *From* Waffen-SS: The Unpublished Photographs, *Verlag Brown Packaging Books Ltd., London, public domain*

Fighting with *Panzerfaust*. *TVP*

Sturmgeschütze schlagen Breschen.

Ein nördlicher Vorort von Warschau: Um jede Häuserecke tobt ein erbitterter Kampf. Schuß um Schuß jagt aus den Sturmgeschützen, dann stoßen die Grenadiere zum Nahkampf vor.

PK-Aufnahme: Kriegsberichter Schlegel

Warschau

A clipping from a German newspaper. *Schlegel, author's collection*

Left and below: Poniatowski Bridge. 88 mm mortar position, St. Kopf, Dni Powstania. *Warszawa 1984 (PAX)*

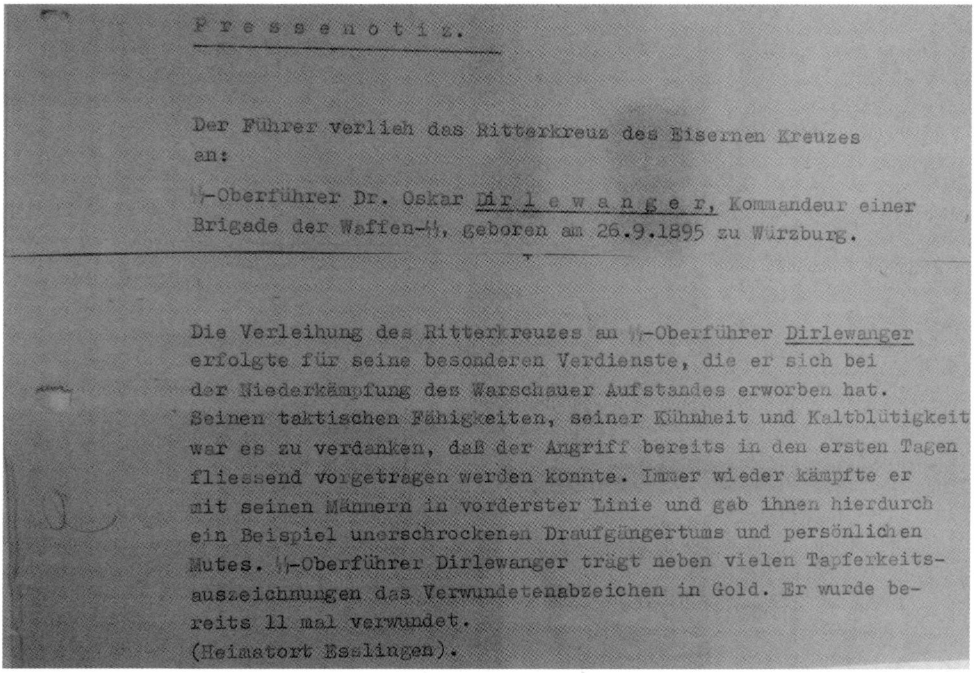

Pressenotiz.

Der Führer verlieh das Ritterkreuz des Eisernen Kreuzes an:

SS-Oberführer Dr. Oskar Dirlewanger, Kommandeur einer Brigade der Waffen-SS, geboren am 26.9.1895 zu Würzburg.

Die Verleihung des Ritterkreuzes an SS-Oberführer Dirlewanger erfolgte für seine besonderen Verdienste, die er sich bei der Niederkämpfung des Warschauer Aufstandes erworben hat. Seinen taktischen Fähigkeiten, seiner Kühnheit und Kaltblütigkeit war es zu verdanken, daß der Angriff bereits in den ersten Tagen fliessend vorgetragen werden konnte. Immer wieder kämpfte er mit seinen Männern in vorderster Linie und gab ihnen hierdurch ein Beispiel unerschrockenen Draufgängertums und persönlichen Mutes. SS-Oberführer Dirlewanger trägt neben vielen Tapferkeitsauszeichnungen das Verwundetenabzeichen in Gold. Er wurde bereits 11 mal verwundet.
(Heimatort Esslingen).

Press release on the awarding of the Knight's Cross of the Iron Cross to Dirlewanger. *Bundesarchiv Berlin, R/9361/III*

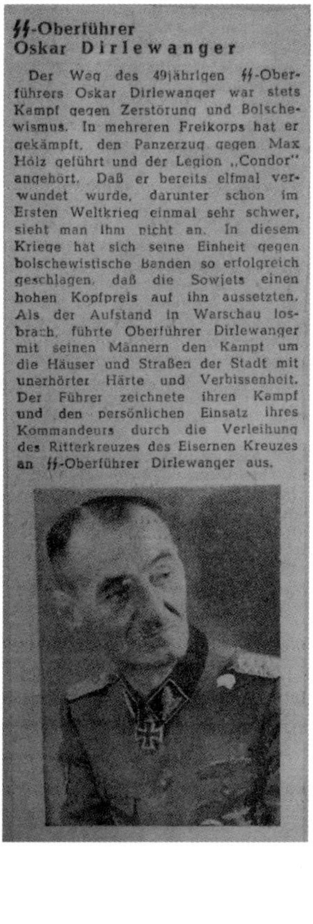

SS-Oberführer Oskar Dirlewanger

Der Weg des 49jährigen SS-Oberführers Oskar Dirlewanger war stets Kampf gegen Zerstörung und Bolschewismus. In mehreren Freikorps hat er gekämpft, den Panzerzug gegen Max Hölz geführt und der Legion „Condor" angehört. Daß er bereits elfmal verwundet wurde, darunter schon im Ersten Weltkrieg einmal sehr schwer, sieht man ihm nicht an. In diesem Kriege hat sich seine Einheit gegen bolschewistische Banden so erfolgreich geschlagen, daß die Sowjets einen hohen Kopfpreis auf ihn aussetzten. Als der Aufstand in Warschau losbrach, führte Oberführer Dirlewanger mit seinen Männern den Kampf um die Häuser und Straßen der Stadt mit unerhörter Härte und Verbissenheit. Der Führer zeichnete ihren Kampf und den persönlichen Einsatz ihres Kommandeurs durch die Verleihung des Ritterkreuzes des Eisernen Kreuzes an SS-Oberführer Dirlewanger aus.

Slovak president Josef Tiso decorates German soldiers who participated in the suppression of the national uprising in Slovakia. *Public domain*

Article from the *Schwarze Korps*, dated November 16, 1944. *Bundesarchiv Berlin, R/9361/III*

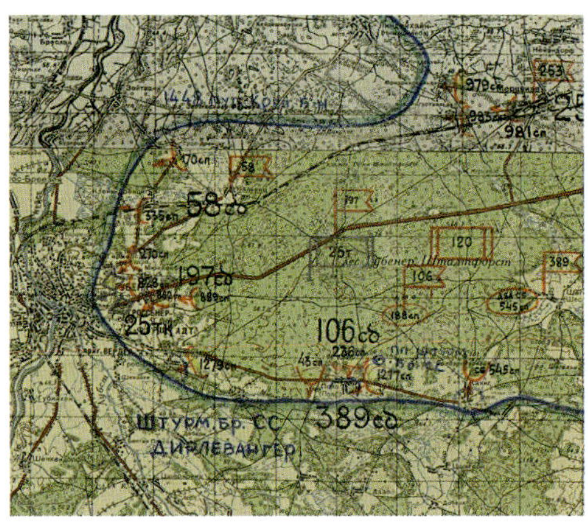

German staff maps depicting the situation on the front during the fighting near Gubin. *Author's collection*

The special collar insignia. On January 26, 1943, new insignia were introduced for the SS-Sonderbataillon "Dirlewanger" by order of Reichsführer-SS Himmler, on which rifles were crossed, and underneath them was a horizontally aligned stick grenade. *Public domain*

Dr. Oskar Dirlewanger, commander of the SS-Sonderkommando "Dirlewanger," as an *SS-Oberführer*. Decorations visible in the photograph: Around his neck is the Knight's Cross of the Iron Cross, awarded for suppressing the Warsaw Uprising; Order of the Slovak Cross, for suppressing the National Uprising in Slovakia; above the left pocket is the Nahkampfspange 1st Class in bronze, awarded for hand-to-hand combat; on the left pocket is the Iron Cross 1st Class, awarded for fighting in World War I, with spangles added for fighting in World War II; on the right sleeve is the V chevron, awarded to those who joined the SS or NSDAP before Hitler came to power (prior to January 30, 1933); on the right pocket is the the German Cross in Gold, awarded in 1943 for antipartisan fighting in Belarus. Below is the Spanish Cross of the Condor Legion for fighting in Spain in 1936–39.
Bundesarchiv Ludwigsburg

Oskar Dirlewanger's grave in the Altshausen cemetery in the 1960s.
BA Ludwigsburg
Gemeindearchiv Altshausen

SS-Untersturmführer Heinz Feiertag. The insignia of the SS Leibstandarte "Adolf Hitler" are visible on the epaulettes. *Yad Vashem*

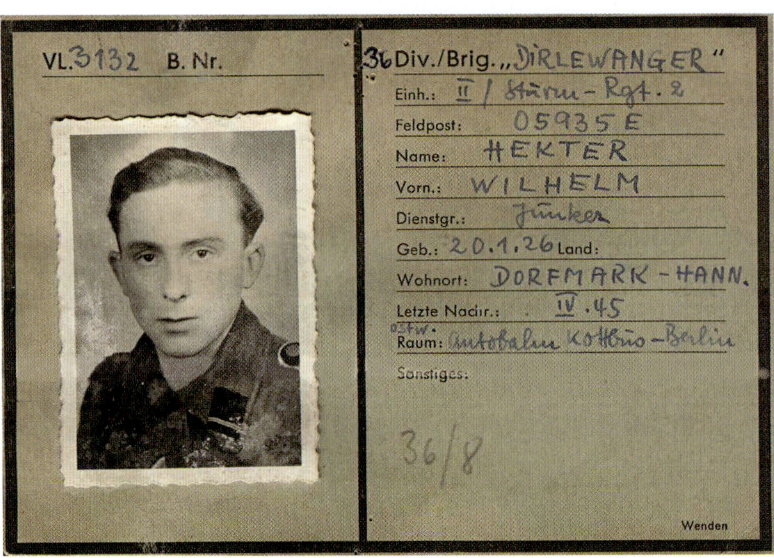

VL. 3132 B. Nr.

36 Div./Brig. „DIRLEWANGER"

Einh.: II / Sturm-Rgt. 2

Feldpost: 05935 E

Name: HEKTER

Vorn.: WILHELM

Dienstgr.: Junker

Geb.: 20.1.26 Land:

Wohnort: DORFMARK-HANN.

Letzte Nachr.: IV.45

ostw. Raum: Autobahn Kottbus–Berlin

Sonstiges:

36/8

Wenden

Dirlewanger's missing subordinate sought after the war by HIAG (Hilfgemeinschaft auf Gegenseitigkeit der Angehörigen der ehemaligen Waffen-SS [Self-Help Association of Former Waffen-SS Members]). Wilhelm Hekter belonged to the 2nd Battalion of the 2nd Assault Regiment of the 36th Waffen-SS Grenadier Division. He was last seen in April 1945 on the Cottbus–Berlin highway. *Public domain*

Zum
Andenken
im Gebete
an den SS
Pz. Gren.

Anton Augustin
Schreiner in Warzenried

welcher am 21.9.1944 bei den Straßenkämpfen
in Warschau im Alter von 35 Jahren
sein Leben opferte.

In weiter Ferne in schwerster Stunde
Gab ich mein junges Leben hin,
Wohl schrecklich war für euch die Kunde
Daß nun auch ich gefallen bin.
O weinet nicht ihr Kinder mein
Lieb' Gattin, laß das Klagen!
Denn Gott wird euer Vater sein,
Und für euch Sorge tragen.
O Kinder bleibt fromm und rein
Mein Weib, o hüt die Kleinen!
Und wenn ihr betet, denket mein
Dann wird uns Gott vereinen.

Memorial death card of a SS-Sonderkommando "Dirlewanger." *Andrzej Skorupski collection*

In Gottes hl. Frieden
ruht fern von seinen Lieben auf
dem Heldenfriedhof zu Warschau
unser lieber Sohn und Bruder

Johann Greiter
Gefreiter in einer Nachr.-Abtlg.
geb. am 17. April 1921 in Apfeltrang
gefallen am 15. September 1944
im Kampfe gegen die Aufständischen in Warschau

Gefallen! Diese Schreckenskunde
Schlug unserm Herzen tiefe Wunde
Er, der so lieb war und so gut,
Hingeben mußte er sein teures Blut.
Du hast uns ja so oft geschrieben,
Macht keine Sorgen euch ihr Lieben,
Ich kehr zurück, auf Wiedersehn.
Doch kann es jetzt nicht mehr geschehn,
Und sollten die Friedensglocken klingen,
Die Sieger jubelnd in die Heimat ziehn,
Dann werden heißer unsere Tränen fließen
Und traurig werden wir zur Seite stehn.

Memorial death card of a SS-Sonderkommando "Dirlewanger"

Kurt Weisse. *Bundesarchiv Ludwigsburg, B 162/16570*

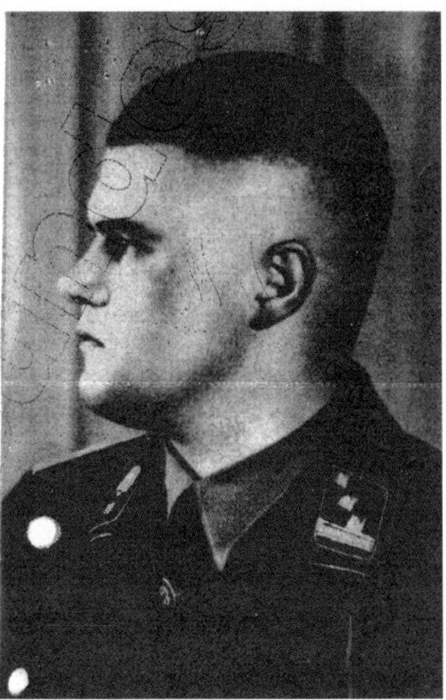

SS-Sturmbannführer Erwin Walser. *AIPN GK 164/1180—Akta w sprawie: Walser Erwin—Obersturmführer SS, dowódca oddziału SS-Dirlewanger w Lublinie. Materiały OKBZN w Lublinie. (1948–49).*

Members of the SS-Sonderkommando "Dirlewanger." The unit's patch is visible on the soldier standing at left. *Public domain*

Member of the SS-Sonderkommando "Dirlewanger." *Public domain*

Photo of an unknown member of SS-Sonderkommando "Dirlewanger" (unit patch visible). Decorations include Iron Cross Second Class and the Winterschlacht im Osten decoration (medal for the 1941–42 Winter Campaign in the East), indicating that he had previously served in a frontline unit and participated in the invasion of the USSR. *Public domain*

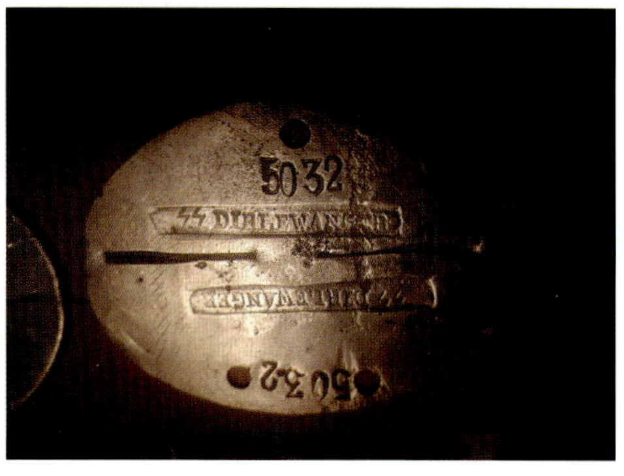

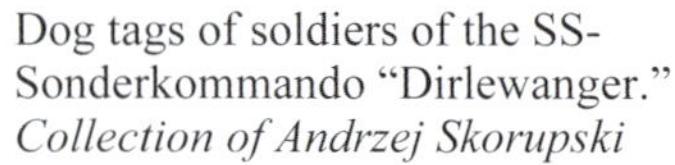

Dog tags of soldiers of the SS-Sonderkommando "Dirlewanger." *Collection of Andrzej Skorupski*

The dog tag (*Erkennungsmarke*) of SS-Sonderkommando "Dirlewanger," found near Gubin. *Author's collection*

Herbert Meyer. *Douglas E. Nash Sr.*

DEUTSCHES ROTES KREUZ · SUCHDIENST MÜNCHEN · VERMISSTENBILDLISTE

Kdo. 36. SS Div. "Dirlewanger"

VPN: 00512

DEUTSCHES ROTES KREUZ · SUCHDIENST MÜNCHEN · VERMISSTENBILDLISTE

Kdo. 36. SS Div. "Dirlewanger"

VPN: 00512

Missing Dirlewanger soldiers sought after the war by the German Red Cross. *Author's collection*

Dog tag with the number 76. This type of dog tag was issued to the first eighty-eight soldiers. Its owner probably joined a unit in Stary Dzików or Lublin. *Collection of Piotr Micielski*

Franz Magill's wallet, which contained "souvenir" photographs of the action and documents. Next to the wallet can be seen the SS-Sonderkommando "Dirlewanger" collar insignia. There is also an Iron Cross First Class and an Iron Cross Second Class ribbon. *Public domain*

Photos found in Magill's wallet; all are captioned on the back. *Left from the top*: "Germans shot by Poles," "Belarusian partisans, 1942," "Russian partisans." *On the right from the top*: "September 1942, actions in the east, 19.09.1942." *Public domain*

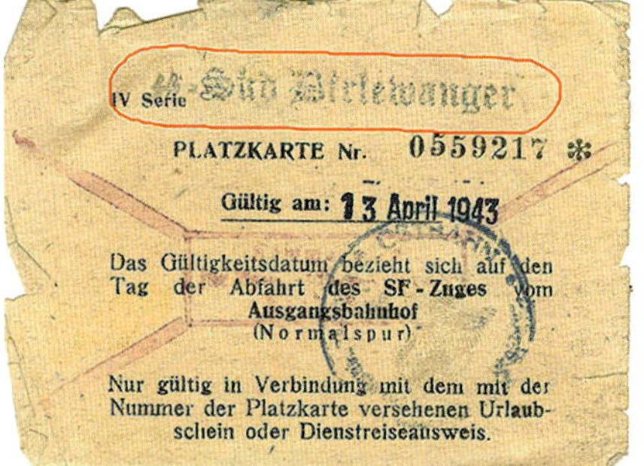

IV Serie Dirlewanger

PLATZKARTE Nr. 0559217 *

Gültig am: 13 April 1943

Das Gültigkeitsdatum bezieht sich auf den Tag der Abfahrt des SF-Zuges vom Ausgangsbahnhof (Normalspur)

Nur gültig in Verbindung mit dem mit der Nummer der Platzkarte versehenen Urlaubschein oder Dienstreiseausweis.

Train ticket valid April 13, 1943, for SS-Sonderkommando "Dirlewanger" (also from Magill's wallet). *Public domain*

Mokotów

After the fall of Upper Czerniaków, the heaviest fighting took place in Mokotów. The main German offensive against this district started on September 24. Mokotów was drowned in a hurricane of artillery fire from multiple rocket launchers (*Nebelwerfer*).[283] At the same time, Gen. Rohr's units together with armored troops from the 19th Panzer Division under Gen. Hans Källner attacked from the south and west, pushing the insurgents into the area of Szuster Street.[284] Dirlewanger's soldiers were engaged in combat in the area of the vinegar factory (Essigfabrik) (now the J. Komicz Villa, Grażyna Street 11).[285]

On September 26, the evacuation of Mokotów started: First the wounded from the Radosław Group left the district, then several dozen AL soldiers, and finally around 4,500 civilians. During the chaotic retreat, a group of people got lost in the sewers and after several dozen hours' hard marching emerged by mistake from a hatch in an area controlled by the Germans. The captured insurgents and civilians were led before a nearby gendarmerie command at Dworkowa Street. There the Germans separated the civilians and part of the female paramedics and couriers from the rest of the prisoners and ordered the AK soldiers to kneel by a fence on the edge of the nearby embankment. When one of them broke under pressure and tried to take a guard's weapon, the *Schutzpolizei* men shot all the insurgents.[286]

At this time, on September 26, a sumptuous birthday celebration was held in the city for the commander of SS-Sturmbrigade Dirlewanger:

> It was Dirlewanger's birthday on October 6 [Vieregge mixed up the days]; it was celebrated in Warsaw, but I don't remember in which building the event took place in; right after his birthday Dirlewanger set off for Hungary.[287]

Strumpf remembered that "the birthday party took place (on 26 September 1944) in the Hospital for Infectious Diseases."[288] A violent quarrel ensued on that occasion between Dirlewanger and Reinefarth;[289] according to Adolf Katz, about decorations: "It was later said that Dirlewanger threw his Knight's Cross at Reinefarth's feet."[290] It is possible that he did indeed throw a medal. This could not have been the Knight's Cross, however, as it was only on September 30, 1944, that the Führer awarded this distinction to Dirlewanger and von dem Bach. Dirlewanger was granted the Knight's Cross of the Iron Cross on October 8, 1944.[291] That was the end of the celebration. Dirlewanger was furious and Reinefarth left the hospital immediately.[292] On September

27, around 1:30 p.m., Mokotów surrendered. Over a thousand soldiers and over five thousand civilians were taken prisoner. From that moment, Żoliborz and Śródmieście were the only remaining insurgent points of resistance.[293]

Żoliborz

The fighting in Żoliborz lasted practically until the very end of the uprising. On September 23, the situation there deteriorated rapidly. The Germans increased their attacks from day to day. The surrender of Żoliborz was signed in the afternoon of September 30. Over 1,500 soldiers, sixty officers, and around 440 wounded insurgents were taken captive.[294]

Śródmieście: Surrender of the Home Army

After the surrender of Czerniaków, Żoliborz, and Mokotów, German forces commanded by Erich von dem Bach-Zelewski attacked the last insurgent stronghold: Śródmieście. Two months before, this district had been the center of a capital city; now it was the picture of misery and despair. Its former splendor had been replaced by smoking debris, ruins, and graves in the streets. In breaks between raids, people would steal by like shades, leaving cellars for a brief moment in search of drinking water and food. Around 200,000 starving civilians were present in the area. On October 2, after sixty-three days of constant combat, Śródmieście capitulated as the longest-fighting district of insurgent Warsaw.[295]

On October 1, the Home Army High Command and the Government Delegation for Poland finally decided to start surrender talks again. They were led to do so by the hopeless situation of the insurgents, the fall of Mokotów and Żoliborz, and no hope of any help from the Allies. Gen. Tadeusz Komorowski "Bór" appointed a committee to hold capitulation negotiations. Its members were as follows:

Chairman: Certified Colonel Kazimierz Iranek-Osmecki "Heller"
Certified Lieutenant Colonel Zygmunt Dobrowolski "Zyndram"
Lieutenant Colonel Franciszek Herman "Bogusławski"
Translator: Captain Alfred Korczyński "Sas"[296]

The Polish losses were enormous. Around 17,000 insurgents and 120,000–170,000 civilians had been killed. The Germans had around two thousand killed and around ten thousand wounded, of which the losses of Korpsgruppe von dem Bach were 1,570 killed and 8,374 wounded (according to Gen. Erich von dem Bach-Zelewski's report of October 5, 1944).[297] In 1947, von dem Bach testified in Warsaw that German losses were ten thousand killed, seven thousand missing, and nine thousand wounded: some historians today question these data, while others believe them to be reliable.[298]

Dirlewanger's subordinate Joseph Rau did not fight in the uprising, but his companions in the unit told him that the fighting in Warsaw was extremely hard and daily brought enormous loss of life.[299] On August 5, there were sixteen officers and 865 soldiers serving in Dirlewanger's 1st Battalion. Over the course of the fighting, the 1st Battalion was constantly replenished, the new soldiers totaling 2,500. On September 20, pursuant to Himmler's decision, around 1,500–1,900 inmates of the Matzkau prison were to join Dirlewanger's unit. It was planned that they would set off within three days, and their goal was Warsaw and suppressing the fighting during the uprising. It is claimed that they were well equipped, armed, and uniformed.[300]

Replenishments were also sent from Wehrmacht prisons in Glatz (Kłodzko), Torgau, Anklam, and Bruchsal. From Anklam there came a transport of four hundred to five hundred people, and from Glatz, of three hundred. At the turn of August and September, further trains arrived with prisoners from Glatz (five hundred to six hundred) and again from Anklam (three hundred). Around three hundred people were most likely also sent from Torgau in mid-September. At the end of September—that is, shortly before the insurgents surrendered—a third transport came from Anklam with around 200–250 Wehrmacht convicts. Around three hundred prisoners arrived from Bruchsal at the same time.[301]

Soldiers from SS-Grenadier Ersatz Bataillon "Ost" Breslau were also sent to Warsaw. In the period between October 15, 1942, and April 15, 1944, this battalion served as a reserve unit commanded by Oskar Dirlewanger. Its purpose was antipartisan and pacification operations.[302] On August 25, 1944, a transport of seventy soldiers who had been on leave arrived in Warsaw from Breslau.[303]

During the suppression of the Warsaw Uprising, concentration camp prisoners were the main group serving in SS-Sturmbrigade Dirlewanger. The poachers who had initially formed the unit's core had become a minority. It is assumed that in 1944, Dirlewanger's soldiers were exclusively criminals, murderers, and offenders. A German general stated that SS-Sturmbrigade Dirlewanger was composed of 50 percent criminals.[304] In 1944, these "criminals" were primarily political prisoners (Communists, opponents of the Nazi regime) from concentration camps, and also people indirectly responsible for the attempt on Adolf Hitler's life on July 20, 1944. Many men who lost their positions because they were suspected of supporting the assassins were punitively placed under Dirlewanger's orders.[305] Col. (Oberst) Harald Momm, from the Wehrmacht cavalry and riding school located in Potsdam-Krampnitz and a friend of Claus von Stauffenberg, may serve as an example. He stated,

> On July 20, 1944, I was arrested by the Gestapo and I was sent to Prinz-Albrecht Street. In October 1944, I was convicted as a political opponent, degraded to the rank of rittmeister, and transferred to Dirlewanger's SS Brigade.[306]

In the last months of the war, he was promoted to the rank of *SS-Hauptsturmführer* in that unit and became a battalion commander. Similarly, Bernhard Klamroth, who was employed in the Reich Ministry for Church Affairs (Reichsministerium für die Kirchlichen Angelegenheiten), was arrested on August 15 for participation in the conspiracy of July 20 and placed under Dirlewanger's orders as a punishment.[307]

Corporal Gerhard F. was sentenced to death for contact with the "White Rose" group and inappropriate statements. Himmler ordered that the penalty be amended to service under Dirlewanger.[308]

Moreover, Wehrmacht and SS soldiers sentenced by military courts for various misdemeanors (defeatism, sleeping on watch, hitting an officer, refusal to follow orders, etc.) were transferred to the unit. As Niclas Sennerteg wrote, during the Warsaw Uprising also, Spanish volunteers belonging to the Blue Division and a contingent of ethnic Germans from Romania drafted into the Waffen-SS served under Dirlewanger's command.[309]

In the last days of the uprising, 648 men remained in Dirlewanger's unit. On this basis, Stachiewicz calculated the battalion's losses during the Warsaw Uprising to have been 2,733.[310]

Around 90 percent of Dirlewanger's soldiers were killed in Warsaw. They were buried in the city in individual and mass graves, and also in the Orthodox (Jewish) cemetery in Wola.[311] In 1947, von dem Bach-Zelewski summarized their activity as follows:

> While Dirlewanger's brigade was characterized by very low moral value, its value in battle should be appreciated appropriately more highly. The brigade was composed exclusively of convicted criminals and political offenders who were promised amnesty if they did well in combat. These were people who had nothing to lose and everything to gain. They thus risked their own lives with no regard to anything.

> They knew they had a terrible reputation both among their own side and among the enemy and could count on no mercy. On the other hand, they showed nobody any mercy either and so did not expect to be shown any. This is why Dirlewanger's brigade sustained losses equal to three times its initial numbers.[312]

Von Krannhals stated,

> Policemen and soldiers did not, therefore, demonstrate in combat the viciousness attributed to them by the Polish side, neither did their fight fiercely for their own skin . . . , but after four days of the uprising saw themselves in the role of the attacked increasingly often. As a mass, they tended to be shy and inexperienced (apart from the SS Dirlewanger regiment).[313]

As the paramedic Karl Wenzel remembered, at the end of the uprising, all SS-Sturmbrigade Dirlewanger personnel assembled in the Brühl Palace. From there, they were transported to Slovakia,[314] where the Slovak National Uprising had started. Meanwhile, the 500th Assault Sapper Battalion was sent to Budapest, and Maj. Reck's group to Poznań. Part of the forces remained in Warsaw to perform special tasks.[315]

Initially, it had been planned that SS-Sturmbrigade Dirlewanger would be withdrawn to the Przytyk-Przysucha-Wolanów area. There it was to rest, and at the same time, "as part of combat exercises, together with the 532nd rear command and the governor of Radom, clear the Przysucha-Opoczno region."[316] The command of the 9th Army intended to preserve the composition of SS-Sturmbrigade Dirlewanger and attach it to the 4th SS Panzer Corps.[317] The factor that caused Dirlewanger's soldiers to be sent to Slovakia was their experience in antipartisan combat.

The successes of Dirlewanger's soldiers in the Warsaw Uprising were strongly appreciated in the Third Reich. During postwar trials, von dem Bach and Reinefarth belittled Dirlewanger's achievements, creating a black legend. They emphasized that Dirlewanger and his subordinates "only" murdered, raped, and looted, and he himself was not under anyone's command. They actually denied any contact with him, placing full blame for all crimes on him.

After the suppression of the Warsaw Uprising in October 1944, his skills were assessed completely differently. Oskar Dirlewanger was present at the capitulation of the Home Army and was awarded the Knight's Cross of the

Iron Cross for combat during the Warsaw Uprising. In his motion of September 10, 1944, for this distinction to be granted, von dem Bach wrote,

> We owe the fact that it was possible to carry out the attack efficiently and achieve the goals set for each day only to SS-Oberscharführer Dirlewanger's tactical abilities, audacity, and cold blood. Moreover, SS-Oberscharführer Dirlewanger showed great zeal and fought at the head of his men with weapon in hand. . . . He was also a model of valor, courage, and fulfillment of one's duties for his people. . . . During the destruction of the enemy in the Old Town encirclement on September 2, 1944, SS-Oberscharführer Dirlewanger demonstrated great military skill, courage, and fearlessness. Together with his people he always fought on the front line, destroying enemy pockets of resistance and sharpshooters. . . . By his many actions, SS-Oberscharführer Dr Dirlewanger showed that he belongs to the bravest of the brave. Thus, I present him as a candidate for the Knight's Cross of the Iron Cross.[318]

On October 16, 1944, at 1:00 p.m., Governor General Hans Frank threw an official banquet in Dirlewanger's honor at Wawel Castle, and the latter gave an account of the fighting in Warsaw. Frank offered him "his thanks and appreciation for the model action of his combat group during the fighting in Warsaw."[319] This was not the only celebration in Dirlewanger's honor after he received the Knight's Cross. Between November 7 and 9, Dirlewanger stayed in his hometown, Esslingen. On November 7, a small function was organized in the office of Klaiber, Esslingen's *Oberbürgermeister*, in which Dirlewanger's family took part. On November 9, Klaiber honored the "true victor of Warsaw"[320] with an entry in the Golden Book of the City of Esslingen.[321]

The press also noticed Dirlewanger's success in suppressing the Warsaw Uprising:

> The Führer awarded the Knight's Cross of the Iron Cross to
>
> SS-Oberscharführer Dr. Oskar Dirlewanger, commander of a Waffen-SS brigade, born on September 26, 1895, in Würzburg.
>
> SS-Oberscharführer Dirlewanger was granted the Knight's Cross of the Iron Cross for his special achievements while putting down the Warsaw Uprising. We owe it to his tactical abilities, audacity, and cold blood that in the first days, the attack was carried out smoothly. He always fought in the first line together with his men and offered

them an example of fearless bravado and personal courage. In addition to many other decorations, SS-Oberscharführer Dirlewanger has been awarded the Gold Wound Badge. He has been wounded eleven times. (Place of residence: Esslingen).[322]

6

Suppression of the Slovak National Uprising

In Slovakia, the first Communist armed groups, called Janosik combat teams, were formed in the summer of 1941. At the end of 1941, partisan and combat groups numbered three hundred soldiers, and a year later, five hundred.[1] The first partisan bases in central Slovakia started to be built, and the first unit was formed in 1942. By 1943, partisan groups were being established all over the country, but until summer 1944, partisan operations were practically nonexistent there.

In 1943, the Communists together with Social Democrats and the Agrarian Party formed the Slovak National Council (SNR). In December, its members signed an agreement on jointly combating the Germans and Dr. Jozef Tiso's regime.[2]

In July 1944, so-called raiding groups from the Soviet partisan movement started operations. These were small units tasked with collecting information about the situation behind German lines, filling gaps in the topography of the area, and "inspiring attitudes of resistance among the populace."[3] The outcome of their activity was that German troops in the rear area felt less and less confident.

In that period, there were already several partisan groups steered by Moscow fighting against the Germans in eastern Slovakia. They primarily focused on sabotage, managing to destroy road and railway transport to a significant extent. The orchestrators of the partisan movement believed this would be effective in weakening the Third Reich's military potential. Communication routes from Germany, Austria, the Protectorate of Bohemia and Moravia, and Hungary to Poland and Russia led through the territory of Slovakia, and their interruption made supplying the Eastern Front more difficult.[4] According to Andrzej Krawczyk, in spring 1944 there operated several groups of deserters and POW camp escapees, who hid in forests and mountain valleys. From a military perspective they had no significance, however.[5]

The partisans also disarmed smaller German patrols, thus obtaining weapons, ammunition, uniforms, and light vehicles. From July 1944 onward, the Ukrainian Headquarters of the Partisan Movement in Kyiv sent partisan groups to Slovakia. They consisted of Soviet citizens and Slovaks who had been taken captive in the USSR.[6] To make partisan operations more effective, Slovak fighters formed small teams of around five or six people (like Dirlewanger's unit in Belarus). They were armed with pistols and machine guns. Their equipment also included spades, picks, axes, pliers, and wire cutters. Packages with explosives weighed around 20–25 kg each. When setting off on missions, partisans took food supplies that were to last around two days. Their tasks included mining railway lines and roads. Because of their small numbers, they were less visible, moving faster and with more ease even through difficult terrain. Usually, two partisans stood guard while three placed explosive charges on the railway tracks or next to the road. Primarily Slovak state infrastructure—that is, state office files, telephone lines, and food warehouses—were destroyed. On this type of expedition, the partisans tried to take as little equipment as possible so as not to be weighed down.[7]

The first group of partisans formed by the Ukrainian Headquarters of the Partisan Movement was deployed in Slovakia near Ružomberok on the night of July 25, 1944, with the goal of organizing a broader partisan movement. It made contact with groups of Slovak military units. Furthermore, it announced the rebuilding of Czechoslovakia and recruited volunteers.[8]

For attacks on German patrols, motorized columns, and telephone and telegraph lines, larger groups of ten to fifteen people were organized. Also assigned to these tasks were the inhabitants of neighboring villages, who knew the area well and were able to cut down telephone posts and cut hanging transmission lines. Like Belarusian partisans, in the daytime the Slovaks hid in huts and mud shanties in the forests.

Small groups usually attacked by night, because under cover of darkness it was easier and safer to disassemble tracks, dismantle sleepers, and pull through the detonating cord that was buried in the ground. However, German patrols were ambushed in the daytime, usually in the afternoon, when visibility was best. Actions were well prepared and planned: They were carried out after a reconnaissance of the area. Everyone had an assigned task. Like in Belarus, the plan took into account potential escape routes and masking methods. This allowed losses to be reduced to a minimum. Also, the Slovaks could quickly disappear among the trees and excelled at camouflage both in forests and in the foothills. Some of the saboteurs had undergone training in Ukraine, Belarus, or Russia under the supervision of the commanders there,[9] which is why so many similarities to operations in Belarus may be seen in the activity of the Slovak partisans.

On July 20, 1944, the Slovak National Council approved a plan for a military uprising. Initially, it was assumed that it would start after Krakow's liberation by the Red Army. From the start of August, Slovak partisan units carried out several spectacular actions, which included blowing up the tracks near Vranov nad Topľou train station and damaging a German locomotive on August 4, and blowing up a railway bridge and attacking a German train station in Kostoľany nad Hornádom on August 9.

At the turn of July and August 1944, the Russians sent fifty-three partisan and reconnaissance groups to Slovakia. They managed to destabilize the functioning of the administration in the Low Tatras, leading Tiso to issue an order on August 9 for antipartisan operations to be undertaken. Because of the intensity and effectiveness of Slovak partisan activity, on August 12 he announced a state of emergency in Slovakia.[10]

On August 13, the commander of the partisan 1st Czechoslovak Štefanik Brigade met the commander of the general staff of the Slovak Ground Forces, Col. Ján Golian.[11] This partisan group was to defend the access route to Slovakia through the valley along the Čadca–Žilina road, and its commander was Col. Wieliczko (surname or pseudonym). On August 28 he executed members of the German military mission evacuating from Romania, precipitating a premature start of the uprising.[12] Veličko's[13] unit had come down from the mountains by August 21, and the number of partisans in it grew gradually. They were joined by workers and soldiers of the Slovak army. On August 2, the Czechoslovakian Republic was proclaimed.[14]

At the end of August, the German army had no available reserves that could immediately be sent to Slovakia. Nevertheless, the situation was so tense that the Germans had to summon all the units located in the vicinity. Hanns Ludin, the German ambassador in Slovakia, reported to Berlin:

> In connection with the situational reports concerning the partisans that I received on August 27, and this morning, accompanied by a German general, I found President Dr. Tiso at 14.00. I explained to him that the development of the partisan movement did not allow us to further delay and that it was necessary to immediately transfer German military units to Slovakia and direct them against the partisans. Next, I proposed the immediate demobilization of unreliable Slovak units. Dr. Tiso substantially agreed to my proposals.

Ludin added that the available German units would be concentrated in the Púchov and Žilina area on August 29. It was planned that in the coming days they would be used to defend the Trenčín–Čadca railway line and the line running through Martin.[15]

After operations in Warsaw ended at the turn of September and October, Dirlewanger's soldiers had no chance to rest. The national uprising broke out in Slovakia by August 29, and partisans attempted to take power in some locations.[16] At 7:00 p.m., the Slovak minister for national defense, Gen. Ferdinand Čatloš, announced on the radio that the Germans had started the occupation of Slovakia:

> You all know that the enemy in the heinous form of partisans has cunningly attacked our beloved free homeland! . . . In consequence, German army units are arriving in Slovakia. . . . Thus, I request that each honest soldier and each honest Slovak welcome German troops everywhere as our allies, and that everyone actively aid them.[17]

A day earlier, on August 28, the order had been issued for the German military to enter Slovakia.

In the face of the Red Army offensive and the coming of the Wehrmacht, Ján Golian, in cooperation with the Czechoslovak government in exile in London and the Communist Slovak National Council, attempted to overthrow President Tiso's collaborationist government. Golian had been appointed coordinator of preparations for the coup by March 1944. Viliam Talský was designated as the commander of the uprising after its start. Previously head of the general staff in the Ministry of Defense, from the first days of August he was the deputy commander of the East Slovak Corps.[18]

On August 29 at 8:00 p.m., Golian issued the order to "start expulsion," which was the signal for the uprising to start. On that day, the partisans fought a battle with the Germans at Žilina.[19] However, their operations were weakly coordinated and slow. The East Slovak Corps, which was to be the insurgents' key force, lacked a commander. Its passivity allowed German units from the 1st Panzer Army to surround the barracks of the corps near Prešov and, by August 31, demand for the troops to lay down weapons and surrender. Two Slovak divisions thus ceased to exist at the very start of the uprising.[20]

On the night of August 29, three partisan units from the Stalin Brigade, the "Janosik" Brigade, and the Ján Nálepka Brigade entered Banská Bystrica. After capturing the town, they took the Three Oaks airport. Other units from those brigades entered Brezno and Poprad. The Upper Nitra Partisan Brigade, led by František Hagar, liberated Novaky and Prievidza.[21]

The Germans sent into combat around fifty thousand soldiers, initially commanded by SS-Obergruppenführer Gottlob Berger. Berger had left Berlin on August 30. Following the initial successes of German soldiers, Berger believed that the uprising would be put down rapidly, but the situation in central Slovakia turned out to be impossible to control. Banská Bystrica became the capital and center of the insurgent state. The insurgents controlled a territory of around 20,000 square miles, inhabited by 1.7 million people. Around eighteen thousand soldiers of the Slovak army were sent into combat, and after the start of the insurrection, regular mobilization was announced. As a result, twenty-nine thousand people were conscripted into the ranks of the insurgents, but most of them did not take part in combat.[22]

The first task that Berger set himself was to clear the Žilina–Košice railway line, which was important for the German front in the east, and then to secure Ružomberok. The next was taking control of the Zbiegi–Prievidza railway line and capturing Zemianske Kostoľany, where depots with petrol and artillery ammunition were located.[23] On August 29, units of the Tatra division crossed the western border of Slovakia in the Čadca area. The division comprised two regiments, and each of them was composed of two infantry battalions, an artillery battalion, and several tanks. On that same day, the first fighting at Žilina and Zlaté Moravce took place,[24] with the outcome that the Germans took the hills on the right bank of the Váh.[25]

On September 5, Golian was appointed general. Together with Gen. Rudolf Viest he was commander of the uprising. Expanding operations to cover the whole country, including Bratislava, proved impossible. The fighting took place mainly in the eastern part of the country and in mountainous areas. The Slovak forces numbered eighteen thousand soldiers from partisan units and the Slovak army, which after mobilization had reached the size of around forty-six thousand. The Slovak insurgents were supported by the Soviet Union. On September 8, the 38th Army launched an offensive toward the Dukla Pass, but now the East Slovak Army Corps could not provide support. Due to a lack of progress and large losses, at the end of October the operation was interrupted.[26]

The reconnaissance unit of the 68th Division and the 1st Assault Regiment of the 1st Panzer Army were sent to fight the insurgents in the east. From the northeast, from the direction of Poland, the SS Schäfer Pioneer Battalion set out toward Kežmarok, Poprad, Mikuláš, and Ružomberok. Furthermore, Heimatschutz groups composed of Germans from Spiš were sent into action. These units quickly captured Spiš and Liptov. Ružomberok was taken on September 5.[27] On the southern stretch (Nitra-Topolčany), operations were conducted by Kampfgruppe Schill.[28]

In mid-September, SS-Obergruppenführer Hermann Höfle[29] received a telegram from Heinrich Himmler ordering him to head to Slovakia.[30] On September 19, he replaced Berger as commander of the German units. He planned to divide operations into two stages. During the first, German forces were to conduct offensive action to systematically combat the insurgent forces and prevent the area covered by the uprising from growing. By taking control of the Žarnovica–Svätý Kríž nad Hronom–Horná Štubňa railway line and moving units from the Tatra division and Kampfgruppe Schill toward each other, he wanted to create a barrier that would stop the insurgents from moving west. He also planned to capture the Handlová area and secure railway communication between Ružomberok and Žilina.

To carry out the second stage, Höfle intended to call in larger forces and then ultimately put down the uprising. He wanted to send German forces into combat also from the east, thus planning to shut the insurgents in an encirclement. After further German units were brought in from the south, a concentric offensive would be carried out from all sides.[31]

Subordinate to Höfle was the 14th Waffen-SS Panzer Division (1st Ukrainian) (14. Waffen Grenadier Division der SS "Halychyna" [ukrainische Nr. 1]), which on September 19, 1944, received the order to form a battle group. Three days later it was re-formed into Kampfgruppe SS Wildner (under the command of SS-Obersturmbannführer Karl Wildner). Its composition was as follows:

3rd Battalion of the 29th Waffen-SS Panzer Division

Battery from the 14th Waffen-SS Artillery Regiment

2 companies from the 14th Waffen-SS Antitank Unit

2 companies from the 14th Waffen-SS Pioneer Battalion

Part of the 14th Waffen-SS Reconnaissance Unit
Part of the 14th Waffen-SS Reserve Regiment[32]

The German army launched its main attack at the end of September from the direction of Hungary, and the fighting lasted around ten days. On both sides, losses in wounded and killed were around ten thousand men.[33] After Kampfgruppe Schill took Novaky and Prievidza, on September 19 the Germans reached the edge of Turiec from the southwest. Following the capture of Turiec, German forces were directed to the west and southwest parts of the front. Some of the Tatra Division units fought against units of the 1st Stalin Brigade. Kampfgruppe Schill attempted to penetrate the defenses of units from the 4th Tactical Group northeast of Handlová and in the direction of Veľké Pole-Žarnovica.[34]

In that period, all of Slovakia was talking about an attack by Soviet forces on the Carpathian passes, which awoke great hopes in the insurgents. The information about Red Army operations turned out to be erroneous and premature. Only a sortie by the 1st Cavalry Corps of the guard took place, which was rapidly encircled by the Germans, and the large Alexander Nevsky partisan group changed the location it was staying in, leaving the Čergov Mountains.[35]

On October 5, Höfle wrote a request for Himmler to send him more units: SS-Sturmbrigade Dirlewanger, the 14th Halychyna Waffen-SS Panzer Division, and the 18th Horst Wessel SS Volunteer Panzer Grenadier Division (18 SS-Freiwilligen Panzergrenadier Division "Horst Wessel") from Hungary.[36]

During an interrogation conducted in Bratislava on February 13, 1947, Höfle maintained that SS-Sturmbrigade Dirlewanger had been brought to Slovakia upon the express request of Berger, who was friends with Dirlewanger. He testified that as the commander of the German units putting down the Slovak National Uprising, he had been against having this unit sent under his command and its use in the fighting, but Himmler had been deaf to his objections.[37]

Like during the Warsaw Uprising, Dirlewanger still had under his command the 13th Company (Postschutzeneinheit), which took part in regular fighting throughout this period.[38] Moreover, Höfle had at his disposal units of the Slovak Hlinka Guard,[39] SS-Jagdgruppe 232 "Slowakei,"[40] and Abwehrgruppe 218.[41]

By October 3, 1944, German troops had pushed through to the region north of Svätý Kríž nad Hronom. They took Šášovské Podhradie—the valley along the Kremnický Stream. The partisans defending the approach to Svätý

Kríž from the south retreated through Vyhne to the Banská Štiavnica area. On October 4, units from the Tatra Division launched a strong offensive against the 1st Tactical Group in the Čremošné region, but the partisans managed to repulse the attack.[42] They retreated from the Banská Štiavnica region on October 8, under pressure from Kampfgruppe Schill.[43]

Most likely between October 10 and 15,[44] SS-Sturmbrigade Dirlewanger was transferred from Warsaw to the area of Trenčín in Slovakia,[45] and then to Ružomberok.[46] A large transport of recruits composed of political prisoners from the Sachsenhausen camp were also sent there.[47] They were trained in the Low Tatras, and then part of them were quartered in the settlements of Diviaky and Laskár.[48]

In Ružomberok, SS-Sturmbrigade Dirlewanger relieved Kampfgruppe SS Schäfer, which returned to its home unit, the 18th Horst Wessel Volunteer Panzer Grenadier Division (18 SS-Freiwilligen Panzergrenadier Division "Horst Wessel") in south Slovakia.

The staffs of the units pacifying the uprising—that is, Sonderkommando z.b.V. 15 (Einsatzgruppe H) and SS-Sturmbrigade Dirlewanger—were stationed in the settlements of Nitra, Topoľčany, Bánovce nad Bebravou, Prievidza, and Zlaté Moravce.[49] Dirlewanger's soldiers were quartered in a school in Turčianske Teplice (Bad Stuben).[50]

In Prievidza, Dirlewanger's unit most likely shot twenty-four men who were political prisoners belonging to the Communist Party of Germany (KPD).[51] When the uprising started, this village became a significant outpost in the defense of the Upper Nitra basin and the command center for the whole region. Its defense was provided by units of the 4th Tactical Group of the insurgent army and the Upper Nitra Partisan Brigade. The area was very rapidly, by September 14, occupied by German units from SS Kampfgruppe Schill.

On October 18, German units initiated an attack from the Poprad direction toward Telgárt against the 2nd Tactical Group Plesnivec. That day, the main goal was to draw the attention of Slovak insurgents.[52] SS-Sturmbrigade Dirlewanger, meanwhile, took part in an offensive on the mountain of Ostrov in Bílý Potok. After four hours of heavy combat, it had to retreat.

It was only on October 19, that the "Horst Wessel" Division initiated the offensive proper. It took Chyžné, and then the settlement of Rimavská Baňa. On October 20, the main German forces attacked: Kampfgruppe Schill in the southwest, SS-Sturmbrigade Dirlewanger from the northwest, Kampfgruppe Wittenmeyer from the north, and the Tatra Division in the west. Over the days of October 18–22, the insurgent troops were encircled. Some symptoms of panic appeared, and members of some units even broke down mentally.[53]

Even though in his testimony Höfle at first said that he was against bringing SS-Sturmbrigade Dirlewanger to Slovakia and sending it in to fight, several sentences later he contradicted himself: "The entire brigade was transferred before the end of the year on my demand by Himmler."[54] At the same time, he still emphasized his dislike both for the unit and for its commander. He described SS-Sturmbrigade Dirlewanger soldiers as completely undisciplined and accepted Dirlewanger only because the latter was a close friend and protégé of Gottlob Berger and moved in Heinrich Himmler's circles.[55]

On October 22, one of Dirlewanger's battalions was involved in heavy combat with partisans in Necpaly in the Martin District. At the same time, another battalion faced the Stalin partisan brigade commanded by Capt. A. S. Jegorow. Next, it clashed with the 6th Tactical Group of the insurgent army commanded by Maj. Miloš Vesel south of Bílý Potok. It was only after heavy fighting that the units reached the area 4 km away from Liptovská Osada in the Ružomberok District.[56] Wolfgang Venohr described the unit's battles thus:

> **October 8, 1944**: On the north stretch, near the settlement of Bílý Potok, a regiment from Dirlewanger's brigade attacked, storming Ostrá Mountain and in the afternoon, after four hours of fierce fighting, it cleared the area. . . .
>
> **October 20, 1944**: In . . . the north, across from the positions of Dirlewanger's brigade and Kampfgruppe Wittenmeyer, the Slovak defense held their positions. . . .
>
> **October 22, 1944**: . . . Near Necpalská Dolina, 9 km southeast of [the settlement] Turč[iansky] Svätý Martin [now Martin], a regiment of Dirlewanger's Brigade gradually approached the Stalin Brigade commanded by Capt. Jegorow, which was putting up strong resistance. South of Bílý Potok the regiment of Dirlewanger's Brigade was stopped by the 6th Tactical Group. . . .
>
> **October 24, 1944**: While Kampfgruppe Schill and the Tatra Division were held up, Dirlewanger's brigade repeatedly attacked Slovak positions at Necpaly and Bílý Potok, without making any progress. It seemed as if the insurgents were unbeatable here. . . .
>
> **October 25, 1944**: . . . At Necpaly and Bílý Potok the assault columns of Dirlewanger's brigade had not even managed to move 6 km after a week of bloody fighting.
>
> **October 26, 1944**: In the evening the Slovak high command moved to Donovaly, a small village in the Low Tatras, 17 km north of Banská Bystrica and 14 km south of the spearhead of the Dirlewanger Brigade,

> which on that day, in heavy fighting against Maj. Vesel's soldiers, pushed through to a location 4 km away from Liptovská Osada, where the command post of the 6th Tactical Group was placed. . . .
>
> **October 27, 1944**: . . . In the north, Miloš Vesel together with his soldiers successfully defended himself in Liptovská Osada against Dirlewanger's brigade.'[57]

After Dirlewanger's men took Liptovská Osada on October 26–27, they started moving on Donovaly and Veľký Šturec.[58]

Following the penetration of the insurgents' defense at Zlatá Studňa by the Tatra Division, on October 27, Gen. Viest gave the order for Banská Bystrica to be abandoned. The fighting was to continue in the mountains.[59]

Milan Mikulovsky remembered in the 1960s that SS-Sturmbrigade Dirlewanger was stationed in the settlement of "Banovce" (probably Bánovce nad Bebravou). "The unit was in this area for the purpose of combating partisans."[60] Mikulovsky went on to describe that

> at the end of October or the start of November 1944, part of the unit arrived in the settlement of Cimenná and early in the morning, around 6, burned down the whole village. Around 100–120 houses were destroyed. At the same time, the inhabitants . . . , only the men, were herded into a square in the village. According to me, around 25–30 men were selected from around 100–120. Members of Dirlewanger's brigade took these men to the cemetery and shot them there after the latter had dug themselves a grave.[61]

Mikulovsky did not witness these events: He knew them from the accounts of survivors. He stated, "When [on the next day] I was going to my grandparents, I saw smoldering ruins, some were still burning."[62] Witnesses told him that around two hundred soldiers from Dirlewanger's unit took part in the action.[63]

These may have been the same events that Franz H., a subordinate of Dirlewanger's and a repeat offender from a concentration camp, described:

> Our task at the time was to fight partisans, and for that reason we searched many villages. . . . On the road, the partisans shot two German soldiers belonging to our unit. That was in the daytime. Soon afterward we received the order: "Everybody who is in the village shall be shot!" . . . As a result, around 20–25 civilians were shot. They included

> women. I did not see children. No military action was ongoing at the time. Some civilians were shot inside the houses, some outside. I saw the shooting that took place outside the houses myself. [People] came out of the houses with their hands up, and then they were shot. . . . I did not see the executions inside the houses, but I heard the shots.[64]

According to Milan Mikulovsky, Dirlewanger's soldiers then moved to the settlement of Zlatníky. They carried out a pacification also there, but

> here they did not destroy the whole village. Here too they gathered all the men in the square and chose seventy of them and took them away. I don't know what happened to them, I only heard that they never came back.[65]

This version was confirmed by Vojtech Zaboj, who survived the action conducted against his village of Zlatníky:

> It was in autumn 1944. It could have been early November or late October. I lived with my parents in Zlatníky. That day, it might have been between 5 and 6, we were forced out of our house. The German soldiers (German uniforms) surrounded the village. Everyone had to leave their home and assemble in the square. Only men. Women, children, and very old men were to stay. All the houses were searched. . . . I had to report in the square too. There I saw three houses burning. Two of them were in the gypsy district. . . . After around two hours we were joined by around 120 men from neighboring villages: Malé Hoste and Velké Hoste. From Zlatníky around 300 men were taken, and then this number grew to around 420 people. . . . Next, we were taken west to the forest, under guard. There was a road leading to a quarry there. I thought they would take us there and shoot us.'[66]

They were saved by an officer who ordered the column to be turned around. They were not set free: The column was marched through several villages, and they could see Cimenná burning as they walked. Part of the men were taken away to a concentration camp, while the others, including Zaboj, were let go.[67] In the 1960s, investigators established that around seventy-five to eighty men were then taken away to a concentration camp in Germany.[68] Zaboj had also heard about the events in Cimenná:

> They assembled [men] in a square in the village, and very many were selected from that group. Those men were shot in the cemetery in Cimenná. I also heard that two or three men died in flames during the action. Those people were pushed into the fire.[69]

Stefan Asverás also survived the German operation in Zlatníky:

> During the war, on October 2, 1944, in the morning hours, the settlements of Zlatníky, Malé Hoste, and Cimenná were violently fired upon by German units that arrived in Slovakia from Hungary. Goal: suppressing the Slovak uprising. However, there were no partisans in these settlements. Later the German units [illegible word] herded the male inhabitants aged 16–60 into a closed building and on that same day we set out for the settlement of [illegible word]. A large group, around 75–80 men [illegible word], [were sent] to camps in Germany. Quite a lot of those people lost their lives in the camps. . . . My uncle Josef Spánik died on March 5, 1945, in the camp in Sachsenhausen.
>
> That day, on October 2, 1944, in the village of Cimenná, seven men—workers and peasants—were dragged from their houses; they were told to take spades and hoes with them. . . . Twelve soldiers led them to the nearby cemetery. Then they had to dig trenches under the crosses. During that job, they were killed by shots to the back of the head. After this incident, German [illegible word] [groups] looted the settlement and set it on fire.[70]

On October 22, 1944, German units penetrated Slovak positions. In effect, on that same day it was decided in Banská Bystrica that further open combat made no sense and that partisan warfare should be undertaken again. On October 30, in Banská Bystrica, Tiso and SS-Obergruppenführer Höfle received a ceremonial parade of German and Slovak units returning from combat. Tiso decorated a group of German soldiers and Slovaks from the Hlinka Guard for combat against the partisans.[71]

SS-Sturmbrigade Dirlewanger remained in action at this time, slowly moving south. Together with the 18th Horst Wessel Volunteer Panzer Grenadier Division and Kampfgruppe Schill, it finally surrounded the last insurgent units in the area between Banská Bystrica and Liptovská Osada. The fighting lasted four days.[72]

Compared to other German units that suppressed the national uprising in Slovakia, losses among Dirlewanger' soldiers were relatively high. Wolf-

Dietrich Heike, who was delegated to the 14th Waffen-SS Grenadier Division Halychyna, which fought together with Kampfgruppe Wittenmeyer and SS-Sturmbrigade Dirlewanger, wrote,

> Dirlewanger had no knowledge of how to command a unit. He commanded brutally and with a lot of stupidity. He often lay in his quarters after a night spent drinking while his unit fought. Unfortunately, due to crazy tactics the unit suffered heavy losses. . . .
>
> During one of the operations, Dirlewanger was briefly attached to the division. He was distinguished by a dislike for carrying out orders, and in key moments of the fighting he lay in bed, unaware of the situation of his units. . . . Moreover, Dirlewanger's unit allowed itself to commit a serious violation of the basic rules of secrecy, providing in the Slovak daily press the military structure, exact numbers and placement of weapons. The division immediately reported this, wanting Dirlewanger to be brought down. However, the latter was not made accountable and kept his position.[73]

Presumably Heike, like Reinefarth during the Warsaw Uprising, had no influence over Dirlewanger. The losses in the unit were quite large. This was due, among other reasons, to the lack of time for training the recruits sent to the front and also to the nature of combat against partisans.

The uprising fell after eight weeks. Losses on the German side numbered around 4,200 German soldiers killed and 5,000 wounded, while the insurgents lost over 1,700 men, with 3,600 wounded. Among those killed were several thousand civilians murdered by the Germans, Tiso's units, and insurgents.[74] From the political point of view, the start of the uprising meant the end of Tiso's regime. While the administration did function until the spring of 1945, it was present only in West Slovakia and Bratislava. Citizens no longer identified with the state directed by Tiso. The president officially condemned the uprising, calling it a "putsch," while German troops occupied the country's territory. Tiso created a mass movement to fight Bolshevism called Domabrana (Home Defense). Around forty thousand people were drafted into it and stationed in the Nitra-Bratislava-Trnava triangle. Half of the soldiers were unarmed.[75]

Despite the fall of the uprising, fighting against partisans hiding in the mountains lasted until the approach of the front in 1945. The Germans formed special *Jagdkommandos*:[76] police and military groups. The fighting was very brutal, and German units applied the principle of collective responsibility against the civilian population. From November 1944 to March 1945, ninety-three villages were affected by reprisals. Some were burned down for supporting the partisans. After the end of the fighting, 211 graves of people killed in shootings were found.[77]

The Red Army entered Slovak territory on September 21, 1944, in the Kalinov commune. Soviet troops took Košice and Prešov on January 19, 1945; Banská Bystrica on March 25; Bratislava on April 4; and the last villages in the Čadca area only on May 3.[78]

After the end of the fighting against Slovak partisans, Dirlewanger's soldiers were transferred to the village of Diviaky nad Nitricou in Slovakia. In that location they were to rest and recover their strength, severely dented by the two uprisings. In November, part of the unit recuperated in Revruka in Slovakia.[79] From the villages of Diviaky and Laskár they were then led along a mountain route to Ipolyság in Hungary.[80]

7

Fighting in Hungary

Initially, the men who were sent to Dirlewanger's brigade were poachers, and later, criminals, repeat offenders, asocial individuals, and SS and Wehrmacht soldiers with criminal records. In late 1944 and early 1945, due to "depleting human resources," politically unreliable persons were also drafted. On October 7, 1944, Dirlewanger wrote to Himmler:

> Regarding: SS-Sturmbannführer Zill's proposal.
>
> . . .
>
> Reichsführer!
>
> During my visits to concentration camps both SS-Gruppenführer Glücks and, in particular, SS-Standartenführer Pister suggested that I attempt to make use of former political opponents.
>
> In the camps there are people who in February 1933 and perhaps also after March 5, 1933, did not pretend to be German nationalists but remained faithful to their previous convictions, thus demonstrating a strong character, unlike hundreds of thousands of those who went with the victor and joined us on March 5, 1933, despite internal reservations.
>
> I support SS-Sturmbannführer Zill's proposal and believe it to be good, and also most obediently request the following order to be given:

> 1. Camp commanders will personally each find 250 former political opponents who according to the commanders' belief have changed internally and desire to prove this in combat for the German Reich. Age up to 45, in exceptional cases up to 50 years of age. If they are deemed fit for combat, they should be treated gently.
>
> 2. The selected recruits will by October 25, 1944, be uniformed suitably for heading into the field. They should be transported to the Sachsenhausen Guard Battalion, where they will form a battalion. Their clothing is at the discretion of the concentration camp.
>
> 3. Depending on the tasks awaiting it, the unit should be armed as follows: small arms or rifles, every 10th man an MP, 8 medium machine guns, 48 light machine guns, . . . 8 medium mortars, 12 flame throwers and 5 field kitchens. . . .
>
> 4. The commanders of the new battalion will be provided by SS-Sonderregiment Dirlewanger [already SS-Sturmbrigade Dirlewanger at the time]. The SS Main Command Office will provide 8 commanders (*Untersturmführers* or *Obersturmführers*) and 50 *Unterführers* from the guard battalion at Sachsenhausen until October 25, 1944. Fifty percent of commanders may be obtained from the concentration camp's supervisory personnel. . . .
>
> 5. Immediately after formation, the battalion is to be attached to SS-Sonderregiment Dirlewanger, where it will be quickly trained in street fighting and combating partisans.
>
> 6. The details will be given by SS-Sturmbannführer Walser (SS Main Office), who is responsible for getting the new unit ready by October 25, 1944.'[1]

Because of the rapidly progressing Red Army forces, which in September 1944 entered Slovakia, 460 Communists incarcerated in the Neuengamme concentration camp were drafted to serve under Dirlewanger. Many of them had spent even up to eleven years in various prisons. In total, 540 convicts were sent to SS-Sturmbrigade Dirlewanger from Neuengamme. Most of them deserted to the Red Army as soon as they got the chance.[2]

It has been assumed that also concentration camp prisoners who volunteered were drafted into the unit. In fact, "volunteering" was not always the case. Fritz Szeglat, a political prisoner at Sachsenhausen remembered:

> Comrades . . . in the camp often raised this issue: "How would we behave . . . in such a situation? Would you go voluntarily?" To which I replied: "Volunteering is absolutely out of the question." "Yes, but if they draft us?" "Then doing otherwise . . . won't be possible. . . . If they give you a rifle, you will take it, learn to use and handle it well. But do not shoot your brothers, . . . use it only against your oppressors. . . ." So I told people and within four weeks such an attitude gained approval . . . in the Lichterfelde camp. . . .
>
> One day: All Germans: come out. . . . In front stood an SS officer, who was giving a speech. He held a list and said, "Everybody listen carefully: I will read out . . . surnames. Those whom I call will march to the left." Then he read out a lot of names, including mine. Nobody had any idea what was going on. But we suspected something. We were all quite young people. . . .
>
> We were called, and friends and comrades asked: "What's going on?" "Did you volunteer?" "Are you crazy?!" The officer said: "If there are any more people who want to volunteer, now . . . they still have the chance." Then he turned to us: "If there is anybody among you who maybe does not want to volunteer, he can also come forward now."[3]

Assemblies during which "volunteers" for Dirlewanger's unit were selected took place at the turn of October and November 1944. Another Sachsenhausen prisoner, Bruno Meyer, described how on November 12, 1944, a campaign encouraging men to join Dirlewanger was carried out:

> Not quite three months earlier, the camp's commander ordered all traitors to assemble and said: "All of you who did not join our side with a loud shout of *Heil Hitler* but proved your loyalty to your own beliefs have shown that you have strong characters. Those who are still here can prove this now that the fatherland is in need. You can volunteer for Dirlewanger's brigade, which is made up of former prisoners, concentration camp prisoners, and convicted officers from police and SS units. You will not be second-class soldiers; you will receive epaulettes and SS badges; moreover, you will get the same equipment as other SS members. This is your only chance. You will fight against partisans. . . .
>
> Do not think you will peacefully await the end of the war here. It is not at all certain that all those present here will survive." . . . The carrot-and-stick approach.[4]

Karl Knabl's description of the situation was similar. In early 1944 he was transferred from the camp in Stutthof to Buchenwald, and in the first days of April, together with several other inmates, he volunteered for "Dirlewanger's division." The prisoners who did not do so were shot.[5]

Willi Müller, a prisoner of Sachsenhausen, stated that at the turn of October and November 1944, political prisoners convicted of high treason were gathered in the assembly grounds and told,

> The German fatherland is in great danger, and every good German is called to fight the Bolshevik *Untermenschen*. Also, we political [prisoners] could now volunteer for Dirlewanger's formation. He ended with the words "Go to the barracks, discuss it, and report of your own free will to the prison office."[6] He mentioned that during the discussion, those in favor made the following arguments: "One would finally have a rifle, could fight with a weapon [in hand], help the Red Army defeat fascism even faster, etc."[7].

Müller did not volunteer for the unit, but no one took any notice. On the next day, both volunteers and those who had expressed no such desire were sent to Dirlewanger's unit.[8]

According to a record from Oranienburg of November 3, 1944, the following numbers of prisoners were sent to Dirlewanger:[9]

Konz.-Lager	Auschwitz	400 men
	Buchenwald	150
	Dachau	300
	Mauthausen	10
	Neuengamme	130
	Floßenbürg	45
	Groß-Rosen	30
	Ravensbrück	80
	Sachsenhausen	750
	Stutthof	15
Total		**1,910**[10]

To speed up their incorporation into the unit, they were to set out by November 10, 1944.

There is a more detailed list of prisoners (table 1) transferred to Dirlewanger, according to which 2,030 prisoners joined the unit:

Table 1. *Source*: YV, JM 2082, ID 3669495, unpag.; Arch. Sachsenhausen, LAG XXX/1, letter from Dirlewanger to Himmler, Gefechtsstand, 7.10.1944, k. 4.

Concentration camp	Protective-custody prisoners (*Schutzhäftlinge*)[11]	Preventive-custody prisoners (*Vorbeugungshäftlinge*)[12]
Auschwitz	108	333
Buchenwald	69	87
Dachau	248	101
Mauthausen	–	4
Neuengamme	117	16
Natzweiler	–	–
Floßenbürg	23	24
Groß-Rosen	14	16
Ravensbrück	11	70
Sachsenhausen	375	400
Stutthof	1	13
Total	966	1,064

In November 1944, SS-Sturmbrigade Dirlewanger numbered around 6,500 men.[13] Newly conscripted prisoners were sent to Krakow, among other locations, for training.[14] Political prisoners were placed in one company.[15]

By February 1937, Himmler had ordered that two thousand "unemployed professional criminals and common criminals be immediately arrested and shut in concentration camps." This was carried out in March 1937, and two thousand previously sentenced persons were indeed arrested and placed in camps. As a result of this operation, the number of "preventive prisoners" rose fourfold. Preventive detention became routine. The action itself was based on the "Fundamental decree on preventive combating of crime by the police," issued by the Reich Minister of the Interior on December 14, 1937. Preventive combating of crime was to be ensured in two ways. The first was "systematic political invigilation" (police restrictions on place of residence, ban on communications, enforced abstinence from alcohol, etc.) of persons with previous convictions. The second form was the broader use of "preventive detention." This decree also pertained to asocials.[16]

In June 1938, the criminal police launched an action against so-called asocial elements ("Workshy Reich"). The services were to focus mainly on tramps, beggars, "Gypsies and other people who travel like gypsies," pimps, and "persons who have previously committed many crimes, such as resisting arrest, bodily harm, brawling, infringing domestic peace, etc., and thus demonstrated that they do not wish to accommodate themselves to the national community."[17] Numerous people incarcerated in preventive detention further to the decrees of 1937 and 1938 were placed under Dirlewanger's command. If the numerous postwar testimonies of his soldiers are compared, it may be observed that many of them were sent to camps in those years and placed in detention, even though their prison sentences had ended. The first of those imprisoned pursuant to the decrees of 1937–38 were sent to SS-Sonderkommando Dirlewanger at the end of 1941, while the unit was operating in the General Government (GG). During the war, transports with the so-called workshy, repeat offenders, and asocials were sent regularly.

In the last days of October 1944, the Red Army managed to penetrate German positions between the Tisa and the Danube in a northerly direction. It thus gained a foothold near Budapest.

From the farewell letter of Paul Lau, a Communist drafted into Dirlewanger's unit in November 1944, it seems that transports of "volunteers" from concentration camps were sent to Strzelce Opolskie (Groß-Strehlitz) in Silesia.[18] Around three hundred political prisoners from the Sachsenhausen concentration camp were sent there along with Lau.[19] This was likely the transport of November 10. The prisoners were supposed to go to Ružomberok in Slovakia; however, after two days' travel, a break in their journey occurred in Strzelce Opolskie, and their train waited in a siding. Finally, on November 15, they reached the settlement of Horna Štubňa. Each carriage filled with "volunteers" was assigned an *SS-Scharführer* from the camp crew. Sometimes the supervisor was appointed from among the prisoners: Willi Röder, disliked by other inmates, was one example.[20] This transport was formed into the 3rd Battalion of SS-Sturmbrigade Dirlewanger.

Three companies were formed within the 3rd Battalion, and each of them was divided into three platoons. The battalion was commanded by Ltn. Nitzkowski (*Oberleutnant der Flak*).[21] Meanwhile, the company's commanders were Wehrmacht officers who had been placed under Dirlewanger's orders for various offences. Command over the 12th Company was assumed by Stockhausen (Stockhaus?), convicted of supporting Claus von Stauffenberg's group, over the 9th Company, by a demoted *SS-Sturmbannführer*, and over the 10th, by an *SS-Obersturmbannführer* demoted to the rank of *SS-Grenadier*. Within several days, supply, sapper and signals companies were also formed.[22]

The 3rd Battalion was equipped and armed as follows: All "recruits" received Kar98k rifles (Karabiner 98) (Czech model); each platoon, one LMG (light machine gun) (Czech model); each company, one MMG (medium machine gun) (Schwarzlose model). Furthermore, each platoon, received one *Panzerbüchse* (*Panzerfaust*).

In total, four rifle companies were established, divided into three rifle platoons and one medium machine gun company. Furthermore, the following were formed:

one mortar battalion with 4 8 cm mortars (Granatwerfer 34)
staff company
supply platoon
sapper platoon (not equipped)
signals platoon (not equipped)

In total, the equipment of the 3rd Battalion comprised five hundred rifles, thirty-six LMGs, eight MMGs, four mortars, and twelve *Panzerbüchsen*. As of November 12, there were around 560 people serving in the 3rd Battalion.[23]

In mid-November 1944, another transport of political prisoners was sent to Horna Štubňa: around 198 men from Dachau. They were assigned to the 10th Company of the 3rd Battalion. Most of them came from Germany or Austria.[24]

In Horna Štubňa, a camp was established for arrested partisans and those suspected of supporting the Slovak partisans. The tasks of soldiers from the 12th Company of the 3rd Battalion included supervising these prisoners. They were not assigned this job for long, however, because they turned a blind eye to escapes. Since the 3rd Battalion was composed of political prisoners with Communist beliefs, they sympathized with the Slovak partisans.[25] The 12th Company of the 3rd Battalion was transferred to the Hungarian border, to the settlement of Laskár, near the town of Nováky.[26]

On November 28, SS-Sturmbrigade Dirlewanger set off from Slovakia to Hungary. On December 12 it crossed the border, and on December 13 it reached the settlement of Lewa.[27] While stationing in Hungary and waiting for the Red Army, the 12th Company of the 3rd Battalion was changed into a heavy-weapons company[28] (i.e., armed with mortars).

On December 9, it was reported that the Soviets had approached Ipolyság (today's Šahy in Slovakia), where part of Dirlewanger's unit was quartered.[29] The Red Army passed Balassagyarmat, and only weak German units were standing in its way.[30] SS-Obergruppenführer Höfle decided to immediately send Dirlewanger's soldiers there, and on December 10, in the morning they set off toward Budapest.[31] SS-Sturmbrigade Dirlewanger left the Tribeč region in the Western Carpathians and entered the neighboring region of Upper Nitra, north of the settlement of Levice. They positioned themselves east of Levice, with Dirlewanger's staff headquarters located in the village of Palást in Hungary (currently Plášt'ovce in Slovakia). Dirlewanger's subordinates were to bear the brunt of the enemy's strike on the Slovak-Hungarian border.[32]

On the night of December 9, 1944, a telephone call was received in the staff headquarters from the general of Wehrmacht panzer troops, Walther Wenck, who passed on Adolf Hitler's instructions.

> 1. German commanders in Slovakia and Army Group South are to cooperate more closely.
>
> 2. The defensive positions east of Ipolyság should to a large extent be expanded by German commanders.
>
> 3. German commanders have free rein as regards the deployment of their forces in combat. This pertains in particular to clearing the southern border.[33]

In the war diary of Army Group South, the date December 10, 1944, contains this entry: "SS-Oberscharführer Dirlewanger believes it necessary to find suitable people from other penal battalions to [support] the combat action because he cannot use Communists to fight the Soviets."[34] Despite this, so-called political prisoners, often convicted back in the 1930s for supporting communism, among other reasons, were regularly drafted into the unit. Hellmuth Auerbach accurately called this an "act of desperation."[35] It was hard to expect that people convicted as opponents of the Nazi regime, held in concentration camps for many years, would suddenly change their beliefs and go fight and die for the Third Reich in the final act of the war.

After receiving the order from Wenck, Höfle deemed that the decision to send SS-Sturmbrigade Dirlewanger to the endangered section was the best. He stated, "Dirlewanger's brigade was most rapidly available for this mission, and besides, it was the only unit."[36]

Because SS-Sturmbrigade Dirlewanger was poorly equipped with artillery, an order was issued for these lacks to be remedied without delay. Moreover, it was decided that

> Oberführer Dirlewanger will personally find out the situation of the brigade from the commander of the general staff of Army Group South on the basis of documents and draw attention to the difficulties arising [for him] from it.[37]

The Tatra Division, stationed in Slovakia, was also prepared for combat. As a report of December 9, 1944, noted, it had no artillery and few weapons.[38]

On December 10, Dirlewanger was given a verbal order to organize command headquarters near the two augmented battalions. All through this time, Dirlewanger maintained telephone contact with SS-Obersturmbannführer Greiner from the Army Group South general staff.[39] On that same day, it was reported that the situation of SS-Sturmbrigade Dirlewanger was deteriorating.[40]

After heavy fighting, on December 11, SS-Sturmbrigade Dirlewanger achieved the objectives set.[41] On December 12, Dirlewanger's 2nd and 3rd Battalions were relieved, by the 2nd Battalion of the 26th Panzer Grenadier Regiment of the 24th Panzer Division, among others. The front ran along the Ipolyság–Bernecebaráti line.[42] Also participating in the heavy combat under Dirlewanger's orders was the 13th Company (Postschutzeneinheit), and as its soldier Karl Keithan remembered, it suffered enormous losses there. The company was almost completely destroyed, and as a result it was withdrawn to Seesen in Lower Saxony (where it had been formed) to regain strength and replenish losses.[43]

On the night of December 12, 1944, the Red Army launched an attack, enveloping the German units. For this reason, the staff of Army Group South decided to withdraw forces toward the border, to the settlements of Dudince and Santov.[44] The situation changed hourly. On December 13 it was reported that the situation in the Ipolyság region was very tense, and a request was made for reinforcements. SS-Sturmbrigade Dirlewanger became a mobile reserve for the defense.[45] Despite this, on December 14 the Red Army took Ipolyság almost without resistance. Dirlewanger's unit was transferred under the orders of the 4th Panzer Corps of Army Group Wohler. The area around Ipolyság had been manned with insufficient forces despite being crucially important for the Red Army.[46]

The situation was critical: as Generaloberst Frießner stated,

> On December 15, I went via time-consuming detours to Palást, to the headquarters of the SS Brigade Dirlewanger, and then to the 24th Panzer Division. In the Dirlewanger headquarters I saw an astonishing sight. I encountered the brigade's commander, an unpleasant, typical bandit, in the command post with a live monkey on his shoulder—which he always had with him, also in Poland—sitting at a desk. The unit's chief of staff (Weisse) made a good impression. Nevertheless, I could only fragmentarily find out what the situation on the front was. When I ascertained that the staff was packing up, I gave the order for them to remain in place. When in the evening after the meeting in the 24th Panzer Division I was returning along the same route, the staff of Dirlewanger was no longer there.[47]

On December 15, Dirlewanger decided to move the staff headquarters due to danger from the Red Army,[48] which on that same day carried out an attack using around fifteen tanks.[49]

The unit suffered heavy losses in Hungary. Ernst Edler remembered that on December 15, he lost a close companion in the fighting at Ipolyság (Ipoltschak).[50] Dirlewanger himself stated at the end of December: "Once again we have a difficult week behind us, and my brigade sustained heavy, bloody losses."[51]

On December 16, 1944, it was reported that on the previous day, SS-Sturmbrigade Dirlewanger had been attached to Army Group South (Heeresgruppe Süd). Defensive combat was still ongoing in the Ipolyság region.[52] Dirlewanger launched a counterattack by five battalions. However, despite several tactical successes in the initial phase of combat, the army group had to use five reserve divisions in the attempt to retake the town and close the ring of defense.[53]

At Ipolyság, Dirlewanger had significant difficulties maintaining discipline. Desertions occurred and soldiers went over to the Red Army. This was because the newly drafted prisoners, particularly those with differing political views, had not been adequately trained, and discipline had lagged. The Third Reich had entered its decline.

Some of the newly drafted political prisoners managed to desert to the Red Army during combat at Ipolyság in Hungary. It is commonly believed that Red Army soldiers shot all the political prisoners from Dirlewanger's unit who went over to their side during the fighting in that area. This is untrue, however: Such an assertion has its sources in Nazi propaganda. "The Russians do not take prisoners but take care of all Germans with a shot to the neck."[54] Most likely between December 11 and 15, 1944, around six hundred of

Dirlewanger's subordinates deserted near the village of Homosk (Homok?) in Hungary. They included 305 prisoners drafted from Sachsenhausen and 198 from the Dachau camp.[55]

On December 22, in the Banská Štiavnica region, SS-Sturmbrigade Dirlewanger was attached to the 18th Horst Wessel Volunteer Panzer Grenadier Division (18. SS-Freiwilligen Panzergrenadier Division "Horst Wessel"). The battalion that was detached to Wehrmacht Battle Group Schenz deserted on December 28. As a result, the commander of Army Group South forbade the mixing of Dirlewanger's men with other units. On that same day, the decision was made to withdraw SS-Sturmbrigade Dirlewanger to calmer positions to allow it to regain strength.[56]

Many political prisoners assigned to the 12th Company (3rd Battalion) went over to the Red Army side, and in subsequent days, soldiers of other companies followed them across the lines.[57] Josef Rupertinger, a political prisoner conscripted into Dirlewanger's unit in November 1944, is one example. He went over to the Soviet side in early December 1944, together with his unit, and was incarcerated in Romania as a POW in October 1945.[58]

Willi Müller described that part of the Sachsenhausen inmates who volunteered to serve under Dirlewanger had planned to join the Red Army from the outset. They believed they would be received with "open arms" and would be able to fight against Fascism. Müller stated that they intended to break through on the night of November 14. These plans came to nothing due to heavy fighting, and those who were captured by the Soviets were treated as SS soldiers and taken captive. Müller summed this up: "The Red Army did not need their help anymore; to the contrary: their action was something of an impediment."[59]

Some had more luck. The first successful desertions took place by December 13, when parts of the 9th and 11th Companies most likely went over to the Red Army.[60] On the next day, the Russians shut all the deserters in a barn in one of the Hungarian villages in the rear area, holding them there until their interrogation and the decision on what to do with them.[61] Hans Grundig, a political prisoner from the Sachsenhausen camp, described that on December 25, 1944, his whole company went over to the Soviet side. He remembered his experience as follows:

> Will they recognize me, will I be dead before I stand before them openly? That was the question. As I approached, I raised my hands with great conviction. I don't know if they understood the only Russian word that I knew; perhaps my whole being shouted louder than my

> tongue, which had become awfully heavy, that one word: "Tovarishch!" For a very long second, five pairs of eyes and five submachine guns were directed at me. And so, it has happened, I thought; nevertheless, the rifles on that side started to be lowered, I was received with friendly laughter. Friends, I went as to a celebration; I crossed the stream and cried, and laughed, and embraced the Soviet soldiers. "Voyna kaput, Voyna kaput," they said and danced with me, or I with them; who can tell today. Next, they led me to their lines, and I soon noticed that I wasn't alone. I sat in their trenches and saw Toni, Willi, and Fred sitting there. . . .
>
> On that day, on December 25, 1944, early in the morning, our whole company went over to the Red Army in the space of two hours.[62]

Arno Händel, meanwhile, remembered that on December 2, 1944, he was taken captive by the Russians, returning only in 1955. Because of his membership in Dirlewanger's unit and participation in the suppression of the Warsaw Uprising, he was interrogated many times. He was sentenced to twenty-five years' deprivation of liberty in Russia for being a soldier of SS-Sondereinheit Dirlewanger.[63]

The soldiers of the unit that deserted to the Red Army were thoroughly interrogated. They were questioned about the location of Dirlewanger's staff and those of other German units and then split into groups. Some were sent to the rear areas, while the rest were used to perform various tasks. Prisoners were transported to the camp in Vác in Hungary and then the POW camp in Fokszany, Romania. Their next stop was Camp 280/2 in Ukraine.[64]

Due to high losses and desertion, on January 4, 1945, SS-Sturmbrigade Dirlewanger was withdrawn to the settlements of Prievidza (Ger. Priwitz) and Novaky in Slovakia to once again replenish its numbers and assemble its scattered groups. According to records, 1,056 soldiers arrived from the 1st Regiment; from the second, 1,151; and from the artillery unit, 292. They reached the area around January 9 and rested there until January 28, 1945.[65]

8

Operations near Gubin

Georg Severa, an inmate of Auschwitz starting on September 3, 1942, was assigned to Dirlewanger's unit on January 19, 1945. He remembered that together with other prisoners, he was sent to Banská Bystrica in Slovakia and underwent a ten-day training there. Because of the rapidly progressing Russian offensive, they were redeployed to the environs of Gubin-Forst (Lausitz). There they underwent "further training in the use of rifles, MGs, antitank guns (*Panzerfaust*),[1] antitank rocket launchers (*Panzerschreck*), and "Kanone 3" (Rudel-Kanone).[2] Otto Hafner was also drafted into the unit from Auschwitz. He confirmed Severa's testimony, adding that they reached Slovakia via Vienna.[3] Both of them were political prisoners.

On January 28, 1945, SS-Sturmbrigade Dirlewanger was dispatched to Gubin on the Oder, reaching it on February 12.[4] It was to support Artillerie-Ersatz-Abteilung (motorisiert) "Großdeutschland."[5] The soldiers were quartered in a village near Gubin, where they could rest for several days and prepare for combat.[6] They also underwent further training there.[7]

In Gubin, heavy fighting lasted until February 28, 1945, destroying 90 percent of the town.[8] Combat was particularly brutal in the Gubin Hills, called the Mountains of Death. In the final clashes, many soldiers, both German and Russian, lost their lives there. On February 12, SS-Sturmbrigade Dirlewanger was attached to the XXXX Panzer Corps. The Germans gradually retreated under the pressure of the attacking Red Army. The fighting was extremely intense. Some settlements such as Lubsko (Sommerfeld) changed hands several times.

In February, SS-Brigadeführer Fritz Schmedes was transferred to SS-Sturmbrigade Dirlewanger as its so-called tactical commander.[9]

On February 13, the 4th Panzer Army set off against Lubsko and Żary. After Bieniów and Jasień were taken, in the evening clashes over Lubsko started, and the settlement was captured on the following day by the 6th Mechanized Corps, commanded by Vasily Orlov. He then headed toward the Lusatian Neisse.[10] On February 15, Oskar Dirlewanger personally led the next attack on the Red Army and was probably wounded again. He was sent to the rear,[11] and Schmedes took command of the unit, keeping this position until the end of the war.

The war diary of Oberkommando der Wehrmacht (OKW) noted in mid-February 1945, that SS-Sturmbrigade Dirlewanger was located near Naumburg in Germany (now Nowogród Bobrzański). The diary indicates that they were relentless in combat. An entry of February 16 states, "At Nauenburg [Naumburg] the enemy was repelled. Dirlewanger's brigade in combat at Nauenburg [Naumburg]." On the next day: "The offensive toward the north has stalled. Sommerfeld [Lubsko] has been retaken by Dirlewanger's group. At Krossen [Krosno Odrzańskie] the enemy has breached the lines."[12] After retaking Lubsko, SS-Sturmbrigade Dirlewanger attacked the Red Army in Bieniów together with the 25th Panzer Division. After bloody fighting, the Russian units of the 102nd Infantry Corps had to retreat toward the Bóbr River. Due to high losses, the commander of the Russian 4th Panzer Army requested all his units to be recalled from the Neisse.[13]

On February 18, 1945, SS-Sturmbrigade Dirlewanger was sent to the first line of the fighting, to the outskirts of Gubin,[14] and on February 20 it was reported that "Dirlewanger's Brigade is attacking from the north."[15] On that day, Dirlewanger's soldiers engaged in heavy combat with the 102nd Infantry Corps in Bieniów. The village changed hands several times. As a result, it was completely destroyed, and the Red Army captured it on February 20.[16]

On February 19, a fierce struggle was once again waged at Sommerfeld. East of this settlement, the clashes lasted until February 20, when the German units started retreating under the pressure of Soviet forces.[17] It was noted on February 20 that "Dirlewanger's brigade is continuing progress toward the southwest. Defense of Gubin."[18]

The unit that fought in Gubin was the 1st Company of the 2nd Battalion of the 2nd Regiment, commanded by Harald Momm.[19] Its members had been trained in the use of *Panzerfausts* only two days before. On the outskirts of Gubin, they defended themselves against the Red Army, which used two T-34 tanks in the attack. One moved off toward the town center but was destroyed by a grenadier from SS-Sturmbrigade Dirlewanger, which was immortalized in a German newsreel.[20]

On the morning of February 22, after several days of intensive combat, Gubin was captured by soldiers of Marshal Ivan Konev's 1st Ukrainian Front[21] and Polish units from Gen. Karol Świerczewski's 2nd Army.[22] Following Dirlewanger's unit, the 24th Panzer Corps under Gen. Walther Nehring also retreated.[23]

In Gubin, SS-Sturmbrigade Dirlewanger was stationed in a textile product factory.[24] During the fighting, three soldiers, Georg Ley, Zieche, and an anonymous soldier from Cologne, were shot for attempting to desert and go over to the Red Army. These three men had been pleased by the approach of the Red Army and the imminent end of the war. They were concentration camp prisoners who had only just been drafted into the unit.[25] According to Otto Hafner, one day around midnight, Zieche shot at Adolf Hitler's portrait and was sentenced to death for this.[26]

On March 3, 1945, pursuant to Heinrich Himmler's order of February19, SS-Sturmbrigade Dirlewanger was transformed into the 36th Waffen-SS Panzer Division (36. Waffen Grenadier Division der SS),[27] whose formation had started in Lower Silesia in February. The unit had suffered heavy losses already during the fighting in Hungary, and they were increasingly difficult to replenish.

As Franz Schmuckerschlag stated, after the unit was transformed into a division, around a hundred graduates of SS officer schools (*SS-Offiziersschule*) were placed under Dirlewanger's orders. They were to organize new regiments and show mettle as their commanders and the commanders of companies.[28] The division was reorganized and expanded to include Kampfgruppe SS-Junkerschule Braunschweig and part of the Hermann Göring Division's recruits.[29] The division was composed of an artillery regiment (*Artillerieregiment*) and two rifle regiments (*Schützenregimentern*): nos. 72 and 73.[30]

The division was nicknamed Knochensturm (*Knochen*, bone) after the symbol of two hand grenades that were the unit's tactical emblem (painted on vehicles, among other objects).[31] These grenades resembled crossed bones. Previously, Dirlewanger's unit had been called the Himmelfahrt (Ascension) Unit[32] due to the high losses sustained among its soldiers, particularly during the fighting in Warsaw. In 1944, the soldiers called themselves the Himmelfahrt Unit also in the context of Kurt Weisse's exploits during Oskar Dirlewanger's absence. As Franz Schmuckerschlag remembered,

> We always tried to keep out of his [Weisse's] way because after Dirlewanger, it was he who had power in the unit, and one could never be sure whether one would not be delegated to the Ascension Unit by Weis[s]e due to some small misstep.[33]

Hermann Schulze, a political prisoner drafted into the unit from Sachsenhausen, described that after arriving in Slovakia in 1944, they were greeted with the statement that Dirlewanger's unit was certainly not the Ascension Unit and that losses were no higher than in other units. Their new commander stated, "Warsaw was an exception."[34]

Georg Severa testified that in March 1945, the unit was redeployed from Gubin to Jamlitz, to a branch of the Sachsenhausen concentration camp—Lieberose.[35] This was confirmed by a prisoner of the Sachsenhausen camp, Oskar Blömer, who at that time together with around three hundred other prisoners from Block 29 was transferred to Lieberose and drafted into Dirlewanger's unit (now commanded by Schmedes).[36] Also others were assigned to the 36th Waffen-SS Grenadier Division. The inmates from that transport underwent a three-week training and were then sent to the front at Gubin and Cottbus.[37]

The Lieberose camp had been evacuated by February 1945, and the SS had shot over a thousand people because they were unfit for transport due to exhaustion and illness.[38] Dirlewanger's soldiers arrived there in March 1945. Descriptions of the camp and what the soldiers encountered and did there differ between testimonies. For this reason I present all the versions. Nevertheless, the accounts are similar as regards the main issues: "The camp was empty apart from one block in which Ukrainian laborers were located."[39] From the Ukrainian laborers, the soldiers found out that all the Jews held there had been shot.[40] Blömer testified that there were around fifteen barracks in the Lieberose camp, and their first task was clearing them of the bodies of gassed Jews. Paper had been glued over the doors and windows. First, they had to open the doors and windows to allow the rest of the gas to escape from the rooms. After putting on gas masks, they started to pull out the bodies of the dead. According to Blömer's estimates, in one barrack there lay 400–450 bodies, which they loaded onto trucks. He assumed that the corpses were taken to Oranienburg (Sachsenhausen), where they were burned. Soldiers were quartered in the barracks thus cleared.[41]

Otto Hafner remembered that in the camp there were around two hundred prisoners from the Wehrmacht and Dirlewanger's unit, "allegedly" convicted of desertion attempts.[42] They were held in overcrowded barracks, which had no bunks or pallets for them. The inmates had to sit on the ground. There were also individual cells for Wehrmacht members in which the prisoner could only stand. Food was provided through a flap placed at the level of the prisoner's head. Moreover, arms and legs were shackled. All physiological needs had to be met in the cell, standing up and clothed. Such prisoners were led out in the morning during assembly to wash themselves. Most of them were sentenced to death by shooting.[43] They were guarded by Dirlewanger's soldiers, each of whom received a rifle and three bullets for the duration of his watch.[44] These prisoners (particularly soldiers from Dirlewanger's unit) were hanged and shot. They had to dig themselves a grave and lie in it face down and were then shot in the neck. Their clothing consisted of only a shirt, old trousers, and shoes and often had to be left behind in the barracks. An execution team consisted of four people.[45]

In this camp, around eighty soldiers from Dirlewanger's unit were still undergoing training. Oskar Blömer remembered that also prisoners from other camps were placed in the barracks where he was quartered. He estimated that around 1,700 inmates convicted of various offences were assembled there: They included "Bible Students" ("Bibelforscher," Jehovah's witnesses).[46]

During their stay in the camp, apart from undergoing training, Dirlewanger's subordinates carried out executions. Deserters and those suspected of desertion attempts were hanged. Execution units consisted mostly of six people, sometimes four, depending on the number of convicts. Georg Severa stated that over that period, around seventy soldiers of the Wehrmacht, SS-Sturmbrigade Dirlewanger, and the Hitlerjugend were killed.[47]

Recruits from the 36th Waffen-SS Grenadier Division received uniforms in feldgrau with added rank designations.[48]

At the turn of January and February 1945, Herbert Maeger, a soldier of Leibstandarte SS Adolf Hitler who questioned the might of Germany and infringed the rules of the Junker academy in Djevice, the western suburb of Prague, was punitively sent to Dirlewanger's unit. In a conversation with a friend, he had said,

> If all this really is to end well, a miracle would probably have to happen. Our strength now lies practically only in the conviction that we are fighting to protect European civilizational values, which we are defending against Bolshevism.[49]

As a paramedic, Maeger was to be assigned to the division's main medical station. His journey was drawn out, and he waited three weeks for transport in the military barracks in Lichterfelde, Berlin. He had already heard about the commander of the 36th Waffen-SS Grenadier Division, Oskar Dirlewanger. He knew Dirlewanger was "the commander of a special penal unit. Chances of surviving under his command were equal to zero."[50] In Trebin he was assigned to an operational team in the 36th Waffen-SS Grenadier Division. He stated that it was composed of remnants of SS-Sturmbrigade Dirlewanger, decimated during combat of the retreat.

Maeger remembered:

> The new unit gave the opportunity to redeem wrongdoings through armed combat to everybody who had been tried by a court, punitively transferred, or incarcerated in a concentration camp. Members of division staffs who were sent here were, however, believed to be "harmless cases" because they had been accused of incompetent command, so they kept their officer's patches. They were thus saved from wearing the discriminatory Knochensturm insignia, and so I too avoided them.[51]

He stated that at the end of March, he was sent to a village school west of Gubin, where the main medical station of the division was located.[52] He most likely meant the village of Pole (east of Gubin), where the wounded from the 36th Waffen-SS Grenadier Division Dirlewanger were placed in a rural hospital. When the area was taken by the Red Army, all the wounded were murdered (presumably around one hundred of Dirlewanger's soldiers).

Maeger mentioned that after some initially calm days in the division's medical point,

> early in the morning on April 16 the Russians commenced an incredibly massed attack of tanks, artillery, and eighteen field armies numbering 2.5 million people, heading for Berlin. They started with violent shelling by all the assembled artillery weapons, around forty-three thousand guns, howitzers, and rocket launchers being available to them. There was one gun per every five meters of front, supported by heavy fire from 6,287 tanks and self-propelled guns.[53]

Ambulances kept bringing more and more wounded to the 36th Waffen-SS Grenadier Division Dirlewanger's medical station. The doctors and paramedics were unable to keep up with their dressing and operating.

> The rows of stretchers amassing before the operation room were placed closer and closer together. Lying on them were people in shock, suffering from loss of blood and sustained injuries. The faces of those who were conscious were a picture of despair; they were aware of how defenseless they were, waiting for their hopeless fate to fulfill itself. Each of us knew that this battle was the last act in the *Götterdämmerung* of the "Thousand Year Reich."[54]

Otto Hafner mentioned that he had been sent to the front on April 10, 1945, to the Cottbus (Chociebuż) area. Heavy artillery fire by the Russians led to the rapid destruction of the unit. Hafner hid in a forest in the Beskow/Spreewald area until the end of the war and was taken into Russian captivity there, remaining a prisoner between April 27 and September 20, 1945.[55]

Even as late as April 29, 1945, 368 prisoners from the concentration camp in Neuengamme were assigned to the division. They were sent to Artlenburg am Elbe, which they were to defend. Some ended up in barracks in the Langenhorn District of Hamburg.[56]

A unit of the 36th Waffen-SS Grenadier Division Dirlewanger, most likely commanded by Kurt Weisse, reached the Halbe area. It participated in extremely fierce fighting there. Presumably on April 25, Weisse together with several companions attempted to lead around five hundred to seven hundred soldiers in a southwesterly direction. Ewald Ehlers, Harald Momm, and Erich Buchmann were presumably with him. On April 28, Weisse gave an order for three civilians to be shot, which was met with the displeasure of his subordinates. As a result, Weisse disappeared during the night and the unit scattered. He was last seen on April 29–30 in the Spreewald region. Ehlers was wounded in the fighting and lost an arm. He died on April 28 at Hermsdorf. Momm was taken prisoner by the Russians on April 30. Buchmann most likely set off toward Luckenwalde with four hundred people. They waited in Wiesenhagen for a chance to break through Red Army lines.[57]

8.1. Fall of the Third Reich, Fighting at Halbe: The Fates of Dirlewanger's Soldiers in Captivity

In February 1945 at Gubin, Heinz Rotheigner was wounded in the right hip. He stayed in the hospital in Landshut until March 11, after which he was entitled to sixteen days' rest to recuperate. After the end of this time, he was supposed to return to SS-Sturmbrigade Dirlewanger, but by that time, transport was no longer functioning, and getting to the front was severely impeded. Having stayed in hiding until the entry of American troops, he reported to their headquarters in Eugenbach near Landshut only on May 2, 1945. He remained in captivity for only a month and was set free by June 2, 1945. He settled in Rottenburg, where he regularly had to report to the police station.[58]

A similar fate met Friedrich Walter, who fought under Dirlewanger's orders from the time of the unit's formation to the final clashes at Gubin. On February 14, 1945, he was wounded in the shin and sent to the hospital in Freising, Bavaria. There he quietly waited until the American army arrived. He was taken captive but did not remain imprisoned long, being released home by June 13, 1946.[59]

The unit of Georg Severa, Otto Hafner, and Karl Gerber (political prisoners drafted from Auschwitz in January 1945) was sent to the front on April 10[60] or 17.[61] Severa was taken captive by the Russians by April 19 in Forst (Lausitz) and remained a Soviet prisoner for three years. He was sent to prison in the USSR and released only on April 16, 1948. He returned to his home region of Upper Silesia but was resettled in 1959.[62]

Otto Hafner, meanwhile, described that he ended up in the Cottbus area, where his unit was destroyed. He hid in the forest for several days and was taken prisoner on April 27, 1945, in "Beeskow/Spreewald" and released by September 20, 1945.[63]

Karl Gerber had the most luck. As he mentioned, in early March 1945, together with an anonymous companion he ended up in the vicinity of Neiße, a settlement between Gubin and Forst. On April 19, he was taken captive by the Russians. His imprisonment did not last long, since he was released by July 18, 1945.[64]

Two paramedics from the 36th Waffen-SS Grenadier Division, Karl Wenzel and Hugo Erbguth, also found themselves in the Spreewald region in April 1945. Wenzel remembered that Erbguth tried to convince him to push deeper into the Third Reich and so avoid Soviet captivity. Wenzel thought this idea pointless. When they parted, Wenzel fell into Red Army hands. He was released from captivity only in 1949. Erbguth managed to escape and avoided imprisonment.[65]

In April 1945, when the great Russian offensive started, the soldiers of the 36th Waffen-SS Grenadier Division were located near the town of Halbe. There they took part in the battle of Halbe and, on April 27, were shut in an encirclement. The division was destroyed, and on April 29 the remaining soldiers surrendered to the Red Army.[66]

This is how Herbert Maeger remembered those days:

> The last weeks on the front by the Oder survive in my memory as wild chaos, rivers of blood, and a sense of defeat and despair. All the brutality of command's ruthless mode of operation now, in the time of total defeat, turned against the fighting troops.[67]

When he saw the approaching Russians through the hospital window, he took the rucksack he had packed, a first-aid kit with bandages and drugs, and started to flee. He planned to join the surviving soldiers of the 9th Army, cross the Elbe, and surrender to the Americans. Like many other marauders, he traveled alone. To the extent possible, he tried to dress the wounds of those he encountered.

Maeger headed toward Halbe. As he mentioned, the Red Army was positioned north and south of the town, while the remains of the German divisions were defending the evacuation route leading through it.

> Anyone who wanted to push through to the west had to pass through the bottleneck in Halbe, which turned out to be a real gateway to hell. . . . In many places the road was densely lined with corpses. For stretches of a hundred or more meters, it was impossible to put your foot on the ground without stepping on a body. . . . Anyone who was shot or tripped was immediately crushed by transporter tracks, from under which fountains of blood literally spurted.

After escaping the Halbe encirclement, Maeger was taken into Russian captivity south of Beelitz on May 1, 1945:

> I was standing in a waterlogged meadow, bogged down almost to the knees in a muddy ditch. Before me, in a tall thicket . . . , I suddenly saw well-masked Russian soldiers with a machine gun. . . . I quickly threw my pistol into the mud and raised my hands. A Russian came out of the bushes and started toward me. He was an impeccably dressed lieutenant, more or less my age, around twenty. . . . At that moment there was a deafening bang; everything went black before my eyes. I moved my hand and looked at the Russian lieutenant again. He was standing in the same place, but now he looked completely different. Like me, he was covered in black mud from head to toe. A

> Russian tank standing on the other side of the mire had fired from a distance of around three hundred meters, and the missile had fallen directly between us, spattering muck all around. . . . The lieutenant raised his clenched fists and shouted a stream of offensive curses at the tankists. . . . To me, exhausted, hungry, defenseless, and stuck in shit literally up to my ears, this whole situation suddenly seemed utterly comical; I couldn't contain myself and I burst out laughing. The Russian, still furious, looked at me, squinting. After a moment he too was pealing with laughter.

Maeger was only an hour late for crossing the Elbe and reaching the West.

As a prisoner of war, Maeger had a lot of luck. During selection in the assembly ground of the POW camp, he was qualified as "ill," which meant being released home. The "healthy" were sent to Siberia. On August 14, 1945, Maeger received a certificate, numbered 299, informing him of his release from the POW camp.[68]

Maeger's companion, a soldier whose name he did not know and who came from Jägerndorf in West Prussia, was qualified as "healthy." He was a Communist imprisoned in a concentration camp, from which he had been sent to Oskar Dirlewanger's unit. He begged to be released, explaining that he was a Communist, which was why he had been in the camp and the penal division. The doctor responded to his requests: "You Communist? Ochen horosho! You Siberia, lots of Communists in Siberia!"[69]

At Halbe, the German units retreating from the Seelow hills were surrounded by the Red Army on April 22, 1945. German soldiers unsuccessfully, in heavy combat, tried to push through to the west "irrespective of the losses." This is how SS-Oberscharführer Herbert Brunneger from the 30th Waffen-SS Grenadier Division "30 Januar" described the events at Halbe:

> The rumble of shots around us intensifies. All around lie the bodies of those who fell recently and those who have been dead for many days already. Sometimes the corpses serve us as a shield as we jump over the enemy's blockades. . . . Who lags behind is lost. . . . When from an elevation I notice the whole encirclement open like the palm of my hand, I stop warily. At least 10,000 of our soldiers are heading west. . . . A tragedy of unimaginable proportions begins. Missiles from artillery batteries detonate one next to the other between soldiers who are looking for shelter. The heavy missiles approach with a rumble and scatter their deathly load into the tightly packed masses.

> In the center of the encirclement, missiles from "Stalin organ" rocket launchers start hitting in waves, killing and maiming tens of people. It seems there is no escaping the encirclement anymore because its edges have suddenly come alive. From cannons and mortars, from machine guns we are hit by deadly fire, which finishes off those who writhe on the ground wounded, rips to pieces the bodies of the living and the already dead. . . . After all eternity—or maybe it was only several minutes—the fire suddenly stops. The valley and its sides now look like a giant field of death. After the artillery fell silent suddenly, the moans and screams of the dying may be heard.[70]

Around thirty thousand German soldiers died in the fighting at Halbe, and according to some estimates, even over forty thousand.[71] In a nearby forest lies one of the largest war cemeteries in Germany, in which around twenty-four thousand soldiers, civilians, and forced laborers who died in the fighting are buried. Around twenty-five thousand Germans managed to push through to the Elbe, where they surrendered to the American army. Among them was the last commander of the 36th Waffen-SS Grenadier Division, Fritz Schmedes.

Karl Vieregge mentioned that together with other soldiers of the 36th Waffen-SS Grenadier Division Dirlewanger, he was taken into American captivity on May 5, 1945, near Tangermünde on the Elbe. He remained in a POW camp for three years and was released only in 1948.[72]

Some of Dirlewanger's subordinates were luckier. Gerhard Hellkamp, a member of SS-Sonderkommando Dirlewanger since its formation in 1940, managed to avoid captivity. As he remembered, at the moment when the war ended, he was in Berlin, but he managed to get home in Örlingshausen.[73]

Georg Geipel, a truck driver attached to the staff of a 1st Battalion company, stated that he took part in the battle at Halle, where they were cut off. In May 1945, several days after the capitulation, he dressed in a Wehrmacht uniform and hid in a pile of timber together with four companions. They were taken captive by the Russians and put in a barn with several women. At night, while the Russians were raping the women, they were able to escape. Geipel managed to get to Lauter in Saxony.[74]

9

Oskar Dirlewanger Remembered: Sadist and "Master of Life and Death," or Valued Commander and "Decent Guy"?

Oskar Dirlewanger was no average man. An excellent soldier and commander, quarrelsome and proud rebel, hothead and alcoholic, he had many friends and still more enemies. He was an individual who found submission hard. Although he had spent most of his life in military service, he obeyed orders only when it suited him.

He can be considered an "original" also as regards appearance. His very characteristic figure has offered many authors, historians among them, a lot of room for the imagination to wander. For example, in her book *Warszawa 1944. Tragiczne powstanie*, Alexandra Richie included the following vivid description:

> Unlike the affable von dem Bach, Dirlewanger actually looked and acted like the murderer he was. His face resembled that of a vulture, with thin lips and deep circles under his cruel, almost mocking eyes, while his hair was cropped closely to his bony, angular head.[2]

His subordinates described him as a "narrow, thin, and bony"[3] and tall man, who was accompanied by a small animal. According to some, this was a small dog: a schnauzer.[4] In fact, it was a so-called organ grinder's monkey, which he took everywhere. It became a kind of mascot for the whole unit and accompanied Dirlewanger from the moment it was formed until the fighting in Hungary, where it was most likely poisoned by accident. Apart from the above, Dirlewanger's golden teeth stuck in many people's heads.[5] One of the commander's attributes was a whip, from which he never parted.[6]

Already at the start of the unit's operations in the General Government, Dirlewanger managed to annoy all the top officials. Friedrich Krüger demanded the immediate removal of SS-Sonderkommando Dirlewanger from the Lublin region. The Gestapo opened criminal proceedings against Dirlewanger, and as a result, the unit was soon transferred to Belarus.

Dirlewanger sometimes ignored Heinrich Himmler's orders. When in August 1944 the latter commanded him to immediately set off from Berlin to Warsaw in the plane that was waiting for him, Dirlewanger went to East Prussia, without a word of explanation, to prepare supplies and equipment for his soldiers. Going against all orders, he reached Warsaw only in mid-August. Despite this, Himmler praised him highly. In his speech of August 3, 1944, to Gauleiters in Poznań, he stated that "Dirlewanger is a decent Swabian; he was wounded ten times; he is an original."[7] The commander whose orders Dirlewanger ignored the most was Heinz Reinefarth, who could not be sure whether he and his unit would move to attack Warsaw as commanded or not. Furthermore, Dirlewanger would sometimes even forbid couriers with orders from Reinefarth entry to his headquarters. During the Warsaw Uprising, Dirlewanger's soldiers would sometimes fire on Erich von dem Bach-Zelewski's quarters on purpose.

It seems that for Dirlewanger, insubordination and showing a lack of respect for one's commanders were something natural. Also, Hermann Höfle, who was in command during the suppression of the Slovak National Uprising, complained about him. He frequently emphasized his dislike both for the unit and for Dirlewanger himself, describing SS-Sturmbrigade Dirlewanger's soldiers as completely undisciplined. As he claimed, he accepted Dirlewanger only because the latter was a close friend and protégé of Gottlob Berger and moved in Heinrich Himmler's circles.[8]

Wolf-Dietrich Heike, who in Slovakia had been delegated to 14. Waffen Grenadier Division der SS Halychyna, which fought together with Kampfgruppe Wittenmeyer and SS-Sturmbrigade Dirlewanger, also had an extremely bad opinion of Dirlewanger. He described him as a useless, brutal commander whose main occupation was drinking.[9]

Despite such opinions, nobody recalled or punished Dirlewanger. Instead, he was decorated for courage and heroism in first-line combat multiple times. Numerous reports emphasized his engagement and manner of command.

SS-Hauptsturmführer Artur Wilke, who was on the staff of Kampfgruppe von Gottberg, stated that he did not have much to do with Dirlewanger but remembered him as an "oddball" and "eccentric" (*Sonderling*) who was a decent *Landsknecht* type.[10]

SS-Gruppenführer Gerret Korsemann,[11] who commanded Kampfgruppe Korsemann during operations in Belarus, also had quite a lot of trouble with Dirlewanger. The first tensions surfaced during Operation Zauberflöte. Korsemann forbade Dirlewanger's unit to loot, threatening them with severe penalties. The order presented Dirlewanger's subordinates as "unmanageable robbers." The situation repeated itself before Operation Günther: In a special order, Korsemann once again warned Dirlewanger against pacifying villages thought to support partisans. Dirlewanger did not fail to respond to his orders: On July 14, he filed a report on his experiences in which a deep contempt for his superior is apparent. Korsemann had ordered some villages to be spared during Operation Günther. According to an SD report, they were allegedly pockets of resistance, and it was demanded that the order to refrain from action against these villages be rescinded. In response, Korsemann replied vaguely that the villages should be spared even if they were a source of gunfire, and the roads were mined. During Operation Günther the 2nd Company of SS-Sonderbataillon Dirlewanger was shot at from one of the villages, inflicting losses (two killed and two wounded). Dirlewanger summed this up, stating, "It would be good if the most-important orders were issued by commanders with experience in *Bandenbekämpfung*: unnecessary losses will then be avoided."[12]

Dirlewanger's close, trusted friends included Gottlob Berger. They met back in Esslingen at the turn of the 1920s and 1930s, and Berger often got his companion out of trouble and saved his good name. He helped the latter in 1934, when he was sentenced to imprisonment in Ludwigsburg, and then got him out of the Welzheim camp. He helped convince Himmler to put Dirlewanger in command of the poacher unit in Oranienburg. Many years after the war and Dirlewanger's death, Berger still talked about him with respect and as a friend. He underlined that he was an excellent, brave soldier. He often described the successes his unit achieved in antipartisan fighting in Belarus. At the same time, he was aware of his faults and weaknesses, which made him enemies:

> Dirlewanger got his nickname because of significant alcohol consumption and strong interest in women. Furthermore, he drew attention by regularly personally attacking officers who were in weaker form, who had not been on the front line.[13]

Dirlewanger's subordinates were in a completely different position than higher commanders. They all knew from the outset that they had been assigned to a penal unit. They were aware that Dirlewanger had the authority to decide their fates, even including about their life and their death.[14] As Franz Stümpfl remembered, it was common knowledge that Dirlewanger gave no "pardon."[15] Even so, his subordinates generally considered Dirlewanger to be a commander who had good contact with them and understood their needs. They described him as a modest but nevertheless very vigorous man. He was described by using epithets such as "old warrior" (*alten Haudegen*),[16] "Gandhi,"[17] etc. The terms "great man" (*prima Mann*) and "a fine man" (*feiner Kerl*)[18] often recur in his people's accounts, even though he was a criminal. Karl Vieregge[19] termed him "fickle and erratic" (*launisch und unberechenbar*) but did not believe him a sadist.[20] Friedrich Walter, who had been in the unit since its formation, testified that Dirlewanger commanded quite efficiently but was feared. Indeed, he himself was afraid of the commander, even though he had not experienced any unpleasantness himself.[21] Peter Erretkamps mentioned that Dirlewanger had a soft spot for good soldiers.[22]

When criminal proceedings were conducted against Dirlewanger in Lublin in 1941, the Gestapo interrogated his subordinates. He was described as a strict, nervous, and terrifying commander already by then. On the other hand, soldiers stated that they had good contact with him and that he was generally liked and respected. Richard Eibl, who had been serving in SS-Sonderkommando Dirlewanger from August 1940 onward, said,

> Dirlewanger is very nervous and quick tempered. He is very strict with us, [often] justly so, but very often also unjustly. I have to admit that we have all complained a lot about Dirlewanger. D. intervened very strongly in matters of trifles but was quite bearable on the other hand. It depends on what mood he was in.[23]

Erich Selzer, also interrogated in 1941, stated that

> our chief D. is nervously disposed, often intervenes strictly, but in my opinion rightly so. He is just in all respects. . . . Our unit is made up of the accused, and it is said from the start that anybody who does not prove himself will return to the concentration camp.[24]

Soldiers who knew him well described him as a just but strict leader. Adalbert Daschner testified that Dirlewanger "was very strict." He also stated that he had to act in such a way if he wanted to maintain discipline.[25] This was confirmed by Walter Escher, who remembered that Dirlewanger often emphasized that a soldier should not steal.[26] Dirlewanger was termed a sadist surprisingly rarely.[27] It was usually soldiers who had been in the unit briefly, mostly those drafted only at the end of 1943 or later, who made negative statements about him.

Heinz Feiertag, who was transferred to SS-Sonderkommando Dirlewanger from Leibstandarte SS Adolf Hitler and held the post of instructor, among others, said this of Dirlewanger's subordinates in 1941:

> Throughout my career I have trained many soldiers, including volunteers, and also Belgians and Dutch in the school at Sennheim, but you cannot deal with the people who are in the Dirlewanger unit in a military fashion. I had to adapt and treat these men as severely as possible. At the same time, I noticed that the more strictly I treated these men, the better the atmosphere and soldierly attitude.[28]

In 1960, Feiertag stated that in Dirlewanger's unit, things were no worse than in others. Dirlewanger was characterized by the ability to maintain strict discipline. Feiertag mentioned that already in Lublin, Dirlewanger often meted out punishments to all his subordinates. When five cases of theft were reported among his subordinates, the whole unit had to lie on their stomachs in the yard for so long that several people died. But no more thefts occurred.[29]

Franz Bauser, who met Oskar Dirlewanger in June 1944 and was sent to his unit by the SS Main Office (SS-Hauptamt) in Berlin as a supplies officer (and not punitively), remembered that the commander made a positive impression on him. Their relationship was polite but cool. He assessed him to be an exceptionally brave soldier, a vigorous but at the same time modest man:

> He was a man who had been born too late. He was a *Landsknecht* who had to live in the period of the wars of the thirties. I told him so once. He did not take it the wrong way.[30]

Not only his subordinates had warm memories of Dirlewanger. The SS man Alfred Koziel said that in 1940 in Lublin, he and nine other SS men were quartered at Chopin Street together with soldiers of SS-Sonderkommando Dirlewanger. Dirlewanger would visit them with bottles of cognac. Koziel remembered him as an "affable" (*leutselig*) man. When he first saw him, Dirlewanger was dressed in an

> SS uniform with an SS-Rottenführer's stripes and the sleeve chevrons of a Wehrmacht second lieutenant. This strange combination of insignia was commonly discussed.[31]

Although he served with the unit, the paramedic Karl Wenzel stated that he had never met Dirlewanger but remembered that his subordinates spoke of and to him by first name. They valued him:

> His soldiers generally spoke well of him because he cared for his people well as regards supplies and decorations. Neither did he have an officer's pride. He spoke normally to each of his subordinates.[32]

Dirlewanger's soldiers had been recruited mostly from among concentration camp prisoners or soldiers of other formations convicted of various offenses. Under Dirlewanger's orders, they had the opportunity to atone for their crimes and rehabilitate themselves during combat. As one of Dirlewanger's subordinates remembered, they were informed that all bad deeds would be forgotten if they made good while serving.[33]

A statement that often recurs in testimonies is that Dirlewanger "cared for each member of his unit."[34] He was very protective toward his subordinates. Interestingly, soldiers remembered that he tried to get to know everybody personally and knew their past and their problems. This is demonstrated in the following account:

> Dirlewanger was not only strict with his people but also very caring. . . . One example can be his writing a letter to my mother, to whom I brought so much worry with my misdeeds. . . . In that letter, he wrote to my mother that I was on the right track to improvement and that when the war ended, she should receive me as a son and restore my right to inherit. I am deeply convinced that if Dirlewanger survived the war, he would have taken care of me, so that I would not be punished again, which is unfortunately happening.[35]

Heinrich Arndt, meanwhile, mentioned that Dirlewanger "showed his soldiers some heart":

> When we were traveling from the Minsk region to Warsaw through East Prussia, I asked him while in Prussia to be allowed to briefly visit my mother, who lived in Lötzen [Giżycko]. He allowed me to do so without any problems. He showed great trust in me.[36]

Heinz Feiertag also mentioned similar behaviors by the commander, saying that he sometimes inquired whether they had children. If they did, he gave them a piece of leather or fabric, telling them to make shoes or clothes for them.[37]

SS-Untersturmführer Paul Zimmermann, who commanded one of the Russian companies in Belarus and a company during the Warsaw Uprising, knew Dirlewanger well. Zimmermann (born in 1888) was older than his commander. He stated, "I cannot say anything bad against Dirlewanger. Toward me, who was older than him, . . . he always behaved correctly and caringly."[38]

In his unit, Dirlewanger introduced a lot of informal, nonhierarchical behaviors unprecedented in the army. The atmosphere among the soldiers was even familial, and Dirlewanger himself was the object of his men's "filial" affection. When talking to old comrades who had joined the unit before the end of 1943, he addressed them with the familiar "du" form, and they called him by his first name.[39] Every member of the unit could talk to him, and he offered cigarettes and vodka to his subordinates.[40] Otto Ruch emphasized Dirlewanger's almost fatherly care.[41]

Feiertag underlined that they never lacked for anything. Dirlewanger always tried to make sure that his subordinates had the best food; he excelled at organization. When the unit received a transfer order, one of the first issues he focused on as a commander was organizing good supplies:

> When we changed quarters and arrived in Lublin, it is quite certain [Oskar Dirlewanger] first went to the Supplies Office to personally talk with the head of the office and personally took care of the food.[42]

Karl Engel mentioned in the 1960s that a soldier was once made to march with an abrasion on his foot. Dirlewanger examined the wound personally and ordered him to ride in a truck.[43] Soldiers told how they received specially prepared provisions from the commander when going home on leave. He also allowed them to send packages with food and other items that they had obtained back to their families.[44] He made a very positive impression on subordinates, even though he was an offender and criminal.

Gustav Strumpf observed that Dirlewanger was better able to understand his men's situation because he himself had been in prison and in a concentration camp. Despite supply problems, he did everything he could to prevent his people from experiencing any shortages. Moreover, Strumpf testified that Dirlewanger had the right disposition for commanding such a unit. He knew how to maintain discipline. The unit had strict rules: Anyone who stole, looted, or behaved brutally or aggressively toward women was subject to severe punishment.[45] Both commanders of similar units and Himmler called the methods applied by Dirlewanger medieval because of the use of corporal punishment. This was a very infrequent and extraordinary method of disciplining soldiers during the Second World War and might engender surprise and outrage today. On the other hand, the medieval methods used by Dirlewanger on people "with a shady past" turned out to be exceptionally effective. Adalbert Daschner claimed that Dirlewanger had to be strict if he wanted to maintain discipline in the unit.[46] Most soldiers indicated that Dirlewanger was a "strict but fair" (*streng aber auch gerecht*) commander.[47]

Dirlewanger could apply the death penalty against a member of his unit for any infringement of discipline.[48] Further to Reichsführer-SS Himmler's order of February 20, 1944, Dirlewanger officially became "master of life and death" in the unit.[49] Gustav Strumpf's testimony was confirmed by one of Dirlewanger's younger soldiers, Friedrich Walter, who protested the terms "rabble" (*Sauhaufen*) and "wild band" (*wilder Haufen*).[50] According to him, the commander's strictness made the unit very disciplined. Also, Arno Händel was outraged at this type of allegation: "They murdered, plundered, and raped; that is a lie. Dirlewanger did not tolerate anything like that."[51] Of course, such statements should be approached with skepticism.

New "recruits" were often welcomed in a very peculiar manner, so that they would immediately understand that any offenses would be severely punished. Johannes Stein, who volunteered from the Neuengamme camp, testified that he was sent to the Minsk area in 1942. He got a shock there right away. After a preliminary speech, the soldier who brought them there was shot. This made a horrifying impression on the arrivals. Dirlewanger was not present at the time. Only later were they informed that their commander was "master of life and death" in the unit.[52]

In Belarus, Dirlewanger's soldiers were categorically forbidden to enter houses, and looting and rape were severely punished.[53] Josef Rau explained that conversations with inhabitants of Belarusian villages were absolutely forbidden because the latter could maintain contact with partisans, and traps and ambushes were a source of fear. Rau believed that Dirlewanger did not abuse the right to issue death sentences, and that the ones that were carried out were justified.[54] An execution near Lahoysk can serve as an example. For "committing indecent acts" on a Russian child, Dirlewanger executed the soldier Rudolf Peter, who was shot.[55]

Heinrich Arndt described that

> I myself once had to escort two deserters belonging to my company within Sonderkommando Dirlewanger to Dirlewanger's headquarters. I left both deserters with "Oskar" and Obersturmbannführer Wei[s]se. Wei[s]se, who found pleasure in beating people with a whip if they did something, whipped and whipped them, after which Dirlewanger ordered the deserters to be taken away because they would be shot. I did not take part in the shooting. However, I don't doubt that the execution took place. Generally, no other penalty than the death penalty was possible in this case.[56]

Adolf Katz testified that the commander did not find it easy to issue death sentences and always considered it for a long time.[57] Johannes Stein told of the execution of two or three unit members for returning from leave after the time set: They were hanged. The convicts belonged to the 3rd Company, and all its soldiers had to witness their deaths. Stein stated,

> I don't know which of the company members had to play hangman. The individuals—from what I remember— . . . stood on a truck and had the noose placed around their necks. The rope was attached to a mast set up specifically for that purpose. The truck moved away and thus the execution was carried out.[58]

The death penalty was to deter and discourage soldiers from breaking regulations: It was the only way to make the unit carry out all orders without problems. Either the whole unit or the company to which the guilty members belonged participated in the punitive executions.

The most strictly forbidden behavior was looting. In Uzda in Belarus, one of Dirlewanger's soldiers robbed a school building and was shot as an example. Dirlewanger punished instances of rape equally severely. In that same village, a subordinate of his raped a young Russian girl. The penalty was high: The soldier was shot.[59]

Four more members of the unit were also sentenced to death in Belarus. The first was shot pursuant to a military court sentence. Before this occurred, Dirlewanger punished him with four days' strict detention:

> Despite frequently repeated orders that truck drivers should not leave quarters, in the village of Sabaschew together with a Russian armed with a rifle he entered different houses in the village for the purpose of "organizing" [items]; i.e., looting.[60]

As a result, "N. was instructed that . . . if he had to be punished again, he would go back where he had come from."[61] N. was most likely punitively sent back to his concentration camp for another infraction and shot for attempting to escape further to a military court sentence.

The second soldier to be shot stole 1 kg of coffee beans from a supply truck. It was also suspected that he took fourteen bottles of rum, 3 kg of sweets, and six boxes of cigarillos.[62] Dirlewanger used the death penalty when discipline in the unit deteriorated.

During operations in Belarus, the local population also trusted the commander of SS-Sonderkommando Dirlewanger. According to the testimony of Adalbert Daschner,

> The people trusted Dirlewanger. In Usda [Uzda] he was not called "Dirlewanger" but "Major." Residents went to the "Major" when they had complaints about unit members. They went to the "Major" also when they had complaints about partisans.[63]

These were doubtless not the residents of villages pacified by the unit.

Friedrich Walter described how in 1943 Dirlewanger shot a soldier called Wächter. His offense was lack of vigilance while guarding a building:

A Ukrainian *Hiwi* deserted on his watch. Walter did not see the execution, being on leave at the time, but his companions told him the whole story when he returned.[64]

Meting out the death penalty came a lot easier to Dirlewanger's deputy, Kurt Weisse. Adalbert Daschner mentioned that while Dirlewanger was affable (*leutselig*) toward his subordinates, Weisse was extremely cool and correct in his behavior.[65] Furthermore, Weisse was described as a "brutal and ruthless" (*brutal und rücksichtslos*) man.[66] Paul Dorn said that the greatest difference between Dirlewanger and Weisse lay in their approach to combat. Weisse did not take part in first-line fighting, while Dirlewanger fought together with his men and was wounded multiple times.[67]

After the war, Karl Engel testified that three of his companions were shot in the village of Katny for moving away from their group unauthorized and leaving a horse cart unattended. Engel had been sitting a sentence in the Dachau, Sachsenhausen, and Auschwitz concentration camps since 1943 for fencing goods.

> In spring 1943 I was unexpectedly drafted into Dirlewanger's unit. . . . During the collapse of the front in the Minsk region, our unit retreated in early July 1944. . . . During the retreat, our company ended up in the village of Katny; this settlement was situated between Grodno and Minsk. . . . I can't say to what extent these allegations were true. However, also other soldiers from our detachment later joined us without horse-drawn vehicles. Given that the company arrived in Grodno in the strength of eighteen soldiers, and others continued coming over many hours and even days, I believe SS-Stabsscharführer Stein's allegations were unjustified. . . . Anyway, in my opinion, SS-Stabsscharführer Stein had some personal issues with those three soldiers and that was why he made a false report to the company commander, Max Schreiner. Schreiner wrestled with himself for a long time, but he could not prevent the whole matter from being reported to the commander of the 1st Regiment, SS-Hauptsturmführer Wei[s]se. Had he failed to do so, Stein himself would probably have made the report. Schreiner was afraid of this.
>
> Anyway, the report reached Weis[s]se, and the three companions were thrown into the cellar in the Katny school building, where our unit was stationed at the time. Some two hours later they were taken from the cellar again and put in the kitchen to peel potatoes. In the evening, they were once again locked in the cellar of the school

> building. On the next day, I personally received an order from company commander Schreiner to take away [those] three companions' valuables and military books. I carried out the order. I got the military books, purses, etc. from them without any trouble, but they were all upset, which I could tell by the question they asked me: "Will we be shot?" I only laughed. But I myself did not know what would happen. Most likely, however, in the past two days that had gone by since the report, company commander Schreiner received an order from Rgt. Kdr. Wei[s]se to take away the valuables and most likely concerning the further fate of the three detainees. . . . The companions were tied up with a rope.
>
> Around 14.00 on that same day—that is, shortly afterward, *Spiess* (Stein) ordered the company to assemble in full gear. We reported, according to my knowledge, around 16.00. . . . Around 14.00 I found out from Schreiner that the three people were to be shot. . . .
>
> The company assembled around 16.00. They appeared without arms. Only the execution unit, consisting of 6 or 9 people, was armed. . . . As soon as the company lined up, SS-Hauptsturmführer Wei[s]se appeared in his jeep together with an adjutant. . . .
>
> The three soldiers, already tied up, were led out from the cellar. They stood with their backs to the school building, around 2 meters away. The distance between the three people was 1 meter. Facing them stood the execution platoon; the company to the left [illegible word] from the company stood Wei[s]se with his adjutant.
>
> Rgt. Kdr. Weis[s]e told the guilty soldiers: "These three have broken the discipline of the unit. Because our situation is critical, we cannot afford to waste petrol to drive these people to a military court. For this reason, a death sentence is pronounced here and now. . . . Egle gave the order to 6 or 9 people and then they were shot before our eyes. Egle took a pistol out of its holster and shot each of them in the head." . . .
>
> I see the whole matter as an arbitrary action by Weis[s]e, who was known to be a "swine."[68]

The events of Katny were confirmed by Paul Dorn. He mentioned that he was not an eyewitness, being on watch duty at the time, but the situation stuck in his mind. The only difference between Engel's and Dorn's testimonies concerns the manner of execution. Engel spoke of shooting, Dorn of hanging. They both agreed that the order had been issued by Kurt Weisse. Dorn added information to Engel's testimony, stating that the events in Katny had taken place in summer 1944, before the Warsaw Uprising. He emphasized that Dirlewanger was not with the unit at the time, and Weisse was acting commander.[69]

Dorn added that Weisse "executed many members of our unit without Dirlewanger's knowledge":[70] for example, a soldier of the 4th Company of the 1st Battalion in the Uzda area at the turn of May and June 1944, as the Soviet army approached. His fault was that he "stole" (took without permission) a razor. He first spent an extended period in detention, and then Weisse issued a declaration that this soldier would be executed by hanging. The order was carried out. The noose was made of telephone wire. The convict was placed on a chair in the central square of the kolkhoz in which they were quartered. A quarter of an hour after the execution, the company was ready to march, and the kolkhoz was set on fire.[71]

On January 10, 1943, Dirlewanger issued the order: "I strictly forbid members of the battalion . . . to requisition cattle and other objects as they see fit and for personal use."[72] Emil Bauer mentioned that in the Minsk region, an *SS-Sturmmann* stole a pig from a farm. He was shot in punishment. Theft and plundering were punished severely.[73]

During the transfer from East Prussia to Warsaw, in the Augustów area Wally Geißmann, a grenadier from Kiel, raped a woman and looted. Dirlewanger had him hanged for these offences.[74]

René Ferderer was sent to Dirlewanger's unit in May 1944, after volunteering from the Ravensbrück camp. He was assigned to the 1st Battalion, which was stationed in Uzda. He described that after his arrival there, the first words he heard were "Everyone who goes over to the Russian side will not be shot, but hanged."[75] By June 13, he witnessed the hanging of two deserters who attempted to go over to the Soviet partisans. That was also when he found out that further to an order by Himmler, the commander of the unit had the authority to punish various infractions with death.[76]

During the suppression of the Warsaw Uprising, the death penalty for theft and rape was also in force. The doctor assigned to the unit on August 1, 1944, testified in 1954:

> Over the several months during which I belonged to the unit, I heard of numerous shootings for abandoning the unit, and I am convinced that only part of these people were intentionally trying to get away [desert]. In this . . . unit, death sentences were decided according to will and whim, with no court order, and the decision was influenced by the quantity of alcohol consumed. In other cases, the punishment

> of flogging was meted out. Two such soldiers came . . . to me for treatment after receiving such a punishment.[77]

Punishments imposed during the Warsaw Uprising were also described by Viktor Zerfaß, who was sent to that city in September 1944 from the Matzkau camp and drafted into Dirlewanger's unit. He testified that before the start of combat, he took part in an assembly during which Dirlewanger informed them that "looting in Warsaw was strictly forbidden," and anyone who broke the ban would be "shot immediately."[78]

In the building in which the unit was quartered during the uprising, there hung a notice informing them that "He who loots will be shot" (*Wer plündert, wird erschossen*).[79] Karl Vieregge remembered that in Warsaw, Dirlewanger said, "You have to fight, but not loot."[80] He testified that under Dirlewanger's orders, discipline was firm, and theft was punished with death.[81]

Like in Belarus, in Warsaw Dirlewanger also punished insubordination with death. Artur Schuldt described:

> During the few days that I spent in Warsaw, I witnessed two of Dirlewanger's soldiers being shot for looting. They had to stand in shirts and trousers, and then it was announced that they were temporarily removed from the unit for looting. Then they were shot.[82]

Despite the strict ban on looting, Dirlewanger permitted his subordinates to obtain provisions in Warsaw "independently." If a building was abandoned, soldiers were allowed to take the foodstuffs they needed, and even to send them back home.[83] This was confirmed by Karl Jochheim-Armin, who testified that they could procure food supplies on their own and obtain and improve their wardrobes in abandoned homes. He emphasized, however, that they were not allowed to take valuables, because this was punishable by shooting:

> I once personally witnessed Dirlewanger shoot a soldier from a foreign unit because the latter had taken a wristwatch from a civilian refugee's arm.[84]

In Belarus, orders concerning antipartisan operations also stated that food supplies should be obtained independently.

During the fighting in Warsaw, soldiers were forbidden to have contact with the Polish population. Heinrich Arndt testified that Dirlewanger did not pay much attention to this order and allowed contact, particularly with women. Rape and using violence against them were forbidden, but if they freely formed a closer relationship with soldiers, he had nothing against it.[85] It may be assumed that Dirlewanger's subordinates often abused these rules.

Paul Dorn said that during operations in Slovakia, offenses were also severely punished. He mentioned an execution carried out by Kurt Weisse in Oberstuben (now Horná Štubňa) near St. Martin (now Martin). Three of his companions (who came from Berlin, Hamburg, and the Netherlands) were shot there for attempting to desert:

> Three men were tied to stakes, with hands behind their backs and eyes blindfolded. The commander of the company, Paulus, granted their request to be untied and have the blindfold taken off. P. commanded the execution platoon. When the shooters took aim, all three extended their hands in the German salute and, standing to attention, shouted, "Heil Hitler!" The shots were fired. Then Paulus approached the individuals lying on the ground and shot each of their heads with his pistol. It seemed that one had only been shot in the arm.
>
> Before that, Paulus had read a notice saying "names went over to the Slovak partisans and for that reason were sentenced to death."[86]

The sentence had been signed by Weisse. The execution platoon was composed of six soldiers belonging to the 4th Company of the 1st Battalion, commanded by SS-Unterscharführer Paulus. Paul Dorn was to have been one of them, but as he testified, he was let off, his pretext being a sty on his eye.[87]

Hermann Schulze described that during antipartisan fighting in Slovakia, discipline was strictly enforced. No infringements were tolerated. He mentioned that one day, one of the men was punished for theft by twenty-five strokes with a stick and then hanged.[88]

Even though the Third Reich was in its decline, in Dirlewanger's unit discipline was strictly maintained until the very end. A transport of political prisoners from the Sachsenhausen camp, which in November 1944 was formed into the 3rd Battalion, was welcomed in Slovakia by an SS man (its later commander) whose name is unknown. In his first sentence, he informed the new members of SS-Sturmbrigade Dirlewanger about the penalties imposed for desertion. He added that in recent days, he had personally shot "several cowardly soldiers and dodgers" (*feiger Soldaten und Drückeberger*), and yet another of his men for insubordination. In a further part of his welcome speech, the SS man presented the situation on the front, stating that it did not seem bad, and that Germany would achieve victory.[89]

During combat, Dirlewanger was very demanding of his soldiers. In the heat of battle, he was a ruthless commander, but he had no leniency for himself either.[90] Gustav Strumpf mentioned that he never expected people to do anything that he himself would not have managed. He said that Dirlewanger went into combat and stormed enemy positions together with his men. According to him, this was why Sondereinheit Dirlewanger "always achieved its military goal."[91] This was confirmed by Heinrich Kraus, who also remembered the commander setting off to fight at the head of his men.[92] As Albert Venderbusch put it, "He never [stayed] behind during combat; [he was] always in front."[93] Karl Jochheim-Armin emphasized that Dirlewanger "not only demanded great courage of his men but also [demonstrated] valor himself."[94] Dirlewanger was a man of action and had spent his whole adult life fighting (he participated in the First World War and served in the Freikorps in the 1920s and the Condor Legion during the Spanish Civil War). His unquestionable bravery and love for warfare fired his subordinates' imaginations and had an enormous impact on them.

Dirlewanger was no stranger to alcohol, and he liked great drunken sprees[95] but did not get visibly drunk or reel.[96] He also invited his soldiers to drink and indulge with him. On special occasions such as promotions and the presentation of decorations, he organized evening gatherings.[97] Soldiers testified that they had the nature of banquets, although they also mentioned that Dirlewanger became quarrelsome and started brawls after consuming alcohol. This had no negative impact on his image and even increased their liking. Such celebrations must have taken place quite often, because many soldiers were awarded decorations.[98]

The atmosphere in the unit was very good:

> Comradeship among the members of Dirlewanger's unit . . . was exemplary. Nobody was reproached for their past. Previous penalties were not mentioned.[99]

People who were drafted into Sondereinheit Dirlewanger in late 1943 and in 1944 mentioned that they initially had a talk with Dirlewanger. During it (or during a general assembly), the commander informed them that theft, looting, and rape were strictly forbidden and that their conduct must be blameless.[100] Apart from the death penalty, flogging was also used to punish rule breaking (usually theft).[101] Those convicted of wrongdoing were beaten with a rubber truncheon until they fainted.[102] In at least one instance, a soldier was hanged for rape.[103]

Dirlewanger also sent soldiers who committed offenses back to the camps. Sometimes they were punished with death only after returning there. Friedrich Börth (arrested for membership in the SPD—Social Democratic Party of Germany—and imprisoned in Sachsenhausen) mentioned such a situation:

> In autumn 1944, one of the criminals from that brigade was sent back to the camp and publicly hanged during the evening assembly. Whether it was for looting or desertion, I am unable to say now. The true reason soon became clear to us.
>
> Several days later, we political prisoners were ordered to stay behind after the evening assembly, and the commander of the camp informed us that we would be given the opportunity to "rehabilitate ourselves" if only we volunteered for Dirlewanger's SS Brigade. We discussed this in the barracks.[104]

A similar event took place on October 30, 1944, in the Neuengamme concentration camp. One of the freshly trained political prisoners was publicly hanged in the assembly ground for a desertion attempt.[105]

10

Oskar Dirlewanger's Death: Myth and Controversy

In early 1945, Oskar Dirlewanger suffered increasingly from his old wounds. According to his oldest sister, Mathilde, he had sustained eleven in total.[1] At this time, he was granted leave, during which he arrived home in Esslingen and visited his family for the last time. He also went through pneumonia.[2] Next, he headed to Berlin, and from there he arrived at Berger's hunting residence in Allgäu on April 22, 1945.[3] Contact with Dirlewanger broke off at the end of April or the beginning of May, when his family received the last of his letters. However, when interrogated in the 1960s, the siblings were unable to remember exactly at what point this occurred.[4]

10.1. Ostarrest Prison in Altshausen[5]

Altshausen is a picturesque town located in Baden-Württemberg in Germany. It was here that the last act of Oskar Dirlewanger's life played out in 1945. At the end of April, the front rolled through Altshausen and its environs, and a battle between the Germans and the French took place in the town. The French army continued pressing south, and only a small unit remained in Altshausen.[6] The occupation of the German town of Altshausen by French forces started on April 22. Not many documents containing eyewitness accounts of those days have been preserved, but they indicate that fear and terror reigned. At that time, one of the routes of mass emigration via which Nazis and German soldiers escaped led through Altshausen. Prisoners released from concentration camps, forced laborers, and other people looking for a better, safer life also arrived in Altshausen.

From June 8, 1945, the mayor of Altshausen appointed by the French occupier was Johann Friedrich Rohrer. His brief period of rule was characterized by terror and anarchy, and much harm was inflicted.[7] In Altshausen, "Rohrer's band" plundered, looted, and even terrorized the inhabitants with beatings and murders. Although the rule of Mayor Rohrer did not last long, it caused a lot of damage. According to witnesses, it was he who was responsible for the terrible conditions in the Ostarrest prison in Altshausen, where Dirlewanger died. Rohrer was held responsible and convicted by the French command. Hugo Riegel was appointed as his successor.

At the turn of April and May, a hospital for French and German soldiers was established in the Realschule building. Lying there were former members of German penal battalions who had ended up in Altshausen as a result of wartime chaos, and also Jews liberated from concentration camps.[8] From this hospital, the food and drugs for prisoners incarcerated in Ostarrest were supplied. According to the postwar testimony of Betty Angele, who was part of the Red Cross, in late April 1945 a Dutch officer came to see her. He told her that prisoners were not getting food or drink.[9] SS-Oberführer Oskar Dirlewanger was most likely brought to the prison in Altshausen a month later. Betty Angele was one of the last people to talk to him.

Near Altshausen, in the town of Blönried lived the parents of Second Lieutenant Anton Füssinger. He had been a Luftwaffe pilot from 1939 to 1945. He had barely managed to return home when, on the very next day, June 1, 1945, a French soldier accompanied by two armed and uniformed Poles appeared. Even though Füssinger had documents issued by the Americans, he was arrested and transported to Ostarrest.[10] He was placed in a cell with men who introduced themselves as "Dirlewanger" and "Gustl Minch from Oberndorf."[11] According to Angele, Dirlewanger arrived in the prison at the turn of May and June.[12] Füssinger mentioned that initially there was mistrust and wariness between them. However, Dirlewanger made a positive first impression on Angele.[13] Apparently, he could still charm women.

The Luftwaffe pilot remembered that Dirlewanger did not say much on the first day. Only on the next day did they find out that he was a colonel (Oberst), and he explained that he had belonged to the Waffen-SS and served in a concentration camp. He had not been its commander, however: his men had served as guards there only temporarily. He did not say which camp or when this had taken place.[14] He added that while traveling through Altshausen, he had been recognized by a Jew who had been imprisoned in the camp. He was arrested immediately afterward.[15] In her conversations with him, Angele was not aware of who he was, his name having told her nothing. She believed he was one of the accidentally arrested travelers who did not have the right documents. She did not even suspect that he was a soldier. She was convinced that he would be released from prison on the next day. On the first day, he informed her that he had recently stayed in a hospital due to a skull fracture. She decided he should not sleep on an empty bunk, and wanting to relieve his suffering, she brought pillows from her own sofa to his cell. That was when the guards told her that Dirlewanger was a war criminal and she should not take such care of him.[16] In further conversations, Dirlewanger explained to Minch and Füssinger that during the war he had commanded one of the penal battalions—Strafregiment 999—and that they were sent on pacification operations.[17] When Angele found out that Dirlewanger was a war criminal, she also started questioning him about the past. She found out that during the First World War, he had been an officer, and in the war that had just ended, he had commanded a penal unit.[18] Both Betty Angele and Anton Füssinger mentioned that the guards were mainly uniformed Poles, and at first there were practically no French soldiers present.

Angele testified that because of his looks, she had believed that he had been arrested accidentally. She had gotten the impression that he was around sixty years old, and she thought that he would no longer have been a soldier at such an age.[19] He was around 1.80 m tall, a robust, sinewy man with an upright, soldierly stance, very thin, with a face with very prominent cheekbones and a high forehead. Füssinger "noticed; large ears." While staying in one cell with him, he assessed Dirlewanger to be forty-five to fifty years old.[20] They both indicated that he wore civilian clothes, a tight jacket or old checked coat, and gray military trousers.

The conditions in the Ostarrest prison were atrocious. Angele stated that initially, there were around twenty to twenty-five prisoners in two cells. They were mainly German soldiers and travelers who did not have the right documents. The French shut them in prison until their situation was clarified.[21] The cells were so full that people could not even sit down; they had to stand. Sanitary and hygienic conditions were at a similarly terrible level. For physiological needs, there was one bucket.[22] At first, Betty Angele could, with the consent of the Polish guards, provide food and drink to the prisoners. She obtained supplies for the inmates mostly from the hospital, but also from farms in Altshausen and kitchens organized by the occupier. She even collected food from the community.[23] It was only in June, after French soldiers started serving as guards, that Angele was forbidden from entering the prison. From that point on, she had to give the meals to the French guards, and they would distribute them among inmates. During interrogations and conversations in the 1960s, she strongly doubted that the food did indeed go to the prisoners. Already in 1945, she wondered whether Dirlewanger and Minch had been beaten so badly that they were unable to eat, or whether they were already dead (Anton Füssinger was released earlier). The guards who received the food returned after around three minutes with empty containers. It was doubtful that the inmates would have managed to finish eating within such a short time.[24]

Dirlewanger's sister Elfriede remembered that the last postcard from her brother had come to the family house in Esslingen.[25] His brother, Paul, added that Oskar had informed them that he was in a French prison and had been wounded. He also wrote that he would be transferred in the following week but did not know where.[26] The wound that Dirlewanger mentioned in the letter was most likely the result of a beating in prison. Angele testified that in the daytime, when she brought food, the prisoners were not beaten. Poles and Jews in civilian clothes performed guard duty. She did not meet French soldiers, particularly at first.[27] This was partly confirmed by Füssinger: "While in prison, I did not see any Frenchman, I saw only armed and uniformed Poles."[28] On the first night, Dirlewanger and Minch were led out into the corridor. There the guards beat them with wooden truncheons, accusing them of belonging to the SS and of Gestapo activity. After that night, Dirlewanger decided that it was time to exchange addresses with his companions in captivity. He foresaw that he would not leave Ostarrest alive.[29] Angele stated that at night, drunken Poles beat the arrestees, and the interrogations conducted by soldiers in the French command in the town hall were also violent. She saw signs of torture only on the faces of people returning from the town hall, usually blue marks. She could not find out much from the prisoners because she had been forbidden to talk to them. Once during a visit, she saw Dirlewanger's back. It was so bloody that she could not distinguish the marks of individual strokes.[30] Füssinger remembered that on the second day, a Jew of around sixteen years was brought to their cell and, under the supervision of Poles, hit them in the face until he had no strength left. Moreover, Dirlewanger and Minch were led out into the corridor every night and tortured there. One morning, Füssinger noticed that they both had open, bleeding wounds on their faces. All of their bodies were covered with wounds that seeped blood.[31] It was then that Betty Angele was forbidden to enter the prison. When she last saw Dirlewanger, he did not have the marks of a beating on his face yet, unlike Minch.[32] On the night of June 4, 1945, Dirlewanger and Minch were taken out of the cell three times. They were tortured and abused each time. The guards hit them with wooden truncheons and rifle butts all over the head and body and kicked them in the lower abdomen. After the last beating, the prisoners were unable to get up or speak and were brought unconscious into the cell. Füssinger remembered that night as the most terrible in his life. All through it he sat in a corner of the cell, afraid even to move so as not to provoke the guards. According to him, Minch died on that same night; his body was dragged out of the cell around thirty minutes later. Dirlewanger was still alive and tried to say something. On June 5 at 8:30 a.m., Füssinger was led out and transferred to the French command in the town hall. There his documents were controlled again, and he was released home.[33] When he left the cell, Dirlewanger was still alive. Betty confirmed that Füssinger had been released from prison several days before Dirlewanger's death, but she was unable to state precisely when the latter died.[34] Füssinger maintained that Dirlewanger and Minch could not have died on June 7 or 8 of natural causes. According to his knowledge, they were both already dead on the night of June 6, 1945. During the interrogation, he was unable to explain why the French would have provided a false date of death.[35] Dirlewanger and Minch were the last prisoners held in the Ostarrest prison in Altshausen. The arrests ended when Mayor Rohrer was dismissed, and Hugo Riegel was appointed his successor in June 1945.

A press article that appeared in the *Schwäbische Zeitung* fifteen years after Dirlewanger's death stated that by June 8, 1945, the register of deaths noted, "Dr. Oskar Dirlewanger, SS colonel, born September 26, 1895, in Würzburg, died June 7, 1945, at 1930 in Ostarrest in Altshausen." The cause of death was given as "Died as a result of a beating by guards."[36] In the death certificate, the French command in Altshausen stated that Dirlewanger died "of natural causes" on June 7, 1945, in Ostarrest in Altshausen at 7:30 p.m.[37]

On the morning of June 8, 1945, a coffin was brought out of the Ostarrest building. The French guards made sure that it was not opened. At 11:00 the parish priest and Capt. Hoffmann arrived.[38] Gravedigger Thaddäus Hund remembered that in early June 1945, he buried the coffin with Dirlewanger's body in the Altshausen cemetery. Two French soldiers armed with rifles witnessed the funeral. Also present were the parish priest, Romer, and the French commander at the time, who told the gravedigger that the deceased had been a highly ranked SS officer. On the grave, the French soldiers placed a cross with his name. The burial site remained unchanged until 1960.[39] Dirlewanger was laid to rest in field M, grave no. 5.[40]

10.2. Exhumation

In 1960, a lot of gossip started to circulate about Oskar Dirlewanger's later fate. Ideas about his postwar doings were quite abundant, some completely unrealistic and even verging on the fantastic. He had been sighted practically the world over. The most reports were made after *Revue* magazine published an article about Dirlewanger that featured two photos. The first showed Oskar Dirlewanger in a long leather coat. The second, contemporaneous photo (taken in 1958) allegedly contained Dirlewanger with a group of acquaintances after the war.[41] The matter gained publicity when on April 2, 1960, a Mr. K. recognized Oskar Dirlewanger in both photos.[42] Following the uproar caused by the article, it was decided that an investigation would be carried out and the body in the Altshausen cemetery exhumed. The photo in question was shown to many people who had known Dirlewanger while he was alive, including his brother and sister (the elder sister did not read the article). Most witnesses failed to recognize Dirlewanger in the 1958 picture. His siblings also denied that this was their brother.[43]

In the 1970s, investigators stated that Oskar Dirlewanger had been arrested on June 7, 1945, by plainclothes French gendarmes and interrogated by the French police (Deuxieme Bureaux colonel Ludman). According to them, he either committed suicide by hanging or (which they thought more likely) was handed over to the Russians.[44]

The most-popular theories, which may still be encountered today, involve Dirlewanger's alleged stay in the Middle East. The press published and still publishes articles about his postwar fate. Some witnesses testified having seen him in Germany (in 1958), among other places.[45]

In the 1960s, a theory about a cooperation between Martin Bormann and Oskar Dirlewanger dominated. Dirlewanger was to have passed through the Bosporus in 1947 and hid in Bormann's safe haven.[46] They allegedly aided Gen. Muhammad Nagib together and later, after the situation changed, Gamal Abdeil Nasser. To help in the takeover of power, they were supposedly given excellent training and equipment. The press claimed that they were promised very high remuneration for their work: Bormann was to receive fifteen million dollars' worth of bonds to be shared with Dirlewanger. The author of the article "Dirlewanger–Hauptquartier: Port Said," who claimed to have participated in the events he described, asserted that Bormann and Dirlewanger actively participated in the conclusion of a deal to buy arms from the USSR. They allegedly also took part in negotiations with Soviet politician Dmitri Shepilov[47] (they were conducted mainly by Dirlewanger). Moreover, Dirlewanger's men supposedly flew MiG-19 planes[48] and trained Egyptian pilots to do so.

According to these sensational reports, in 1956, on an assignment from Nasser, Dirlewanger negotiated with Josip Tito for the latter to remain neutral and not join international military pacts. Furthermore, Oskar Dirlewanger conducted unofficial talks with him about arms supplies to Yugoslavia. He even allegedly went to Yugoslavia in person to finalize the armament negotiations. According to these accounts, he visited Yugoslavia again several months later and met Tito in Zagreb. It was said that they formed such a strong friendship that at the end of the 1950s, Dirlewanger visited Tito, accompanied by Bormann and several of his soldiers, and even spent his free time in Split (Dalmatia) and Dubrovnik. During these holidays, wartime memories were revisited.[49]

A further part of the article indicated that Dirlewanger (who would then have been sixty-one years old) fought at the head of Waffen-SS soldiers during the so-called Suez crisis in 1956,[50] when war broke out between Egypt and an Israeli-British-French coalition, ending in Egypt's defeat.[51] During this conflict, the headquarters of Dirlewanger's organization was allegedly located in Port Said in Egypt. The author of the text claimed that after Bormann's death (he gave no date), Dirlewanger, together with the author and a person called Schedle, lived in a villa in Port Fuad. According to the daily, apart from advisory services for President Nasser, Dirlewanger's company also offered tourist services. The author added that three large hotels in Port Said and a bar with the intriguing name of Genickschußdiele ("Shot to the neck") were under Dirlewanger's control, and he also had several taxis, which made it possible to see over the whole town.[52] The article was accompanied by a photo in which the author marked the venues he described.

Carl Friedrichs, arrested in 1933 by the Nazis for his political convictions, testified in 1948 in Nuremberg that on Sunday, April 22, 1945, Oskar Dirlewanger appeared on the border in Tirol. He was wearing a uniform, which he soon exchanged for civilian clothes, and set off toward Tannheim. According to this statement, Dirlewanger did not arrive alone: He was accompanied by two women. Friedrichs did not witness these events himself—he had been told this story by a friend. Friedrichs had also heard that "Dirlewanger was currently in the French Foreign Legion in Indochina," but added that this information was unconfirmed.[53]

Gottlob Berger told historians from the Institut für Zeitgeschichte that in his opinion, Dirlewanger had found a haven in Syria or Egypt as a secret advisor to the people in power. He testified that his friend was certainly alive and that the grave in Altshausen held somebody else's corpse (despite the results of the exhumation). Like Carl Friedrichs, he claimed that Dirlewanger had been detained in Tannheim in Tyrol and then brought to France. There he ended up in a POW camp, from which he joined the Foreign Legion before finding shelter with the great mufti of Jerusalem.[54]

After the war, Dirlewanger was most frequently sighted in the Middle East. Additionally, people claimed that he was staying in his hometown of Esslingen. Some met him in the streets of Bonn.[55]

Numerous stories about Oskar Dirlewanger's alleged escape and further fate still circulate today. Oskar's brother, Paul Dirlewanger, cited many of them in his testimony. He had never been to Altshausen and never looked for information about his brother's fate. However, tales reached him via acquaintances. He himself described some of them as improbable. According to one, Oskar escaped from Germany to Spain while dressed as a nun. One friend informed Paul that he had seen his brother in Echterdingen Airport (Stuttgart) about to fly to Egypt.[56] Egypt is where he was seen the most often.

Peter Erretkamps remembered that many years after the war, he heard a broadcast in English about Egypt's King Farook I[57] and Dirlewanger's unit on the radio. The host stated that "Dirlewanger was currently Farook's tactical officer."[58]

After the war, some members of SS-Sonderkommando Dirlewanger looked for their former commander, believing him to still be alive. His soldier Walter Zeppenfeld testified in 1962 that he now knew that Dirlewanger was dead. However, earlier, Herbert Meyer (*SS-Obersturmführer*), a friend from the unit, had told him that Dirlewanger was in Indochina.[59]

Meanwhile, Paul Dorn was convinced in the 1960s that his former commander was still alive. He said that after the war (from January 14 to September 1960), he had searched for him for a long time. He traveled around Italy, France, and Spain, trying to find some trace of him. In Genoa, a Jesuit (he did not know his name) told him that he had helped Nazis escape to Egypt and that the former commander of SS-Sonderkommando Dirlewanger had been among them. According to his story, Dirlewanger traveled from Italy to Egypt and worked there as Muhammad Nagib's advisor. Next, he served Gamal Naser in the rank of general.[60] These were not the only stories by Oskar Dirlewanger's former soldiers.

In 1962, unit member Paul Rass testified that according to his knowledge, Dirlewanger was alive. He claimed that at the turn of 1947 and 1948, he had hosted Dirlewanger in his home in Hamburg. Rass believed that his former commander probably found the address with the help of the Association of Persecutees of the Nazi Regime (Vereinigungen der Verfolgten des Naziregimes, or VVN). Dirlewanger did not visit him alone: He was accompanied by two Polish soldiers (one was called Sokołowski), who according to Rass were stationed in the Hamburg District of Wandsbek.[61]

In 1956 the subject of Oskar Dirlewanger's postwar fate was raised during the World Jewish Congress. On the basis of press information from France and Mexico, suspicions were voiced that Dirlewanger was staying in Cairo, handling the personal security of President Nasser. Apart from newspaper articles, Prof. Raul Hilberg's publication *The Destruction of European Jews* (p. 705) was also referenced, with its information that in 1952, Dirlewanger had been present in Cairo.[62]

In connection with the increasingly great doubts concerning Dirlewanger's death and the numerous tales about his further fate and happy postwar life, the Ravensbrück prosecution opened an investigation to establish whether Dirlewanger really did die in the Ostarrest prison in Altshausen, and whether it was his corpse that lay in the grave in the town cemetery. The prosecution thus described the circumstances of the criminal offense (*Tathergang*):

> According to witness statements, at the end of May / start of June 1945, while traveling through Altshausen, Dirlewanger was recognized by a former concentration camp prisoner as the commander of the concentration camp. Dirlewanger was shut in the Altshausen prison and beaten to death by the Altshausen auxiliary police, composed of former Polish and Jewish concentration camp prisoners.
>
> The death was recorded in the register of deaths under no. 3/45 in the Altshausen civil registry. The entry was made by Hoffman, a military security officer, under the date of June 16, 1945, and according to it, Dirlewanger died of natural causes on June 7, 1945, at 19.30.[63]

The exhumation was carried out on Saturday, November 12, 1960, at 10:30 a.m. in the Altshausen cemetery. Its participants were prosecutor general Dr. Zoller, Prof. Dr. Weyrich from the Court Medicine Institute of the university in Freiburg im Breisgau, court-appointed physician Dr. Landenberger, and the gravedigger Thaddäus Hund, who had taken part in Oskar Dirlewanger's funeral.[64] After the grave was opened, it was established that the coffin was 1.85 m long. The remains were transported to the abovementioned Court Medicine Institute and thoroughly examined there.[65] It was ascertained that the skeleton belonged to a tall adult male whose height was preliminarily assessed at around 1.87–1.88 m. These data were in accordance with witness testimonies from the case files. Age was estimated at forty-five to fifty-five years. Injuries to the skull were found, sustained as the result of a strong blow to the head with a blunt instrument right before death or immediately after. Such a blow might not have caused death right away but may have caused later edema of the brain. The second injury to the skull that was found was consistent with the surface wound that Dirlewanger had sustained in 1921. The faciocranial bones featured visible, prominent cheekbones. In further investigations, a bone deformation in the right metatarsus was also found, consistent with a wound sustained during the First World War ("a shot through the foot, as a result of which a bone was broken"). The summary stated that the bones had been lying in the ground for around fifteen years. They belonged to a strong, tall man aged around forty-five to fifty-five and around 1.86 m tall. The circumference of the head was 54 cm. It was established that all the parameters were consistent with information provided by Dirlewanger's siblings and other witnesses. Bone damage agreed with data about the injuries he had sustained during the two wars. Thus, it was indisputably confirmed that the body buried in the cemetery in Altshausen belonged to Dr. Oskar Dirlewanger.[66] Several days after the examination was conducted, his siblings confirmed in a survey that the data were correct.[67]

After the exhumation, prosecutor general Dr. Zoller said in a conversation with journalists from Baden-Württemberg that "it is conclusively established that the exhumed body is the corpse of SS-Brigadeführer Dirlewanger."[68] The press wrote that despite the information in the register of deaths of the Altshausen prison about a natural cause of death, the court-appointed physician found damage to the skull during the examination. According to specialists, it may have contributed to Dirlewanger's death. Dr. Zoller stated that eleven traces of war wounds had been found (found wounds to the head, one in the left toe, and one to the left arm, clearly visible on the skeleton) that confirmed the deceased's identity beyond doubt. Moreover, it was established that in February 1945, he had two gold teeth put in in his lower jaw. They were found during the exhumation.[69]

The results of the specialist opinion did not satisfy everybody. In 1962, members of the Association of Persecutees of the Nazi Regime (Vereinigungen der Verfolgten des Naziregimes) questioned its results in a letter to Dr. Zoller. They maintained that Dirlewanger was alive and had been seen in 1952 in Heidelberg and Frankfurt. Furthermore, they criticized the experts, saying that the length of the skeleton did not match Dirlewanger's actual height.[70]

Also, the editors of *QUICK* magazine doubted the results of the exhumation. In a letter to the prosecutor, its editor, Zeug, wrote that he had consulted with a BBC London journalist (who had made a program about the Nazis in Egypt), and they had reached the conclusion that the body in Dirlewanger's grave probably belonged to Sergeant (Scharführer) Georg Dasch, a member of the unit who had been taken captive together with him. According to the English friend of the letter's author, this was supported by the fact that Dirlewanger's death certificate stated "died of natural causes," while the exhumed corpse had a bullet wound to the stomach.[71]

Dirlewanger's soldier Paul Rass did not believe the exhumation results either, stating that the doctors identifying the body and examining the remains must have made a mistake. He was not a reliable witness. Even if his tale about Oskar Dirlewanger's visit to his house is ignored, other elements are incorrect too. During an interrogation in 1962, he said that Kurt Weisse had a stiff leg and walked with a cane.[72] Nobody else mentioned Weisse having any disability.

Although the specialists examining the case and witnesses of the events repeatedly stated that the body in the Altshausen grave belonged to Dr. Oskar Dirlewanger, many people have doubts even to this day and spin far-fetched tales about him. Dirlewanger's legend is so strong that it has survived longer than the unit's commander himself.

Oskar Dirlewanger had three siblings: two sisters and a brother. In their testimony, they all described him as a family man who was attached to his parents and siblings. They were convinced that if he were alive, he would certainly have attempted to contact them.[7]

Conclusion

Oskar Dirlewanger's death brought the story of SS-Sonderkommando Dirlewanger to a close. Although at the end of the war the unit was renamed the 36th Waffen-SS Grenadier Division (36. Waffen Grenadier Division der SS), it never achieved the strength of a division.

In many respects, it was a curious unit. It was composed of people of extremely varied origin, from poachers to real criminals and offenders, from concentration camp prisoners who were given no choice in the matter to first-rate soldiers from elite Waffen-SS units. The individual fates and life stories of each SS-Sonderkommando Dirlewanger member are in themselves fascinating, and separate book chapters could be written about them.

Contrary to common belief, not only brutal criminals and sadists were sent to Dirlewanger's penal unit. A large part were soldiers, who had been trained for frontline units and were transferred for minor military infractions. One example may be the soldier mentioned by Stanisław Likiernik "Stach" from the Warsaw Uprising, who was guilty of having slapped his lieutenant in Normandy. He had some justification: His French fiancée had cheated on him with that officer. His conduct certainly violated military regulations, but it was understandable. Was the punishment commensurate with the offense?

Also, soldiers who had no records or convictions were placed under Dirlewanger's command. Part of them had been transferred to the unit due to personnel shortages; others volunteered. Many of SS-Sonderkommando Dirlewanger's soldiers were with the unit from its formation to its end: from 1940 to 1945. A large part of them were taken captive by the Russians or Americans in the last days of the war. Most of them managed to regain their liberty within several days, months, or a year. Some were less lucky and were transported to POW camps in the USSR and returned only in the mid-1950s. Others did not survive imprisonment.

Oskar Dirlewanger proved capable of gathering and integrating a diverse multitude and forming them into a well-functioning unit. He built his companies according to a specific plan. One company was composed only of poachers, the next of criminals, another of asocials, etc. Thus, different types of criminals became faithful companions in arms, and the phenomenon of "hazing" present in the military did not occur. The soldiers considered themselves brothers-in-arms because they came from the same camps and had often known each other previously. This also influenced the atmosphere in the unit. Walter Escher remembered that "camaraderie in the unit was exceptional. Everybody was responsible for everybody else."[1] Moreover, nobody revisited the offenses they had been sentenced for: They all started with a "blank slate."

In the final days of the war, this strategy turned against Dirlewanger. Political prisoners were conscripted into one company,[2] and during the fighting in Hungary they went over to the Red Army. Over its five-year history, the unit committed many terrible crimes, distinguishing itself by its particular cruelty in Belarus while pacifying villages and combating partisans. Similar methods of operation, both exceptionally effective and brutal, were also observed during the suppression of the Warsaw Uprising and the Slovak National Uprising.

Many different cruel offenses have been attributed to Dirlewanger's unit. For years, investigators who documented their actions added all instances of extermination of the Polish, Jewish, Belarusian, and Slovak population to the history of Dirlewanger's soldiers. In the 1970s, they were ascribed, for instance, the extermination of the Polish leadership and intelligentsia carried out within Operation Tannenberg.[3] Investigators failed to take into account that this operation was carried out from September to October 1939, while the Oranienburg Poachers' Unit, later SS-Sonderkommando Dirlewanger, was formed on July 1, 1940.

As I have shown in my book, they committed many crimes: starting from operations in the General Government, through the pacifications of around two hundred Belarusian villages conducted during numerous antipartisan operations in the years 1942–44, to massacres during the suppression of the Warsaw Uprising and the Slovak National Uprising.

Robberies and looting were strictly forbidden in Dirlewanger's brigade and in many instances were punished with flogging or death. Despite this, they commonly occurred both in occupied Poland and in Belarus. In many instances, they took place with the tacit consent of Oskar Dirlewanger himself. However, contrary to popular belief, this was not the result of his "criminal" or "bandit nature." The looting of inhabitants, both during antipartisan operations in Belarus and during the fighting in Warsaw, was chiefly the result of the head command's orders. According to these orders, during antipartisan operations, soldiers from participating units (not only Dirlewanger's) were to secure supplies "individually." Of course, this does not justify all the looting and stealing carried out by Dirlewanger's unit, but it does explain many situations.

As staff employee Leo Mletzko stated, the unit was always sent into the most-difficult and most-challenging areas.[4] This was confirmed by SS-Gruppenführer Graf von Pückler, who in 1942 wrote, "SS-Sonderkommando Dirlewanger is working out very well here. No other unit is as suitable for combat against partisans in difficult terrain."[5]

SS-Sonderkommando Dirlewanger was reasonably well trained and equipped, which is demonstrated by its numerous successes during antipartisan actions in Belarus and the suppression of the Warsaw Uprising. In the context of the fighting in Warsaw, they are presented as drunken criminals who focused on rape and looting, which is not completely true. They bore the brunt of combat efforts, being constantly on the front lines, and as the insurgents themselves stated, they were exceptionally difficult opponents. Dirlewanger's unit undoubtedly had the greatest combat value of all the German formations fighting in Warsaw. The insurgents underlined that Dirlewanger's soldiers attacked in a thought-out and organized manner. That Dirlewanger's unit was the chief German force in Warsaw is indicated also by the fact that most soldiers heard the names of Reinefarth and von dem Bach-Zelewski only during postwar interrogations. Many of them believed that it was Oskar Dirlewanger who was in command of all the German troops and responsible for suppressing the uprising.[6]

SS-Sonderkommando Dirlewanger had military value. In addition to the soldiers' training and special skills, their effectiveness was also a result of the amnesty they had been promised. Dirlewanger's subordinates became people who had nothing to lose and everything to gain. The poachers drafted into the unit demonstrated first-rate shooting skills. To them, the only thing that counted was to accurately target the enemy, often from a large distance. The soldiers of SS-Sonderkommando Dirlewanger were perfectly aware that both Germans and their opponents believed them to be "rabble." That was why they fought without mercy and did not expect any quarter from their enemies.

During his trial, Erich von dem Bach-Zelewski said of the fighting in Warsaw that "withdrawing [SS-Sturmbrigade Dirlewanger] from combat would have been equal to refraining from all offensive operations."[7] He also stated,

> Although their qualities left much to be desired in moral terms, their ability to fight was particularly high. They had nothing to lose and everything to win. They showed no mercy in battle and did not expect it for themselves.[8]

In his book *Kat Warszawy*, Sennerteg described Oskar Dirlewanger as follows:

> For somebody like Dirlewanger there was no place in society, but in the heat of battle he was in his element. He usually led his soldiers himself amid approaching bullets and left his members of staff to direct the action. Soldiers surely believed him an immortal demon, but he too could be hit by bullets. The long list of wounds sustained during the First World War was added to by further injuries from the Second.[9]

I believe that this brief portrayal aptly reflects Dirlewanger's character and his life. Aware that he would not return home from Altshausen, he made no attempt to lie and absolve himself of guilt. He helped the guards when they needed a translator, and his attitude earned respect until the end. Persons who knew him praised his tough, soldierly attitude. German war correspondent Horst B. described him thus:

> Dirlewanger was a ruthless careerist type who treated his men equally ruthlessly. He carried a pistol with the safety catch off everywhere but did not do anything by halves either. His soldiers regarded him with a combination of love and hate. They knew he did not demand more of them than he would demand of himself. At the same time, however, they looked forward to the day when they would return to their old units.[10]

Oskar Dirlewanger was hardened by his experiences in the First World War. Right after finishing school, he set off for the front. This must have made an indelible impression on a young man. As a result of the war, he suffered a permanent 40 percent loss of health. We cannot establish how great a toll this armed conflict had on his psyche, but he never managed to return to civilian life. Dirlewanger himself stated in 1944 that those who held positions in the rear areas during the war and did not fight at the front were "scoundrels" (*Lumpen*).[11] His experience from the Great War, later combat in the Freikorps, and problems with the law (two years of heavy imprisonment in Ludwigsburg and a stint in the Welzheim concentration camp) made him become the perfect commander of a penal unit. Himmler could not have managed to find a better man for this position. The assessment written by investigators in the 1960s after interrogations of the former soldiers of SS-Sonderkommando Dirlewanger can serve as a summary:

> He is assessed positively by the interrogated witnesses practically without exception, whether they belong to the category of nonconvicts, poachers, convicted by military courts, or repeat convicts. He was generally liked by his unit. . . . [During interrogations] the following features were emphasized: old warrior (Lewandowski), rake (Rau), vigorous, humble *Landsknecht* of exceptional courage (Bauser), in combat he demanded that his people gave of themselves everything that he gave of himself (Strumpf), he was always in front [in the first line] with his people (Jochheim, Kraus, Venderbusch) . . . , he had a big heart for his subordinates (Arndt), he stood up for his men (Vieregge) . . . , a strict but correct and just superior (Strumpf, Ruch, Escher, Venderbusch, Katz), maintained strict discipline (Strumpf, Händel), who did not tolerate . . . theft, looting and rape (Racher, Vieregge, Strumpf, Walter, Zerfaß, Daschner), and did not decide to apply the death penalty lightly . . . (Katz).[12]

They also stated,

> Dirlewanger drank much and often (Lewandowski, Katz, Rau) . . . , but nobody saw him reeling or lying on the ground (Katz), although he became fickle and erratic while drunk (Vieregge), and it was better to keep out of his way then (Lewandowski).[13]

Dirlewanger was a war criminal, but his military training cannot be denied. Thanks to his leadership skills, SS-Sonderkommando Dirlewanger achieved good effects in the fighting against partisans. He also achieved military success earlier, during the First World War. In 1919, Hauptmann Ritter von Molo, an adjutant of the 7. Landwehr Division, wrote, "Thanks to his resourcefulness, fearlessness, and valor, he became a wonderful example for his subordinates."[14]

Dirlewanger was an intelligent and educated man. He completed his studies with the title of doctor of political science and knew at least three foreign languages (French, English, Spanish), being fluent in two (Spanish and French). He had an extraordinary facility in "making" enemies, particularly among other commanders and people working in the führer's Chancellery: For example, they forbid him to contact them in any way. This was also apparent when the unit, termed a "plague," was withdrawn from Lublin. Even during social events, he sometimes offended others with his direct statements. One example is a party held on June 8, 1944, in Belarus at SS-Gruppenführer von Gottberg's dacha, to which commanders serving in Belarus were invited (they included Oberstquartiermeister der Heeresgruppe Mitte Oberst Georg von Unold, Hauptbannführer Nickel, and SS-Hauptsturmführer Walter Brandenburg). The last-mentioned felt extremely injured by what Dirlewanger said about various types of draft dodgers. Dirlewanger had addressed himself to Brandenburg, saying he was a "strange bird" (*schräger Vogel*) who had "shirked" for five years of the war by working at the Reich Ministry for the Occupied Eastern Territories in Berlin.[15] Dirlewanger's behavior offended Brandenburg so badly that he wrote complaints to Gottlob Berger and SS-Obergruppenführer Ernst Kaltenbrunner.[16] Dirlewanger was a unique and very original figure. He became a commander who inspired his soldiers by his personality and courage but, at the same time, irritated other officers with his behavior.

Dirlewanger turned out to be an effective leader. He formed the individuals under his command into an extremely effective special-purposes military unit. However, all his merits and skills are overshadowed by the scale of the crimes committed by SS-Sonderkommando Dirlewanger. As a unit, they do not bear responsibility for all the crimes attributed to them. Nevertheless, the acts they committed are so horrifying and on such a large scale that Dirlewanger should be considered one of the worst war criminals of his time.

Endnotes

Introduction

1. BA Ludwigsburg, B 162/5926, Betrifft: Sammelvorgang Strafsache Dirlewanger, Weiße, Heinsen Rußland-Polen-Ungarn-Tschecho-Slowakei u. Deutschland verbrechen, Berlin 44, May 12, 1972, 1511; and P. Stachiewicz, *"Parasol": Dzieje oddziału do zadań specjalnych Kierownictwa Dywersji Komendy Głównej Armii Krajowej* (Warsaw, Poland, 1984), 499.

2. S. Podlewski, *Przemarsz przez piekło* (Warsaw, Poland, 1957), 138.

3. S. Ozimek, *Stare Miasto 1944* (Warsaw, Poland, 1971), 71.

4. "Die rote Peitsche," *Frankfurter Illustrierte* 48 (1961), after P. Marti, *Sprawa Reinefartha: Kat Powstania Warszawskiego czy szacowny obywatel* (Warsaw, Poland, 2016), 212.

5. P. Longerich, *Himmler: Buchalter śmierci* (Warsaw, Poland, 2014), 426.

6. Ibid., 427.

7. M. Winstone, *Generalne Gubernatorstwo: Mroczne serce Europy* (Poznań, Poland, 2015), 81.

8. BAB, R/9361/III, t. 521445, Untersuchungsbogen (SS-UB), May 18, 1940, 793–94.

9. J. Hernández, *Nazistowskie bestie: Kaci z SS* (Warsaw, Poland, 2016), 191 (the source for Morgen's testimony quoted there is not provided).

10. BA Ludwigsburg, B 162/5924, 45 Js 30/64, Verfügung, Dortmund, October 15, 1964, 1143; and BA Ludwigsburg, B 162/16570, Das Urteil im Wilhelmstrassen-Prozess, 316. His testimony varies slightly depending on the date it was given.

11. BA Ludwigsburg, B 162/5924, 45 Js 30/64, Verfügung, Gottlob Berger, Dortmund, October 15, 1964, 1149–50.

12. W. Bartoszewski, *Prawda o von dem Bachu* (Warsaw and Poznań, Poland, 1961), 61.

13. Ibid.

14. P. Marti, *Sprawa Reinefartha*, 171.

15. Postwar investigations concerning Heinz Reinefarth are an example. For more on the subject: P. Marti, *Sprawa Reinefartha*.

16. R. Bechtle, *Die Ulmer Grenadier an der Ostfront: Die württembergischen Regimenter im Weltkrieg 1914–1918*, vol. 6, *Das Grenadier Regiment König Karl (5 Württ.) No. 123* (Stuttgart, 1920); and K. Stein, *Die württembergischen Regimenter im Weltkrieg 1914–1918: Das Württembergische Landw. Infanterie Regiment Nr. 121 im Weltkrieg 1914–1918*, vol. 37 (Stuttgart, 1925).

17. BAB, R/9361/III 521445, Personalangaben: Schulbildung und Beruf, 744. Apart from Spanish, Dirlewanger also spoke English and French.

Chapter 1

1. Reinsurance Treaty (1887) was a secret agreement concluded between Germany and Russia for three years, guaranteeing its parties mutual neutrality in the event of war between one of them and any other power. It was to become void if Russia attacked Austria or Germany attacked France; a completion protocol required Germany not to hinder Russia in taking control of the Turkish Straits (http://encyklopedia.pwn.pl/haslo/reasekuracyjny-traktat-1887;3966460.html, accessed 12.8.2016).

2. K. Grünberg, *SS. Gwardia Hitlera* (Warsaw, Poland, 1994), 18.

3. L. Rees, *Naziści: Ostrzeżenie historii* (Warsaw, Poland, 1997), 26.

4. Ibid.

5. Ibid.

6. Sta Ludwigsburg, E 356 d III Bü 9, Aktenzeichen 6131, Zuchthaus Ludwigsburg mit Zweiganstalt Hohenasperg, December 1, 1936.; and BAB, R/9361/III, vol. 521445, document from Dirlewanger's personal file, n.d., 755.

7. R. Laschet, *Dr. Oskar Dirlewanger: Die schwarze Gestalt unserer Schulgeschichte*, in Schelztor-Gymnasium 1838–2013, Festschrift, 175 Jahre (Esslingen, Germany, 2013), 45.

8. All data were found by Iris Sonnenstuhl-Fekete from Stadtarchiv Esslingen and made available to me by Rolf Laschet, a teacher at the Schelztor-Gymnasium in Esslingen, which I am very grateful for.

9. Sta Ludwigsburg, E 356 d III Bü 9, Aktenzeichen 6131, Zuchthaus Ludwigsburg mit Zweiganstalt Hohenasperg, December 1, 1936.

10. According to Oskar's school documents, August Dirlewanger started working as an attorney only in 1912, and up to that time his social position (profession) was listed as merchant.

11. All data were found by Iris Sonnenstuhl-Fekete from Stadtarchiv Esslingen and made available to me by Rolf Laschet, a teacher at the Schelztor-Gymnasium in Esslingen, for which I am very grateful.

12. BA Ludwigsburg, B 162/16592, Kriminalkommissariat Ulm, Kriminalaussenstelle Göppingen. Tgb. Nr. G5/405/60 Da, testimony of Mathilde H., Göppingen, July 15, 1960.

13. BA Ludwigsburg, B 162/16569, Bisheriges Ermittlungsergebnis über das Sonderkommando "Dirlewanger," n.d., 127.

14. Dirlewanger gave this as his home address until the end of his life in 1945 (e.g., BAB, R/9361/III, vol. 521445, document from Dirlewanger's personal file, n.d., 755).

15. R. Laschet, *Dr. Oskar Dirlewanger*, 45; and Oskar Dirlewanger als Esslinger Symbolfigur bei der Zerstörung gewerkschaftlicher und menschlicher Grundwerte, Vortrag am Ort des früheren Gewerkschaftshauses in Esslingen, June 24, 2014.

16. R. Laschet, *Dr. Oskar Dirlewanger*, 45–46.

17. Reifeprüfung 1913: Anmeldungs und Zeugnisliste, Oberrealschule Esslingen.

18. R. Laschet, *Dr. Oskar Dirlewanger*, 46. For unknown reasons, in the 1970s investigators recorded that Oskar Dirlewanger completed the Würzburg Oberrealschule and after his matriculation exam in 1913 enrolled in the Stuttgart School of Commerce to study political economics (BA Ludwigsburg, B 162/5926, Betrifft: Sammelvorgang Strafsache Dirlewanger, Weiße, Heinsen Rußland-Polen-Ungarn-Tschecho-Slowakei u. Deutschland verbrechen, Berlin 44, May 12, 1972, 1503).

19. Sta Ludwigsburg, E 356 d III Bü 9, Aktenzeichen 6131, Zuchthaus Ludwigsburg mit Zweiganstalt Hohenasperg, December 1, 1936.

20. BA Ludwigsburg, B 162/16569, Bisheriges Ermittlungsergebnis über das Sonderkommando "Dirlewanger," n.d., 130. According to SS personal files, he belonged to the 123rd Machine Gun Company (MG Kompanie 123) from October 1, 1913, to December 31, 1918. He was at the front from August 2, 1914, to 1918 (BAB, R/9361/III 521445, Personal Bericht, 732).

21. H. Stuttgart, M 430/3 Bü 1975, Personal-Bogen des Oskar Dirlewanger, n.d.

22. BA Ludwigsburg, B 162/16592, Die Oberste SA–führung: Führer–Fragebogen, March 20, 1934, 20; and H. Stuttgart, M 430/3 Bü 1975, Personal-Bogen des Oskar Dirlewanger, n.d.

23. YV, JM 2088, ID 3672138, The personal file of Dirlewanger, August 9, 1943.

24. H. Stuttgart, M 430/3 Bü 1975, Personal-Bogen des Oskar Dirlewanger, n.d.

25. Ibid.

26. R. Bechtle, *Die Ulmer Grenadier*, 5–6.

27. Ibid., 175.

28. H. Stuttgart, M 430/3 Bü 1975, Personal-Bogen des Oskar Dirlewanger, n.d.

29. R. Bechtle, *Die Ulmer Grenadier an der Ostfront*, 6.

30. For more information about the fighting at Bleid, see *Die Ulmer Grenadier an der Ostfront*, 6–11.

31. Ibid., 7.

32. Ibid., 8.

33. H. Stuttgart, M 430/3 Bü 1975, Personal-Bogen des Oskar Dirlewanger, n.d.

34. Ibid.

35. Ibid.

36. YV, JM 2088, ID 3672138, the personal file of Dirlewanger, August 9, 1943.

37. For more information about the fighting in the Forest of Argonne on September 8, 1914, see R. Bechtle, *Die Ulmer Grenadier*, 45–48.

38. H. Stuttgart, M 430/3 Bü 1975, Personal-Bogen des Oskar Dirlewanger, n.d., unpag.; BA Ludwigsburg, B 162/16592, Abschrift 7, Württ, Landwehr-Division Abwicklungsstelle, Stuttgart, June 20, 1919, 16; and BAB, R/9361/III, vol. 521445, motion to decorate SS-Obersturmbannführer Oskar Dirlewanger with the German Cross in Gold, August 15, 1943, 766.

This must be the event that Dirlewanger's sister Mathilde recalled. According to her, Oskar participated in the action at Argonne on the Western Front, where he was injured for the first time on August 24, 1914: he was shot in the foot and the bone was damaged; moreover, a piece of shrapnel wounded him in the head (BA Ludwigsburg, B 162/16592, Tgb. Nr. G5/405/60 Da, Ermittlungssache gegen Dr. Oskar Dirlewanger, früherer SS-Oberst, geb. 26 IX 1895 in Würzburg, July 15, 1960, 139).

Meanwhile, according to documents from 1943, his wound to the foot and forehead were from August 22, while on August 23, 1914, he was once again injured in the head by a piece of shrapnel (BAB, R/9361/III, vol. 521445, motion to decorate SS-Obersturmbannführer Oskar Dirlewanger with the German Cross in Gold, August 15, 1943, 766).

According to yet another document, his convalescence took almost a year, and in June 1915, Dirlewanger returned to the first line of fighting in France (BA Ludwigsburg, B 162/16592, Abschrift 7, Württ, Landwehr-Division Abwicklungsstelle, Stuttgart, June 20, 1919, 16).

39. R. Bechtle, *Die Ulmer Grenadier*, 175–76.

40. BA Ludwigsburg, B 162/16592, Die Oberste SA–führung. Führer–Fragebogen, March 20, 1934, 20; and BA Ludwigsburg, B 162/16592, Abschrift der politischen Beurteilung des Dr. Oskar Dirlewanger durch den SD–Oberabschnitt Süd-West, Stuttgart, May 14, 1938, 139.

41. BA Ludwigsburg, B 162/16592, Die Oberste SA–führung. Führer–Fragebogen, March 20, 1934, 20. Another document indicates that from December 1, 1916, to December 29, 1916, he worked in the general staff of the 7th Infantry Division (7. Inf. Div.) in the west as a machine gun officer—MG-Offizier (YV, JM 2088, ID 3672138, the personal file of Dirlewanger, August 9, 1943).

42. BA Ludwigsburg, B 162/16592, Abschrift 7, Württ, Landwehr-Division Abwicklungsstelle, Stuttgart, June 20, 1919, 16.

43. BA Ludwigsburg, B 162/16592, Abschrift der politischen Beurteilung des Dr. Oskar Dirlewanger durch den SD–Oberabschnitt Süd-West, May 14, 1938, 23.

44. YV, JM 2088, ID 3672138, the personal file of Dirlewanger, August 9, 1943.

45. H. Stuttgart, M 430/3 Bü 1975, Personal-Bogen des Oskar Dirlewanger, n.d.

46. Ch. Ingrao, *Czarni myśliwi: Brygada Dirlewangera* (Wołowiec, Poland, 2011), 86–87.

47. BA Ludwigsburg, B 162/16592, Abschrift 7, Württ, Landwehr-Division Abwicklungsstelle, Stuttgart, June 20, 1919, 16; and YV, JM 2088, ID 3672138, the personal file of Dirlewanger, August 9, 1943.

48. H. Stuttgart, M 430/3 Bü 1975, Personal-Bogen des Oskar Dirlewanger, n.d., unpag. For more information about fighting on the Stokhid and in Ukraine, see K. Stein, *Die Württembergischen Regimenter im Weltkrieg 1914–1918: Das Württembergische Landw. Infanterie Regiment Nr. 121 im Weltkrieg 1914–1918* (Stuttgart, 1925).

49. H. Stuttgart, M 430/3 Bü 1975, Personal-Bogen des Oskar Dirlewanger, n.d.

50. Ibid.; and K. Stein, *Die Württembergischen Regimenter im Weltkrieg 1914–1918: Das Württembergische Landw. Infanterie Regiment Nr. 121 im Weltkrieg 1914–1918* (Stuttgart, 1925), 180.

51. BAB, R/9361/III, vol. 521445, motion to decorate SS-Obersturmbannführer Oskar Dirlewanger with the German Cross in Gold, August 15, 1943, 766.

52. H. Stuttgart, M 430/3 Bü 1975, Personal-Bogen des Oskar Dirlewanger, n.d.

53. Ibid.

54. Ibid. According to other documents, he received the Iron Cross, 1st Class, on July 13, 1915 (i.a., BA Ludwigsburg, B 162/5926, Betrifft: Sammelvorgang Strafsache Dirlewanger, Weiße, Heinsen Rußland-Polen-Ungarn-Tschecho-Slowakei u. Deutschland verbrechen, Berlin 44, May 12, 1972, 1503).

55. YV, JM 2088, ID 3672138, the personal file of Dirlewanger, August 9, 1943.

56. H. Stuttgart, M 430/3 Bü 1975, Personal-Bogen des Oskar Dirlewanger, n.d.

57. For more about the First World War, see A. Chwalba, *Samobójstwo Europy: Wielka Wojna 1914–1918* (Kraków, Poland, 2014); J. Piekałkiewicz, *Pierwsza wojna światowa* (Warsaw, Poland, 1988); J. Pajewski, *Pierwsza wojna światowa 1914–1918* (Warsaw, Poland, 2014); and M. Gilbert, *Pierwsza wojna światowa* (Poznań, Poland, 2003).

58. BA Ludwigsburg, B 162/16592, Abschrift eines Artikels der "Sangerhäuser Kreiszeitung" vom 14 VII 1932, 17; information confirming this event: BA Ludwigsburg, B 162/16592, Abschrift der politischen Beurteilung des Dr. Oskar Dirlewanger durch den SD–Oberabschnitt Süd-West, May 14, 1938, 23).

59. H. Stuttgart, M 430/3 Bü 1975, Personal-Bogen des Oskar Dirlewanger, n.d.

60. Sta Ludwigsburg, E 356 d III Bü 9, Urteil, L 87/34, January 24, 1935.

61. BA Ludwigsburg, B 162/16592, Abschrift 7, Württ, Landwehr-Division Abwicklungsstelle, Stuttgart, June 20, 1919, 16.

62. Stadtarchiv Heilbronn, "Prozeß Dr. Dirlewanger: Der Mann, der an der Türe horchte: Wird das Gericht diesem Zeugen glauben?," *Heilbronner Tagblatt*, September 21, 1934, 7.

63. BA Ludwigsburg, B 162/16569, Bisheriges Ermittlungsergebnis über das Sonderkommando "Dirlewanger," n.d., 127.

64. Some documents contain the term "Volkswirt"—macroeconomist (BA Ludwigsburg, B 162/16569, Bisheriges Ermittlungsergebnis über das Sonderkommando "Dirlewanger," n.d., 127).

65. For more information about the organization Deutschvölkische Schutz und Trutzbund, see J. Leicht, *Der Deutschvölkische Schutz- und Trutzbund*, https://www.dhm.de/lemo/kapitel/weimarer-republik/antisemitismus/der-deutschvoelkische-schutz-und-trutzbund.html (accessed March 7, 2019).

66. Ch. Ingrao, *Czarni myśliwi*, 97–98.

67. BA Ludwigsburg, B 162/15141, V 502 AR 875/72, July 7, 1972, 16–17; and BA Ludwigsburg, B 162/15141, V 502 AR 875/72, September 29, 1972, 18–19.

68. BA Ludwigsburg, B 162/16593, letter from Oskar Dirlewanger to Prof Dr Arndt, Frankfurt, July 22, 1922, 230–33.

69. BA Ludwigsburg, B 162/16593, O. Dirlewanger, Zur Kritik des Gedankens einer planmässigen Leitung der Wirtschaft, 269.

70. The dissertation consisted of the following chapters: "Vorwort"; "Orientierende Systematik der Sozialisierungsmassnahmen: Versuch der Eingliederung des Gedankens einer planmässigen Leitung der Wirtschaft in die Sozialisierungmassnahmen"; "Wesen, Aufbau und Ziele einer planmässig geleiteten Wirtschaft"; "Planwirtschaft und Marxismus"; "Die Propagierung der planwirtschaftlichen Idee: Untersuchung der Berechtigung der Gründe, mit die Forderung nach Planwirtschaft motiviert wird"; "Wirtschaft und Ethik"; "Über die dem Gedanken einer planmässigen Leitung der Wirtschaft zugrunde liegende Auffassung vom Staate"; "Planwirtschaft und Individuum"; "Planwirtschaft und Persönlichkeitsbildung"; "Die wirtschaftlichen Auswirkungen der Verwirklichung des Gedankens einer planmässigen Leitung der Wirtschaft"; "Fixierung der wirtschaftlichen Massnahmen, die eine Planwirtschaft sich logischerweise zu stellen hätte: Untersuchung der Wirkung derselben auf die Erhöhung des nationalen Produktionsumfangs und der produktiven Kräfte, sowie des individuellen Produktionsanteils"; (a) "Rohstoffverteilung und Güterproduktion nach der Dringlichkeit des Bedarfs unter Berücksichtigung des ursächlichen Zusammenhangs zwischen Arbeitsintensität und Luxus"; (b) "Einfluss auf die Preisbildung durch Beherrschung des Presaufbaus"; (c) "Begelung des Absatzes"; "Die Kosten der Organisation einer Planwirtschaft"; "Der Gedanke einer planmässigen Leitung der Wirtschaft vom nationalen Standpunkt betrachtet"; "Bemerkungen"; "Über die Notwendigkeit einer Planwirtschaft im Kriegsfalle"; "Planwirtschaft und Reichseinheit"—original emphasis

(BA Ludwigsburg, B 162/16593, O. Dirlewanger, Zur Kritik des Gedankens einer planmässigen Leitung der Wirtschaft, 272–73).

71. Ibid., 274–76.

72. Ibid., 274–367.

73. Ibid., 365.

74. Ibid., 365–66.

75. BA Ludwigsburg, B 162/16593, Letter from the university, March 10 [?], 244.

76. Sta Ludwigsburg, E 356 d III Bü 9, Aktenzeichen 6131, Zuchthaus Ludwigsburg mit Zweiganstalt Hohenasperg, December 1, 1936.

77. Sta Ludwigsburg, E 356 d III Bü 9, Urteil, Abschrift: L 87/34, 24.1.1935, unpag.; and BAB, R/9361/III vol. 571150, Begründung, n.d.

78. P. Longerich, *Himmler*, 86.

79. K. Grünberg, *SS*, 18.

80. P. Longerich, *Himmler*, 86.

81. On the evening of November 8, 1923, Gustav von Kahr had been invited to the Bürgerbräukeller beer cellar to give a speech announcing his program. Also invited to the rally were government members, Gen. Otto von Lossow, the chief of the Bavarian police Hans von Seisser, the highest officials and representatives of business, and, furthermore, the leaders of patriotic associations. Hitler convinced von Kahr, von Lossow, and von Seisser to support the revolution. In the morning, all three reneged on their promises to him. For more, see D. Irving, *Wojna Göringa*, 60–90.

82. Feldernhalle is a monumental portico in Munich's Odeonsplatz. Commissioned in 1841 by King Ludwig I (for more, see https://www.schloesser.bayern.de/deutsch/schloss/objekte/mu_feldh.htm, accessed February 18, 2021).

83. P. Longerich, *Himmler*, 88.

84. H. P. Klausch, *Antifaschisten in SS-Uniform* (Bremen, Germany, 1993), 39–40.

85. Freikorps (Freiwillige Landesjägerkorps). Nationalist German volunteer units formed in 1918. They were used in the fighting to annex Saarland and the Baltic States to Germany, among other battles. They were also employed to put down revolutionary movements and against Polish insurgents; for example, in Silesia (https://encyklopedia.pwn.pl/haslo/Freikorps;3902703.html, accessed March 8, 2019); for more, see T. Kotłowski, *Historia Republiki Weimarskiej 1919–1933* (Poznań, Poland, 2004).

86. BAB, R/9361/III 521445, Personal Bericht, n.d., 732.

87. Sta Ludwigsburg, E 356 d III Bü 9, Urteil, Abschrift: L 87/34, January 24, 1935; and BA Ludwigsburg, B 162/5926, Betrifft: Sammelvorgang Strafsache Dirlewanger, Weiße, Heinsen Rußland-Polen-Ungarn-Tschecho-Slowakei u. Deutschland verbrechen, Berlin 44, May 12, 1972, 1503.

88. BA Ludwigsburg, B 162/5926, Betrifft: Sammelvorgang Strafsache Dirlewanger, Weiße, Heinsen Rußland-Polen-Ungarn-Tschecho-Slowakei u. Deutschland verbrechen, Berlin 44, May 12, 1972, 1503.

89. Stadtarchiv Heilbronn, "Pg. Dirlewanger zum Ehrenbürger der Stadt Sangerhausen ernannt," *Heilbronner Tagblatt*, May 31, 1934.

90. YV, JM 2088, ID 3672138, the personal file of Dirlewanger, August 9, 1943.

91. BA, NS 19/1207, Abschrift der politischen Beurteilung des Dr. Oskar Dirlewanger durch den SD—Oberabschnitt Süd-West, Stuttgart, May 14, 1938, H. P. Klausch, Antifaschisten, 36.

92. YV, JM 2088, ID 3672138, the personal file of Dirlewanger, August 9, 1943.

93. BAB, R/9361/III, vol. 521445, Abschrift, Freiwilligen-Abteilung "Sprösser," Unna, April 18, 1920, 884.

94. Stadtarchiv Heilbronn, D027-3, Materialsammlung zur Geschichte des Bahnschutzes in Württemberg von Reichsbahnoberinspektor Rudolf Behne, Anlage 34b. Leitung der Verkehrswehr, Tagesbefehl Nr. 2, Stuttgart, March 18, 1920. Meanwhile, according to a document issued by the Württemberg Ministry of the Interior, from August 24, 1920, Dirlewanger commanded his own platoon and together with its members took part in suppressing riots and strikes (BAB, R/9361/III, vol. 521445, Abschrift, Württ. Ministerium des Innern Polizeibefehlsstelle. Ib, Stuttgart, November 1,1920, Altes Schloss, 885).

95. Stadtarchiv Heilbronn, D027-3, Materialsammlung zur Geschichte des Bahnschutzes in Württemberg von Reichsbahnoberinspektor Rudolf Behne, Anlage 34b. Leitung der Verkehrswehr, Tagesbefehl Nr. 2, Stuttgart, March 18, 1920, unpag.; and Stadtarchiv Heilbronn, D027-3, Materialsammlung zur Geschichte des Bahnschutzes in Württemberg von Reichsbahnoberinspektor Rudolf Behne, Anlage 34c, Verkehrswehrbann, Tagesbefehl Nr 3, Stuttgart, March 23, 1920.

96. Stadtarchiv Heilbronn, D027-3, Materialsammlung zur Geschichte des Bahnschutzes in Württemberg von Reichsbahnoberinspektor Rudolf Behne, Anlage 34c, Verkehrswehrbann, Tagesbefehl Nr. 3, Stuttgart, March 23, 1920.

97. Kapp Putsch—an attempted monarchist coup in the Weimar Republic of March 1920. Its failure was caused by a lack of support from the commander of the Reichswehr, Hans von Seeckt, and mass workers' demonstrations (https://encyklopedia.pwn.pl/haslo/Kappa-Luettwitza-pucz;3920099.html, accessed March 8, 2019; for more, see D. Charlwood, *Rok 1920: Świat po wielkiej wojnie* (Warsaw, Poland, 2020); and https://de.wikipedia.org/wiki/Kapp-Putsch (accessed March 8, 2019).

98. H. P. Klausch, *Antifaschisten*, 36.

99. Stadtarchiv Heilbronn, D027-3, Materialsammlung zur Geschichte des Bahnschutzes in Württemberg von Reichsbahnoberinspektor Rudolf Behne, Anlage 34 b. 1, Stuttgart, August 26, 1920.

100. Ibid., Anlage 48 b, Verkehrswerbahnn, Bannbefehl Nr. 2, Stuttgart, August 29, 1920.

101. Ibid., Anlage 48 d, Verkehrswehrbann, Bannbefehl Nr. 4, Stuttgart, August 30, 1920.

102. Ibid., Anlage 48 h, Verkehrswehrbann, Bannbefehl Nr. 8, Stuttgart, September 2, 1920.

103. Ibid., Anlage 48 d, Verkehrswehrbann, Bannbefehl Nr. 9, Stuttgart, September 3, 1920.

104. Ibid., Anlage 48 l, Verkehrswerbahnn, Bannbefehl Nr. 11, Stuttgart, September 4, 1920, unpag.; and ibid., Anlage 48 q, Verkehrswehrbann, Bannbefehl Nr. 16, Stuttgart, September 7, 1920.

105. Ibid., Anlage 48 q. Verkehrswehrbann, Bannbefehl Nr. 16, Stuttgart, September 7, 1920.

106. Ibid., Anlage 48 n, Verkehrswehrbann, Bannbefehl Nr. 13, Stuttgart, September 5, 1920.

107. Ibid., Anlage 48 o, Verkehrswehrbann, Bannbefehl Nr. 14, Stuttgart, September 6, 1920.

108. Ibid., Anlage 48 q. Verkehrswehrbann, Bannbefehl Nr. 16, Stuttgart, September 7, 1920.

109. Ibid., Anlage 48 r. Verkehrswehrbann, Bannbefehl Nr. 17, Stuttgart, September 9, 1920.

110. For more on the March Action of 1921 and Max Hölz, see Stadtarchiv Heilbronn, "Wer denkt noch an Max Hölz? Der Panzerzug der Württ. [illegible word]," *Heilbronner Tagblatt*, April 14, 1934, 5; Stadtarchiv Heilbronn, D027-3, Materialsammlung zur Geschichte des Bahnschutzes in Württemberg von Reichsbahnoberinspektor Rudolf Behne; Stadtarchiv Heilbronn, "Aufruf! Arbeiter! Genossen! Pg. Dirlewanger zum Ehrenbürger der Stadt Sangerhausen ernannt," *Heilbronner Tagblatt*, May 31, 1934; J. Leicht, *Die Märzkämpfe in Mitteldeutschland 1921*, https://www.dhm.de/lemo/kapitel/weimarer-republik/innenpolitik/maerzkaempfe (accessed July 12, 2016); A. Peschel, *Hoelz (Hölz) Max*, http://saebi.isgv.de/biografie/Max_Hoelz_(1889–1933), accessed July 12, 2016; and Max Hoelz, DDR 1989, dir. J. Günter.

111. Stadtarchiv Heilbronn, D027-3, Materialsammlung zur Geschichte des Bahnschutzes in Württemberg von Reichsbahnoberinspektor Rudolf Behne, Anlage Nr. 67, Gefecht der Württ. Verkehrswehr gegen Hoelz-Banden auf Bahnhof Sangerhausen am Karsamtag, den 26. März 1921.

112. Stadtarchiv Heilbronn, "Pg. Dirlewanger zum Ehrenbürger der Stadt Sangerhausen ernannt," *Heilbronner Tagblatt*, May 31, 1934.

113. Stadtarchiv Heilbronn, D027-3, Materialsammlung zur Geschichte des Bahnschutzes in Württemberg von Reichsbahnoberinspektor Rudolf Behne, Anlage Nr. 68. Liste über die bei dem Gefecht Sangerhausen am 26./27. März 1921 gefallenen und verwundet Verkehrswehrleute; and BAB, R/9361/III, vol. 521445, motion to decorate SS-Obersturmbannführer Oskar Dirlewanger with the German Cross in Gold, August 15, 1943, 766.

114. Kyffhäuser Monument—built in the years 1890–96 according to a design by architect Bruno Schmitz. It depicts two emperors: Wilhelm I Hohenzollern on a horse and Frederick I Barbarossa enthroned. It is the third-largest monument in Germany and was intended to symbolize the German Empire as a continuation of the medieval Holy Roman Empire (for more, see http://www.kyffhaeuser-denkmal.de/, accessed August 9, 2017).

115. Stadtarchiv Heilbronn, D027-3, Materialsammlung zur Geschichte des Bahnschutzes in Württemberg von Reichsbahnoberinspektor Rudolf Behne, Anlage Nr. 95, An die Kameraden des ehemaligen Panzerzugs, Esslingen, June 22, 1932.

116. Stadtarchiv Heilbronn, "Pg. Dirlewanger zum Ehrenbürger der Stadt der Stadt Sangerhausen ernannt," *Heilbronner Tagblatt*, May 31, 1934; and BAB, R/9361/III vol. 571150, Begründung, n.d.

117. Ortsgruppenleiter. After the Nazi seizure of power, this title meant the chief of an urban area and region.

118. Stadtarchiv Heilbronn, "Uebererreichung der Ehrenbürger: Urkunde der Stadt Sangerhausen an Pg. Dirlewanger," *Heilbronner Tagblatt*, June 11, 1934.

Because on May 5, 1934, he was sent on mandatory leave and forbidden to wear the SA uniform due to disciplinary proceedings (more on this further in the chapter), Dirlewanger applied for this punishment to be suspended on June 10, 1934. The response to his request was likely positive (BAB, R/9361/III, vol. 521445, Dirlewanger's letter to SA-Gruppe Südwest, Heilbronn, May 29, 1934, 923).

119. BA Ludwigsburg, B 162/5926, Betrifft: Sammelvorgang Strafsache Dirlewanger, Weiße, Heinsen Rußland-Polen-Ungarn-Tschecho-Slowakei u. Deutschland verbrechen, Berlin 44, May 12, 1972, 1503; and Stadtarchiv Heilbronn, "Pg. Dirlewanger zum Ehrenbürger der Stadt Sangerhausen ernannt," *Heilbronner Tagblatt*, May 31, 1934.

120. YV, JM 2088, ID 3672138, the personal file of Dirlewanger, August 9, 1943.

121. BA Ludwigsburg, B 162/5926, Betrifft: Sammelvorgang Strafsache Dirlewanger, Weiße, Heinsen Rußland-Polen-Ungarn-Tschecho-Slowakei u. Deutschland verbrechen, Berlin 44, May 12, 1972, 1503.

122. For more about the Silesian Uprisings and the plebiscite: T. Jędruszczak, *Powstania śląskie 1919–1920–1921* (Katowice, Poland, 1981); W. Dobrzycki, *Powstanie Śląskie* (Warsaw, Poland, 1971); K. Popiołek, *Trzecie Powstanie Śląskie* (Katowice, Poland, 1971); W. Dąbrowski, *Trzecie powstanie śląskie: rok 1921* (London, 1973); *Encyklopedia powstań śląskich*, ed. F. Hawranek (Opole, Poland, 1982); and http://www.muzeumpowstanslaskich.pl/ (accessed August 10, 2016).

123. BA Ludwigsburg, B 162/5926, Betrifft: Sammelvorgang Strafsache Dirlewanger, Weiße, Heinsen Rußland-Polen-Ungarn-Tschecho-Slowakei u. Deutschland verbrechen, Berlin 44, May 12, 1972, 1503–04.

124. Ibid., 1504.

125. Manfred von Killinger: b. July 14,1886; d. September 2, 1944 (for more, see https://de.wikipedia.org/wiki/Manfred_von_Killinger (accessed March 8, 2019).

126. Hermann Ehrhardt: b. November 29, 1881; d. September 27, 1971 (for more, see https://de.wikipedia.org/wiki/Hermann_Ehrhardt, accessed 8.3.2019).

127. *Święta wojna bękartów Weimaru*, http://www.newsweek.pl/wiedza/historia/republika-weimarska-od-konca-1918-r-,artykuly,393452,1.html (accessed December 28, 2017).

128. H. W. Koch, *In the Name of the Volk: Political Justice in Hitler's Germany* (London, 1997), 12.

129. W. Wette, *The Wehrmacht: History, Myth, Reality*, 51.

130. T. Kotłowski, *Niemcy 1919–1923* (Poznań, Poland, 1986), 185.

131. *Święta wojna bękartów Weimaru.*

132. BA Ludwigsburg, B 162/5926, Betrifft: Sammelvorgang Strafsache Dirlewanger, Weiße, Heinsen Rußland-Polen-Ungarn-Tschecho-Slowakei u. Deutschland verbrechen, Berlin 44, May 12, 1972, 1504.

133. In March 1921, Dirlewanger was granted the professional title of qualified economist (*Diplomkaufmann*) in Mannheim. From 1922, he lived at Leipzigstrasse in Frankfurt am Mein and studied in that city until August 1925.

134. Sta Ludwigsburg, E 356 d III Bü 9, Urteil, Abschrift: L 87/34, January 24, 1935.

135. Sta Ludwigsburg, E 356 d III Bü 9, Aktenzeichen 6131, Zuchthaus Ludwigsburg mit Zweiganstalt Hohenasperg, December 1, 1936.

136. Ibid.

137. Sta Ludwigsburg, E 356 d III Bü 9, Urteil, Abschrift: L 87/34, January 24, 1935.

138. BA Ludwigsburg, B 162/5926, Betrifft: Sammelvorgang Strafsache Dirlewanger, Weiße, Heinsen Rußland-Polen-Ungarn-Tschecho-Slowakei u. Deutschland verbrechen, Berlin 44, May 12, 1972, 1504; and Sta Ludwigsburg, E 356 d III Bü 9, Aktenzeichen 6131, Zuchthaus Ludwigsburg mit Zweiganstalt Hohenasperg, December 1, 1936.

139. Sta Ludwigsburg, E 356 d III Bü 9, Aktenzeichen 6131, Zuchthaus Ludwigsburg mit Zweiganstalt Hohenasperg, December 1, 1936. The website http://forum.valka.cz/topic/view/64593/Dirlewanger-Oskar-Paul (accessed March 17, 2016) contains the information that Dirlewanger was an independent tax advisor from December 31, 1931, until July 1933. Court documents confirm that he conducted such activity until July 1933 (BAB, R/9361/III, vol. 571150, Begründung, unpag.). Meanwhile, in the 1970s, investigators noted that he worked as a volunteer in Esslingen at the company S., a metal article manufacturer. It was Jewish owned, and Dirlewanger embezzled from it and was let go as a result. Investigators also stated that this occurred immediately after he passed his matriculation examination in 1913 (BA Ludwigsburg, B 162/5926, Betrifft: Sammelvorgang Strafsache Dirlewanger, Weiße, Heinsen

Rußland-Polen-Ungarn-Tschecho-Slowakei u. Deutschland verbrechen, Berlin 44, May 12, 1972, 1503).

140. BA Ludwigsburg, B 162/5926, Betrifft: Sammelvorgang Strafsache Dirlewanger, Weiße, Heinsen Rußland-Polen-Ungarn-Tschecho-Slowakei u. Deutschland verbrechen, Berlin 44, May 12,1972, 1504. According to still other sources, Dirlewanger pocketed a large amount of money belonging to Kornicker. He underpaid employees and transferred the remaining sums to his own account. He was likely forced to resign from his position because of this. The issue was settled amicably, no court proceedings were started, and according to the agreement, Dirlewanger reimbursed the stolen funds to the company (http://www.mauspfeil.com/Oskar_Dirlewanger.html, accessed March 17, 2016).

141. L. Rees, *Naziści*, 14.

142. Ibid., 15–16.

143. Ibid., 38; and P. Longerich, *Himmler*, 173.

144. BAB, R/9361/III 521445, Personalangaben, n.d., 743. A court judgment from 1935 recorded the party number as 1,000,172 (Sta Ludwigsburg, E 356 d III Bü 9, Urteil, Abschrift L 87/34, January 24, 1935), and the Personal Bericht as 1,092,492 (BAB, R/9361/III 521445, Personal Bericht, n.d., 747).

145. Sta Ludwigsburg, E 356 d III Bü 9, Aktenzeichen 6131, Zuchthaus Ludwigsburg mit Zweiganstalt Hohenasperg, December 1, 1936. According to the SS file entry, Dirlewanger belonged to the SA from March 1, 1932, to July 1, 1934 (BAB, R/9361/III 521445, Personal Bericht, n.d., 732).

146. P. Longerich, *Himmler*, 173.

147. Ibid., 174.

148. R. Laschet, *Dr. Oskar Dirlewanger*, 46; and BA Ludwigsburg, B 162/5926, Betrifft: Sammelvorgang Strafsache Dirlewanger, Weiße, Heinsen Rußland-Polen-Ungarn-Tschecho-Slowakei u. Deutschland verbrechen, Berlin 44, May 12, 1972, 1504.

149. BA Ludwigsburg, B 162/5926, Betrifft: Sammelvorgang Strafsache Dirlewanger, Weiße, Heinsen Rußland-Polen-Ungarn-Tschecho-Slowakei u. Deutschland verbrechen, Berlin 44, May 12, 1972, 1505.

150. Brown House (Braunes Haus). Name of the NSDAP headquarters from 1930 to 1945, located at Briennerstraße 45 in Munich.

151. BAB, NS 19/1207, letter from Oskar Dirlewanger to SS Reichsführer, July 4, 1939, 3.

152. R. Laschet, *Oskar Dirlewanger als Esslinger Symbolfigur bei der Zerstörung gewerkschaftlicher und menschlicher Grundwerte, Vortrag am Ort des früheren Gewerkschaftshauses in Esslingen*, June 24, 2014; http://www.mauspfeil.com/Oskar_Dirlewanger.html (accessed March 17, 2016).

153. Sta Ludwigsburg, E 356 d III Bü 9, Urteil, Abschrift: L 87/34, January 24, 1935. According to a different document, he assumed leadership of I/122 by 1928

(BA Ludwigsburg, B 162/5926, Betrifft: Sammelvorgang Strafsache Dirlewanger, Weiße, Heinsen Rußland-Polen-Ungarn-Tschecho-Slowakei u. Deutschland verbrechen, Berlin 44, May 12, 1972, 1504). The date February 20, 1934, is sometimes also provided (BA Ludwigsburg, B 162/16569, Bisheriges Ermittlungsergebnis über das Sonderkommando "Dirlewanger," n.d., 129). However, the year 1933 cited by me seems more reliable, given the time the document was written (1935).

154. Sta Ludwigsburg, E 356 d III Bü 9, Aktenzeichen 6131, Zuchthaus Ludwigsburg mit Zweiganstalt Hohenasperg, December 1, 1936.

155. Stadtarchiv Heilbronn, "Erneuter großer Erfolg des Arbeitsamts Heilbronn: Sämtliche Kriegsbeschädigten in Arbeit!," *Heilbronner Tagblatt*, April 14, 1934, 5.

156. Stadtarchiv Heilbronn, "Wer denkt noch an Max Hölz? Der Panzerzug der Württ. [illegible word]," *Heilbronner Tagblatt*, April 14, 1934, 5.

157. Sta Ludwigsburg, E 356 d III Bü 9, Urteil, Abschrift: L 87/34, January 24, 1935.

158. "Haus Fleischmann," https://de.wikipedia.org/wiki/Haus_Fleischmann (accessed June 20, 2016).

159. Sta Ludwigsburg, E 356 d III Bü 9, Aktenzeichen 6131, Zuchthaus Ludwigsburg mit Zweiganstalt Hohenasperg, December 1, 1936.

160. F. MacLean, *The Cruel Hunters: SS-Sonderkommando Dirlewanger; Hitler's Most Notorious Anti-Partisan Unit* (Atglen, PA, 1998), 28–31; and A. Richie, *Warszawa 1944: Tragiczne powstanie* (Warsaw, Poland, 2013), 53.

161. F. MacLean, *The Cruel Hunters*, 27; and A. Richie, *Warszawa 1944*, 53.

162. Sta Ludwigsburg, E 356 d III Bü 9, Urteil, Abschrift: L 87/34, January 24, 1935.

163. "Heute vor der Großen Strafkammer: Prozeß gegen Dr. Dirlewanger," *Heilbronner Tagblatt*, September 20, 1934; "Prozeß Dr. Dirlewanger: Der Mann, der an der Türe horchte; Wird das Gericht diesem Zeugen glauben?," *Heilbronner Tagblatt*, September 21, 1934, 7; "2 Jahre Zuchthaus: Das Urteil gegen Dr. Dirlewanger," *Heilbronner Tagblatt*, September 22, 1934; and "2 Jahre Zuchthaus für Dr. Dirlewanger: Die Plädoyers," *Neckar-Zeitung*, September 22, 1934. All the newspapers may be found in Stadtarchiv Heilbronn.

164. Sta Ludwigsburg, E 356 d III Bü 9, Urteil, Abschrift: L 87/34, January 24, 1935, unpag.; and Stadtarchiv Heilbronn, "Prozeß Dr. Dirlewanger: Der Mann, der an der Türe horchte; Wird das Gericht diesem Zeugen glauben?," *Heilbronner Tagblatt*, September 21, 1934, 7.

165. Sta Ludwigsburg, E 356 d III Bü 9, Urteil, Abschrift: L 87/34, January 24, 1935.

166. Ibid.

167. Ibid.

168. Ibid.

169. Ibid.

170. Stadtarchiv Heilbronn, "Prozeß Dr. Dirlewanger: Der Mann, der an der Türe horchte; Wird das Gericht diesem Zeugen glauben?," *Heilbronner Tagblatt*, September 21, 1934, 7.

171. Sta Ludwigsburg, E 356 d III Bü 9, Urteil, Abschrift: L 87/34, January 24, 1935; and Stadtarchiv Heilbronn, "Heute vor der Großen Strafkammer: Prozeß gegen Dr. Dirlewanger," *Heilbronner Tagblatt*, September 20, 1934.

172. Sta Ludwigsburg, E 356 d III Bü 9, Urteil, Abschrift: L 87/34, January 24, 1935.

173. Sta Ludwigsburg, E 356 d III Bü 9, Aktenzeichen 6131, Zuchthaus Ludwigsburg mit Zweiganstalt Hohenasperg, December 1, 1936; Sta Ludwigsburg, E 356 d III Bü 9, Urteil, L 87/34, January 24, 1935; Stadtarchiv Heilbronn, "2 Jahre Zuchthaus. Das Urteil gegen Dr. Dirlewanger," *Heilbronner Tagblatt*, September 22, 1934; and BA Ludwigsburg, B 162/16569, Bisheriges Ermittlungsergebnis über das Sonderkommando "Dirlewanger," n.d., 128.

174. BAB, R/9361/III vol. 571150, Begründung, Stuttgart, May 22, 1940.

175. For more on Kreisleiter Richard Drauz, see http://www.stadtgeschichte-heilbronn.de/ausstellung/nationalsozialismus/richard-drauz.html (accessed November 3, 2017); and S. Schlösser, *Die Heilbronner NSDAP und ihre "Führer": Eine Bestandsaufnahme zur nationalsozialistischen Personalpolitik auf lokaler Ebene und ihren Auswirkungen "von Ort"* (Stadtarchiv Heilbronn, 2003).

176. For more on Gauleiter Wilhelm Murr, see S. Schlösser, *Die Heilbronner NSDAP*.

177. H. P. Klausch, *Antifaschisten*, 42.

178. Sta Ludwigsburg, E 356 d III Bü 9, Aktenzeichen 6131, Zuchthaus Ludwigsburg mit Zweiganstalt Hohenasperg, December 1, 1936.

179. Sta Ludwigsburg, E 356 d III Bü 9, Der Oberstaatsanwalt bei dem Landgericht Stuttgart. Verfügung vom 12. März 1936, March 14, 1936.

180. Ibid.

181. BA Ludwigsburg, B 162/16570, Das Urteil im Wilhelmstrassen-Prozess, n.d., 316.

182. BAB, R/9361/III, vol. 521445, SA der NSDAP Brigade 155 (Hohenlohe-Obenwald), Abt. Iia 1b, B.B. Nr. 3252/3[?], Betrifft: Disziplinarverfahren gegen Stuf. Dirlewanger, Heilbronn, May 9, 1934, 899.

183. BAB, R/9361/III, vol. 521445, Abschrift, SA. Gruppe Südwest Standarte 122 Abt. Ia 1b, Betrifft Stab der Brigade 155, Heilbronn, April 30, 1934, 891.

184. BAB, R/9361/III, vol. 521445, II alb 3076/34, Iia Za BB Nr.2890/34 v. 30.4.34, Heilbronn, May 5, 1934, 897; BAB, R/9361/III, vol. 521445, An die SA-Standarte 122 Heilbronn, Heilbronn, May 9, 1934, 898; H. P. Klausch, *Antifaschisten*, 41; BAB, R/9361/III, vol. 521445, protocols from questioning of SA-Brigade 155 members of May 2–4, 1934, 892–94; BAB, R/9361/III, vol. 521445, SA der NSDAP Brigade 155 (Hohenlohe-Obenwald), Abt. Iia 1b, B.B. Nr. 3252/3[?], Betrifft:

Disziplinarverfahren gegen Stuf. Dirlewanger, Heilbronn, May 9, 1934, 899; and BAB, R/9361/III, vol. 521445, Dirlewanger's letter to SA-Gruppe Südwest, Heilbronn, May 29, 1934, 923.

185. BAB, R/9361/III, vol. 521445, Dirlewanger's letter to Oberführer Ziegler, commander of SA brigade 155, Heilbronn, May 11, 1934, 901–05.

186. Sta Ludwigsburg, E 356 d III Bü 9, Urteil, Abschrift: L 87/34, January 24, 1935.

187. BAB, R/9361/III, vol. 521445, S.A. Gruppe Südwest, Stuttgart, August 8, 1934, 931.

188. Dirlewanger was expelled from the SA as a result of an earlier disciplinary proceedings caused by "bad behavior," among other things, which had nothing to do with the court proceeding (described further in this chapter). The motion to expel him was made by May 1934 (BAB, R/9361/III, vol. 521445, SA der NSDAP Brigade 155 (Hohenlohe-Obenwald), Abt. Iia 1b, B.B. Nr. 3252/3[?], Betrifft: Disziplinarverfahren gegen Stuf. Dirlewanger, Heilbronn, May 9, 1934, 899).

189. Sta Ludwigsburg, E 356 d III Bü 9, Urteil, Abschrift: L 87/34, January 24, 1935.

190. BAB, R/9361/III, vol. 521445, Abschrift, SA. Gruppe Südwest Standarte 122 Abt. Ia 1b, Betrifft Stab der Brigade 155, Heilbronn, April 30, 1934, 891.

191. Stadtarchiv Heilbronn, "2 Jahre Zuchthaus: Das Urteil gegen Dr. Dirlewanger," *Heilbronner Tagblatt*, September 22, 1934.

192. Sta Ludwigsburg, E 356 d III Bü 9, Landes . . . Ludwigsburg, 6131, October 16, 1936.

193. Sta Ludwigsburg, E 356 d III Bü 9, Aktenzeichen 6131, Zuchthaus Ludwigsburg mit Zweiganstalt Hohenasperg, December 1, 1936. Cf. "Die Strafe trug er ruhig . . . : Er war ernst und verständig, willig und geschickt, anständig und verträglich mit den Mitgefangenen. Korrekt im Verkehr mit den Beamten. Immer zeigte er sich als aufrichtiger und Ehrlicher Mann" (H. P. Klausch, *Antifaschisten*, 42).

194. BAB, R/9361/III, vol. 521445, Gaugericht Württemberg-Hohenzollern der NSDAP, Aktenzeichen: 501/34, Stuttgart, February 26, 1936, 942–45.

195. H. Stuttgart, M 430/3 Bü 1975, Wehrbezirks—Kommando Heilbronn Abt. II a Az. 22 b/e, Heilbronn, July 13, 1937.

196. P. Longerich, *Himmler*, 426.

197. BA Ludwigsburg, B 162/16592, Abschrift der politischen Beurteilung des Dr. Oskar Dirlewanger durch den SD—Oberabschnitt Süd-West, May 14, 1938, 24; and BA Ludwigsburg, B 162/16569, Bisheriges Ermittlungsergebnis über das Sonderkommando "Dirlewanger," n.d., 128.

198. YV, JM 2088, ID 3672136, recommendation letter from the personal file of Dirlewanger, June 4, 1940. For information about Dirlewanger's incarceration in the Welzheim camp, see http://www.mauspfeil.com/Oskar_Dirlewanger.html (accessed March 17, 2016).

199. BA Ludwigsburg, B 162/16592, letter from Dirlewanger to *SS Reichsführer* and chief of German police, Berlin, July 4, 1939, 26. According to some sources, he served in the Condor Legion from April 1937 to May 1939 (BA Ludwigsburg, B 162/16569, Bisheriges Ermittlungsergebnis über das Sonderkommando "Dirlewanger," n.d., 130) or to June 1939 (BAB, R/9361/III 521445, Personal Bericht, n.d., 732, 746).

200. The Condor Legion was formed on November 7, 1936. On October 31, 1936, General Hugo Sperrle flew to Spain, taking command as "Sander." The legion's air units were organized as follows: command, bomber group (three squadrons of Ju 52 airplanes), fighter group (three He 51 squadrons), a reconnaissance unit equipped with He 70 and He 45 planes, a naval reconnaissance squadron with He 59 and He 60 seaplanes, an experimental bomber squadron, an experimental fighter squadron and a battalion of antiaircraft artillery (three batteries of 88 mm antiaircraft guns, two batteries of 20 mm antiaircraft guns, and a battery of reflectors), a signals unit (radiotelegraph company, telephone company, observation company, and a surveillance company), an airfield ground crew company, repair workshops, munitions depot, a meteorological unit, a field hospital, and a medical battalion. Furthermore, it had a small ground force under its command: the Imker. The Condor Legion never numbered more than 6,500 soldiers. Service in Spain lasted nine months on average, and from the second half of 1937, volunteer intake for the legion was abandoned. Only Imker-Ausbilder instructors stayed there longer, sometimes for the whole war—for more information, see T. Nowakowski and M. Skotnicki, *Legion Condor: Hiszpańska wojna Hitlera* (Warsaw, Poland, 2011); and M. Skotnicki, T. Nowakowski, and K. Zalewski, *Legion Condor* (Warsaw, Poland, 1994).

201. YV, JM 2088, ID 3672136, recommendation letter from the personal file of Dirlewanger, June 4, 1940.

202. Sonderstab W, set up by Gen. Erhard Milch on July 26, 1936, was to coordinate support for rebel forces. Its first commander was Gen. Helmut Wilberg (for more on Sonderstab W, see T. Nowakowski and M. Skotnicki, *Legion Condor*).

203. For more on the situation in 1930s Spain and the start of the putsch and civil war, see T. Nowakowski and M. Skotnicki, *Legion Condor*; A. Beevor, *Walka o Hiszpanię 1936–1939: Pierwsze starcie totalitaryzmów* (Kraków, Poland, 2009); and T. Zubiński, *Wojna domowa w Hiszpanii 1936–1939* (Poznań, Poland, 2015).

204. T. Nowakowski and M. Skotnicki, *Legion Condor*, 17–21.

205. D. Irving, *Wojna Hitlera* (Warsaw, Poland, 2005), 62–63.

206. A. Beevor, *Walka o Hiszpanię*, 569.

207. Ibid., 568–69.

208. Ibid., 281.

209. T. Nowakowski and M. Skotnicki, *Legion Condor*, 43.

210. A. Beevor, *Walka o Hiszpanię*, 293.

211. YV, JM 2088, ID 3672138, the personal file of Dirlewanger, August 9, 1943, unpag.; and BA Ludwigsburg, B 162/16592, letter from Dirlewanger to *SS Reichsführer* and chief of German police, Berlin, July 4, 1939, 26.

212. BAB, R/9361/III, vol. 521445, *Oberst Ritter v. Thoma*, Bestätigung, November 20, 1939, 786.

213. H. P. Klausch, *Antifaschisten*, 44.

214. BAB, R/9361/III, vol. 521445, letter from Oskar Dirlewanger to Heinrich Himmler, Stuttgart, July 4, 1939, 809, after the Polish translation by J. Kalemba.

215. T. Nowakowski and M. Skotnicki, *Legion Condor*, 52.

216. Ibid., 53.

217. Spanish Cross—*Spanienkreuz*—on April 14, 1939, Hitler issued this decree: "To express my appreciation and gratitude for the merits of German volunteers who contributed to the victory over Bolshevism during the Spanish war of liberation." Two versions of the decoration were introduced: with swords and without. The Spanish Cross with Swords—gold, silver, and bronze—was awarded for merit in combat (in face of the enemy and within the field of enemy operations). The cross without swords could be bronze or silver and was awarded to crews of courier planes, members of armed forces who had served at least three months in Spain without taking an active part in the fighting, civilian employees of the Condor Legion or other German institutions in Spain, and aviation industry workers. All participants of the Spanish war were decorated with the Bronze Cross. The Spanish Cross was worn on the right breast at midpocket level (Ibid., 176–78).

218. The Military Merit Cross—Cruz del Mérito—had four classes. The first, with a diamond-encrusted star, was rarely awarded. The fourth-class cross was given the most often. The Spanish commonly used the term Cruz Rojo del Mérito Militar, and thus the name popularly used by the Germans: Rotes Kriegsverdienstkreuz; that is, the Red Cross of Military Merit. It had the shape of a Greek cross with rectangular arms, the upper being topped with a golden crown. The central field contained the coat of arms of Castile and Leon on the front, and the initials "MM" for Mérito Militar on the verso. The arms of the cross were enameled red on both sides. Higher-class-order badges were gold, and the fourth class of gold-plated silver (Ibid., 182–83).

219. BA Ludwigsburg, B 162/16592, Personalangaben, n.d., 35; and BAB, R/9361/III vol. 571150, Begründung, Stuttgart, May 22, 1940.

220. T. Nowakowski and M. Skotnicki, *Legion Condor,* 53–54.

221. R. Michaelis, *Dirlewanger* (Warsaw, Poland, 2005), 69.

222. BAB, R/9361/III, vol. 521445, letter from Oskar Dirlewanger to Heinrich Himmler, Stuttgart, July 4, 1939, 809.

223. T. Nowakowski and M. Skotnicki, *Legion Condor*, 5, 146.

224. A. Beevor, *Walka o Hiszpanię*, 569.

225. T. Nowakowski and M. Skotnicki, *Legion Condor*, 55.

226. Ibid., 147–49, 153.

227. YV, JM 2088, ID 3672136, recommendation letter from the personal file of Dirlewanger, June 4, 1940.

228. BAB, R/9361/III 521445, Personalangaben. Schulbildung und Beruf, n.d., 744.

Chapter 2

1. BAB, R/9361/III, vol. 521445, letter from Oskar Dirlewanger to Heinrich Himmler, Stuttgart, July 4, 1939, 808–10, translated by K. Kupiszewska from the Polish translation by J. Kalemba and S. Kuklińska.

2. Gottlob Berger, born July 16, 1896, in Gerstetten, Württemberg, died in January 1975. He held the function of chief of the SS Main Office (SS-Hauptamtes) from April 1, 1940. In the early 1930s, he was active in the Esslingen Education Board, which was when he met Oskar Dirlewanger (R. Laschet, *Oskar Dirlewanger als Esslinger Symbolfigur bei der Zerstörung gewerkschaftlicher und menschlicher Grundwerte, Vortrag am Ort des früheren Gewerkschaftshauses in Esslingen*, June 24, 2014; for more about Berger, see A. Lasik, *Sztafety ochronne w systemie niemieckich obozów koncentracyjnych: Rozwój organizacyjny, ewolucja zadań i struktur oraz socjologiczny obraz obozowych załóg SS* (Oświęcim, Poland, 2007), 456–57; BA Ludwigsburg, B 162/5924, 45 Js 30/64, Verfügung, Gottlob Berger, Dortmund, October 15, 1964, 1146–54; and http://www.leo-bw.de/web/guest/detail/-/Detail/details/PERSON/kgl_biographien/118837419/Berger+Gottlob+Christian, accessed February 18, 2017).

3. BAB, R/9361/III, vol. 521445, Gottlob Berger's letter to Reichsführer-SS, Gomaringen, July 28, 1939, 779.

4. BAB, R/9361/III, vol. 521445, /6/77/39, August 16, 1939, 842.

5. BAB, R/9361/III, vol. 521445, "Stuttgarter NS-Kurier," May 25, 1940, 819.

6. BA Ludwigsburg, B 162/16592, Kanzlei des Führers der NSDAP, Aktenzeichen II c 80459, May 17, 1940, 30–31; and H. P. Klausch, *Antifaschisten*, 45.

7. BAB, R/9361/III, vol. 521445, Oskar Dirlewanger's letter to Vorberg of the Führer's Chancellery, Esslingen, May 28, 1940, 891; BAB, R/9361/II, vol. 169257, Nationalsozialistische Deutsche Arbeiterpartei. Gauleitung Württemberg-Hohenzollern, October 30, 1942, unpag.; and BAB, R/9361/II, vol. 169257, KvaSchn/De/Gl 1.43 Le/Vo, January 23, 1943.

8. YV, JM 2088, ID 3672137, the personal file of Dirlewanger, August 16, 1941; BA Ludwigsburg, B 162/16569, Bisheriges Ermittlungsergebnis über das Sonderkommando "Dirlewanger," n.d., 130; BAB, R/9361/III, vol. 521445, Personalnachweis, n.d., 741–47; and BA Ludwigsburg, B 162/16592, V 502 AR 875/72, September 3, 1940, 34.

9. BAB, R/9361/III, vol. 521445, Ergänzungsamt der Waffen-SS, Berlin, June 22, 1940, 811.

10. YV, JM 2088, ID 3659572, Ha/Fu. Tgb. No. 995/41, Beförderung des SS-Standartenführers Dirlewanger, Hauptsturmführer d.R. zum Sturmbannführer d.R., Lublin, August 5, 1941.

11. BAB, R/9361/III, vol. 521445, letter, 805.

12. BAB, R/9361/III, vol. 521445, Gottlob Berger's letter to Oskar Dirlewanger, Berlin, May 25, 1940, 792.

13. BAB, R/9361/III, vol. 521445, Oskar Dirlewanger's letter to Gottlob Berger, Stuttgart, May 29, 1940 r., 889.

14. BAB, NS 19/1207, Ergänzungsamt der Waffen-SS Abt. III Az.: 16, June 4, 1940, 1; and BA Ludwigsburg, B 162/5924, 45 Js 30/64, Verfügung, Gottlob Berger, Dortmund, October 15, 1964, 1147.

15. YV, JM 2088, ID 3672136, recommendation letter from the personal file of Dirlewanger, June 15, 1940.

16. BAB, R/9361/III, vol. 521445, Ergänzungsamt der Waffen-SS, Berlin, June 22, 1940, 811.

17. BAB, R/9361/III, vol. 521445, letter, August 19, 1940, 804.

18. Fragments of this chapter are from my previous book: S. Kuklińska, *Działalność jednostki SS-Sonderkommando "Dirlewanger" (1940–1945)* (Kraków, Poland, 2017), 19–26.

19. H. Hoffmann, *Mój przyjaciel Hitler: Wspomnienia fotografa Hitlera* (Warsaw, Poland, 2015), 223–27.

20. BA Ludwigsburg, B 162/5924, 45 Js 30/64, Verfügung, Gottlob Berger, Dortmund, October 15, 1964, 1147; see also BA Ludwigsburg, B 162/4250, Geschäfts-Nr. 147 Js 11/77 U, 87.

21. Der Reichsführer SS Tgb. No. AR /617/15, March 29, 1940, after H. P. Klausch, *Antifaschisten*, 32.

22. Aktenvermerk des Ministerialrats Sommer, March 26, 1940, after H. P. Klausch, *Antifaschisten*, 27.

23. Also Hermann Göring, the marshal of the Third Reich (*Reichsmarschall*), was in favor of forming a unit composed of poachers that would fight against partisans. As Irving wrote, "Out of the forests and marshes behind the advancing German armies there now rose hordes of Soviet partisans. Göring suggested releasing convicted poachers and smugglers into special units of desperadoes to combat partisans with their own irregular methods—they could 'burn and ravish,' as he put it, in their assigned operational zones. To this suggestion he then added the idea of conscripting Dutchmen willy-nilly into two anti-partisan regiments." This occurred in 1942. (D. Irving, *Göring: A Biography*, http://www.fpp.co.uk/books/Goering/Goering_better.pdf, 529, accessed August 15, 2023).

24. Henry the Fowler, German king reigning in the years 919–936.

25. R. Girtler, *Wilderer: Rebellen in den Bergen* (Vienna and Cologne, 2003), 106.

26. E. Hobusch, *Wilddieberei und Förstermorde*. vol. 3, *Kriminalkommissar Otto Busdorf—Sein letzter Fall* (Berlin, 2002), 252–53.

27. P. Longerich, *Himmler*, 11, 139, 143.

28. Ibid., 11, 39.

29. Ibid., 141, 372.

30. For more on the SS Main Office, see A. Lasik, *Sztafety ochronne*, 55–58.

31. K. Grünberg, *SS*, 101.

32. Ibid.

33. P. Longerich, *Himmler*, 372–73.

34. Aktennotiz von Kammergerichtsrat Westphal, April 5, 1940, after H. P. Klausch, *Antifaschisten*, 32.

35. Professor K. Schulz from Berlin University, who conducted studies on race, prepared a nine-point system of anthropological assessment. The SS accepted only those candidates who were in one of the top four categories: ideal, perfect, very good, and good. Applicants were questioned about their parents' and siblings' political views and their family tree up to 1750, and they were also required to have a descent certificate issued by an office of the Commission for Racial Issues (K. Grünberg, *SS*, 101).

36. Aktenvermerk 4055/4—Iva—1279.42 im Reichsjustizministerium, after H. P. Klausch, *Antifaschisten*, 32.

37. Ibid., 32. Karl Vieregge mentioned that in Sachsenhausen around a hundred poachers were assembled, of whom fifty were chosen (BA Ludwigsburg, B 162/16573, LKA-NW-Dez.15, Wilhelm Karl Vieregge, Plettenberg, July 11, 1962, 456).

38. H. P. Klausch, *Antifaschisten*, 32–33.

39. Ibid., 33.

40. BA Ludwigsburg, B 162/5922, Polizeipräsidium Koblenz—III/A (NSG), Josef Rau, Kamp-Bornhofen, July 31, 1963, 730. Heinz Feiertag gave this number as around sixty to seventy (BA Ludwigsburg, B 162/29251, Gespräch zwischen Herrn Heinz Feiertag, ehemals Hauptsturmführer der LAH und Herrn Fritz Langeur [illegible word], am Sonntag dem 22. Mai 1960, 52).

41. Miejsce Pamięci i Muzeum Sachsenhausen: Zarys historyczny i plan sytuacyjny, 2012.

42. For more information about the Sachsenhausen concentration camp, see G. Finn, *Sachsenhausen 1936–1950: Geschichte eines Lagers* (Berlin, 1988); A. Lasik, *Sztafety ochronne*; http://www.stiftung-bg.de/gums/de/index.htm (accessed February 9, 2018); and T. Cieślak, *Oranienburg-Sachsenhausen: Hitlerowskie obozy koncentracyjne 1933–1945* (Warsaw, Poland, 1972).

43. G. Schwarz, *Żony SS-manów: Kobiety w elitarnych kręgach III Rzeszy* (Warsaw, Poland, 2016), 143–44.

44. P. Longerich, *Himmler*, 297.

45. Ibid., 298.

46. Miejsce Pamięci i Muzeum Sachsenhausen.

47. Theodor Eicke, *SS-Obergruppenführer*, born October 17, 1892, in Hudingen (Hampont), Alsace. He designed the camp system and was the concentration camps inspector, commandant of Dachau, and creator and commandant of the SS Totenkopf

Division. He died on February 26, 1943, during combat in Russia. For more information on this figure, see S. Kuklińska, *SS-Obergruppenführer Theodor Eicke: Projektodawca obozów koncentracyjnych i dowódca dywizji SS "Totenkopf,"* typescript; A. Lasik, *Sztafety ochronne*; J. Solarz, *Totenkopf 1939–1943* (Warsaw, Poland, 2008); and Ch. W. Sydnor Jr., *Żołnierze zagłady: Dywizja SS "Totenkopf" 1933–1945* (Warsaw, Poland, 1998).

48. BA Ludwigsburg, B 162/4249, K 424 Hamburg, 147 p11/71, Georg Kraus, Bamberg, April 9, 1976 r., 997; and Ibid., Peter Gossens, Kevelaer, May 20, 1976, 1003.

49. BA Ludwigsburg, B 162/4249, K 424 Hamburg, 147 p11/71, Georg Kraus, Bamberg, April 9, 1976 r., 997; and BA Ludwigsburg, B 162/16573, LKA-NW-Dez.15, Wilhelm Karl Vieregge, Plettenberg, July 11, 1962 r., 456. The training was conducted by soldiers from 5. SS-Totenkopf-Standarte (BA Ludwigsburg, B 162/16570, Dr. Klietmann, *Die Waffen-SS: Eine Dokumentation*, 1965, 319).

50. Arch. Sachsenhausen, LAG XXX/3, Abschrift, "SS-Sonder-Bataillon-Dirlewanger."

51. Gerhard Hellkamp mentioned that around sixty poachers underwent training, and Dirlewanger appeared in Sachsenhausen in September 1940. They were then transported to Lublin (BA Ludwigsburg, B 162/28392, Sonderkommission–Hamburg, 147 Js 11/71 U, Gerhard Hellkamp, Wattenscheid, June 28, 1973, 460).

52. BAB, R/9361/III, vol. 521445, Der Reichsführer-SS, SS-Personalhauptamt, Schm/O., Berlin, July 1, 1940, 806.

53. BAB, R/9361/III 521445, Personal Bericht, n.d., 747.

54. The MG 34 machine gun (Maschinengewehr 34), a 7.92 × 57 mm caliber machine gun. It was characterized by atypical construction solutions: Depending on the need, it could be fed from magazines or from a belt. The modification of the feeding system required the feed cover to be changed (one feedway had a magazine holder, the other a belt feed mechanism). It was the basic team machine weapon of the German armed forces. Because of its rapid rate of fire, a good shooter could make it impossible for enemy soldiers to approach German positions; for more about this gun and training of recruits, see Ch. McNab, *Armia Hitlera* (Warsaw, Poland, 2014), 42–55.

55. Mauser Gewehr 98k, rifle adapted to 7.92 × 57 mm ammunition. The magazine contained five cartridges; the weapon was equipped with a backsight and a traditional ramrod (more: Ibid.).

56. The log of the 2nd Battalion of SS-Sonderregiment "Dirlewanger," June 12, 1944, after R. Michaelis, *Dirlewanger*, 11.

57. BA Ludwigsburg, B 162/5924, 45 Js 30/64, Verfügung, Gottlob Berger, Dortmund, October 15, 1964, 1147.

58. BA Ludwigsburg, B 162/16573, LKA-NW-Dez.15, Wilhelm Karl Vieregge, Plettenberg, July 11, 1962, 456.

59. BA Ludwigsburg, B 162/16569, Bisheriges Ermittlungsergebnis über das Sonderkommando "Dirlewanger," n.d., 133.

60. Ch. Ingrao, *Czarni myśliwi*, 25. Heinz Feiertag in turn said that sixty to seventy people were chosen in Oranienburg (BA Ludwigsburg, B 162/29251, Gespräch zwischen Herrn Heinz Feiertag, ehemals Hauptsturmführer der LAH und Herrn Fritz Langeur [illegible word], am Sonntag dem 22. Mai 1960, 52).

61. BA Ludwigsburg, B 162/16569, Verfügung, 45Js 30/64, Dortmund, December 15, 1967, 5; and BAB, ZM 1454, SS IIA I3, Vernehmungsniederschrift, Lublin, August 26, 1941, 134.

62. In an order of January 29, 1942, Himmler pronounced it a Waffen-SS volunteer unit and named it SS-Sonderkommando Dirlewanger (BA Ludwigsburg, B 162/16569, Verfügung, 45Js 30/64, Dortmund, December 15, 1967, 5).

63. H. P. Klausch, *Antifaschisten*, 33.

64. According to document R 22/1009 from the Bundesarchiv, in July 1940, up to five poachers joined (H. P. Klausch, *Antifaschisten*, 33 and 423n31).

65. BA Ludwigsburg, B 162/5922, Tgb. Nr. SK. Zst. I/3-180/62, Friedrich Walter, Mörsch, May 21, 1963, 617.

66. BA Ludwigsburg, B 162/5926, Landeskriminalamt NW, Wilhelm Schlauter, Duisburg, November 28, 1965, 1554.

67. BA Ludwigsburg, B 162/5924, 45 Js 30/64, Verfügung, Gottlob Berger, Dortmund, October 15, 1964, 1147.

68. BA Ludwigsburg, B 162/5922, Polizeipräsidium Koblenz—III/A (NSG), Josef Rau, Kamp-Bornhofen, July 31, 1963, 730; in it, Josef Rau describes the insignia of the later 36th Dirlewanger Waffen-SS Grenadier Division: crossed grenades. See also H. P. Klausch, *Antifaschisten*, 34.

69. BA Ludwigsburg, B 162/5926, Zahl: 18/69, Franz Wegscheider, Mayrhofen, September 16, 1969, 1452.

70. H. P. Klausch, *Antifaschisten*, 46.

71. Ibid., 52.

Chapter 3

1. Gustav Brusberg, Georg Kraus, and Peter Gossens stated that in early autumn 1940, they continued training in Lviv and were only later sent to Lublin (BA Ludwigsburg, B 162/4249, K 424, Gustav Brusberg, Stade, December 18, 1975, 837; BA Ludwigsburg, B 162/4249, K 424 Hamburg, 147 p11/71, Georg Kraus, Bamberg, April 9, 1976, 997; and BA Ludwigsburg, B 162/4249, K 424 Hamburg, 147 p11/71, Peter Gossens, Kevelaer, May 20, 1976, 1003). Meanwhile, Erich Illing claimed that at the beginning of 1941, they were sent to Lviv or Lublin (BA Ludwigsburg, B 162/4248, Sonderkommission Hamburg, Paul Erich Illing, Wanne-Eickel, August 31, 1972, 249).

2. For more on Globocnik, see B. Rieger, *Odilo Globocnik*.

3. H. P. Klausch, *Antifaschisten*, 47.

4. In the 1960s, investigators established that from September 1, 1940, to February 25, 1942, the unit was stationed in the Lublin District (BA Ludwigsburg, B 162/16569, Verfügung, 45Js 30/64, Dortmund, December 15, 1967, 5).

5. S. Kuklińska, *Działalność*, 43.

6. BA Ludwigsburg, B 162/5922, Tgb. Nr. SK. Zst. I/3-180/62, Friedrich Walter, Mörsch, May 21, 1963, 618.

7. BA Ludwigsburg, B 162/5926, Landeskriminalamt NW, Wilhelm Schlauter, Duisburg, November 28, 1965, 1554. Meanwhile, Friedrich Walter stated that they stayed in Lublin for two to three weeks before being transferred to Stary Dzików (BA Ludwigsburg, B 162/5922, Sonderkommission Zentrale Stelle—I/3-180/62, Friedrich Walter, Ludwigsburg, May 27, 1963, 614; and BA Ludwigsburg, B 162/5922, Tgb. Nr. SK. Zst. I/3-180/62, Friedrich Walter, Mörsch, May 21, 1963, 618). Both of them may have been right, because the unit was divided into smaller detachments, which were sent to different places at various times, as I further describe in more detail.

8. BA Ludwigsburg, B 162/5920, Auszugsweise Abschrift von Blatt 206 bis 214 der Akten 29 Js 46/62 der Staatsanwaltschaft Essen, July 24, 1962, 198.

9. BA Ludwigsburg, B 162/5926, Landeskriminalamt NW, Wilhelm Schlauter, Duisburg, November 28, 1965, 1556.

10. BA Ludwigsburg, B 162/5926, Zahl: 18/69, Franz Wegscheider, Mayrhofen, September 16, 1969, 1454; BA Ludwigsburg, B 162/5922, Sonderkommission Zentrale Stelle—I/3-180/62, Friedrich Walter, Ludwigsburg, May 27, 1963, 614; and other testimonies.

SS-Unterführer, equivalent of *Unterscharführer* in the Waffen-SS. *SS-Unterscharführer* was the lowest NCO rank in the Waffen-SS and equivalent to an *Unteroffizier* in the Wehrmacht. The rank insignia of an *Unterscharführer* was one square star worn on the left collar patch.

11. BA Ludwigsburg, B 162/5922, Sonderkommission Zentrale Stelle—I/3-180/62, Friedrich Walter, Ludwigsburg, May 27, 1963, 614.

12. BA Ludwigsburg, B 162/5922, Polizeipräsidium Koblenz—III/A (NSG), Josef Rau, Kamp-Bornhofen, July 31, 1963, 730.

13. Franz Wegscheider was sent to Riga as part of a four-person group (BA Ludwigsburg, B 162/5926, Zahl: 18/69, Franz Wegscheider, Mayrhofen, September 16, 1969, 1454). Also, Konrad Morgen testified that a detachment of SS-Sonderkommando Dirlewanger ended up in this city (BA Ludwigsburg, B 162/5924, Eidesstattliche Erklärung, Konrad Morgen, Nuremberg, December 16, 1947, 1133).

14. BA Ludwigsburg, B 162/5926, Landeskriminalamt NW, Wilhelm Schlauter, Duisburg, November 28, 1965, 1557.

15. BA Ludwigsburg, B 162/5922, Tgb. Nr. SK. Zst. I/3-180/62, Friedrich Walter, Mörsch, May 21, 1963, 625.

16. SS-Brigadeführer Walther Schröder, born February 26, 1902, in Lübeck, died October 31, 1973. He held the position of SS and police leader in Riga from August 4, 1941 (see more: "Walter Schröder," https://de.wikipedia.org/wiki/Walther_Schr%C3%B6der, accessed March 19, 2019).

17. BA Ludwigsburg, B 162/5926, Zahl: 18/69, Franz Wegscheider, Mayrhofen, September 16, 1969, 1454.

18. Ibid.

19. BA Ludwigsburg, B 162/5922, Tgb. Nr. SK. Zst. I/3-180/62, Friedrich Walter, Mörsch, May 21, 1963, 618. They could not have guarded the Riga ghetto, because it was formed pursuant to a decree of August 23, 1941, and in October of that year the Reich Security Main Office issued an order for the ghettos in Riga and in Minsk to divide fifty thousand newly arriving Jews between themselves.

20. BA Ludwigsburg, B 162/4249, V 424 AR 875/72, December 18, 1975, 837; BA Ludwigsburg, B 162/4249, K 424 Hamburg, 147 p11/71, Georg Kraus, Bamberg, April 9, 1976, 997; ibid., Peter Gossens, Kevelaer, May 20, 1976, 1003; and BA Ludwigsburg, B 162/4248, Sonderkommission Hamburg, Paul Erich Illing, Wanne-Eickel, August 31, 1972, 249.

21. M. Winstone, *Generalne Gubernatorstwo*, 232.

22. For more information about the Janowska camp in Lviv, see *Obóz janowski—Niemiecki obóz pracy przymusowej i obóz koncentracyjny (ul. Janowska 134; ob. Szewczenki 134)*, https://sztetl.org.pl/pl/miejscowosci/l/703-lwow/116-miejsca-martyrologii/47981-oboz-janowski-niemiecki-oboz-pracy-przymusowej-i-oboz-koncentracyjny-ul-janowska-134-ob-szewczenki (accessed April 22, 2018); and *Janowski obóz we Lwowie*, http://www.jhi.pl/psj/janowski_oboz_we_Lwowie (accessed April 22, 2018).

23. BA Ludwigsburg, B 162/5922, Polizeipräsidium Koblenz—III/A (NSG), Josef Rau, Kamp-Bornhofen, July 31, 1963, 730–31.

24. Ibid., 731.

25. BA Ludwigsburg, B 162/16569, Ausfertigung, 2 Ks 1/65, 28 a 9/64, March 6, 1967, 211–12.

26. H. P. Klausch, *Antifaschisten*, 54–55.

27. BA Ludwigsburg, B 162/16569, Ausfertigung, 2 Ks 1/65, 28 a 9/64, March 6, 1967, 211.

28. H. P. Klausch, *Antifaschisten*, 55.

29. The Otto plan assumed the construction of a network of labor camps from spring 1940 and the erection of fortifications along the demarcation line with the Soviet Union. The performance of this task was dependent on the creation of a complex of camps, which were built in settlements along the border, such as Bełżec, Cieszanów, Dzików, Lipsko, Narol, and Płazów. These were the so-called fortification camps. Implementation of the plan was halted in autumn 1941, probably due to preparations for the offensive in the east within Operation Barbarossa (for more on the Otto plan,

see J. Marszałek, *Obozy pracy w Generalnym Gubernatorstwie 1939–1945* (Lublin, Poland, 1998); *Akcja Reinhardt: Zagłada Żydów w Generalnym Gubernatorstwie*, ed. D. Libionka (Warsaw, Poland, 2004); and J. Chmielewski, *Obozy pracy w dystrykcie lubelskim*, http://teatrnn.pl/leksykon/node/1668#2, accessed February 22, 2017).

30. S. Kuklińska, *Działalność*, 44.

31. BA Ludwigsburg, B 162/5926, Zahl: 18/69, Franz Wegscheider, Mayrhofen, September 16, 1969, 1453.

32. *Dzików*, http://teatrnn.pl/leksykon/kalendarium/wydarzenie_miejsce/1708 (accessed September 14, 2016).

33. M. Winstone, *Generalne Gubernatorstwo*, 172.

34. AIPN, GK 103/72, Sara Bergmann's testimony, Lublin, September 6, 1941; Ibid., Mendel Rosenberg's testimony, z. Zt. Josefow, September 23, 1941; Ibid., Izaak Flomenbaum's testimony, z. Zt. Josefow, September 23, 1941; Ibid., Josef Tintenfisch's testimony, z. Zt. Josefow, September 24, 1941; and Ibid., Moszek Wassermann's testimony, z. Zt. Josefow, September 24, 1941.

35. Ibid., SS-Rottenführer Erich Selzer's testimony, Lublin, October 9, 1941, 42–45.

36. B. Musiał, *Deutsche Zivilverwaltung und Judenverfolgung im Generalgouvernement: Eine Fallstudie zum Distrikt Lublin 1939–1944* (Wiesbaden, Germany, 1999), 164.

37. J. Grechuta, "Obozy pracy dla Żydów w południowo-wschodniej części dystryktu lubelskiego w 1940 r. (Bełżec, Lipsko, Płazów, Cieszanów, Dzików Stary)," in *Polska-Ukraina: Wspólna przeszłość, Materials from the Session "Dziedzictwo kulturowe pogranicza polsko-ukraińskiego"* [Cultural Heritage of the Polish-Ukrainian Borderlands] (Cieszanów, Poland, September 29, 2006) and the conference "Polska Ukraina: Wspólna przeszłość" [Poland Ukraine: A Common Past] (Cieszanów, Poland, 25–November 26, 2006) (Cieszanów, Poland, 2007), 50.

38. BA Ludwigsburg, B 162/5926, Zahl: 18/69, Franz Wegscheider, Mayrhofen, September 16, 1969, 1453; BA Ludwigsburg, B 162/5926, Landeskriminalamt NW, Wilhelm Schlauter, Duisburg, November 28, 1965, 1555; and BA Ludwigsburg, B 162/5922, Tgb. Nr. SK. Zst. I/3-180/62, Friedrich Walter, Mörsch, May 21, 1963, 618.

39. BA Ludwigsburg, B 162/5926, Landeskriminalamt NW, Wilhelm Schlauter, Duisburg, November 28, 1965, 1555.

40. J. Grechuta, *Obozy pracy dla Żydów*, 36–37.

41. AIPN, GK 103/72, SS-Hauptsturmführer Dirlewanger's testimony, Lublin, October 14, 1941; Ibid., SS-Rottenführer Erich Selzer's testimony, Lublin, October 9, 1941; Ibid., Sara Bergmann's testimony, Lublin, September 6, 1941; Ibid., Mendel Rosenberg's testimony, z. Zt. Josefow, September 23, 1941; Ibid., Izaak Flomenbaum's testimony, z. Zt. Josefow, September 23, 1941, 27; Ibid., Josef Tintenfisch's testimony, z. Zt. Josefow, September 24, 1941; and Ibid., Moszek Wassermann's testimony, z. Zt. Josefow, September 24, 1941.

42. Ibid., SS-Rottenführer Erich Selzer's testimony, Lublin, October 9, 1941, 42–45.

43. BA Ludwigsburg, B 162/5924, 45 Js 30/64, Verfügung, Gottlob Berger, Dortmund, October 15, 1964, 1148).

44. BA Ludwigsburg, B 162/5926, Landeskriminalamt NW, Wilhelm Schlauter, Duisburg, November 28, 1965; and BA Ludwigsburg, B 162/5926, Wilhelm Schlauter, Duisburg, November 28, 1965, 1555. The lack of officers in the initial period of the unit's operation and the arrival of Schlauter (Schleuder) was confirmed by Friedrich Walter. He testified that Schlauter acted as Oskar Dirlewanger's deputy for some time (BA Ludwigsburg, B 162/5922, Tgb. Nr. SK. Zst. I/3-180/62, Friedrich Walter, Mörsch, May 21, 1963, 621).

45. http://www.belzec.pl/index.php?historia,0,0,pl (accessed January 30, 2016).

46. S. Kuklińska, *Działalność.*, 48–49.

47. BA Ludwigsburg, B 162/5926, Landeskriminalamt NW, Wilhelm Schlauter, Duisburg, November 28, 1965, 1555.

48. AIPN, GK 103/72, Sara Bergmann's testimony, Lublin, October 30, 1941, 63; and BA Ludwigsburg, B 162/5922, Tgb. Nr. SK. Zst. I/3-180/62, Friedrich Walter, Mörsch, May 21, 1963, 618. SS-Hauptscharführer Reinhold Kluß stated that SS-Sonderkommando Dirlewanger came to Lublin in April or May 1941 (AIPN, GK 103/72, Vernehmungsniederschrift, Lublin, December 13, 1941, 98).

49. BA Ludwigsburg, B 162/5922, Tgb. Nr. SK. Zst. I/3-180/62, Friedrich Walter, Mörsch, May 21, 1963, 618; and BA Ludwigsburg, B 162/5922, Sonderkommission Zentrale Stelle- I/3-180/62, Friedrich Walter, Ludwigsburg, May 27, 1963, 614.

50. BA Ludwigsburg, B 162/5926, Zahl: 18/69, Franz Wegscheider, Mayrhofen, September 16, 1969, 1452–53. Friedrich Walter, meanwhile, gave the address as Chopin Street 19 (BA Ludwigsburg, B 162/5922, Tgb. Nr. SK. Zst. I/3-180/62, Friedrich Walter, Mörsch, May 21, 1963, 625. See also BA Ludwigsburg, B 162/5922, Polizeipräsidium Koblenz—III/A (NSG), Josef Rau, Kamp-Bornhofen, July 31, 1963, 731; and BA Ludwigsburg, B 162/5924, Tgb. No. SK. Zst. I/14-180/62, Vernehmungsniederschrift, Curt Karl Vollmer, Ludwigsburg, May 27, 1964, 1093).

51. Alfred Paul Koziel, born June 26, 1904, in Katowice (Kattowitz). He worked as an official in the tax office in Kamienna Góra in Silesia (Landeshut, Schlesien) until April 1940. He then entered the Waffen-SS in Krakow and was transferred to Radom after about three months. There he underwent thorough training, which lasted until autumn 1940. In October 1940 he was sent to Lublin, where he was to supervise guards in the camp at Lipowa Street. He additionally had sentry duty in the Majdanek concentration camp. Together with nine other SS men, he was quartered in a flat on the ground floor of the house at Chopin Street, in which Dirlewanger's soldiers were stationed (BA Ludwigsburg, B 162/5923, Bayerisches Landeskriminalamt IIIa/SK K 6259, Alfred Paul Koziel, Ansbach, March 15, 1964, 977–981).

52. Ibid., 977–78; and BA Ludwigsburg, B 162/5924, Tgb. No. SK. Zst. I/14-180/62, Vernehmungsniederschrift, Curt Karl Vollmer, Ludwigsburg, May 27, 1964, 1093.

53. AIPN, GK 103/72, Vernehmungsniederschrift, Lublin, December 13, 1941, 98–99.

54. BA Ludwigsburg, B 162/5926, Zahl: 18/69, Franz Wegscheider, Mayrhofen, September 16, 1969, 1453; and BA Ludwigsburg, B 162/5922, Polizeipräsidium Koblenz—III/A (NSG), Josef Rau, Kamp-Bornhofen, July 31, 1963, 731.

55. BA Ludwigsburg, B 162/5922, Polizeipräsidium Koblenz—III/A (NSG), Josef Rau, Kamp-Bornhofen, July 31, 1963, 731.

56. Ibid., 731, 740.

57. BA Ludwigsburg, B 162/5926, Zahl: 18/69, Franz Wegscheider, Mayrhofen, September 16, 1969, 1453.

58. Based on interviews given to Rieger by Rickheim: B. Rieger, *Odilo Globocnik, twórca nazistowskich obozów śmierci* (Zakrzewo, Poland, 2009), 111; and S. Kuklińska, *Działalność*, 50–51.

59. M. Szabłowska-Zaremba, *Getta w Lublinie*, http://teatrnn.pl/leksykon/node/609/getta_w_lublinie?kat=907 (accessed September 14, 2016).

60. Ibid., http://teatrnn.pl/leksykon/node/609/getta_w_lublinie?kat=907 (accessed 14.9.2016); and S. Kuklińska, *Działalność*, 52.

61. B. Rieger, *Odilo Globocnik*, 83.

62. P. Longerich, *Himmler*, 714.

63. For more about this camp, see *Obóz pracy dla Żydów przy ulicy Lipowej 7 w Lublinie* (http://teatrnn.pl/leksykon/artykuly/oboz-pracy-dla-zydow-przy-ulicy-lipowej-7-w-lublinie/#p5, accessed April 22, 2018; and *Nazistowski obóz pracy przymusowej przy ul. Lipowej 7*, https://sztetl.org.pl/pl/miejscowosci/l/264-lublin/116-miejsca-martyrologii/47898-nazistowski-oboz-pracy-przymusowej-przy-ul-lipowej-7, accessed April 22, 2018).

64. B. Rieger, *Odilo Globocnik*, 87.

65. Ibid.

66. AIPN, GK 103/72, Verhandelt!, Sara Elka Rozencwajg, Lublin, September 5, 1941; and ibid., Sara Bergmann's interrogation, Lublin, September 6, 1941.

67. Werner Schindler, born in 1912. He was held as a prisoner in the labor camp at Lipowa Street in Lublin. On March 23, 1943, he managed to escape together with eight other prisoners and went to Warsaw. Two days before the start of the uprising (1943), he ended up in the Warsaw ghetto, from which he escaped to the Aryan side through the sewers and hid in the city under a false name until January 19, 1945. He fought in the Warsaw Uprising in 1944 (BA Ludwigsburg, B 162/1708, Michalsen Files, Werner Schindler's report on survivors: "Ich habe Lublin und Majdanek überlebt," 2297–98).

68. Ibid., 2300.

69. YV, JM 2088, ID 3659572, Ha/Fu. Tgb. No. 995/41, Beförderung des SS-Standartenführers Dirlewanger, Hauptsturmführer d.R. zum Sturmbannführer d.R, Lublin, August 5, 1941, proposal to promote Dirlewanger, unpag. According to some

sources, Dirlewanger was promoted on November 9, 1941 (BAB, R/9361/III, vol. 521445, Heinrich Himmler's letter to Oskar Dirlewanger, n.d., 803).

70. YV, JM 2088, ID3672137, the personal file of Dirlewanger, September 27, 1941; and BAB, R/9361/III, v. 521445, Pers. Stelle I 2a/Az.: 16 d/H/Pae, Berlin, September 27, 1941, 798.

71. S. Kuklińska, *Działalność*, 54.

72. BA Ludwigsburg, B 162/16569, Verfügung, 45Js 30/64, Dortmund, December 15, 1967, 5.

73. According to some testimonies, this may have occurred in Lublin. However, all the soldiers questioned about it answered very vaguely, attempting to escape punishment. Most of them held that nothing of the sort had taken place, while several of Dirlewanger's subordinates said that they had heard of it but had not taken part and did not know who may have participated. Investigators in the 1960s and 1970s also asked about the SS doctor who administered the injections to the Jews. None of those questioned were able to indicate him. The fact is that, at the time, no doctor was assigned to SS-Sonderkommando Dirlewanger, and in the event of medical problems, the help of other units was sought. The conclusion is that the SS doctor described by investigators belonged to a similar unit operating in that area at the time (for a sample of a testimony on this matter: BA Ludwigsburg, B 162/5924, Tgb. No. SK. Zst. I/14-180/62, Vernehmungsniederschrift, Curt Karl Vollmer, Ludwigsburg, May 27, 1964, 1093).

Josef Rau mentioned that around three times he had seen naked corpses being taken to trucks from the cellar of the tenement house at Chopin Street in Lublin in which Dirlewanger's soldiers were quartered. He assessed that there may have been around forty to fifty bodies, mostly of men but sometimes also women. There were no children. The loading was done by men from the transport division (BA Ludwigsburg, B 162/5922, Polizeipräsidium Koblenz—III/A (NSG), Josef Rau, Kamp-Bornhofen, July 31, 1963, 733–37).

74. Dr. Konrad Morgen (*SS-Sturmbannführer*), SS judge and lawyer investigating crimes committed among others in concentration camps (for more about this person, see H. Pauer-Studer and J. D. Velleman, *Konrad Morgen: The Conscience of a Nazi Judge*, 2015).

75. BA Ludwigsburg, B 162/5924, Eidesstattliche Erklärung, Konrad Morgen, Nuremberg, December 16, 1947, 1133.

76. In the second half of the 1960s, several proceedings were conducted concerning this matter. Many witnesses were questioned in order to establish the name of the SS doctor who injected prisoners with strychnine. In 1967 the Vienna prosecutor's office ascertained that the crime had been committed by Dr. Dominik Romani (BA Ludwigsburg, B 162/5925, 55.223-18/67, Dortiges Aktenzeichen 29 Js 46/62, Wien, July 28, 1967, 1343–44; for more about the medical services and doctors operating in Lublin in 1941, see BA Ludwigsburg, B 162/5925, 45 Js 30/64, Dortmund, December 15, 1967, 1373–81).

77. BA Ludwigsburg, B 162/16569, Verfügung, 45Js 30/64, Dortmund, December 15, 1967, 2–3; and BA Ludwigsburg, B 162/5925, 45 Js 30/64, Dortmund, December 15, 1967, 1374.

78. BA Ludwigsburg, B 162/16569, Verfügung, 45Js 30/64, Dortmund, December 15, 1967, 19.

79. BA Ludwigsburg, B 162/5925, Landeskriminalamt NW—Dezernat 15—Tgb. Nr. (4300)-6357/64-Re, Peter Erretkamps, Kevelaer, December 15, 1964, 1191; and BA Ludwigsburg, B 162/16569, Verfügung, 45Js 30/64, Dortmund, December 15, 1967, 3. As I mentioned, also SS-Unterscharführer Josef Rau witnessed the bodies (around forty to fifty) being carried out of the cellar (BA Ludwigsburg, B 162/16569, Verfügung, 45Js 30/64, Dortmund, December 15, 1967, 4; and BA Ludwigsburg, B 162/5925, 45 Js 30/64, Dortmund, December 15, 1967, 1373–75).

80. BA Ludwigsburg, B 162/5925, Landeskriminalamt NW—Dezernat 15—Tgb. Nr. (4300)-6357/64-Re, Peter Erretkamps, Kevelaer, December 15, 1964, 1192.

81. BA Ludwigsburg, B 162/5925, Landeskriminalamt NW—Dezernat 15—Tgb. Nr. (4300)-6357/64-Re, Peter Erretkamps, Kevelaer, December 15, 1964, 1190–91.

82. BA Ludwigsburg, B 162/5922, Polizeipräsidium Koblenz—III/A (NSG), Josef Rau, Kamp-Bornhofen, July 31, 1963, 732.

83. P. Longerich, *Himmler*, 714–15; and M. Winstone, *Generalne Gubernatorstwo*, 260–61.

84. H. P. Klausch, *Antifaschisten*, 50–51.

85. BA Ludwigsburg, B 162/5926, Zahl: 18/69, Franz Wegscheider, Mayrhofen, September 16, 1969, 1454.

86. This was mentioned by, among others, Curt Vollmer, a dentist by education. He entered the Allgemeine-SS in Stuttgart in 1936, and on September 2, 1939, he joined the 6. SS Inf.-Rgt. (later the Nord Division). He encountered Dirlewanger and his soldiers while staying in Lublin: He was quartered in the house at Chopin Street 19 and spent six to eight weeks there. When interrogated after the war, he stated, "Man munkelte davon, er [Dirlewanger] habe ein Verhältnis mit einer Judin" (BA Ludwigsburg, B 162/5924, Tgb. No. SK. Zst. I/14-180/62, Vernehmungsniederschrift, Curt Karl Vollmer, Ludwigsburg, May 27, 1964, 1089–94).

87. BA Ludwigsburg, B 162/5925, Landeskriminalamt NW—Dezernat 15—Tgb. Nr. (4300)-6357/64-Re, Gottlob Berger, Gerstetten, July 29, 1965, 1198.

88. BA Ludwigsburg, B 162/16570, Das Urteil im Wilhelmstrassen-Prozess, n.d., 316; and P. Stachiewicz, *"Parasol,"* 500n65. Konrad Morgen confirmed Krüger's statement in his testimony (BA Ludwigsburg, B 162/5924, Eidesstattliche Erklärung, Konrad Morgen, Nuremberg, December 16, 1947, 1134).

89. BAB, R/9361/III, vol. 521445, Pers. Stelle I 2a/Az.: 16 d/H/Pae, Berlin, September 27, 1941, 798.

90. In Lublin, Johannes Müller held the function of commander of the Security Police and the Security Service (*Der Kommandeur der Sicherheitspolizei und des Sicherheitsdienst*)

for the Lublin District from June 1940 to December 1943. He was subordinate to the commander of the Security Police and the Security Service (*Der Befehlshaber der Sicherheitspolizei und des Sicherheitsdiensts*) in the General Government, and through him, to the Reich Security Main Office (Reichssicherheitshauptamt, or RSHA), and at the local level, to the SS and police leader of the Lublin District. In 1940, this office was divided into Division I (administration), Division II (Security Service), Division IIIA (internal policy), Division IIIB (internal policy), Division IIIC (intelligence), and Division IV (Criminal Directorate), and in the years 1943–44 into Department I/II (law and administration), Department III (Security Service; leader: SS-Sturmbannführer Biegelmeyer), Department IV (Geheime Staatspolizei; that is, the Gestapo), and Division V (Kriminalpolizei). Under it were regional outposts (*Aussendienststellen*) and criminal police (*Kriminalkommisariaten*) units in Biała Podlaska, Biłgoraj, Chełm, Hrubieszów, Krasnystaw, Kraśnik, Lublin, Puławy, Radzyń, Tomaszów, Włodawa, and Zamość; border stations (*Grenzpolizeiposten*); prisons; and detention facilities in the town and the district, and also an ad hoc court (*Standgericht*). The tasks of the Security Police and the Security Service included observing and combating underground organizations and matters of nationality and religion, and surveying the sentiment of the population and of their own personnel in the area of their jurisdiction. The command ceased existence as a result of Lublin's liberation by the Red Army between July 21 and 25, 1944, when the Germans left the town (for more on Johannes Müller, see teatrnn.pl/leksykon/artykuly/lublin-19391944/, accessed January 18, 2018; and http://szukajwarchiwach.pl/35/511/0#tabZespol, accessed January 18, 2018).

91. BA Ludwigsburg, B 162/5924, Eidesstattliche Erklärung, Konrad Morgen, Nuremberg, December 16, 1947, 1133.

92. BAB, R/9361/III, vol. 521445, Fernspruch Nr. 344, n.d., 775.

93. AIPN, GK 103/72, SS-Hauptsturmführer Dirlewanger's testimony, Lublin, October 14, 1941; AIPN, GK 103/72, SS-Rottenführer Erich Selzer's testimony, Lublin, October 9,1941; AIPN, GK 103/72, Sara Bergmann's testimony, Lublin, September 6, 1941; AIPN, GK 103/72, Mendel Rosenberg's testimony, z. Zt. Josefow, September 23, 1941; AIPN, GK 103/72, Izaak Flomenbaum's testimony, z. Zt. Josefow, September 23, 1941; AIPN, GK 103/72, Josef Tintenfisch's testimony, z. Zt. Josefow, September 24, 1941; and AIPN, GK 103/72, Moszek Wassermann's testimony, z. Zt. Josefow, September 24, 1941.

94. BAB, ZM 1454, letter to Heinrich Himmler, Lublin, July 23, 1941, 3–4; and AIPN, GK 103/72.

95. According to the Nuremberg Laws of September 15, 1935—the Law for the Protection of German Blood and German Honor of September 15, 1935 (article 2: "Extramarital relations between Jews and citizens of German or related blood are forbidden"; article 5, point 2: "A male who violates the prohibition under article 2 will be punished with jail or imprisonment." For more on this subject, see https://www.dhm.de/lemo/kapitel/ns-regime/ausgrenzung/nuernberg/ (accessed February 15, 2019); and https://www.1000dokumente.de/index.html?c=dokument_de&dokument=0007_nue&l=de (accessed February 15, 2019).

96. AIPN, GK 103/72, letter to Heinrich Himmler, Lublin, August 3, 1941.

97. Ibid., Der Kommandeur der Sicherheitspolizei und des SD für den Distrikt Lublin, Vermerk, Lublin, September 2, 1941.

98. In the original: "In Jozefow habe ich einen Polen namens Michael Terlecki als Bräutigam gehabt und mit diesem habe ich auch geschlechtlich verkehrt. Mit anderen Personen als mit diesen Polen habe ich bisher keinen Geschlechts—oder intimen Verkehr gepflegt" (Ibid., Sara Bergmann's interrogation, Lublin, September 6, 1941.).

99. Ibid., Sara Bergmann's interrogation, Lublin, September 6, 1941.

100. Ibid., Sara Bergmann's interrogation, Lublin, September 6, 1941.

101. Ibid., Sara Bergmann's interrogation, Lublin, September 6, 1941; ibid., Izaak Flomenbaum's interrogation, Josefow, September 23, 1941; ibid., Josef Tintenfisch's testimony, z. Zt. Josefow, September 24, 1941; and ibid., Moszek Wassermann's testimony, z. Zt. Josefow, September 24, 1941.

102. Ibid., Mendel Rosenberg's testimony, September 23, 1941; ibid., Josef Tintenfisch's testimony, z. Zt. Josefow, September 24, 1941; and ibid., Moszek Wassermann's testimony, z. Zt. Josefow, September 24, 1941.

103. Ibid., Hugo Kannegiesser's testimony, Riga, September 26, 1941.

104. Ibid., Hugo Kannegiesser's testimony, Riga, September 26, 1941.

105. Ibid., Erich Selzer's testimony, Lublin, September 9, 1941.

106. In the original: "Nachdem mir jetzt die von mir ausgestellt Quittung vom 7.2.41 der Jüdin Wassermann aus Olowice über eine eingezahlte Geldstrafe von 1000, zl vorgelegt wurde, entsinne ich mich, daß von Dirlewanger doch verschiedentlich Geldstrafen bei Juden verhängt und eingezogen wurde"; ibid., Erich Selzer's testimony, Lublin, October 9, 1941.

107. Ibid., Erich Selzer's testimony, Lublin, October 9, 1941.

108. Ibid., Franz Hunke's testimony, Lublin, September 25, 1941.

109. Ibid., Hugo Kannegiesser's testimony, Riga, September 26, 1941.

110. Ibid., Erich Selzer's testimony, Lublin, October 9, 1941.

111. Ibid., Abt. III-A-3, Aktenvermerk, Lublin, October 7, 1941.

112. Ibid., Erich Selzer's testimony, Lublin, October 9, 1941.

113. Ibid., Hugo Kannegiesser's testimony, Riga, September 26, 1941.

114. Ibid., Sara Bergmann's interrogation, Lublin, September 6, 1941.

115. Ibid., Sara Elka Rozencwajg's interrogation, Lublin, September 5, 1941.

116. Ibid., Sara Elka Rozencwajg's interrogation, Lublin, September 5, 1941.

117. Ibid., Hugo Kannegiesser's testimony, Riga, September 26, 1941.

118. Ibid., Richard Eibl's testimony, Lublin, October 8, 1941.

119. Ibid., Erich Selzer's testimony, Lublin, October 9, 1941.

120. Ibid., Hugo Kannegiesser's testimony, Riga, September 26, 1941.

121. Ibid., Richard Eibl's testimony, Lublin, October 8, 1941; and ibid., Erich Selzer's testimony, Lublin, October 9, 1941.

122. Ibid., SS-Hauptsturmführer Dirlewanger's interrogation, Lublin, October 14, 1941.

On August 24, 1941, Dirlewanger was interrogated about the accusations made in anonymous letters. He denied the allegation that he sold goods in the canteen and that he sent sausages, butter, and large amounts of money to his mother and sister. He confirmed that he sent his mother 150 marks a month. He questioned the amounts from 40,000 to 60,000 and said he did not know where he would have gotten them from. Furthermore, he called the information about his intimate relationship with Sara Bergmann an infamous lie (infame Lüge) (see BAB, ZM 1454, Vernehmungsniederschrift, Lublin, August 26, 1941, 141–45).

123. AIPN GK, 103/72, SS-Hauptsturmführer Dirlewanger's interrogation, Lublin, October 14, 1941.

124. Ibid.

125. Ibid.

126. Ibid.

127. AIPN GK, 103/72, Der Kommandeur der Sicherheitspolizei und des SD für den Distrikt Lublin, III A 597/41g, Lublin, October 30, 1941.

128. Rheinhold Kluss, born April 4, 1893, in Breslau (Wrocław), and died June 21, 1955, in Elmshorn; member of the camp staff in Auschwitz. He joined the SS on April 11, 1932 (for more, see http://www.tenhumbergreinhard.de/1933-1945-taeter-und-mitlaeufer/personal-auschwitz-i-u-ii/auschwitz-i-u-ii-buchstabe-k.html, accessed February 22, 2019; and AIPN GK, 103/72, SS-Hauptscharführer Rheinhold Kluss' interrogation, Groß-Rosen, November 4, 1941).

129. AIPN GK, 103/72, 597/41g—IIIA—Schlußbericht, Lublin, November 14, 1941, unpag. SS-Sonderkommando Dirlewanger; Kommando Kluss (around seventy men who arrived in Lublin in October 1940) and Kommando Schneidt were stationed in one neighborhood, at the same street (see more: Ibid., Vernehmungsniederschrift, Lublin, December 13, 1941).

130. Ibid., SS-Hauptscharführer Rheinhold Kluss's interrogation, Groß-Rosen, November 4, 1941.

131. Ibid., SS-Hauptscharführer Rheinhold Kluss's interrogation, Groß-Rosen, November 4, 1941.

132. Ibid., SS-Hauptscharführer Rheinhold Kluss's interrogation, Groß-Rosen, November 4, 1941.

133. Ibid., SS-Unterscharführer Oswald Egger's testimony, Lublin, November 10, 1941.

134. Ibid., Gustav Strumpf's testimony, Lublin, November 10, 1941.

135. Ibid., SS-Hauptscharführer Hermann Tetzel's testimony, Lublin, November 11, 1941.

From *Kommando Kluss*, also the SS man Xaver Bühler was interrogated, who confirmed having heard gossip about dissatisfaction among Dirlewanger's subordinates and about the Jewish woman Sara Bergmann. He said that she was sometimes seen in the window of Dirlewanger's room, both in the daytime and at night, but was unable to add anything else (Ibid., Xaver Bühler's testimony, Lublin, November 11, 1941).

136. BA Ludwigsburg, B 162/5924, 45 Js 30/64, Verfügung, Gottlob Berger, Dortmund, October 15, 1964, 1150–51.

137. H. P. Klausch, *Antifaschisten*, 58.

138. BAB, R/9361/III, vol. 521445, Fernschreiben Nr. 535, 534, 526, 523, pp. 768–71.

Chapter 4

1. Ch. McNab, *Armia Hitlera* (Warsaw, Poland, 2014), 174.

2. P. Longerich, *Himmler*, 645.

3. B. Musiał, *Sowieccy partyzanci 1941–1944: Mity i rzeczywistość* (Poznań, Poland, 2014), 32.

4. P. Longerich, *Himmler*, 644.

5. Wilhelm Keitel (born 1882), field marshal, chief of the German Supreme Command (OKW). Sentenced to death in the Nuremberg proceedings: The sentence was carried out on October 16, 1946 (for more on the subject, see G. Mueller, *Wilhelm Keitel, the Forgotten Field Marshal* (New York, 2003).

6. Field Marshal Wilhelm Keitel issued the order on September 16, 1941; see more in P. Longerich, *Himmler*, 644; and P. W. Blood, *Siepacze Hitlera: Oddziały specjalne SS do zwalczania partyzantki* (Warsaw, Poland, 2008), 93.

7. Der Untermensch, publication by Reichsführer-SS and SS Main Office (Berlin, 1942), after P. Longerich, *Himmler*, 767.

8. For more about *Bandenbekämpfung*, see P. W. Blood, *Siepacze Hitlera.*

9. B. Musiał, *Sowieccy partyzanci*, 180.

10. S. Kuklińska, *Działalność*, 59.

11. For more about von Gottberg, see P. Longerich, *Himmler*, 427–30.

12. B. Musiał, *Sowieccy partyzanci*, 33–34.

13. S. Kuklińska, *Działalność*, 60.

14. Ch. Gerlach, *Kalkulierte Morde: Die deutsche Wirtschafts- und Vernichtungspolitik in Weissrussland, 1941 bis 1944* (Hamburg, Germany, 1999), 955–58; and B. Musiał, *Sowieccy partyzanci*, 534.

15. K. D. Slepyan, *Partyzanci Stalina: Radziecki ruch oporu w czasie II wojny światowej* (Poznań, Poland, 2008), 76.

16. B. Musiał, *Sowieccy partyzanci*, 10.

17. Ibid., 115.

18. BA Ludwigsburg, B 162/16569, Verfügung, 45Js 30/64, Dortmund, December 15, 1967, 5.

19. Erich von dem Bach-Zelewski, born March 1, 1899, in Lębork and died March 8, 1972, in Munich. From June 22, 1942, he held the position of higher SS and police leader in Army Group Center's (Mitte) area of operation. For more on von dem Bach-Zelewski, see W. Bartoszewski, *Prawda o von dem Bachu* (Poznań, Poland, 1961); "Von dem Bach-Zelewski: Die Toten stehen auf," *Der Spiegel* 2 (1959); and O. von Loewenstern, *Noch heute—des Teufels General: Nachkriegsporträt eines hohen SS-Führers—Zum Urteil über Bach-Zelewski*, February 17, 1961, http://www.zeit.de/1961/08/noch-heute-des-teufels-general/komplettansicht (accessed February 18, 2017).

20. Zeznania Ericha von dem Bacha-Zelewskiego podczas procesów norymberskich [Erich von dem Bach-Zelewski's testimony during the Nuremberg proceedings], after J. Heydecker and J. Leeb, *Trzecia Rzesza w świetle Norymbergi: Bilans tysiąca lat* (Warsaw, Poland, 1979), 437.

21. GPU—from 1934, the People's Commissariat for Internal Affairs; that is, Naródnyi Komissariát Vnútrennikh Del—NKWD.

22. For more on the subject, see B. Musiał, *Sowieccy partyzanci*, 38–43.

23. B. Musiał, *Sowieccy partyzanci*, 59.

24. Ibid.; see also Ch. Ailsby, *Piekło na froncie wschodnim* (Warsaw, Poland, 2001), 134–35).

25. Ch. Ailsby, *Piekło*, 136–37.

26. B. Musiał, *Sowieccy partyzanci*, 103.

27. Ibid., 103n243.

28. Ibid., 108.

29. *Nazism, 1919–1945*, vol. 3, *Foreign Policy, War and Racial Extermination: A Documentary Reader*, ed. J. Noakes and G. Pridham (Liverpool, UK, 2001), 489.

30. BA Ludwigsburg, B 162/16569, Bisheriges Ermittlungsergebnis über das Sonderkommando "Dirlewanger," n.d., 137; and BAB, NS 19/1, Der Reichsführer-SS—Persönlicher Stab Tgb. No. A 35/39/42, n.d.

31. BA Ludwigsburg, B 162/28392, Sonderkommission Hamburg, 147 Js 11/71 U, Gerhard Hellkamp, Wattenscheid, June 28, 1973, 460.

32. P. Longerich, *Himmler*, 663.

33. BA Ludwigsburg, B 162/5922, Sonderkommission Zentrale Stelle—I/3-180/62, Friedrich Walter, Ludwigsburg, May 27, 1963, 614; and BA Ludwigsburg, B 162/5922, Tgb. Nr. SK. Zst. I/3-180/62, Friedrich Walter, Mörsch, May 21, 1963, 619.

34. BAB, R70 Sowjetunion/38, Der Höhere SS- und Pol-Führer Russland-Mitte, June 20, 1942, 272. Gerhard Hellkamp remembered it as a guesthouse located outside town, in the forest. He may have been right, since the old people's home was in the

neighborhood of the hospital for SS soldiers and police (BA Ludwigsburg, B 162/28392, Sonderkommission Hamburg, 147 Js 11/71 U, Gerhard Hellkamp, Wattenscheid, June 28, 1973, 460).

35. BA Ludwigsburg, B 162/5924, Niederschrift, Dr. Med. Heinz Hartlieb, Wien, February 28, 1964, 1028–29.

36. W. Bartoszewski, *Prawda*, 41.

37. S. Kuklińska, *Działalność*, 62.

38. B. Musiał, *Sowieccy partyzanci*, 381.

39. BA Ludwigsburg, B 162/5924, Niederschrift, Dr. Med. Heinz Hartlieb, Wien, February 28, 1964, 1028. One of Dirlewanger's soldiers, Georg Kraus, stated that in summer 1942 their strength was that of a company (around 100–150 people); BA Ludwigsburg, B 162/4249, K 424 Hamburg, 147 p11/71, Georg Kraus, Bamberg, April 9, 1976, 998.

40. R. Michaelis, *Das SS-Sonderkommando "Dirlewanger": Der Einsatz in Weißrussland 1941–1944* (Berlin, 1999), 8–11.

41. The forerunner of the motorcyclist platoon was formed already in Lublin (BA Ludwigsburg, B 162/5922, Polizeipräsidium Koblenz—III/A (NSG), Josef Rau, Kamp-Bornhofen, July 31, 1963, 731).

42. BA Ludwigsburg, B 162/5922, Tgb. Nr. SK. Zst. I/3-180/62, Friedrich Walter, Mörsch, May 21, 1963, 619. Meanwhile, Waldemar Wilhelm stated they had four or five B-Kräder motorcycles at their disposal (BA Ludwigsburg, B 162/28392, Sonderkommission Hamburg 147 Js 11/71 U, Waldemar Wilhelm, Bad Dürkheim, May 11, 1973, 453).

43. BA Ludwigsburg, B 162/16569, Bisheriges Ermittlungsergebnis über das Sonderkommando "Dirlewanger," n.d., 137.

44. BA Ludwigsburg, B 162/21001, Persönliche Stab Reichsführer-SS [illegible words], Akt. [illegible word] Geh./127, n.d., 16.

45. YV, JM 2083, ID 3669870, letter from Rascher to Suchanek, July 27, 1942, München.

46. BA Ludwigsburg, B 162/3324, Vernehmung Nr. 1844 A, Erich von dem Bach-Zelewski, b.d., 105.

47. BA Ludwigsburg, B 162/16572, Der Oberstaatsanwalt 2 Js 700/61, Paul Zimmermann, Stuttgart, July 1, 1963, 263.

48. BA Ludwigsburg, B 162/4249, V 424 AR 875/72, December 18, 1975, 839.

49. BA Ludwigsburg, B 162/4250, Geschäfts-Nr. 147 Js 11/77 U, n.d., 92–93.

50. BA Ludwigsburg, B 162/4249, V 424 AR 875/72, December 18, 1975, 839.

51. BA Ludwigsburg, B 162/29251, Gespräch zwischen Herrn Heinz Feiertag, ehemals Hauptsturmführer der LAH und Herrn Fritz Langeur [illegible word], am Sonntag dem 22. Mai 1960, 53. Johannes Stein stated that in his company (3rd) there were around 120 soldiers (BA Ludwigsburg, B 162/29251, LKA-NW-Dez.15, Stein Johannes, Bochum, July 3, 1962, 71).

52. BA Ludwigsburg, B 162/16572, Der Oberstaatsanwalt 2 Js 700/61, Paul Zimmermann, Stuttgart, July 1, 1963, 263.

53. BA Ludwigsburg, B 162/16569, Bisheriges Ermittlungsergebnis über das Sonderkommando "Dirlewanger," n.d., 138; and BA Ludwigsburg, B 162/16572, Der Oberstaatsanwalt 2 Js 700/61, Paul Zimmermann, Stuttgart, July 1, 1963, 263. At the start of October 1942, Dirlewanger formed one Russian company and one Ukrainian platoon of around 230 soldiers (H. P. Klausch, *Antifaschisten*, 64).

54. BA Ludwigsburg, B 162/16572, Der Oberstaatsanwalt 2 Js 700/61, Paul Zimmermann, Stuttgart, July 1, 1963, 263.

55. H. P. Klausch, *Antifaschisten*, 73.

56. BA Ludwigsburg, B 162/16634, "Hohe Strafen für Kollaborateure," *Die Welt*, December 5, 1968, 5.

57. BA Ludwigsburg, B 162/5922, Tgb. Nr. SK. Zst. I/3-180/62, Friedrich Walter, Mörsch, May 21, 1963, 619.

58. Paul Lau's letter from Groß-Strehlitz, November 12, 1944, after H. P. Klausch, *Antifaschisten*, 23.

59. P. W. Blood, "Hitler's Bandit Hunters: The SS and the Nazi Occupation of Europe," https://www.academia.edu/44812858/Hitlers_Bandit_Hunters_The_SS_and_the_Nazi_occupation_of_Europe p. 223 (accessed August 15, 2023).

60. BA Ludwigsburg, B 162/29251, Gespräch zwischen Herrn Heinz Feiertag, ehemals Hauptsturmführer der LAH und Herrn Fritz Langeur [illegible word], May 22, 1960, 54.

61. In a previous publication, I wrote that SS-Sonderkommando Dirlewanger participated in twenty-seven antipartisan operations (S. Kuklińska, *Działalność*, 66), but during the course of further work I found documents confirming that there were more of them.

62. Ch. Ingrao, *Czarni myśliwi*, 34–35; and BA Ludwigsburg, B 162/5922, Tgb. Nr. SK. Zst. I/3-180/62, Friedrich Walter, Mörsch, May 21, 1963, 619.

63. BA Ludwigsburg, B 162/29251, Gespräch zwischen Herrn Heinz Feiertag, ehemals Hauptsturmführer der LAH und Herrn Fritz Langeur [illegible word], May 22, 1960, 53.

64. Zusatzbefehl für Unternehmen Lenz-Süd, March 31, 1943, after H. P. Klausch, *Antifaschisten*, 59.

65. BA Ludwigsburg, B 162/29251, Gespräch zwischen Herrn Heinz Feiertag, ehemals Hauptsturmführer der LAH und Herrn Fritz Langeur [illegible word], May 22, 1960, 53–54.

66. *Jednostki Waffen-SS: 1939–1945* (Warsaw, Poland, 1996), 84; and S. Kuklińska, *Działalność*, 67.

67. S. Kuklińska, *Działalność*, 68.

68. *Jednostki Waffen-SS*, 89–90.

69. BAB, R/9361/III 521445, Personalangaben, 743. Moreover, it is visible on photographs of Oskar Dirlewanger.

70. S. Kuklińska, *Działalność*, 68–69.

71. BA Ludwigsburg, B 162/29251, Gespräch zwischen Herrn Heinz Feiertag, ehemals Hauptsturmführer der LAH und Herrn Fritz Langeur [illegible word], May 22, 1960, 55.

72. Ibid.

73. H. C. Verton, *W piekle frontu wschodniego: Byłem holenderskim ochotnikiem Waffen-SS* (Warsaw, Poland, 2010), 122.

74. A. Beevor, *Druga wojna światowa* (Kraków, Poland, 2013), 269.

75. S. Kuklińska, *Działalność*, 69–70.

76. Wytyczne dla oddziałów myśliwskich, załącznik Naczelnego Dowództwa Grupy Armii B [Instructions for hunting units, appendix of Supreme Command of Army Group B], Ia nr 7142/42g, 4.9.1942, after V. Koop, *Werwolf: Ostatni zaciąg Himmlera* (Warsaw, Poland, 2016), 32.

77. BAB, R70 Sowjetunion/38, Grundsätzliche Bestimmungen für den Erkennungs- und Verständigungsdienst zwischen Truppenteilen am boden und fliegenden Verbänden, July 21, 1943.

78. This was done in accordance with instructions from Franz Halder, the chief of the Army's General Staff. The Jagdkommandobefehl order initiated *Aufklärung*; that is, tactical intelligence gathering. *Aufklärung* effectively combined reconnaissance during combat with intelligence gathering (P. W. Blood, *Siepacze Hitlera*, 159–60).

79. B. Musiał, *Sowieccy partyzanci*, 104.

80. Ibid.

81. S. Kuklińska, *Działalność*, 70.

82. BA Ludwigsburg, B 162/29251, Gespräch zwischen Herrn Heinz Feiertag, ehemals Hauptsturmführer der LAH und Herrn Fritz Langeur [illegible word], May 22, 1960, 54.

83. P. W. Blood, *Siepacze Hitlera*, 159–60.

84. BA Ludwigsburg, B 162/4249, V 424 AR 875/72, December 18, 1975, 838.

85. B. Musiał, *Sowieccy partyzanci*, 105.

86. BA Ludwigsburg, B 162/5922, Tgb. Nr. SK. Zst. I/3-180/62, Friedrich Walter, Mörsch, May 21, 1963, 619.

87. Ibid.

88. Ibid.

89. BA Ludwigsburg, B 162/4249, K 424 Hamburg, 147 p11/71, Georg Kraus, Bamberg, April 9, 1976, 998–99.

90. BA Ludwigsburg, B 162/29251, Gespräch zwischen Herrn Heinz Feiertag, ehemals Hauptsturmführer der LAH und Herrn Fritz Langeur [illegible word], May 22, 1960, 56.

91. Ibid., 57.

92. Ibid., 56.

93. B. Musiał, *Sowieccy partyzanci*, 122–23; Befehl des Polizei-Regiments Mitte zur Partisanenbekämpfung zwischen drut und Beresina, March 31, 1942; and R. Michaelis, *Das SS-Sonderkommando "Dirlewanger,"* 56–7.

94. B. Musiał, *Sowieccy partyzanci*, 122.

95. Brygada Zabezpieczenia: Operacja "Bamberg"—propozycja przeprowadzenia akcji [Security Brigade: Operation Bamberg—proposal for conducting the action], March 10, 1942, after B. Musiał, *Sowieccy partyzanci*, 529.

96. 102. pułk Kozaków: Raport z akcji Kozaków, Sonderführer (nazwisko nieczytelne) [102nd Cossack regiment: Report from Cossack action, Sonderführer (name illegible)], April 25, 1942, after B. Musiał, *Sowieccy partyzanci*, 529.

97. BAB, R/9361/III, vol. 521445, motion to award SS-Obersturmbannführer Oskar Dirlewanger with the German Cross in Gold, August 15, 1943, 761.

98. YV, JM 2088, ID 3672138, the personal file of Dirlewanger, August 9, 1943; R. Michaelis, *Das SS-Sonderkommando "Dirlewanger,"* 40; and BAB, R70 Sowjetunion/22, Polizeiregiment Mitte Ia, Regimentsbefehl Nr. 4, March 31, 1942.

99. BAB, R/9361/III, vol. 521445, motion to award SS-Obersturmbannführer Oskar Dirlewanger with the German Cross in Gold, August 15, 1943, 761.

100. YV, JM 2088, ID 3672138, the personal file of Dirlewanger, August 9, 1943.

101. BAB, R70 Sowjetunion/22, Polizeiregiment Mitte Ia, Regimentsbefehl Nr. 4, 31.3.1942; and Befehl des Polizei-Regiments Mitte zur Partisanenbekämpfung zwischen drut und Beresina, March 31, 1942, after R. Michaelis, *Das SS-Sonderkommando "Dirlewanger,"* 56–8.

102. BAB, R70 Sowjetunion/22, Polizeiregiment Mitte I, Regimentsbefehl Nr. 4, March 31, 1942.

103. B. Musiał, *Sowieccy partyzanci*, 122.

104. Krótki raport na temat działalności oddziału partyzanckiego im. Stalina, Tichomirow [Brief report on the activity of the Stalin partisan unit, Tichomirov], August 25, 1942, after B. Musiał, *Sowieccy partyzanci*, 126.

105. Meldunek generała dowodzącego grupami zabezpieczenia i dowódcy Obszarów Tyłowych Grupy Armii "Środek" do OKH [Report of the general commanding the security groups and the commander of the Rear Area of Army Group Center to the OKH], April 24, 1942, after B. Musiał, *Sowieccy partyzanci*, 126.

106. BAB, R70 Sowjetunion/22, Polizeiregiment Mitte Ia, Regimentsbefehl Nr. 4, March 31, 1942.

107. B. Musiał, *Sowieccy partyzanci*, 124.

108. Ibid., 82.

109. For more about Stalin Partisan Unit no. 208, see ibid., 117–164.

110. BAB, R/9361/III, vol. 521445, motion to award SS-Obersturmbannführer Oskar Dirlewanger with the German Cross in Gold, August 15, 1943, 761.

111. B. Musiał, *Sowieccy partyzanci*, 127.

112. BAB, R/9361/III, vol. 521445, motion to award SS-Obersturmbannführer Oskar Dirlewanger with the German Cross in Gold, August 15, 1943, 762; and YV, JM 2088, ID 3672138, the personal file of Dirlewanger, August 9, 1943.

113. BAB, R/9361/III, vol. 521445, motion to award SS-Obersturmbannführer Oskar Dirlewanger with the German Cross in Gold, August 15, 1943, 761.

114. Ibid., 766.

115. B. Musiał, *Sowieccy partyzanci*, 128.

116. BAB, R/9361/III, vol. 521445, motion to award SS-Obersturmbannführer Oskar Dirlewanger with the German Cross in Gold, August 15, 1943, 762.

117. BAB, R70 Sowjetunion/19, Polizeiregiment Mitte, Gefechtsbericht v. 9-12.5.42, May 16, 1942, unpag.; and B. Musiał, *Sowieccy partyzanci*, 128.

118. YV, JM 2088, ID 3672138, the personal file of Dirlewanger, August 9, 1943; and BAB, R/9361/III, vol. 521445, motion to award SS-Obersturmbannführer Oskar Dirlewanger with the German Cross in Gold, August 15, 1943, 762.

119. BAB, R70 Sowjetunion/19, Polizeiregiment Mitte, Gefechtsbericht v. 9-12.5.42, May 16, 1942.

120. B. Musiał, *Sowieccy partyzanci*, 128. Musiał also stated that the Germans burned them down. SS-Sonderkommando Dirlewanger and a company of the 11th Police Battalion (Pol.Batls. 11) were left behind in Razvadovo as reserve forces (BAB, R70 Sowjetunion/19, Polizeiregiment Mitte, Gefechtsbericht v. 9-12.5.42, May 16, 1942).

121. BAB, R70 Sowjetunion/19, Polizeiregiment Mitte, Gefechtsbericht v. 9-12.5.42, May 16, 1942.

122. Ibid.

123. OKH was the German Army High Command from 1936 to 1945.

124. B. Musiał, *Sowieccy partyzanci*, 131.

125. BAB, R70 Sowjetunion/19, Polizeiregiment Mitte, Gefechtsbericht v. 9-12.5.42, May 16, 1942; and 1. pułk policji "Mitte": Sprawozdanie z walki, 9–12.05.1942 [1st police regiment Miite: Combat report, May 9–12, 1942], May 16, 1942, after B. Musiał, *Sowieccy partyzanci*, 128–29.

126. B. Musiał, *Sowieccy partyzanci*, 129.

127. YV, JM 2088, ID 3672138, the personal file of Dirlewanger, August 9, 1943; and BAB, R/9361/III, vol. 521445, motion to award SS-Obersturmbannführer Oskar Dirlewanger with the German Cross in Gold, August 15, 1943, 762.

128. B. Musiał, *Sowieccy partyzanci*, 130.

129. This was the village of Susha situated near the Mogilev–Asipovichy railway line.

130. B. Musiał, *Sowieccy partyzanci*, 130.

131. BAB, R/9361/III, vol. 521445, motion to award SS-Obersturmbannführer Oskar Dirlewanger with the German Cross in Gold, August 15, 1943, 762; and YV, JM 2088, ID 3672138, the personal file of Dirlewanger, August 9, 1943.

132. B. Musiał, *Sowieccy partyzanci*, 131.

133. Ibid., 132.

134. Ibid., 137.

135. Niederschrift der Vernehmung des Albin V. vom 19.03.1948, 2, after H. P. Klausch, *Antifaschisten*, 62–64, translated by K. Kupiszewska from the Polish translation by J. Kalemba.

136. BA Ludwigsburg, B 162/4249, V 424 AR 875/72, December 18, 1975, 840–41.

137. Ibid., 841.

138. Ibid.

139. BAB, R70 Sowjetunion/38, SS-Sonderkommando, June 16, 1942, 277.

140. Ibid.

141. R. B. Birn, "'Zaunkönig' an 'Uhrmacher': Grosse Partisanenaktion 1942/43 am Beispiel des "Unternehemns Winterzauber," *Militärgeschichtliche Zeitschrift* 1 (2001): 111.

142. P. Longerich, *Himmler*, 767; and Ch. Gerlach, *Kalkulierte Morde*, 1055.

143. YV, JM 2088, ID 3672138, the personal file of Dirlewanger, August 9, 1943; and BAB, R/9361/III, vol. 521445, motion to award SS-Obersturmbannführer Oskar Dirlewanger with the German Cross in Gold, August 15, 1943, 762.

144. YV, JM 2088, ID 3672138, the personal file of Dirlewanger, August 9, 1943.

145. BA Ludwigsburg, B 162/21001, Dirlewanger's letter, Esslingen, July 27, 1942, 31–32; and BAB, NS 19/1, 5–6.

146. BAB, R/9361/III, vol. 521445, motion to award SS-Obersturmbannführer Oskar Dirlewanger with the German Cross in Gold, August 15, 1943, 766.

147. BAB, R70 Sowjetunion/21, Der Höhere SS- und Polizeiführer Russland Mitte, Stabsbefehl Nr. 39, July 16, 1942. He was granted this decoration in April 1942.

148. For more about Carl Friedrich Graf von Pückler-Burghauss, see https://de.wikipedia.org/wiki/Carl_Friedrich_von_P%C3%BCckler-Burghauss (accessed February 1, 2019). While Erich von dem Bach-Zelewski was in the hospital, von Pückler-Burghauss acted as his deputy (P. W. Blood, *Siepacze Hitlera*, 101).

149. BA Ludwigsburg, B 162/21001, Dirlewanger's letter, Esslingen, July 27, 1942, 31–2; and BAB, NS 19/1, Dirlewanger's letter, July 27, 1942, 5–6.

150. BA Ludwigsburg, B 162/21001, Dirlewanger's letter, Esslingen, July 27, 1942, 32; and BAB, NS 19/1, Dirlewanger's letter, July 27, 1942, 5–6.

151. W. Bartoszewski, *Prawda*, 38.

152. B. Musiał, *Sowieccy partyzanci*, 141–42.

153. YV, JM 2088, ID 3672138, the personal file of Dirlewanger, August 9, 1943.

154. BAB, R/9361/III, vol. 521445, motion to award SS-Obersturmbannführer Oskar Dirlewanger with the German Cross in Gold, August 15, 1943, 763. Musiał stated that Operation Adler started on July 19, 1942 (B. Musiał, *Sowieccy partyzanci*, 142).

155. Johann-Georg Richert, born April 14, 1890, was hanged in Minsk on January 30, 1946 for war crimes (see more at http://www.lexikon-der-wehrmacht.de/Personenregister/R/RichertJG-R.htm, accessed March 10, 2019).

156. B. Musiał, *Sowieccy partyzanci*, 142.

157. Ibid., 143.

158. Ibid.

159. Ibid.

160. Ibid., 145.

161. Ibid.

162. E. von dem Bach, Dziennik wojenny [War diary], July 28, 1942, after B. Musiał, *Sowieccy partyzanci*, 145.

163. Ibid., 145–48.

164. Ibid., 151.

165. Ibid.

166. Ibid.

167. Ibid., 152.

168. Ibid.

169. BAB, R70 Sowjetunion/38, Polizei-Regiment 2 Gruppe Buchmann, August 8, 1942, 271.

170. B. Musiał, *Sowieccy partyzanci*, 154.

171. BAB, R/9361/III, vol. 521445, motion to award SS-Obersturmbannführer Oskar Dirlewanger with the German Cross in Gold, August 15, 1943, 763; and YV, JM 2088, ID 3672138, the personal file of Dirlewanger, August 9, 1943. Meanwhile, Musiał stated that Operation Greif lasted from August 17 to 29, 1942 (B. Musiał, *Sowieccy partyzanci*, 193).

172. BAB, R70 Sowjetunion/38, Polizei-Regiment 14, September 1, 1942, 451.

173. B. Musiał, *Sowieccy partyzanci*, 193.

174. Ibid., 194.

175. Ibid., 195. As Musiał wrote, "Slightly earlier, Danukalov claimed quite the opposite; namely, that his brigade fought very effectively against the German units."

176. Ibid., 196.

177. Ibid.

178. YV, JM 2088, ID 3672138, the personal file of Dirlewanger, August 9, 1943.

179. BAB, R/9361/III, vol. 521445, motion to award SS-Obersturmbannführer Oskar Dirlewanger with the German Cross in Gold, August 15, 1943, 763.

180. Marshal Voroshilov was dismissed by Stalin from this position after two months, on November 19, 1942.

181. B. Musiał, *Sowieccy partyzanci*, 239–40.

182. Generał Schenckendorff, dowodzący grupami zabezpieczenia i dowódca Obszarów Tyłowych Grupy Armii "Środek," Ia, do OKH [General Schenckendorff, commanding security groups and commander of the Rear Areas of Group Army Center], October 10, 1942, after B. Musiał, *Sowieccy partyzanci*, 201–02.

183. B. Musiał, *Sowieccy partyzanci*, 202. Heinrich Himmler wanted the population of the occupied territories to cut down trees and bushes in a 400–500-meter-wide strip on either side of roads and railways, so that partisans would have nowhere to hide (see P. Longerich, *Himmler*, 764).

184. D. Irving, *Wojna Hitlera*, 444.

185. B. Musiał, *Sowieccy partyzanci*, 527; and P. Longerich, *Himmler*, 655.

186. BAB, NS 33/226, Abschrift von Abschrift, Tgb. No. Ia 492/g.Kdos, Richtlinien für die Durchführung der Aktion gegen Partisanen und sonstige Banditen in Oberkain und Untersteiermark, June 25, 1942.

187. BAB, R70 Sowjetunion/77, Der Bevollmächtigte des Reichsführers-SS für Bandenbekämpfung, Richtlinien für die Maßnahmen zur Bandenbekämpfung, February 26, 1943, 1668.

188. Ibid.

189. BA Ludwigsburg, B 162/4248, Sonderkommission Hamburg, Paul Erich Illing, Wanne-Eickel, August 31, 1972, 251.

190. BA Ludwigsburg, B 162/4250, Geschäfts-Nr. 147 Js 11/77 U, n.d., 117.

191. BA Ludwigsburg, B 162/4249, FD 724 Hamburg, 147 Js 11/71, Friedrich Noweck, Herten, January 17, 1978, 966.

192. Ibid., Wilfried Höfling, Bielefeld, June 19, 1978; and BA Ludwigsburg, B 162/4249, Wilfried Höfling, n.d., 972. Similar phrasing was used by another soldier, Paul Rumschewitsch: "dort, wo die Dörfer brannten, Dirlewanger am 'Werke' sei" (BA Ludwigsburg, B 162/28392, K 424 Hamburg, 147 Js 11/71 U, Paul Rumschewitsch, Osnabrück, June 10, 1974, 659).

193. BA Ludwigsburg, B 162/4249, FD 724 Hamburg, Edmund Berke, Leutkirch, November 10, 1976, 1088.

194. BA Ludwigsburg, B 162/28392, Sta Hamburg, 147 Js 11/714, Werner Weber-Bergfeldt, October 25, 1973, 368.

195. B. Musiał, *Sowieccy partyzanci*, 530–31.

196. Ibid., 526.

197. A. Beevor, *Druga wojna światowa*, 269.

198. B. Musiał, *Sowieccy partyzanci*, 105.

199. Ibid., 400.

200. Zapiski partyzanta J. D. Rudki z Brygady Nikitina [Notes of the partisan J. D. Rudka from the Nikitin Brigade], summer-autumn 1942, after B. Musiał, *Sowieccy partyzanci*, 401–02.

201. Działalność 2. Białoruskiej Brygady Partyzanckiej towarzysza Diaczkowa w okresie od 6.07.1941 do 2.07.1942 [Activity of comrade Diachkov's 2nd Belarusian Partisan Brigade in the period July 6, 1941, to July 2, 1942], after B. Musiał, *Sowieccy partyzanci*, 182.

202. B. Musiał, *Sowieccy partyzanci*, 470.

203. Dowódca Obszarów Tyłowych Grupy Armii "Środek", Ia, do OKH [Commander of the Rear Area of Army Group Center, Ia, to OKH], February 5, 1942, after B. Musiał, *Sowieccy partyzanci*, 372.

204. Wykład z 29.05.1942 generała Schenckendorffa, dowódcy Obszarów Tyłowych Grupy Armii "Środek"[Lecture of May 29, 1942, by General Schenckendorff, Commander of the Rear Area of Army Group Center], June 2, 1942, after B. Musiał, *Sowieccy partyzanci*, 372.

205. Protokół nr 19 posiedzenia komitetu obwodowego KP(b)B w Witebsku [Minutes no. 19 from the session of the oblast CP(b)B committee in Vitebsk], March 14, 1943, after B. Musiał, *Sowieccy partyzanci*, 270.

206. Fragment sprawozdania z działalności komisarza politycznego w Brygadzie "Leninskij Komsomoł" w okresie od 15.02 do 25.03.1943 [Fragment of a report on the activity of the political commissar in the "Leninskiy Komsomol" Brigade in the period February 15 to March 25, 1943], March 25, 1943, after B. Musiał, *Sowieccy partyzanci*, 512.

207. B. Musiał, *Sowieccy partyzanci*, 375.

208. Rozkaz nr 18 Mowczanskiego, sekretarza komitetu obwodowego KP(b)B w Mohylewie, do brygad i grup operacyjnych z obwodu mohylewskiego [Order no. 18 of Movchanski, secretary of the oblast CP(b)B committee in Mogilev, directed to brigades and operation groups in the Mogilev oblast], April 25, 1943, after B. Musiał, *Sowieccy partyzanci*, 359.

209. B. Musiał, *Sowieccy partyzanci*, 359–60.

210. W. Bartoszewski, *Prawda*, 37–38.

211. BAB, R/9361/III, vol. 521445, motion to award SS-Obersturmbannführer Oskar Dirlewanger with the German Cross in Gold, August 15, 1943, 763.

212. Arthur Nebe, born November 13, 1894, and executed March 4, 1945, commander of Einsatzgruppe B operating in the USSR (see more at https://encyklopedia.pwn.pl/haslo/Nebe-Arthur;3946388.html, accessed February 2, 2019; and https://de.wikipedia.org/wiki/Arthur_Nebe, accessed February 2, 2019).

213. BAB, NS 19/1, Der Reichsführer-SS Chef des SS-Hauptamtes, Cd SS HA/ Be/Vo. Vs-Tgb.Nr. 3795/42 geh., October 3, 1942, 11.

214. BAB, R70 Sowjetunion/38, SS-Sonderkommando Dirlewanger, October 4, 1942, 435.

215. P. W. Blood, *Siepacze Hitlera*, 140.

216. B. Musiał, *Sowieccy partyzanci*, 203.

217. P. W. Blood, *Siepacze Hitlera*, 140.

218. P. Longerich, *Himmler*, 766.

219. In some sources, its duration is given as November 18–19 to 25–27, 1942 (BA Ludwigsburg, B 162/4248, Die Kampfgruppe von Gottberg, n.d., 40).

220. BAB, R70 Sowjetunion/63, 1. SS-Infanterie-Brigade (mot) Ia/Nr. 655/42 geh., Angriffsbefehl Nr. 1 Unternehmen "Nürnberg," November 20, 1942, 1421.

221. This was established in order no. 1. In the original: "Bandenfreundliche und bandenverdächtige Orte, die nach schriftlich bekanntgegeben oder im Verlauf des Unternehmens durch die den Rgt. Zugeteilten Komandos des SD und der Landwirtschaftsführer werden oder eine feindliche Haltung zeigen, sind gründlich zu überholen und rücksichtslos zu behandeln. In diesen Ortschaften sind unter Heranziehung des Gemeindeältesten (Starosten) oder sonstiger geeigneter Persönlichkeiten die Banden verdächtigen und Bandenfreundlichen Bewohner festzustellen und Juden und Zigeneur zu vernichten. Jeder Berittene ist zu erschiessen, dasgleichen als Kundschafter oder Posten anzusehende halbwüchsige oder andere Bevölkerung" (Ibid., 1421).

222. B. Musiał, *Sowieccy partyzanci*, 203.

223. BA Ludwigsburg, B 162/4248, Die Kampfgruppe von Gottberg, n.d., 40.

224. BAB, R70 Sowjetunion/38, Sonderkommando Dirlewanger, October 28, 1942, 390.

225. BA Ludwigsburg, B 162/4248, Die Kampfgruppe von Gottberg, Abschlußbericht des Unternehmens "Nürnberg," November 30, 1942, 44. Musiał gave the number of alleged partisans and their supporters killed as 3,800 (see B. Musiał, *Sowieccy partyzanci*, 203), Gerlach as 2,974, and Cüppers as 2,984 (Ch. Gerlach, *Kalkulierte Morde*, 900; and M. Cüppers, *Wegbereiter der Shoah: Die Waffen-SS, der Kommandostab Reichsführer-SS und die Judenvernichtung 1939–1945* [Darmstadt, 2005], 258, 278–79). According to report no. 46, of December 1, 1942, conveyed by Himmler to Hitler, the number of victims was 2,984 (given by Cüppers). "798 Tote, 340 Gefangene, erschossen wurden: 1,833 Bandenhelfer, 353 Bandenverdächtige" (BA Ludwigsburg, B 162/4248, Die Kampfgruppe von Gottberg, Meldungen an den Führer über Bandebekämpfung—Meldung Nr. 46—Gebiet Rußland Mitte vom 1.12.1942, 44).

226. BA Ludwigsburg, B 162/28392, Fortsetzung der Vernehmung vom 5 VI 1974, SS-Hauptsturmführer Wilke, Peine, June 6, 1974, 646; and BA Ludwigsburg, B 162/4248, Die Kampfgruppe von Gottberg, n.d., 46.

227. Wspomnienia mieszkańców byłego postawskiego powiatu [Memories of residents of the former Pastavy poviat], http://postawyiokolice.blogspot.com/2011/05/wspomnienia-mieszkancow-byego.html, May 29, 2011 (accessed March 28, 2018).

228. BA Ludwigsburg, B 162/4248, Die Kampfgruppe von Gottberg, n.d., 46.

229. For more about the CSPD, see B. Musiał, *Sowieccy partyzanci*, 205–48.

230. Ibid., 210.

231. Ibid.

232. Ibid., 211.

233. Ibid., 252.

234. BAB, R70 Sowjetunion/38, SS-Sonderbataillon Dr. Dirlewanger, December 2, 1942, 373–74.

235. Letter from engineer Karl B. of July 24, 1942, to NSDAP Kreisleiter in Esslingen, after H. P. Klausch, *Antifaschisten*, 71–72.

236. Information on this may be found in Stadtarchiv Esslingen, after R. Laschet, *Dr. Oskar Dirlewanger*, 51.

237. BA Ludwigsburg, B 162/16569, Verfügung, 45Js 30/64, Dortmund, December 15, 1967, 57.

238. Kurt von Gottberg, born February 11, 1896, fought in the First World War and joined the NSDAP and SS (no. 45923) in 1932. He arrived in Belarus in November 1942 and replaced SS-Brigadeführer Walter Schimana as SS and police leader in Belarus (*SS- und Polizeiführer Weißruthenien*). He committed suicide on May 31, 1945 (BA Ludwigsburg, B 162/4248, Die Kampfgruppe von Gottberg, n.d., 26; and S. Kuklińska, *Działalność*, 83).

239. BA Ludwigsburg, B 162/4248, Sonderkommission Hamburg, Adolf Rübe, Karlsruhe, September 15, 1972, 283.

240. BA Ludwigsburg, B 162/28392, Fortsetzung der Vernehmung vom 5 VI 1974, SS-Hauptsturmführer Wilke, Peine, June 6, 1974, 640.

241. P. Longerich, *Himmler*, 766. For detailed numbers, see Ch. Gerlach, *Kalkulierte Morde*, 900.

242. In a previous publication I wrote that SS-Sonderkommando Dirlewanger participated in eleven operations over the course of the year, one per month on average, and that each lasted around three weeks (S. Kuklińska, *Działalność*, 83–84). During further research, I corrected these data.

243. According to some documents, on August 10, 1943, Himmler ordered the transformation of SS-Sonderkommando Dirlewanger into SS-Sonderbataillon Dirlewanger (BA Ludwigsburg, B 162/16569, Bisheriges Ermittlungsergebnis über das Sonderkommando "Dirlewanger," n.d., 141). According to Himmler's order, on August 10, 1943, SS-Sonderkommando (SS-Sonderbataillon) Dirlewanger was transformed into SS-Sonderregiment Dirlewanger (BA Ludwigsburg, B162/21001, SS-Führungshauptamt, Kdo. Amt d. Waffen-SS, Org. Tgb. Nr. II/5868/43 geh, SS-Sonderkommando Dirlewanger, Berlin-Wilmersdorf, August 10, 1943, 11–12).

244. BA Ludwigsburg, B 162/28392, Sonderkommission Hamburg, 147 Js 11/71, Erwin Walser, Stuttgart, May 10, 1973, 445.

245. S. Kuklińska, *Działalność*, 84.

246. BA Ludwigsburg, B 162/28392, Sta Hamburg, 147 Js 11/71U, Hans Richard Wiechert, n.d., 419–20.

247. E. Hesse, *Der sowjetrussische Partisanenkrieg 1941 bis 1944 im Spiegel deutscher Kampfanweisungen und Befehle* (Göttingen, Germany, 1969), 264.

248. B. Musiał, *Sowieccy partyzanci*, 378–79.

249. SS-Oberführer Hermann Pister, born February 21, 1885, in Lübeck, was sentenced to death by hanging but died earlier (September 28, 1948) of a heart attack in Landsberg am Lech. He belonged to the Allgemeine-SS from 1932 and was active in Organization Todt as a manager of labor camps in western Europe from 1939. In 1940, he received the rank of *SS-Sturmbannführer* in the Waffen-SS. He was the commander of the concentration camp in Buchenwald from 1942 (for more about Pister, see YV, JM 2095, ID 3675709, testimony of Pister about recruitment to Dirlewanger unit, January 14, 1947).

250. Amtsgruppe D: Konzentrationslager, one of the five bodies under the SS Main Economic and Administrative Office (SS-Wirtschafts- und Verwaltungshauptamt, or SS-WVHA), which concentration camps were subordinate to. The latter were administered by the Concentration Camp Inspectorate. Office D was headed by SS-Gruppenführer Richard Glücks.

251. YV, JM 2095, ID 3675709, testimony of Pister about recruitment to Dirlewanger unit, January 14, 1947.

252. H. P. Klausch, *Antifaschisten*, 75–76.

253. Ibid., 82.

254. R. Michaelis, *Das SS-Sonderkommando "Dirlewanger,"* 11.

255. BAB, R70 Sowjetunion/38, Dirlewanger's letter to SS-Gruppenführer von Gottberg], February 26, 1944.

256. BA Ludwigsburg, B 162/21001, SS-Führungshauptamt Ia, Berlin-Wilmersdorf, January 21, 1943, 27.

257. BA Ludwigsburg, B 162/21001, Der Reichsführer-SS, Persönlicher Stab, Tgb. Nr. 35/109/43, Me/Bn, Feld-Kommandostelle, January 26, 1943, 26; and BA Ludwigsburg, B 162/16569, Bisheriges Ermittlungsergebnis über das Sonderkommando "Dirlewanger," n.d., 139.

258. BA Ludwigsburg, B 162/5922, Polizeipräsidium Koblenz—III/A (NSG), Josef Rau, Kamp-Bornhofen, July 31, 1963, 730.

259. BA Ludwigsburg, B 162/5922, Tgb. Nr. SK. Zst. I/3-180/62, Friedrich Walter, Mörsch, May 21, 1963, 624.

260. Stadtarchiv Heilbronn, Nachlass Hellmut Riegraf D037-54. Nachforschungen zum Schicksal von Herbert Koeber, standrechtlich erschossen am 6 IV 1945 bei Schmeden. Brief von Herbert Koeber an seine Eltern, Lazarett Goisern, December 21, 1944.

261. BA Ludwigsburg, B 162/29251, Bayerisches Landeskriminalamt IIIa/SK, Tgb.Nr. 489/62, Dr. Franz Schmuckerschlag, München, May 29, 1962, 35–36.

262. BA Ludwigsburg, B 162/16569, Bisheriges Ermittlungsergebnis über das Sonderkommando "Dirlewanger," n.d., 140.

263. BA Ludwigsburg, B 162/29251, Bayerisches Landeskriminalamt IIIa/SK, Tgb.Nr. 489/62, Dr. Franz Schmuckerschlag, München, May 29, 1962, 36.

264. BAB, R70 Sowjetunion/38, Der Bevollmächtigte des Reichsführer-SS für Bandenbekämpfung Ia, Betr.: Organisation und Schriftverkehr, March 25, 1943, 323.

265. B. Musiał, *Sowieccy partyzanci*, 277.

266. Ibid.

267. Fritz Sauckel, born in 1894. Plenipotentiary for Labor Deployment, he orchestrated the exploitation of forced laborers from countries occupied or held by forces of the Third Reich, creating a system of slave labor. On March 21, 1942, he was assigned the task of "using all available labor force, including laborers from abroad and POWs." The working and living conditions of such people were terrible. He was sentenced to death in a trial in Nuremberg and executed on October 16, 1946 (for more about this subject, see "Fritz Sauckel (1894–1946)," http://www.erfurt-web.de/Fritz_Sauckel_English, accessed February 12, 2018).

268. P. Longerich, *Himmler*, 798.

269. Ch. Gerlach, *Kalkulierte Morde*, 1010, 1034.

270. BA Ludwigsburg, B 162/5926, Betrifft: Sammelvorgang Strafsache Dirlewanger, Weiße, Heinsen Rußland-Polen-Ungarn-Tschecho-Slowakei u. Deutschland verbrechen, Berlin 44, May 12, 1972, 1508; and BA Ludwigsburg, B 162/16570, Das Urteil im Wilhelmstrassen—Prozess, n.d., 317.

271. Interrogation of Albin V., March 19, 1948, after Ch. Ingrao, *Czarni myśliwi*, 210.

272. BAB, R70 Sowjetunion/78, SS Sonderbataillon Dirlewanger, May 25, 1943, 1672.

273. D. Pohl, *Die Herrschaft der Wehrmacht: Deutsche Militärbesatzung und einheimische Bevölkerung in der Sowjetunion 1941–1944* (Frankfurt am Main, Germany, 2011), 293.

274. BA Ludwigsburg, B 162/16569, "Cottbus," Dortmund, December 15, 1967, 93.

275. BA Ludwigsburg, B 162/16570, Einsatzbefehl für "Unternehmen Dirlewanger," Mińsk, March 2, 1943, 227.

276. BA Ludwigsburg, B 162/28392, Sonderkommission Hamburg, 147 Js 11/71 U, Gerhard Hellkamp, Wattenscheid, June 28, 1973, 462.

277. BA Ludwigsburg, B 162/16574, Leseabschrift NO 887, n.d., 274.

278. BAB, R/9361/III, vol. 521445, motion to award SS-Obersturmbannführer Oskar Dirlewanger with the German Cross in Gold, August 15, 1943, 763; YV, JM

2088, ID 3672138, the personal file of Dirlewanger, August 9, 1943; and BA Ludwigsburg, B 162/16569, Erntefest, 72. According to data from BA Ludwigsburg, Operation Erntefest I lasted from January 18 to 26, 1943, and Erntefest II, from January 28 to February 9, 1943 (B 162/16569, Verfügung, 45Js 30/64, Dortmund, December 15, 1967, 72; and ibid., 162/4248, Die Kampfgruppe von Gottberg, 54).

279. BA Ludwigsburg, B 162/16569, Erntefest, n.d., 72.

280. Ibid., 74.

281. YV, JM 2088, ID 3672138, the personal file of Dirlewanger, August 9, 1943; and BAB, R/9361/III, vol. 521445, motion to award SS-Obersturmbannführer Oskar Dirlewanger with the German Cross in Gold, August 15, 1943, 764.

282. BA Ludwigsburg, B 162/16569, Erntefest, n.d., 75.

283. BA Ludwigsburg, B 162/16569, "Hornung," n.d., 77; and BA Ludwigsburg, B 162/4248, "Hornung," n.d., 59.

284. BAB, R/9361/III, vol. 521445, motion to award SS-Obersturmbannführer Oskar Dirlewanger with the German Cross in Gold, August 15, 1943, 763.

285. BA Ludwigsburg, B 162/16569, "Hornung," n.d., 77.

286. P. W. Blood, *Siepacze Hitlera*, 221–22.

287. BA Ludwigsburg, B 162/28392, Fortsetzung der Vernehmung vom 5·VI 1974, SS-Hauptsturmführer Wilke, Peine, June 6, 1974, 632–33.

288. BAB, R/9361/III, vol. 521445, motion to award SS-Obersturmbannführer Oskar Dirlewanger with the German Cross in Gold, August 15, 1943, 763–64.

289. BA Ludwigsburg, B 162/4248, "Hornung," n.d., 64. Some authors—among them, A. Richie, *Warszawa 1944*: *Tragiczne Powstanie* (Warsaw, Poland, 2013)—state that Dirlewanger's unit was responsible for burning this and the neighboring villages, but documents point to the Latvian battalion.

290. "Słuck," https://encyklopedia.pwn.pl/haslo/Sluck;3976606.html (accessed March 28, 2018); and BA Ludwigsburg, B 162/4248, "Hornung," n.d., 61–62.

291. BA Ludwigsburg, B 162/16569, "Hornung," n.d., 78–80.

292. BAB, R70 Sowjetunion/98, Einsatzbefehl für "Unternehmen Dirlewanger," Mińsk, March 2, 1943, 146.

293. Ibid.

294. S. Kuklińska, *Działalność*, 75.

295. Pjotr Grigorjewitsch Lis, born in 1901 in Kozyri near Lahoysk (BA Ludwigsburg, B 162/16636, II 202 AR 1957/68, Übersetzung Bl.-Nr. 19–23, Pjotr Grigorjewitsch Lis, January 31, 1961).

296. BA Ludwigsburg, B 162/16636, II 202 AR 1957/68, Übersetzung Bl.-Nr. 19–23, Pjotr Grigorjewitsch Lis, January 31, 1961.

297. Josif Josifowitstsch Kaminskij, born in 1887 in the village of Gani, near Lahoysk. During the German occupation, he lived with his family in Khatyn near Pleshchanitsy until March 22, 1943 (BA Ludwigsburg, B 162/16636, II 202 AR

1957/68, Übersetzung Bl.-Nr. 197–201, Josif Kaminskij, January 31, 1961).

298. Ibid.

299. BA Ludwigsburg, B 162/16636, II 202 AR 1957/68, Übersetzung Bl.-Nr. 19–23, Pjotr Grigorjewitsch Lis, January 31, 1961.

300. Ibid.

301. BA Ludwigsburg, B 162/16636, II 202 AR 1957/68, Übersetzung Bl.-Nr. 197–201, Josif Kaminskij, January 31, 1961.

302. Ibid.

303. Ibid.

304. "The Tragedy of Khatyn," http://khatyn.by/en/tragedy/ (accessed July 23, 2016). For more about the fates of the children who survived, see http://khatyn.by/en/tragedy/trage/witnesses/ (accessed July 23, 2016).

305. H. P. Klausch, *Antifaschisten*, 403, translated by K. Kupiszewska from Polish translation by J. Kalemba.

306. BA Ludwigsburg, B 162/16636, II 202 AR 1957/68, Übersetzung Bl.-Nr. 197–201, Josif Kaminskij, January 31, 1961.

307. "The Tragedy of Khatyn," http://khatyn.by/en/about/excursion/step1/ (accessed July 23, 2016); Памяць Беларусі, 1941–1945, Мінск 2005, 528–29; and S. Kuklińska, *Działalność*, 79.

308. "W Kanadzie zmarł kat Chatynia," http://kresy24.pl/w-kanadzie-zmarl-kat-chatynia/ (accessed July 23, 2016).

309. For more on Walter Schimana, see https://de.wikipedia.org/wiki/Walter_Schimana (accessed January 31, 2019).

310. BAB, R70/Sowjetunion/21, Der Bevollmächtigte des RFSS für Bandenbekämpfung Abtlg. Ia Tgb. Nr. 387/43 geh. Tagesbefehl Nr. 2, March 24, 1943.

311. Dokument 55: Einsatzbefehl für das Unternehmen "Zauberflöte" 15. April 1943, after R. Michaelis, *Das SS-Sonderkommando "Dirlewanger,"* 125–30; and BAB, R/9361/III, vol. 521445, document from Dirlewanger's personal file, n.d., 763.

312. P. W. Blood, *Siepacze Hitlera*, 226–27.

313. R. Michaelis, *Erinnerungen an das SS-Sonderkommando "Dirlewanger"* (Berlin, 2010), 35. I give the numbers on the basis of the memories of one of Dirlewanger's soldier, although they are untrue.

314. P. W. Blood, *Siepacze Hitlera*, 228.

315. BAB, R70 Sowjetunion/38, Der Führer des Unternehmens "Zauberflöte," Befehl für den Apell und Vorbeimarsch im Anschluß an "Zauberflöte," Minsk, April 22, 1943, 360–61.

316. BAB, R/9361/III, vol. 521445, motion to award SS-Obersturmbannführer Oskar Dirlewanger with the German Cross in Gold, August 15, 1943, 763.

317. BA Ludwigsburg, B 162/16569, "Cottbus," n.d., 87.

318. Ibid.

319. Meldung der D-Kompanie an das Bataillon, 5.5.1943 r., after H. P. Klausch, *Antifaschisten*, 66.

320. "Molodetschno/Weißrußland—GUS," http://www.esslingen.de/,Lde/start/es_themen/Molodetschno.html (accessed July 23, 2016).

321. S. Kuklińska, *Działalność*, 81.

322. BAB, R/9361/III, vol. 521445, Der Reichsführer-SS—Adjutant—288/43, Feld-Kommandostelle, May 13, 1943, 859.

323. P. W. Blood, *Siepacze Hitlera*, 241.

324. Ibid.

325. BA Ludwigsburg, B 162/16569, "Cottbus," n.d., 86.

326. BAB, R/9361/III, vol. 521445, motion to award SS-Obersturmbannführer Oskar Dirlewanger with the German Cross in Gold, August 15, 1943, 766; and BA Ludwigsburg, B 162/4248, "Cottbus," n.d., 68. Operation Cottbus lasted from May 20 to June 23, 1943 (see B. Musiał, *Sowieccy partyzanci*, 278). Dates differ depending on the source: It started around May 20–22 and ended on June 21–23 (BA Ludwigsburg, B 162/16569, "Cottbus," n.d., 86).

327. Ch. Gerlach, *Kalkulierte Morde*, 902.

328. BA Ludwigsburg, B 162/16569, "Cottbus," n.d., 87–88; and BA Ludwigsburg, B 162/4248, "Cottbus," n.d., 69.

329. B. Musiał, *Sowieccy partyzanci*, 279–82.

330. B. Musiał, *Sowieccy partyzanci*, 282. The report concerns spring 1943. In April the "Mstitiel" unit moved to the Baranavichy oblast.

331. Ibid., 283.

332. Ibid.

333. BA Ludwigsburg, B 162/16574, Der Oberstaatsanwalt 2 Js 700/61, April 5, 1962, 29.

334. B. Musiał, *Sowieccy partyzanci*, 285.

335. BAB, R/9361/III, vol. 521445, motion to award SS-Obersturmbannführer Oskar Dirlewanger with the German Cross in Gold, August 15, 1943, 764.

336. Ibid., 293.

337. Dirlewanger's letter to SS-Gruppenführer Berger (Chef des SS-Hauptamtes), June 8, 1943, after H. P. Klausch, *Antifaschisten*, 68.

338. BAB, R/9361/III, vol. 521445, motion to award SS-Obersturmbannführer Oskar Dirlewanger with the German Cross in Gold, August 15, 1943, 766.

339. BA Ludwigsburg, B 162/4248, "Cottbus," n.d., 72; and BAB, R 70 Sowjetunion/14, Ergebnis des Unternehmens "Cottbus," Minsk, June 18, 1943.

340. BA Ludwigsburg, B 162/4248, "Cottbus," n.d., 72–73. On June 18, 1943, SS-Hauptsturmführer Wilke gave enemy losses as 9,796 killed, 599 prisoners, and

over 6,000 "registered labor force, and German losses as 5 officers, 83 NCOs and soldiers killed, 11 officers and 364 NCOs and officers wounded, and 3 missing. Furthermore, he recorded 40 killed, 152 wounded, and 4 missing members of eastern units. Also, 3,626 cattle, 2,182 sheep, 904 horses, and 153 pigs were "secured" (B. Musiał, *Sowieccy partyzanci*, 278).

341. B. Musiał, *Sowieccy partyzanci*, 287.

342. Ibid., 288–89.

343. Ibid., 291.

344. BA Ludwigsburg, B 162/16569, "Cottbus," n.d., 95.

345. Ibid.

346. BAB, R70 Sowjetunion/95, SD-Kommando-Lahojsk, Lahojsk, June 29, 1943, 112. Günther's operation area was also described as the environs of the Manila Forest (Manila-Waldes) (BAB, R/9361/III, vol. 521445, motion to award SS-Obersturmbannführer Oskar Dirlewanger with the German Cross in Gold, August 15, 1943, 763), and it was stated that it had been conducted in the Pleshchanitsy area (BAB, R70-Sowjetunion/95, Kampfgruppe Korsemann, Ia, June 28, 1943, 105).

347. Spelling according to the German original.

348. BAB, R70-Sowjetunion/95, Kampfgruppe Korsemann, Ia, June 28, 1943, 104.

349. BAB, R70 Sowjetunion/95, SD-Kommando-Lahojsk, Lahojsk, June 29, 1943, 112.

350. Ibid., 113.

351. Ibid., 113–14.

352. BAB, R70 Sowjetunion/95, Kampfgruppe Korsemann, Ia, June 28, 1943, 105.

353. BAB, R70 Sowjetunion/95, Der Kommandeur der Sicherheitspolizei u.d.SD. Weissruthenien Einsatzstab, Einsatzbefehl für das Unternehmen "Günther," Mińsk, June 29, 1943, 110–11.

354. Ibid., 111.

355. BAB, R70 Sowjetunion/95, Kampfgruppe Korsemann, Ia, June 28, 1943, 105–06.

356. BAB, R70 Sowjetunion/95, Kampfgruppe Korsemann Ia, Befehl zur Beendigung des Unternehmen "Günther," July 3, 1943, 115.

357. B. Musiał, *Sowieccy partyzanci*, 532.

358. Wilhelm Kube, komisarz generalny na Białorusi, do dyrektora ministerialnego Riekego [Wilhelm Kube, commissar general in Belarus to ministerial director Rieke], June 29, 1943, after B. Musiał, *Sowieccy partyzanci*, 532.

359. BA Ludwigsburg, B 162/16569, "Hermann," n.d., 97; and BAB, R70 Sowjetunion/14, Einsatzbefehl für das Unternehmen "Hermann," July 7, 1943.

360. BA Ludwigsburg, B 162/28392, Fortsetzung der Vernehmung vom 5 VI 1974, SS-Hauptsturmführer Wilke, Peine, June 6, 1974, 634.

361. BAB, R/9361/III, vol. 521445, motion to award SS-Obersturmbannführer Oskar Dirlewanger with the German Cross in Gold, August 15, 1943, 764; and P. Duffy, *Bracia Bielscy: Historia żydowskich partyzantów, którzy rzucili wyzwanie nazistom* (Kraków, Poland, 2009), 194. Meanwhile, Musiał stated that Operation Hermann lasted from July 13 to August 11, 1943 (B. Musiał, *Sowieccy partyzanci*, 303).

362. B. Musiał, *Sowieccy partyzanci*, 302; and P. Duffy, *Bracia Bielscy*, 193. The following took part in the Operation "Hermann": 1. SS-Inf. Brig. (mot); SS-Pol. Rgt. 2; Pol. Schützen-Rgt. 31; SS-Sdr. Btl. Dirlewanger; Gend. Züge (mot) Nr 7, 13, and 19; Gend. Einsatzkommando z. b. V. Kreikenbom; 12. Pol. Pz. Kompanie; Schutzmannschafts-Btle. 11, 15, 57, and 115; 4 Btle. Wermachtseinheiten der OFK (Oberfeldkommandanturen) 392; and Einsatzgruppe Körner—8,800 people in total (BA Ludwigsburg, B 162/16569, "Hermann," n.d., 97; BA Ludwigsburg, B 162/4248, "Hermann," n.d., 79; and BAB, R70 Sowjetunion/14, Einsatzbefehl für das Unternehmen "Hermann," July 7, 1943).

363. B. Musiał, *Sowieccy partyzanci*, 296.

364. Ibid.

365. BAB, R70 Sowjetunion/14, Einsatzbefehl für das Unternehmen "Hermann" July 7, 1943.

366. Valery Chkalov, born in 1904, Soviet stunt and test pilot. In 1937 he completed the first flight over the North Pole, from Moscow to Vancouver, Canada. He died on December 15, 1938, in Moscow (more on the subject, see http://www.warheroes.ru/hero/hero.asp?Hero_id=511, accessed October 4, 2017).

367. B. Musiał, *Sowieccy partyzanci*, 296–99.

368. For more about Vasilii Chernyshov "Platon," see P. Duffy, *Bracia Bielscy*, 186–88.

369. BAB, R70 Sowjetunion/14, Einsatzbefehl für das Unternehmen "Hermann," July 7, 1943.

370. Ibid.

371. B. Musiał, *Sowieccy partyzanci*, 302.

372. BA Ludwigsburg, B 162/28392, Fortsetzung der Vernehmung vom 5 VI 1974, SS-Hauptsturmführer Wilke, Peine, June 6, 1974, 634.

373. For more about the Bielski brothers and their activity, see P. Duffy, *Bracia Bielscy*.

374. B. Musiał, *Sowieccy partyzanci*, 301.

375. P. Duffy, *Bracia Bielscy*, 191.

376. BA Ludwigsburg, B 162/28392, Fortsetzung der Vernehmung vom 5 VI 1974, SS-Hauptsturmführer Wilke, Peine, June 6, 1974, 634.

377. BAB, R70 Sowjetunion/14, Einsatzbefehl für das Unternehmen "Hermann," July 7, 1943.

378. BAB, R70 Sowjetunion/14, Unternehmung "Hermann"—Zusatzbefehl Nr. 1 zum Einsatzbefehl für des Unternehmen "Hermann Ia Tgb. Nr. 398/43 II (g), July 7, 1943. On July 25, 1943, corrections were made to order no. 1 Ia Tgb. Nr. 398/43 III (g) of July 18. According to them, Battalion Schuma 57 was not under Dirlewanger's command (BAB, R70 Sowjetunion/14, Kampfgruppe v. Gottberg Ia Tgb. Nr. 398/43 IV (g), Zusatzbefehl Nr. 2, July 25, 1943).

379. BAB, R70 Sowjetunion/14, Kampfgruppe v. Gottberg Ia, August 5, 1943.

380. BAB, R70 Sowjetunion/14, Einsatzbefehl für das Unternehmen "Hermann," July 7, 1943.

381. YV, JM 2088, ID 3672138, the personal file of Dirlewanger, August 9, 1943. According to another version, "The third bullet knocked the cigarette out of his hand" (BAB, R/9361/III, vol. 521445, motion to award SS-Obersturmbannführer Oskar Dirlewanger with the German Cross in Gold, August 15, 1943, 764).

382. Johann Görgen, born August 15, 1914, in Saarbrücken. He was not part of Dirlewanger's unit but often cooperated with it in Belarus (and also with Kampfgruppe von Gottberg as a whole). He served as a pilot. He participated in antipartisan activities in Belarus, performing reconnaissance flight and transporting ammunition and the wounded from Minsk. Near the settlement of Pleshchanitsy (possibly Pleshchytsy), there was an airfield. There he collected wounded *Hiwis* and policemen and then transported them to Minsk. A medical point was located next to the airfield, because only two injured people could be evacuated at a time. He also transported important figures, including Kurt von Gottberg and his adjutant Herzig. Furthermore, he transported commanders of other units operating in the area to Dirlewanger's headquarters, to allow them to discuss the military situation. He stated that he carried Dirlewanger in 1944, but this likely occurred during Operation "Hermann" (BA Ludwigsburg, B 162/4249, K 424 Hamburg, Johann Görgen, Saarbrücken, May 6, 1976, 1072).

383. BAB, R70 Sowjetunion/14, Einsatzbefehl für das Unternehmen "Hermann," July 7, 1943.

384. Ibid.

385. B. Musiał, *Sowieccy partyzanci*, 303, 304.

386. B. Musiał, *Sowieccy partyzanci*, 304.

387. Ibid.

388. P. Duffy, *Bracia Bielscy*, 191–203.

389. B. Musiał, *Sowieccy partyzanci*, 304–05.

390. Ibid., 305.

391. BA Ludwigsburg, B 162/16569, "Hermann," n.d., 99–100; and B. Musiał, *Sowieccy partyzanci*, 307.

392. BAB, R70 Sowjetunion/14, Kampfgruppe v. Gottberg Ia, August 1, 1943.

393. BA Ludwigsburg, B 162/4248, "Hermann," 80.

394. B. Musiał, *Sowieccy partyzanci*, 309.

395. BA Ludwigsburg, B 162/4248, "Hermann," n.d., 81.

396. BAB, R70 Sowjetunion/14, Kampfgruppe v. Gottberg Ia, August 1, 1943.

397. BAB, R70 Sowjetunion/38, Der Höhere SS- und Polizeiführer Rußland-Mitte und Weißruthenien Ic, Minsk, August 24, 1943, 295.

398. B. Musiał, *Sowieccy partyzanci*, 309–11.

399. Relacja z rozmowy przeprowadzonej w dniu 07.03.2007 r. przez Stanisława Karlika z panią Marią Chilicką [Report from a conversation conducted on March 7, 2007, by Stanisław Karlik with Maria Chilicka], http://www.iwieniec.eu/martyrologia/naliboki.htm (accessed October 4, 2017).

400. BA Ludwigsburg, B 162/4250, Geschäfts-Nr. 147 Js 11/77 U, n.d., 122.

401. Anna Iwanowna Zhdanowitsch, born in 1892 in the village of Priluki in the Minsk region (BA Ludwigsburg, B 162/16636, 202 AR 1957/68, Übersetzung B, Nr. 65–70, Anna Iwanowna Zhdanowitsch, February 18, 1961).

402. Ibid.

403. Ibid.

404. Anna Aleksandrona Tichonowitsch, born in 1922 in the village of Swidnoje in the Lahoysk area (BA Ludwigsburg, B 162/16636, II 202 AR 1957/68, Übersetzung Bl.-Nr. 76–80, Anna Aleksandrowna Tichonowitsch, January 26, 1961).

405. Ibid.

406. BA Ludwigsburg, B 162/16569, "Heinrich," n.d., 101.

407. BAB, R 70 Sowjetunion/14, Einsatzgruppe von Gottberg, Abtlg. Ia Tgb. Nr. 19/43 g, October 25, 1943.

408. Friedrich Jeckeln, born in 1895, joined the NSDAP at the start of 1929, and the SS a year later (for more on Jeckeln, see P. Longerich, *Himmler*; and Friedrich Jeckeln, https://de.wikipedia.org/wiki/Friedrich_Jeckeln (accessed February 1, 2018).

409. BA Ludwigsburg, B 162/16569, "Heinrich," n.d., 101.

410. For more about Sich. Rgt. 64, see http://www.lexikon-der-wehrmacht.de/Gliederungen/SichReg/Gliederung.htm (accessed February 1, 2018).

411. BA Ludwigsburg, B 162/16569, "Heinrich," n.d., 101.

412. BA Ludwigsburg, B 162/4249, K 424, Gustav Brusberg, Stade, December 18, 1975, 837; BA Ludwigsburg, B 162/28392, Sonderkommission Hamburg, 147 Js 11/71 U, Gerhard Hellkamp, Wattenscheid, June 28, 1973, 460; and BA Ludwigsburg, B 162/28392, Fortsetzung der Vernehmung vom 5 VI 1974, SS-Hauptsturmführer Wilke, Peine, June 6, 1974, 638–39.

413. BAB, R 70 Sowjetunion/14, Einsatzgruppe von Gottberg, Abtlg. Ia Tgb. Nr. 19/43 g, October 25, 1943. According to a document dated November 20, 1943, Kampfgruppe von Gottberg comprised SS-Pol.Rgt.2 (3. and 8. Komp. SS-Jäger-Abt. Pannier, 1 Komp. Bau-Pi. Batl. 18, 2. Battr. Leichte Flak Abt. 995), SS-Pol.Rgt.13 (1 Komp. Bau-Pi.-Batl. 18, TN-Bau-Komp., Panzer-Komp. Mitte, Battr. Der OFK 392, Flak Kampftrupp Wegner), SS-Pol.Rgt. 24 (SS-Sdr.Btl.Dirlewanger, 2. Komp.

SS-Jäger Abtlg. Pannier, 1 Komp. Bau-Pi.-Btl. 18, 9. Pol.Pz.-Komp., 2. Batterie der 1.SS-Inf.Brigade, Flak Kampftruppe Bruns), Schm.Btl. 57 (Schm. Btl. 255, Schm. Btl 11), and Gend. Eins.Kdo. z.b.V. Kreikenbom (Flak Kampftruppe Vogel); moreover, also available were 12.Pol.Pz.-Komp., Flak-Abtlg. RFSS, SS-Jäger Abtlg. Pannier, Bau.-Pi.-Btl. 18 and 7. Komp. SS-Jäger Abtlg. Pannier (as a supply company), and as reserves, 1 Komp. Gend.Eins.Kdo.z.b.V. Kreikenbom, Gend. Züge (mot) 13, 19 and 49, and Flak Kampftruppe Bernard (BAB, R 70 Sowjetunion/14, Kampfgruppe von Gottberg Ia- Tgb.-Nr. 94/43, November 20, 1943).

414. BAB, R 70 Sowjetunion/14, Einsatzgruppe von Gottberg, Abtlg. Ia Tgb. Nr. 19/43 g, October 25, 1943.

415. BAB, R 70 Sowjetunion/14, Kampfgruppe von Gottberg Ia- Tgb.-Nr. 94/43, November 20, 1943. Konnyi Bor is located around 10 km from Dretun.

416. D. Irving, *Wojna Hitlera*, 537.

417. BA Ludwigsburg, B 162/29251, LKA-NW-Dez.15, Stein Johannes, Bochum, July 3, 1962, 73.

418. BAB, R 70 Sowjetunion/14, Kampfgruppe von Gottberg Ia- Tgb.-Nr. 94/43, November 20, 1943.

419. BA Ludwigsburg, B 162/29251, LKA-NW-Dez.15, Stein Johannes, Bochum, July 3, 1962, 73.

420. Arch. Sachsenhausen, LAG XXX/8, Deutsche Konzentrationslager. Aus der schriftlichen Erklärung des Grenadiers René Gaston Ferderer vom Sonderkommando der SS "Dirlewanger" vom 12 VII 1944. Biografische Angaben, July 31, 1944, 15.

421. B. Musiał, *Sowieccy partyzanci*, 409.

422. K. J. Arnold, *Die Wehrmacht und die Besatzungspolitik in den besetzten Gebieten der Sowjetunion: Kriegsführung und Radikalisierung im "Unternehmen Barbarossa"* (Berlin, 2005), 477–80.

423. Ch. Gerlach, *Kalkulierte Morde*, 865–66.

424. BAB, R/9361/III, vol. 521445, motion to award SS-Obersturmbannführer Oskar Dirlewanger with the German Cross in Gold, August 15, 1943, 764.

425. BAB, R/9361/III, vol. 521445, document from Dirlewanger's personal file, n.d., 764; BA Ludwigsburg, B 162/16570, Das Urteil im Wilhelmstrassen—Prozess, n.d., 317; and YV, JM 2088, ID 3672138, the personal file of Dirlewanger, August 9, 1943.

426. BAB, R/9361/III, vol. 521445, motion to award SS-Obersturmbannführer Oskar Dirlewanger with the German Cross in Gold, August 15, 1943, 764; and YV, JM 2088, ID 3672138, the personal file of Dirlewanger, August 9, 1943.

427. BAB, R/9361/III, vol. 521445, motion to award SS-Obersturmbannführer Oskar Dirlewanger with the German Cross in Gold, August 15, 1943, 764.

428. YV, JM 2088, ID 3672138, the personal file of Dirlewanger, August 9, 1943; BAB, R/9361/III, vol. 521445, Aktennotiz, January 19, 1944, 785; and BAB, R/9361/III, vol. 521445, 759, 801.

429. BA Ludwigsburg, B 162/5924, 45 Js 30/64, Verfügung, Gottlob Berger, Dortmund, October 15, 1964, 1148.

430. As P. Longerich informs us, on the basis of the "Order on presenting the death's head signet" of April 10, 1934, all SS commanders from Sturmführer upward received a Totenkopf ring if they had joined the organization before 1933 and belonged to it for at least two years or joined after January 30, 1933, and had been members for three years, as did all SS commanders who, due to their affiliation with the Reichswehr or police, could not join before January 30, 1933: they received it after two years of membership. The SS leadership group was, according to Himmler's guidelines, supposed to wear it "always on the ring finger of the left hand. . . . Presentation of the signet is an external indication of internal value achieved through combat and service, as well as fellowship, tried and tested over years of loyalty to the Führer and his vision. . . . The death's head reminds us to be ready at each moment to sacrifice our individual lives for the life of the whole community. The runes on the other side of the death's head are sacred symbols of our past, with which we have again reconnected. . . . The signet is surrounded by leaves of the oak, the ancient Germanic tree." The signet could not be purchased and could not "fall into third-party hands," so after an SS member's death or his departure from the SS, it was to be returned to the Reichsführer-SS and stored in a special room in Wewelsburg Castle. Honor swords, meanwhile, were given as presents by Himmler to selected SS commanders. "I present you with the SS sword. Never draw it needlessly! Never place it in its scabbard without honor! Preserve your honor as unconditionally as you are unconditionally obligated to respect the honor of others and chivalrously protect the defenseless!" It was possible to "keep [the sword] in one's clan if one wore it without disgrace all one's life." In other cases, Himmler demanded its return. For more on symbols and Himmler's presents, see P. Longerich, *Himmler*, 353–67; and K. D. Patzwall, *Der SS-Totenkopfring: Seine illustrierte Geschichte 1933–1945* (Norderstedt, Germany, 2002).

431. BA Ludwigsburg, B 162/5926, Betrifft: Sammelvorgang Strafsache Dirlewanger, Weiße, Heinsen Rußland-Polen-Ungarn-Tschecho-Slowakei u. Deutschland verbrechen, Berlin 44, May 12, 1972, 1509.

432. *Diensaltersliste der Schutzstaffel der NSDAP (SS-Oberst-Gruppenführer—SS Standartenführer) Stand vom 9. November 1944* (Berlin, 1944), 31; and *Diensaltersliste der Schutzstaffel der NSDAP (SS-Obersturmbannführer und SS-Sturmbannführer) Stand vom 1. Oktober 1944)* (Berlin, 1944), 94.

433. BA Ludwigsburg, B162/21001, SS-Führungshauptamt, Kdo. Amt d. Waffen-SS, Org. Tgb. Nr. II/5868/43 geh, SS-Sonderkommando Dirlewanger, Berlin-Wilmersdorf, August 10, 1943, 11–12.

434. H. P. Klausch, *Antifaschisten*, 88–89.

435. BA Ludwigsburg, B 162/4249, K 424 Hamburg, Franz Stümpfl, Grafenau, June 25, 1976, 981.

436. BAB, R70 Sowjetunion/38, Oskar Dirlewanger's letter to Kurt von Gottberg, February 26, 1944, 421.

437. BA Ludwigsburg, B 162/16572, Der Oberstaatsanwalt Flensburg, 2 Js 700/61, Rudi Fiedler, Lippstadt, May 7, 1963, 252. Walter Fentzahn, one of Dirlewanger's soldiers, stated that the 2nd Battalion was formed in mid-1944 (BA Ludwigsburg, B 162/16574, Der Oberstaatsanwalt, 2 Js 700/61, Walter Fentznahn, Flensburg, November 23, 1961, 17).

438. H. P. Klausch, *Antifaschisten*, 92; BA Ludwigsburg, B 162/16574, Der Oberstaatsanwalt, 2 Js 700/61, Walter Fentznahn, Flensburg, November 23, 1961, 11; and BA Ludwigsburg, B 162/16574, Der Oberstaatsanwalt 2 Js 700/61, Karl Engel, Flensburg, October 25, 1961, 47–48.

439. BA Ludwigsburg, B 162/16574, Der Oberstaatsanwalt 2 Js 700/61, Karl Engel, Flensburg, October 25, 1961, 48.

440. B. Musiał, *Sowieccy partyzanci*, 429–30.

441. BA Ludwigsburg, B 162/16569, Bisheriges Ermittlungsergebnis über das Sonderkommando "Dirlewanger," n.d., 142. In later years it was reported that in this period, they numbered three thousand people (BA Ludwigsburg, B 162/16569, Bisheriges Ermittlungsergebnis über das Sonderkommando "Dirlewanger," n.d., 141; and BA Ludwigsburg, B 162/4250, "Hermann," n.d., 95). Meanwhile on April 30, 1944, SS-Sonderregiment Dirlewanger had 17 officers (*Führers*), 87 NCOs (*Unterführers*), and 867 soldiers. This was 971 people in total.

442. Persönlicher Stab Reichsführer-SS, Schriftgutverwaltung, Geheim 127, after R. Michaelis, *Dirlewanger*, 7.

443. BA Ludwigsburg, B 162/29251, LKA-NW-Dez. 15, Paul Dorn, Lüdenscheid, July 4, 1962, 78.

444. H. P. Klausch, *Antifaschisten*, 89.

445. BA Ludwigsburg, B 162/4250, Geschäfts-Nr. 147 Js 11/77 U, n.d., 95; and S. Kuklińska, *Działalność*, 91.

446. BA Ludwigsburg, B 162/21001, Der Reichsführer-SS, RF/M. 35/26/44g, Feld-Kommandostelle, February 9, 1944, 24; and BAB, NS 19/1, Der Reichsführer-SS, RF/M. 35/26/44 G, n.d., 18.

447. S. Kuklińska, *Działalność*, 93.

448. YV, JM 2082, ID 3669432, Der Reichsführer SS RF/M, 35/26/44 g, February 20, 1944, unpag.; and BA Ludwigsburg, B 162/16569, Bisheriges Ermittlungsergebnis über das Sonderkommando "Dirlewanger," n.d., 142–43.

449. BA Ludwigsburg, B 162/5924, Niederschrift, Dr. Med. Heinz Hartlieb, Wien, February 28, 1964, 1029.

450. BAB, NS 19/1, Der Reichsführer SS RF/M, 35/26/44g, February 19, 1944. Friedrich Walter mentioned that the doctor who had been assigned to the unit as a punishment had according to gossip been demoted. He did not remember the reason, however (BA Ludwigsburg, B 162/5922, Tgb. Nr. SK. Zst. I/3-180/62, Friedrich Walter, Mörsch, May 21, 1963, 625).

451. The SS dentists were assigned there for "*mißlungener Anstiftung zur Abtreibung*" and "*Volltrunkenheit*" (H. P. Klausch, *Antifaschisten*, 93; and BA Ludwigsburg, B 162/16569, Bisheriges Ermittlungsergebnis über das Sonderkommando "Dirlewanger," n.d., 148).

452. The SS and police penal camp in Matzkau (I will use an abbreviated form from now on) was the largest facility of this type in the Third Reich. It operated from 1939. From July 21, 1941, it was subject to the SS Court Main Office (Hauptamt SS-Gericht). Convicts from the SS and the police were sent there because the authorities believed that incarceration of SS members with other prisoners was undesirable. From Matzkau they were sent to penal units, such as the one under Oskar Dirlewanger's command or SS-Fallschirmjäger 500. Only in 1942 were 1,100 prisoners from this camp sent to special units. Similar facilities functioned in Berlin-Ludwigsfelde, Dachau, the Latvian Salaspil, Mosbach (in Baden-Württemberg), and Allach, near Munich. For more about the camp in Matzkau, see J. Daniluk, *SS w Gdańsku* (Gdańsk, Poland, 2013), 139–52.

453. BA Ludwigsburg, B 162/21001, Niederschrift, Dr. Dirlewanger SS-Obersturmbannführer an den Chef des SS-Hauptamts, March 14, 1944, 19; and BAB, NS 19/1, letter, March 14, 1944, 30.

454. YV, JM 2085, ID 3670809, document concerning recruitment of 1,500 criminals from Matzkau to Dirlewanger's unit, September 20, 1944; and BA Ludwigsburg, B 162/16569, Bisheriges Ermittlungsergebnis über das Sonderkommando "Dirlewanger," n.d., 153 (see appendix 14).

455. R. Michaelis, *Dirlewanger*, 10.

456. H. P. Klausch, *Antifaschisten*, 90.

457. BAB, R70 Sowjetunion/38, Der Höhere SS-und Polizeiführer Rußland Mitte und Weißruthenien Abt.II/33,30 b/44, Verleihung des EK.2.Klasse, April 1, 1944, 209.

458. YV, JM 2088, ID 3671956, recruitment from Waffen-SS to Dirlewanger's unit, March 20, 1944.

459. H. P. Klausch, *Antifaschisten*, 90.

460. B. Musiał, *Sowieccy partyzanci*, 435.

461. Ibid.

462. Ibid., 436–37.

463. Ibid., 438.

464. Ibid.

465. Mikhail V. Frunze, born in 1885 and died in 1925, was a military commander in the Red Army and Bolshevik activist (for more, see https://encyklopedia.pwn.pl/haslo/Frunze-Michail-W;3902934.html, accessed October 5, 2017).

466. B. Musiał, *Sowieccy partyzanci*, 438–41.

467. Ibid., 444.

468. The press even claimed that this was the number of villages burned and civilians killed by Dirlewanger's unit only over the course of 1943 in the Mogilev and Minsk regions. For one year of activity, these data are significantly exaggerated. They were published by the Soviet propaganda newspaper *Pravda* (BA Ludwigsburg, B 162/16634, Hohe Strafen für Kollaborateure, *Die Welt*, December 5, 1968, 5). According to some estimates, this was the number of victims of the unit's activity in Belarus from 1942 to 1944.

469. BA Ludwigsburg, B 162/4250, Geschäfts-Nr. 147 Js 11/77 U, n.d., 112.

470. H. P. Klausch, *Antifaschisten*, 91.

471. Initially, Obersturmbannführer Andreas Meyer-Mader was made commander of the 1st Eastern Muslim SS Regiment; for more on the subject, see Ch. Bishop, *Zagraniczne formacje SS: Zagraniczni ochotnicy w Waffen-SS 1940–1945* (Warsaw, Poland, 2005).

472. BA Ludwigsburg, B 162/16574, Der Oberstaatsanwalt 2 Js 700/61, Karl Engel, Flensburg, October 25, 1961, 48; BA Ludwigsburg, B 162/29251, Tgb. Nr. SK. Zst. III/2-157/61, Karl Richard Engel, Pforzheim, August 24, 1961, 8; and R. Michaelis, *Dirlewanger*, 11.

473. BAB, R/9361/III, vol. 521445, Begründung und Stellungnahme des Zwischenvorgesetzen, September 10, 1944, 756.

474. BA Ludwigsburg, B 162/16574, Der Oberstaatsanwalt 2 Js 700/61, Albert Venderbusch, Flensburg, April 5, 1962, 136.

475. BA Ludwigsburg, B 162/21001, 2 AR 1140/60, December 5, 1960, 52.

476. BAB, R/9361/III vol. 521445, message from Reichsführer-SS Himmler to SS-Standartenführer Dirlewanger with an order to immediately join the SS assault regiment commanded by him, sent to suppress the Warsaw Uprising, August 4, 1944. I quote the telegram in the chapter on the Warsaw Uprising.

477. Reiner Stahel, born January 15, 1892, in Bielefeld, served in the Imperial German Army during the First World War. He was commander of Rome from 1943 and, in July 1944, was appointed commander of Vilnius, and then military commander of Warsaw. After the war he remained in Soviet custody, and he died there in 1955. For more on Stahel, see Sawicki, *Wyrok na miasto: Berlin i Moskwa wobec Powstania Warszawskiego* (Warsaw, Poland, 1993); and Sawicki, *Rozkaz: Zdławić powstanie; Niemcy i ich sojusznicy w walce z powstaniem warszawskim* (Warsaw, Poland, 2010).

Chapter 5

1. Paul Otto Geibel, born June 10, 1898, in Dortmund, was an NSDAP member from 1931 and SS member from 1938. After the death of Franz Kutschera, Himmler appointed him SS and police leader in the Warsaw District on March 3, 1944. When the Warsaw Uprising started, he was in charge of defending the police district. After the war, he was sentenced to life imprisonment in Poland and committed suicide in prison in 1961 (for more on the subject, see *Zbrodnie okupanta w czasie*

powstania warszawskiego w 1944 r. (w dokumentach) (Warsaw, Poland, 1962); and A. Borkiewicz, *Powstanie Warszawskie 1944: Zarys działań natury wojskowej* (Warsaw, Poland, 1957).

2. S. Kuklińska, *Działalność*, 99.

3. T. Sawicki, *Rozkaz: zdławić powstanie*, 9.

4. A. Borkiewicz, *Powstanie warszawskie 1944*, 42–43.

5. Nikolaus von Vormann, born December 24, 1895, in Nowe Miasto Lubawskie and died October 26, 1959, in Berchtesgaden. He commanded the 9th Army from June 28, 1944; for more on the subject, see J. Kirchmayer, *Powstanie Warszawskie* (Warsaw, Poland, 1984).

6. S. Kuklińska, *Działalność*, 100.

7. J. Kirchmayer, *Powstanie*, 165.

8. A. Borkiewicz, *Powstanie warszawskie 1944*, 35.

9. J. M. Ciechanowski, "Pierwsza relacja gen: Bora-Komorowskiego o AK i powstaniu warszawskim," *Zeszyty Historyczne* 49 (1979): 49.

10. A. Borkiewicz, *Powstanie Warszawskie 1944*, 12–13; and J. Kirchmayer, *Powstanie*, 160.

11. J. Sidorowicz, "Powstanie warszawskie—bez niedomówień," *Pro Memoria* 5 (2004), in *Kulisy katastrofy Powstania Warszawskiego 1944: Wybrane publikacje i dokumenty* (New York, 2009), 30.

12. S. Kuklińska, *Działalność*, 102.

13. T. Sawicki, *Rozkaz: Zdławić powstanie*, 22.

14. Heinz Guderian, born June 17, 1888, in Chełmno. *Generaloberst* (colonel-general) of the Wehrmacht, inspector general of panzer troops, chief of the general staff of Oberkommando des Heeres (Army High Command), military theorist, and author of the Blitzkrieg concept. In May 1945, he was taken into American custody, but no charges were made against him. He died on May 14, 1954, in Schwangau. For more, see H. Guderian, *Wspomnienia żołnierza* (Warsaw, Poland, 2008); and H. Guderian, *Achtung Panzer! Uwaga czołgi!* (Warsaw, Poland, 2012).

15. S. Podlewski, *Przemarsz przez piekło*, 138.

16. BA Ludwigsburg, B 162/16569, Bisheriges Ermittlungsergebnis über das Sonderkommando "Dirlewanger," September 21, 1944, 177.

17. Ibid.

18. Ibid.

19. Gen. Stahel's report, August 2, 1944, after T. Sawicki, *Rozkaz: Zdławić powstanie*, 24.

20. N. Sennerteg, *Kat Warszawy* (Warsaw, Poland, 2009), 15, 19.

21. S. Kuklińska, *Działalność*, 104.

22. *Zburzenie Warszawy: Zeznania generałów niemieckich przed polskim prokuratorem, członkiem polskiej delegacji przy Międzynarodowym Trybunale*

Wojennym w Norymberdze, Główna Komisja Badania Zbrodni Niemieckich w Polsce (Katowice, Poland, 1946), 91.

23. S. Kopf, *Dni powstania: Kronika fotograficzna walczącej Warszawy* (Warsaw, Poland, 1984), 48.

24. S. Kuklińska, *Działalność*, 109–10.

25. N. Sennerteg, *Kat Warszawy*, 18.

26. W. Bartoszewski, *Prawda*, 46–47.

27. P. Marti, *Sprawa Reinefartha*, 62.

28. Ibid., 378 (fn 295).

29. P. Stachiewicz, *"Parasol,"* 499.

30. Ibid., 499–500.

31. P. Marti, *Sprawa Reinefartha*, 63.

32. Heinz Reinefarth, born December 26, 1903, in Gniezno. From 1932, a member of the NSDAP (no. 1,268,933) and the SS. *SS-Gruppenführer* and police lieutenant general. He took part in the September campaign and the campaign in France. From December 1943, higher SS and police leader in the Wartheland. Decorated with Oak Leaves to the Iron Cross for combat in the Warsaw Uprising. After the war, he held the function of mayor in the town of Westerland on the island of Sylt. He died in 1979 in his residence on Sylt. For more on the subject, see K. Leszczyński, *Heinz Reinefarth* (Poznań, Poland, 1961); and N. Sennerteg, *Kat Warszawy*.

33. RONA (Русская освободительная народная армия, Russian National Liberation Army). Its commander was Bronislaw Vladislavovich Kaminski. RONA took part in antipartisan actions in Belarus. Like Dirlewanger's unit, it was withdrawn to East Prussia to recuperate and rest in summer 1944. After the start of the Warsaw Uprising, it was directed to Warsaw, where it committed numerous war crimes. In 1944, Kaminski was most likely placed before a military court in Łódź, which sentenced him to death. The sentence was carried out. For more on the formation, see G. H. Stein, *Geschichte der Waffen-SS* (Düsseldorf, 1967); Ch. Bishop, *Zagraniczne formacje SS: Zagraniczni ochotnicy w Waffen-SS 1940–1945* (Warsaw, Poland, 2015); G. Reitlinger, *Die SS: Tragödie einer deutschen Epoche*, Munich, 1957; and I. Kowtun and D. Żukow, *29. Dywizja Grenadierów SS Kamiński* (Zakrzewo, Poland, 2017).

34. R. Michaelis, *Die SS-Sturmbrigade "Dirlewanger": Vom Warschauer Aufstand bis zum Kessel von Halbe* (Berlin, 2003), 25. Meanwhile, Sennerteg informed that Kampfgruppe Reinefarth officially numbered 3,997 people, of which 48 percent were soldiers from other countries (N. Sennerteg, *Kat Warszawy*, 37).

35. H. von Krannhals, *Powstanie Warszawskie 1944: Der Warschauer Aufstand 1944* (Warsaw, Poland 2017), 173–74.

36. P. Stachiewicz, *"Parasol,"* 501.

37. T. Sawicki, *Rozkaz: Zdławić powstanie*, 25.

38. H. von Krannhals, *Powstanie Warszawskie*, 175.

39. BA Ludwigsburg, B 162/16571, Der Oberstaatsanwalt 2 Js 700/61, Heinrich Kraus, Bamberg, April 3, 1962, 104.

40. BA Ludwigsburg, B 162/16571, Der Oberstaatsanwalt 2 Js 700/61, Flensburg, z. Zt. Plettenberg, November 30, 1961, 79–80.

41. Hanns von Krannhals stated that Dirlewanger's unit came to Warsaw from Ełk (H. von Krannhals, *Powstanie Warszawskie*, 172, 175). According to a teleprint message from the Supreme Command of Army Group Center, it set off for Warsaw from Olecko via Ełk, Szczytno, and Modlin on the night of August 3, 1944 (Odpis maszynowy z dalekopisu: Do D-twa 9. Armii, August 5, 1944, after H. von Krannhals, *Powstanie Warszawskie*, 470).

42. BA Ludwigsburg, B 162/16572, Der Oberstaatsanwalt Flensburg 2 Js 700/61, Karl Keithan, Witzenhausen, May 9, 1963, 258.

43. Albert Venderbusch, who probably reached Warsaw in the same transport, testified that they went to Bielany airport and spent the night in the barracks there (BA Ludwigsburg, B 162/16574, Der Oberstaatsanwalt 2 Js 700/61, Albert Venderbusch, Flensburg, April 5, 1962, 136). However, Karl Jochheim-Armin was most likely correct in saying that they spent the night of August 4, 1944, at Okęcie airport.

44. BA Ludwigsburg, B 162/16574, Der Oberstaatsanwalt 2 Js 700/61, Albert Venderbusch, Flensburg, April 5, 1962, 136.

45. BA Ludwigsburg, B 162/16574, Der Oberstaatsanwalt 2 Js 700/61, Karl Jochheim-Armin, Flensburg, February 1, 1962, 111, 113–14.

46. Wolska Street was renamed Litzmannstädter Straße (or Litzmannstadtstrasse) at the start of the German occupation. It was the exit road leading to Łódź, which the Germans called Litzmannstadt in 1939. The thoroughfare was around 5 km long. After August 1, 1944, it was partly controlled by the Germans, while its west stretch remained in partisan hands.

47. BA Ludwigsburg, B 162/16572, Der Oberstaatsanwalt 2 Js 700/61, Paul Zimmermann, Stuttgart, July 1, 1963, 263–64.

48. BA Ludwigsburg, B 162/16571, Der Oberstaatsanwalt—2 Js 700/61, Flensburg, z Zt. Hannover, January 17, 1962, 95. Marti stated, meanwhile, that Dirlewanger came to Warsaw on August 8, 1944 (P. Marti, *Sprawa*, 381n308). The period between August 8 and 10 seems the most likely. Zimmermann indicated that he reported to Dirlewanger immediately after arriving in Warsaw (August 8–9) (BA Ludwigsburg, B 162/16572, Der Oberstaatsanwalt 2 Js 700/61, Paul Zimmermann, Stuttgart, July 1, 1963, 264).

49. BA Ludwigsburg, B 162/16571, Der Oberstaatsanwalt 2 Js 700/61, Adolf Katz, Flensburg, z. Zt. Eutingen, April 7, 1962, 129–30; and BA Ludwigsburg, B 162/16569, Bisheriges Ermittlungsergebnis über das Sonderkommando "Dirlewanger," n.d., 172–73.

50. BA Ludwigsburg, B 162/16569, Bisheriges Ermittlungsergebnis über das Sonderkommando "Dirlewanger," n.d., 174–75.

51. Ibid., 175. Helmut Lewandowski informed that the Azerbaijani Battalion was placed under Dirlewanger while he was staying in the Brühl Palace (BA Ludwigsburg, B 162/16572, Anlage zur Vernehmung vom 20. Februar, Helmut Lewandowski, n.d., 192).

52. BA Ludwigsburg, B 162/16572, Anlage zur Niederschrift, Oskar Henning, March 5, 1962, 200.

53. BAB, R/9361/III vol. 521445, letter from Reichsführer-SS Himmler to SS-Standartenführer Dirlewanger with an order to immediately join the SS assault regiment commanded by him, sent to suppress the Warsaw Uprising, August 4, 1944.

54. BA Ludwigsburg, B 162/16571, Der Oberstaatsanwalt 2 Js 700/61, Flensburg, z. Zt. Eutingen, April 7, 1962, 130.

55. BA Ludwigsburg, B 162/16569, Bisheriges Ermittlungsergebnis über das Sonderkommando "Dirlewanger," n.d., 173–74.

56. Ibid., 174.

57. N. Sennerteg, *Kat Warszawy*, 34.

58. BA Ludwigsburg, B 162/16571, Der Oberstaatsanwalt—2 Js 700/61, Flensburg, z Zt. Hannover, January 17, 1962, 101.

59. Zeznania gen. Ernsta Rode, szefa sztabu von dem Bacha, z przesłuchania dnia 28 stycznia 1946 r., [Testimony of Gen. Ernst Rode, von dem Bach's chief of staff, from the interrogation of January 28, 1946], after N. Sennerteg, *Kat Warszawy*, 39 (fn 43).

60. BA Ludwigsburg, B 162/16569, Bisheriges Ermittlungsergebnis über das Sonderkommando "Dirlewanger," n.d., 178.

61. H. von Krannhals, *Der Warschauer Aufstand*, 250.

62. N. Sennerteg, *Kat Warszawy*, 148–49.

63. А. Пишенков, *Штрафники СС: Зондеркоманда "Дирлевангер" (*Москва, 2009), 181–82.

64. Sz. Datner and K. Leszczyński, *Zbrodnie okupanta hitlerowskiego na ludności cywilnej w czasie powstania warszawskiego w 1944 roku (w dokumentach)* (Warsaw, Poland, 1962, 315.

65. N. Sennerteg, *Kat Warszawy*, 35.

66. H. von Krannhals, *Powstanie Warszawskie*, 183.

67. *1944, sierpień 13, Warszawa—Raport SS-Hauptsturmführera A. Feuchta do W. Bierkampa, dowódcy policji bezpieczeństwa w Krakowie, o działalności Einsatzkommando na Woli i Ochocie, przekazany za pośrednictwem komendanta policji bezpieczeństwa w Radomiu* [1944, August 13, Warsaw—SS-Hauptsturmführer A. Feucht's report to W. Bierkamp, security police commander in Krakow, on the operations of Einsatzkommando in Wola and Ochota, transmitted via the commander of security police in Radom], in *Exodus Warszawy—Ludzie i miasto po powstaniu 1944*, vol. 3, *Archiwalia* (Warsaw, Poland, 1994), 38–45.

68. H. von Krannhals, *Powstanie Warszawskie*, 188–89.

69. BA Ludwigsburg, B 162/16572, Anlage zur Niederschrift, Oskar Henning, March 5, 1962, 198.

70. BA Ludwigsburg, B 162/5925, Bisheriges Ermittlungsergebnis über das Sonderkommando "Dirlewanger," n.d., 1275–76.

71. P. Stachiewicz, *"Parasol,"* 501.

72. Ibid., 496–97.

73. Batalion "Parasol," I kompania 3–5 sierpnia 1944 rok. Pałacyk Michla i Wenecja (obrona Wolskiej), after J. Wróblewski, *Gryf: Pałacyk Michla, Żytnia, Wola* (Warsaw, Poland, 2016), 244–55, 263–65.

74. P. Stachiewicz, *"Parasol,"* 496–97.

75. Ibid., 510–11.

76. H. von Krannhals, *Powstanie Warszawskie*, 184.

77. P. Stachiewicz, *"Parasol,"* 515.

78. BA Ludwigsburg, B 162/16569, Bisheriges Ermittlungsergebnis über das Sonderkommando "Dirlewanger," n.d., 169.

79. Ibid., 150.

80. BA Ludwigsburg, B 162/16571, Der Oberstaatsanwalt 2 Js 700/61, Flensburg, z. Zt. Plettenberg, November 30, 1961, 80.

81. BA Ludwigsburg, B 162/16574, Der Oberstaatsanwalt 2 Js 700/61, Karl Jochheim-Armin, Flensburg, February 1, 1962, 112.

82. BA Ludwigsburg, B 162/16571, Der Oberstaatsanwalt 2 Js 700/61, Flensburg, z. Zt. Plettenberg, November 30, 1961, 81.

83. BA Ludwigsburg, B 162/16574, Der Oberstaatsanwalt 2 Js 700/61, Karl Jochheim-Armin, Flensburg, February 1, 1962, 112. They reached Brühl Palace and the Saxon Garden on August 6, 1944, in the afternoon. Part of the troops from Dirlewanger's unit (the vanguard of the assault) remained in the Saxon Garden. Fischer received the relief almost as his salvation. At that time, the resistance of the gendarmerie unit and armed officials had started to break down (W. Bartoszewski, *Prawda*, 52; and T. Sawicki, *Rozkaz: Zdławić powstanie*, 34). Meanwhile, on August 7 the connection between Wolska Street and the Brühl Palace, recaptured on the previous day, was secured (P. Marti, *Sprawa*, 68; and H. von Krannhals, *Powstanie Warszawskie*, 190). By August 5, Reinefarth announced that Kaminski had taken Ochota and Dirlewanger had reached the railway crossing in Wola, which, however, turned out to be untrue. The staff of the 9th Army corrected: "Our attack from the south and west on the city has not yet reached Ochota and the railway line east of Wola, where the opponent is putting up extremely strong resistance from behind barricades." (T. Sawicki, *Rozkaz: Zdławić powstanie*, 33).

84. On August 6, 1944, Reinefarth's units and Dirlewanger's unit, supported by artillery and aviation, opened a route through Wolska and Chłodna Streets and the Saxon Garden to Krakowskie Przedmieście Street and Kierbedź Bridge; see T.

Sumiński, *Pamiętniki żołnierzy baonu AK "Zośka": Powstanie Warszawskie*, vol. 3, *Czerniaków* (Warsaw, Poland, 1997), 253–54.

85. BA Ludwigsburg, B 162/16571, Der Oberstaatsanwalt 2 Js 700/61, Flensburg, z. Zt. Plettenberg, November 30, 1961, 81.

86. BA Ludwigsburg, B 162/16571, Der Oberstaatsanwalt 2 Js 700/61, Adolf Katz, Flensburg, z. Zt. Eutingen, April 7, 1962, 132.

87. BA Ludwigsburg, B 162/16571, Der Oberstaatsanwalt 2 Js 700/61, z. Zt. Kevelaer, February 28, 1963, 148–49.

88. BA Ludwigsburg, B 162/16572, Anlage zur Niederschrift, Oskar Henning, March 5, 1962, 199–200.

89. P. Stachiewicz, *"Parasol,"* 520.

90. BA Ludwigsburg, B 162/16569, Bisheriges Ermittlungsergebnis über das Sonderkommando "Dirlewanger," n.d., 169.

91. N. Sennerteg, *Kat Warszawy*, 150.

92. P. Stachiewicz, *"Parasol,"* 521.

93. BA Ludwigsburg, B 162/16569, Bisheriges Ermittlungsergebnis über das Sonderkommando "Dirlewanger," n.d., 170.

94. Many of Dirlewanger's soldiers have described insurgents creeping along Wola's sewers. They were interrogated in the 1960s and most likely meant operations in the Old Town or even later ones.

95. P. Stachiewicz, *"Parasol,"* 522–23.

96. Ibid., 524.

97. "Janusz Brochwicz-Lewiński 'Gryf,'" https://www.1944.pl/archiwum-historii-mowionej/janusz-brochwicz-lewinski,449.html (accessed October 19, 2017).

98. J. Wróblewski, *Gryf*, 271.

99. P. Zychowicz, *Obłęd 44* (Poznań, Poland, 2013), 317–18.

100. BA Ludwigsburg, B 162/16571, Der Oberstaatsanwalt 2 Js 700/61, Flensburg, z. Zt. Plettenberg, November 30, 1961, 81–82.

101. BA Ludwigsburg, B 162/16571, Der Oberstaatsanwalt—2 Js 700/61, Flensburg, z Zt. Hannover, January 17, 1962, 98.

102. T. Sawicki, *Rozkaz: Zdławić powstanie*, 33–4, 51.

103. N. Sennerteg, *Kat Warszawy*, 277–78.

104. BA Ludwigsburg, B 162/16571, Der Oberstaatsanwalt—2 Js 700/61, Flensburg, z Zt. Hannover, January 17, 1962, 99.

105. BA Ludwigsburg, B 162/16574, Der Oberstaatsanwalt 2 Js 700/61, Walter Hardt, Hamburg, January 23, 1963, 195–96.

106. BA Ludwigsburg, B 162/16574, Der Oberstaatsanwalt, 2 Js 700/61, Adalbert Daschner, Flensburg, April 5, 1962, 196.

107. BA Ludwigsburg, B 162/16571, Der Oberstaatsanwalt 2 Js 700/61, z. Zt. Kevelaer, February 28, 1963, 149.

108. BA Ludwigsburg, B 162/16574, Der Oberstaatsanwalt 2 Js 700/61, Franz Haschäcker, Brakel, January 29, 1963, 182–83.

109. J. Sawicki, *Przed polskim prokuratorem* (Warsaw, Poland, 1958).

110. H. von Krannhals, *Powstanie Warszawskie*, 401.

111. N. Sennerteg, *Kat Warszawy*, 21.

112. Ibid. (fn 21).

113. Friedrich Peterburs's interrogation, February 22, 1962, after P. Marti, *Sprawa*, 65–66.

114. Max Reck's interrogation, December 11, 1962, after P. Marti, *Sprawa*, 66.

115. H. von Krannhals, *Powstanie Warszawskie*, 400–401.

116. I. Kowtun and D. Żukow, *29. Dywizja*, 175.

117. Alfred Spilker (Spielker), SD-Hauptamt official until 1939. In September 1939 he became part of Einsatzkommando 1/I and then combated the Polish resistance movement as the head of a department attached to the SiPo and SD command in Krakow. In 1943 he was delegated to Warsaw as the representative of the SiPo and SD commander in the GG. He was transferred to Krakow in October (K. Grünberg, *SS*, 265–66n59). It is uncertain who commanded these units on August 5, 1944, but from August 10 to 13, at the latest, their commander was Spilker. The command was stationed in the clergy house of St Wojciech's Church. Spilker went missing after the end of the war, and in 1961 the German authorities pronounced him dead (N. Sennerteg, *Kat Warszawy*, 363; and P. Marti, *Sprawa*, 384n329).

118. N. Sennerteg, *Kat Warszawy*, 159 (fn 28); and P. Marti, *Sprawa*, 68.

119. In August and September 1944, Sonderkommando 7a of Einsatzkommando B was most likely stationed in Błonie or Włochy, near Warsaw, together with Russian auxiliary units. This commando, in accordance with the OKH's decree of April 28, 1941, had the right to use various measures against the civilian population, at its discretion (Załącznik nr 2, Uniewinnienie Reinefartha, 1967 r., after N. Sennerteg, *Kat Warszawy*, 424).

120. Ibid., 159. Sonderkommando 7a (Einsatzgruppe B) had permission to apply "executive measures" against the civilian population without requesting consent from anyone, pursuant to an agreement between the security police and the high command of the army, OKH. In spring 1944, Sonderkommando 7a was commanded by Gerhard Bast, a lawyer by education, born in 1911. In 1947 he was killed by a guide with whom he was crossing the border between Austria and Italy. For more on the subject, see M. Pollack, *Śmierć w bunkrze: Opowieść o moim ojcu* (Wołowiec, Poland, 2010).

121. S. Biernacki, "Działalność hitlerowskiej policji bezpieczeństwa w okresie powstania w Warszawie i dystrykcie warszawskim," in *Powstanie Warszawskie: Sesja w 40 rocznicę* (Warsaw, Poland, 1987), 331.

122. P. Marti, *Sprawa*, 384 (fn 321).

123. Ibid.

124. A. Richie, *Warsaw 1944: Hitler, Himmler, and the Warsaw Uprising* (New York, 2013), 284.

125. Ibid., 288; and W. Nowak and A. Kuźniak, *Mój warszawski szał: Druga strona powstania.*

126. BA Ludwigsburg, B 162/16571, Der Oberstaatsanwalt 2 Js 700/61, Flensburg, z. Zt. Eutingen, April 7, 1962, 132.

127. N. Sennerteg, *Kat Warszawy*, 43.

128. Ibid., 48–49.

129. BA Ludwigsburg, B 162/16572, Der Oberstaatsanwalt Flensburg, 2 Js 700/61, Rudi Fiedler, Lippstadt, May 7, 1963, 254.

130. Sz. Datner, K. Leszczyński, *Zbrodnie okupanta*, 47.

131. J. Mańkowska, J. Janowski, and M. Janaszek-Seydlitz, *Rzeź Woli*, http://www.sppw1944.org/index.html?http://www.sppw1944.org/powstanie/wola_rzez.html (accessed March 12, 2019).

132. P. Gursztyn, *Rzeź Woli* (Warsaw, Poland, 2014), 92.

133. J. Kirchmayer, *Powstanie*, 282.

134. BA Ludwigsburg, B 162/16574, Der Oberstaatsanwalt, 2 Js 700/61, Adalbert Daschner, Flensburg, April 5, 1962, 32.

135. BA Ludwigsburg, B 162/16574, Der Oberstaatsanwalt 2Js 700/61, Bauer Emil, Flensburg, October 24, 1961, 66.

136. BA Ludwigsburg, B 162/16574, Der Oberstaatsanwalt 2 Js 700/61, Artur Schuldt, Kiel, January 22, 1963, 203.

137. BA Ludwigsburg, B 162/16574, Der Oberstaatsanwalt 2 Js 700/61, Karl Jochheim-Armin, Flensburg, February 1, 1962, 113.

138. BA Ludwigsburg, B 162/16574, Anlage zur Niederschrift, Paul Wilhelm Rass, March 16, 1962, 125–29.

139. BA Ludwigsburg, B 162/16574, Der Oberstaatsanwalt 2 Js 700/61, Franz Haschäcker, Brakel, January 29, 1963, 182.

140. BA Ludwigsburg, B 162/16569, 2 Js 272/65, Flensburg, July 13, 1967, 201.

141. "Lucyna Lange, lat 47, siostra miłosierdzia, pielęgniarka Szpitala Wolskiego przy ul: Płockiej 26" [Lucyna Lange, 47 years old, Sister of Mercy, nurse in the Wolski Hospital at Płocka Street 26], in *Exodus Warszawy: Ludzie i miasto po Powstaniu 1944*, vol. 1, *Pamiętniki: Relacje* (Warsaw, Poland, 1992), 384.

142. "Stefan Wesołowski," in *Encyklopedia medyków powstania warszawskiego*, http://lekarzepowstania.pl/osoba/stefan-wesolowski-2/ (accessed July 23, 2017).

143. Janusz Zeyland (1897–1944), pediatrician and pulmonologist, professor at the University in Poznań; during the war he was the organizer of antituberculosis surgeries for children in Warsaw and the children's tuberculosis ward in the Wolski Hospital (*Exodus Warszawy*, 229).

144. Marian Józef Piasecki (1894–1944), doctor; before the war he worked in the Hospital of the Sisters of Saint Elizabeth and in the Childhood Diseases Clinic at the University of Warsaw. From 1936 he was the organizer and chief of the surgical ward at the Wolski Hospital, and the hospital's director during the occupation. Within it, he ran an academic training center and conducted underground work; a soldier of the AK (*Exodus Warszawy*, 229).

145. "Leokadia Ciekanowska, z domu Grochowiecka, lat 32, zamieszkała przy ul. Twardej 46; Przed wojną urzędniczka w Warszawskiej Spółce Myśliwskiej, w czasie okupacji barmanka w barze-jadłodajni "Zielona" przy ul. Wolskiej 11" [Leokadia Ciekanowska, née Grochowiecka, age 32, residing at ul. Twarda 46; a clerk at the Warsaw Hunting Company before the war, a barwoman in the "Zielonka" bar and canteen at Wolska Street 11 during the occupation], in *Exodus Warszawy*, 216.

146. "Stefan Wesołowski," in *Encyklopedia medyków powstania warszawskiego*, http://lekarzepowstania.pl/osoba/stefan-wesolowski-2/ (accessed July 23, 2017).

147. Account of Stefan Wesołowski, pseudonym Chirurg (http://www.1944.pl/archiwum-historii-mowionej/stefan-wesolowski,428.html, accessed July 23, 2017); and account of Eugeniusz Trepczyński (http://www.1944.pl/archiwum-historii-mowionej/eugeniusz-trepczynski,1019.html, accessed July 23, 2017).

148. "Leokadia Ciekanowska," in *Exodus Warszawy*, 218–21.

149. "Jerzy Górski, lat 16, zamieszkały przy ul. Górczewskiej 45; uczeń szkoły powszechnej, gazeciarz, z rodziny robotniczej; preparator materiałów analitycznych w Instytucie Geologicznym" [Jerzy Górski, age 16, residing at Górczewska Street 45; primary school pupil, newspaper boy from a working-class family; technician preparing material for analysis at the Geological Institute], in *Exodus Warszawy*, 216.

150. "Stefan Wesołowski," in *Encyklopedia medyków powstania warszawskiego*, http://lekarzepowstania.pl/osoba/stefan-wesolowski-2/ (accessed July 23, 2017).

151. N. Sennerteg, *Kat Warszawy*, 45–46.

152. BA Ludwigsburg, B 162/16572, Protokoll einer Zeugenvernehmung, Warschau, March 14, 1947, 217.

153. Bronisław Paczyński's account of August 30, 2007, http://www.1944.pl/archiwum-historii-mowionej/bronislaw-paczynski,1248.html (accessed July 24, 2017).

154. P. Gursztyn, *Rzeź*, 153.

155. BA Ludwigsburg, B 162/16571, Der Oberstaatsanwalt—2 Js 700/61, Flensburg, z Zt. Hannover, January 17, 1962, 95. Meanwhile, in the 1967 verdict that found Reinefarth not guilty, issued in Flensburg, the court stated that Dirlewanger arrived in Warsaw on August 8, 1944 (Załącznik nr 2, Uniewinnienie Reinefartha, 1967 r., after N. Sennerteg, *Kat Warszawy*, 426).

156. BA Ludwigsburg, B 162/16571, Der Oberstaatsanwalt 2 Js 700/61, Flensburg, z. Zt. Eutingen, April 7, 1962, 130.

157. *Ludność cywilna w powstaniu warszawskim*, vol. 1, part 1, *Pamiętniki, relacje, zeznania* (Warsaw, Poland, 1974), 319. Oskar Dirlewanger's arrival at the

Infectious Diseases Hospital was also confirmed by Heinrich Arndt (BA Ludwigsburg, B 162/16574, Der Oberstaatsanwalt 2Js 700/61, Heinrich Arndt, Flensburg, January 30, 1961, 84). As I wrote above, the precise date of Dirlewanger's arrival is unknown, but it occurred between August 8 and 15.

158. "Stefan Wesołowski," in *Encyklopedia medyków powstania warszawskiego*, http://lekarzepowstania.pl/osoba/stefan-wesolowski-2/ (accessed July 23, 2017).

159. BA Ludwigsburg, B 162/16574, Der Oberstaatsanwalt 2Js 700/61, Heinrich Arndt, Flensburg, January 30, 1961, 83.

160. Ibid., 86.

161. BA Ludwigsburg, B 162/16574, Der Oberstaatsanwalt 2 Js 700/61, Franz Haschäcker, Brakel, January 29, 1963, 183.

162. Nürnbergdokument USSR-313, zaprzysiężone oświadczenie von dem Bacha-Zelewskiego [Nürnbergdokument USSR-313, von dem Bach-Zelewski's statement made under oath], February 3, 1946, after N. Sennerteg, *Kat Warszawy*, 401.

163. Ibid., 405.

164. Ibid., 407.

165. P. Marti, *Sprawa*, 91–92.

166. Ibid., 160–61, 168.

167. Ibid., 169–70.

168. For more about Hanns von Krannhals, see ibid., 203–05.

169. Załącznik nr 2, Uniewinnienie Reinefartha, 1967, after N. Sennerteg, *Kat Warszawy*, 425.

170. P. Marti, *Sprawa*, 387–88 (fn 343).

171. In many people's accounts, Joanna Kryńska is called a student. In a testimony made in 1947 before the Warsaw Commission for Investigation of German Crimes, she herself stated that she was in St. Stanislaus Hospital "as a doctor" (P. Gursztyn, *Rzeź*, 151n264; and BA Ludwigsburg, B 162/16569, Bisheriges Ermittlungsergebnis über das Sonderkommando "Dirlewanger," n.d., 175). Joanna Ewa Kryńska was born on September 19, 1915, in Charbin. She was a doctor by education (BA Ludwigsburg, B 162/16572, Protokoll einer Zeugenvernehmung, Warschau, April 14, 1947, 215).

172. After the war, all Russian-speaking units participating in the Warsaw Uprising came to be referred to as Vlasov's soldiers, which is untrue. It is quite improbable for Dirlewanger or his officers to have used this phrase during the uprising.

173. BA Ludwigsburg, B 162/16572, Protokoll einer Zeugenvernehmung, Warschau, April 14, 1947, 215.

174. Ibid.

175. Ibid.; A. D. Sławińska, *Przeżyłam to: Wola 1944* (Edmond, OK: Gondwana, 2015), 31; and B. Urbanek, *Pielęgniarki i sanitariuszki w Powstaniu Warszawskim w 1944 r.* (Warsaw, Poland, 1988), 89–90.

176. BA Ludwigsburg, B 162/16572, Protokoll einer Zeugenvernehmung, Warschau, March 14, 1947, 215–16.

177. B. Urbanek, *Pielęgniarki i sanitariuszki w Powstaniu Warszawskim w 1944 r.*, 333; *Ludność cywilna*, 264, 320; and BA Ludwigsburg, B 162/16572, Protokoll einer Zeugenvernehmung, Warschau, March 14, 1947, 216.

178. N. Sennerteg, *Kat Warszawy*, 16.

179. BA Ludwigsburg, B 162/16574, Der Oberstaatsanwalt 2Js 700/61, Heinrich Arndt, Flensburg, January 30, 1961, 85.

180. BA Ludwigsburg, B 162/16574, Der Oberstaatsanwalt, 2 Js 700/61, Adalbert Daschner, Flensburg, April 5, 1962, 85.

181. P. Marti, *Sprawa*, 298.

182. S. Kuklińska, *Działalność*, 116.

183. W. Bartoszewski, *Prawda*, 47.

184. Himmler sent a telephonogram to von dem Bach: "Return immediately. Great devilry in the General Government" (T. Sawicki, *Wyrok na miasto*, 44).

185. As Sennerteg wrote, von dem Bach received Himmler's order on August 2, during his stay in Sopot. He flew immediately to Giżycko (Lötzen), thence on August 3 to Wrocław (the weather in Krakow was inappropriate for landing), and from Wrocław, he went to Warsaw by car (N. Sennerteg, *Kat Warszawy*, 59n74).

186. S. Podlewski, *Przemarsz przez piekło*, 144.

187. BA Ludwigsburg, B 162/16571, Der Oberstaatsanwalt 2 Js 700/61, z. Zt. Kevelaer, February 28, 1963, 150.

188. Zeznania Ericha von dem Bacha-Zelewskiego przed prokuratorem Sawickim w Norymberdze [Erich von dem Bach-Zelewski's testimony before prosecutor Sawicki in Nuremberg], January 26, 1946, after W. Bartoszewski, *Prawda*, 49.

189. P. Padfield, *Himmler*, 561.

190. S. Kuklińska, *Działalność*, 117–18.

191. Status as of August 8, 1944, after H. von Krannhals, *Powstanie Warszawskie*, 318.

192. A. Przygoński, *Powstanie warszawskie w sierpniu 1944*, vol. 1 (Warsaw, Poland, 1980), 425.

193. R. Michaelis, *Dirlewanger*, 18.

194. H. Krannhals, *Powstanie Warszawskie*, 322 (fn 649).

195. Protokół przesłuchania Joanny Kryńskiej, March 14, 1947, after H. P. Klausch, *Antifaschisten*, 118.

196. BA Ludwigsburg, B 162/16574, Der Oberstaatsanwalt 2Js 700/61, Bauer Emil, Flensburg, October 24, 1961, 64.

197. Sz. Datner, K. Leszczyński, *Zbrodnie okupanta*, 157–58; and *Ludność cywilna*, 578.

198. E. Serwański and I. Trawińska, *Zbrodnia niemiecka w Warszawie 1944 r.* (Poznań, Poland, 1946), 151–52.

199. M. Motyl and S. Rutkowski, *Powstanie Warszawskie—rejestr miejsc i faktów zbrodni* (Warsaw, Poland, 1994), 163–64; and A. Przygoński, *Powstanie*, 430.

200. BA Ludwigsburg, B 162/16572, Der Oberstaatsanwalt 2 Js 700/61, Paul Zimmermann, Stuttgart, July 1, 1963, 264–65.

201. W. Bartoszewski, *Prawda*, 54.

202. BA Ludwigsburg, B 162/16569, Bisheriges Ermittlungsergebnis über das Sonderkommando "Dirlewanger," n.d., 171.

203. T. Sawicki, *Rozkaz: Zdławić powstanie*, 41.

204. BA Ludwigsburg, B 162/16569, Bisheriges Ermittlungsergebnis über das Sonderkommando "Dirlewanger," n.d., 171.

205. T. Sawicki, *Rozkaz: Zdławić powstanie*, 41.

206. S. Ozimek, *Stare Miasto 1944* (Warsaw, Poland, 1971), 92.

207. E. F. Ziemke, *Sowiecki walec* (Warsaw, Poland, 2001), 160.

208. R. Michaelis, *Dirlewanger*, 28.

209. N. Sennerteg, *Kat Warszawy*, 170.

210. BA Ludwigsburg, B 162/16569, Bisheriges Ermittlungsergebnis über das Sonderkommando "Dirlewanger," n.d., 171.

211. T. Sawicki, *Rozkaz: Zdławić powstanie*, 42.

212. S. Ozimek, *Stare Miasto*, 104.

213. The Maltese Hospital was located between German outposts in the Saxon Garden, the Wehrmacht command in Teatralny Square, and the insurgent Old Town. Both wounded Germans and insurgents were cared for there. On August 4 the heads of the sanitary division of the Home Army High Command (KG AK) reached the hospital, including its chief, Col. Dr. Leon Strehl, pseudonym "Feliks," who on August 5 became the commander of the Maltese Hospital. From August 4 the number of wounded coming in from Wola rose significantly. On August 7 the hospital was shelled from Senatorska Street by a German tank.

214. St. Podlewski, *Przemarsz przez piekło* (Warsaw, Poland, 1971), 226–28; Służba sanitarna w Powstaniu Warszawskim, http://www.sppw1944.org/index.html?http://www.sppw1944.org/powstanie/sanitariat_06.html (accessed May 14, 2021); and Szpital Maltański, http://www.szpitale1944.pl/i/28,szpital-maltanski (accessed May 14, 2021).

215. N. Sennerteg, *Kat Warszawy*, 169.

216. Willi Schmidt, Wehrmacht colonel. At the start of the Warsaw Uprising, he was sent to Warsaw at the head of the 608th Regiment, which he commanded during the fighting in Wola. This was a frontline unit, and Willi Schmidt had plentiful combat experience (for more on the subject, see P. Stachiewicz, *"Parasol"*).

217. T. Sawicki, *Rozkaz: Zdławić powstanie*, 37; and P. Stachiewicz, *"Parasol,"* 514.

218. H. von Krannhals, *Powstanie Warszawskie*, 177–78. Furthermore, Krannhals wrote that on August 11, Dirlewanger's and Kaminski's units were assigned sapper units and three assault guns each from the alarm battery of the 200th Reserve Battalion; Reck's units were allocated the 201st Positional Battery of Heavy Rocket Launchers, and Schmidt's group the 5th Armored Train in addition to sappers. The sappers, meanwhile, were assigned a platoon of Taifuns (ibid., 195). The Goliaths and Taifuns were used by August 14. The Taifun was used in the sewer system, in which destruction of 500–900 meters was later ascertained. On August 17 the OKH sent Maj. Herzog to Warsaw along with two motorized sapper battalions: the 46th and 627th. Moreover, on that day the mortar Karl arrived, and ammunition for it was sent a day later. On August 21 the 501st Mechanized Assault Sapper Battalion came (T. Sawicki, *Rozkaz: Zdławić powstanie*, 45).

219. S. Kuklińska, *Działalność*, 120.

220. N. Sennerteg, *Kat Warszawy*, 175.

221. Rozkaz bojowy gen. Reinefartha z 18 sierpnia 1944 r., godz. 17.30 [Gen. Reinefarth's operational order of August 18, 1944, 5.30 p.m.], after P. Stachiewicz, *"Parasol,"* 550.

222. P. Stachiewicz, *"Parasol,"* 551. Moreover, as von Krannhals stated, Dirlewanger's unit was equipped with Russian medium machine guns and eight Russian antitank guns (H. Krannhals, *Powstanie Warszawskie*, 320).

223. P. Stachiewicz, *"Parasol,"* 553.

224. Ibid.

225. P. Marti, *Sprawa*, 72.

226. BA Ludwigsburg, B 162/16571, Der Oberstaatsanwalt—2 Js 700/61, Flensburg, z Zt. Hannover, January 17, 1962, 98.

227. Ibid., 98, 101.

228. M. Grzechocińska, *Historia Szpitala Zakaźnego w Warszawie*, http://www.zakazny.pl/historia?showall=1 (accessed September 18, 2016); according to information on the website, Dirlewanger had moved in by August 6, 1944.

229. Battalion *Czwartacy* was an assault unit of the People's Guard (Gwardia Ludowa) and then the People's Army (Armia Ludowa, or AL), intended for special tasks and formed in October 1943. During the Warsaw Uprising, it was referred to as the 4th AL Battalion Czwartacy; for more on the subject, see Strzembosz, *Oddziały szturmowe konspiracyjnej Warszawy 1939–1944* (Warsaw, Poland, 1983); and J. Gargas, *Oddziały Gwardii Ludowej i Armii Ludowej 1942–1945* (Warsaw, Poland, 1974).

230. *Czwartacy: Wspomnienia byłych żołnierzy Szturmowego Batalionu im. "Czwartaków" 1943–1945*, ed. J. Bednarczyk et al. (Warsaw, Poland, 1977), 276–77.

231. BAB, R70 Polen/76, Der Befelshaber de Sicherheitspolizei und des SD in Generalgouvernment, IV 1—1976/44g, Krakau, August 24, 1944.

232. T. Sawicki, *Rozkaz: Zdławić powstanie*, 65.

233. BA Ludwigsburg, B 162/16571, Der Oberstaatsanwalt 2Js 700/61, Flensburg, z. Zt. Hannover, January 18, 1962, 122–23.

234. Ibid., 124.

235. T. Sawicki, *Rozkaz: Zdławić powstanie*, 68.

236. Ibid., 71.

237. W. Bartoszewski, *Prawda*, 55.

238. R. Michaelis, *Dirlewanger*, 19.

239. T. Sawicki, *Rozkaz: Zdławić powstanie*, 75.

240. Ibid.

241. Ibid., 77–78.

242. Ibid., 79.

243. N. Sennerteg, *Kat Warszawy*, 178. In six hospitals the wounded were burned, and shootings were carried out next to the wall in Wąski Dunaj Street (T. Sawicki, *Rozkaz: Zdławić powstanie*, 79). One of the *Einsatzcommandos* attached to Maj. Reck's group stated that on September 2, 1944, they shot fifty-four people and burned fifty-one, as cited in "Meldunek jednostki "Einsatzkommando," 3.9.1944," in *Mocarstwa wobec Powstania*: *Wybór dokumentów i materiałów*, ed. M. M. Drozdowski (Warsaw, Poland, 1994), 198–99).

244. "Zofia Krauze, z domu Głuska, lat 51, wykształcenie wyższe; w czasie Powstania—na Starym Mieście i w szpitalu przy ul. Długiej 7" [Zofia Krauze, née Głuska, aged 51, higher education; during the Uprising: in the Old Town and in the hospital at Długa Street 7], in *Exodus Warszawy*, 349.

245. "Stefania Krosnowska, z domu Ruszczykowska, lat 31, wykształcenie wyższe, bibliotekarka, zamieszkała na Powiślu ul. Lipowa 4a, w powstaniu sanitariuszka szpitala przy ul. Długiej 7" [Stefania Krosnowska, née Ruszczykowska, aged 31, higher education, librarian, residing in Powiśle, Lipowa Street 4a, a paramedic in the hospital at Długa Street 7 during the uprising], in *Exodus Warszawy*, 355–56.

246. T. Sawicki, *Rozkaz: Zdławić powstanie*, 79.

247. Meldunek, September 2, 1944, after T. Sawicki, *Rozkaz: Zdławić powstanie*, 79.

248. J. Kurdwanowski, *Mrówka na szachownicy* (Warsaw, Poland, 2014), 227.

249. N. Sennerteg, *Kat Warszawy*, 178.

250. T. Sumiński, *Pamiętniki żołnierzy*, vol. 3, *Czerniaków*, 255.

251. BA Ludwigsburg, B 162/16574, Der Oberstaatsanwalt, 2 Js 700/61, Walter Fentzahn, Flensburg, November 23, 1961, 11.

252. BA Ludwigsburg, B 162/16574, Az: 2 Js 700/61, November 28, 1961, 1; and BA Ludwigsburg, B 162/16574, Der Oberstaatsanwalt, 2 Js 700/61, Walter Fentzahn, Flensburg, November 23, 1961, 11.

253. BA Ludwigsburg, B 162/16574, Der Oberstaatsanwalt, 2 Js 700/61, Walter Fentzahn, Flensburg, November 23, 1961, 11.

254. Gen Rohr's group took Sadyba-Czerniaków almost at the same time as the Old Town was captured (T. Sumiński, *Pamiętniki żołnierzy*, vol. 3, *Czerniaków*, 255).

255. W. Bartoszewski, *1859 dni Warszawy* (Kraków, Poland, 1974), 668.

256. Sonderausführungen des Kriegstagebuchs zum Warschauer Aufstand, August 21, 1944, after H. von Krannhals, *Powstanie Warszawskie*, 206.

257. BA Ludwigsburg, B 162/16574, Der Oberstaatsanwalt 2 Js 700/61, Wilhelm Pohl, Flensburg, April 17, 1962, 157–58.

258. T. Sawicki, *Rozkaz: Zdławić powstanie*, 86.

259. Von dem Bach's diary, entry for September 5, 1944, after T. Sawicki, *Rozkaz: Zdławić powstanie*, 87.

260. Ibid.

261. "Leszek Łacheta, lat 12, uczeń, zamieszkały z rodzicami przy ul. Grzybowskiej 56" [Leszek Łacheta, aged 12, pupil, residing with his parents at Grzybowska Street 56], in *Exodus Warszawy*, 446–47.

262. T. Sawicki, *Rozkaz: Zdławić powstanie*, 88.

263. "Jerzy Rowiński, lat 38, lekarz medycyny, zamieszkały przy ul. Tamka 25" [Jerzy Rowiński, aged 38, medical doctor, residing at Tamka Street 25], in *Exodus Warszawy*, 535.

264. R. Michaelis, *Dirlewanger*, 35.

265. T. Sawicki, *Rozkaz: Zdławić powstanie*, 90.

266. P. Stachiewicz, *"Parasol,"* 582.

267. Ibid., 582–83.

268. BA Ludwigsburg, B 162/16574, Der Oberstaatsanwalt 2 Js 700/61, Wilhelm Pohl, Flensburg, April 17, 1962, 157–58.

269. BA Ludwigsburg, B 162/16574, Der Oberstaatsanwalt, 2 Js 700/61, Walter Fentzahn, Flensburg, November 23, 1961, 12.

270. Ibid., 12–14.

271. BA Ludwigsburg, B 162/16574, Az: 2 Js 700/61, November 28, 1961, 1.

272. BA Ludwigsburg, B 162/16573, Der Oberstaatsanwalt 2 Js 700/61, Viktor Zerfaß, April 4, 1962, 334.

273. BA Ludwigsburg, B 162/16574, Der Oberstaatsanwalt, 2 Js 700/61, Adalbert Daschner, Flensburg, April 5, 1962, 31.

274. P. Stachiewicz, *"Parasol,"* 583. At this time, SS-Sonderregiment Dirlewanger numbered 33 officers and 2,221 soldiers (T. Sawicki, *Rozkaz: Zdławić powstanie*, 104).

275. S. Likiernik, *Diabelne szczęście czy palec boży?* (Warsaw, Poland, 1994), 138–41.

276. For more information on the subject, see T. Sawicki, *Rozkaz: Zdławić powstanie*, 106–07.

277. Ibid., 107.

278. Ibid., 109.

279. "Notatka z rozmowy telefonicznej mjr. Voekela z szefem sztabu 9 A z 17.9.1944, godz. 9.35" [Note from telephone conversation between Maj. Voekel and 9th Army chief of staff of September 17, 1944, 9.35 a.m.], in M. J. Kwiatkowski, *"Tu mówi powstańcza Warszawa": Dni powstania w audycjach Polskiego Radia i dokumentach niemieckich* (Warsaw, Poland, 1994), 480.

280. T. Sawicki, *Rozkaz: Zdławić powstanie*, 1118.

281. P. Stachiewicz, *"Parasol,"* 596.

282. T. Sawicki, *Rozkaz: Zdławić powstanie*, 121–22.

283. S. Kuklińska, *Działalność*, 122–23.

284. S. Kopf, *Dni powstania*, 330; and N. Sennerteg, *Kat Warszawy*, 183.

285. BA Ludwigsburg, B 162/16574, Der Oberstaatsanwalt 2 Js 700/61, Wilhelm Pohl, Flensburg, April 17, 1962, 157–58.

286. A. Borkiewicz, *Powstanie warszawskie 1944*, 502.

287. BA Ludwigsburg, B 162/16571, Der Oberstaatsanwalt 2 Js 700/61, Flensburg, z. Zt. Plettenberg, November 30, 1961, 83.

288. BA Ludwigsburg, B 162/16571, Der Oberstaatsanwalt—2 Js 700/61, Flensburg, z Zt. Hannover, January 17, 1962, 101.

289. Ibid.

290. BA Ludwigsburg, B 162/16571, Der Oberstaatsanwalt 2 Js 700/61, Flensburg, z. Zt. Eutingen, April 7, 1962; and BA Ludwigsburg, B 162/16571, Adolf Katz, April 7, 1962, 134. Marti stated that the decorations were granted both to Reinefarth and to Dirlewanger on September 30 (P. Marti, *Sprawa*, 388n344), and to von Krannhals, and that Dirlewanger was awarded the Knight's Cross of the Iron Cross on October 17, 1944 (H. Krannhals, *Powstanie Warszawskie*, 320). Sawicki wrote that von Vormann sent the motion for him to be decorated by August 12, 1944, Reinhardt seconded it on the next day, and the letter was received by the OKH Personnel Division on August 15. The decoration was awarded on September 30, and the order to this effect was issued on October 8 (T. Sawicki, *Rozkaz: Zdławić powstanie*, 157). According to SS personal files, the decoration was awarded on September 30, 1944 (BAB, R/9361/III 521445, Personal Bericht, n.d. 732).

291. Fernschreiben, October 8,1944, BAB, R/9361/III 521445, 753; Vorschlag für die Verleihung des Ritterkreuzes des Eisernen Kreuzes, September 10, 1944; BAB, R/9361/III 521445, 754; Aktennotiz, Berlin, November 8, 1944; and BAB, R/9361/III, vol. 521445, 784. Reinefarth proposed that Dirlewanger be granted the Knight's Cross of the Iron Cross on September 10, 1944, and the motion was received by the *Reichsführer-SS*'s staff on September 12, 1944 (BAB, R/9361/III, vol. 521445, 754).

292. BA Ludwigsburg, B 162/16571, Der Oberstaatsanwalt 2 Js 700/61, Flensburg, z. Zt. Eutingen, April 7, 1962, 134.

293. S. Kuklińska, *Działalność*, 125.

294. Ibid.

295. Ibid.

296. Ibid., 126.

297. A. Solak, "Powstanie warszawskie—mitologia zrywu," in *Kulisy katastrofy powstania*, 52.

298. *Nowa Encyklopedia Powszechna PWN*, vol. 6 (Warsaw, Poland, 2004), 756; and T. Sawicki, *Rozkaz: Zdławić powstanie*, 189.

299. BA Ludwigsburg, B 162/16571, Der Oberstaatsanwalt 2 Js 700/61, Flensburg, z. Zt. St. Go[?], April 14, 1962, 140.

300. YV, JM 2085, ID 3670809, document concerning recruitment of 1,500 criminals from Matzkau to Dirlewanger's unit, n.d.

301. H. P. Klausch, *Antifaschisten*, 122; and BA Ludwigsburg, B 162/16569, Bisheriges Ermittlungsergebnis über das Sonderkommando "Dirlewanger," n.d., 152–54.

302. A. Lasik, *Sztafety ochronne*, 206.

303. BA Ludwigsburg, B 162/16569, Bisheriges Ermittlungsergebnis über das Sonderkommando "Dirlewanger," n.d., 152.

304. P. Stachiewicz, *"Parasol,"* 500 (fn 65).

305. BA Ludwigsburg, B 162/29251, Bayerisches Landeskriminalamt IIIa/SK, Tgb.Nr. 489/62, Dr. Franz Schmuckerschlag, München, May 29, 1962, 36.

306. Kriminalpolizeiliche Vernehmung des Harald Momm, May 28, 1962, after H. P. Klausch, *Antifaschisten*, 128.

307. Ibid., 456 (fn 82).

308. Ibid., 128.

309. N. Sennerteg, *Kat Warszawy*, 30–31.

310. P. Stachiewicz, *"Parasol,"* 500 (fn 65). These data have been confirmed by H. von Krannhals, *Powstanie Warszawskie*, 175, 318 (fn 637). However, the data provided after Stachiewicz are not completely correct.

311. BA Ludwigsburg, B 162/16574, Der Oberstaatsanwalt 2Js 700/61, Heinrich Arndt, Flensburg, January 30, 1961, 82. This was most likely the Jewish cemetery at Okopowa Street in Warsaw.

312. N. Sennerteg, *Kat Warszawy*, 164–65.

313. H. von Krannhals, *Powstanie Warszawskie*, 213.

314. BA Ludwigsburg, B 162/16573, Der Oberstaatsanwalt 2 Js 700/61, Karl Wenzel, Weißenbrunn, April 2, 1962, 324.

315. T. Sawicki, *Rozkaz: Zdławić powstanie*, 192.

316. "Telegram szefa sztabu 9 A z 9.10.1944, godz. 14.00" [Telegram from the chief of staff of 9th A of October 9, 1944, 14:00], in M. J. Kwiatkowski, *"Tu mówi powstańcza Warszawa,"* 633.

317. T. Sawicki, *Rozkaz: Zdławić powstanie*, 192.

318. BAB, R/9361/III, vol. 521445, Begründung und Stellungnahme des Zwischenvorgesetzen, n.d., 756–57; see also S. Ozimek, *Stare Miasto 1944*, 71–72.

319. *Okupacja i ruch oporu w dzienniku Hansa Franka 1939–1945*, vol. 2, *1943–1945* (Warsaw, Poland, 1971), 557; and M. Winstone, *Generalne Gubernatorstwo*, 320.

320. Hitler's words after Dirlewanger was awarded the Knight's Cross of the Iron Cross (R. Laschet, *Dr. Oskar Dirlewanger*, 48).

321. In the original: "Die besondere soldatische Laufbahn des neuen Esslinger Ritterkreuzträgers, der seine Auszeichnung direkt aus der Hand des Führers erhalten hat, umriß mit herzlichen Worten Oberbürgermeister Dr. Klaiber, der mit seinen Dankesworten zum Anwalt der Gefühle der gesamten Einwohnerschaft wurde. . . . Daß Dirlewanger 1939 in den Reihen gerade der Waffen-SS stand, rundet das Bild eines Mannes ab, wie er ihn verkörpert. Er wurde dank seiner Art, eisern und unerbittlich durchzufahren, geradezu zum Spezialisten der Bandenbekämpfung. Auszeichnungen wie das Deutsche Kreuz in Gold und andere Anerkennungen sprechen äußerlich von seinen Verdiensten.

Was Dirlewanger aber in der Bekämpfung der polnischen Aufständischen in Warschau leistete, krönt seine militärischen Leistungen in besonderem Maße. . . .

Es gibt kaum einen Ritterkreuzträger, der eine solch permanente Linie des Soldatenlebens nachweisen kann wie Dirlewanger. Sein Dasein ist jenes Opfer an der Idee, die von bedeutenden Männern gefordert wird!

Diese Idee aber ist

Deutschland,

und nur Deutschland.

Deutschland heißt nichts anderes

als Adolf Hitler!

Mit den Worten des Dankes und des Stolzes darüber, dass Dirlewanger Esslinger ist, schloß der Oberbürgermeister seine Ausführungen" (entry in the Golden Book of the City of Esslingen of November 9, 1944, after R. Laschet, *Dr. Oskar Dirlewanger*, 48).

322. BAB, R/9361/III 521445, Personalangaben, n.d., 758.

Chapter 6

1. P. Matusak, *Europa walcząca 1939–1945* (Siedlce, Poland, 2005), 147.

2. Jozef Tiso, born October 13, 1887, in Veľká Bytča; Catholic priest, doctor of theology, and leader of the Slovak People's Party. During the Second World War,

he held the office of president of Slovakia. Sentenced to death after the war by the Czechoslovakian government for treason and participation in war crimes, he was hanged on April 18, 1947. For more on this subject, see A. Krawczyk, *Słowacja księdza prezydenta: Jozef Tiso 1887–1947* (Kraków, Poland, 2015).

3. Ibid., 219.

4. S. Cosban-Woytycha, "Dywersja i sabotaż kolejowy na Słowacji w latach 1943–1944," *Słupskie Studia Historyczne* 19 (2013): 203–04.

5. A. Krawczyk, *Słowacja księdza*, 205.

6. Ibid.

7. S. Cosban-Woytycha, *Dywersja i sabotaż*, 203–04.

8. A. Krawczyk, *Słowacja księdza*, 205–06.

9. S. Cosban-Woytycha, *Dywersja i sabotaż*, 204–05.

10. A. Krawczyk, *Słowacja księdza*, 206–07.

11. Ján Golian, born January 26, 1906, in Dombóvár; cooperated with the antifascist underground movement and the Czechoslovak government in exile from 1943. He was appointed commander of the underground Military Center in Slovakia. He was promoted to brigade general on September 5, 1944. On November 3 the Third Reich's security services arrested him, and he was incarcerated in the Flössenburg concentration camp in Germany, where he died in 1945 (for more on Golian, see Generál Ján Golian, http://www.muzeumsnp.sk/historia/osobnosti/general-jan-golian/, accessed February 22, 2017).

12. A. Krawczyk, *Słowacja księdza*, 206.

13. The names Wieliczko (*above*) and Veličko may refer to the same person, the first being the Polish and the second the Slovak spelling. This could not be established for certain, however, since they are mentioned in only two sources (footnotes 12 and 14, respectively).

14. *Ruch oporu*, ed. J. Lubiński (Warsaw, Poland, 2009), 115.

15. F. Beer, *Słowacja na przełomie: Powstanie słowackie 1944 r.* (Warsaw, Poland, 1969), 421.

16. S. Kuklińska, *Działalność*, 134.

17. Ibid., 423; cf. A. Krawczyk, *Słowacja księdza*, 222.

18. A. Krawczyk, *Słowacja księdza*, 217.

19. S. Kuklińska, *Działalność*, 134.

20. Ibid., 222–23.

21. F. Beer, *Słowacja*, 429.

22. A. Krawczyk, *Słowacja księdza*, 225–26.

23. F. Beer, *Słowacja*, 445.

24. Ibid., 422–23.

25. Ibid., 452.

26. A. Krawczyk, *Słowacja księdza*, 223.

27. F. Beer, *Słowacja*, 453–54.

28. Ibid., 456.

29. Hermann Höfle, born September 12, 1898, in Augsburg; fought in the First World War. He participated in the Munich Putsch in 1923. In 1943, he joined the SS and was promoted to *SS-Obergruppenführer und General der Waffen-SS und Polizei* on April 20, 1944. He previously distinguished himself during action Reinhardt. He had his own *Einsatzgruppe*, which persecuted Slovakia's Jewish community. Responsible for suppressing the uprising in this country in 1944, he was handed over to the Czechoslovak authorities after the war and sentenced to death for war crimes. He was shot on December 9,1947. For more on this subject, see W. Venohr, *Aufstand für die Tschechoslowakei: Der slowakische Freiheitskampf von 1944* (Hamburg, Germany, 1969); and P. Longerich, *Himmler*, 854.

30. YV, JM 2089, ID 3672426, Testimony of Höfle, February 13, 1947.

31. F. Beer, *Słowacja*, 495.

32. R. Michaelis, *Dirlewanger*, 43–44.

33. A. Krawczyk, *Słowacja księdza*, 227.

34. F. Beer, *Słowacja*, 490, 493.

35. Ibid., 489.

36. R. Michaelis, *Dirlewanger*, 45. During Höfle's meeting with Himmler in Vienna, the *Reichsführer-SS* accepted the combat plan in Slovakia and assigned new units to fight there. Among others, he promised that Höfle would get Dirlewanger's unit. Höfle obtained further reinforcements by accident. SS-Brigadeführer Wilhelm Trabandt, commander of the 18th Horst Wessel Volunteer Panzer Grenadier Division, stationed in Hungary, was present at the briefing. Since the unit had no specific assignment, Trabandt proposed to Höfle that it be used to suppress the uprising in Slovakia, which Himmler approved (see ibid., 497–98).

37. YV, JM 2089, ID 3672426, Testimony of Höfle, February 13, 1947.

38. BA Ludwigsburg, B 162/16572, Der Oberstaatsanwalt Flensburg 2 Js 700/61, Karl Keithan, Witzenhausen, May 9, 1963, 258.

39. Hlinka Guard, a paramilitary formation of the Slovak People's Party operating in the years 1938–45. Its name comes from its founder, Andriej Hlinka. On March 14, 1939—that is, the moment when the Slovak state was formed—it obtained the status of the official state police. It was to be the Slovak elite and help merge the Slovak population with ethnic Germans. During the suppression of the Slovak uprising, it took part in mass executions (for more on the subject, see A. Krawczyk, *Słowacja księdza*, 209; and *Gwardia Hlinki*, https://pl.wikipedia.org/wiki/Gwardia_Hlinki, accessed February 22, 2017).

40. SS-Jagdgruppe "Slowakei," a volunteer armed formation composed of Slovaks and Germans (for more on this subject, see "SS-Jagdgruppe 232 'Slowakei,'" https://pl.wikipedia.org/wiki/SS-Jagdgruppe_232_Slowakei, accessed February 22, 2017).

41. Abwehrgruppe 218 (Kampfgruppe "Edelweiß"), a volunteer formation within the SS for special tasks, composed of Slovaks, Don Cossacks, inhabitants of the Caucasus, and Germans (for more on its subject, see "Abwehrgruppe 218," https://pl.wikipedia.org/wiki/Abwehrgruppe_218, accessed February 22, 2017).

42. F. Beer, *Słowacja*, 496.

43. Ibid., 497.

44. Ibid., 541.

45. BA Ludwigsburg, B 162/4249, K 424 Hamburg, Karl Knabl, München, January 8, 1976, 845.

46. YV, JM 2089, ID 3672426, Testimony of Höfle, February 13, 1947.

47. Arch. Sachsenhausen, P3 Schulze, Hermann, Hermann Schulze. Fortsetzung zum Bericht vom Okt./Nov. 1978 und Ergänzung das Strafbataillon Dirlewanger, March 1979.

48. Ibid.

49. BA Ludwigsburg, B 162/19061, V 505 AR 96/79, August 31, 1980, 777.

50. Arch. Sachsenhausen, P3 Schulze, Hermann, Hermann Schulze. Fortsetzung zum Bericht vom Okt./Nov. 1978 und Ergänzung das Strafbataillon Dirlewanger, March 1979.

51. BA Ludwigsburg, B 162/5926, Betrifft: Sammelvorgang Strafsache Dirlewanger, Weiße, Heinsen Rußland–Polen–Ungarn–Tschecho-Slowakei u. Deutschland verbrechen, Berlin 44, May 12, 1972, 1512–14.

52. F. Beer, *Słowacja*, 546.

53. Ibid., 546–47.

54. YV, JM 2089, ID 3672426, Testimony of Höfle, February 13, 1947.

55. Ibid.

56. R. Michaelis, *Dirlewanger*, 45; and H. P. Klausch, *Antifaschisten*, 130.

57. H. P. Klausch, *Antifaschisten*, 130.

58. F. Beer, *Słowacja*, 550.

59. A. Krawczyk, *Słowacja księdza*, 227; and F. Beer, *Słowacja*, 550.

60. BA Ludwigsburg, B 162/19061, Landeskriminalamt Baden-Württemberg Sonderkommission—Zentrale Stelle, z. Zt. Bruchsal, May 27, 1964, 818.

61. Ibid.

62. Ibid.

63. Ibid. Alternatively, Sonderkommando z.b.V. 15, a part of Einsatzgruppe H, which operated in the same area as Dirlewanger's unit, may have been responsible for pacifying Cimenná (BA Ludwigsburg, B 162/19061, I 505 AR-Z 96/79—Schlußvermerk, Ludwigsburg, October 31, 1980, 781).

64. H. P. Klausch, *Antifaschisten*, 132.

65. BA Ludwigsburg, B 162/19061, Landeskriminalamt Baden-Württemberg Sonderkommission—Zentrale Stelle, z. Zt. Bruchsal, May 27, 1964, 818–19.

66. BA Ludwigsburg, B 162/19061, Landeskriminalamt NW—Dezernat 15, z. Zt. Solingen, September 9, 1964, 829–30.

67. Ibid.

68. BA Ludwigsburg, B 162/19061, 5 AR 601/63, Vermerk, Ludwigsburg, November 24, 1964, 840.

69. BA Ludwigsburg, B 162/19061, Landeskriminalamt NW—Dezernat 15, z. Zt. Solingen, September 9, 1964, 829.

70. BA Ludwigsburg, B 162/19061, 5 AR-Nr. 601/63, Buchsal, June 20, 1963, 808–09.

71. A. Krawczyk, *Słowacja księdza*, 228.

72. R. Michaelis, *Dirlewanger*, 45.

73. H. P. Klausch, *Antifaschisten*, 131.

74. S. Kuklińska, *Działalność*, 142.

75. A. Krawczyk, *Słowacja księdza*, 207–08.

76. A *Jagdkommando* was a motorized, militarized pursuit unit. It was also called an emergency expeditionary service. It carried out instant arrests and executions of persons indicated to it, and also antipartisan operations.

77. A. Krawczyk, *Słowacja księdza*, 228.

78. Ibid., 210.

79. BA Ludwigsburg, B 162/16574, Leseabschrift NO-259, Heinz Rotheigner, Freising, August 29, 1945, 296.

80. Arch. Sachsenhausen, P3 Schulze, Hermann, Hermann Schulze. Fortsetzung zum Bericht vom Okt./Nov. 1978 und Ergänzung das Strafbataillon Dirlewanger, March 1979.

Chapter 7

1. Arch. Sachsenhausen, LAG XXX/1, letter from Dirlewanger to Himmler, Gefechtsstand, October 7, 1944, 2–3; and BAB, NS3/401, letter.

2. Arch. Sachsenhausen, LAG XXX/5, Herausgegeben von der Deutschen Lagergemeinschaft Neuengamme der politisch, rassisch und religiös Verfolgten des Naziregimes, Sitz Hamburg, 20 Jahre danach, 1965.

3. H. P. Klausch, *Antifaschisten*, 146.

4. Ibid., 147.

5. BA Ludwigsburg, B 162/16574, DD 2, Vernehmungsniederschrift, Karl Knabl, München, February 1962, 169. According to information gathered by Prof. Dr. Walter Bartel in Buchenwald, drafting prisoners to serve in penal companies of the SS was made highly difficult by the convicts' unwillingness (Arch. Sachsenhausen, LAG

XXX/6, letter from Prof. Dr. Walter Bartel to Rudi Wunderlich, n.d.).

6. Arch. Sachsenhausen, LAG XXX/7, Willi Müller ehem. Häftling im KZ Sachsenhausen Nr. 56538, Zu Dirlewanger? Nein oder Ja?, Berlin, April 24, 1973, 51.

7. Ibid., 52.

8. Ibid., 51.

9. This was a response to Oskar Dirlewanger's letter to Heinrich Himmler of October 7, 1944, and a letter from the *Reichsführer-SS*'s adjutant dated October 15, 1944.

10. YV, JM 2082, ID 3669495, Oranienburg, November 3, 1944.

11. Protective-custody prisoners (*Schutzhäftlinge*)—the institution of protective custody (*Schutzhaft*) was derived from the "Decree for the Protection of People and the Reich" signed by President Paul von Hindenburg on February 28, 1933, the day after the Reichstag fire. It was a penal sanction that was rooted in the nineteenth-century German judicial tradition. However, while previous acts concerning protective custody provided for control of its application by authorized institutions, the procedures introduced by the Nazis did not envisage any supervision over it on the part of national judicial or administrative bodies. This was because it was to be a means of police repression, applied for an undefined period, against which there was no recourse or appeals procedure; neither were any claims for damages possible. The first official legal interpretation concerning protective custody was placed in the Official Monitor of the Prussian Ministry of Justice in connection with the decree of its minister on May 5, 1933. That document indicated the general procedure for restricting personal freedom by police authorities. Because these normative acts did not provide for the prisoner's right to defense, no appeal procedures were foreseen for individuals; neither were time limits for its application precisely defined. The Ministry of the Interior attempted to institute control over *Schutzhaft*, but, faced with an unyielding attitude by the heads of the Gestapo, who wanted to have free rein over its application, on December 17, 1936, the chief of the political police issued a memo according to which *Schutzhaft* was not to be treated as a normative legal category, for the application of which it was unnecessary to prove before the courts that it was justified, but exclusively as a means of eliminating persons deemed to be enemies of the Nazi state and the so-called community of German folk (*Volksgemeinschaft*) from society. On August 28, 1939, the chief of the SS Security Police and the Security Service, SS-Gruppenführer Reinhard Heydrich, issued a memo regarding the necessity to relatively rapidly broaden the institution of *Schutzhaft* to include Poles placed on proscription lists, and to simplify procedures for using protective custody. In wartime, the regulations on *Schutzhaft* were successively modified, the direction of the changes being constant broadening to take into account the growing role of concentration camps in German industry. This was why, for example, on August 27, 1941, the Reich Security Main Office issued another directive, which simplified procedures in this respect: "The

Reichsführer-SS and chief of German police, faced with the fact of increasingly frequent acts and statements hostile to the state and their manifestation after the start of the war against the Soviet Union, has taken radical decisions according to which all instigator priests, Czechs and Poles hostile to Germans, Communists, and also the remaining rabble should without exception be imprisoned for a long time in concentration camps." From 1941, those imprisoned via "protective custody" were given triangles (*winkel*) in only one color: red, which meant the broadly understood category of "political prisoner." For more on the subject, see *KL Lublin 1941–1944*, http://www.majdanek.com.pl/slowniczek/slowniczek%20obozowy.html, accessed December 3, 2017).

12. Preventive-custody prisoners (*Vorbeugungshäftlinge*)—preventive custody was another means of repression, next to protective custody, introduced by the Reich Criminal Police Office (Reichskriminalpolizeiamt, or RKPA) in order to incarcerate further population groups in concentration camps. The rules for its application were harmonized and set out in a decree of the Reich minister of the interior of December 14, 1937, concerning crime prevention. These rules were confirmed in a decree of the Reich minister of the interior on January 25, 1938. They allowed to preventively intern persons who had previously (at least three times) been arrested on counts of political crimes, those convicted of such offenses for at least six months of deprivation of liberty, so-called professional and habitual criminals, and also those who were suspected that they might return to criminal activity, those using false names, without a profession or steady employment, displaying "asocial" behaviors, and those endangering the population by their behavior. This group also included Jehovah's Witnesses and also some traveling Gypsy clans. In practice, people could be interned again even after they had sat their sentence: It was possible for a released prisoner to remain free no longer than several minutes before returning to undergo a prison or camp term of undetermined length, without any input from the prosecution. For more on the subject, see *KL Lublin 1941–1944*, http://www.majdanek.com.pl/slowniczek/slowniczek%20obozowy.html, accessed 3.12.2017; and K. Grünberg, *SS: Gwardia Hitlera* (Warsaw, Poland, 1994).

13. BA Ludwigsburg, B 162/16569, Bisheriges Ermittlungsergebnis über das Sonderkommando "Dirlewanger," n.d., 154.

14. Arch. Sachsenhausen, LAG XXX/4, April–June 1970.

15. Arch. Sachsenhausen, LAG XXX/7, Willi Müller ehem. Häftling im KZ Sachsenhausen Nr. 56538, Zu Dirlewanger? Nein oder Ja?, Berlin, April 24, 1973, 52.

16. Preventive combating of crime pertained to "beggars, tramps (Gypsies), prostitutes, alcoholics, the contagiously ill, particularly those with STDs, persons attempting to elude measures undertaken by the health authorities," and "the workshy and work avoidant" (P. Longerich, *Himmler*, 280–81).

17. Ibid., 281.

18. Paul Lau's letter from Groß-Strehlitz, 12.11.1944, after H. P. Klausch, *Antifaschisten*, 23.

19. H. P. Klausch, *Antifaschisten*, 24. The prisoners most likely numbered 305 (Arch. Sachsenhausen, KAW K16M6, B. Behnke, "Ein Beitrag zur Geschichte des antifaschistischen Widerstandskampfes in Deutschland: Das III. Bataillon des 2. Regiments der Waffen-SS 'Brigade Dirlewanger,'" May 1976, 19).

20. Arch. Sachsenhausen, KAW K16M6, B. Behnke, "Ein Beitrag zur Geschichte des antifaschistischen Widerstandskampfes in Deutschland: Das III. Bataillon des 2. Regiments der Waffen-SS 'Brigade Dirlewanger,'" May 1976, 15–16, 18–19.

21. Ibid., 59.

22. Ibid., 20–22.

23. Ibid., 59.

24. Ibid., 22.

25. Ibid., 27.

26. Ibid.

27. BA Ludwigsburg, B 162/16574, Leseabschrift NO-259, Heinz Rotheigner, Freising, August 29, 1945, 296.

28. Arch. Sachsenhausen, KAW K16M6, B. Behnke, "Ein Beitrag zur Geschichte des antifaschistischen Widerstandskampfes in Deutschland: Das III. Bataillon des 2. Regiments der Waffen-SS 'Brigade Dirlewanger,'" May 1976, 29.

29. Arch. Sachsenhausen, P3 Schulze, Hermann, Hermann Schulze. Fortsetzung zum Bericht vom Okt./Nov. 1978 und Ergänzung das Strafbataillon Dirlewanger, March 1979.

30. BA Ludwigsburg, B 162/21001, 376/45 geh., Meldung über den Einsatz der SS-Brigade Dirlewanger im Raum Ipolysag ab 9.12.1944, 45.

31. Arch. Sachsenhausen, KAW K16M6, B. Behnke, "Ein Beitrag zur Geschichte des antifaschistischen Widerstandskampfes in Deutschland: Das III. Bataillon des 2. Regiments der Waffen-SS 'Brigade Dirlewanger,'" May 1976, 36–37.

32. BA Ludwigsburg, B 162/21001, 376/45 geh., Meldung über den Einsatz der SS-Brigade Dirlewanger im Raum Ipolysag ab 9.12.1944, 45.

33. Ibid.

34. Kriegstagebuch Ia Heeresgruppe Süd, December 10, 1944, after H. P. Klausch, *Antifaschisten*, 142.

35. H. Auerbach, "Viertelsjahrshefte für Zeitgeschichte," in *Die Einheit Dirlewanger*, 1962, 3.

36. BA Ludwigsburg, B 162/21001, 376/45 geh., Meldung über den Einsatz der SS-Brigade Dirlewanger im Raum Ipolysag ab 9.12.1944, 46.

37. Ibid.

38. Ibid.

39. Ibid., 46–47.

40. Military History Archive (M.H. Arch.), "Slovenské národné povstanie," i. é. 297, Nr. 326/44 geh. Kdos. Feindlageoffizier, Betr.: Lage in der Slowakei, Prag, December 11, 1944, 34.

41. BA Ludwigsburg, B 162/21001, 376/45 geh., Meldung über den Einsatz der SS-Brigade Dirlewanger im Raum Ipolysag ab 9.12.1944, 47.

Apart from Dirlewanger's unit, located in these positions were two augmented battalions, a staff regiment (*Rgt. Stab*), 1 artillery unit (1 Art. Abt.), Gr. W. Kp., s.Pak 2/ ungar. Pz. Div. (M.H. Arch., "Slovenské národné povstanie," i. é. 296, Nr. 328/44 geh. Kdos. *Feindlageoffizier*, Betr.: Lage in der Slowakei, Prag, December 12, 1944, 33).

42. H. P. Klausch, *Antifaschisten*, 57.

43. BA Ludwigsburg, B 162/16572, Der Oberstaatsanwalt Flensburg 2 Js 700/61, Karl Keithan, Witzenhausen, May 9, 1963, 258.

44. BA Ludwigsburg, B 162/21001, 376/45 geh., Meldung über den Einsatz der SS-Brigade Dirlewanger im Raum Ipolysag ab 9.12.1944, 47.

45. M.H.Arch., "Slovenské národné povstanie," i. é. 294, Nr. 331/44 geh. Kdos. *Feindlageoffizier*, Betr.: Lage in der Slowakei, Prag, December 14, 1944, 31.

46. Ch. Ingrao, *Czarni myśliwi*, 75.

47. Generaloberst Frießner, Zdradzone bitwy, after R. Michaelis, *Dirlewanger*, 57–58.

48. BA Ludwigsburg, B 162/21001, 376/45 geh., Meldung über den Einsatz der SS-Brigade Dirlewanger im Raum Ipolysag ab 9.12.1944, 48.

49. https://live.warthunder.com/post/690555/en/ (accessed November 18, 2019).

50. BA Ludwigsburg, B 162/15449, Ernst Edler's testimony, n.d.

51. BAB, R/9361/III, letter from Oskar Dirlewanger to Gottlob Berger, December 30, 1944, 843.

52. M.H. Arch., "Slovenské národné povstanie," i. é. 292, Nr. 334/44 geh. Kdos. *Feindlageoffizier*, Betr.: Lage in der Slowakei, Prag, December 16, 1944, 29.

53. Ch. Ingrao, *Czarni myśliwi*, 75.

54. Arch. Sachsenhausen, KAW K16M6, B. Behnke, "Ein Beitrag zur Geschichte des antifaschistischen Widerstandskampfes in Deutschland: Das III. Bataillon des 2. Regiments der Waffen-SS 'Brigade Dirlewanger,'" May 1976, 50.

55. Ibid., 60. Karl Jochheim-Armin testified after the war that the 3rd Battalion, composed mainly of Communists, deserted. He stated that two *Unterführers* who tried to prevent this were shot at the time. This is not confirmed in other archival sources, however (BA Ludwigsburg, B 162/16571, KK III A 4, Vernehmungsniederschrift, Karl Jochheim-Armin, München, April 30, 1971, 12). The event was confirmed by the author of the article "The Mass Deserting of Ipolysag" (https://live.warthunder.com/post/690555/en/, accessed November 18, 2019).

56. BA Ludwigsburg, B 162/21001, 376/45 geh., Meldung über den Einsatz der SS-Brigade Dirlewanger im Raum Ipolysag ab 9 XII 1944, 48.

57. Arch. Sachsenhausen, P3 Schulze, Hermann, Hermann Schulze. Fortsetzung zum Bericht vom Okt./Nov. 1978 und Ergänzung das Strafbataillon Dirlewanger, March 1979.

58. BA Ludwigsburg, B 162/16571, Bayerische Landpolizei 8433 Parsberg, Landpoliceiispektion, Zeugen—Vernehmung zur LPI Parsberg, June 23, 1971, 19–22.

59. Arch. Sachsenhausen, LAG XXX/7, Willi Müller ehem. Häftling im KZ Sachsenhausen Nr. 56538, Zu Dirlewanger? Nein oder Ja?, Berlin, April 24, 1973, 53.

60. Arch. Sachsenhausen, KAW K16M6, B. Behnke, "Ein Beitrag zur Geschichte des antifaschistischen Widerstandskampfes in Deutschland: Das III. Bataillon des 2. Regiments der Waffen-SS 'Brigade Dirlewanger,'" May 1976, 48.

61. Ibid., 52.

62. Arch. Sachsenhausen, LAG XXX/9, "Hans Grundig erzählt von der Fraternisierung deutscher und sowjetischer Truppen, M. Hugk," *Dessauer Kulturspiegel* 11 (1959): 3.

63. BA Ludwigsburg, B 162/16574, Der Oberstaatsanwalt 2 Js 700/61, Arno Händel, Flensburg, April 11, 1962, 146.

64. Arch. Sachsenhausen, P3 Schulze, Hermann, Hermann Schulze. Fortsetzung zum Bericht vom Okt./Nov. 1978 und Ergänzung das Strafbataillon Dirlewanger, March 1979; and Arch. Sachsenhausen, KAW K16M6, B. Behnke, "Ein Beitrag zur Geschichte des antifaschistischen Widerstandskampfes in Deutschland: Das III. Bataillon des 2. Regiments der Waffen-SS 'Brigade Dirlewanger,'" May 1976, 53.

65. M.H.Arch., "Slovenské národné povstanie," i. é. 307, Nr. 45/45 geheim. *Feindlageoffizier*, Betr.: Lage in der Slowakei, Prag, January 6, 1945, 17; BA Ludwigsburg, B 162/21001, Der deutsche Befehlshaber in der Slowakei, 376/45 geh., Preßburg, January 6, 1945, 44; and BA Ludwigsburg, B 162/16574, Leseabschrift NO-259, Heinz Rotheigner, Freising, August 29, 1945, 296.

Chapter 8

1. The *Panzerfaust* is a single-shot, recoilless antitank gun. It was a cheap, easy-to-use, and effective weapon.

2. Kanone 3: German siege gun; and BA Ludwigsburg, B 162/27187, Landeskriminalamt Baden-Württemberg Sonderkommission Zentral Stelle, Tgb. Nr. SK. Zst. III/15-153/65, Georg Severa, Lörrach, May 6, 1965, 25.

3. BA Ludwigsburg, B 162/27187, Landeskriminalamt Baden-Württemberg, Sonderkommission Zentrale Stelle, Otto Hafner, Karlsruhe, June 9, 1965, 39–40.

4. BA Ludwigsburg, B 162/16574, Leseabschrift NO-259, Heinz Rotheigner, Freising, August 29, 1945, 296.

5. https://live.warthunder.com/post/640610/en/ (accessed November 18, 2019).

6. BA Ludwigsburg, B 162/16574, Leseabschrift NO-259, Heinz Rotheigner, Freising, August 29, 1945, 296. This was most likely the Radów camp, located in the vicinity of Lubsko.

7. BA Ludwigsburg, B 162/27187, Landeskriminalamt Baden-Württemberg, Sonderkommission Zentrale Stelle, Otto Hafner, Karlsruhe, June 9, 1965, 40.

8. Sources give different dates for the capture of Gubin. According to some, fighting for the town lased from February 19 to 26, 1945. Heavy battles for the Gubin Hills, called the Mountains of Death, went on until February 28 (see also "Gubin," http://www.gubin.pl/index.php?g=2&p=14, accessed January 29, 2019). Others state that the fighting for Gubin lasted until April: the right-bank part of the town Guben (now Gubin) was finally captured by the Red Army on April 20, 1945, while left-bank Guben was captured on April 24, 1945 (*Czy 24 kwietnia 1945 zdobyto Gubin?*, https://gazetalubuska.pl/czy-24-kwietnia-1945-zdobyto-gubin/ar/7850653, accessed February 7, 2019).

9. Fritz Schmedes, born October 7, 1894, in Schwarme and died in February 1952 in Springe. *SS-Brigadeführer* in the Waffen-SS and police from November 9, 1943, he earlier served in the 4th SS Panzer Grenadier Division Polizei (Kdr. 4. SS-Pol.Pz.Gr.Div.). His party number was 5,240,168, and in the SS, 420,790: see *Diensaltersliste der Schutzstaffel der NSDAP (SS-Oberst-Gruppenführer–SS Standartenführer) Stand vom 9. November 1944* (Berlin, 1944), 21; and S. Kuklińska, *Działalność*, 155.

10. M. Olejniczak, *Jak wyzwalano nasze ziemie*, http://krzystkowice.eisp.pl/artykuly/a04.html (accessed November 18, 2019); and M. Kaźmierczak, *Bitwa o Bieniów: Operacja Dolnośląska; Bitwa nad Bobrem*, http://bieniow.cba.pl/bitwa_o_benau.htm (accessed November 18, 2019).

11. Karl Vieregge claimed that according to gossip, Dirlewanger left the unit in March 1945 in the settlement of "Weiszak/Neisse" (on the Neisse) because he wanted to evacuate his mother (BA Ludwigsburg, B 162/16573, LKA-NW-Dez.15, Wilhelm Karl Vieregge, Plettenberg, July 11, 1962, 458).

12. R. Michaelis, *Das SS-Sonderkommando "Dirlewanger,"* 13.

13. *70 rocznica zajęcia miasta Sommerfeld (późniejszego Lubska)*, http://www.stacjalubsko.pl/70-rocznica-zajecia-miasta-sommerfeld-pozniejszego-lubska/ (accessed January 29, 2019); M. Kaźmierczak, *Bitwa o Bieniów: Operacja Dolnośląska; Bitwa nad Bobrem*, http://bieniow.cba.pl/bitwa_o_benau.htm (accessed November 18, 2019); and M. Olejniczak, *Jak wyzwalano nasze ziemie*, http://krzystkowice.eisp.pl/artykuly/a04.html (accessed November 18, 2019).

14. BA Ludwigsburg, B 162/16574, Leseabschrift NO-259, Heinz Rotheigner, Freising, August 29, 1945, 297.

15. R. Michaelis, *Das SS-Sonderkommando "Dirlewanger,"* 13.

16. B. Dolata, *Wyzwolenie Dolnego Śląska w 1945 r.* (Wrocław, Poland, 1985); and M. Kaźmierczak, *Bitwa o Bieniów: Operacja Dolnośląska; Bitwa nad Bobrem*, http://bieniow.cba.pl/bitwa_o_benau.htm (accessed November 18, 2019).

17. *70 rocznica zajęcia miasta Sommerfeld (późniejszego Lubska)*, http://www.stacjalubsko.pl/70-rocznica-zajecia-miasta-sommerfeld-pozniejszego-lubska/ (accessed January 29, 2019).

18. R. Michaelis, *Das SS-Sonderkommando "Dirlewanger,"* 13.

19. BA Ludwigsburg, B 162/16571, Bayerisches Landeskriminalamt IIIa/SK Tgb.Nr. 489/62, Harald Momm, n.d., 45–7; and https://live.warthunder.com/post/640610/en/ (accessed November 18, 2019).

20. https://live.warthunder.com/post/640610/en/ (accessed November 18, 2019); 1945, *Walki o Guben*, https://www.youtube.com/watch?v=nbe_VRy1CMY (accessed September 15, 2018); and "Die Deutsche Wochenschau," 1945, nr. 754.

21. Ivan Konev, born December 28, 1897, and died May 21, 1973. Soviet military commander, marshal, one of the commanders in chief during the Berlin operation (for more, see https://de.wikipedia.org/wiki/Iwan_Stepanowitsch_Konew, accessed February 7, 2019).

22. Karol Świerczewski, born February 22, 1897, and died March 28, 1947. Colonel general of the Red Army and general of the branch in the Polish People's Army. For more, see https://de.wikipedia.org/wiki/Karol_%C5%9Awierczewski (accessed February 7, 2019); http://muzhp.pl/pl/e/1844/smierc-generala-karola-swierczewskiego (accessed February 7, 2019); and *Czy 24 kwietnia 1945 zdobyto Gubin?*, https://gazetalubuska.pl/czy-24-kwietnia-1945-zdobyto-gubin/ar/7850653 (accessed 7.2.2019).

23. *70 rocznica zajęcia miasta Sommerfeld (późniejszego Lubska)*, http://www.stacjalubsko.pl/70-rocznica-zajecia-miasta-sommerfeld-pozniejszego-lubska/ (accessed January 29, 2019). For more about Walther Nehring, see https://de.wikipedia.org/wiki/Walther_Nehring (accessed January 29, 2019).

24. BA Ludwigsburg, B 162/27187, Landeskriminalamt Baden-Württemberg Sonderkommission Zentral Stelle, Tgb. Nr. SK. Zst. III/15-153/65, Georg Severa, Lörrach, May 6, 1965, 25. Otto Hafner stated that it was a factory that produced hats (Hutfabrik) (BA Ludwigsburg, B 162/27187, Landeskriminalamt Baden-Württemberg, Sonderkommission Zentrale Stelle, Otto Hafner, Karlsruhe, June 9, 1965, 40).

25. BA Ludwigsburg, B 162/27187, Landeskriminalamt Baden-Württemberg Sonderkommission Zentral Stelle, Tgb. Nr. SK. Zst. III/15-153/65, Z. Zt. Lörrach, May 6, 1965, 26.

26. BA Ludwigsburg, B 162/27187, Landeskriminalamt Baden-Württemberg, Sonderkommission Zentrale Stelle, Otto Hafner, Karlsruhe, June 9, 1965, 41.

27. From summer 1944, *Volksgrenadier* divisions had started to be formed. They were, in terms of organizational structure, "ordinary infantry divisions, whose manpower being very similar to their manpower, 'model 1945.'" According to it, a *Volksgrenadier* division was to number 11,197 people, including around 691 *Hiwi* personnel. They were distinguished by the epithet 'folk' (*volks*), which had begun to be given at this time to many units, both infantry and other troop types, and primarily newly formed or reorganized ones. They were to be an external manifestation of the alleged democratization of the army. They held a deeper significance, however. The staff of the *Reichsführer-SS*—at the SS Main Office (SS-Führungshauptamt)—played a significant part in the formation of *Volksgrenadier* divisions. It was responsible, as

an order of July 17, 1944, emphasized for the selection of National Socialist officers and NCO staff for these divisions. "The objective was for command positions to be occupied by people who declared their attachment to National Socialism, and thus to strengthen these units' morale. Pursuant to the aforementioned order, the whole personnel of the grenadier division was subject to SS disciplinary regulations and courts and had a special chain of command, and the commanding staff could be transferred only to positions within SS units. . . . In total, fifty *Volksgrenadier* divisions were organized." T. Sawicki, *Niemieckie wojska lądowe na froncie wschodnim, czerwiec 1944–maj 1945 (struktura)* (Warsaw, Poland, 1987), 66–67; BA Ludwigsburg, B 162/21001, Der Reichsführer-SS Chefadjutant, Tgb. Nr. 2084/45 geh., February 19, 1945, 14; and BA Ludwigsburg, B 162/16569, Bisheriges Ermittlungsergebnis über das Sonderkommando "Dirlewanger," n.d., 155.

28. BA Ludwigsburg, B 162/29251, Bayerisches Landeskriminalamt IIIa/SK, Tgb.Nr. 489/62, Dr. Franz Schmuckerschlag, München, May 29, 1962, 36.

29. BA Ludwigsburg, B 162/16570, Dr. Klietmann, *Die Waffen-SS: eine Dokumentation*, 1965, 320.

30. BA Ludwigsburg, B 162/29251, Bayerisches Landeskriminalamt IIIa/SK, Tgb.Nr. 489/62, Dr. Franz Schmuckerschlag, München, May 29, 1962, 37.

31. Patches contained crossed rifles with a grenade instead of the SS runes.

32. H. Maeger, *Utracony honor, zdradzona wiara: Relacja żołnierza Leibstandarte SS Adolf Hitler* (Międzyzdroje and Kraków, Poland, 2008), 227–28.

33. BA Ludwigsburg, B 162/29251, Bayerisches Landeskriminalamt IIIa/SK, Tgb.Nr. 489/62, Dr. Franz Schmuckerschlag, München, May 29, 1962, 39.

34. Arch. Sachsenhausen, P3 Schulze, Hermann, Hermann Schulze. Fortsetzung zum Bericht vom Okt./Nov. 1978 und Ergänzung das Strafbataillon Dirlewanger, March 1979.

35. BA Ludwigsburg, B 162/27187, Landeskriminalamt Baden-Württemberg Sonderkommission Zentral Stelle, Tgb. Nr. SK. Zst. III/15-153/65, Georg Severa, Lörrach, May 6, 1965, 31–32.

36. BA Ludwigsburg, B 162/27187, LKA/NW Dez. 15, Oskar Blömer, Bonn, January 6, 1967, 128.

37. Ibid.

38. Ch. Kreutzmüller, *Lieberose—Centrum Dokumentacji KZ*, http://www.miejscapamieci.org/obozy/mpc/Memorial/mpa/show/mp-place/lieberose-centrum-dokumentacji-kz/ (accessed April 3, 2018).

39. BA Ludwigsburg, B 162/27187, Landeskriminalamt Baden-Württemberg Sonderkommission Zentral Stelle, Tgb. Nr. SK. Zst. III/15-153/65, Georg Severa, Lörrach, May 6, 1965, 32.

40. Ibid., 31–32.

41. BA Ludwigsburg, B 162/27187, LKA/NW Dez. 15, Oskar Blömer, Bonn, January 6, 1967, 128–29.

42. BA Ludwigsburg, B 162/27187, Landeskriminalamt Baden-Württemberg, Sonderkommission Zentrale Stelle, Otto Hafner, Karlsruhe, June 9, 1965, 45, 48. Oskar Blömer estimated that these prisoners may have numbered even up to a thousand (BA Ludwigsburg, B 162/27187, LKA/NW Dez. 15, Oskar Blömer, Bonn, January 6, 1967, 129).

43. BA Ludwigsburg, B 162/27187, LKA/NW Dez. 15, Oskar Blömer, Bonn, January 6, 1967, 130.

44. In the original: "Für diesem Zweck erhielten die Wachposten 1 Gewehr und 3 Schuss Munition." (ibid., 129).

45. BA Ludwigsburg, B 162/27187, Landeskriminalamt Baden-Württemberg, Sonderkommission Zentrale Stelle, Otto Hafner, Karlsruhe, June 9, 1965, 45, 48; and BA Ludwigsburg, B 162/27187, LKA/NW Dez. 15, z. Zt. Bonn, January 6, 1967, 130. Oskar Blömer added that every day during the morning assembly, the names of the convicts and members of the 36th Waffen-SS Grenadier Division assigned to perform the executions were read out (BA Ludwigsburg, B 162/27187, LKA/NW Dez. 15, Oskar Blömer, Bonn, January 6, 1967, 129–30).

46. BA Ludwigsburg, B 162/27187, LKA/NW Dez. 15, Oskar Blömer, Bonn, January 6, 1967, 129.

47. BA Ludwigsburg, B 162/27187, Landeskriminalamt Baden-Württemberg Sonderkommission Zentral Stelle, Tgb. Nr. SK. Zst. III/15-153/65, Georg Severa, Lörrach, May 6, 1965, 33–34.

48. BA Ludwigsburg, B 162/27187, LKA/NW Dez. 15, Oskar Blömer, Bonn, January 6, 1967, 129.

49. H. Maeger, *Utracony honor, zdradzona wiara*, 224.

50. Ibid., 239.

51. Ibid., 239–40.

52. Ibid., 241.

53. Maeger cited data after J. Piekałkiewicz, *Druga wojna światowa* (Augsburg, Germany, 1993); and P. Yong, *Wielki Atlas II wojny światowej* (Monachium, Germany, 1974); quotation from H. Maeger, *Utracony honor, zdradzona wiara*, 241.

54. H. Maeger, *Utracony honor, zdradzona wiara*, 241–42.

55. BA Ludwigsburg, B 162/27187, Landeskriminalamt Baden-Württemberg, Sonderkommission Zentrale Stelle, Otto Hafner, Karlsruhe, June 9, 1965, 47.

56. Arch. Sachsenhausen, LAG XXX/4, April–June 1970.

57. https://live.warthunder.com/post/693225/en/ (accessed November 18, 2019); A. Lasik, *Führerliste Waffen-SS*, typescript; H. [illegible]lausch, *Antifaschisten*; BA Ludwigsburg, B 162/16571, Bayerisches Landeskriminalamt IIIa/SK Tgb.Nr. 489/62, Harald Momm, n.d., 45–46; BA Ludwigsburg, B 162/29251, Tgb. Nr. SK. Zst. III/2-157/61, Karl Richard Engel, Pforzheim, August 24, 1961, 14; BA Ludwigsburg, B 162/16574, Der Oberstaatsanwalt, 2 Js 700/61, Walter Fentznahn, Flensburg, November

23, 1961, 15; and BA Ludwigsburg, B 162/16571, Der Oberstaatsanwalt—2 Js 700/61, Gustav Strumpf, Flensburg, January 17, 1962, 90.

58. BA Ludwigsburg, B 162/16574, Leseabschrift NO-259, Heinz Rotheigner, Freising, August 29, 1945, 297.

59. BA Ludwigsburg, B 162/5922, Tgb. Nr. SK. Zst. I/3-180/62, Friedrich Walter, Mörsch, May 21, 1963, 617.

60. BA Ludwigsburg, B 162/27187, Landeskriminalamt Baden-Württemberg, Sonderkommission Zentrale Stelle, Otto Hafner, Karlsruhe, June 9, 1965, 47.

61. BA Ludwigsburg, B 162/27187, Landeskriminalamt Baden-Württemberg, Sonderkommission Zentral Stelle, Tgb. Nr. SK. Zst. III/15-153/65, Z. Zt. Lörrach, May 6, 1965, 35.

62. BA Ludwigsburg, B 162/27187, Landeskriminalamt Baden-Württemberg, Sonderkommission Zentral Stelle, Tgb. Nr. SK. Zst. III/15-153/65, Georg Severa, Lörrach, May 6, 1965, 25, 33–35.

63. BA Ludwigsburg, B 162/27187, Landeskriminalamt Baden-Württemberg, Sonderkommission Zentral Stelle, z. Zt. Karlsruhe, June 9, 1965, 39, 47.

64. BA Ludwigsburg, B 162/27187, Landeskriminalamt Baden-Württemberg, Sonderkommission Zentrale Stelle, Karl Gerber, Nürtingen, July 6, 1965, 59–60.

65. BA Ludwigsburg, B 162/16573, Der Oberstaatsanwalt 2 Js 700/61, Karl Wenzel, Weißenbrunn, April 2, 1962, 323.

66. BA Ludwigsburg, B 162/16570, Dr. Klietmann, Die Waffen-SS—eine Dokumentation, 1965, 319.

67. H. Maeger, *Utracony honor, zdradzona wiara*, 243.

68. Ibid., 245–71.

69. Ibid., 266.

70. H. Brunnegger, *Kto sieje wiatr . . . Opowieść żołnierza dywizji SS Totenkopf* (Kraków, Poland, 2005), 311–12.

71. *Cmentarz leśny w Halbe*, https://liberationroute.pl/germany/spots/h/halbe-forest-cemetery (accessed October 16, 2017).

72. BA Ludwigsburg, B 162/16573, LKA-NW-Dez.15, Wilhelm Karl Vieregge, Plettenberg, July 11, 1962, 456.

73. BA Ludwigsburg, B 162/28392, Sonderkommission Hamburg, 147 Js 11/71 U, Gerhard Hellkamp, Wattenscheid, June 28, 1973, 460.

74. BA Ludwigsburg, B 162/16574, Zentrale Stelle der Landesjustizverwaltungen 11 AR 1210/62, Ludwigsburg, August 30, 1962, 217–18.

Chapter 9

1. In the original: "ordentlicher Kerl" (BA Ludwigsburg, B 162/16572, Anlage zur Niederschrift, Oskar Henning, May 5, 1962 r., 196.

Fragments of this chapter appeared in S. Kuklińska, *Działalność*, 161–73.

2. A. Richie, *Warsaw 1944*, 45

3. BA Ludwigsburg, B 162/29251, LKA-NW-Dez.15, Stein Johannes, Bochum, July 3, 1962, 71.

4. Ibid.

5. Ibid.

6. Ibid.

7. BA Ludwigsburg, B 162/16570, Reichsführer-SS Himmler auf der Gauleitertagung am 3. August 1944 in Posen, 255.

8. YV, JM 2089, ID 3672426, Testimony of Höfle, February 13, 1947.

9. H. P. Klausch, *Antifaschisten*, 131.

10. BA Ludwigsburg, B 162/28392, Fortsetzung der Vernehmung vom 5 VI 1974, SS-Hauptsturmführer Wilke, Peine, June 6, 1974, 638.

11. Gerret Korsemann—SSPF in the Stanisławów and Rostov District. He replaced Carl Pückler-Burghaus in this position on March 24, 1943. In 1943 (after being recalled in July by Himmler), he held the post of HSSPF Russland-Mitte. He planned Operations Zauberflöte, Cottbus, and Günther.

12. P. W. Blood, *Siepacze*, 248.

13. BA Ludwigsburg, B 162/5924, 45 Js 30/64, Verfügung, Gottlob Berger, Dortmund, October 15, 1964, 1148, translated by K. Kupiszewska after Polish translation by J. Kalemba.

14. BA Ludwigsburg, B 162/16574, Der Oberstaatsanwalt 2Js 700/61, Bauer Emil, Flensburg, October 24, 1961, 65.

15. BA Ludwigsburg, B 162/4249, K 424 Hamburg, Franz Stümpfl, Grafenau, June 25, 1976, 982.

16. BA Ludwigsburg, B 162/16572, Anlage zur Vernehmung vom 20. Februar, Helmut Lewandowski, n.d., 189.

17. Ch. Ingrao, *Czarni myśliwi*, 119.

18. BA Ludwigsburg, B 162/16574, Der Oberstaatsanwalt 2 Js 700/61, Albert Venderbusch, Flensburg, April 5, 1962, 135.

19. Dirlewanger was his commander from 1940 until the fall of the Third Reich.

20. BA Ludwigsburg, B 162/5920, Abschrift, Der Oberstaatsanwalt 2 Js 700/61, November 30, 1961, 318.

21. BA Ludwigsburg, B 162/5922, Tgb. Nr. SK. Zst. I/3-180/62, Friedrich Walter, Mörsch, May 21, 1963, 621.

22. BA Ludwigsburg, B 162/29251, LKA-NW-Dez. 15, Peter Erretkamps, Kevelaer, July 24, 1962, 128.

23. AIPN GK, 103/72 SS-Hauptsturmführer Dirlewanger's interrogation, Lublin, October 14, 1941.

24. Ibid., Erich Selzer's testimony, Lublin, October 9, 1941.

25. BA Ludwigsburg, B 162/16574, Der Oberstaatsanwalt, 2 Js 700/61, Adalbert Daschner, Flensburg, April 5, 1962, 28.

26. BA Ludwigsburg, B 162/16573, Der Oberstaatsanwalt 2 Js 700/61, Walter Escher, Lengfeld, January 28, 1962, 317.

27. One of those who termed him thus was Walter Fentzahn, who joined Dirlewanger's unit in mid-1943, was wounded and returned only at the end of that year, and was wounded again in 1944 (BA Ludwigsburg, B 162/16574, Der Oberstaatsanwalt, 2 Js 700/61, Walter Fentzahn, Flensburg, November 23, 1961, 15).

28. BAB, ZM 1454, Heinz Feiertag's testimony, Lublin, November 18, 1941, 115.

29. BA Ludwigsburg, B 162/29251, Gespräch zwischen Herrn Heinz Feiertag, ehemals Hauptsturmführer der LAH und Herrn Fritz Langeur [illegible word], May 22, 1960, 60.

30. BA Ludwigsburg, B 162/16572, Der Oberstaatsanwalt 2 Js 700/61, Franz Bauser, Flensburg, z. Zt. Göppingen, February 5, 1962, 182–85.

31. BA Ludwigsburg, B 162/5923, Bayerisches Landeskriminalamt IIIa/SK K 6259, Alfred Paul Koziel, Ansbach, March 15, 1964, 978.

32. BA Ludwigsburg, B 162/16573, Der Oberstaatsanwalt 2 Js 700/61, Karl Wenzel, Weißenbrunn, April 2, 1962, 326.

33. BA Ludwigsburg, B 162/16574, Der Oberstaatsanwalt 2Js 700/61, Bauer Emil, Flensburg, October 24, 1961, 65.

34. BA Ludwigsburg, B 162/5920, Abschrift, Der Oberstaatsanwalt 2 Js 700/61, November 30, 1961, 320.

35. BA Ludwigsburg, B 162/16574, Der Oberstaatsanwalt, 2 Js 700/61, Adalbert Daschner, Flensburg, April 5, 1962, 29.

36. BA Ludwigsburg, B 162/16574, Der Oberstaatsanwalt 2Js 700/61, Heinrich Arndt, Flensburg, January 30, 1961, 80.

37. BA Ludwigsburg, B 162/29251, Gespräch zwischen Herrn Heinz Feiertag, ehemals Hauptsturmführer der LAH und Herrn Fritz Langeur [illegible word], May 22, 1960, 63.

38. BA Ludwigsburg, B 162/16572, Der Oberstaatsanwalt 2 Js 700/61, Paul Zimmermann, Stuttgart, July 1, 1963, 265.

39. BA Ludwigsburg, B 162/16574, Der Oberstaatsanwalt, 2 Js 700/61, Adalbert Daschner, Flensburg, April 5, 1962, 29; and BA Ludwigsburg, B 162/16574, Der Oberstaatsanwalt 2Js 700/61, Heinrich Arndt, Flensburg, January 30, 1961, 80.

40. BA Ludwigsburg, B 162/16574, Der Oberstaatsanwalt 2 Js 700/61, Karl Engel, October 25, 1961, 49.

41. BA Ludwigsburg, B 162/16571, Der Oberstaatsanwalt 2 Js 700/61, January 18, 1962, 119.

42. BA Ludwigsburg, B 162/29251, Gespräch zwischen Herrn Heinz Feiertag, ehemals Hauptsturmführer der LAH und Herrn Fritz Langeur [illegible word], May 22, 1960, 61–62.

43. BA Ludwigsburg, B 162/16574, Der Oberstaatsanwalt 2 Js 700/61, Karl Engel, Flensburg, October 25, 1961, 49.

44. BA Ludwigsburg, B 162/16571, Der Oberstaatsanwalt 2 Js 700/61, April 7, 1962, 129; and BA Ludwigsburg, B 162/16574, Der Oberstaatsanwalt 2Js 700/61, Heinrich Arndt, Flensburg, January 30, 1961, 81.

45. BA Ludwigsburg, B 162/5920, Abschrift, Der Oberstaatsanwalt 2 Js 700/61, November 30, 1961, 320.

46. BA Ludwigsburg, B 162/16574, Der Oberstaatsanwalt 2 Js 700/61, April 5, 1962, 28.

47. BA Ludwigsburg, B 162/16574, Der Oberstaatsanwalt 2 Js 700/61, Arno Händel, April 11, 1962, 144.

48. BA Ludwigsburg, B 162/5920, Der Oberstaatsanwalt 2 Js 700/61, April 14, 1962, 323.

49. BA Ludwigsburg, B 162/5920, Abschrift, Der Oberstaatsanwalt 2 Js 700/61, November 30, 1961, 320.

50. BA Ludwigsburg, B 162/5920, Der Oberstaatsanwalt 2 Js 700/61, April 9, 1962, 322.

51. BA Ludwigsburg, B 162/16574, Der Oberstaatsanwalt 2 Js 700/61, Arno Händel, April 11, 1962, 144.

52. BA Ludwigsburg, B 162/29251, LKA-NW-Dez.15, Stein Johannes, Bochum, July 3, 1962, 70.

53. BA Ludwigsburg, B 162/5920, Der Oberstaatsanwalt 2 Js 700/61, April 9, 1962, 322.

54. BA Ludwigsburg, B 162/5920, Der Oberstaatsanwalt 2 Js 700/61, Josef Rau, April 14, 1962, 323–24.

55. BA Ludwigsburg, B 162/29251, LKA-NW-Dez. 15, Peter Erretkamps, Kevelaer, July 24, 1962, 128.

56. BA Ludwigsburg, B 162/16574, Der Oberstaatsanwalt 2Js 700/61, Heinrich Arndt, Flensburg, January 30, 1961, 82.

57. BA Ludwigsburg, B 162/16571, Der Oberstaatsanwalt 2 Js 700/61, April 7, 1962, 129.

58. BA Ludwigsburg, B 162/29251, LKA-NW-Dez.15, Stein Johannes, Bochum, July 3, 1962, 72.

59. Adalbert Daschner witnessed these punitive executions (BA Ludwigsburg, B 162/16574, Der Oberstaatsanwalt, 2 Js 700/61, Adalbert Daschner, Flensburg, April 5, 1962, 28–29).

60. H. P. Klausch, *Antifaschisten*, 69.

61. Ibid.

62. Ibid.

63. BA Ludwigsburg, B 162/16574, Der Oberstaatsanwalt, 2 Js 700/61, Adalbert Daschner, April 5, 1962, 29–30.

64. BA Ludwigsburg, B 162/5922, Tgb. Nr. SK. Zst. I/3-180/62, Friedrich Walter, Mörsch, May 21, 1963, 621.

65. BA Ludwigsburg, B 162/16574, Der Oberstaatsanwalt, 2 Js 700/61, Adalbert Daschner, Flensburg, April 5, 1962, 30.

66. BA Ludwigsburg, B 162/29251, LKA-NW-Dez. 15, Paul Dorn, Lüdenscheid, July 4, 1962, 79.

67. Ibid., 82.

68. BA Ludwigsburg, B 162/29251, Vernehmungsniederschrift. Karl Richard Engel, Pforzheim, August 24, 1961, 7–13.

69. BA Ludwigsburg, B 162/29251, LKA-NW-Dez. 15, Paul Dorn, Lüdenscheid, July 4, 1962, 85.

70. Ibid., 79.

71. Ibid., 83–84.

72. H. P. Klausch, *Antifaschisten*, 70.

73. BA Ludwigsburg, B 162/16574, Der Oberstaatsanwalt 2Js 700/61, Bauer Emil, Flensburg, October 24, 1961, 65.

74. BA Ludwigsburg, B 162/16574, Der Oberstaatsanwalt 2 Js 700/61, Artur Schuldt, Kiel, January 22, 1963, 203.

75. Arch. Sachsenhausen, LAG XXX/8, Deutsche Konzentrationslager: Aus der schriftlichen Erklärung des Grenadiers René Gaston Ferderer vom Sonderkommando der SS "Dirlewanger" vom 12 VII 1944, Biografische Angaben, July 31, 1944, 15–16.

76. Ibid., 16.

77. H. P. Klausch, *Antifaschisten*, 134.

78. BA Ludwigsburg, B 162/16573, Der Oberstaatsanwalt 2 Js 700/61, Viktor Zerfaß, April 4, 1962, 331–32.

79. Ibid., 332.

80. BA Ludwigsburg, B 162/16571, Der Oberstaatsanwalt 2 Js 700/61, Flensburg, z. Zt. Plettenberg, November 30, 1961, 84.

81. Ibid.

82. BA Ludwigsburg, B 162/16574, Der Oberstaatsanwalt 2 Js 700/61, Artur Schuldt, Kiel, January 22, 1963, 203.

83. BA Ludwigsburg, B 162/16574, Der Oberstaatsanwalt 2 Js 700/61, Heinrich Arndt, Flensburg, January 30, 1961, 81.

84. BA Ludwigsburg, B 162/16574, Der Oberstaatsanwalt 2 Js 700/61, Karl Jochheim-Armin, Flensburg, February 1, 1962, 115.

85. BA Ludwigsburg, B 162/16574, Der Oberstaatsanwalt 2Js 700/61, Heinrich Arndt, Flensburg, January 30, 1961, 81.

86. BA Ludwigsburg, B 162/29251, LKA-NW-Dez. 15, Paul Dorn, Lüdenscheid, July 4, 1962, 86.

87. Ibid., 86–87.

88. Arch. Sachsenhausen, P3 Schulze, Hermann, Hermann Schulze. Fortsetzung zum Bericht vom Okt./Nov. 1978 und Ergänzung das Strafbataillon Dirlewanger, March 1979.

89. Arch. Sachsenhausen, KAW K16M6, B. Behnke, "Ein Beitrag zur Geschichte des antifaschistischen Widerstandskampfes in Deutschland: Das III. Bataillon des 2. Regiments der Waffen-SS 'Brigade Dirlewanger,'" May 1976, 20.

90. BA Ludwigsburg, B 162/16574, Der Oberstaatsanwalt 2Js 700/61, Heinrich Arndt, Flensburg, January 30, 1961, 80.

91. BA Ludwigsburg, B 162/5920, Abschrift, Der Oberstaatsanwalt 2 Js 700/61, November 30, 1961, 320.

92. BA Ludwigsburg, B 162/5920, Abschrift, Der Oberstaatsanwalt 2 Js 700/61, April 3, 1962, 321. This is confirmed in other soldiers' testimonies, including "er war selbst mit vorne bei der kämpfenden Truppe" (BA Ludwigsburg, B 162/16574, Der Oberstaatsanwalt 2Js 700/61, Heinrich Arndt, Flensburg, January 30, 1961, 80).

93. BA Ludwigsburg, B 162/16574, Der Oberstaatsanwalt 2 Js 700/61, Albert Venderbusch, Flensburg, April 5, 1962, 135.

94. BA Ludwigsburg, B 162/16574, Der Oberstaatsanwalt 2 Js 700/61, Karl Jochheim-Armin, Flensburg, February 1, 1962, 115.

95. Drunkenness and revelry were nothing exceptional in the SS. Himmler often had to call his commanders to order and punish them for abusing alcohol. For instance, SS-Obergruppenführer Friedrich Jeckeln, higher SS and police leader in Brunswick, received a warning for drunk driving in 1939 ("He rushed through towns and villages in his car at a speed of 80–100 kph, with "no heed to drivers and pedestrians"). Jeckeln explained that he had drunk only "four, maybe five glasses of Moselle wine," "three of four schnappses at the most," and another "three glasses of beer at the most." Himmler took no consequences. In 1936, an altercation took place between SS-Brigadeführer Kaul and SS-Oberführer Unger, who were drunk and spilled beer and wine over each other's uniforms. Von dem Bach wanted to initiate formal proceedings, but Himmler only reprimanded them. Kurt von Gottberg, the commander of Kampfgruppe von Gottberg, had a big alcohol problem. By 1936 he was banned from consuming it for three years after he lost his foot in an accident caused by alcohol abuse. These were not the only cases. Alcohol problems in the SS were so serious that Himmler issued decrees forbidding alcohol consumption, believing this to be the best method for disciplining alcoholics. More examples: P. Longerich, *Himmler*; and Ch. W. Sydnor, *Żołnierze zagłady: Dywizja SS "Totenkopf" 1933–1945* (Warsaw, Poland, 1998).

96. BA Ludwigsburg, B 162/5920, Der Oberstaatsanwalt 2 Js 700/61, April 14, 1962, 323.

97. BA Ludwigsburg, B 162/16574, Der Oberstaatsanwalt, 2 Js 700/61, Adalbert Daschner, April 5, 1962, 29.

98. BA Ludwigsburg, B 162/16574, Der Oberstaatsanwalt 2Js 700/61, Bauer Emil, Flensburg, October 24, 1961, 65.

99. BA Ludwigsburg, B 162/16574, Der Oberstaatsanwalt 2 Js 700/61, Albert Venderbusch, Flensburg, April 5, 1962, 136.

100. BA Ludwigsburg, B 162/16574, Der Oberstaatsanwalt 2 Js 700/61, Arno Händel, April 11, 1962, 143.

101. Ibid.

102. BA Ludwigsburg, B 162/16571, Bayerisches Landeskriminalamt IIIa/SK, Tgb.Nr. 489/62, Harald Momm, n.d., 48.

103. Artur Schulde also mentioned this in his testimony: "Dieser [Wally Geißmann] hatte eine Frau vergewaltigt und geplündert. Er ist in meiner Gegenwart aufgehangen worden." (BA Ludwigsburg, B 162/16574, n.d., 203).

104. H. P. Klausch, *Antifaschisten*, 144.

105. Arch. Sachsenhausen, LAG XXX/4, April–June 1970.

Chapter 10

1. BA Ludwigsburg, B 162/16592, Tgb. No. G5/405/60 Da, Ermittlungssache gegen Dr. Oskar Dirlewanger, früherer SS-Oberst, geb. 26 IX 1895 in Würzburg, 15 VII 1960, 140.

2. Ibid.

3. Ch. Ingrao, *Czarni myśliwi*, 257.

4. S. Kuklińska, *Działalność*, 177.

5. This chapter appeared in the book: ibid., 178–88.

6. W. Radlow, *Altshausen: Opfer des Todesmarches*, http://www.dsk-nsdoku-oberschwaben.de/de/erinnerungswege/ergaenzungsheft-neu-2015/altshausen-opfer-des-todesmarsches.html (accessed September 11, 2015).

7. Ibid.

8. Sta Ludwigsburg, EL 317 III Bü 142, Az.: II/Mi/3355/60, Ermittlungsverfahren gegen Dr. Dirlewanger Oskar, wegen Mord, July 8, 1960.

9. Ibid.

10. BA Ludwigsburg, B 162/16592, 6. Füssinger Anton, n.d., 101.

11. BA Ludwigsburg, B 162/16592, 2 Js 6366/60, Staatsanwaltschaft Ravensburg: Geschehen am 30. Juni 1960, June 30, 1960, 107.

12. Sta Ludwigsburg, EL 317 III Bü 142, Az.: II/Mi/3355/60, Ermittlungsverfahren gegen Dr. Dirlewanger Oskar, wegen Mord, July 8, 1960.

13. Ibid.

14. BA Ludwigsburg, B 162/16592, 2 Js 6366/60, Staatsanwaltschaft Ravensburg. Geschehen am 30. Juni 1960, June 30, 1960, 107–08.

15. BA Ludwigsburg, B 162/16592, 6. Füssinger Anton, n.d., 102.

16. Sta Ludwigsburg, EL 317 III Bü 142, Az.: II/Mi/3355/60, Ermittlungsverfahren gegen Dr. Dirlewanger Oskar, wegen Mord, July 8, 1960.

17. BA Ludwigsburg, B 162/16592, 2 Js 6366/60, Staatsanwaltschaft Ravensburg. Geschehen am 30. Juni 1960, June 30, 1960, 108.

18. Sta Ludwigsburg, EL 317 III Bü 142, Az.: II/Mi/3355/60, Ermittlungsverfahren gegen Dr. Dirlewanger Oskar, wegen Mord, July 8, 1960.

19. Ibid.

20. BA Ludwigsburg, B 162/16592, 2 Js 6366/60, Staatsanwaltschaft Ravensburg. Geschehen am 30. Juni 1960, June 30, 1960, 108.

21. Sta Ludwigsburg, EL 317 III Bü 142, Az.: II/Mi/3355/60, Ermittlungsverfahren gegen Dr. Dirlewanger Oskar, wegen Mord, July 8, 1960.

22. BA Ludwigsburg, B 162/16592, 5. Angele Betty, n.d., 99–100.

23. Sta Ludwigsburg, EL 317 III Bü 142, Az.: II/Mi/3355/60, Ermittlungsverfahren gegen Dr. Dirlewanger Oskar, wegen Mord, July 8, 1960, unpag.; and BA Ludwigsburg, B 162/16592, 5. Angele Betty, n.d., 99.

24. Sta Ludwigsburg, EL 317 III Bü 142, Az.: II/Mi/3355/60, Ermittlungsverfahren gegen Dr. Dirlewanger Oskar, wegen Mord, July 8, 1960.

25. BA Ludwigsburg, B 162/16592, Tgb! No. SK. Zst. I/5-117/60, Vernehmungsniederschrift, August 19, 1960, 161.

26. Ibid., 157–58.

27. BA Ludwigsburg, B 162/16592, 5. Angele Betty, n.d., 99.

28. BA Ludwigsburg, B 162/16592, 6. Füssinger Anton, n.d., 103.

29. Ibid., 102.

30. Sta Ludwigsburg, EL 317 III Bü 142, Az.: II/Mi/3355/60, Ermittlungsverfahren gegen Dr. Dirlewanger Oskar, wegen Mord, July 8, 1960, unpag.; and BA Ludwigsburg, B 162/16592, 5. Angele Betty, n.d., 99.

31. BA Ludwigsburg, B 162/16592, 6. Füssinger Anton, n.d., 102.

32. Sta Ludwigsburg, EL 317 III Bü 142, Az.: II/Mi/3355/60, Ermittlungsverfahren gegen Dr. Dirlewanger Oskar, wegen Mord, July 8, 1960.

33. BA Ludwigsburg, B 162/16592, 6. Füssinger Anton, n.d., 103–04.

34. Sta Ludwigsburg, EL 317 III Bü 142, Az.: II/Mi/3355/60, Ermittlungsverfahren gegen Dr. Dirlewanger Oskar, wegen Mord, July 8, 1960.

35. BA Ludwigsburg, B 162/16592, 6. Füssinger Anton, n.d., 105.

36. BA Ludwigsburg, B 162/16592, "Das Rätsel um Strafbrigadeführer Dr. Dirlewanger," *Schwäbische Zeitung*, April 22, 1960, 92.

37. BA Ludwigsburg, B 162/16592, Anmeldung eines Sterbefalles, June 16, 1945, 94; and BA Ludwigsburg, B 162/21001, Beglaubigte Abschrift aus dem Sterbebuch des Standesamts Altshausen, Nr. 63, Altshausen, July 17, 1959, 81.

38. BA Ludwigsburg, B 162/16592, "Das Rätsel um Strafbrigadeführer Dr. Dirlewanger," *Schwäbische Zeitung*, April 22, 1960, 92.

39. BA Ludwigsburg, B 162/16592, Gs 183/60, Amtsgericht Saulgau, Geschehen am 12. November 1960 auf dem Friedhof in Altshausen, November 12, 1960, 178–79.

40. Sta Ludwigsburg, EL 201 VI Bü 1980—Gräberliste, Kriegsgräberliste, Friedhof Altshausen, n.d.

41. The original photographs are located in Sta Ludwigsburg, EL 317 III, 142, pp. 17, 18. The first was taken in Lahoysk, Belarus.

42. BA Ludwigsburg, B 162/16592, Eidesstattliche Erklärung, April 2, 1960, 98.

43. BA Ludwigsburg, B 162/16592, Tgb! No. SK. Zst. I/5-117/60, Vernehmungsniederschrift, August 19, 1960, 159, 162–63.

44. BA Ludwigsburg, B 162/5926, Betrifft: Sammelvorgang Strafsache Dirlewanger, Weiße, Heinsen Rußland-Polen-Ungarn-Tschecho-Slowakei u. Deutschland verbrechen, Berlin 44, 12 V 1972, 1516.

45. BA Ludwigsburg, B 162/16592, "Das Rätsel um Strafbrigadeführer Dr. Dirlewanger," *Schwäbische Zeitung*, April 22, 1960, 90.

46. BA Ludwigsburg, B 162/16592, Und Dirlewanger lebt doch!, n.d., 197.

Martin Bormann, born June 17, 1900, in Halberstadt. From May 1941 he held the post of head of the NSDAP chancellery and was Adolf Hitler's deputy and secretary. According to Artur Axmann's testimony, he died on May 2, 1945, in an attempt to escape Berlin. In 1972, during construction work at Invalidenstraße, the skeletons of two men were found. On the basis of their sets of teeth and other anatomical features, they were identified as Bormann and Dr. Ludwig Stumpfegger. For more about Bormann and his death, see A. Beevor, *Berlin 1945: Upadek* (Kraków, Poland, 2003), 490–2; and V. Koop, *Bormann: Pierwszy po bestii* (Warsaw, Poland, 2015).

47. Dmitri Shepilov (1905–95), Soviet politician and minister of foreign affairs of the USSR.

48. BA Ludwigsburg, B 162/5924, Dirlewanger—Haupquartier: Port Said, n.d., 1166–73.

49. Ibid.

50. Ibid.

51. For more on the subject, see K. Schultze, *Konflikt arabsko-izraelski* (Warsaw, Poland, 2010).

52. BA Ludwigsburg, B 162/5924, Dirlewanger—Haupquartier: Port Said, n.d., 1166–73.

53. YV, JM 2095, ID 3675813, n.d.

54. BA Ludwigsburg, B 162/5925, Landeskriminalamt NW—Dezernat 15—Tgb. Nr. (4300)-6357/64-Re, Gottlob Berger, Gerstetten, July 29, 1965, 1199.

55. BA Ludwigsburg, B 162/5924, "Fall Dirlewanger durch Identität erledigt, Nachrichten aus Baden-Württemberg," *Stuttgarter Nachrichten*, December 2, 1960, 1185a.

56. BA Ludwigsburg, B 162/16592, Tgb! No. SK. Zst. I/5-117/60, Vernehmungsniederschrift, August 19, 1960, 158.

57. Farook I, born in 1920 in Cairo. King of Egypt in the years 1936–1952 and of Sudan. He rejected democracy. His decision deepened the economic crisis in the country, which caused a fall in support by the population. The situation was so tense that conspirators decided to overthrow the rulers. Standing at the head of the conspiracy were Muhammad Nagib and Gamal Abdel Nasser (for more on the subject, see *Faruk I: Ostatni król Egiptu*, https://www.polskieradio.pl/39/1240/Artykul/1595071,Faruk-I-ostatni-krol-Egiptu, accessed May 2, 2018).

58. BA Ludwigsburg, B 162/29251, LKA-NW-Dez. 15, Peter Erretkamps, Kevelaer, July 24, 1962, 126.

59. BA Ludwigsburg, B 162/16573, Przesłuchanie Waltera Zeppenfelda, January 20, 1962 r., 308–14.

60. BA Ludwigsburg, B 162/29251, LKA-NW-Dez. 15, Paul Dorn, Lüdenscheid, July 4, 1962, 82.

61. BA Ludwigsburg, B 162/16574, Anlage zur Niederschrift, Paul Wilhelm Rass, March 16, 1962, 125–26.

62. BA Ludwigsburg, B 162/5924, letter from Dr. Oscar Karbach (Institute of Jewish Affairs) to prosecutor general Dr. E. Schuele, April 20, 1965, 1160.

63. BA Ludwigsburg, B 162/5924, Kriminalkommissariat Ravensburg Az.: II D1/Mi/794/69, Ravensburg, April 11, 1969, 1185b–c.

64. BA Ludwigsburg, B 162/16592, Gs 183/60, Amtsgericht Saulgau, November 3, 1960, 177.

65. BA Ludwigsburg, B 162/16592, Gs 183/60, November 12, 1960, 179.

66. BA Ludwigsburg, B 162/16592, Ermittlungsverfahren gegen Dr. Oskar Dirlewanger wegen Mordverdacht, November 24, 1960, 181–92. According to SS personnel data, Dirlewanger was 183 cm tall (BAB, R/9361/III 521445, Personalangaben, n.d., 743).

67. BA Ludwigsburg, B 162/16592, Ludwigsburg nr 18, November 30, 1960, 193–94.

68. BA Ludwigsburg, B 162/5924, "Fall Dirlewanger durch Identität erledigt, Nachrichten aus Baden-Württemberg," *Stuttgarter Nachrichten*, December 2, 1960, 1185a.

69. Ibid.

70. BA Ludwigsburg, B 162/16592, Vereinigungen der Verfolgten des Naziregimes, January 18, 1962, 198–99.

71. BA Ludwigsburg, B 162/16592, Verlag Th. Martens & Co. GMBH München, Redaktion Quick, July 24, 1964, 211–12.

72. BA Ludwigsburg, B 162/16574, Anlage zur Niederschrift, Paul Wilhelm Rass, March 16, 1962, 126.

73. BA Ludwigsburg, B 162/16592, Tgb! No. SK. Zst. I/5-117/60, Vernehmungsniederschrift, August 19, 1960, 159, 162; and BA Ludwigsburg, B 162/16592, Tgb. Nr. G5/405/60 Da, Ermittlungssache gegen Dr. Oskar Dirlewanger, früherer SS-Oberst, geb. 26 IX 1895 in Würzburg, August 15, 1960, 141.

Conclusion

1. BA Ludwigsburg, B 162/16573, Der Oberstaatsanwalt 2 Js 700/61, Walter Escher, Lengfeld, January 28, 1962, 319.

2. Such a division into companies was confirmed by the political prisoner Willi Müller, who was under Dirlewanger's command from November 1944. He said that political prisoners were grouped together and that repeat offenders were also put with them. He mentioned that the inmates who volunteered planned to go over to the Red Army and fight against Fascism (Arch. Sachsenhausen, LAG XXX/7, Willi Müller ehem. Häftling im KZ Sachsenhausen Nr. 56538, Zu Dirlewanger? Nein oder Ja?, Berlin, April 24, 1973, 52–53).

3. BA Ludwigsburg, B 162/5926, Betrifft: Sammelvorgang Strafsache Dirlewanger, Weiße, Heinsen Rußland-Polen-Ungarn-Tschecho-Slowakei u. Deutschland verbrechen, Berlin 44, May 12, 1972, 1506.

4. BA Ludwigsburg, BA 162/28392, Sta Hamburg, 147 Js 11/71U, Leo Mletzko, Ettlingen, April 10, 1973, 409.

5. BAB, NS 19/1, Der Höhere SS und Polizeiführer Rußland-Mitte, March 23, 1942, 7.

6. BA Ludwigsburg, B 162/16573, Der Oberstaatsanwalt 2 Js 700/61, Viktor Zerfaß, April 4, 1962, 334.

7. Ch. Hale, *"Kaci Hitlera": Mroczne serce Europy* (Poznań, Poland, 2012), 420.

8. Ibid.

9. N. Sennerteg, *Kat Warszawy*, 34.

10. Przesłuchanie Horsta B., September 4, 1958, after N. Sennerteg, *Kat Warszawy*, 149n12.

11. BAB, R/9361/III, vol. 521445, Meldung! SS-Hauptsturmführer Walter Brandenburg, Berlin, June 9, 1944, 816.

12. BA Ludwigsburg, B 162/16569, Bisheriges Ermittlungsergebnis über das Sonderkommando "Dirlewanger," n.d., 155–56.

13. Ibid., 157.

14. BAB, R/9361/III, vol. 521445, Abschrift 7, Württ, Landwehr-Division Abwicklungsstelle, Stuttgart, June 20, 1919, 789.

15. BAB, R/9361/III, vol. 521445, Meldung! SS-Hauptsturmführer Walter Brandenburg, Berlin, June 9, 1944, 815.

16. BAB, R/9361/III, vol. 521445, letter from Walter Brandenburg to Ernst Kaltenbrunner, Berlin, June 9, 1944, 813; BAB, R/9361/III, vol. 521445, Meldung! SS-Hauptsturmführer Walter Brandenburg, Berlin, June 9, 1944, 815; and BAB, R/9361/III, vol. 521445, letter from Walter Brandenburg to Gottlob Berger, Berlin, June 9, 1944, 824–25.

Bibliography

Archival material

Archiv Gedenkstätte und Museum Sachsenhausen (Stiftung Brandenburgische Gedenkstätten) (Arch. Sachsenhausen).

LAG XXX/1, LAG XXX/2, LAG XXX/3, LAG XXX/4, LAG XXX/5, LAG XXX/6, LAG XXX/7, LAG XXX/8, LAG XXX/9, P3 Schulze, "Hermann"/1, P7 Wiesenthal, Simon/1, KAW K16 M6.

Archive of the Yad Vashem Holocaust Martyrs' and Heroes' Remembrance Authority in Jerusalem (YV).

JM 2095, ID 3675813; Testimony of Friedrichs about Dirlewanger after the war (March 30, 1948).

JM 2095, ID 3675709; Testimony of Pister about recruitment to Dirlewanger unit (January 14, 1947).

JM 2094, ID 3674792; Himmler's order to recruit to Dirlewanger's unit (March 28, 1943).

JM 2089, ID 3672426; Testimony of Hoefle (February 13, 1947).

JM 2088, ID 3672138; From the personal file of Dirlewanger (August 9, 1943).

JM 2088, ID 3672137; From the personal file of Dirlewanger (September 27, 1941).

JM 2088, ID 3672136; Recommendation letter from the personal file of Dirlewanger (June 4, 1940).

JM 2088, ID 3671956; Recruitment form Waffen-SS to Dirlewanger's unit (March 20, 1944).

JM 2087, ID 3671849; Letter from Berger to Himmler's office (June 17, 1942).

JM 2085, ID 3670809; Document concerning recruitment of 1,500 criminals from Matzkau to Dirlewanger's unit (September 20, 1944).

JM 2083, ID 3669870; Letter from Rascher to Suchanek (July 27, 1942).

JM 2082, ID 3669495; Letter concerning moving prisoners to Dirlewanger's unit (November 3, 1944).

JM 2082, ID 3669469; Letter from Dirlewanger (October 7, 1944).

JM 2082 ID 3669432; לש ריכזת Himmler לע תדיחי Dirlewanger (February 20, 1944).

JM 2088, ID 3659572; Proposal to promote Dirlewanger (August 5, 1941).

ID 3659324, Testimony of Morgen (January 28, 1947).

Baden-Württemberg Landesarchiv, Hauptstaatsarchiv Stuttgart (H. Stuttgart) branch.

M 430/3 Bü 1975.

Bundesarchiv Berlin-Lichterfelde; formerly the American Berlin Document Center (BAB).

R/9361/II, vol. 169257; R/9361/III, vol. 521445; R/9361/III, vol. 566487; R/9361/III, vol. 571150; R/9354/224; ZM 1454; NS3/401; NS 19/1; NS 19/1207; NS33/226; R70 Polen/75; R70 Polen/76; R70 Polen/124; R 70 Polen/179; R70 Sowjetunion/14; R70 Sowjetunion/19; R70 Sowjetunion/21; R70 Sowjetunion/22; R70 Sowjetunion/23; R70 Sowjetunion/38; R70 Sowjetunion/51; R70 Sowjetunion/63; R70 Sowjetunion/69; R70 Sowjetunion/76; R70 Sowjetunion/77; R70 Sowjetunion/78; R70 Sowjetunion/95; R70 Sowjetunion/96; R70 Sowjetunion/98.

Bundesarchiv Ludwigsburg (BA).

B 162 Zentrale Stelle der Landesjustizverwaltungen zur Aufklärung nationalsozialistischer Verbrechen:

B 162/3324; B 162/4248; B 162/4249; B 162/4250; B 162/4251; B 162/4252; B 162/4253; B 162/4254; B 162/4255; B 162/4256; B 162/4257; B 162/4258; B 162/4259; B 162/4260; B 162/4261; B 162/4262; B 162/4263; B 162/4264; B 162/4265; B 162/4266; B 162/5919; B 162/5920; B 162/5921; B 162/5922; B 162/5923; B 162/5924; B 162/5925; B 162/5926; B 162/15140; B 162/15141; B 162/15449; B 162/16569; B 162/16570; B 162/16571; B 162/16572; B 162/16573; B 162/16574; B 162/16592; B 162/16593; B 162/16634; B 162/16635; B 162/16636; B 162/16743; B 162/16907; B 162/19061; B

162/19797; B 162/19799; B 162/19830; B 162/21001; B 162/21202; B 162/26290; B 162/27187; B 162/28392; B 162/29251; B 162/29456; B 162/1708.

Institute of National Remembrance. Commission for the Prosecution of Crimes against the Polish Nation.

AIPN, 1834/11; AIPN, 1836/13; AIPN, 2727/1; AIPN GK, 103/72AIPN GK, 103/76; AIPN GK, 103/78; AIPN GK, 164/906 vol. 1; AIPN GK, 164/1711; AIPN GK, 164/906 vol. 2; AIPN GK, 164/906 vol.7; AIPN GK, 164/906 vol. 8; AIPN GK, 164/906 vol. 14; AIPN GK, 164/906 vol. 15; AIPN GK, 164/906 vol. 18; AIPN GK, 164/906 vol. 19; AIPN GK, 164/906 vol. 20; AIPN GK, 164/906 vol. 21; AIPN GK, 164/906 vol. 61; AIPN GK, 164/906 vol. 62; AIPN GK, 164/906 vol. 63; AIPN GK, 164/906 vol. 64; AIPN GK, 164/1180; AIPN GK, 164/1716; AIPN GK, 164/2280; AIPN GK, 661/7; S 1/06/Zn.

Landesarchiv Baden-Württemberg, Staatsarchiv Ludwigsburg (Sta Ludwigsburg) branch.

E 356 d III Bü 9; EL 48/2 I 1193; EL 48/2 I 1343; EL 48/2 I 1636; EL 48/2 I 2562; EL 48/2 901; EL 48/2 931; EL 48/2 1478; EL 48/2 2811; EL 201 VI Bü 1980; EL 302 V 104; EL 317 III Bü 142.

National Archive USA; Documents made available by the Yad Vashem Authority.

Staatliche Archive Bayerns, Staatsarchiv München (Sta München).

Staatsanwaltschaft 3468/3.

Staatsanwaltschaft 34865/59.

Stadtarchiv Esslingen; material used thanks to the kindness of Rolf Laschet.

Stadtarchiv Heilbronn.

"2 Jahre Zuchthaus: Das Urteil gegen Dr. Dirlewanger." *Heilbronner Tagblatt*, September 22, 1934.

"2 Jahre Zuchthaus für Dr. Dirlewanger: Die Plädoyers." *Neckar-Zeitung*, September 22, 1934.

D027-3, Materialsammlung zur Geschichte des Bahnschutzes in Württemberg von Reichsbahnoberinspektor Rudolf Behne.

"Erneuter großer Erfolg des Arbeitsamts Heilbronn: Sämtliche Kriegsbeschädigten in Arbeit!" *Heilbronner Tagblatt*, April 14, 1934, 5.

"Generalversammlung des Svar- und Konsumvereins Heilbronn." *Neckar-Zeitung*, March 27, 1934, 5.

"Heute vor der Großen Strafkammer: Prozeß gegen Dr. Dirlewanger." *Heilbronner Tagblatt*, September 20, 1934.

Nachlass Hellmut Riegraf D037-54. Nachforschungen zum Schicksal von Herbert Koeber, standrechtlich erschossen am 6 IV 1945 bei Schmeden. Brief von Herbert Koeber an seine Eltern, Lazarett Goisern, December 21, 1944 r.

"Pg. Dirlewanger zum Ehrenbürger der Stadt der Stadt Sangerhausen ernannt." *Heilbronner Tagblatt*, May 31, 1934.

"Prozeß Dr. Dirlewanger: Der Mann, der an der Türe horchte; Wird das Gericht diesem Zeugen glauben?" *Heilbronner Tagblatt*, September 21, 1934, 7.

"Uebererreichung der Ehrenbürger: Urkunde der Stadt Sangerhausen an Pg. Dirlewanger." *Heilbronner Tagblatt*, June 11, 1934.

"Wer denkt noch an Max Hölz? Der Panzerzug der Württ. [illegible word]." *Heilbronner Tagblatt*, April 14, 1934, 5.

The Military History Archive in Bratislava, Slovenská republika (M.H. Arch.).

"Slovenské národné povstanie."

Dokumentations- und Informationszentrum (DIZ) Torgau

List of Wehrmacht and Waffen-SS prisoners sent from the prison in Torgau to SS-Sonderkommando Dirlewanger.

Source material

Bechtle, Richard. *Die Ulmer Grenadier an der Ostfront: Die württembergischen Regimenter im Weltkrieg, 1914–1918*. Vol. 6, *Das Grenadier Regiment König Karl (5 Württ.) Nr. 123*. Stuttgart: Belsersche Verlagsbuchhandlung Stuttgart, 1920.

Lasik, Aleksander. *Führerliste Waffen-SS*. Typescript (Aleksander Lasik's collection).

Lasik, Aleksander. *Oficerowie SS w niemieckich obozach koncentracyjnych w latach, 1933–1945: Słownik biograficzny*. Typescript (Aleksander Lasik's collection).

Seniority List of Waffen-SS officers, 1 October 1934 (Dienstaltersliste der Schutzstaffel der N.S.D.A.P., 1.10.1934). Berlin: Buchdruckerei Birkner, 1934.

Seniority List of Waffen-SS officers, 1 July 1935 (Dienstaltersliste der Schutzstaffel der N.S.D.A.P., 1.07.1935). Berlin: Gedruckt in der Reichsdruckerei, 1935.

Seniority List of Waffen-SS officers, 1 December 1936 (Dienstaltersliste der Schutzstaffel der N.S.D.A.P., 1.12.1936). Berlin: Gedruckt in der Reichsdruckerei, 1936.

Seniority List of Waffen-SS officers, 1 December 1937 (Dienstaltersliste der Schutzstaffel der N.S.D.A.P., 1.12.1937). Berlin: Gedruckt in der Reichsdruckerei, 1937.

Seniority List of Waffen-SS officers, 1 October 1944 (Diensaltersliste der Schutzstaffel der NSDAP (SS-Obersturmbannführer und SS-Sturmbannführer) Stand vom 1. Oktober 1944). Berlin: Gedruckt in der Reichsdruckerei, 1944.

Seniority List of Waffen-SS officers, 9 November 1944 (Diensaltersliste der Schutzstaffel der NSDAP SS-Oberst-Gruppenführer—SS-Standartenführer), Stand vom 9. November 1944. Berlin: Gedruckt in der Reichsdruckerei, 1944.

Scheinost, Jan, Antonín J., Kožišek, and Karel Werner. *Banská Bystrica*. Prague: Orbis, 1944.

Stein, Kurt. *Die württembergischen Regimenter im Weltkrieg, 1914–1918: Das Württembergische Landw. Infanterie Regiment Nr. 121 im Weltkrieg, 1914–1918, Band 37*. Stuttgart: Belser, Verlagsbuchchandlung Stuttgart, 1925.

Zottmann, Karl Otto. *Zánik Varšavy: Ličeni válečného zpravodaje*. Prague: Orbis, 1944.

Studies

Ailsby, Christopher. *Die geschichte der Waffen-SS*. Vienna: Tosa Verlag, 1999.

Ailsby, Christopher. *Piekło na froncie wschodnim*. Warsaw, Poland: Bellona, 2001. [*SS: Hell on the Eastern Front; The Waffen-SS War in Russia*. Osceola, WI: MBI, 1998.]

Arnold, Klaus Jochen. *Die Wehrmacht und die Besatzungspolitik in den besetzten Gebieten der Sowjetunion: Kriegsführung und Radikalisierung im "Unternehmen Barbarossa."* Berlin: Duncker & Humblot, 2005.

Auerbach, Hellmuth. "Die Einheit Dirlewanger." *Viertelsjahrshefte für Zeitgeschichte* 10, no. 3 (July 1962): 250–63.

Bączyk, Norbert. *Panzertruppen a Powstanie Warszawskie*. Warsaw, Poland: Pegaz-Bis, 1999.

Bartoszewski, Władysław. *1859 dni Warszawy*, Kraków, Poland: Znak, 1974.

Bartoszewski, Władysław. *Dni walczącej stolicy: Kronika Powstania Warszawskiego*. Warsaw, Poland: Świat Książki, 1989.

Bartoszewski, Władysław. *Prawda o von dem Bachu*. Poznań, Poland: Wydawnictwo Zachodnie, 1961.

Beer, Ferdinand. *Słowacja na przełomie: Powstanie słowackie 1944 r*. Warsaw, Poland: Spóldzielnia Wydawniczo-Handlowa "Książka i Wiedza," 1969. [*Dejinná križovatka: Slovenské narodné povstanie—predpoklady a výsledky*. Vydavatel'stvo politickej literatúry, 1964.]

Beevor, Antony. *Berlin 1945: Upadek*. Kraków, Poland: Znak, 2003. [*Berlin: The Downfall, 1945*. London: Penguin Books, 2002.]

Beevor, Antony. *Druga wojna światowa*. Kraków, Poland: Znak, 2013. [*The Second World War*. London: Weidenfeld & Nicolson, 2014.]

Beevor, Antony. *Walka o Hiszpanię 1936–1939: Pierwsze starcie totalitaryzmów*. Kraków, Poland: Znak, 2009. [*The Battle for Spain: The Spanish Civil War, 1936–1939*. London: Weidenfeld & Nicolson, 2007.]

Bielecki, Robert. *"Gustaw"—"Harnaś," dwa powstańcze bataliony*. Warsaw, Poland: Państwowy Instytut Wydawniczy, 1989.

Bishop, Chris. *Zagraniczne formacje SS: Zagraniczni ochotnicy w Waffen-SS 1940–1945*. Warsaw, Poland: Muza SA, 2006. [*SS: Hitler's Foreign Divisions; Foreign volunteers in the Waffen-SS, 1940–45*. Amber Books, 2015.]

Blood, Philip W. *Siepacze Hitlera: Oddziały specjalne SS do zwalczania partyzantki*. Warsaw, Poland: Bellona, 2008. [*Hitler's Bandit Hunters: The SS and the Nazi Occupation of Europe*. Dulles, VA: Potomac Books, 2006.]

Borkiewicz, Adam. *Powstanie warszawskie 1944: Zarys działań natury wojskowej*. Warsaw, Poland: Instytut Wydawniczy "Pax," 1957.

Borkiewicz-Celińska, Anna. *Batalion "Zośka."* Warsaw, Poland: Wydawnictwo P.I.W., 1990.

Brighton, Terry. *Gry wojenne: Patton, Monty, Rommel*. Kraków, Poland: Znak, 2011. [*Patton, Montgomery, Rommel: Masters of War*. New York: Crown, 2008.]

"Broń pancerna w Powstaniu Warszawskim." *Wozy Bojowe Świata*, special no. 2 (2018).

Bryja, Marcin, and Janusz Ledwoch. *Jednostki Waffen-SS 1939–1945*. Warsaw, Poland: Militaria, 1996.

Buchheim, Hans. *SS und Polizei im Nationalsozialistischen Staat*. Duisdorf bei Bonn, Germany: Studiengesellschaft für Zeitprobleme, 1964.

Bullock, Allan. *Hitler: Studium tyranii*. Warsaw, Poland: Iskry, 1969. [*Hitler: A Study in Tyranny*. London: Odhams, 1952.]

Casas de la Vega, Rafael. *Franco: żołnierz*. Krzeszowice, Poland: Dom Wydawniczy "Ostoja," 2001. [*Franco: Militar*. Madrid: Fenix, 1995.]

Charlwood, David. *Rok 1920: Świat po wielkiej wojnie*. Warsaw, Poland: Bellona, 2020. [*1920: A Year of Global Turmoil*. Barnsley, UK: Pen & Sword Books, 2020.]

Chiari, Bernhard. *Alltag hinter der Front: Besetzung, Kollaboration und Widerstand in Weissrussland, 1941–1944*. Düsseldorf: Droste Verlag, 1998.

Chwalba, Andrzej. *Samobójstwo Europy: Wielka Wojna 1914–1918*. Kraków, Poland: Wydawnictwo Literackie, 2014.

Ciechanowski, Jan M. *Powstanie warszawskie*. Pułtusk and Warsaw, Poland: Bellona, 2009.

Cieślak, Tadeusz. *Oranienburg-Sachsenhausen: Hitlerowskie obozy koncentracyjne 1933–1945*. Warsaw, Poland: Książka i Wiedza, 1972.

Cosban-Woytycha Stefan. "Dywersja i sabotaż kolejowy na Słowacji w latach 1943–1944." *Słupskie Studia Historyczne* 19 (2013).

Crowe, David M. *Oskar Schindler: Prawdziwa historia*. Warsaw, Poland: Prószyński i Ska, 2015. [*Oskar Schindler: The Untold Account of His Life, Wartime, Activities, and the True Story Behind the List*. Cambridge, MA: Westview, 2004.]

Cubała, Agnieszka. *Sten pod pachą, bimber w szklance, dziewczyna i . . . Warszawa: Życie codzienne powstańczej Warszawy*. Warsaw, Poland: Bellona, 2015.

Cüppers, Martin. *Wegbereiter der Shoah: Die Waffen-SS, der Kommandostab Reichsführer-SS und die Judenvernichtung 1939–1945*. Darmstadt: Wissenschaftliche Buchgesellschaft, 2005.

Dąbrowski, Włodzimierz. *Trzecie powstanie śląskie: Rok 1921*. London: Odnowa, 1973.

Daniluk, Jan. "Obóz karny SS i policji w Maćkowach pod Gdańskiem." *Pamięć i Sprawiedliwość* 18, no. 2 (2011). https://bazhum.muzhp.pl/media/files/Pamiec_i_Sprawiedliwosc/Pamiec_i_Sprawiedliwosc-r2011-t10-n2_(18)/Pamiec_i_Sprawiedliwosc-r2011-t10-n2_(18)-s217-232/Pamiec_i_Sprawiedliwosc-r2011-t10-n2_(18)-s217-232.pdf.

Daniluk, Jan. *SS w Gdańsku*. Gdańsk, Poland: Wydawnictwo IPN, 2013.

Datner, Szymon, and Kazimierz Leszczyński. *Zbrodnie okupanta hitlerowskiego na ludności cywilnej w czasie powstania warszawskiego w 1944 roku (w dokumentach)*. Warsaw, Poland: Wydawnictwo Ministerstwa Obrony Narodowej, 1962.

Datner. Szymon. *Zbrodnie okupanta w czasie powstania warszawskiego w 1944 r. (w dokumentach)*. Warsaw, Poland: Wydawnictwo Ministerstwa Obrony Narodowej, 1962.

Davies, Norman. *Powstanie '44*. Kraków, Poland: Znak, 2004. [*Rising '44: The Battle for Warsaw*. London: Pan Books, 2004.]

Dobrzycki, Wiesław. *Powstanie Śląskie*. Warsaw, Poland: PZWS, 1971.

Dolata, Bolesław. *Wyzwolenie Dolnego Śląska w 1945 r*. Wrocław, Poland: Ossolineum, 1985.

Drobisch, Klaus. "Theodor Eicke: Verkörperung des KZ-Systems." In *Sturz ins Dritte Reich: Historische Miniaturen und Portraits 1933–1935*. Leipzig: Urania Verlag, 1983.

Drozdowski, Marian M., ed. *Mocarstwa wobec Powstania: Wybór dokumentów i materiałów*. Warsaw, Poland: Bellona, 1994.

Dybicz. Paweł, ed. *Zakłamana historia powstania*. Vol. 1, *Kto odpowiada za śmierć 200 tysięcy cywilów*. Warsaw, Poland: Fundacja Oratio Recta, 2014.

Dybicz. Paweł, ed. *Zakłamana historia powstania*. Vol. 2, *Błędy dowódców: Poufne rozkazy i dokumenty*. Warsaw, Poland: Fundacja Oratio Recta, 2018.

Dybicz. Paweł, ed. *Zakłamana historia powstania*. Vol. 3, *Obłęd i głód: Nieznany "Dziennik powstańczy."* Warsaw, Poland: Fundacja Oratio Recta, 2018.

Eberle, Henrik. *Teczka Hitlera*. Edited by Matthias Uhl. Warsaw, Poland: Świat Książki, 2005. [*Das Buch Hitler*. Cologne: Bastei Lübbe, 2006.]

Färber, Mathias. *Zweiter Weltkrieg in Bildern*. Stuttgart: Unipart, 1995.

Finn, Gerhard. *Sachsenhausen 1936–1950: Geschichte eines Lagers*. Berlin: Westkreuz Verlag, 1988.

Gargas, Józef. *Oddziały Gwardii Ludowej i Armii Ludowej 1942–1945*. Warsaw, Poland: Wydawnictwo Ministerstwa Obrony Narodowej, 1974.

Geber, Halina, and Halina Halweg. *Szpital dobrej woli: Szpital Wolski 1939–1945*. Warsaw, Poland: Czytelnik, 2004.

Gerlach, Christian. *Kalkulierte Morde: Die deutsche Wirtschafts- und Vernichtungspolitik in Weissrussland 1941 bis 1944*. Hamburg, Germany: Hamburger Edition, 1999.

Gilbert, Martin. *Pierwsza wojna światowa*. Poznań, Poland: Zysk i S-ka, 2003. [*First World War*. New York: Henry Holt, 1994.]

Girtler, Roland. *Wilderer: Rebellen in den Bergen*. Vienna and Cologne: Böhlau Wien, 2003.

Goldsworthy, Terry. *Valhalla's Warriors: A History of the Waffen-SS on the Eastern Front, 1941–1944*. Indianapolis, IN: Dog Ear, 2007.

Grechuta, J. "Obozy pracy dla Żydów w południowo-wschodniej części dystryktu lubelskiego w 1940 r. (Bełżec, Lipsko, Płazów, Cieszanów, Dzików Stary)." In *Polska-Ukraina: Wspólna przeszłość, Material from the Session "Dziedzictwo kulturowe pogranicza polsko-ukraińskiego"* [*Cultural Heritage of the Polish-Ukrainian borderlands*] (Cieszanów, Poland, September 29, 2006) and the conference Polska Ukraina: Wspólna przeszłość [Poland Ukraine: A Common Past] (Cieszanów, November 25–26, 2006). Cieszanów, Poland, 2007.

Grünberg, Karol. *SS: Gwardia Hitlera*. Warsaw, Poland: Książka i Wiedza, 1994.

Guderian, Heinz. *Achtung Panzer! Uwaga czołgi!* Warsaw, Poland: Erica, Tetragon, 2012. [*Achtung Panzer!* Stuttgart: Union deutsche Verlagsgesellschaft, 1937.]

Gursztyn, Piotr. *Rzeź Woli*. Warsaw, Poland: Demart, 2014.

Hale, Christopher. *"Kaci Hitlera": Brudny sekret Europy*. Kraków, Poland: Znak, 2012. [*Hitler's Foreign Executioners: Europe's Dirty Secret*. Stroud, UK: History Press, 2011.]

Hawranek Franciszek, ed. *Encyklopedia powstań śląskich*. Opole, Poland: Wydawnictwo Instytutu Śląskiego, 1982.

Heck, Roman, and Marian Orzechowski. *Czechosłowacja*. Wrocław, Warsaw, and Kraków, Poland: Ossolineum, 1969.

Hernández, Jesus. *Nazistowskie bestie: Kaci z SS*. Warsaw, Poland: Bellona, 2016. [*Bestias Nazis*. Barcelona: Melusina, 2013.]

Hesse, Erich. *Der sowjetrussische Partisanenkrieg 1941 bis 1944 im Spiegel deutscher Kampfanweisungen und Befehle*. Göttingen, Germany: Musterschmidt-Verlag, 1969.

Heydecker, Joe, and Johannes Leeb. *Trzecia Rzesza w świetle Norymbergi: Bilans tysiąca lat*. Warsaw, Poland: Książka i Wiedza, 1979. [*Der Nürnberger Prozess: Bilanz der Tausend Jahre*. Cologne and Berlin, Kiepenheuer & Witsch, 1958.]

Hilberg, Raul. *The Destruction of the European Jews*. Chicago: Quadrangle Books, 1960.

Hobusch, Erich. *Wilddieberei und Förstermorde*. Vol. 3, *Kriminalkommissar Otto Busdorf: Sein letzter Fall*. Berlin: Morschen, 2002.

Höhne, Heinz. *Zakon Trupiej Czaszki*. Warsaw, Poland: Wołoszański, 1997. [*Der Orden unter dem Totenkopf: Die Geschichte der SS*. Munich: Goldmann, 1979.]

Hoppe, Bert. *Die Verfolgung und Ermordung der europäischen Juden durch das nationalsozialistische Deutschland 1933–1945*. Vol. 8, *Sowjetunion mit annektierten Gebieten II*. Berlin: Bundesarchiv, Institut für Zeitgeschichte and Lehrstuhl für Neuere und Neueste Geschichte der Universität Freiburg, 2016.

Hryciuk, Grzegorz. "Represje niemieckie na Kresach Wschodnich II Rzeczypospolitej 1941–1944." *Pamięć i Sprawiedliwość* 12, no. 1 (2008): 79–112.

Ingrao, Christian. *Czarni myśliwi: Brygada Dirlewangera*. Wołowiec, Poland: Wydawnictow Czarne, 2011. [*Les chasseurs noirs: Essai sur la Sondereinheit Dirlewanger*. Paris: Éditions Perrin, 2006.]

Irving, David. *Wojna Göringa: Biografia Marszałka Rzeszy*. Kraków, Poland: Arkadiusz Wingert, 2011. [*Göring: A Biography*. London: Focal Point, 1991.]

Irving, David. *Wojna Hitlera*. Warsaw, Poland: Arkadiusz Wingert, 2005. [*Hitler's War*. London: Focal Point, 2002.]

Jędruszczak, Tadeusz. *Powstania śląskie 1919-1920-1921*. Katowice, Poland: Wydawnictwo Śląsk, 1981.

Katzan, P. *Politische Häftlinge in der SS-Formation Dirlewanger*. Heft 44. Lieberose Germany: KZ-Nebenlager Lieberose.

Kershaw, Ian. *Hitler: Hybris 1889–1936*. Poznań, Poland: Dom Wydawniczy Rebis, 2001. [*Hitler: Hubris, 1889–1939*. London: Allen Lane, 1998.]

Kirchmayer, Jerzy. *Powstanie warszawskie*. Warsaw, Poland: Książka i Wiedza, 1984.

Kitchen, Martin. *Pustynna wojna Rommla*. Warsaw, Poland: Książka i Wiedza, 2014. [*Rommel's Desert War: Waging World War II in North Africa*. Cambridge, UK: Cambridge University Press, 2009.]

Klausch, Hans-Peter. *Antifaschisten in SS-Uniform: Schicksal und Widerstand der deutschen politischen KZ-Häftlinge, Zuchthaus- und Wehrmachtsgefangenen in der SS-Sonderformation Dirlewanger*. Bremen, Germany: Temmen, 1993.

Koch, Hannsjoachim W. *In the Name of the Volk: Political Justice in Hitler's Germany*. London: I. B. Tauris, 1997.

Koehl, Robert Lewis. *The Black Corps: The Structure and Power Struggles of the Nazi SS*. Madison: University of Wisconsin Press, 1983.

Kogon, Eugen. *Państwo SS: Organizacja i funkcjonowanie niemieckiego obozu koncentracyjnego*. Poznań, Poland: Replika, 2017. [*Der SS-Staat: Das System der deutschen Konzentrationslager*. Munich: W. Heyne, 1988.]

Komorowski, Krzysztof. *Bitwa o Warszawę '44: Militarne aspekty Powstania Warszawskiego*. Warsaw, Poland: Rytm, 2004.

Koop, Volker. *Bormann: Pierwszy po bestii*. Warsaw, Poland: Prószyński i S-ka, 2015. [*Martin Bormann: Hitler's Executioner*. Barnsley, UK: Pen & Sword Books, 2021.]

Koop, Volker. *Werwolf: Ostatni zaciąg Himmlera*. Warsaw, Poland: Prószyński i S-ka, 2016. [*Himmler's letztes Aufgebot: Die NS-Organization "Werwolf."* Göttingen, Germany: Vandenhoeck & Ruprecht, 2008.]

Kopf, Stanisław. *Dni powstania: Kronika fotograficzna walczącej Warszawy*. Warsaw, Poland: Państwowy Instytut Wydawniczy, 1984.

Kościelak, Lech. *Historia Słowacji*. Wrocław, Poland: Ossolineum, 2010.

Kotłowski, Tadeusz. *Niemcy 1919–1923*. Poznań, Poland: UAM, 1986.

Kowtun, Iwan, and Dmitrij Żukow. *29. Dywizja Grenadierów SS "Kamiński."* Poznań, Poland: Replika, 2017. [*29-я гренадерская дивизия СС 'Каминский'*. Вече, 2009.]

Krannhals von, Hanns. *Powstanie Warszawskie 1944: Der Warschauer Aufstand 1944*. Warsaw, Poland: Bellona, 2017. [*Der Warschauer Aufstand 1944*. Frankfurt am Main, Germany: Bernard & Graefe, 1962.]

Krausnick, Helmut, Hans Buchheim, Martin Broszat, and Hans Adolf Jacobsen. *Anatomie the SS Staates*. Vols. 1–2. Freiburg im Breisgau, Germany, and Olten, Switzerland: Walter, 1965.

Krausnick, Helmut. *Hitlers Einsatzgruppen: Die Truppe des Weltanschauungskrieges 1938–1942*. Frankfurt am Main, Germany: Fischer Taschenbuch, 1985.

Krawczyk, Andrzej. *Słowacja księdza prezydenta: Jozef Tiso 1887–1947*. Kraków, Poland: Znak, 2015.

Siuklińska, Soraya. *Działalność jednostki SS-Sonderkommando "Dirlewanger" (1940–1945)*. Kraków, Poland: Ridero, 2017.

Kulisy katastrofy Powstania Warszawskiego 1944: Wybrane publikacje i dokumenty. New York: Nieformalna grupa b. Powstańców Warszawskich, 2009.

Kunert, Andrzej. K. *Kronika Powstania Warszawskiego*. Warsaw, Poland: Zysk i S-ka, 2004.

Kwiatkowski, Maciej J. *"Tu mówi powstańcza Warszawa . . .": Dni powstania w audycjach Polskiego Radia i dokumentach niemieckich*. Warsaw, Poland: Państwowy Instytut Wydawniczy, 1994.

Lacko Martin. *Dwuramienny krzyż w cieniu swastyki: Republika Słowacka 1939–1945*. Lublin, Poland: Oficyna Wydawnicza El-Press s.c. 2012. [*Slovenská republika, 1939–1945*. Bratislava, Slovakia: Perfekt, 2008.]

Langerbein, Helmut. *Szwadrony śmierci Hitlera: Einsatzgruppen i logika masowej zbrodni*. Zakrzewo, Poland: Replika, 2017. [*Hitler's Death Squads: The Logic of Mass Murder*. College Station: Texas A&M University Press, 2004.]

Laschet, Rolf. "Dr. Oskar Dirlewanger: Die schwarze Gestalt unserer Schulgeschichte." In *Schelztor-Gymnasium 1838–2013: Festschrift, 175 Jahre*. Esslingen, Germany: Schelztor-Gymnasium Esslingen, 2013.

Laschet, Rolf. *Oskar Dirlewanger als Esslinger Symbolfigur bei der Zerstörung gewerkschaftlicher und menschlicher Grundwert*. Esslingen, Germany: Vortrag am Ort des früheren Gewerkschaftshauses in Esslingen, 2014.

Lasik, Aleksander. *Sztafety ochronne w systemie niemieckich obozów koncentracyjnych: Rozwój organizacyjny, ewolucja zadań i struktur oraz socjologiczny obraz obozowych załóg SS*. Oświęcim, Poland: Państwowe Muzeum Auschwitz-Birkenau, 2007.

Lenarczyk, Wojciech, and Dariusz Libionka. *Erntefest, zapomniany epizod Zagłady*. Lublin, Poland: Państwowe Muzeum na Majdanku, 2009.

Leszczyński, Kazimierz. *Heinz Reinefarth*. Poznań, Poland: Wydawnictwo Zachodnie, 1961.

Lewandowska, Stanisława. *Powstanie Warszawskie 1944*. Edited by Martin Bernd. Warsaw, Poland: Wydawnictwo Polsko-Niemieckie, 1999.

Libionka, Dariusz, ed. *Akcja Reinhardt: Zagłada Żydów w Generalnym Gubernatorstwie*. Warsaw, Poland: Wydawnictwo IPN, 2004.

Longerich, Peter. *Goebbels: Apostoł diabła*. Warsaw, Poland: Prószyński i S-ka, 2014. [*Goebbels: Biographie*. Munich: Siedler, 2010.]

Longerich, Peter. *Himmler: Buchalter śmierci*. Warsaw, Poland: Prószyński i S-ka, 2014. [*Heinrich Himmler: Eine Biographie*. Munich: Siedler, 2008.]

Lubiński, Józef, ed. *Ruch oporu*. Warsaw, Poland: Rzeczpospolita, 2009.

Lucas, John. *Handbuch der Wehrmaht 1939–1945: Ein Nachschlage Werk*. Vienna: Tosa, 2001.

Lukas, Richard C. *Zapomniany Holocaust: Polacy pod okupacją niemiecką 1939–1944*. Kielce, Poland: Wydawnictwo jenośċ, 1995. [*The Forgotten Holocaust: The Poles Under German occupation, 1939–1944*. New York: Hippocrene Books, 1997.]

Lumsden, Robin. *SS Regalia*. Edison, NJ: Chartwell Books, 1996.

Lumsden, Robin. *Waffen-SS*. Warsaw, Poland: Militaria, 1999. [*A Collector's Guide to the Waffen-SS*. Shepperton, UK: Ian Allan, 1994.]

MacLean, French. *The Cruel Hunters: SS-Sonderkommando Dirlewanger; Hitler's Most Notorious Anti-partisan Unit*. Atglen, PA: Schiffer, 1998.

Majewski, Jerzy, and Tomasz Urzykowski. *Przewodnik po powstańczej Warszawie*. Warsaw, Poland: Świat Książki, 2014.

Maršalek, Hans. *Die Geschichte des Konzentrationslagers Mauthausen*. Vienna: Österreichische Lagergemeinschaft Mauthausen, 1974.

Marszałek, Józef. *Obozy pracy w Generalnym Gubernatorstwie 1939–1945*. Lublin, Poland: Państwowe Muzeum na Majdanku, 1998.

Marti, Philipp. *Sprawa Reinefartha: Kat Powstania Warszawskiego czy szacowny obywatel*. Warsaw, Poland: Świat Książki, 2016. [*Der Fall Reinefarth: Eine biografische Studie zum öffentlichenund juristischen Umgang mit der NS-Vergangenheit*. Neumünster, Germany: Wachholtz, 2014.]

Matusak, Piotr. *Europa walcząca 1939–1945*. Siedlce, Poland: Wydawnictwo Akademii Podlaskiej, 2005.

McNab, Chris. *Armia Hitlera*. Warsaw, Poland: RM, 2014. [*Hitler's Armies: A History of the German War Machine, 1939–45*. Oxford: Osprey, 2011.]

McNab, Chris. *Elita Hitlera: Waffen-SS*. Warsaw, Poland: RM, 2016. [*Hitler's Elite: The SS, 1939–44*. Oxford: Osprey, 2015.]

McNab, Chris. *SS 1923–1945: Fakty, liczby i dane statystyczne*. Poznań, Poland: Vesper, 2011. [*The SS, 1923–1945*. London: Amber Books, 2009.]

McQueen, Victor. *The 10 Worst Psychopaths: The Most Depraved Killers in History*. London: Arcturus, 2015.

Michaelis, Rolf. *Das SS-Sonderkommando "Dirlewanger": Der Einsatz in Weißrussland 1941–1944*. Berlin: Michaelis Verlag, 1999.

Michaelis, Rolf. *Die SS-Sturmbrigade "Dirlewanger": Vom Warschauer Aufstand bis zum Kessel von Halbe*. Berlin: Michaelis Verlag, 2003.

Michaelis, Rolf. *Dirlewanger*. Warsaw, Poland: Militaria, 2005.

Miejsce Pamięci i Muzeum Sachsenhausen: Zarys historyczny i plan sytuacyjny. 2012.

Mierecki, Piotr. *Powstanie Warszawskie 1944 w dokumentach z archiwów służb specjalnych*. Warsaw, Poland: Instytut Pamięci Narodowej, Komisja Ścigania Zbrodni przeciwko Narodowi Polskiemu, Ministerstwo Spraw Wewnętrznych i Administracji Rzeczypospolitej Polskiej, 2007.

Mollo, Andrew. *Uniforms of the SS*. Vol. 1, *Allgemeine SS 1923–1945*. London: Historical Research Unit, 1969.

Montefiore, Simon S. *Stalin: Dwór czerwonego cara*. Warsaw, Poland: Magnum, 2013. [*Stalin: The Court of the Red Tsar*. New York: Vintage, 2005.]

Mórawski, Karol, Krzysztof Oktabiński, and Lidia Świerczek. *Wola: Warszawskie Termopile 1944*. Warsaw, Poland: Fundacja Wystawy "Warszawa Walczy 1939–1945," 2000.

Mueller, Gene. *Wilhelm Keitel, the Forgotten Field Marshal*. New York: Cooper Square, 2003.

Musiał, Bogdan. *Deutsche Zivilverwaltung und Judenverfolgung im Generalgouvernement: Eine Fallstudie zum Distrikt Lublin 1939–1944*. Wiesbaden, Germany: Harrassowitz Verlag, 1999.

Musiał, Bogdan. *Sowieccy partyzanci 1941–1944: Mity i rzeczywistość*. Poznań, Poland: Zysk i Ska, 2014. [*Sowjetische Partisanen, 1941–1944: Mythos und Wirklichkeit*. Paderborn, Germany: Schöningh, 2009.]

Musiał, Filip. *Od Września do Norymbergi*. Edited by Jarosław Szarek. Kraków, Poland: Instytut Pamięci Narodowej i Ośrodek Myśli Politycznej, 2012.

Niżyński, Leszek K. *Batalion Miotła: W dywersji, sabotażu i powstaniu warszawskim*. Warsaw and Kraków, Poland: Mireki, 2014.

Noakes, Jeremy. *Documents on Nazism, 1918–1945*. Edited by Geoffrey Pridham. London: Jonathan Cape, 1974.

Nowak, Szymon. *Ostatni szturm: Ze Starówki do Śródmieścia 1944*. Gdańsk, Poland: Finna, 2012.

Nowak, Szymon. *Przyczółek czerniakowski 1944*. Zabrze, Poland: Inforteditions, 2011.

Nowakowski, Tomasz, and Mariusz Skotnicki. *Legion Condor: Hiszpańska wojna Hitlera*. Warsaw, Poland: Instytut Wydawniczy Erica, 2011.

Nowakowski, Tomasz, Mariusz Skotnicki, and Krzysztof Zalewski. *Legion Condor*. Warsaw, Poland: Lampart & Bellona, 1994.

Nowożycki, Bartosz. *Batalion Armii Krajowej "Czata 49" w Powstaniu Warszawskim*. Warsaw, Poland: Rytm, 2008.

Nowożycki, Bartosz. *Zgrupowanie AK Radosław*. Warsaw, Poland: Rytm, 2014.

Olejko, Andrzej, ed. *Powstanie Warszawskie i Słowackie Powstanie Narodowe 1944: Cienie alianckiej pomocy*. Rzeszów, Poland: Wydawnictwo Uniwersytetu Rzeszowskiego, 2006.

Orth, Karin. *Das System der nationalsozialistischen Konzentrationslager: Eine politische Organizationsgeschichte*. Hamburg, Germany: Hamburger Edition, 1999.

Orth, Karin. *Die Konzentrationslager-SS: Sozialstrukturelle Analysen und biographische Studien*. Göttingen, Germany: Wallstein Verlag, 2000.

Ostrowska, Elżbieta. *Z tajemnic powstańczej Warszawy: Kanały; Łączność dowodzenia i ewakuacje na trasach południowych*. Warsaw, Poland: Wydawnictwo Naukowe ASKON, 2003.

Ozimek, Stanisław. *Stare Miasto 1944*. Warsaw, Poland: Wydawnictwo Ministerstwa Obrony Narodowej, 1971.

Padfield, Peter. *Himmler: Reichsführer-SS*. Warsaw, Poland: Iskry, 2005. [*Himmler*. New York: MJF Books, 1996.]

Pajewski, Janusz. *Pierwsza wojna światowa 1914–1918*. Warsaw, Poland: Wydawnictwo Naukowe PWN, 2014.

Patterson, David. *A Genealogy of Evil: Anti-Semitism from Nazism to Islamic Jihad*. New York: Cambridge University Press, 2011.

Patzwall, Klaus. *Der SS-Totenkopfring: Seine illustrierte Geschichte 1933–1945*. Norderstedt, Germany: Patzwall, 2002.

Piekałkiewicz, Janusz. *Kalendarium II wojny światowej*. Warsaw, Poland: Wydawnictwo Morex, 1999. [*Der Zweite Weltkrieg*. Düsseldorf: Econ-Verlag, 1988.]

Piekałkiewicz, Janusz. *Kalendarium wydarzeń I wojny światowej*. Warsaw, Poland: Wydawnictwo Morex, 1988. [*Der Erste Weltkrieg*. Düsseldorf: Econ-Verlag, 1985.]

Pohl, Dieter. *Die Herrschaft der Wehrmacht: Deutsche Militärbesetzung und einheimische Bevölkerung in der Sovjetunion 1941–1944*. Frankfurt am Main, Germany: S. Fischer, 2011.

Popiołek, Kazimierz. *Trzecie Powstanie Śląskie*. Katowice, Poland: Wydawnictwo Śląsk, 1971.

Powstanie Warszawskie: Sesja w 40 rocznicę. Warsaw, Poland: Główna Komisja Ścigania Zbrodni, 1987.

Przygoński, Antoni. *Powstanie warszawskie w sierpniu 1944*. Vol. 1. Warsaw, Poland: Wydawnictow PWN, 1980.

Rees, Laurence. *Naziści: Ostrzeżenie historii*. Warsaw, Poland: Prószyński i S-ka, 1997. [*The Nazis: A Warning from History*. London: BBC Books, 1998.]

Reitlinger, Gerald. *Die SS: Tragödie einer deutschen Epoche*. Munich: Desch, 1957.

Rhodes, Richard. *Mistrzowie śmierci: Einsatzgruppen*. Warsaw, Poland: Bellona, 2007. [*Masters of Death: The SS-Einsatzgruppen and the Invention of the Holocaust*. New York: Vintage, 2003.]

Richie, Alexandra. *Warszawa 1944*. Warsaw, Poland: Muzeum Powstania Warszawskiego, 2013. [*Warsaw 1944*. London: William Collins Book, 2014.]

Rieger, Bernd. *Odilo Globocnik, twórca nazistowskich obozów śmierci*. Zakrzewo, Poland: Replika, 2009. [*Creator of Nazi Death Camps: The Life of Odilo Globonik*. London: Vallentine Mitchell, 2006.]

Salvado, Francisco Romero. *Wojna domowa w Hiszpanii 1936–1939*. Warsaw, Poland: Bellona, 2009. [*The Spanish Civil War*. New York: Palgrave Macmillan, 2005.]

Sawicka, Irena, ed. *Oddziały i żołnierze NSZ w Powstaniu Warszawskim*. Warsaw, Poland: Związek Żołnierzy Narodowych Sił Zbrojnych, 1998.

Sawicki, Tadeusz. *Niemieckie wojska lądowe na froncie wschodnim, czerwiec 1944–maj 1945 (struktura)*. Warsaw, Poland: PWN, 1987.

Sawicki, Tadeusz. *Rozkaz zdławić powstanie: Niemcy i ich sojusznicy w walce z powstaniem warszawskim*. Warsaw, Poland: Bellona, 2013.

Sawicki, Tadeusz. *Wyrok na miasto: Berlin i Moskwa wobec Powstania Warszawskiego*. Warsaw, Poland: Bellona, 1993.

Scheinost, Jaromil, Antonin J. Kožišek, and Karel Werner. *Banská Bystrica*. Prague: Orbis, 1944.

Schlösser, Susanne. *Die Heilbronner NSDAP und ihre "Führer": Eine Bestandsaufnahme zur nationalsozialistischen Personalpolitik auf lokaler Ebene und ihren Auswirkungen "von Ort."* Heilbronn, Germany: Stadtarchiv Heilbronn, 2003.

Schultze, Kirsten. *Konflikt arabsko-izraelski*. Warsaw, Poland: Wydawnictwo Naukowe PWN, 2010. [*The Arab-Israeli Conflict*. Upper Saddle River, NJ: Addison Wesley, 2008.]

Schwarz, Gudrun. *Żony SS-manów: Kobiety w elitarnych kręgach III Rzeszy*. Warsaw, Poland: Pószyński i S-ka, 2016. [*Die Frau an seiner Seite: Die Ehefrauen in der "SS- Sippengemeinschaft."* Hamburg, Germany: Hamburger Edition, 1997.]

Segev, Tom. *Die Soldaten des Bösen: Zur Geschichte der KZ-Kommandanten*. Hamburg, Germany: Rowohlt Taschenbuch Verlag, 1992.

Seidel, Jutta. *Das grosse Dilemma: Leipziger Antifaschisten in der SS-Sturmbrigade "Dirlewanger."* Sachsen, Germany: Rosa-Luxemburg Stiftung, 1999.

Sennerteg, Niclas. *Kat Warszawy*. Warsaw, Poland: Wołoszański, 2003. [*Warszawas bödel: Ett tyskt öde*. Lund, Sweden: Historiska Media, 2017.]

Serwański, Edward, and Irena Trawińska. *Zbrodnia niemiecka w Warszawie 1944*. Poznań, Poland: Wydawnictwo Instytutu Zachodniego, 1946.

Shirer, William L. *Powstanie i upadek Trzeciej Rzeszy*. Kraków, Poland: Kluszczyński, 1995. [*The Rise and Fall of Third Reich*. New York: Simon & Schuster, 1960.]

Skibiński, Paweł. *Państwo generała Franco: Ustrój Hiszpanii w latach 1936–1967*. Kraków, Poland: Arkana, 2004.

Slepyan, Kenneth D. *Partyzanci Stalina: Radziecki ruch oporu w czasie II wojny światowej*. Poznań, Poland: Rebis, 2008. [*Stalin's Guerrillas: Soviet Partisans in World War II*. Lawrence: University Press of Kansas, 2006.]

Słowiński, Przemysław. *Otto Skorzeny: Pierwszy komandos Trzeciej Rzeszy*. Warsaw, Poland: Bellona, 2016.

Solarz, Jacek. *Totenkopf 1939–1943*. Warsaw, Poland: Militaria, 2008.

Stachiewicz, Piotr. *"Parasol": Dzieje oddziału do zadań specjalnych Kierownictwa Dywersji Komendy Głównej Armii Krajowej*. Warsaw, Poland: Instytut Wydawniczy PAX, 1984.

Stachiewicz, Piotr. *Starówka 1944: Zarys organizacji i działań bojowych Grupy "Północ" w powstaniu warszawskim*. Warsaw, Poland: Wydawnictwo Ministerstwa Obrony Narodowej, 1983.

Stang, Knut. "Dr. Oskar Dirlewanger: Protagonist der Terrorkriegsführung." In *Karrieren der Gewalt: Nationalsozialistische Täterbiographien*. Darmstadt: Wissenschaftliche Buchgesellschaft (WBG), 2004.

Stang, Knut. *Ritter, Landsknecht, Legionär, Militärmythische Leitbilder in der Ideologie der SS*. Frankfurt am Main, Germany: Peter Lang GmbH, Internationaler Verlag der Wissenschaften, 2008.

Stein, George H. *Geschichte der Waffen-SS*. Düsseldorf: Droste, 1967.

Stein, George H. *The Waffen-SS: Hitler's Elite Guard at War*. Ithaca, NY: Cornell University Press, 1986.

Strzembosz, Tomasz. *Oddziały szturmowe konspiracyjnej Warszawy 1939–1944*. Warsaw, Poland: Państwowe Wydawnictwo Naukowe, 1983.

Suhling, Ursula. *999er-Strafsoldaten: Deportiert vom Hannoverschen Bahnhof; Hamburger Antifaschisten in Wehrmachts-Uniform*. Hamburg, Germany: VSA, 2014.

Sumiński, Tadeusz, ed. *Pamiętniki żołnierzy baonu AK "Zośka": Powstanie Warszawskie*. Warsaw, Poland: Społeczny Komitet Opieki nad Grobami Poległych Żołnierzy Batalionu "Zośka," 1997.

Sydnor, Charles W., Jr. *Żołnierze zagłady: Dywizja SS "Totenkopf" 1933–1945*. Warsaw, Poland: Wydawnictwo Oskar, 1998.

Tomaszewski, Jerzy. *Słowacja*. Warsaw, Poland: Wydawnictwo Trio, 2011.

Trang, Charles. *The "Florian Geyer" Division*. Bayeux, France: Heimdal, 2000.

Tuchel, Johannes. *Konzentrationslager: Organizationsgeschichte und Funktion der "Inspektion der Konzentrationslager" 1934–1938*. Boppard am Rhein, Germany: H. Boldt, 1991.

Urbanek, Bożena. *Pielęgniarki i sanitariuszki w Powstaniu Warszawskim w 1944 r.* Warsaw, Poland: Wydawnictwo PWN, 1988.

Utracka, Katarzyna. *Powstańcze miejsca pamięci: Wola 1944*. Warsaw, Poland: Urząd Dzielnicy Wola m. st. Warszawy, 2009.

Venohr, Wolfgang. *Aufstand für die Tschechoslowakei: Der slowakische Freiheitskampf von 1944*. Hamburg, Germany: Christian Wegner Verlag, 1969.

Von Weimar und Bonn: Esslingen 1919–1949. Esslingen, Germany: Sigmaringen, Jan Thorbecke Verlag, 1991.

Wachsmann, Nikolaus. *Historia nazistowskich obozów koncentracyjnych*. Warsaw, Poland: Świat Książki, 2016. [*KL: A History of the Nazi Concentration Camps*. New York: Farrar, Straus & Giroux, 2015.]

Walther, Herbert. *Die Waffen-SS: Eine Bilddokumentation*. Utting am Ammersee, Germany: Dörfler Verlag, 2006.

Weise, Niels. *Eicke: Eine SS-Karriere zwischen Nervenklinik, KZ-System und Waffen-SS*. Paderborn, Germany, and Munich: Ferdinand Schöningh Verlag, 2013.

Wenn alle Brüder schweigen: Großer Bildband über die Waffen-SS. Selent, Germany: Edition Zeitgeschichte im Pour le Mèrite-Verlag, 2014.

Wette, Wolfram. *The Wehrmacht: History, Myth, Reality*. Cambridge, MA: Harvard University Press, 2006.

Whiting, Charles. *Skorzeny: Najbardziej niebezpieczny człowiek w Europie*. Gdańsk, Poland: Finna 1999. [*Skorzeny: The Most Dangerous Man in Europe*. Oxford: Pen & Sword Books, 1997.]

Wieczorkiewicz, Paweł. *Historia polityczna Polski 1935–1945*. Poznań, Poland: Zyska i s-ka, 2014.

Wieliński, Bartosz T. *Źli Niemcy: Zbrodniarze, geniusze, fanatycy, wizjonerzy*. Warsaw, Poland: Agora SA, 2014.

Williamson, David G. *Polski ruch oporu 1939–1947*. Poznań, Poland: Dom Wydawniczy Rebis, 2015.

Williamson, Gordon. *Die Waffen-SS 1933–1945*. Vienna: Tosa, 2003.

Williamson, Gordon. *SS: Gwardia Adolfa Hitlera; Pełna historia Schutzstaffel od ulicznych bojówek do Waffen-SS*. Warsaw, Poland: Espadon, 1995. [*Die SS: Hitlers Instrument der Macht; Die Geschichte der SS von der Schutzstaffel bis zur Waffen-SS*. Fränkisch-Crumbach, Germany: Neuer Kaiser, 2013.]

Winstone, Martin. *Generalne Gubernatorstwo: Mroczne serce Europy Hitlera*. Poznań, Poland: Dom Wydawniczy Rebis, 2015. [*The Dark Heart of Hitler's Europe*. London: Bloomsbury, 2020.]

Wiśniewska, Maria, and Małgorzata Sikorska. *Szpitale powstańczej Warszawy*. Warsaw, Poland: Oficyna Wydawnicza RYTM, 1991.

Wołoszański, Bogusław. *Encyklopedia II wojny światowej*. Warsaw, Poland: Amber, 1997.

Wyganowska-Eriksson, Anna. *Pluton pancerny batalionu 'Zośka' w powstaniu warszawskim*. Gdańsk, Poland: FINNA, 2010.

Yeger, Mark C. *Allgemeine-SS: The Commands, Units and Leaders of the General SS*. Atglen, PA: Schiffer, 1997.

Zamojski, Henryk. *Tragiczne decyzje: Jak wywołano Powstanie Warszawskie?* Warsaw, Poland: Bellona, 2013.

Zburzenie Warszawy: Zeznania generałów niemieckich przed polskim prokuratorem, członkiem polskiej delegacji przy Międzynarodowym Trybunale Wojennym w Norymberdze, Główna Komisja Badania Zbrodni Niemieckich w Polsce. Katowice, Poland: Awir, 1946.

Ziemke, Earl F. *Sowiecki walec*. Warsaw, Poland: Amber, 2001. [*The Soviet Juggernaut*. Chicago: Time Life Books, 1980.]

Zubiński, Tadeusz. *Wojna domowa w Hiszpanii 1936–1939*. Poznań, Poland: Wydawnictwo poznańskie, 2015.

Zychowicz, Piotr. *Obłęd '44*. Poznań, Poland: Rebis, 2013.

Жуков, Дмитрийv А., and Иван Ковтун. *Охотники за Партизанами Бригада Дирлевангера*. Москва: Вече Год, 2013.

Памяць Беларусі, 1941–1945. Мінск: Белорусская энциклопедия, 2005.

Пишенков, Алексей. *Штрафники СС: Зондеркоманда "Дирлевангер."* Москва: Яуза-Пресс, 2009.

Memoirs

Adamowicz, Aleś. *Oprawcy*. Warsaw, Poland: Współpraca, 1988. [*Karatieli*. Mastackaja Literatura, 1981.]

Brunnegger, Herbert. *Kto sieje wiatr . . . Opowieść żołnierza dywizji SS Totenkopf*. Kraków, Poland: Arkadiusz Wingert, 2005. [*Saat In den Sturm: Ein Soldat der Waffen-SSv berichtet*. Graz, Austria: Leopold Stocker Verlag, 2000.]

Brzezinski, Matthew. *Armia Izaaka: Walka i opór polskich Żydów*. Kraków, Poland: Znak, 2013. [*Isaac's Army: A Story of Courage and Survival in Nazi-Occupied Poland*. New York: Random House, 2012.]

Bukalska, Patrycja, in cooperation with Stanisław Aronson. *Rysiek z Kedywu: Niezwykłe losy Stanisława Aronsona*. Kraków, Poland: Znak, 2009.

Czwartacy: Wspomnienia byłych żołnierzy Szturmowego Batalionu AL im "Czwartaków" 1943–1945. Edited by J. Bednarczyk et al. Warsaw, Poland: Książka i Wiedza, 1977.

Damski, Zbigniew. *Najmłodsi od "Parasola."* Warsaw, Poland: Oficyna Wydawnicza Rytm, 2005.

Duffy, Peter. *Bracia Bielscy: Historia żydowskich partyzantów, którzy rzucili wyzwanie nazistom*. Kraków, Poland: Wydawnictwo Literackie, 2009. [*The Bielski Brothers: The True Story of Three Men Who Defied the Nazis, Built a Village in the Forest, and Saved 1,200 Jews*. New York: Harper Perennial, 2004.]

Engels, Willi. *Kellner, Koch, Kommunist: Erinnerungen*. Berlin: Lukas Verlag, 2016.

Exodus Warszawy: Ludzie i miasto po Powstaniu 1944. Vol. 1, *Pamiętniki*, and vol. 2, *Relacje*. Warsaw, Poland: PIW, 1992.

Exodus Warszawy: Ludzie i miasto po Powstaniu 1944. Vols. 3–4, *Archiwalia*. Warsaw, Poland: PIW 1994.

Exodus Warszawy: Ludzie i miasto po Powstaniu 1944. Vol. 5, *Prasa*. Warsaw, Poland: PIW, 1994.

Guderian, Heinz. *Wspomnienia żołnierza*. Warsaw, Poland: Bellona, 2008. [*Erinnerungen eines Soldaten: Autobiografie*. Heidelberg, Germany: K. Vowinckel Verlag, 1951.]

Guth, Karin. *Z 3105: Der Sinto Walter Winter überlebt den Holocaust*. Hamburg, Germany: VSA, 2009.

Hoffmann, Heinrich. *Mój przyjaciel Hitler: Wspomnienia fotografa Hitlera*. Warsaw, Poland: RM, 2015. [*Hitler wie ich ihn sah: Aufzeichnungen seines Leibfotografen*. Munich and Berlin: Herbig, 1974.]

Iberszer, Czesław. *Sachsenhausen*. http://www.fpnp.pl/swiadkowie/materialy/sachsenhausen.pdf.

Jastrzębski, Stanisław. *Zaczęło się pod Arsenałem*. Warsaw, Poland: Agencja Omnipress: Spółdzielnia Pracy Dziennikarzy i Państwowe Przedsiębiorstwo Wydawnicze "Rzeczpospolita," 1988.

Kaczyńska, Danuta. *Byli żołnierzami Parasola*. Warsaw, Poland: Młodzieżowa Agencja Wydawnicza, 1985.

Kaczyńska, Danuta. *Dziewczęta z Parasola*. Warsaw, Poland: Oficyna Wydawnicza Wiesław R. Kufirski, 1993.

Komornicki, Stanisław. *Na barykadach Warszawy*. Warsaw, Poland: MON, 1964.

Kotłowski, Tadeusz. *Historia Republiki Weimarskiej 1919–1933*. Poznań, Poland: Wydawnictwo Poznańskie, 2004.

Kulesza, Juliusz. *Powstańcza Starówka: Ludzie i ulice*. Warsaw, Poland: Askon, Attyka, 2007.

Kulesza, Juliusz. *Z tasiemką na czołgi*. Warsaw, Poland: Czytelnik, 1979.

Kurdwanowski, Jan. *Mrówka na szachownicy: Powstanie Warszawskie 1944, wspomnienia żołnierza z batalionu Chrobry I*. Warsaw, Poland: Muzeum Powstania Warszawskiego, 2014.

Likiernik, Stanisław. *Diabelne szczęście czy palec boży?* Warsaw, Poland: Czytelnik, 1994.

Ludność cywilna w powstaniu warszawskim. Vol. 1, part. 1, *Pamiętniki, relacje, zeznania.* Warsaw, Poland: Państwowy Instytut Wydawniczy, 1974.

Maegor, Herbert. *Utracony honor, zdradzona wiara: Relacja żołnierza Leibstandarte SS Adolf Hitler.* Międzyzdroje and Kraków, Poland: Arkadiusz Wingert, 2008.

Marat, Emil, and Michał Wójcik. *Made in Poland.* Warsaw, Poland: Wielka Litera, 2014.

Michaelis, Rolf. *Erinnerungen an das SS-Sonderkommando "Dirlewanger."* Berlin: Michaelis Verlag, 2010.

Nowak, Włodzimierz. *Obwód głowy.* Wołowiec, Poland: Wydawnictwo Czarne, 2007.

Nowożycki, Bartosz. *"Czata 49": Relacje i wspomnienia żołnierzy batalionu Armii Krajowej w zasobie Archiwum Akt Nowych.* Warsaw, Poland: Wydawnictwo historyczna.com.pl, 2011.

Polubiec, Zofia, ed. *Okupacja i ruch oporu w dzienniku Hansa Franka 1939–1945.* Vol. 2, *1943–1945.* Warsaw, Poland: Książka i Wiedza, 1971.

Pauer-Studer, Herlinde, and James D. Velleman. *Konrad Morgen: The Conscience of a Nazi Judge.* Basingstoke, UK: Palgrave Macmillan, 2015.

Podlewski, Stanisław. *Przemarsz przez piekło.* Warsaw, Poland: Instytut Wydawniczy PAX, 1957.

Pollack, Martin. *Śmierć w bunkrze: Opowieść o moim ojcu.* Wołowiec, Poland: Wydawnictwo Czarne, 2010. [*Der Tote im Bunker: Bericht über meinen Vater.* Munich: Deutscher Taschenbuch Verlag, 2006.]

Rommel, Erwin. *Piechota atakuje.* Warsaw, Poland: Erica, 2015. [*Infanterie greift an.* Potsdam, Germany: Voggenreiter, 1937.]

Sajer, Guy. *Zapomniany żołnierz.* Gdańsk, Poland: Gdański Kantor Wydawniczy, 2009. [*Le soldat oublié.* Paris: Robert Laffont, 1976.]

Sawicki, Jerzy. *Przed polskim prokuratorem.* Warsaw, Poland: ISKRY, 1958.

Schliwski, Kurt, and Regina Scheer. *Kurt Schliwski: Mein Leben; Autobiografischer Bericht.* Schwerin, Germany: VVN-BdA Landesvereinigung MV, 2014.

Seltmann von, Uwe. *Gabi i Uwe: Mój dziadek zginął w Auschwitz; A mój był esesmanem.* Warsaw, Poland: Wydawnictwo Naukowe PWN, 2012. [*Todleben: Eine deutsch-polnische Suche nach der Vergangenheit.* Munich: Herbig, 2019.]

Sławińska, Anna D. *Przeżyłam to: Wola 1944.* Edmond, Oklahoma: Gondwana, 2015.

Szepansky, Wolfgang. *Dennoch ging ich diesen Weg.* Berlin: Trafo, 2000.

Troński, Bronisław. *Tędy przeszła śmierć: Zapiski z Powstania Warszawskiego.* Warsaw, Poland: Krajowa Agencja Wydawnicza, 1957.

Verton, Hendrik C. *W piekle frontu wschodniego: Byłem holenderskim ochotnikiem Waffen-SS*. Warsaw, Poland: Bellona, 2010. [*In the Fire of the Eastern Front: The Experiences of a Dutch Waffen-SS Volunteer on the Eastern Front 1941–45*. Mechanicsburg, PA: Stackpole Books, 2010.]

Wachowicz, Barbara. *To "Zośki" wiara!* Vol. 4, *cz. 2*. Warsaw, Poland: Oficyna Wydawnicza Rytm, 2005.

Wróblewski, Jarosław. *Gryf: Pałacyk Michla, Żytnia, Wola*. Warsaw, Poland: Fronda, 2016.

Articles and reports

Birn, Ruth. B. "'Zaunkönig' an 'Uhrmacher,' Grosse Partisanenaktion 1942/43 am Beispiel des 'Unternehemns Winterzauber.'" *Militärgeschichtliche Zeitschrift* 1 (2001).

Böhnisch, Georg, Axel Frohn, Christian Siepmann, and Klaus Wiegrefe. "Ein braver Schwabe." *Der Spiegel* 30 (2008).

Ciechanowski, Jan. "Pierwsza relacja gen. Bora-Komorowskiego o AK i powstaniu warszawskim." *Zeszyty Historyczne* 49 (1979).

Dannenbaum, Uwe. "Historische Kriminalfälle: Schöngeist, Muttermörder, Massenmörder." *Spiegel Online*, December 28, 2009.

Herbich, Anna. "Cel: Kobiety; Polki, które przeszły przez piekło." *Do Rzeczy Historia* 8 (2014).

Mix, Andreas. "Kriegsverbrechen: Männer mit Vergangenheit." *Spiegel Online*, June 29, 2008.

"Niepokonani: Powstanie Warszawskie '44." *Superalbum* 4 (2014).

Nowak, Włodzimierz, and Angelika Kuźniak. "Mój warszawski szał: Druga strona powstania." Duży Format, addition to *Gazeta Wyborcza* 197 (June 23, 2004).

"Powstanie Warszawskie 1944." *Polityka* 7 (special issue) (2014).

Rakowiecki, Jerzy. "Ech, Wania . . ." *Newsweek Polska Historia* 8–9 (2018).

Rakowiecki, Jerzy. "Schowany w pomniku marszałka." *Newsweek Polska Historia* 8–9 (2018).

Rosalak, Maciej. "Męczeństwo Warszawy: Ofiary niemieckiego mordu." *Do Rzeczy Historia* 8 (2014).

Rybińska, Aleksandra, and Cezary Gmyz. "Ścigając dirlewangerowców, oprawców Warszawy." *Rzeczpospolita*, June 10, 2008.

"'Sie haben etwas gutzumachen': Ein Tatsachenbericht vom Einsatz der Strafsoldaten." *Spiegel Online*, April 4, 1951.

Stańczyk, Tomasz. "Bestie w mieście: Pułk specjalny SS 'Dirlewanger'; Szlak zbrodni od Woli do Czerniakowa." *Do Rzeczy Historia*, 8 (2014).

Urzykowski, Tomasz. "Urodzony 20 sierpnia." *Gazeta Wyborcza*, August 8, 2013.

"Von dem Bach-Zelewski. Die Toten stehen auf." *Der Spiegel* 2 (1959).

Węgłowski, Adam. "Dopaść rzeźnika Warszawy." *Focus.pl*, July 31, 2014.

Wieliński, Bartosz T. "Pan burmistrz z SS." *Gazeta Wyborcza*, August 3, 2013.

Włoczyk, Piotr. "Ocaleni z rzezi mówią." *Do Rzeczy Historia* 8 (2014).

Zychowicz, Piotr. "Niemiecka oferta dla "'Bora': Nieoczekiwany zwrot Berlina." *Do Rzeczy Historia* 8 (2014).

Zychowicz, Piotr. "Swołocz '44." *Do Rzeczy Historia* 8 (2014).

Novels

Hassel, Sven. *Gestapo*. Warsaw, Poland: Erica, 2007.

Hassel, Sven. *Królestwo piekieł: Powstanie warszawskie*. Warsaw, Poland: Erica, 2009.

Kerr, Philipp. *Był pan w Smoleńsku, kapitanie?* Warsaw, Poland: W.A.B., 2013.

Mastalerz, Marcin. *Miasto 44 (na podstawie scenariusza filmu Miasto 44 J. Komasy)*. Warsaw, Poland: PWN, 2014.

Websites

Abwehrgruppe 218. https://pl.wikipedia.org/wiki/Abwehrgruppe_218.

Archiwum Historii Mówionej. http://www.1944.pl/archiwum-historii-mowionej.html.

Archiwum Historii Mówionej. http://www.audiohistoria.pl/web/.

Attentat auf Himmler. "Pariser Tageblatt." June 25, 1934. https://portal.dnb.de/bookviewer/view/1026571014#page/1/mode/1up.

"Biszop" Biskup M. Brygada potworów. http://polimaty.pl/2014/07/brygada-potworow/.

Boguch, W. To zwierzę Dirlewanger. http://www.tunguska.pl/to-zwierze-dirlewanger/.

Święta wojna bękartów Weimaru. http://www.newsweek.pl/wiedza/historia/republika-weimarska-od-konca-1918-r-,artykuly,393452,1.html.

Index

Wildner, Karl, 237
Wilhelm, Waldemar, SS-Obersturmbannführer, 340

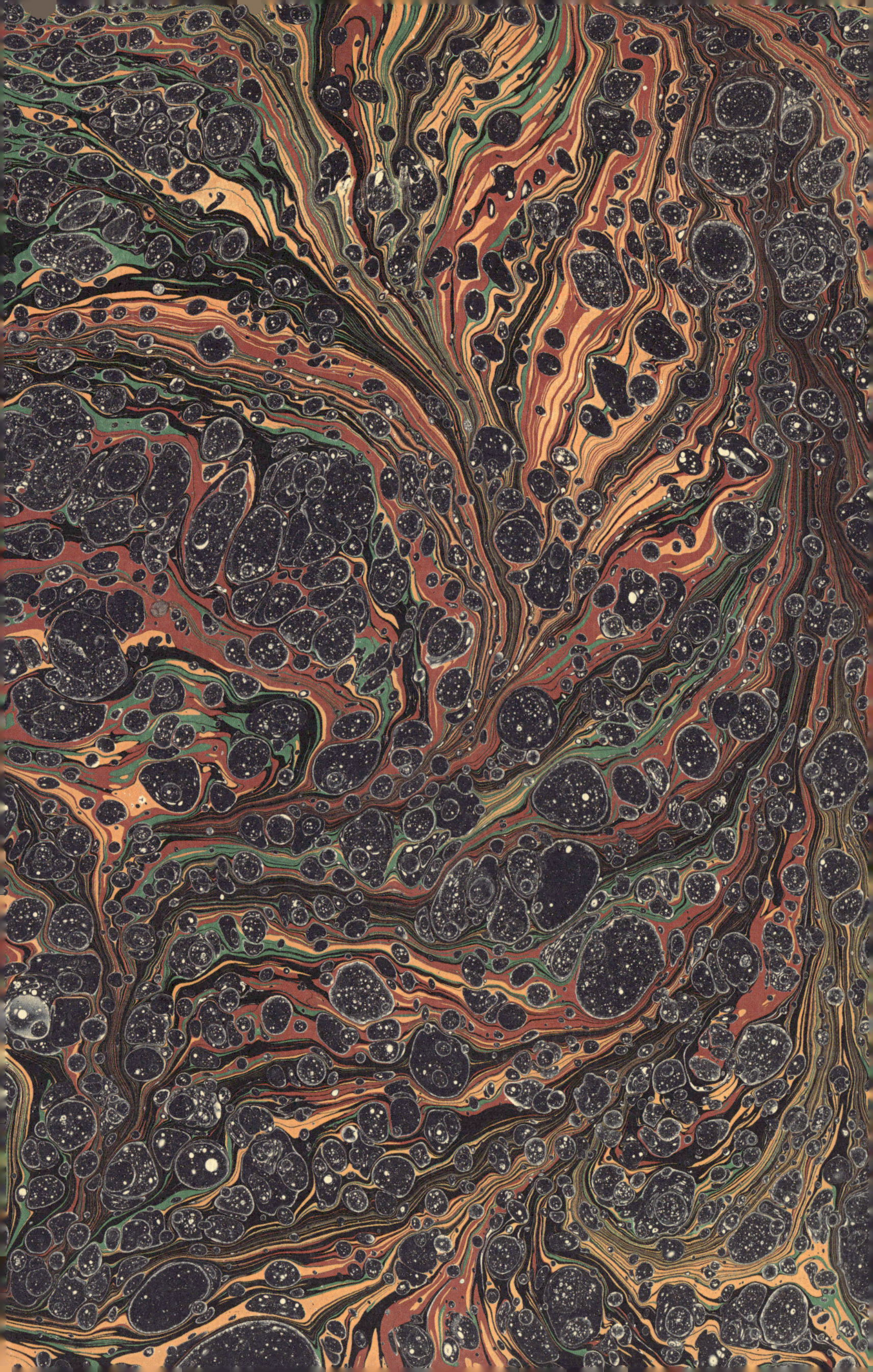